PIONEERS' JOURNEY F
WINTER QUARTERS TO SALT LAKE, 1847

rossing
Deer Creek
Natural Bridge
Scotts Bluff
Missouri River
Laramie River
North Platte
Chimney Rock
WINTER QUARTERS
Loup Fork River
Ash Hollow
Platte River
South Platte
Courthouse and Jail Rocks

THE WORK AND THE GLORY

All Is Well

Miracle of the Quail

VOLUME 9

THE WORK AND THE GLORY

All Is Well

A HISTORICAL NOVEL

Gerald N. Lund

BOOKCRAFT
Salt Lake City, Utah

THE WORK AND THE GLORY

Volume 1: Pillar of Light
Volume 2: Like a Fire Is Burning
Volume 3: Truth Will Prevail
Volume 4: Thy Gold to Refine
Volume 5: A Season of Joy
Volume 6: Praise to the Man
Volume 7: No Unhallowed Hand
Volume 8: So Great a Cause
Volume 9: All Is Well

Copyright © 1998 by Gerald N. Lund and
Kenneth Ingalls Moe

All rights reserved. No part of this book may be reproduced in any form or by any means without permission in writing from the publisher, Bookcraft, Inc., 2405 W. Orton Circle, West Valley City, Utah 84119.

Bookcraft is a registered trademark of Bookcraft, Inc.

Library of Congress Catalog Card Number: 98-74085
ISBN 1-57008-563-3

First Printing, 1998

Printed in the United States of America

For behold, this is my work and my glory—to bring to pass the immortality and eternal life of man.

—Moses 1:39

To my mother—
Evelyn Mortensen Lund—
whose gentle spirit and manner
have influenced me more deeply
than even I fully recognize

Preface

The story told by *The Work and the Glory* series began in the spring of 1827 in Palmyra Township in western New York. There we were introduced to the family of Benjamin and Mary Ann Steed. In looking for help to clear his newly acquired farmland, Benjamin Steed hired two brothers, Hyrum and Joseph Smith, who lived on a farm a short distance south of the city of Palmyra. Thus did the lives of the Steeds come to be intertwined with Joseph Smith, the work of the Restoration, and the unfolding destiny of The Church of Jesus Christ of Latter-day Saints.

We moved with the Steeds to Kirtland, Ohio, and Jackson County, Missouri; to Far West and Adam-ondi-Ahman and Haun's Mill. We went with them as they were driven from Missouri to Commerce, Illinois, and watched them help transform a swamp into Nauvoo, the City Beautiful. Then, when once again their enemies threatened to exterminate them, we saw them abandon that beloved city in the spring of 1846 and start across the muddy vastness of Iowa Territory.

Through the eyes of the Steeds we have watched as the Book of Mormon came forth, as the Church was organized, as persecution and ridicule against Joseph Smith swelled in a bitter crescendo. We marched with them on Zion's Camp, took hammer and saw and trowel in hand with them as they built first the Kirtland Temple and then the magnificent edifice called the Nauvoo Temple. Through their eyes we came to know the Prophet Joseph Smith and saw his quick humor, his deep love of people, his great vision, and his tragic end in a jail in Carthage, Illinois. We accompanied the Steeds on missions, trekked with them as they were driven by their enemies, laughed with them in their times of joy, and wept with them in their times of sorrow.

In *So Great a Cause*, volume 8 of the series, we left the Steeds on the banks of the Missouri River at Council Bluffs, Iowa. They had no permanent homes. Thousands upon thousands of Saints were leaving Nauvoo and its surrounding communities and heading west to join Brigham Young and the Twelve. They started out from Nauvoo thinking they would go all the way to the Rocky Mountains that year. They soon learned that there was no choice but to change their minds. The three hundred twenty-seven miles across Iowa in the spring rains took them one hundred and nine days! They averaged only three miles per day. If they had continued at that rate it would have taken them almost another full year to cover the remaining one thousand sixty-seven miles to the Salt Lake Valley.

Throughout the series, the events of the Restoration led the Steed family down numerous roads. Often these roads separated and went in different directions. Then, at Nauvoo, the paths began to converge again, and for a wonderful time of peace and happiness the family was together. But it was not to last. The golden years in the City Beautiful were quickly coming to an end in sharp, hostile, violent jerks. Once again fate began to have its way with the family, and once again the Steeds began to be pulled in different directions. Peter and Kathryn Ingalls decided to find another way west so that they would not be a burden to the family. They hired on with the family of James Reed and started west with the Donner Party, a name that would forever be linked with tragedy. Will and Alice were asked by Brigham Young to go to New York and join the group led by Samuel Brannan. Their road would be across the sea, a ten-thousand-mile journey around the southern tip of South America.

In *All is Well*, volume 9, we quickly see that the forces of divergence have not yet run their course in the family. Within a few days of their arrival at Council Bluffs, Iowa, Captain James Allen rides in and asks Brigham Young for five hundred of their best men to march to California. Can the Steed men ignore such a call? When the time finally comes for the move west in the spring of 1847, Brigham decides that a Pioneer Company must lead the way for the thousands who will follow. Other companies will come later that same season. The majority will wait until 1848, 1849, even as late as 1852. What does all of this mean for the Steeds? Nor does the fact that the Saints are in exile set aside the duty to proclaim the gospel to the world. Even as they struggle for survival, some Latter-day Saints are called to the eastern states, the southern states, England, the Sandwich Islands. The Steeds have been separated by the call to serve before. Will it once again set some on roads that lead far away from the family?

In many ways, volume 9 will be significantly different from previous volumes. For one thing, most of this volume covers a people on the move. Any sense of permanence is gone. Even when they stop to build cabins and houses, there is no purpose but to make shelter until it is time to move again. Canvas and open sky become the norm now. The days are counted in miles and landmarks. The nights are spent preparing for the next day's march.

In some ways—particularly from the perspective of a novelist—the story of Brigham Young's Pioneer Company of 1847 is anticlimactic. After Iowa, it is almost deadly dull. There are no deaths. No battles. No tragedies. They moved forward with endless monotony across a thousand miles of plains and deserts and mountains, with nothing more exciting happening than having to ferry across the river or lock the wagon wheels when they went down a particularly sharp decline. But this is exactly what Brigham hoped for. This was the result of his months of careful planning and preparation. In the novel, whole blocks of days are completely skipped because there is not much to say except that they kept moving on. So complete and thorough were President Young's preparations that not until 1856, when the Willie and Martin Handcart Companies left very late in the season, would any real tragedy strike the Mormon pioneer trains, even though thousands upon thousands would follow across the trail blazed by the Pioneer Company.

Divergence and convergence. Separation and reunion. The Pioneer Company. The Mormon Battalion. The Donner-Reed Party. The *Brooklyn* Saints. The Big Company. Each has its own unique part to play in the gathering, and the Steeds will be swept up in grand events just as they have been so many times before. In volume 9, it has been twenty years since Joseph and Hyrum Smith came to the Steed farm in Palmyra, New York, to help clear the land. The family then consisted of Benjamin, Mary Ann, and their five surviving children. Now the family has swelled to almost forty people. Now the third generation of Steeds begins to come forth to take part in the great saga of finding a place of refuge in the Rocky

Mountains. It will not be an easy task. It will demand sacrifice and separation. It will take determination and dedication. It will require that covenants take precedence over convenience. But when it is done, the family—along with so many others—will be able to say without hesitation or reservation, "All is well."

With the completion of volume 9, the series known as *The Work and the Glory* will come to a close for a time. Personally, it will have covered ten years of my life. As previously noted in the preface to volume 8, Kim Moe and I signed our agreement to begin working on this project in November 1988. Perhaps it was just as well that neither of us could foresee that the project on which we embarked with such bold naivete would still be going a full ten years later. Sadly, Kim did not live to see it come to fruition. He died of cancer in October 1996.

Having finished volume 9, I am going to set the series aside for a time. There are a couple of reasons for this. For one thing, with the arrival of the Saints in the Salt Lake Valley, the Restoration era comes to a close. What follows is a period of isolation in which the Church is given time to consolidate, grow, and strengthen its roots. From there, it moves step by step until it becomes what we see today, a worldwide kingdom experiencing remarkable growth and global recognition. Those are exciting eras too, but my desire was to tell the story of the Restoration. (As a side note, it even feels to me as though the Steeds are saying, "All right. We've let you into our lives for these twenty years. Now we'd like a little time to ourselves.")

A second reason for stopping for a time now is that for ten years I have had to put many other projects and assignments on hold in order to produce one book in the series each year. After that long, it is time to step back, take a breath, and catch up on some other things. Then, after a time, I would like to finish the series by writing another volume that jumps forward approximately one hundred and fifty years to take a look at the descendants of the Steeds in the closing years of this century. From the beginning, Kim Moe had strong feelings that we needed to tell our readers what it's like to be a Latter-day Saint in the modern world. Before his death, I committed to Kim that once I got the Saints to the Salt Lake Valley, I would take some time off but then would complete the series by doing something with the Steeds in modern times.

I look forward to that. I have already started a file of ideas that I would like to include in that volume. Like Kim, I feel strongly that it is a story that needs to be told. A century and a half in time will have elapsed. We will have moved from the world of wagons and carts to a world of jetliners, automobiles, and the Internet. We will have gone from an age of faith to an age of high tech and low morals and widespread self-indulgence. Yet it is my deep conviction that the gospel of Jesus Christ, restored through the Prophet Joseph Smith, provides the answers to our age and our dilemmas and our challenges just as it did for those early Saints whom Benjamin and Mary Ann Steed and their family are intended to represent.

As the series comes to a close for a time, I should once again like to thank those who have played such an important part in taking this project from concept to reality. First and foremost I would like to thank my wife, Lynn, who has been not only my untiring partner over ten years of effort and sacrifice but also my first reader and most-valued critic. Though she herself would deny this, her mark—though not visible—is found throughout the series. As mentioned several times before, without Kim Moe's vision and dogged commitment to the importance of this project, I would likely have continued doing other things with my writing for some time to come and this series would not have moved forward as it has. His wife, Jane, continues on with the work, as determined to see it through as Kim was during his life.

Russell Orton, president of Bookcraft, now retired, along with Cory Maxwell, editorial manager at Bookcraft, saw almost instantly the potential for the series while I was still struggling to make volume 1 a reality. Not only did Russell's support and vision make him a valued associate, but through it all he and his wife, Ann, became treasured friends.

Kristin Johnson—whose work on the Donner-Reed Party entitled *"Unfortunate Emigrants": Narratives of the Donner Party* was especially valuable—also provided important consultation and many helpful suggestions on the manuscript. Her help has increased the accuracy of the references to that important group. There are many others who have been mentioned before in previous volumes—historians, designers, artists, editors, researchers, marketing personnel, secretaries, and readers. Each one could—though none of them ever will—easily step forward and say, "I had a hand in the success of this project."

Last of all I should like to thank them whose work and glory is the subject of the series. Before I ever began, I had a testimony of the Father and the Son and of their great, ever-watchful love and concern for each of us. I knew about and loved the Prophet Joseph Smith. I had a strong conviction that the restoration of the Church and the gospel on the earth was one of the most significant events in all of human history. All of that I knew and knew it strongly.

Now, after ten years of constantly pouring over the sources, of reading and rereading, of checking and cross-checking, of trying to wiggle into the heads of these great people who made the Restoration a reality, my testimony has deepened beyond my greatest expectations. The work of the restored Church is God's work, and from it comes his glory. Of that there is not the slightest shadow of doubt.

Recently I came across a statement by Joseph F. Smith, sixth President of the Church, that epitomizes what I have come to know and feel after ten years of writing this series. He said: "The hand of the Lord may not be visible to all. There may be many who can not discern the workings of God's will in the progress and development of this great latter-day work, but there are those who see *in every hour and in every moment* of the existence of the Church, from its beginning until now, the overruling, almighty hand of Him who sent His Only Begotten Son to the world to become a sacrifice for the sin of the world" (in Conference Report, April 1904, p. 2; emphasis added).

GERALD N. LUND

Bountiful, Utah
September 1998

Characters of Note in This Book

The Steed Family

Mary Ann Morgan, widow of Benjamin Steed, and mother and grandmother; not quite sixty as the story opens.

Joshua, the oldest son (thirty-nine), and his wife, **Caroline Mendenhall** (almost forty).

William ("Will"), from Caroline's first marriage (twenty-two), and his wife, Alice Samuelson (nineteen).

Savannah; nine.

Charles Benjamin; six.

Livvy Caroline; two years old as the book opens.

Jessica Roundy Garrett (forty-two), Joshua's first wife, widow of John Griffith, and her husband, **Solomon Garrett** (forty-one).

Rachel, from marriage to Joshua; fourteen.

Luke and Mark, sons from John Griffith's first marriage; thirteen and eleven, respectively.

John Benjamin, from marriage to John; eight.

Miriam Jessica, from marriage to Solomon; almost three.

Solomon Clinton; fourteen months.

Nathan, the second son (thirty-seven), and his wife, **Lydia McBride** (about the same age).

Joshua Benjamin ("Josh"); fifteen.

Emily; not quite fourteen.

Elizabeth Mary; eight.

Josiah Nathan; five.

Nathan Joseph (called Joseph); nearly three.

Patricia (Tricia) Ann; just over two months as the book opens.

Melissa, the older daughter (thirty-five), and her husband, **Carlton ("Carl") Rogers** (thirty-six).

Carlton Hezekiah; fourteen.
David Benjamin; almost twelve.
Caleb John; nearly ten.
Sarah; seven.
Mary Melissa; almost two.

Rebecca, the younger daughter (twenty-eight), and her husband, **Derek Ingalls** (twenty-eight).

Christopher Joseph; seven.
Benjamin Derek; four.
Leah Rebecca; fifteen months.

Matthew, the youngest son (almost twenty-six), and his wife, **Jennifer Jo McIntire** (twenty-four).

Betsy Jo; four.
Emmeline; fifteen months.

Peter Ingalls, Derek's younger brother (twenty-two), and his wife, **Kathryn Marie McIntire,** Jennifer Jo's sister (twenty).

Note: Deceased children are not included in the above listing.

The Smiths

*Lucy Mack, the mother.
*Mary Fielding, Hyrum's widow.
*Emma Hale, Joseph Smith's widow.

Others

*Samuel Brannan, leader of the group that sailed to California on the *Brooklyn*.
*Jim Bridger, famous mountain man and trapper.

*Designates actual people from history.

- * William Clayton, an English convert; clerk to Brigham Young and an accomplished musician.
- * George and Jacob Donner, well-to-do farmers from Springfield, Illinois, who decide to go to California in 1846.
- * Heber C. Kimball, friend of Brigham Young's and a member of the Quorum of the Twelve Apostles.
- * Orson Pratt, member of the Quorum of the Twelve Apostles.
- * Parley P. Pratt, member of the Quorum of the Twelve Apostles.
- * James Reed, wealthy businessman who heads for California with the Donner brothers and his own family.
- * Willard Richards, member of the Quorum of the Twelve Apostles.
- * George A. Smith, member of the Quorum of the Twelve Apostles.
- * John Sutter, Swiss emigrant and founder of Sutter's Fort in Upper California.
- * John Taylor, member of the Quorum of the Twelve Apostles.
- * Wilford Woodruff, member of the Quorum of the Twelve Apostles.
- * Brigham Young, President of the Quorum of the Twelve Apostles and head of the Church; forty-five as the novel opens.

Though too numerous to list here, there are many other actual people from the pages of history who are mentioned by name in the novel. James and Drusilla Hendricks, Ezra T. Benson, Thomas Rhoads and family, Levinah Murphy, Colonel Philip St. George Cooke, and many others mentioned in the book were real people who lived and participated in the events described in this work.

*Designates actual people from history.

The Benjamin and Mary Ann Steed Family

Shown below are the various Steed family groups. The chart for Benjamin and Mary Ann is followed by separate charts for their children—actual and "adopted." (These charts do not include those deceased children who play no part in the novel.)

Benjamin and Mary Ann

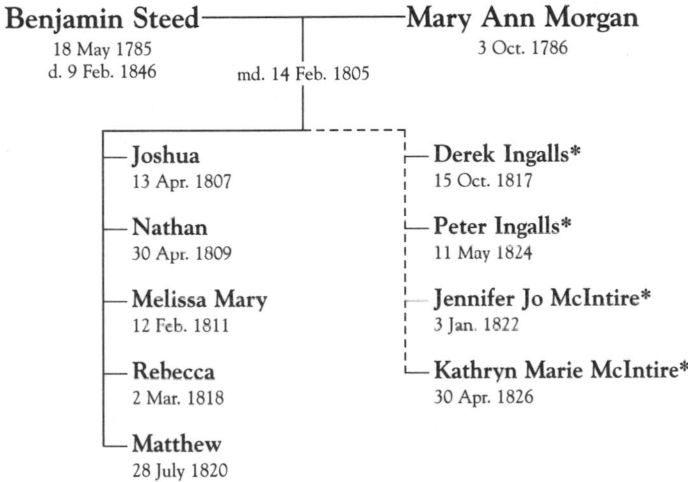

Joshua and Caroline

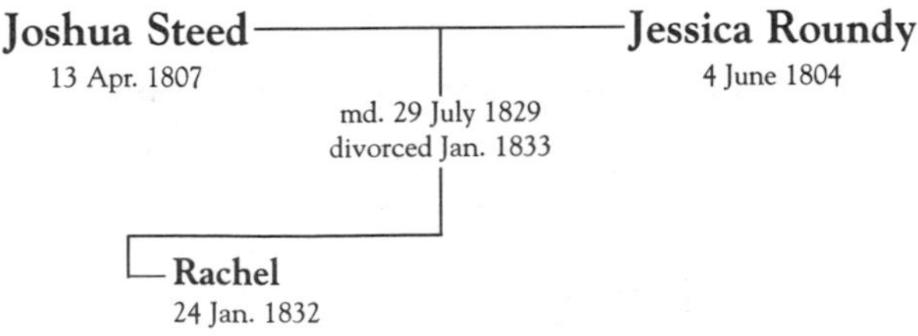

* Indicates a person who, though never legally adopted, became a part of the Steed family.

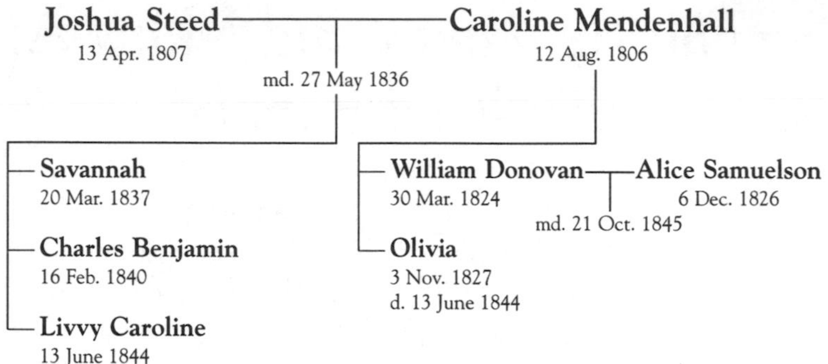

Jessica and Solomon

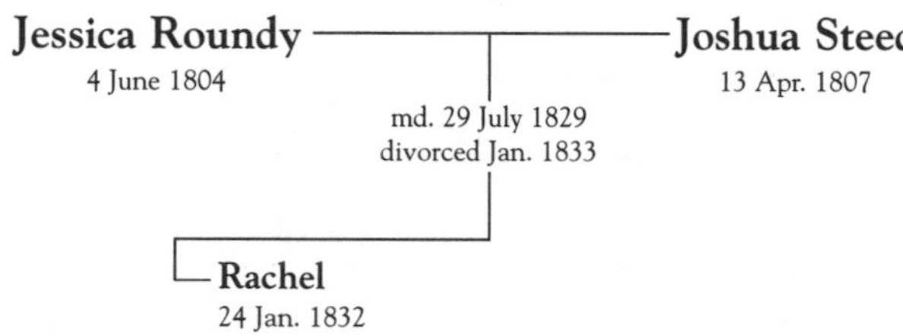

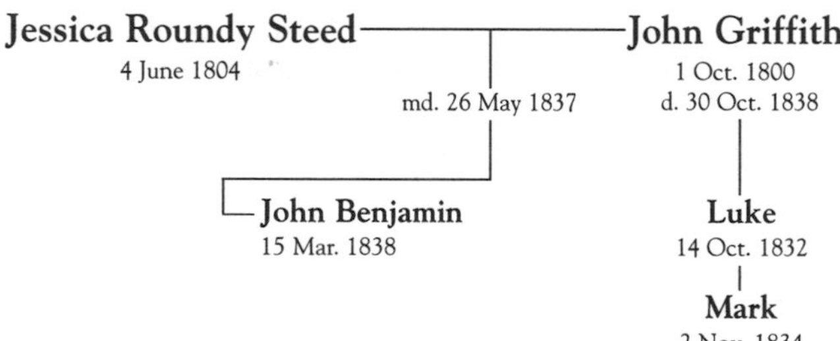

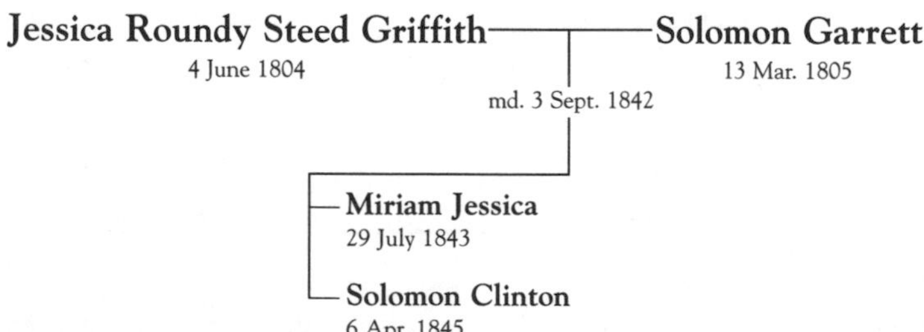

Nathan and Lydia

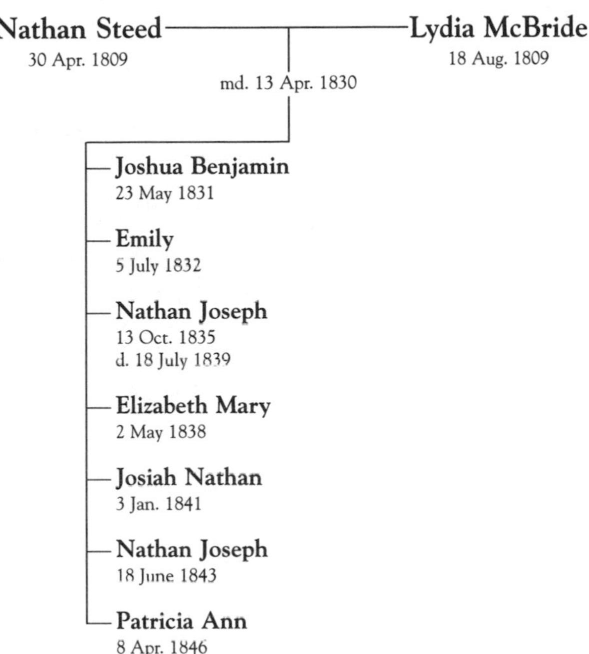

Melissa and Carl

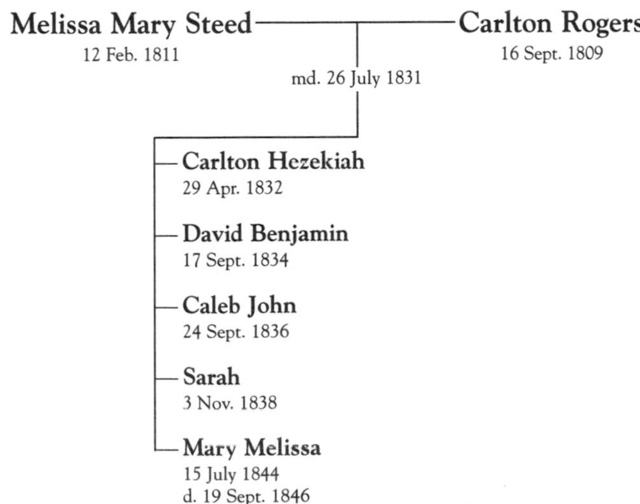

Rebecca and Derek

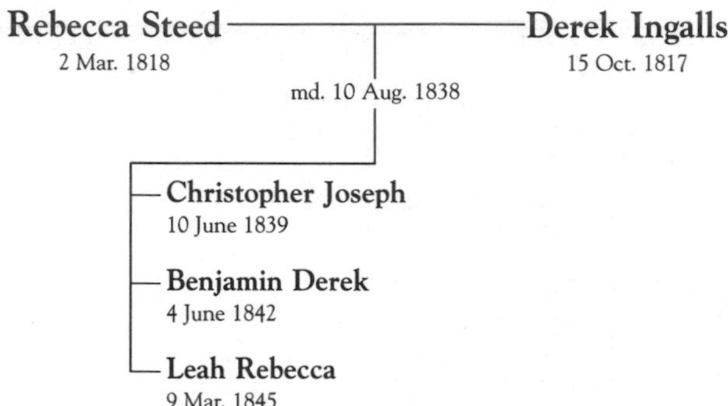

Matthew and Jenny

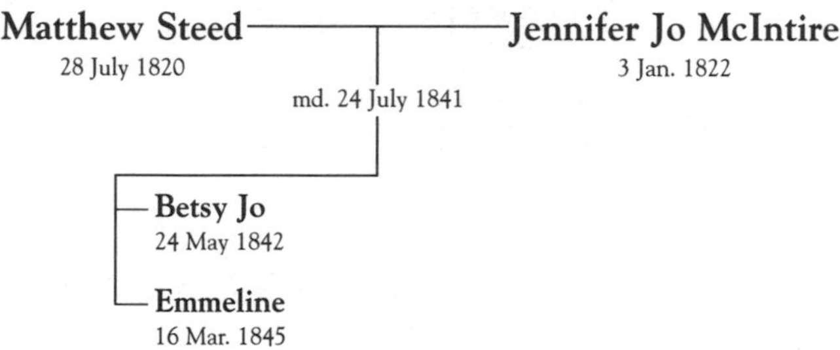

Peter and Kathryn

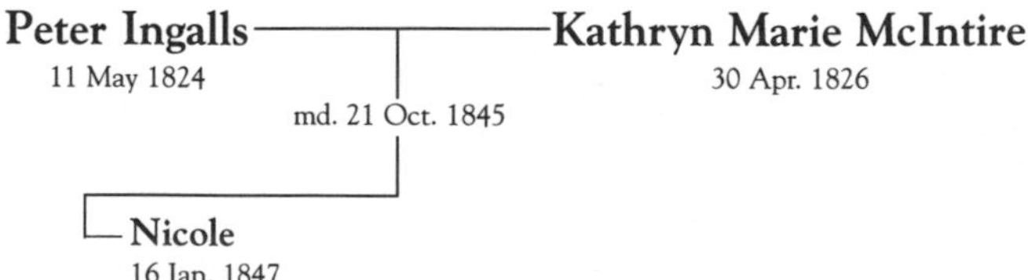

WILL AND ALICE

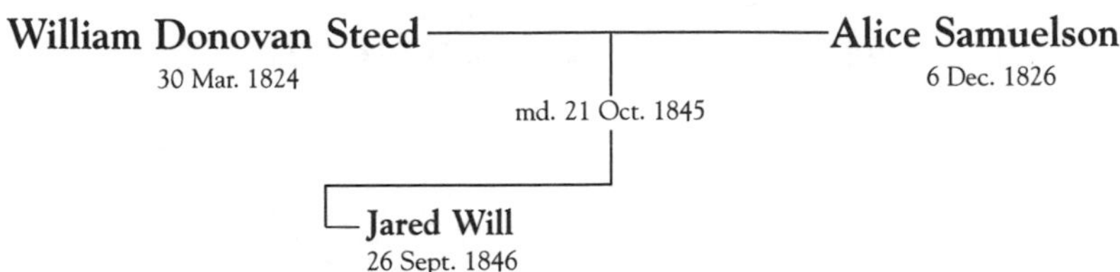

Key to Abbreviations Used in Chapter Notes

Throughout the chapter notes, abbreviated references are given. The following key gives the full bibliographic data for those references.

CHMB	Daniel Tyler, *A Concise History of the Mormon Battalion in the Mexican War, 1846–1847* (1881; reprint, Glorieta, N.Mex.: Rio Grande Press 1969.)
Chronicles	Frank Mullen Jr., *The Donner Party Chronicles: A Day-by-Day Account of a Doomed Wagon Train, 1846–1847* (Reno: Nevada Humanities Committee, 1997.)
CS	Richard O. Cowan and William E. Homer, *California Saints: A 150-Year Legacy in the Golden State* (Provo, Utah: Religious Studies Center, Brigham Young University, 1996.)
MB	Norma Baldwin Ricketts, *The Mormon Battalion: U.S. Army of the West, 1846–1848* (Logan, Utah: Utah State University Press, 1996.)
MHBY	Elden J. Watson, ed., *Manuscript History of Brigham Young, 1846–1847* (Salt Lake City: Elden J. Watson, 1971.)
OBH	George R. Stewart, *Ordeal by Hunger: The*

	Story of the Donner Party (Boston: Houghton Mifflin Co., 1988.)
Overland in 1846	Dale Morgan, ed., *Overland in 1846: Diaries and Letters of the California-Oregon Trail* (1963; reprint, Lincoln: University of Nebraska Press, 1993.)
"Pioneer Journeys"	John Zimmerman Brown, ed., "Pioneer Journeys: From Nauvoo, Illinois, to Pueblo, Colorado, in 1846, and Over the Plains in 1847; Extracts from the Private Journal of the Late Pioneer John Brown. . . . ," *Improvement Era* 13 (July 1910): 802-10.
SW	David R. Crockett, *Saints in the Wilderness: A Day-by-Day Pioneer Experience*, vol. 2 of LDS-Gems Pioneer Trek Series (Tucson, Arizona: LDS-Gems Press, 1997.)
UE	Kristin Johnson, ed., *"Unfortunate Emigrants": Narratives of the Donner Party* (Logan, Utah: Utah State University Press, 1996.)
"Voyage"	Lorin K. Hansen, "Voyage of the Brooklyn," *Dialogue* 21 (Fall 1988): 47-72.
WFFB	J. Roderic Korns, comp., *West from Fort Bridger: The Pioneering of Immigrant Trails Across Utah, 1846–1850*, ed. J. Roderic Korns and Dale Morgan; revised and updated by Will Bagley and Harold Schindler (Logan, Utah: Utah State University Press, 1994.)
What I Saw	Edwin Bryant, *What I Saw in California* (1848; reprint, Lincoln: University of Nebraska Press, 1985.)

All Is Well

Why should we mourn or think our lot is hard?
'Tis not so; all is right.
Why should we think to earn a great reward
If we now shun the fight?
Gird up your loins; fresh courage take.
Our God will never us forsake;
And soon we'll have this tale to tell—
All is well! All is well!

We'll find the place which God for us prepared,
Far away in the West,
Where none shall come to hurt or make afraid;
There the Saints will be blessed.
We'll make the air with music ring,
Shout praises to our God and King;
Above the rest these words we'll tell—
All is well! All is well!

—William Clayton

Chapter One

"Are you still awake?"

Joshua spoke in a low murmur. Caroline had stirred a moment before, but he wasn't sure if she was, like him, lying there in the darkness far from sleep. But there was no answer, and as he listened carefully he could hear her breathing softly but deeply. His mouth softened and he turned his head toward her, resisting the temptation to reach out and gently caress her face. He could see nothing, not even the outline of her, but he was sure that if suddenly a light were to illuminate the inside of the tent, Caroline Mendenhall Steed would be smiling softly in her sleep. And rightly so. She had waited a long time for what had happened this day.

He grinned in the darkness as he remembered Brigham Young's words to the people who had gathered to witness Joshua's baptism. "A giant in the forest has fallen." And then there was Brigham's droll smile. "And he has fallen right into our hands."

He closed his eyes. O God. *How did you ever see fit to take mercy on one whose heart was so hardened? What ever possessed thee to reach out and save me from my own blindness?*

The answer was simple. How many times had Caroline prayed in his behalf? How many tears had she shed? But then, he thought, it went back further than that. Joseph and Hyrum Smith had first come to the Steed farm back in New York in the spring of 1827. Within a year, Nathan and Mary Ann were convinced that Joseph's fantastic account of the Father and the Son appearing to him in a grove of trees and of angels and golden plates was true, and Joshua had bitterly turned against it. How many times had his mother been on her knees?

He was staggered now by the sheer number of prayers that must surely have been offered in his behalf. Will. Alice. Sweet and stubborn Savannah. Derek and Rebecca. Matthew and Jenny. His father. He turned away, eyes burning. And Olivia. This was the greatest pain for him. Even now it was as fresh and excruciating as when he learned that there had been an accident and Olivia had been killed.

Oh, Father, I would give my all—there was a sudden, fleeting smile as he realized that at the moment that wasn't much of an offer—*I would give everything if I could walk those paths again. If I could rectify some of the pain and the hurt and the loss.*

His thoughts came back to Caroline. He had caused a lot of suffering for many people over the last twenty years, but Caroline had endured the most. His mind turned to those who didn't know yet. Oh, how he longed to be present when they first learned the news that Joshua Steed was now a member of the Church! Jessica and Solomon back at Garden Grove, Peter and Kathryn somewhere out on the trail ahead of them, *Carl and Melissa.* That thought stopped him for a moment. He would have to send a letter back to Nauvoo with the news. Carl would be stunned. Joshua had been his one ally in the family, the one other holdout against their beliefs. Now Carl was alone.

Joshua sighed. Most of all he wanted to share his news with Will. Where were he and Alice by now? He thought of the vastness of their sea voyage and felt a little sick. Had there been any problems? Was Alice with child yet? Had they reached Upper California? How long before they would see them again? It was a terrible frustration knowing that he couldn't even send them a letter. But then he shook his head. No, this news could not come by letter. Not for Will. That had to be face to face, no matter how long it took before they were reunited.

And with that, he slid closer to his wife, gently putting one arm around her and pulling in closer. She stirred, snuggling in against him. She half turned her head. "You still awake?" she mumbled.

He grinned. "No."

"That's good." It was a faraway murmur.

He pressed his face against the back of her head. "I love you, Caroline Steed," he whispered.

"Hmm." And she was gone again.

He smiled, knowing that she would remember none of this in the morning. But it was all right. He closed his eyes and lay back. Tonight, everything was all right.

When they were stretched out in one great line—as they were today—the Russell wagon train, with its forty-plus wagons, covered almost a full mile of trail. If you added the large herd of oxen and cattle that trailed behind, it was closer to a mile and a half from lead scouts to last cow. Not that Kathryn Ingalls could tell any of that from sight alone. Through the great curtains of dust which veiled the train she was fortunate if she could see more than two wagons ahead.

Summer had finally come. The pleasant spring temperatures were gone, and the earth was battered relentlessly by a sun that shone out of a cloudless sky. What had once been mud was now brick-hard soil, so that those riding aboard the wagons were jolted and jarred with numbing consistency. By an almost constant repetition of wagon wheels that had passed over the ground, the hardpan was chewed into a fine powder that lay ankle deep and exploded upward with the slightest provocation.

When the terrain allowed it, the company would spread out across the prairie horizontally, each wagon or small group of wagons choosing its own way so as to stay out of the endless dust of those before them. Often, however, the trail narrowed to a single track and the dust became unbearable.

Kathryn Ingalls had an especially difficult time. She, like everyone else, buttoned her collars and sleeves as tightly as possible. She wore a bonnet over her hair and a scarf across her face. That alone was enough to make the heat almost intolerable. But she had no choice except to ride in the wagon. Others could get out and walk and escape the worst of the dust. Kathryn could not. Though she could tell that the exercise she was getting was strengthening her legs, there was no possibility of her walking alongside the wagons.

She had heard stories that the Indians out here complained that the white people carried an unbearable odor about them. At first Kathryn had dismissed that as another of the unending rumors that made their way up and down the trail. Now she no longer doubted it. If the only whites the natives ever met were those traversing the trail, it was no wonder they complained. She tried to wash off as best she could each night. But privacy was limited, and she could do no more than use a cloth. Occasionally they would stop long enough to cordon off a place of privacy along the river and let the women bathe and wash their clothing. But that was rare. It was mid-June already, and they still had a thousand miles to go. Colonel Russell was not of a mind to spend a lot of time on making women comfortable.

She did have to admit that Russell's determination was paying off. Though it seemed as if they were barely crawling, they were three hundred miles west of Independence and making twenty or sometimes twenty-five miles per day. The people were toughened up now, and so were the teams. Kathryn marveled when Peter removed his boots and socks and she saw the bottoms of his feet. The calluses were half an inch thick and almost as tough as the leather soles of his boots. She too had toughened. She knew that, and it gave her pride. If she could just relieve the endless misery of the dust and heat . . .

Not that the Platte was a great place to bathe. It was a broad, shallow river that meandered sluggishly eastward across the nearly flat plains. Its waters were heavily silted and ran a chocolate to a reddish brown color. Unlike the Mississippi and the Missouri Rivers, which inspired such names as "the Wide Missouri," "the Father of Waters," and "the Mighty Mississippi," the Platte brought forth a host of more whimsical quips. "It's a mile wide and an inch deep." "It's too thick to drink and too thin to plow." "It's the only water you have to chew." But right now Kathryn would gladly take an opportunity to bathe, no matter what the river was like.

Fighting off the gloomy mood, she lifted her head. Peter walked stolidly along at the head of the oxen. In one hand he carried the light whip, which he rarely used, even to pop over the heads of the animals. Instead he spoke constantly to the eight oxen that pulled the oversized wagon that James Reed had built for his wife and family. Peter would call softly, coaxing, praising, geeing and hawing when they needed to turn. The animals responded like children to a beloved parent, rarely giving him a moment's problems. She smiled softly. Kathryn was proud to know that her husband was not one whit behind the other "bullwhackers" in skill and effectiveness.

She stuck her fingers inside her collar and rubbed at the grit that was there. "Peter?"

He turned. "Yes?"

"I don't care what it takes. I want you to find me a place where I can bathe tonight."

He looked surprised, then nodded. "I'll talk to Mr. Reed."

As it turned out, they camped on a small stream that was almost three miles from the river. Not even Mr. Reed, as considerate as he was, would consent to a six-mile round-trip for a bath. So once again Kathryn settled for her cloth and basin of water.

Now, with the children finally asleep, Kathryn came out of

the wagon and saw that a group had gathered around the campfire. By the firelight she recognized George and Jacob Donner; Mr. Reed; Hiram Miller, one of the Donners' teamsters; and Edwin Bryant, from the Russell camp. Mrs. Reed sat quietly beside her husband, so Kathryn moved over and sat down beside Peter. He smiled briefly at her. Then he turned back to listen carefully as Edwin Bryant was speaking. She smiled at that. Mr. Bryant was a newspaper editor from Louisville, Kentucky. He was going to California with the specific intent to return the following year and write a book concerning his travels. Anything associated with newspapers and newspapermen was of interest to Peter, and the two of them had quickly struck up a warm bond.

"So," George Donner suddenly asked of no one of them in particular, "how is Colonel Russell?"

Bryant shook his head. "Still very sick. He told me tonight he's thinking of resigning as wagon captain."

"No!" Reed exclaimed. "Is he really that ill?"

"It's dysentery," Bryant replied. "He's also tired of all the squabbling and problems."

That came as no surprise to Kathryn. The train was made up of parties going to both Oregon and California, and while they traveled together for protection, there was considerable contention between the two different groups. It had finally gotten so bitter that they split into two parties—the Oregon group and the California group. They were only a day apart from each other and often passed one another on the trail.

"I think you'll see them elect Boggs as captain if Russell withdraws," Jacob Donner said.

"Boggs!" Peter blurted. Then instantly he realized his mistake and blushed deeply.

"Boggs is a natural choice," George Donner said. "After all, he's been a governor twice, once in Kentucky and once in Missouri."

Peter glanced at Kathryn, who looked stricken. When they had first heard that Lilburn W. Boggs was among their traveling companions they had almost withdrawn. It was Boggs who had issued the infamous extermination order against the Mormons in Missouri. He made no secret of his hatred for Mormons and still was a potentially dangerous enemy.

Reed was looking at the two of them closely, suddenly understanding. "Boggs is highly respected by many in the train, though I find him to be more bluster and blow than substance."

Bryant had seen their reaction too and now was openly curious. "Where did you say you were from, Mr. Ingalls?"

"Most recently from Springfield, Illinois." Peter was suddenly wary.

"And before that?"

There was a moment's hesitation. He and Kathryn had talked about this possibility when they first decided to try to hire on with the Donner-Reed group. They had concluded that they would not flaunt their religious affiliation to anyone, but neither were they going to try to hide the fact that they were Latter-day Saints. "Originally I'm from England." He paused. "But before Springfield, we lived upriver at Nauvoo."

Bryant nodded slowly, not surprised. "You Mormons?"

Peter's head bobbed once. He glanced sideways at George Donner. He was sure Mr. Reed knew of their Church membership, but he wasn't sure if the Donner brothers did. But George Donner merely looked bored.

"Is it true that your people are heading for the Rocky Mountains?" Bryant asked.

"Yes. With the 'encouragement' of the state of Illinois." Peter pronounced the one word with soft mockery. "We are being driven out."

"That's what I understand. Shameful business."

"We haven't heard any word since we left Springfield, but we know they're out here ahead of us somewhere. My wife and I both have family with them. We hope to catch them before we reach Fort Laramie."

"And are they armed with rifles and bowie knives, and do they march with ten brass fieldpieces?"

"What?"

There was a twinkle in Bryant's eyes. "That's the story going around Independence. Supposedly five thousand Mormons crossed the Kansas River, armed to the teeth. They intend to catch and murder every emigrant they find and expropriate property for their own use."

Peter snorted in disgust. "Ha!" was all he said.

"That's what I thought," Bryant said. Then he grinned. "But I'll tell you this, that story sure has His Excellency, Lilburn W. Boggs, looking over his shoulder. I'm told he sleeps with a brace of pistols beneath his pillows every night."

"Well, first of all, we don't believe in taking revenge," Peter said, relieved to see that Bryant gave the tale no credence. "Second, the last we heard, our people were going by way of Iowa Territory. That's a long way from the Kansas River."

"Sure is," Bryant agreed. "By the way, did you know there are some other Mormons traveling with the party?"

Peter was startled. The widow Levinah Murphy, who with her family had joined the Russell train about three weeks ago, was a Latter-day Saint, but she had specifically told Peter that her fellow travelers didn't know about her religious faith and she wasn't going to say anything to anyone about it. He decided to temporize. "Really? And who might that be?"

"Thomas Rhoads and his family. Ironically they're with the Missourians." Bryant chuckled. "I asked Rhoads if the governor knows about his religion and he just laughed. He said if he did, there wouldn't be enough room under his pillows for more pistols."

"Oregon or California?" Peter asked.

"California. But they're already talking about going on ahead with some of the faster groups."

Bryant clearly felt bad that he had gotten Peter's ire up a little. "Let me tell you the other story I heard while I was in Independence, and then you'll know how much stock I put in those rumors." His smile broadened and he began to chuckle again. "I swear this is just the way it was told to me."

"Another story about the Mormons?" Reed said, feeling a little protective of Peter and Kathryn.

"No, this one is about California. But it's worth the telling."

"Like what?" Hiram Miller and Margret Reed asked at the same moment.

"Well, according to the story, which is supposed to come from an impeccable source—" He stopped and grinned sardonically. "Pardon me if I seem a little skeptical as I share it with you." He was still smiling as he went on. "Seems that there was this man who had lived his whole life in California. The climate there, which we have all heard about, was so life-giving and youth-preserving, that after two hundred and fifty years of life, he was still in the perfect enjoyment of his health and every faculty of mind and body he had ever possessed."

"Two hundred and fifty years?" Reed cried.

"Exactly," Bryant drawled. "But after having lived so long in a turbulent and unquiet world, he anxiously desired some new state of existence, unencumbered with its cares and unruffled by its passions and its strifes. In other words, he decided he wanted to die. But notwithstanding all his efforts to produce the results for which he so much wished and prayed, health and vigor and life still clung to him."

Bryant leaned back now, fully into his story and showing the gifts that made him a successful journalist. "He sometimes contemplated suicide, but the holy padres, to whom he confessed his thoughts, admonished him that down such a path lay sure damnation. Being a devout Christian, he would not disobey their injunctions.

"Then a friend of the old gentleman"—he smiled wryly—"an heir, no doubt, made a suggestion for how the man could obtain the desired results. He should make a will and complete his other final arrangements and travel into a far country."

Reed laughed aloud, seeing at least in part what was coming.

Bryant nodded, chuckling openly. "This suggestion was pleasing to our venerable California patriarch, and as soon as things were in order he departed. Sure enough, not long after he left California he took sick and died, much to his great relief."

"So that did it?" Kathryn asked, smiling. She was enjoying this.

"Well, not exactly," Bryant replied. "Seems that the old man in his will had insisted that his heir prepare his body and return it to California for burial on pain of disinheritance if his wishes were not carried out. The fellow did so, but what a disappointment that proved to be. No sooner was the old man interred in California soil, with the health-breathing California zephyrs rustling over his grave, than the energies of life were immediately restored to the inanimate corpse."

"No!" Reed slapped his leg and chortled in delight.

"Yes," Bryant said, straight-faced now. "Herculean strength was imparted to his frame, and bursting the prison walls of death, he appeared before his crestfallen heir reinvested with all the vigor and beauty of early manhood. Resigned now to his fate, he determined to live out his appointed time."

Peter was shaking his head. "Surely they didn't believe such a wild story."

"But that is what is so delightful," Bryant responded. "The man who told it to me swore that every word was true. And he was highly incensed when I seemed doubtful."

"I've heard similar things," James Reed answered, "not that wild, but they sound pretty exaggerated. The climate is supposed to be delightfully pleasant year round. You never have to light a fire except to cook food. Cabbages grow too large to fit in a cart. Lumber wagons are needed to carry half a dozen carrots or so."

Bryant nodded, then turned to Peter. "So anyway, you can see that I have some question about five thousand Mormons bearing down on us with murder in their eyes."

"I think we're safe," Reed added.

They fell silent for a few moments, still savoring the yarn that the journalist had shared with them. Then Reed turned to Bryant. "How many buffalo did the hunters see across the river today?"

He shrugged. "Eight or nine, maybe. Two big bulls, a few cows, and a couple of calves."

Reed grunted. "I think I'll go hunting tomorrow."

George Donner looked a little surprised. "We have hunters, James. And good ones."

"The 'stars,' you mean?" Reed asked with mild disdain.

Edwin Bryant said nothing but was watching the interchange with interest. Peter smiled. Two men in the train had been given the specific assignment of bringing in meat. Colonel Russell and others bragged that they were the two best buffalo hunters west of the Missouri, real stars. But in a hunt the day before, they had killed only two. James Reed, bored with the tedium of the long days, had recently taken up hunting. Three days before, he bagged a beautiful two-year-old elk. The meat had been tender and sweet, a welcome addition to their regular stores. When the two hunters announced they had shot only two buffalo from the large herd which had been visible from the train, Peter's employer started referring to them as the "perfect stars." His tone left no doubt about whether or not it was meant as a compliment.

"Now, James," George said patiently. "They're doing fine. They're going out again in the morning. If you're of a mind to hunt, why don't you go with them?"

Reed considered that, then shook his head. He turned to Peter. "How would you like to go hunting tomorrow?"

Peter was startled. "Me?" Kathryn too was surprised and stared at her husband.

"Why not? You've become a good horseman now, Peter. Hiram and I are going to try our hand at this. With Glaucus, I think I can show them perfect stars a thing or two."

"Glaucus?" Bryant broke in with surprise. "I thought your horse was a mare."

Reed grinned. "She is."

"But Glaucus is a masculine name in Latin," Bryant replied.

"That horse is so fast," Reed said proudly, "she needed a name that was worthy of her, and somehow Claudia just didn't do it. You're welcome to come too, Edwin."

Bryant raised his hands. "Not me, thank you anyway."

"Well, what do you say?" Reed said, turning back to Peter.

Peter hesitated, then nodded. This would be an exciting change of pace. "Why not?"

Chapter Notes

Edwin Bryant, a journalist and coeditor of a paper in Louisville, Kentucky, went to California in 1846. Though eventually he grew impatient and went on ahead with a pack train of mules, for a time he traveled in the same train with the Donner-Reed group and became a close friend to James Reed. He returned to the States the following year and wrote what became a highly popular book and one of the "trail bibles" for other emigrants, especially the California Forty-niners. The rumors and wild tales circulating in Independence at this time, including much of the actual wording of the story about the California patriarch, come from Bryant's book. (See *What I Saw*, pp. 15–17.) In the novel Bryant is depicted as visiting with the Reeds on the night of 14 June. Actually, he had gone ahead to help another company that night but was with the Russell train on both 13 and 15 June.

On 18 June 1846, Colonel William H. Russell did resign as captain, and it appears that Lilburn W. Boggs became the company's leader (see *What I Saw*, p. 96). Boggs eventually split off from the Donners and went to California by a different route, and thus did not participate in the tragedy that took place in the Sierra.

Chapter Two

The two hired buffalo hunters left immediately after breakfast, taking along more than half a dozen others of those they considered to be "acceptable" for their hunting party. James Reed was invited but begged off, admitting that he and a small party would be hunting on their own. That brought a disdainful laugh from the designated hunters, and they rode off still chuckling at his naivete. Reed's expression was bemused and he said nothing as he watched them ride away, but the moment they were all but out of sight he got to his feet. "Peter. Get the horses."

"Yes, sir, Mr. Reed."

Hiram Miller and Milt Elliott were waiting behind the last of Reed's wagons. They were already mounted and had Peter's horse and Glaucus. Peter took the reins and they moved forward. Milt Elliott, like Peter, was one of Reed's hired drivers. Hiram Miller was a Donner teamster but had been a longtime friend of Reed's back in Springfield.

As they returned, Peter saw Margret Reed standing close to her husband, speaking in a low voice. Peter and the others stopped, not wanting to interfere, but Reed motioned them forward.

"It will be all right, Mrs. Reed," he said, addressing her more formally as he usually did when there were others nearby. "Glaucus will serve me well."

She glanced quickly at the three who now stood just beyond them. "Yes, I know, James," she said, "but they say the bulls will charge without provocation. Tamsen Donner said she heard that a bull charged a wagon and knocked it clear over."

He smiled and kissed her gently on the cheek. "I seriously doubt that. And no bull, however determined, will be able to outrun Glaucus. We shall be fine. And tonight we shall have some tender buffalo veal for dinner."

She saw that there was no changing his mind and gave in. She nodded, pressed her cheek against his, and then stepped back.

"The other hunting party is going mostly north, so we'll ride west for a time. Just keep going and we'll find you. I expect we'll be back by noon."

"Yes, Mr. Reed," his wife said.

He turned back and looked at his three companions. "Do you know what those 'perfect stars' are calling us, boys? We're the 'sucker hunters.' What say we go remove a few of those stars from off their brows?"

Miller gave a whoop and Milt Elliott uttered an oath. As Reed swung up in the saddle, Peter walked over to Kathryn, the horse trailing behind him. He touched her cheek briefly with his free hand. "We'll be back before long."

Her eyes were large and pleading. "Be careful, Peter."

"Me?" he said gruffly. "You're worried about the world's most accomplished buffalo hunter? I find that difficult to comprehend."

She laughed and gave him a gentle shove. "Go, brave hunter," she said, shaking her head. "Just don't fall off your horse."

After crossing the river, Reed turned immediately west. He wanted to be completely clear of the other hunting party so that they could in no way take credit for his planned triumph. He and his companions had the horses at a steady, mile-eating walk, wanting to save their running strength for when it would be needed most.

"Is it true, Mr. Reed," Milt Elliott asked, "that you can't kill a buffalo by shooting it in the head?"

"That's what they say," came the reply. "They claim that the hair on the front lock of a buffalo bull is so shaggy and so matted that you can shoot a ball at five or six paces and it will merely bounce off." He was clearly warming to the subject. "While we were in Independence I spoke with some professional hunters. Allowing for exaggeration, I still think it is safe to say that the buffalo is a difficult animal to kill."

"They say they weigh about a ton," Miller piped in.

"More like seventeen or eighteen hundred pounds. They say there are only two ways to 'throw a buffalo in his tracks'—that means bringing him down with one clean shot. Either you have to cut his spine with your ball—a very difficult thing to do—or you aim a few inches above the brisket. Only then will you pierce his vitals. Even if you hit his lungs, he may run another mile or two." He slapped the horn of his saddle with delight. "That's what makes the hunt so exhilarating. Experienced hunters claim buffalo hunting is the finest sport in the world."

They rode on easily, talking through the dangers and the possibilities and savoring the expected triumphs. They had come about four miles, angling away from the river until it was no longer in sight. As they crested a gentle rise, they saw them, a large black splotch against the green expanse of prairie about a mile ahead.

Reed went up in his stirrups, squinting. "I count about thirty bulls, twice that many cows, and a lot of calves." A wide grin split his face. "What say, boys? Are you game?"

"Yes!" Miller and Elliott exclaimed. Peter nodded, but without the same enthusiasm.

As they moved slowly forward, each man began to check his weapons. Reed carried two heavy Craddock's pistols, plus a rifle in a scabbard. Miller and Elliott both had breech-loading Remington rifles. Peter carried an older-model pistol Reed had bought for him back in Springfield. Peter checked the cylinder quickly, seeing that all the chambers were loaded. He decided this wasn't the time to remind his boss that as yet he had never fired the gun and wasn't sure he could remember the instructions Reed had given him about how to do so.

Reed flashed a huge smile. "Okay, boys, let's see what us 'sucker hunters' can do."

They moved ahead at a steady walk, no longer talking. At about five hundred yards, the first bull lifted its head and turned in their direction. After a moment, the others did the same. Reed slowed them even more, fingers to his lips. At three hundred yards, the buffalo began to edge away from them. The sound of the animals' snorting carried clearly to the hunters now. What fascinated Peter was how the bulls moved to encircle the cows and calves. Like huge, shaggy watchmen, they formed a rough barrier around their charges.

Suddenly, at just over two hundred yards, the herd bolted. Off they went in a cloud of dust and flying clods of dirt, their hoofbeats rumbling like distant thunder. "Here we go, boys," Reed shouted, digging his heels into Glaucus's flanks. The thoroughbred leaped forward like a rock shot from a sling. Peter and the other two spurred after him, Miller and Elliott cutting to the right to try and head the herd off. Peter decided his safest bet was to stay close to his employer and learn from the master.

As they drew up on them, the herd was running hard now, the bulls driving the cows and calves with grunts and bellows. With a shout, all four men gave the horses their heads and plunged into the herd. As they did so, Peter had three simultaneous perceptions pop into his head. The first was the thickness of the dust. Instantly he was enveloped in a blinding cloud. He tried to pull the bandanna up and over his mouth and nose, but the horse was running so hard that he didn't dare let go of the reins. Second was the sudden keen awareness of the thundering danger on every side of him. The dark bulk of rushing animals appeared and disappeared in the murk. A cow cut suddenly left, trying to escape Reed's pursuit and nearly crashed into Peter's horse. Ahead a huge dark shape whirled and charged, deciding that attack was the best defense against the predators. Peter's horse saved him. It sidestepped quickly and the old bull lumbered past them, no more than two feet away from Peter's leg. With unbelievable clarity Peter suddenly understood that this was not child's play. It was an extremely dangerous game they were playing.

And with that realization came the third perception, and that was the sheer, intoxicating exhilaration of the hunt. The noise roared in his ears. Clods of dirt peppered his face. He was choking on the dust. But this was like nothing else he had ever experienced. Without conscious thought he clamped his legs more tightly against his horse, guiding it with a nudge this way or that. Off to his left he saw Elliott or Miller—he wasn't sure which—coming in fast, stretched forward over the saddle, rifle up and aiming. There was a puff of smoke, followed by the sound of the gunshot. Then he remembered his own pistol. He drew it out. "H'yah!" he shouted, kicking his heels into the horse's flanks and causing it to leap forward.

Reed had said that the meat of the buffalo cow was much more succulent and tender than that of the bulls. A cow was directly ahead of Peter, running at full speed, darting first one way and then another. He turned his horse in her direction. He too leaned forward, hugging the horse's neck. "Go, boy! Go!"

In a moment they were alongside. Her eyes were wild, and flecks of foam flew from her mouth. Peter raised his arm, took aim at the center of the great mass—now no more than five feet away—and fired. The pistol bucked in his hand, and there was a momentary impression of a red splotch in the dark fur. The cow grunted and veered away, running all the harder. *Shoot for the vitals*. Reed's words flashed through his mind. He cocked the hammer back again, bringing the cylinder with a fresh bullet beneath the firing pin. Yelling and shouting, barely conscious that he was doing so, he drove alongside the animal again. This time he leaned over so that the muzzle of the pistol was only three feet away from the animal's body. Again the pistol bucked in his hand, and the explosion nearly deafened him. There was a great *whoosh* from the animal's mouth. Her front legs buckled beneath her, and down she went, plowing up grass and dust like an overturned freight wagon.

Peter shot away from her, and it took him a second or two to grope for the reins and wheel his horse around. He couldn't believe it. There lay his quarry, hind legs twitching convulsively, eyes rolling in its final death struggles.

Breathing hard, he reined in again, taking in the scene around him. Ahead the prairie was a wheeling, churning mass of dust and brute beast. He could see the two teamsters spurring hard to get out ahead of a large group. There was another rifle shot, but he couldn't see through the dust who had done it. Then suddenly there was another dark shape down and kicking. He looked around for Reed but couldn't see him. Then he noticed a cloud of dust coming from behind a slight rise in the prairie.

As Peter came to the top of the rise, he pulled up. Just below him was a remarkable sight. About a quarter of the herd had come to a halt in the confines of a gentle gully. Half a dozen bulls had decided they couldn't outrun their four-legged pursuers and had stopped to fight, just as they would do if a pack of wolves ran them to ground. The cows and calves milled wildly, bawling and snorting. The bulls formed a half circle around them, shoulder to shoulder, placing themselves squarely between their charges and their enemy—the honorable James F. Reed astride his blooded mare Glaucus.

Reed had promised his wife buffalo veal for dinner tonight, and that meant he had to take one of the calves. He started in, trying to get around the bulls, but they whirled as if directed by a single head. Reed darted in another direction, Glaucus responding to his urgings. Again they wheeled and blocked his access to the herd.

"Go get 'em!" Peter yelled, sensing that this was his employer's moment and that he didn't want help. Reed lifted his head and waved, then tried again. This time he spurred hard, racing around the wall of protection, and succeeded in cutting a yearling calf away from its mother. Reed shouted, sending the young animal spurting off in panic. Away they went, only again the bulls were not to be denied their role as protectors. Three of them—one a huge old monster with patches of shaggy hair across his massive shoulders—lunged forward with incredible speed. Up and over the other side of the gully they went, cutting in between the yearling and the hunter.

Peter gave spur to his own horse, wanting to see how this turned out. Stretched out in a full lope, he came up the other side of the hill in time to see that Reed had managed to outrun two of the bulls, but the old monster still ran hard between Glaucus and the yearling, cheating Reed of the shot he wanted. They were wheeling in a large circle as the contest of wills went on, and in a few moments they were headed back in Peter's direction. He reined in, realizing he had the perfect seat for watching the unfolding drama.

Reed raced forward, trying to cut in between the yearling and the bull. In a sudden burst of speed, the bull nearly drove his horns into Glaucus's belly. Reed fell back for a moment, then shot forward again, trying to come in from the other side. In an instant the bull had changed positions and blocked him again. Peter laughed in delight. He was now cheering for the bull.

Seeing that he couldn't win this one, Reed raised one of the Craddock's and, as the old bull charged him again, placed a carefully aimed shot into the great hump of flesh. At first Peter thought he had missed the vital spot, but in a moment the bull faltered and slowed. Reed shouted triumphantly as he raced passed him and closed in on the yearling, lifting the other pistol.

This was much easier. The yearling was tiring now. Reed moved in, took aim, and fired off one shot. The calf went down, nose plowing into the dirt, and then went end over end once before slamming to the earth and coming to a halt. Without waiting to see if it got up again, Reed turned and rode back to the massive old bull.

Peter spurred forward and in a minute was at his employer's side. They both dismounted, Reed reloading his pistols. "He just wouldn't give up," Reed gasped between breaths.

"I saw." Peter watched the buffalo warily, afraid that he might charge again, but the bull was mortally wounded. It stood with its feet splayed out, swaying back and forth like some great ship at anchor. Its head was down; its black tongue lolled out of the side of its mouth. Blood was coming from its nostrils and mouth. It was likely that the bullet had gone through his lungs, for there was a wheezing sound as he breathed. His body swayed from side to side more noticeably now. The great, shaggy head lifted and the animal bellowed once more in pain and rage. Then it lowered its head again and the eyes half closed. The feet spread even farther apart as the weight became too much for it to bear.

Reed stepped forward. "I'll finish him. No sense letting him suffer." As he approached, one great cloven hoof pawed the ground, and the head swung back and forth ominously.

"Watch him," Peter called.

Nodding, Reed moved slowly forward, poised for a charge. But the great beast had charged its last. From about ten feet away Reed raised his pistol and fired. For a moment nothing happened; then the old bull slowly sank to its knees. With one final grunt, it collapsed and rolled over onto its side. The eyes closed. The old bull was dead.

For several moments the two men stared at the beast, a sudden sadness upon them. They had won, but it had been over a formidable enemy. Then Reed turned to Peter and smiled. "I can hardly wait to get back to camp. We'll see who the 'sucker hunters' are now."

Contest on the Plains

That night Peter found Kathryn a bathing spot. It was a place where some long-ago flood had scoured out a large pool near the bank. The water was almost three feet deep and quite still. Thick stands of willows and underbrush provided privacy. Unfortunately it was almost a full mile from where they were camped, and he was worried about how he would get Kathryn there and back. But when Mrs. Reed learned about what he had found, she told her husband that all of the women were going and to take them in a wagon. When word spread through the camp, they ended up with three wagons filled with women.

By the time darkness settled in—even the bravest of women would never have dreamed of bathing out-of-doors in broad daylight—there were some twenty or so women and girls frolicking in the river. Several hundred yards away the men stood beside their oxen or horses, talking quietly, smoking pipes or chewing plugs of tobacco. Peter settled on a long stem of stiff prairie grass. From time to time they would stop, looking up and smiling at each other as the sounds of girlish laughter or wild squeals floated across the stillness to them. The women had chanced into paradise and romped happily and without restraint for the limited time they would have there.

The talk among the men was mostly about the hunt. About a dozen men had gone out with the professional hunters and brought in meat from two buffalo. When Reed announced that the four of them had killed eight, including three bulls, his triumph was complete. Now the men who had come to the river wanted every detail. Peter had to tell about the killing of the bull again and again.

Finally about nine o'clock there was a call from the willows. They turned and saw a figure step out and wave. "James!" It was Margret Reed. "We're ready."

The men moved quickly to the wagons. When they reached the stand of willows, most of the others had come out to stand beside Mrs. Reed. In the pale light of a half moon, Peter saw that each of the ladies had changed to a different dress and each carried her wet laundry over her arm. Their hair was wet and stringy, but their faces were scrubbed and glowing. They were still giggling like a group of four-year-old girls as the wagons stopped for them.

Peter turned to his employer. "I say, Mr. Reed. Is that anyone you recognize?"

Reed squinted in the moonlight, leaning forward, then shook his head slowly. "The one face does look familiar, but the name escapes me."

The women laughed merrily, then trooped around to the back of the wagons and climbed in. As Peter turned the oxen around and started back, Kathryn called out from the wagon. "Mr. Reed. Peter. We have an idea how you can both become very rich."

"What is it?" Reed asked.

"Let's stop here and build a tavern," Margret Reed came in. "We'll dig a large pool out back and let the river water fill it in. Then we'll offer bathing facilities as well as a hot meal and feather beds to all the emigrant trains passing by."

Reed chuckled. "Now, there's an idea for you, Peter."

"But the baths would be only for women," Margret said.

"Yes, only women," Tamsen Donner, George's wife, chimed in.

"But," Reed protested, "how could we make a profit if only women can use it?"

"Charge five dollars a bath," Kathryn said in a matter-of-fact tone.

"Five dollars a bath!" Peter cried. "Who would pay that kind of money?"

"Only every woman who ever passed by here," Kathryn said sweetly. "That's all."

Chapter Notes

In June of 1846, James Frazier Reed wrote a letter to his brother-in-law James W. Keyes that was later published in a Springfield, Illinois, newspaper (see *Overland in 1846*, pp. 274–77). In that letter he described a buffalo hunt he had been on. Many of this chapter's details—including the use of the phrase "perfect stars," the idea of the "sucker hunters," and the killing of one old bull—come from that letter. Other details of the nature of the buffalo and of buffalo hunts of that time are taken from other early writers. The author drew heavily upon a particularly vivid description by Frederick Ruxton, a contemporary pioneer (see Bernard DeVoto, *Across the Wide Missouri* [Boston: Houghton Mifflin, 1947], pp. 35–40).

Chapter Three

Melissa Steed Rogers was alone in the store, working in the back room sorting through the latest collection of bartered goods she had acquired over the last two days. She glanced at the small clock on the fireplace mantel. It was a quarter past nine o'clock. She was startled a little by the lateness of the hour. Normally she closed the store at eight, unless she had customers, but she had become so absorbed in her task that time had been forgotten.

She quickly began to gather up the china set that she had taken in trade for fifty pounds of sugar and a small slab of bacon. Carefully placing the blue-and-white plates and saucers in the box, she saw how chipped and faded they were. It had not been a good trade, at least not for her. But the woman had looked so forlorn, so desperate. The china had been her grandmother's. It had come from Boston and been carried from Kirtland to Far West and then to Nauvoo. Now it would be left behind. Melissa simply didn't have the heart to say no.

Her shoulders lifted and fell. How she needed Carl to advise her! How she hated facing these things alone! But Carl wasn't waiting for her at home. Nor was he at the brickyard where she could go to him if she needed him. She bit her lip. *Stop it! Stop it this very moment!*

When Joshua decided to go west and help his mother, he had offered Carl the rights to his lumber business in Wisconsin. He and Melissa could keep whatever profit they could make, he said. It was an incredibly generous offer and they needed that money desperately. They hadn't received an order of any consequence at the brickyard for over a month. And the store was barely profitable. Melissa kept busy there, but mostly it was barter, and then only for peripheral goods like this set of china. Essentials were more scarce now in Nauvoo than the finest of luxuries had been before.

Carl had delayed going to Wisconsin because of the tensions in the city and the dread it had brought to Melissa. He hadn't blamed her. He said that he didn't feel he could leave with all that was going on. But there was the letter from Jean Claude Dubuque, Joshua's foreman and partner in the logging operation. The lumber, he said, would be ready for floating downriver by the first week of June. Even with Dubuque's urging, Carl had not left until the fourteenth, six days earlier, way past the time when he should have been up there.

A knock on the door brought her up with a jerk. Again she glanced at the clock and felt a little twinge of anxiety. Had something happened at home? She closed the box and grabbed her shawl, wrapping it around her shoulders, then hurried down the hall and into the main room of the store. The lamp was turned low there and shed little light through the windows. She could see that there were two large dark shapes at the door, but nothing more. At least it wasn't one of the children with news of problems at home.

Feeling a little uneasy, she moved to the door, unlocked it, and opened it a crack. "Yes?"

One of the shapes moved closer, and in the faint light of the moon she saw a bearded face beneath a broad hat. "We're looking for Carl Rogers." The voice was gruff, and she caught a whiff of cigar smoke and whiskey.

"I'm sorry, but my husband has left town and—" With a lurch of fear, she realized her mistake. "The store is closed now. You'll have to come back tomorrow." She started to shut the door again but the man shoved his foot against it.

"We have business with him. When do you expect him back?"

Her heart was thumping wildly now and her mouth felt dry. "Tomorrow," she stammered. "Maybe even tonight."

The second man hooted.

"Really?" the first man said sarcastically, showing discolored teeth through his beard. He put his shoulder against the door and shoved it open, pushing Melissa back like a small child.

"Please. The store is closed for the evening."

"Of course it is." The man stepped inside, followed immediately by his companion. The second man peered out the door, then quickly shut it. He pulled the blind down.

Now Melissa felt genuine fear. One glance at them in the light told her exactly who they were. The riffraff that rode the riverboats up and down the Mississippi all had that same look to them. A year ago Brigham Young had finally dealt with the problem by creating the "whistling and whittling brigades." But Brigham was gone now, and so were the boys who followed after the strangers, whittling on their sticks and whistling some nameless tune until the person couldn't stand it any longer and left. Clutching at her shawl, she moved back until she bumped up against the counter. "What do you want?"

The second man was looking around, his porcine eyes dark and tiny, darting here and there, taking eager inventory. The first held out his hands in a gesture of amiability. "Now, missy," he said with a condescending sneer, "we just want to look around."

"My . . . I have a neighbor who is coming to escort me home. I think you'd better go."

There was a disdainful laugh. “I don’t think so,” said the second man as he moved around behind the counter.

Melissa half turned, her head swinging back and forth to keep both men in sight. “I’ll scream,” she said, but it came out weakly.

The first man’s eyes narrowed dangerously. “You don’t want to do that.”

The second man was at the register where normally she kept what little cash came in. He pulled open the drawer and swore softly. “There’s nothing here, Jeb.”

Melissa fumbled wildly in the pocket of her apron, pulling out one crumpled bill and a few coins. “This is all I have,” she said, fighting to get control of her lower lip, which had started to tremble. Jeb came to her and looked at what she held in her palm. “We don’t do much business anymore,” she said in a small voice. “And most of that is done in trade.”

He took it from her and shoved it into his trouser pocket. “You go sit in the corner there and don’t make a peep. Then we’ll be gone”—he laughed contemptuously—“and you can wait for your neighbor to come take you home.”

Afraid that her legs might not carry her that far, Melissa meekly obeyed. She moved to the corner and sank slowly into a seat that allowed her to watch them.

Jeb found a bag of potatoes and dumped them out across the floor, then moved to the shelves. The second man went into the back room, looked around for a moment, then brought back one of the empty flour sacks Melissa had folded and stacked on the sorting counter. They worked swiftly, taking only that which was of greatest value and easily carried—two cans of gunpowder, an old pistol that no longer worked but which Carl had agreed to take because it might be fixable, some small bags of lead shot, a larger bag of salt, some women’s jewelry. If they picked something up and then decided they didn’t want it, instead of putting it back on the shelf or in a box, they flung it disdainfully aside. Soon the floor was littered with what little goods the store still had.

The one called Jeb raised his finger at her in warning to stay still, then went back into the storage area. She could hear him thumping around and an occasional crash. A few moments later he came out, his sack lumpy and hanging heavily from his hand. "All right, Levi, let's get out of here," he growled.

Melissa felt a great surge of relief. Maybe they would simply go. Maybe they . . .

Her heart dropped as Jeb gave her a long, sensuous look, then moved slowly toward her. His partner grabbed three knives from beneath a counter and shoved them in his sack. Melissa shrank back as Jeb reached her and leaned down, shoving his face close to hers. His breath was foul and she saw flecks of tobacco in his beard. "For a storekeeper, you're not a bad looker."

He reached out his hand to touch her hair. She jerked away. "Please! Take what you want. Just go."

The second man was finished now. He started toward the door. "Come on, Jeb. Let's get out of here."

"Maybe I ain't finished quite yet," he said, leering at Melissa.

"Come on," the other snapped. "What if she does have someone comin'?"

Jeb's free hand shot out and grabbed Melissa at the back of her neck. She pulled back, but he easily pulled her in closer. "Now, why you fightin' me, missy? If your hubby's gone, maybe what you need is—"

Suddenly the door flew open, crashing back against the wall with a sharp crack. "Get away from her!"

The two men jumped and whirled around. The one called Jeb let go of Melissa as if her skin had suddenly become red hot.

"Get back. Drop the sack!"

The voice came from out on the porch, beyond the light, and though it was gruff-sounding, Melissa recognized it instantly. It was the voice of young Carl, and with that realization, the instant relief that had washed over her fled.

Levi peered at the door. "We dropped the sack, mister. Show yourself."

"Keep your hands high." Now it was unmistakable. It didn't

matter how hard he was trying to sound older; this was a young boy's voice. "I've got a shotgun on you."

"It's my neighbor," Melissa managed, standing now, her voice shaky. "I told you he was coming."

Jeb and Levi looked at each other. "Ain't no more than a boy," Jeb whispered.

Levi nodded. "Bet he ain't even got a gun."

The blast of the shotgun caused both men to yelp in fear and jump wildly. Melissa also gave a startled cry. Dust and wood chips rained down from the ceiling. She looked up and saw the tight pattern of buckshot peppered into the ceiling.

"Next one's for your britches, mister. Now, git!" There was no attempt to disguise the voice now. The roar of the shotgun had suddenly made Carl old enough. "Get out of there before I lose my temper."

"Don't shoot! Don't shoot!" Jeb raised his hands even higher and started shuffling toward the door. Levi was right behind him, using Jeb as a shield. They eased out the door, then took off running. *Bam!* Another shot blasted off. There was a cry of fear and the fading sound of men running hard.

Melissa felt her knees go weak and had to reach out and steady herself against the chair. "Carl?"

"Mama," came the hoarse whisper. "Turn out the lamp so they can't see nothing."

She obeyed, fighting the trembling in her hands. The moment the light was out, she heard his footsteps on the porch. "Lock the door, Mama. We'll put the stuff away tomorrow."

She did so, still half-numb with the shock of it all. "How did you know, Carl?"

He stepped beside her, holding his finger to his lips. He double-checked the door, then took her by the elbow and guided her off the porch in the opposite direction that her invaders had fled. Only then did he answer. "Papa said I was to keep you safe."

"But how did you know there was trouble?"

He seemed puzzled. "I just suddenly had this really bad feeling, Mama. And something told me to get the shotgun."

She reached out and took his arm, suddenly unable to speak. She glanced up at his face in the dim light. He had turned fourteen in April. At twelve he had caught and then passed her in height. In the last year, whiskers had started to show—surprisingly red and soft, much like his father's, though his hair was dark. But not until this moment had she really considered him a man.

"Did they hurt you, Mama?" he said, suddenly anxious.

"No, Carl. I'm fine. Thank you for coming. I . . ." She couldn't finish, and she had to look away. Her shoulders started to shake.

He shifted the shotgun to his other hand and laid his arm across her shoulders, patting her gently. "It's all right, Mama. They're gone now."

Melissa shot up, grasping at the bedclothes, thinking for a moment that the sound was part of the nightmare she had been having—a nightmare no doubt prompted by the ordeal she had experienced earlier at the store. But now as she stared around wildly in the darkness, seeing the square of window only slightly less dark than the walls, she heard the sound again. There were three sharp bangs, then three or four more. Someone was pounding on her front door.

As she swung out of bed and groped for her robe, she heard young Carl's footsteps go past her door, moving swiftly. The pounding started again, this time followed by the faint cry of a man's voice. "Mrs. Rogers! Wake up!"

Fully awake now, heart pounding with a sudden clutch of fear, she threw her robe on and stepped out in the hallway. They kept a small candle burning there during the night because Mary Melissa was terrified of the darkness. To her surprise, the clock on the wall showed half past three. Another door opened and David looked out, eyes wide, hair wildly tousled. "What is it, Mama?"

She shook her head. "Stay here, David. Watch the children."

By the time she started down the stairs, she saw that Carl was moving across the main room toward the door. She also saw that he had the shotgun in his hand again. Melissa moved quickly and reached the door just behind him.

"Mrs. Rogers. It's Jeremiah Ogletree. Wake up!"

She recognized her neighbor's voice and motioned to Carl. He unlocked the door and opened it, stepping aside enough for his mother to move up beside him.

"What is it?" Melissa asked, alarmed now by the urgency in Ogletree's voice.

He grabbed her by the hand and pulled her out on the porch. "Look."

She turned and looked up the street. For a moment she saw nothing because she was looking straight up Granger Street. Then suddenly she gasped. To the right, in a direct diagonal line through the block, she saw an orange-red glow against the black sky.

Her hand flew to her mouth. She couldn't be positive. There were houses in between. But then she was sure, and she went as cold as death. With a cry, she plunged off the porch and began to run, her nightgown flying out behind her.

By the time they reached the store, there was nothing to be done. The flames had totally engulfed the building, crackling and roaring in the otherwise still night. People were running from everywhere, and someone shouted for a bucket brigade. But they were far too late for a bucket brigade now.

She jumped as one of the rafters collapsed into the inferno and sent up a towering ball of sparks and flames. She stared in numbed horror as flames licked the sign, which was now barely readable. The Steed Family Dry Goods and General Store. Even as she watched, the rope holding the sign burned through and it fell into the flames. With one great sob of pain, Melissa Rogers turned and buried her face against her son's shoulder.

"Oh, Will," Alice breathed, leaning her head against his shoulder, "it's as beautiful as Robinson Crusoe Island."

"I told you it would be."

"I can't wait to get off the ship and be on dry land again."

"Well, don't get too impatient. We'll have to drop anchor outside the reef and wait for a pilot to come take us into the harbor."

She groaned. "How long will that take?"

He glanced up at the sun. "It's already almost midday. By the time we get into place and anchored, it will probably be too late for today. Hopefully tomorrow."

Her mouth turned down and she looked away glumly. "Another whole day?"

He lifted her chin. "I know, I know, but after almost five months, we can stand one more day, can't we?"

"You can if there's no choice," said a cheerful voice.

They turned to see Samuel Brannan, the leader of their little group of emigrants.

"Hello, Brother Brannan." Will turned back to look at the lush green hills and the snow-white beaches that they could see beyond the breakers washing over the reef. "This is a welcome sight, wouldn't you say?"

"Indeed it is. And what makes it all the sweeter is knowing this will be our last stop before we set foot on California soil."

"Do you know yet how long we'll stay here, Brother Brannan?" Alice asked.

Brannan shrugged. "Hard to say. The captain says we have five hundred barrels of freight down below that need unloading. Then, of course, we'll have to restock the ship." He shrugged. "A week. Maybe ten days."

Alice smiled for the first time. Ten days would be a welcome boon. Their stop at the Juan Fernández Islands had given the group's morale a tremendous boost, but six more weeks at sea had faded the memory all too quickly. "And then how long to California?"

Brannan turned to Will. "You'll know that better than me."

"Captain Richardson estimates four or five more weeks, depending on the winds."

Alice turned back to look over the railing toward the approaching harbor. "It doesn't seem possible that we'll ever actually get there, does it?"

Suddenly Will leaned forward, his eyes narrowing. "I think that's a United States ship there," he said.

Alice and Brannan turned to look at the ship that rode at anchor just outside the reef. It was still about a mile away, but there was no mistaking the Stars and Stripes hanging from its halyards at the rear of the ship.

"Well, maybe we'll have some company of our own kind for a—"

"It's a warship, Brother Brannan."

If the Latter-day Saints had reservations about the sight of a U.S. warship anchored off the reef, Captain Richardson did not share them. To the dismay of his passengers, he brought the *Brooklyn* within a few rods of the USS *Congress* and dropped anchor there. Sailors lined the rail of the man-of-war and peered curiously, though for the most part silently, at the Saints who now filled the upper decks and peered back at them. The sense of misgiving was strong among the Saints, but like their captain, Will did not share it, though he understood it.

Back in January, as they prepared to depart from New York, there were growing rumors that the United States might go to war with Mexico. Because of that, there had been talk of government intervention to stop the Saints' planned voyage. Having a colony of disgruntled Latter-day Saints sailing to Mexican California was seen by some as running counter to the interests of the United States. But nothing had come of such rumors, and they had sailed without incident. Was it possible now, after five months at sea, that they were to be stopped short of their final destination? That was the question on everyone's mind.

Everyone's except Will's. In his years of sailing Will had seen more than one warship at close range, and at the moment this one was neither manned nor rigged for possible trouble. The sailors, notably subdued, showed no anger or hostility. There had been no flurry of activity when the *Brooklyn* pulled up within a few yards of the *Congress*. If they planned to give the Mormons trouble, it certainly wasn't today. Of that, Will was confident.

The anxieties of the Latter-day Saints only deepened when a man in full dress uniform—obviously the ship's captain—ordered a small boat prepared for launching, and then he and two other officers, accompanied by an armed escort, climbed aboard and were lowered to the water. Will and Alice were near the railing on the port side of the ship where they could see clearly what was happening.

Alice reached out and clutched at his arm. "What do they want, Will?" She unconsciously held the roundness of her stomach as she stared down at the approaching men. She was now just three months away from delivery of their child and worried constantly about anything that might threaten the baby. "Do you think they're coming for us?"

"Well," he said soberly, letting his voice broaden into the deep southern drawl he had mastered as a boy in Savannah, "if they ah, it sho nuff is gonna take a lawt of trips in that there little teeny boat to get us all across."

Startled, she laughed aloud. Others nearby turned in surprise. In the tense atmosphere, her laugh exploded like someone dropping an iron kettle in a church meeting. Embarrassed, she immediately suppressed a smile, giving Will a sideward look. He had done it. His absolute calm settled her fears. He was not worried in any way, and that was a tremendous relief to her.

Captain Richardson appeared, also dressed in full uniform now, something they had seen only once or twice since leaving the East Coast. He pushed his way to the rope ladder where the small boat was tying up to the *Brooklyn*. The first mate and the bosun were also there with him, standing at attention. There was a definite air of excitement and anticipation.

A moment later, the rope ladder stretched taut and began to creak. Then a plumed hat appeared, and the man Alice had assumed was the captain climbed over the rail and dropped lightly to the deck. He snapped a crisp salute at Captain Richardson, who returned it just as smartly. "Welcome aboard the *Brooklyn*, sir. Captain Abel W. Richardson at your service."

The naval officer nodded formally, then extended his hand. "Thank you. Commodore Robert F. Stockton, United States Navy, commander of the USS *Congress*." He stepped back as the other officers climbed aboard, and he introduced each one as they did so. Only two of the armed escorts came aboard. To Alice's relief, the rest stayed in the boat that had ferried them across.

Commodore Stockton looked around. "I understand you have come around the Horn with a load of emigrants from America."

Captain Richardson nodded, then turned to where Samuel Brannan and his counselors stood nearby. "Yes, sir. Let me introduce you to Mr. Samuel Brannan, Commodore Stockton. He's the leader of these good people and the one who organized the charter of the ship in New York City."

They shook hands and Brannan introduced his two counselors, E. Ward Pell and Isaac Robbins. Then to Will's surprise, Brannan motioned him forward. "And this is Will Steed, one of the leaders of our company and a sailor in his own right."

The naval officer extended his hand. "A pleasure, Mr. Steed. Whom have you sailed with?"

"Jonathan Sperryman, out of Boston, sir, on the China trade route around the Cape of Good Hope."

"Oh, yes, I know Sperryman. Met him in New Orleans a few years back. He has a fine sailing reputation."

"He was a great sailor, sir. I learned a lot from him." He turned his head. "And that's a fine ship you're sailing, sir. Forty-four guns?"

Stockton's eyebrows lifted slightly. "Exactly. You know your ships, son."

"Thank you, sir."

Stockton turned back to Samuel Brannan. "Mr. Brannan, our report says that you have about three hundred emigrants sailing for Oregon or Upper California."

Brannan nodded slowly, obviously somewhat wary. "Not quite that many, Commodore. Closer to about two hundred forty, I'd say."

"Well, Mr. Brannan, I have news that I dare say you have not heard as yet. We are at war with Mexico."

There was a collective gasp from the crowd, who had pushed in closer to hear the interchange. "War, sir?" Brannan exclaimed.

"Yes. Our two countries have already engaged in armed combat, and we are at full war now. I fully expect that our government intends to seize California from the Mexicans. We are waiting for a stores barque to join us and resupply our ship. Then we'll sail for Monterey on the California coast. I fully expect that when we arrive, the order to capture the seaport towns will already have been given."

War? For the first time Will felt a lurch of concern. The Latter-day Saints were fleeing the United States precisely because their government—county, state, and federal—had not offered them protection or allowed them to defend their rights as citizens. They were not anxious to reenter U.S. territory, nor were they comfortable with the idea of taking their families into a combat zone.

"And what is to become of us?" Brannan said, visibly rocked by the news.

"I am told that the supply ship has extra muskets and ammunition. We shall be happy to sell arms to your group if that is of interest to you."

Again there was a startled response from the listening Saints. The fear was that the navy had come to seize what arms they already owned. Now the military was offering to sell them more? That was a good sign.

"I would suggest you continue as planned," Stockton went

on. "Only I would strongly recommend that instead of sailing for Oregon you set sail for Yerba Buena, on the Bay of San Francisco, north of Monterey. There is a small Anglo-American colony there, and your people would be a welcome addition to help them hold it for the United States. Of that I am sure."

Brannan nodded slowly. The relief was evident in his eyes, but there was still some wariness as well. "We appreciate your advice, Commodore, and shall take it under consideration. We also appreciate your offer of arms and are interested in taking advantage of your kindness." He hesitated for a moment. "As you may know, sir, we have come in peace. We have no intention of joining forces with Mexico in these hostilities. Of that you can be assured, but we would like to be prepared to protect ourselves if necessary."

"That is good to hear, Mr. Brannan. I was led to believe that such would be the case."

Captain Richardson spoke up. "I believe Mr. Brannan speaks the truth, Commodore Stockton. And I can vouchsafe for these good people that they are no threat to the United States of America."

"I was not of any other opinion," the commander of the *Congress* said pleasantly.

Chapter Notes

After one hundred and thirty-six days at sea and six weeks after leaving the Juan Fernández Islands off the coast of Chile, on 20 June 1846 the *Brooklyn* arrived at Hawaii, then known as the Sandwich Islands. While waiting for a pilot to guide them to the port of Honolulu, island of Oahu, they anchored outside of the reef. There, as described in this chapter, they were met by a warship, the USS *Congress*, which was about to depart for California and participate in the war with Mexico. The *Brooklyn* did not enter the actual port for two days, 21 June being a Sunday. (See "Voyage," pp. 60–61; CS, pp. 36–38.)

Chapter Four

Even though it was not yet ten o'clock, Solomon Garrett was pouring sweat. The headband of the straw hat Jessica had woven for him was soaked, and some of the straws were working loose. The front of his shirt was darkened halfway down his chest, and though he couldn't see it, from the stickiness he suspected the back of it was the same.

He set the sickle on the ground and straightened, holding his back as he did so. Taking off his hat, he mopped at his brow with a rag he carried in his back pocket. It wasn't just the heat, though the sun was already hot. It had rained for most of the week and the air was still heavy with moisture. Just walking out to the meadow from the main center of Mount Pisgah had left him feeling clammy and prickly around his shirt collar. He arched his back, still pushing against it with his hands, trying to stretch out the stiffness in his muscles. Solomon had passed his forty-first birthday in March. He was still in excellent health, and five months on the trail had left him trim and fit. But two hours of harvesting meadow grass took it out of the best of men.

He turned and looked back, then sighed. He had cut a swath about ten feet wide and no more than fifty to sixty feet long. It looked pitifully small considering how hard he had worked. There was a brief burst of intense longing as he thought of the McCormick harvesting machine he had jointly owned with one of his neighbors back in Hancock County. Or the one Benjamin Steed had once owned, a gift from Joshua. That one had been destroyed during the 1838 Missouri persecutions. His and his partner's was sold for a pittance to help raise money for teams and a wagon. Solomon sighed again, replaced his hat, then reached for the wooden rake he had brought with him. In long, even strokes he pulled the newly cut grass into small windrows.

As they had inched their way across Iowa Territory, Brigham had decided to create semi-temporary way stations for his people. Garden Grove was the first, and because he was an excellent farmer, Solomon had been asked to stay behind to help put some crops in. He had been promised that it would be only a short time and then he could continue on to rejoin his family. The promise had been half kept. They stayed at Garden Grove for almost two weeks, and then John Taylor had said that Solomon and Jessica could move on, but not to Council Bluffs. Solomon's skills were needed in Mount Pisgah. Would he consent to stopping there for a time as well?

Solomon wasn't cutting this meadow hay for himself. He had contracted with three families who were going to winter over here at Mount Pisgah. He would cut enough hay to help see their stock through the winter. In return he would get a side of pork, a hundred pounds of cornmeal, a hundred pounds of wheat, and three gallons of molasses. That would be a great boon to the family, whether they stayed in Council Bluffs for the winter or went across the plains. Two more days, maybe three, and he would be done, and he and Jessica could take their family on. He bent over, grabbed a bunch of the meadow grasses, and went to work again.

It was an hour later when Jessica appeared. On her back in a canvas pouch that Solomon had made for her she carried little Solomon, now fourteen months old. She also carried a wicker basket in one hand. Solomon dropped the sickle and turned to watch her come across the swath he had mowed. She moved lightly. There was no touch of gray in her hair as yet, and her skin was still smooth and clear. She looked five or six years younger than him, even though she was actually almost a year older.

He smiled as he watched her. How fortunate they had been that Joshua had decided to do a little unannounced matchmaking! Solomon had been supervisor of "common schools" for Hancock County, Illinois. The state was vigorously trying to launch schools that were financed out of public funds to compete with the schools offered in the homes of individual schoolteachers. Joshua, then a successful businessman, had met Solomon in Ramus one day, and before their conversation was through he had suggested that Solomon come to Nauvoo to observe a school run by a woman named Jessica Griffith. He spoke so highly of her that Solomon had agreed.

What Joshua hadn't mentioned then was that she had been married twice before—once to Joshua himself, and once to John Griffith, who had been brutally killed at Haun's Mill. Not that it would have made a difference to Solomon. He was also a widower. So he went to Nauvoo and sat in on Jessica's school, and that, as they say, was that.

Solomon's eyes softened now as he watched her walk toward him. They both owed Joshua a great debt for his foresight.

He removed his hat and swiped at his forehead with the sleeve of his shirt. "Hello."

Jessica smiled as she came up, then turned her back to him. He lifted little Solomon out of the carrier. "You're making good progress," she said.

"I think I've got about half a load, but it's coming. I think I can have a full load by tonight. If the weather holds, I can get another one tomorrow. Then we can rest up on Sunday and leave on Monday."

"I hope so, Solomon. I'm so anxious." She held out the basket. "I brought you some food and some cool milk."

"Wonderful."

She went down to her knees and opened the basket and began to take out some bread and cheese, slices of ham, and a crock of milk. He sat down beside her. "Actually," she said with a smile, "there's news. I couldn't wait for you to come in."

"From the family?"

"From east and west."

He looked puzzled, and she laughed lightly. "A new group of families arrived from Nauvoo about an hour ago. They brought a letter from Melissa."

"Good. How are she and Carl doing?"

"I'll talk about that in a minute. Two riders also came in from Council Bluffs this morning." She was smiling now, almost laughing.

"Oh." That explained her comment about east and west. "And they also brought news of the family?"

There were sudden tears in her eyes, and she clasped her hands together in an expression of great joy. "Joshua was baptized a week ago, Solomon."

He nearly dropped the baby. "*What?*"

"Can you believe it? But the man swears it's true. He was there."

"Joshua? *Our* Joshua?" He set the baby down, who immediately toddled over to examine Solomon's wooden rake.

"Yes. He said that Joshua had been secretly reading the Book of Mormon and finally he decided it was true."

He sat back, leaning on his hands. "Well, I'll be."

"Isn't that wonderful? Caroline must be so happy. And Mother Steed."

"It seems too good to be true."

"I know. I can scarcely believe it myself." Then she frowned. "But Melissa's letter is not so good. Someone burned the store down."

He jerked forward, shocked deeply. "They what?"

"I'll let you read her letter. It was awful. Two men came and threatened her at the store. Young Carl drove them off with a shotgun. That night the store was burned to the ground."

"How terrible!"

"Melissa is really frightened, but she doesn't think Carl will hear any talk of leaving. He was still up at the pineries getting lumber when she wrote."

Just then there was a shout from behind them. Both of them turned to see.

"It's Mark," Jessica said, getting to her feet now. Her son was running hard toward them, waving his hands.

Solomon stood up beside her, feeling a sudden pull of anxiety. It was obvious that something had Mark stirred up.

"Mama, Papa!" As he reached them and pulled up short, he bent over, breathing hard.

"What is it, son?" Solomon asked. "What's the matter?"

"Brother Woodruff sent me, Pa. He wants you and Mama to come quick."

Jessica reached out and grabbed his arm. "Why, Mark? What's the matter?"

"Soldiers. There're soldiers in camp, Mama."

To say that Mount Pisgah was in an uproar would be a grave understatement. The meadow where Solomon had been cutting hay was no more than a mile from the main camp of Mount Pisgah, and they walked swiftly. By the time he and Jessica arrived back, people lined the dusty streets or stood outside the rows of cabins talking excitedly or pointing up the street. They were calling back and forth to one another. Some men had rifles.

Solomon grabbed the nearest man. "Are there really soldiers here?"

"Absolutely."

"How many?"

"Five or six," came the reply, "plus a supply wagon."

"Where are they?" Solomon asked.

"Meetin' with President Huntington and Elder Woodruff," the man responded. "Been in there for near quarter of an hour now."

"Were they armed?" Solomon asked.

"Just side arms," another man volunteered. "They didn't have them out or anything."

"Mark," Jessica said, taking her son by the shoulder. "Get Luke; then you two find Miriam and John. Stay with them until we come."

"Ah, Ma, I—"

"Do it, son," Solomon said softly.

Grumbling, he turned and trotted away. Solomon, still carrying the baby, motioned to Jessica and they started toward Wilford Woodruff's tent. They had gone only a few steps when the flap to the tent opened and William Huntington, president of the Mount Pisgah settlement, stepped outside. There was instant silence, and Solomon and Jessica stopped where they were. A moment later an officer dressed in the blue uniform of the United States Army appeared. He was followed by four more officers, and then Elder Wilford Woodruff. The officers stopped, standing close together. Elder Woodruff conferred briefly with President Huntington, who nodded, and then he turned toward the people.

"Brethren and sisters," Elder Woodruff called in a loud voice. "Would you gather in closer, please. We have an announcement to make."

The people immediately obeyed and began to push forward. In a moment, there was a tightly packed crowd of a hundred or more. There was much murmuring and whispering as the people got a closer look at the army officers. Then Elder Woodruff raised his hands for silence.

"Brothers and sisters, as most of you can see we have visitors today. They have come from Fort Leavenworth, in Indian Territory. They come on assignment from the president of the United States."

That sent a ripple through the group, and it was not purely a favorable one. There was some grumbling and a few angry mutters. Elder Woodruff ignored them. "President Huntington and I have listened to what they have to say. We think you need to hear it for yourselves. I therefore introduce to you Captain James Allen of the United States Army. Please give him your kind attention."

He stepped down and one of the officers took his place. Solomon could see the two gold captain's bars sewn onto his shoulders. Once up, he looked around. It was clear that he had sensed the mood of the crowd and was not entirely comfortable. He glanced quickly at Wilford Woodruff, smiled, though it seemed a little strained, then turned back to the crowd.

"Thank you, Mr. Woodruff. I appreciate your willingness to let us speak directly to your people." He straightened to his full height, then reached inside his jacket and withdrew a folded piece of paper. "Ladies and gentlemen, as you all know now, as of May thirteenth of this year, the United States of America is at war with Mexico. It is that circumstance which brings me to you. As your leader has indicated, I am Captain James Allen of the First Dragoons of Fort Leavenworth, which is the headquarters of the Army of the West. I come under authority of my commanding officer, who received his orders from the secretary of war in Washington. I am told that these orders originated directly from President James K. Polk himself."

He stopped, but no one moved. No one spoke. Three or four hundred pairs of eyes were fixed on him. Three or four hundred impassive faces waited to see what was coming. He unfolded the paper. "I have drafted a circular explaining things. I should like to read it to you, and then we shall leave you to consider it. We understand that your leader, Brigham Young, is at Council Bluffs, and we shall take this matter on to him. Mr. Woodruff and Mr. Huntington concur in that action, and Mr. Woodruff has agreed to send a letter of introduction with me."

Again he paused for a moment. Again there was no response. So he lifted the paper and began to read. " 'Circular to the Mormons. I have come among you, instructed by Colonel S. W. Kearny of the U.S. Army, now commanding the Army of the West, to visit the Mormon camps, and to accept the service, for twelve months, of four or five companies of Mormon men—' "

That did get a reaction. At the mention of companies of Mormon men, a buzz of surprise and dismay swept across the audience. Allen stopped, not surprised, and waited until it died out again. " 'To accept the service,' " he started again, " 'for twelve months, of four or five companies of Mormon men who may be willing to serve their country for that period in our present war with Mexico; this force to unite with the Army of the West at Santa Fe, and be marched thence to California, where they will be discharged.' "

Now the crowd was alive with sound, and Wilford Woodruff stepped up beside the captain. "Quiet, brothers and sisters," he shouted. "Please let Captain Allen finish."

"Thank you, Mr. Woodruff." He waited a moment, then lifted the paper again. " 'They will receive pay and rations, and other allowances, such as volunteers or regular soldiers receive, from the day they shall be mustered into the service, and will be entitled to all comforts and benefits of regular soldiers of the army, and when discharged, as contemplated, at California, they will be given, gratis, their arms and accoutrements, with which they will be fully equipped at Fort Leavenworth.

" 'This is offered to the Mormon people now. This gives an opportunity of sending a portion of their young and intelligent men to the ultimate destination of their whole people, and entirely at the expense of the United States, and this advanced party can thus pave the way and look out the land for their brethren to come after them.

" 'The pay of a private volunteer is seven dollars per month, and the allowance for clothing is the cost price of clothing of a regular soldier. Those of the Mormons who are desirous of serving their country, on the conditions here enumerated, are requested to meet me without delay at their principal camp at Council Bluffs, whither I am now going to consult with their principal men, and to receive and organize the force contemplated to be raised. I will receive all healthy, able-bodied men of from eighteen to forty-five years of age.' "

He looked up. "The circular is signed by myself, Captain J. Allen, and marked as being drafted at the Camp of the Mormons, at Mount Pisgah, one hundred and thirty-eight miles east of Council Bluffs, and dated with today's date, Friday, June twenty-sixth, 1846."

"It's a ruse." "A pack of lies." "How can we trust them?" "What has the United States ever done for us?" "I think they're spies, come to search out our camps before they attack us." "I say we don't let 'em go."

At that point Elder Woodruff finally raised his hands. "Brethren, brethren," he soothed. "Let's keep our emotions in check here. Our purpose is to decide what to do, not get ourselves in a lather."

The venerable William Huntington, who had been appointed by Brigham to serve as president of the Mount Pisgah settlement, turned to the Apostle. "What are your feelings, Elder Woodruff? What shall we do?"

Wilford Woodruff sat back in his chair, his piercing gray eyes thoughtful, his mouth twisted slightly in concentration. Finally, his shoulders lifted and fell. "Well, to be honest, I am inclined to wonder if they are not spies from the army. It's barely been six weeks since the Congress declared war on Mexico. I find it hard to believe that the government could move that swiftly. I also have doubts that the president of the United States is really in this."

"That's right," someone shouted. "They are spies."

"I'm glad that the United States is at war with Mexico," another one muttered. "It's God's hand in it, and I hope the government will be utterly overthrown in retribution for what they allowed to happen to us."

Wilford Woodruff shook his head slowly. "On the other hand, I am also inclined to believe that Captain Allen is a man of integrity and of his word. I trust his honor as an officer and believe that he is sincere."

"Didn't President Young have someone in Washington trying to talk to President Polk?" Solomon asked.

"That's correct, Brother Garrett," the Apostle agreed. "Brother Jesse Little, who presides over our Eastern States Mission, was asked by the Twelve to see if he couldn't get a contract from the government for us to build forts along the trail. That's why we cannot act too hastily here, brethren. We must be wise in our response. This all may be part of Elder Little's doing."

Huntington wasn't convinced. "Why would we send our best young men off with the army? We need them now more than ever."

Elder Woodruff looked around the room until his eyes stopped on Thomas Grover. He motioned him forward. "This decision is not in our hands, brethren," he said thoughtfully. "We need to take the matter before President Young. As you heard, I'm sending Captain Allen to meet with President Young." Grover was up beside him now. "Thomas, would you be willing to take a swift horse and ride for Council Bluffs ahead of our military delegation and take a letter to President Young?"

Grover nodded. "I would be happy to, Elder Woodruff."

"Good. Be prepared to leave first thing in the morning. I'll have a letter prepared." He looked around. "Brethren, please send word through the camp that our visitors are to be treated with courtesy and respect. I want no provocations while they're here. Understood?"

There were nods throughout the group, and he was satisfied. "Thank you. We shall just have to be patient and see what this latest development shall bring."

When all but David and Carl were asleep, Melissa left them in charge and slipped out of the house. She told them she needed some air, which was only partially true. When she reached the street, she turned left, or south, knowing exactly where it was she wanted to go. She walked swiftly, not lifting her head. The sun was down now, but it wouldn't be full dark for another ten or fifteen minutes. In the softening light, she couldn't bear to look to either side. This block had once brought her so much joy. Now it was a never-ending source of painful memories and poignant longings.

Due to the fact that all six of the houses along both sides of the street once belonged to members of the Steed family, it had come to be known all over town as Steed Row. Now she and Carl were the only remnants of the Steeds left in Nauvoo. Directly to the west across from her own home was the house and school that Jessica had run along with Jenny and Kathryn McIntire. Then Solomon had come, and it became Solomon and Jessica's house. Now it was owned by a man from Peoria who had opened up a tavern down on River Street. The yard was weed infested, and the fence had several slats missing.

On her left she was passing the house once occupied by Joshua and Caroline. Now the families of Calvin and Jacob Weller lived there. Two months ago they had driven up with a written bill of sale from Joshua and Caroline saying the house had been taken in trade for their wagons and ox teams. They were nice enough people, but Melissa didn't see them much. Now they had sold the house and would be leaving for Tennessee in the next few weeks.

On her right, the house that once belonged to Lydia and Nathan stood empty. She had tried to keep the flowers weeded and the grass trimmed somewhat, but with running the store—at least up to a few days ago—and trying to keep her own house and yard up, she had let it slip. She was grateful in that one small way, that Lydia wasn't here to see it.

She hunched down, walking faster. There was the home where her mother and father had first lived. Here was the place where Rebecca had given birth to her last two children. Both now stood empty and forlorn. Everywhere there were memories—of warm summer nights out on someone's porch, the children playing night games and the adults talking lazily; of winter romps and snowball fights; of sitting around the fire with her father as he told the grandchildren yet another Bible or Book of Mormon story.

Where was the Nauvoo they had known before? Where was the laughter, the smiling couples out for a walk, the children playing tag or kick the bucket in one of the paddocks? Where was the utter sense of safety, even alone on the streets at midnight? It wasn't just the fact that house after house sat empty, that here and there windows were broken or boarded up, or that once rich farmland lay unplowed and unplanted. Gardens were laid waste, fences were down, loose stock wandered through the city at will. It was as if the city itself had fallen. Everywhere you turned, taverns, pawnshops, tenpin alleys, tobacco stores now met the eye. There were even five or six houses of ill repute down on River Street, if the rumors were true. Drunkards reeled up and down the boardwalks; the scum from the river boldly whistled and jeered at women who passed by.

Finally she reached her destination. Across the street from where she stood was the two-story log house known as the Homestead, the original home of Joseph and Emma Smith in Nauvoo. It was nearly dark now, and for that she was glad. Maybe Emma was up visiting with Mother Smith or at the home of one of the neighbors. She turned, looking up and down the street to make sure she was alone, then moved quickly across the street and into the shadows of another tree that filled the corner of the Homestead's yard. She stood there for a moment, letting her eyes move slowly and the memories come swiftly. There on the east side of the house was the well. More than once she had stood there with Joseph or Emma and drunk from the cool, sweet water. She and Carl had eaten supper in that home on more than one occasion.

"Oh, Joseph," she whispered. If only she knew where he and Hyrum were buried . . . She had thought about bringing flowers, but in the first place she was afraid someone might see her and ask what they were for. In the second place, where would she put them? The Saints had gone through the elaborate deception of burying two coffins up at the temple block, but from her father and Nathan she knew the two martyred brothers were not in them. Fear that the enemies who had slain them would try to disturb the graves had caused a few trusted friends to bury them secretly. She suspected her father had known where that was and that he had told Nathan, but neither would discuss it, even in general terms.

It had been two years ago now. She glanced at the sky, now showing only lingering traces of light. It was almost eight o'clock, she guessed. John Taylor's watch had taken one of the balls fired through the window of the jail and stopped at sixteen minutes after five o'clock on the afternoon of June twenty-seventh, 1844. Two years and not quite three hours ago Joseph and Hyrum had been martyred. How many in the city would remember that today? How many would come to spend a quiet moment of memoriam?

She took a step closer to the old house. "I've come back to the faith, Joseph," she whispered. "I'm so sorry I faltered. I'm sorry I was so blind. Now the family is gone. My father is dead." She looked up guiltily. "But you would know that, wouldn't you?"

She heard men's voices, barely a murmur, coming from up the street. She stiffened, peering into the darkness, straining to hear. It seemed to come from around Joseph's stables, another half block up Water Street.

She wrapped the summer shawl more tightly around her shoulders.

"I'm sorry I didn't trust you, Joseph. But I wanted you to know I'm back." Tears welled up suddenly. "If you see Papa, will you tell him for me?"

This time there was a bark of a man's laughter. She wiped at her eyes, then turned, moving swiftly now for the lonely desolation of Steed Row.

Chapter Notes

The arrival of Captain James Allen and a few other officers at Mount Pisgah near the end of June was the first word the Church had that the United States was interested in forming a Mormon battalion. Elder Jesse C. Little knew this was an official request, but he was still on his way west with the news. The orders to the army preceded him, and thus Captain Allen's proclamation, reproduced here in its entirety based on published versions of the original, came as a tremendous shock to the Saints. (See *MHBY*, pp. 196–98; David R. Crockett, *Saints in Exile: A Day-by-Day Pioneer Experience*, vol. 1 of *LDS-Gems Pioneer Trek Series* [Tucson, Ariz.: LDS-Gems Press, 1996], pp. 396–97; *CHMB*, pp. 112–15.)

Chapter Five

Somewhere on the Oregon Trail

Dear Family,

Greetings from Peter and Kathryn, the old bullwhacker and the itinerant prairie schoolteacher. Hello to all of you. We have no way of knowing if this letter will ever reach you, but Peter and I decided we must try to get word to you. I know that you will be worried about us and we are also worried about you. Several times each day I ask myself if we were wise to leave you and find a way west with another group, but it is a great satisfaction to me to know that I am earning my own way by tutoring the children and not being totally dependent on others to care for me. Peter too is proving his value, as he has now become an experienced "bullwhacker."

I am pleased to report that trail life has been good for me. Peter and I are as brown as a couple of Indians, and getting quite used to traveling all day. With this regimen, I find myself getting a little stronger with every passing day. I can now move about the campsite with only a cane. I still use my crutches for longer distances, but I have feeling in both of my legs now and I even had some tingling in my toes the other day. The Lord has been merciful to us.

What is not good is that we recently learned that you are not out ahead of us as we have thought all along. A few nights ago, a party of trappers and mountain men coming from Oregon and headed for St. Louis arrived in our camp. They told us that there are no Mormons on the trail west of here. So the rumors we heard that you were still in Iowa are likely true. This is very disheartening, since our plan has been that once we caught up with you I would leave the Reeds and join you while Peter went on with them to California. Now it looks as though I shall have to go on to California as well until we learn where you are. I have thought about writing to you many times but despaired of finding a way to get a letter to you. But today we arrived at a well-known stopping place along the trail. It is called Ash Hollow. There is an abandoned cabin here, left by some previous trappers. It has been turned into some sort of a general post office by the emigrants. The whole outside wall is covered with notes and bulletins announcing lost horses or cattle. Inside, a recess in the wall is filled with letters which have been deposited there in hopes that someone going east will pick them up and carry them with them. That got us to thinking that maybe we could write to Melissa in Nauvoo, then ask her to send it on to you.

I was determined to write a letter and leave it at Ash Hollow, but then Mr. Reed suggested we would meet others going east, and that would be more sure than leaving it at Ash Hollow. This will give me more time to write to you.

Since you shall soon be following behind us, I should like to talk about life on the trail. I don't mean to discourage you, but out here there is a saying, "I have seen the elephant." At first I didn't know what it meant. Now I understand. Crossing the continent is like meeting a huge elephant which blocks the way. It always seems to be in your path, no matter what you do. This is not child's play out here and only the hardy seem to survive.

Some in our party have already turned back or just stopped at some creek or another and said, "This is far enough."

I am sure we are experiencing things that you will not. Our wagon train consists of different parties who have banded together more for protection than out of a sense of unity. Out here where the elephant lives, contention is easily come by. Our group is constantly bickering and fighting over trivial things. It reached a state some time back where we finally split off from one another. How this happened gives much insight into the character of our group.

Two men in the Oregon portion of our company were in partnership with one another—one had furnished the oxen and the other the wagon for the trip west. Why they ever agreed to be partners is a mystery, for they did not get along and fought with each other constantly. One night, there was a bitter argument because one of them wanted to take his oxen and go on ahead. It turned so ugly that they disrupted the whole camp. It was decided that something had to be done. Out here it is a simple democracy—the majority rules—and so a vote was taken. We in the California company outnumber those going to Oregon, and our men decided to give the wagon and team to the partner who had a wife and who was willing to work. The other man, being a bachelor, and quarrelsome and lazy as well, was to get nothing. But this decision made the Oregon party angry and they said we had no say in the matter. They took their own vote and chose another solution.

You will think I am telling a tall tale, but I saw this with my own eyes. The Oregon group decided to divide the property evenly between the two men. How do you do this when the property includes a wagon and oxen? Well, they sawed the wagon in two, right down the middle, leaving each man with half the oxen and half a wagon. The married man had the front half of the wagon and the bachelor got the back half. We drove off the next morning, leaving him standing there with the back half of a wagon, his oxen, and no way to hitch them up. Such is the folly that we have seen manifest. Our people were so disgusted, that was when we who are going to California and those going to Oregon split from each other.

Then we learned more disturbing news. Colonel Russell and others, most notably a Mr. Edwin Bryant, have left us. Mr. Bryant is a newspaper editor from Kentucky who is traveling to California so he can write a book. He is a fine man and a true gentleman. He has become good friends with Mr. Reed and also Peter. Bryant and the colonel and several others were greatly concerned that our progress was too slow. We are nearly through June and we haven't even reached Fort Laramie yet. Those with experience say that if we are not to Independence Rock (which is two hundred miles west of Fort Laramie) by the Fourth of July, there is danger of having the mountains of the Upper California closed by the snow. We will be lucky to reach Fort Laramie by Independence Day, and that is a great worry. But instead of everyone working together to help the slow ones—the very thing President Young did when we were driven out of Far West—these men are going to leave and strike out on their own. Bryant is apologetic to Mr. Reed but will not change his mind.

This leaves me sick with worry. I think even Peter is beginning to be concerned, though he tries hard not to let me see it. Mr. Reed however is still optimistic. In the book called "The Emigrants' Guide to Oregon and California," Mr. Lansford Hastings describes another route to California which bypasses Fort Hall and the Oregon Trail. It is much shorter and will save us a month. So Mr. Reed says we will be fine, though we are behind the normal schedule.

As we pass some of the more notable landmarks, I cannot help but think that you soon will be seeing these same wonders. Chimney Rock, for example. It was the most stirring sight we had seen since our departure. We first saw it at a distance of about 35 or 40 mi., standing out like some great sentinel guarding the way. It lies a mile or so south of the river and is well named. Peter says that it looks much like the great chimneys on the cotton mills around his home of Preston, England. At the base it is a rounded hill, much like a pyramid in shape, but out of the center of that rises a shaft of rock like some giant's needle rising to what Peter guesses is four hundred fifty to five hundred feet above the plains.

Then there was what is called Scotts Bluff, a few miles farther west from Chimney Rock. Some say these bluffs mark the end of the Great Plains and the very beginnings of the Rocky Mountains. How it gets its name is another interesting story about life on the trail. According to what Peter was told, a few years ago there was a party of fur trappers headed downriver for the States. There was some kind of accident near here and a Mr. Scott was severely injured and could not walk. The others left him, promising to send for him when they caught up with a larger party at a rendezvous. But when they reached the rendezvous site, they told the others that Scott had died. It was late in the season, and they feared that if they went back they would all die. They supposed that he would be dead anyway, even if they went back.

The next spring, they found Scott's bones at the rendezvous site. What is so awful and remarkable is that the rendezvous site was about sixty-five miles from where they left him. Because of his injuries, they could only suppose that he must have crawled all of that way, only to find no one there waiting for him. This is what they mean about seeing the elephant.

Buffalo play a more important part in our lives than ever I dreamed. Everywhere the eye turns there is evidence of the great beasts. We see live ones in the distance quite often, but one can scarcely turn this way or that without seeing bleached skeletons of long-dead animals on the prairie. We have left any trees behind, except for the meager stands of timber along the rivers and creeks. The prairie is as featureless as the sea. So in addition to eating buffalo meat, we use "buffalo chips"—their dried dung—as firewood. These chips are everywhere and are easily gathered, even by the children. They catch fire easily and burn quite hot and without as much odor as you might think. Without them, we would find it difficult to build cooking fires out here.

Fort Laramie, Saturday, June 27th

I have been writing this letter since mid-June, but late this afternoon we arrived at Fort Laramie, which is near the junction of the Laramie River and the North Fork of the Platte. This is a wonderful day. Though by any other standards this would seem like an outpost of the rudest and simplest sort, here in the midst of the wilderness it is the most welcome sight we have seen since leaving Independence. But the more important news is that there is a small party of trappers and emigrants from California led by a Mr. James Clyman, who is an acquaintance of Mr. Reed. They fought together in the Black Hawk War. They are returning to the States, and Mr. Reed says he is sure that his friend will carry our letter back with him. At last we have our "postman." He is going to St. Louis and will take it there. From St. Louis, it should be only a few days upriver to Nauvoo into Melissa's hands. Then I hope she will send it on to you as soon as possible.

Therefore, I shall finish quickly. We love you. We pray for you every day. We also pray for Will and Alice, who, like us, are taking a different route to the place of gathering.

All our love,
Kathryn and Peter

Kathryn handed the thick envelope to Peter, then held on to it for a moment so as to catch his attention. "Will you tell him how important this is to us, Peter?"

He nodded, and she finally let go. "Mr. Clyman seems like a decent man," he said. "I think we can trust him to see that it gets back to the States."

"Even if he wants money, Peter," she went on, the anxiety clouding her eyes, "it's urgent that we let your family know that we are now ahead of them."

"I know, Kathryn. I promise I'll talk to him. Now, you've had a long day. Try to get some rest. I'll return as soon as I can."

She smiled at him through her tiredness and nodded. "I am weary, but I am so pleased to know that someone will take our letter back."

"As am I," he said. He bent down and kissed her, blew out the lamp, then pushed through the flap. He paused for a moment, letting his eyes adjust to the darkness. Their tent was a short distance away from where the largest of the three Reed wagons was parked. He could see the lamplight through the canvas and the shadows behind it. Margret Reed was getting the children ready for bed, he guessed. Then, beyond the wagon, he saw two dark figures silhouetted against the light of Reed's campfire. Pleased, he moved forward, slowing as he approached the fire.

James Reed looked up at the sound of his footsteps. "Ah, Peter. Come join us."

"Thank you." He stepped over a log and sat down across from the two men.

He saw now that both men were smoking cigars. James Clyman reached inside his breast pocket and withdrew another one, holding it toward Peter. "Cigar?"

Reed laughed before Peter could respond. "No, Peter here is a Mormon. As you may know, Mormons don't believe tobacco is good for you."

Clyman looked surprised. "Really? Why is that?"

A little flustered, and certainly not wanting to offend the man he was about to ask a favor of, Peter hesitated for a moment. "Well," he began, "we believe that it is not good for the body."

The man from California considered that, then nodded. "You're probably right. Filthy habit, but hard to break." He put the offered cigar away again. "A Mormon, eh? Heard a lot about them, but never met one before."

"Peter's as fine as they come, Clyman. I'll vouch for that."

Pleased and surprised, Peter inclined his head. "Thank you, Mr. Reed." Then he looked to Clyman again. "You've come from California?"

"Yes siree, all the way from Mr. Sutter's fort on the American River."

"And you saw no other Mormons ahead of us on the trail?"

He shook his head. "Reed told me that you were expecting your people to be ahead of you, but there's none that we met, at least none that were admitting to being Mormons."

"It would be a large party, maybe even a thousand people."

This time the shake of his head was emphatic. "Nothing like that. You're the largest group so far. Sorry." Then he saw the envelope in Peter's hand. "A letter for the States?"

"Yes, sir. My wife was wondering—"

"Be happy to," Clyman said, cutting him off.

Peter stood and handed it to him. "If there's any charge . . ."

He gave a curt wave of his hand. "I said I'd be happy to."

"Much obliged," Peter said gratefully. "If our people are still behind us we'd like to get word to them."

"Consider it done."

James Reed was watching the other man. "Mr. Clyman and I are acquaintances from some years back. What I didn't know then was how distinguished a reputation he has out here. Mr. John Baptiste Reshaw, at Fort Bernard last night, was telling me that you were part of William Henry Ashley's Rocky Mountain Fur Company. Is that true, Clyman?"

There was a brief nod. "I'm afraid John Reshaw talks a little too much."

Reed turned to Peter. "That may not mean much to you, Peter, being from England, but Ashley was one of the pioneers in the fur trading business here in America, a competitor to John Jacob Astor's American Fur Company. Those who worked with Ashley are almost legendary in America—Jedediah Smith, William Sublette, Tom Fitzpatrick."

"Just men," Clyman said quietly. "Good men, but still just men."

"Is it true that you were one of those who discovered South Pass?" Reed asked.

"Well, *rediscovered* might be a better word. Some of the earlier explorers had talked of a broad, gentle pass over the Continental Divide. But yes, me and Jedediah found it in eighteen twenty-four."

"The Continental Divide?" Peter asked.

"Yes, where the waters are divided. Everything this side of the divide flows into the Atlantic Ocean eventually. Everything on the other side goes to the Pacific."

"Oh." It was a concept Peter had never heard before.

"Peter says that Brigham Young, the leader of the Mormons, is planning to settle around the Great Salt Lake," Reed said. "You know that territory?"

There was an amused laugh. "Sure do. In '26 me and some other trappers circumnavigated the Great Salt Lake in a bull boat. First white men to do it, far as I know. Proved there's no outlet to it. That's why it's so salty."

"It really is salty?" Peter inquired, fascinated now. "I always thought it was just a name it was given."

"Whoo-ee," the trapper said. "Take a swallow of that, and a man can choke to death. Go swimming in it and you bob like a cork in a tub of water. Can't sink."

"Really?" Reed said, looking a little dubious. Mountain men were renowned for their whopping exaggerations.

Clyman saw his look and crossed his chest. "It's true, I swear it. Don't get it in your eyes, though. Darn near blinded me." He looked at Peter. "The Valley of the Salt Lake ain't no place for a home. Nothing with two legs is gonna live there very long excepting them Utah Indians."

Peter said nothing. He wasn't about to argue with a man as knowledgeable as this one. "So when did you leave California, Mr. Clyman?" he asked.

"Well, I met up with Hastings and Hudspeth at Johnson's Ranch, which is about forty miles from Sutter's Fort, and we left there April twenty-third, just over two months ago now."

Peter's employer jerked forward. "Hastings? Not Lansford Hastings."

"Yep. One and the same."

"The same that wrote the book?"

There was a frown. "'Fraid so. Why do you ask?"

Reed had become quite animated, surprising both Peter and Clyman. "Is he traveling with you now?"

"No. We planned to rest up and recruit our stock at Jim Bridger's fort on the Black's Fork of the Green, but when we got there the place was deserted. Old Jim and his partner, Vasquez, had gone somewhere, probably up the Green to a rendezvous."

"What did you do?" Peter asked, fascinated by the man's account now.

"Well, there was some consternation among us. Hastings had planned to wait at Fort Bridger for the incoming emigrants to guide them across his new route to California and—"

"Yes!" Reed exclaimed. "He wrote about that route. We've talked much about trying it ourselves. It saves four hundred miles, they say."

Clyman was shaking his head before Reed finished. "Don't do it."

"What?"

"Don't take his new route."

Reed sat back, clearly shocked and dismayed.

"Look," Clyman went on, "you take the regular wagon track and never leave it. It's barely possible to get through if you follow it, and it may be impossible if you don't."

Reed's voice turned testy now. "There is a nigher route, and it seems to me it is no use to take such a roundabout course."

"I admit as much," Clyman said doggedly, "but that nigher route crosses a great desert and the height of the Sierra Nevada. A straighter route might turn out to be impracticable."

Stubbornness was written clearly across Reed's face. "Hastings crossed it last year. He says it is not that hard. We go around the south end of the Great Salt Lake and then head straight for California."

"Hastings doesn't know of what he speaks," Clyman shot right back. "He didn't come that way last season, though he hints that he did, especially not with wagons. He came another way to California."

"But—"

"It is true that once he reached Sutter's place he met Captain John Frémont of the U.S. Army survey party. Frémont had brought a group through a new route that cut across the great desert, then followed Mary's River and the Truckee River to the Sierra. There's a pass there—Truckee's Pass, it's called. It's high and rough terrain, but manageable by wagon. We came that way ourselves this trip and—"

Again Reed cut him off. "You took the new route coming here?"

"Yes."

"Then why do you say not to take it? Isn't it shorter?"

"We didn't have wagons, and shorter ain't always the best way, Mr. Reed," the man said flatly. "There are long stretches without water, and if you don't make that last pass over the Sierra in time . . ." He shook his head.

There were several seconds of silence. Peter watched the man who was making it possible for him and Kathryn to cross the plains. It was Lansford Hastings's book that had fired the imagination of James Reed and the Donner brothers and motivated them to form a party to go to California. Now to hear that name maligned and his proposal treated with open skepticism was clearly unsettling.

"Where is Hastings now?" Reed finally asked after the awkward silence had stretched on.

Clyman shrugged, sensing Reed's coolness. "We all figgered that it wasn't safe to stay at Bridger's fort when there was no one there. I dropped back a little and caught up with some more of our party, and then came on here. Hastings said he was going north to the Greenwood Cutoff. That bypasses Bridger's fort and cuts straight for Fort Hall. He was going to try and convince them to follow him and take his new route. Haven't seen him since."

He withdrew the stub of his cigar, now chewed into a flat, rubbery mass, and flipped it into the fire. "You do what you think is best, Reed. But I'm telling you, his route is not proven, not with wagons and a large company."

When Peter slipped beneath the covers, Kathryn stirred beside him, then rolled over, flopping one arm across his chest. "Hi," she murmured sleepily.

"Hi." He turned to her and brought her into his arms. "Sorry I woke you up."

"I wasn't asleep," she mumbled. "I was only sleeping."

"Oh." He chuckled. "Well, now you can go to sleep."

There was a soft murmur which could have meant anything. Then after a moment her head rose, and the sleepiness in her voice largely disappeared. "Did he take the letter?"

"Yes. He said he would post it in St. Louis."

"Good. Any charge?"

"None. He's a fine man. I liked him very much."

"Good."

The silence stretched on for several moments, and he wondered if he had lost her again, but then she snuggled in closer. "You were gone a long time. What did you talk about?"

"Oh, the trail, which way to go, what it's like out there. He's been a mountain man and a fur trapper. He knows the West well."

"Really? That must have been interesting."

"Yeah." He lay back on the pillow, remembering the change of mood in James Reed.

After a moment, she came up on one elbow. "What's wrong, Peter?"

He laughed in spite of himself, then kissed her nose. "Is it because you're Irish?"

"What?"

"This second pair of eyes you seem to have that sees right through me."

"Aye, that it is," she said, a lilting brogue now in her voice. "So, tell me what's bothering you."

He sighed and found her hand. "Not a lot, but just . . . I don't know. I just have this general feeling of uneasiness about things."

"Like what?"

"I'm not sure. All the bickering and contention. The fact that we've split into separate parties. Governor Boggs being our leader."

"None of that is new, Peter. What happened tonight?"

He sighed again. "Mr. Clyman thinks it is a bad mistake to take this shorter route that Lansford Hastings is proposing. Mr. Reed didn't like what he heard."

"Will he change his mind about it?"

"I don't think so."

She lay back, and he could sense her concern in the darkness.

"I trust Mr. Reed a lot, Kathryn. But . . . I don't know. It's just that everything is changing. The family is not here like we expected. We may have to go all the way to California. Now this." Then, realizing that he was only adding to her worry, he tried to lighten his voice. "I'm just tired. It'll be all right in the morning."

She rose up and kissed him softly. "I love you, Peter Ingalls."

"You do?" he said in surprise. "How come?"

"I can't think of a single reason," she answered.

He reared back. "Hey!" he cried with offended pride.

She laughed. "But isn't that the best reason of all? I don't need a reason to love you. I just do."

Chapter Notes

The details of life on the trail are taken from the various journals and reminiscent accounts of those who were there (see, for example, *Chronicles*, pp. 70–78; Boyd Gibbons, "Life and Death on the Oregon Trail: The Itch to Move West," *National Geographic*, August 1986, pp. 147–77; *What I Saw*, pp. 80, 86–91, 97–98). The sawing of the wagon in two is reported by George McKinstry, who also traveled with the Donners for a time (see *Overland in 1846*, pp. 210, 405–6). The story of Scotts Bluff as related by Kathryn here is the most common version that was told to the emigrants, but there were several variations, and there may be some legendary aspects to the tale. Incidentally, Chimney Rock, which is about thirty miles east of the present Wyoming-Nebraska border, is the most frequently mentioned landmark along the Oregon-California Trail. Today it measures 474 feet in height, having lost some thirty feet between 1846 and the present time.

James Clyman, an experienced mountain man and fur trapper, was returning to the United States from Upper California in the summer of 1846. He arrived at Fort Laramie on the same day as the Donner-Reed party and in his journal notes that "several of us continued the conversation untill [*sic*] a late hour." He and James Reed knew each other from before, having been associates in the Black Hawk War. Another of their companions in that campaign was known as Abraham Lincoln. Clyman strongly warned Reed against the proposed shortcut to California (see *Overland in 1846*, pp. 58–59; see also *WFFB*, pp. 23–29, 46–48; and *Chronicles*, pp. 82–83). Hastings's book about Oregon and California was a major factor in encouraging the great migration of 1846, and therefore Hastings was held in high esteem. Also, John C. Frémont, who was likewise held in high esteem after his military explorations, had taken the same route as Hastings was proposing. Though it was foolish to do so, this helps explain why the emigrants would trust Hastings's word over that of more experienced men like James Clyman.

The Reshaw mentioned here was actually John Baptiste Richard, an American-born trapper and mountain man who, his ancestors being French, used the French pronunciation of his last name.

Chapter Six

The first of the Saints arrived at Council Bluffs on the banks of the Missouri River late in the afternoon on Saturday, June thirteenth, a full two months later than had been originally planned. It was clear to Brigham Young and the Twelve that it was far too late in the season to take everyone across the plains to the Rocky Mountains. Even as wagon after wagon poured in from the east, the chief Apostle set to work on three primary tasks. First, they had to find a place for a winter settlement where the great majority of the Saints could wait for spring. That required negotiating with Peter Sarpy, the local Indian agent, and the tribal leaders for permission to stay on Indian lands. Fortunately the Indians—Potawatomis on the east side of the river, and Otoe and Omaha on the west—were friendly to the white man. There was no threat of hostilities except from the Pawnees, who lived farther west along the Platte River.

The second task was to find a way across the river. Deep, muddy, swift—the Missouri was too wide to bridge and too deep and treacherous to ford. There was an existing ferry at Traders Point downstream a few miles, but with close to a thousand wagons either already here or somewhere east along the trail in Iowa Territory, there was no way the Church could afford to pay to have them all ferried across. With typical pragmatism Brigham convened a council meeting on the afternoon of June twenty-first, their second Sabbath day in the area, and called for carpenters, hewers, and other laborers to begin immediate construction on a ferry of their own.

With possibilities for winter camps being investigated and a ferry under construction, that left one major task undone. At half past eleven a.m. on the twenty-eighth of June—their third Sabbath day and only the sixteenth day after arriving—the Saints assembled at Mosquito Creek for worship services. To no one's great surprise, after prayer and some brief preliminary business Brigham Young rose and began to speak on the third primary task facing the Saints.

The Steed family found a spot near the temporary rostrum and spread out their blankets on the grass. The ground was still damp from a brief but violent thundershower that ripped through the camp shortly after midnight. While it had made for a miserable night, for the moment at least it had left the air cool.

Nathan watched as Brigham came to the makeshift podium. Behind him were seven other members of the Twelve—Heber C. Kimball, Orson Hyde, Parley P. and Orson Pratt, John Taylor, George A. Smith, and Willard Richards—and Father John Smith, uncle to the Prophet Joseph and Patriarch to the Church. As Brigham moved to his place, Nathan noted the thinness of his face and the fact that his coat hung on him loosely. The last few months had taken their toll. About five foot ten inches high, Brigham had always been somewhat portly. Back in Nauvoo he rarely buttoned his coat because it couldn't quite contain his girth. Now that same coat could easily overlap its buttons by an inch or two. Nathan guessed that the chief

Apostle had lost thirty or thirty-five pounds since they had crossed the Mississippi and started west. He had also become more serious. He could still be lighthearted, displaying his razor-sharp sense of humor, but those times came less frequently now, testimony to the weight of responsibility which he carried on his shoulders. Still clean shaven when many men were letting their beards grow, Brigham looked younger than his forty-five years. As the Apostle's head came up, Nathan could see the somberness in the blue-gray eyes and the lines around his mouth.

"Brethren and sisters, I should like to speak to you of a matter relating to the situation of the Church, of the gathering of Israel, and of the building up of the kingdom of God. It is my firm testimony that God controls all things for the perfecting of the Saints and the overthrow of the wicked. I know that while an evil deed may be overruled for good, yet a good deed may bring a greater good."

He stopped and his shoulders seemed to stoop a little. He looked around, letting his eyes move from face to face. Then he seemed to sigh inwardly before straightening again. "As you know, we have come to this place much more slowly than we originally planned. Many of our brethren and sisters have yet to join us. Some have not even left Nauvoo as yet. In two days it will be the first day of July, well into the summer season.

"It is clear that we cannot, as a body, continue on to the Rocky Mountains. We do not have the means to take all of our people there this season. We have not the food. We have not the teams. We have not the strength."

Nathan saw Joshua give him a look, half of surprise, half of self-acknowledgment. Joshua had been saying that there was no way they could continue on to the West without facing major disaster.

"Something must be done and be done quickly," Brigham went on, his voice rising a little as he spoke firmly. "I feel that it is time for a good deed to be done which can bring about a greater good. I would like to propose that a vanguard company be formed and sent across the mountains immediately."

It didn't come as a total surprise. Their leader had spoken in such terms before, but for the last two weeks little had been said concerning any further western movement, and many had begun to wonder if the plans would be canceled.

The Apostle's shoulders pulled back and his voice grew stronger. "The companies must prepare teams and grain and implements of husbandry to send over the mountains immediately. The season is so far advanced that if we are going to do something, it must be done quickly. The people are not willing to let the Twelve go ahead any faster than themselves, and so we are here and can go no farther. We must send on men and teams to prepare a place for us, to plow and plant in preparation to receive us. If we do not send men ahead now, it will throw us back another year and we shall have to buy another year's provisions for our people."

He stopped. The whispering among the people had become a low undercurrent of sound. He waited a moment to let the group quiet down again, then went on. Now his voice was steady but filled with determination. "We shall take mules and horses and swift cattle. We shall travel thirty miles a day. I believe that if we choose carefully and move forward with diligence, we can make our destination in thirty-five days, time enough to plant our seed and reap at least *some* crops before the winter snows come."

Lydia's hand stole across the space between her and Nathan and took his. He looked at her. She didn't turn, but in profile he could see the gravity in her eyes. As he looked farther, he saw that same gravity on Caroline's face, in the thin line of Rebecca's mouth, in the pinched look around Jenny's eyes. A vanguard company moving thirty miles a day meant no women or children. There was no question about that.

"How many are willing to go over the mountains?" Brigham called out. "How many are willing to leave your families for a time to accomplish what must be done? I would like to put it to the vote."

For a moment nothing happened as the crowd considered

what he had said. Then one by one men started raising their hands. Nathan hesitated only a moment, then raised his. He was not surprised to see Joshua, Derek, and Matthew follow suit.

"Good, good!" Brigham exclaimed. "Let me count your numbers, for I am determined to leave my family and go if I can get any volunteers to go with me."

A few more hands lifted. There were three or four dozen hands up now.

"Wonderful, brethren. This gives me great satisfaction. I am determined that we must go."

Though it rained again that afternoon, the showers passed quickly, and by evening, when supper was done and the babies were put to bed, the air was pleasantly cool. The Steeds gathered around their main fire, sitting on chests or lengths of log because of the wet ground. The younger children were allowed to play quietly within sight of the wagons, but the older children were considered part of the family council.

By unspoken agreement, Nathan was in charge. He called on Rachel to begin the meeting with prayer, then immediately launched the discussion when she sat down again. "You know why we're here. Brigham wants volunteers for the vanguard company. We need to decide who of us should go."

Caroline's hand immediately shot up. Nathan gestured toward her. "How many?"

Nathan nodded somberly. It was the question directly on his mind as well. He looked around the circle. "That's a critical question. What do you think?"

Rebecca looked at Derek, then half raised her hand.

"Becca?" Nathan said.

"President Young said that if a man goes west with the vanguard company, other men—probably those older or younger—would be asked to help care for the families left behind."

"Yes."

"What does that mean? For example, is Matthew considered a younger man?"

Savannah giggled suddenly, looking at Joshua. "Uncle Matthew's young, but Papa's not. He's old. Maybe they'll let him stay."

"Hey!" Joshua growled, grabbing for her. She squealed and jumped away. That brought laughs from the family, but they quickly died away.

Young Joshua Steed and Luke Griffith Garrett sat next to each other. Josh was Nathan's oldest and had turned fifteen the month before. Luke was Jessica's stepson from her marriage with John Griffith. He would be fourteen in the fall. Along with his half sister, Rachel, he had come ahead with the family when Solomon and Jessica had stayed behind to help build Garden Grove and then Mount Pisgah. Josh straightened, looking solemn. "I'm almost sixteen now. I'm old enough to go."

Lydia smiled sadly at her son. "Josh, you won't be sixteen for eleven more months." Her voice caught. "If your father goes—and I think he will—then who will take care of us?"

His shoulders slumped and he sat back.

Nathan was looking at Lydia. "You think I should go?"

She nodded, suddenly near tears.

"And Matthew too," Jenny said, her own voice sounding strained.

There were several nods at that. Matthew Steed had been partners with Brother Brigham in a cabinetry business back in Nauvoo. Not only was there a warm affection between the two, Brigham almost treating Matthew as his own son, but Matthew was a skilled carpenter and a hard worker. Brigham had already drawn heavily upon his skills.

Now Derek spoke up. "I don't see how we can send more than two of us. I think we have to leave two men with the family. There's a lot to do here to get ready for winter."

Rachel, sitting beside Emily, raised one hand.

"Yes, Rachel," Nathan said.

"Mama and Papa should be here soon from Mount Pisgah, don't forget that."

Matthew jumped in. "That's right, so that makes five adult men. I think Brigham would agree to have two of us stay."

"Isn't Uncle Solomon the oldest of any of you?" Josh asked.

Now Joshua spoke. "I'm thirty-nine and Solomon is two years older than me. So yes, he's the oldest."

Caroline took his hand. "If we left the two oldest here, then—"

Joshua was shaking his head before she could finish. Caroline looked dismayed. "What?"

"We have to make the decision based on who it is best to have go, not just by age." There was a fleeting smile, tinged with sadness. "You know, if this had come three weeks ago, it would be a lot harder decision."

Nathan turned to him. "How so?"

Now the smile broadened and any touch of sorrow was gone. "Because I would have had a choice then, not being a member of the Church. Now I'm under covenant. I'm here to do whatever you and Brigham ask, Nathan." He shrugged. "Just tell me what you want me to do."

Nathan had to stop. It had come out so simply and so accepting. And this from the man who had once led the mob at Independence as they tarred and feathered the Mormons and drove them from the state.

Mary Ann stood up, eyes shining, and walked over to Joshua. She put her arms around him and held him tightly. Joshua looked surprised, then hugged her back. When she pulled away, her voice was a bare whisper. "That was for your father, Joshua. If he was here, that's what he would have done." She smiled through the tears. "He would be so proud of you."

Completely taken aback by that, Joshua could only nod. "Thank you, Mama."

Several around the fire, including Caroline, were a little teary-eyed now as well. Finally, Nathan cleared his throat. "I have a proposal. When Solomon and Jessica arrive we'll have to talk with them about it, but I propose that we send three of us with our best wagon and team."

"And the three are?" Derek asked slowly.

Nathan looked around, then let his breath out slowly in a long sigh. "I think that me and Matthew"—he glanced quickly at Caroline—"and Joshua should go with the vanguard company."

Rebecca looked up. "Nathan, are you suggesting Derek stay just because of me and the children?"

His answer was immediate and firm. "No. Solomon and Derek are our best farmers. You're going to need food to see you through the winter here. Matthew needs to go because of his skills in bridge and ferry building." There was a moment's hesitation, then a floppy grin. "And me? Well, Joshua and Matthew need someone to do the grunt work for them."

Matthew laughed shortly, shaking his head. "Me and Joshua both know why Nathan needs to go, don't we? Who else would keep us out of trouble?"

Joshua was sober. "Yes, and who else can answer all my gospel questions out there?"

The wives around the circle were nodding now, though not with any joy. Nathan looked around the circle for one last time. "Any other questions before we take a vote?"

Emily, who sat beside Rachel, tentatively raised her hand. "Papa?"

"Yes, Emmy?"

"Won't you need some young women to go with the vanguard company and cook and wash for you? Rachel and I could do that."

Though her mother looked startled, Nathan was not surprised. The vanguard company sounded like adventure, and Emily was never one to let an adventure pass her by. "Next season, Emmy. For now, you and Rachel will be as valuable to the family here as will Luke and Mark and Josh. But thank you for thinking about us."

Her head bobbed. She had already known the answer, but still had to ask.

"By show of hands, how many of you accept the proposal that three of us go."

There was only a moment's delay, and then every person raised a hand so that Nathan could see.

For the past several days they had seen rain off and on, usually accompanied by strong, blustery winds. But this Monday morning the unsettled weather had moved east. The sky was a brilliant blue, the sun already warm upon their faces as they looked out from the wagon in which they rode. Margret Reed, Virginia, and Kathryn were seated inside one of the smaller Reed family wagons, the canvas top being rolled up partway so that they could get a better view as well as catch a breeze. Milt Elliott was walking alongside the oxen, urging them forward. Laramie River—or Laramie Fork, as many of the locals called it—was off to their right about a hundred yards. Even at that distance, they could make out the sound of birds singing lustily in the trees along the banks.

"Isn't this a glorious morning?" Margret Reed said to no one in particular. There was an instant murmur of complete agreement from Virginia and Kathryn. Part of that gloriousness was being near a point of civilization again. It was just a point, and quite rudimentary at that, Kathryn thought, but after six weeks without seeing anything but animals and each other, Fort Laramie was indeed glorious.

Virginia Reed, who had turned thirteen years old the day before, sat between her mother and Kathryn inside the wagon. "Are you excited?" Kathryn asked her. "It's not every girl who gets to celebrate her birthday at a place like this." Though Virginia's birthday was past, Mrs. Reed was determined that they would find something and buy it for her. With everything that needed attention in camp the day before, they had seen but very little of the fort itself. So even though their company had left Fort Laramie yesterday afternoon and traveled on two miles, last night Margret talked her husband into letting her take Virginia and Kathryn back to the fort early this morning. Milt Elliott volunteered to unload a few things from one of the smaller wagons to make room for the three women, then agreed to drive the wagon for them. They planned to do some quick shopping and then return to the group before it moved on.

"Oh, yes," Virginia cried in response to Kathryn's question. "This is so wonderful. Just look." She waved her arm in the direction of what lay before them.

Their heads nodded. It *was* a fascinating scene, Kathryn agreed. Directly ahead of them was the fort itself. It stood all by itself on the flat plain. It was a large quadrangle, the walls of which were made of what they called "adobes," or sun-dried bricks. It enclosed an area of about three-quarters of an acre. The walls were high and surmounted by three towers, one over the front gate, and then one each at opposite corners of the walls.

But it was the scene around that main building that was so fascinating. The grounds around the fort were teeming with activity—Indians, whites, emigrants, trappers, traders, men, women, children, horses, dogs, and an occasional milk cow all moved about with great purpose. There were wagons and tents and small willow shelters. Bull boats—round craft that were made of a framework of sticks and covered with buffalo hides and which were used to carry furs downriver—were turned upside down against one wall of the fort. It was enough to give one a stiff neck, Kathryn thought, as she tried to take it all in.

"Look," Margret said, pointing toward the south. The night before last, as they had come in they had seen a huge assembly of Indian tepees—conical tents fifteen feet high made from long poles covered by brightly decorated animal skins. There must have been two or three hundred of them. Now they were all but gone. A few remained, and there were a few more of the skeletal frameworks, but that was all. Now, where they had been, Indian women and young girls swarmed everywhere. They were striking the camp, taking down the skins from the frameworks, bundling them quickly and neatly into piles. Then the poles came down. Horses stood patiently as men tied two of the long poles across their backs, and then the bundles of robes and personal belongings were piled upon them in what was known as the travois, which was dragged behind the horses. Here and there, smaller children were making miniature travois and tying them to some of the larger dogs.

"They look like they're preparing to move," Kathryn said.

"Do you think we're safe, Mama?" Virginia whispered, scooting a little closer to her mother.

"Yes, dear," Margret smiled. "Your father says the Indians here are very friendly. We have nothing to fear from them. They're probably off to hunt buffalo or something."

They had nearly reached the gate, and that now drew their attention. Through the high doors, which were tied back now, they could see inside the fort. Immediately inside was a large, open courtyard. Here both animals and people milled noisily. Around the courtyard on three sides of the fort, various buildings extended from the walls themselves—stores, mechanical shops, storerooms, offices.

"Well, Virginia," laughed Mrs. Reed. "Let's go see if we can't leave your father a little poorer today, shall we?"

Kathryn was shocked, but not really surprised, by the prices. She was wise enough to know that when all the essentials were brought upriver from Independence or St. Joseph, they would not be cheap. But she wasn't prepared for what she saw. Coffee, sugar, and tobacco were each selling for one dollar per pound. Flour was fifty cents a pint. She shook her head, calculating quickly. Two pints to the quart and four quarts to the gallon meant flour was going for four dollars per gallon measure. In Independence she had been shocked when Peter reported that flour there was selling for an outrageous two dollars a barrel for super fine and one seventy-five for fine. She wasn't sure what a barrel held, but she supposed fifteen or twenty gallons.

A slab of rock-hard bacon hung from a hook. One dollar a pound! Mr. Reed had complained of scalpers' prices in

Independence when he paid three dollars and thirty-five cents a hundred weight.

And yet if anyone was discouraged by the outrageous prices, she certainly couldn't tell. The store was like a madhouse. Every aisle was jammed with piles of skins, stacks of buffalo robes, barrels and boxes and kegs of everything from nails to smoked cod from Boston. There were well over a hundred people crammed into every inch of free space, each shouting for attention or haggling over prices at what seemed to Kathryn at the top of their lungs. She blushed at the stream of profanity that came from the mouth of one emigrant and was pleased to see that the grizzled old clerk, bearded and looking as though he had spent a thousand winters behind the counter, found it as distasteful as she did.

As she watched the bedlam around her, she saw that most of the trading by the Indians or those who looked like mountain men or trappers was done in buffalo or deer skins or in shirts, pantaloons, and moccasins made of buckskin. But the emigrants were another matter. Here the storekeepers asked for cash wherever possible, probably so they could use it to purchase more goods from the States. The travelers were also trading watches, pocketknives, tools, and the like.

Kathryn stopped where a large box of bottles sat precariously on a counter beside a case of knives and whetstones. She wrinkled her nose in obvious distaste. Whiskey! And at one dollar a pint. Eight dollars a gallon! It was shameless and tragic. She had heard the stories about how the whites were corrupting whole Indian tribes with the sale of liquor.

"Not much of a bargain, is it?"

She turned to see who had spoken to her; then her eyes widened in surprise. "Mr. Bryant."

"Hello, Mrs. Ingalls. I see you made it to wonderful Fort Laramie." There was a touch of bitterness in his voice.

"Yes, we arrived the night before last and actually moved on a couple of miles yesterday. But I thought that you had gone on ahead."

"We did, at least this far."

"Is Colonel Russell with you?"

There was a deep frown. "Kind of. Let's just say he's under the weather." He pulled a face. "Corn liquor weather."

"Oh?" Kathryn said.

"Yes," he grunted. "He was supposed to be trading our horses for mules and packs at Fort Bernard, which is downriver about eight miles. But a group of Mexicans came in with what is known as 'Taos lightning,' and when I got there Colonel Russell was as drunk as a polecat."

Kathryn couldn't hide the surprise she felt. Bryant had often been at their campfire before he had gone on ahead, but he had rarely spoken directly to her. His candor as well as his vehemence took her aback somewhat. She nodded sympathetically, not quite sure how to respond to that. Then they both caught sight of Margret Reed and Virginia. Virginia had a bolt of red velvet and a large bonnet.

"Oh," Bryant said. "There's Mrs. Reed. I'll go say hello."

"Will you tell her I'll be outside?" Kathryn said. "All of this is giving me a headache."

He laughed pleasantly. "I will." He watched her as she brought her crutches up and started away. "You manage very well with your handicap, Mrs. Ingalls. Your husband has real cause to be proud of you."

"Why, thank you, Mr. Bryant. What a kind thing to say!"

He tipped his hat. "Give my best to Peter. If there's time, I'd like to get over to your group and visit for a while; Peter and I can swap some old newspaper stories together. I'd also like to see Mr. Reed one more time before we move out ahead."

She laughed. "Peter would like that very much, and I'm sure Mr. Reed would be pleased to see you again."

To Kathryn's surprise, when Margret and Virginia Reed came out of the store ten minutes later they were accompanied by Edwin Bryant, who carried Mrs. Reed's two packages.

Seeing her look, Margret smiled. "You remember Mr. Bryant, Kathryn?"

"Yes. We had a chance to visit for a moment inside the store."

"He is going to try to visit our group out on the trail today."

"That will be good."

As they started toward the wagon, where Milt Elliott stood waiting, Bryant fell in step with them. "Well," he asked, "what do you think of Fort John?"

"I think it's wonderful. I—" Mrs. Reed stopped in midsentence, her mouth dropping open. "Look!" she exclaimed, pointing with one hand, even though she was constantly reminding her children that pointing was impolite.

They turned. Just ahead of them and to the left a column of Indians was approaching. They came on slowly but in complete silence. Around them, the whites were calling out to each other and pointing at this remarkable sight.

"What is it?" Virginia cried.

Bryant took Margret's arm and stopped their progress. The lead rider, still some thirty or so yards away, was headed so that the column would pass between them and where Milt Elliott waited with the wagon. "Sioux," he said quietly. "Let's wait here."

Kathryn shifted her weight, letting the crutches find a new place under her arms so that they were more comfortable, but she was barely conscious of what she did. She looked to the south and then understood. Now all the tepees were gone. The camp was no more. The Indians had formed into groups of a hundred or so, with the first party leading the way and the second group forming up about fifty yards behind them.

What caught her eye was the lead rider. It was not an Indian chief or warrior. It was a young maiden. She was mounted on one of the finest of their horses. She wore a dress of simple buckskin that came to her knees and left her legs bare. But the dress was gorgeously decorated with beads, ribbons, dyed porcupine quills, painted designs, and other items that Kathryn could not identify. On her feet were brightly adorned moccasins. In her hand she held a long pole. From the point of it were suspended additional decorations—a gilt ball, brightly colored feathers, freshly picked wildflowers, brass trinkets.

With her wide dark eyes and bronzed skin, she was a striking sight, as beautiful as any royalty Kathryn could imagine. She rode in complete silence, glossy black hair tied in braids, eyes fixed directly to the front, turning neither to the left nor to the right. She barely seemed to blink. Had it not been for the movement of the horse, she might have passed for a vividly realistic statue. Without even thinking about it, as the Indian maiden neared the four of them, Kathryn bowed slightly, acknowledging her passing. There was not a flicker of recognition or acknowledgment.

Directly behind the lead rider came three of what looked like their chiefs. These too were richly adorned in their ceremonial finery—feathered headdresses, bows, arrows, spears, and tomahawks held at attention, as though they were passing in review. Like their ensign bearer, they held their heads high and stared straight forward.

After the chiefs came the women and children and the old men. They directed the packhorses that pulled the travois or were loaded with packs on their backs. But here too Kathryn was struck by what a handsome people they were. They looked well fed and healthy. The women wore dresses of buckskin for the most part, but these were neatly sewn and were ornamented with beads and dyed porcupine quills. The seams of their sleeves were trimmed with long fringes. Like the maiden, their hair, black and long, was clean and well combed. Even the children were remarkably disciplined. Though here and there Kathryn saw them turn their heads to look at the gathering crowd of whites, they showed no emotion, no recognition. There was not a sound from any of them except for the quiet shuffle of hooves and the creak of harnessing. Even the dogs trailed along without barking.

Finally, bringing up the rear of the party were the warriors. Kathryn shuddered as she looked up into their implacable faces.

Slashes of brilliantly colored paint stood out on their cheeks, their chins, or their foreheads. Hair was pulled back into tight locks. All carried their weapons in utter silence. This was the stuff of which nightmares were made, she thought, for there was nothing but the coldness of death in their eyes.

"What is it, Mr. Bryant?" Margret Reed whispered. "Where are they going?"

"I think they're going to war," Bryant finally said. "Look how the warriors are painted."

"That's right," said a voice just behind them. They turned. A man with a heavy beard and dressed in fringed buckskins had come up behind them. He was nodding as he watched the marchers file past them. "They're off to make war with their most hated enemies—the Snakes and the Crows."

"With their women and children?" Kathryn asked in surprise.

"Nope. They'll go upriver about fifty miles and make camp. They'll leave the women and children in care of the old men, then head into enemy country."

"They're beautiful," Kathryn exclaimed softly. "I've never seen anything so majestic."

He nodded, seemingly pleased by her reaction. "These are the mighty Sioux. What you see are the tribal groupings—the Lakotas, the Arikaras, the Assiniboines, the Oglalas, the Tetons. You rarely see an assembly like this in one place."

"And they're all going to battle?" Bryant asked softly.

"Not just battle. This is a major war against their longtime enemies."

Now the second group was approaching, and the whites fell silent as they came abreast of them. Their interpreter nudged Kathryn gently. "See that lead chief, just behind the girl?"

"Yes." He was a fierce-looking man. His headdress of eagle feathers attached to a crown of buffalo horns spilled down past the belly of his horse. The buckskin shirt was half bloodred and half brown. Designs were painted across his chest. He carried a lance adorned with even more eagle feathers.

"With the Dakotas, or the Sioux, as we call them," the old mountain man went on, "their dress tells you all about them. It's there for either friend or enemy to read."

Bryant looked dubious. "Like what?"

"See there on his shirt? There are black lines with heads drawn above them. That means he has taken many scalps. And can you see the painted hand there below his waist?"

"Yes," Virginia said, leaning forward.

"That means he's killed someone in hand-to-hand combat."

Virginia stared at the man, and an involuntary shudder ran through her body.

"That's right," the man went on. "The tip of his lance is red to show that he has killed with it. The eagle feathers tied to his lance also are signs. A feather with a black dot means that he has killed an enemy. If the feather has a notch near the end, it means he cut someone's throat or scalped them."

Kathryn looked away, feeling sick, no longer wanting to read the "book" the man was describing. "If the feather is split down the middle, like that one near the bottom of the shaft, it means that this man has suffered many wounds in battle."

"You say they're going upriver?" Bryant asked. It was clear that even he was subdued.

"Yes."

"Will we be in danger if we continue on that way?"

The older man shook his head, his eyes somber. "Not now. It's the Crow they're after. But Lord help us if they ever decide to turn against us."

Chapter Notes

Still unaware that Captain James Allen was on his way to Council Bluffs with orders to recruit a battalion of men from the Mormons, Brigham Young spoke to the assembled Saints on Sunday, 28 June 1846, about forming a vanguard company to go west (see *MHBY*, pp. 198–201, 586–87).

The description of Fort Laramie and the prices of goods and other details all come from contemporary accounts (see *Overland in 1846*, pp. 108–9; *What I Saw*, pp. 112–13; LeRoy R. Hafen and Francis Marion Young, *Fort Laramie and the Pageant of the West, 1834–1890* [1938; reprint, Lincoln: University of Nebraska Press, 1984], pp. 119–20). It was Edwin Bryant who saw and described the procession of Sioux leaving Fort Laramie to go out to do battle with their traditional enemies, though it actually happened a few days before the Donners arrived (*What I Saw*, pp. 111–12). Having Bryant at the fort trading post on 29 June is also a liberty of the author's. The description of a chief's war dress and the symbols found thereon are also authentic (see Jules B. Billard, ed., *The World of the American Indian* [Washington D.C.: National Geographic Society, 1989], p. 277).

Several forts were built in this vicinity over the years. They were called variously Fort William, Fort John, Fort Platte, Fort Bernard, and Fort Laramie. Laramie evidently comes from the name of an early French trapper, Jacque La Ramie (various spellings), who was supposedly killed by Indians in this area about 1821. (See Hafen and Young, *Fort Laramie*, pp. 18–94.)

Chapter Seven

To Will's surprise, Alice did not look back as the wind caught the sails and the *Brooklyn* began to pick up speed. He watched her, wondering when she would, betting himself that there would come that moment when she would turn around and look back with longing on the land. It was a temptation that all but a sailor found hard to resist, that one last, longing look at dry land before surrendering to the endless vastness of the sea.

But he was wrong. They were in the bow of the boat, and as it picked up speed they could hear the hiss as its timbers slipped through the water. Almost ten minutes had passed now since clearing the reef and waving off their pilot boat. Off to their left, the majesty of what the natives called Diamond Head, a spectacularly green mountain that formed the southernmost tip of the island of Oahu, was dazzling in the morning sunlight. But even that did not turn her head. As it moved by slowly on the port side she never once turned. She reached up, gripping part of the rigging to brace herself, then leaned far forward, letting the wind blow back her hair. The breeze was stiff enough that it blew against her clothing, showing the roundness of her stomach. They were now down to three months from the time when they would be parents.

A little piqued that she wasn't cooperating with his prediction for her, he turned, looking back toward the island and the white line of surf that marked the reef. "It is a beautiful place, isn't it?"

There was a soft murmur, but she didn't turn. He leaned forward and saw that her eyes were closed as she swayed softly back and forth. "Do you smell it, Will?"

He moved to stand closer to her. "Smell what?"

She opened her eyes and looked at him in surprise. "California!"

He laughed. "We're barely ten miles out of port and you think you can smell California?"

"*Think?* I know it!" She threw out her arms, tipped back her head, and breathed deeply. "I know it."

He laughed and took her in his arms. She leaned against him and closed her eyes again. For a long moment they stood there; then she stirred slightly. "Today is June thirtieth?"

"Yes."

"And you said it should take no more than a month from here?"

He pulled a face. "Well, about that. It depends on how the winds are."

"Oh no you don't, Will Steed. You told me no more than a month, and no more than a month is what I am going to hold you to."

He chuckled softly. "Yes, dear."

"You have July, my husband, and that is all. Then I want to be in California."

"Brother Nathan Steed! Brother Nathan Steed!"

Nathan straightened. "Here." He leaned down, scraping the

last of the soap from his chin as he looked in the small square of mirror he had propped up against the tin bowl. He rinsed the razor, swabbed at his face with his towel, then hurriedly put on his shirt.

"My pa is around here," he heard Elizabeth Mary say. Buttoning his shirt, he stepped around the wagon.

It was Heber Kimball. He sat astride a horse that was still breathing heavily from having run up the bluffs from the camps below.

"Good morning, Heber."

"Mornin', Brother Nathan. I've come at the request of President Young."

He nodded, trying not to look surprised. "What can I do for you?"

Lydia had come to the tent flap and was listening closely. She held little Tricia in her arms. He glanced at her and saw the concern in her eyes.

"There'll be a meeting at ten o'clock. The President would like you there if you can."

"Certainly. Have they crossed the river yet?"

"No. They're still down in the river bottoms, but the meeting won't be there. It'll be at Elder Taylor's tent on Mosquito Creek. Know where that is?"

"I do," Nathan said. The new ferry had finally been completed on Monday afternoon, with considerable fanfare at its launching. Yesterday the leading brethren had moved their families down to the river bottoms in anticipation of moving across to the west side. That had been delayed by a heavy afternoon shower, but he expected that they would go across this morning. John Taylor, however, was still camped up here on the bluffs.

The Apostle started to rein his horse around.

"Any truth to the rumors we're hearing about Thomas Grover riding in late yesterday?"

Heber C. Kimball stopped, his face grave. "Isn't just a rumor. It's true enough."

"Are there really supposed to be army officers on their way here?" Nathan asked, disappointed that it had not proven to be just another of the many rumors that went up and down the camps.

"No," he retorted flatly. "They are not *supposed* to be coming. They got here shortly before dark last night. That's what the meeting's all about." He reined his horse around and slapped its neck. "See you there," he called as he rode away.

Lydia came out to stand beside him. Nathan took the baby from her as they both watched Elder Kimball disappear. "The army?" she said in disbelief. "Would they really dare come asking for men after all they've done to us?"

"I don't know," he said shortly, "but if they do, President Young will send them packing soon enough. We're not part of the United States anymore. We owe them nothing."

There were four other officers with the captain of the First Dragoons from Fort Leavenworth. Though they had ridden well over two hundred miles, they looked as clean and fresh as if they had just come from an officer's ball. Their blue uniforms were crisply pressed, their boots were polished until they gleamed, and their hair and mustaches were neatly trimmed.

Elders Heber Kimball, Willard Richards, and Orson Pratt had ridden up with President Young from the bottoms. Others of the Twelve, including Orson Hyde, John Taylor, and George A. Smith, were still camped on the bluffs and were also present. In addition, there were other leaders. President Young greeted the officers warmly, though with some formality, and invited them to sit in the chairs at the front inside the large tent.

The others then found places to sit on the beds or stood behind their leaders. For a moment there was an awkward silence; then Brigham cleared his throat. "Captain Allen, I understand that you have something to present to us. We are now at your service."

Allen got up, standing firmly, though not rigidly, at attention. "I do, sir. Thank you for your courtesy in receiving us." He reached inside his jacket. "I have a letter of introduction from

Colonel Stephen W. Kearny, commanding officer of the First Dragoons at Fort Leavenworth. With your permission, I should like to read that, sir."

"Proceed."

He unfolded it. "This was addressed to me and dated June nineteenth of this year."

Brigham nodded and motioned for him to go on.

" 'Sir: It is understood that there is a large body of Mormons who are desirous of emigrating to California for the purpose of settling in that country, and I have therefore to direct that you will proceed to their camps, and endeavor to raise from amongst them four or five companies of volunteers to join me in my expedition to that country.' "

There was a quiet ripple of surprise in the tent, and Captain Allen stopped for a moment. Nathan was one of those who had taken in a sharp breath. Four or five companies meant four or five hundred men—four or five hundred of their best men, because that would be what the army required.

"Go on, Captain," Brigham said quietly, giving his people a warning look.

"Thank you, sir." Allen began to read again. The facts were clear, though written in typical army formality. Each of the companies would have from seventy-three to one hundred and nine men. They would have three officers, elected by the men, and would be allowed to pick their own non-commissioned officers. Once mustered in, they were to be marched to Fort Leavenworth, where Captain Allen was to secure all necessary equipment and supplies to turn them into soldiers—uniforms, weapons, tents and traveling gear, horses, mules, wagons, and so forth.

" 'You will have the Mormons distinctly so understand that I wish to take them as volunteers for twelve months, that they will be marched to California, receiving pay and allowances during the above time, and at its expiration they will be discharged, and allowed to retain, as their private property, the guns and accouterments to be furnished to them at this post.

" 'Each company will be allowed four women as laundresses, who will travel with the company, receiving rations and the other allowances given to the laundresses of our army.

" 'With the foregoing conditions which are hereby pledged to the Mormons and which will be faithfully kept by me and other officers in behalf of the Government of the United States, I cannot doubt but that you will in a few days be able to raise five hundred young and efficient men for this expedition. Very respectfully, your obedient servant, S. W. Kearny, Colonel of First Dragoons.' "

He folded the paper, returned it inside his uniform, then straightened again to attention.

For a long moment, total silence filled the tent. Every eye was on President Young. Some seemed not at all surprised by what they had heard. Others were clearly agitated. Nathan watched their leader's face for any signs of anger or disgust. But Brigham seemed only thoughtful, almost pensive. After a few moments, he looked up. "Captain Allen, may I ask you a question?"

"Of course, sir."

"As you know, if we were to send five hundred men with you as requested, that will leave many families here without their breadwinners and protectors."

"Yes, sir." Allen seemed a little wary.

"As you also know, here and across the river from where we now sit is land that has been designated by the government as Indian land."

"Yes, sir, that's true, sir."

"Would an officer who has come to enlist men in the United States Army have the right to say to those men's families, 'You can stay on these lands till your husbands return'?"

Nathan started at that. It was something that hadn't crossed his mind. Already there had been considerable negotiations with the local Indian agent about the Saint's right to stay on Indian land, or even to trade with the Indians without working through the agent. It was clearly a subject that weighed heavily on Brigham's mind.

Captain Allen did not hesitate. "Sir, as an officer in the U.S. Army, I am an official representative of James K. Polk, the president of the United States. As his representative, I am empowered to act until I notify him of my actions and he can either ratify the decisions I make or indemnify your people for any possible damages. And I would say it is safe to say that, under the current circumstances, the president might give his permission to travel through the Indian country, stopping whenever and wherever circumstances required."

Brigham nodded thoughtfully, but Nathan could see the satisfaction in his eyes. "Thank you for that clarification."

He looked around at his leadership. "Brethren, I know there are many questions in your minds about this course of action. You should know that Brother Kimball and Brother Richards and I met last night in council on this matter, knowing that Captain Allen had arrived. I am therefore recommending that we accept this invitation and immediately proceed to help Captain Allen and his officers recruit the necessary numbers requested."

There was a collective gasp. Several looked stunned. There wasn't even going to be a discussion on this? Brother Brigham had already made up his mind? And in favor of the army?

He smiled at the looks on some of their faces. "Captain Allen, we shall send word through the camp for all of our brethren to gather near what we call the wagon stand at fifteen minutes of noon today. There I shall ask you to address them with your proposal and read to them Colonel Kearny's letter."

"Yes, sir!" There was no mistaking the relief and pleasure in his voice. "We shall be prepared. Thank you, Mr. Young. Your treatment of our request will not go without notice." He snapped to attention and threw Brigham a salute, and then he and his fellow officers left the tent.

Brigham stood slowly, looking around at those he had called. "Brethren, you shall hear my reasoning on this subject later. I'd like you all now to spread the word through the camp. I want all the brethren who are here to assemble at forty-five minutes past eleven o'clock. That is just over an hour from now, so please move quickly through the camp and extend the call."

It wasn't just men who came. Many wives came with their husbands, and the whole camp was buzzing with excitement, anger, frustration, and bewilderment. Back at his family's camp, Nathan fended off all queries. He was still a little dazed by it all, but that one simple question put by Brigham Young to the army captain had opened his eyes to a whole different way of looking at it. "Let's go hear what Brother Brigham has to say," was all he would say.

By eleven-thirty the area around what they called the wagon stand—a wagon had been stripped of its cover and a temporary podium nailed inside its bed—was crowded with people. Brigham and the Twelve were there ten minutes before the appointed hour, as were the army officers. At a quarter to twelve President Young stood and introduced Captain Allen to the people, then turned the stand over to him. The captain spoke clearly and calmly. He explained who he was and under what authority he had come. He read the letter from Colonel Kearny again and also the circular he had read to the Saints at Mount Pisgah. He paused for a moment, offered his thanks for their attention, and then sat down.

It was precisely noon when Brigham stood up again. "Brothers and sisters," he began, "I'm sure all of this has taken many of you by surprise, just as it did us. I know that there are many in this congregation, even some among our leadership, who are dismayed at what is happening. They are asking many questions about why we would grant a hearing to such a request when we have been treated so unjustly by our government in times past."

"That's right," someone called out from the back.

Brigham turned in the direction of the sound, his brows lowering. It silenced anything further. Finally he went on. "I wish you to make a distinction between this action of the general government and our former oppressions in Missouri and Illinois.

I know that many are asking, 'Is it prudent to enlist to defend our country?' I also know that if we answer in the affirmative, all will be ready to go."

He stopped for a moment. Then, nodding as if he were agreeing with his own thoughts, he went on. "Suppose we were admitted into the Union as a state, once we reach our destination. If the government did not call upon us then for service, would we not feel ourselves neglected? I say yes, we would. So let the Mormons be the first to set their feet on the soil of California. Let us answer this call for men as faithful citizens."

He turned and looked for a moment at the army officers, then back at the group of Saints. "I want you to think for a moment of the advantages that shall accrue to us in benefit for our obedience. Many of you know that some time ago I sent Brother Jesse Little to Washington to petition the United States to help us move west. We offered to build a series of forts and maintain them for the government. That has not come to pass. But Brother Little met with President Polk and put our case before him. I'm sure this opportunity to enlist men in the army is the result of his labors.

"Do you understand what that means for us? We shall send some five hundred men to the West at the expense of the United States government. Perhaps they shall even reach our final destination before we do. They will be given food and clothing and weapons, all of which they shall be able to keep as their own once their service is done. We are nearly destitute, my brothers and sisters, as you well know. And we have many more still coming, many with nothing but what they wear on their backs and feet.

"These five hundred men will receive army pay for their service. Seven dollars a month. Multiply that by five hundred and then multiply that by twelve months and you have a substantial sum of cash, cash which we desperately need to help us prepare for the winter and to see our way west. The army has agreed to send a goodly portion of those wages back to us in advance. We shall ask the battalion members to contribute much of their pay to care for their families who are left behind and also to help the Church care for our people.

"Now, there is one more thing which comes as a great advantage to us. Captain Allen has agreed to give our people permission to stay on Indian lands until we can move on to the West. Brothers and sisters, open your eyes and your hearts to what the Lord has done for us here. This is the first offer we have ever had from the government which will benefit us at the same time that we offer our services to them."

Nathan looked around. People were nodding everywhere. The anger was gone. Many seemed a little sheepish, as he himself was, that they had not seen beyond their own emotional reaction to this new development.

"My dearly beloved fellow Saints," Brigham went on, his voice softer now, "I propose that we raise those five hundred volunteers and muster them into service. If you are one of those who is willing to volunteer, I promise you that your families will be brought forward with the rest of us when it is time for us to move on. They will not be neglected in your absence. I will feed them myself, so long as my family and I have anything to eat."

He stopped, and Heber C. Kimball got up instantly to stand beside him. "Brethren, I move that five hundred men be raised immediately for service in the United States Army for the war against Mexico."

"Second that motion," Willard Richards cried from behind him.

"All in favor." Heber's fierce dark eyes scanned the congregation. Then finally he turned back to President Young, smiling in satisfaction. "The voting has been unanimous, President. I believe we can begin recruiting immediately."

By that evening the reality of the call for five hundred of their best men had finally settled in on the camps that lined the eastern bluffs of the Missouri River and the bottoms below. It was no longer a question of acceptance. There were still a few grumblers here and there, but Brigham's stirring speech that afternoon had convinced the majority that this was not only the Lord's will but also part of his plan for his people.

Around the campfires and supper tables, the talk was subdued and solemn. Families assessed what this new development meant for them. Who would volunteer? How would they get on without husbands and fathers? What did this mean for the future? Would they have to fight? They were somber questions and carried no easy answers.

For the Steeds, the main question of who would volunteer was easier. In their previous family council they had determined who would go in the vanguard company. Now they simply transferred that decision to who would go with the army. As Brigham came down from the stand and began signing up volunteers, the men of the Steed family got into line. Ten minutes later Nathan, Joshua, and Matthew had added their names to the list. Derek would stay behind with Solomon, once he and Jessica arrived from Mount Pisgah.

Now, around the campfire, they talked quietly about what this would mean. Lydia and Caroline and Jenny were especially quiet. They did not question the decision, but its impact was now all too terribly real. The vanguard company was bad enough, but now there was the possibility of war as well.

During a lull, Jenny raised her head. "I'm going to volunteer as a laundress and go with you."

Matthew jerked up as if he had been slapped. "What?"

"The letter said that each company could have four laundresses. I will be one of them."

"You're not serious!" Matthew's face had actually paled at the thought.

"I am most serious, Matthew. If you have to go, then the children and I shall go with you."

Mary Ann watched her youngest and his wife stare at each other—he in shock, she in determination.

"The letter also said that it will be a march of a thousand miles, Jenny," Matthew pointed out. "Betsy Jo is only four and little Emmeline is but fifteen months."

Her head was up and there was a touch of fire in her green Irish eyes. "And how far will I have to march with my children next spring? A thousand miles? It's not like this is our permanent home, remember. If I have to go a thousand miles one way or the other, I'll choose going with you."

"She's right, Matthew," Rebecca spoke up. "Let her go with you."

Now it was Derek's turn to be shocked. "Rebecca, this is between Matthew and Jenny."

She tossed her head, the dark hair bouncing. "No, this is a family council. We all have a right to say what we think."

"That's right," Nathan said. He too was still reeling a little from Jenny's proposal, but Rebecca was correct in calling for her voice to be heard.

Matthew was glaring at Rebecca. She didn't flinch. "Why not, Matthew? Why shouldn't Jenny go with you?"

He was shaking his head, his mouth set. "Because this is going to be a very difficult march. Going with an army is not the same as traveling with a wagon company."

"Then why do they allow laundresses to go?" Jenny shot back.

"I . . ." He shook his head again, at a loss for an answer to that. "No, Jenny. Just get it out of your head. It is not—" He stopped again, but this time it wasn't because he didn't know what to say. A figure had stepped quietly into the edge of the firelight, just behind Nathan and his mother. Matthew leaned forward, gaping. "Jessica?"

Luke's head snapped up; then his mouth dropped open. "Mama?"

Now a second figure joined the first and they both came into the full light. It was Solomon and Jessica Garrett, looking tired but smiling broadly. There were gasps, then cries of joy. Rachel shot to her feet. "Mama! Papa!"

Jessica opened her arms, and her daughter flew around the

fire and threw herself into them. Luke came right behind her, nearly knocking them both down as he joined his sister.

Now they were all up and swarming around the new arrivals. Joshua grabbed Solomon's hand and pumped it vigorously. "Solomon, what a surprise! When did you get here?"

Jessica let go of her children and stepped forward to face Joshua. "And what is this we hear about you?" she said, her voice suddenly soft with emotion. "Can it really be?"

Embarrassed, Joshua dropped his head. "It's true. Can you believe it?"

She reached out and touched his arm. "Yes, I can."

Suddenly he swept her up and pulled her close to him. "Oh, Jessie, if only I could have done this years ago. I hurt you so much."

She held him tightly in return, tears glistening in her eyes. "It has all worked out for the best, Joshua, and we are so happy for you and Caroline. So happy."

"Thank you."

As they parted again, Nathan clapped Solomon on the shoulder. "Where's your wagon?"

"About a mile from here. We weren't sure where you were."

"Then let's go get it," Derek exclaimed. "There are going to be some very happy cousins tonight."

"Oh, by the way," Solomon remembered, "I have a message for you, Nathan. I brought some letters for President Young. When I delivered them, he asked me to tell you that he'd like to see you first thing in the morning."

Again? Nathan's face showed his surprise. But then he nodded. "All right."

"They're going to start ferrying across the river in the morning."

He nodded again, still puzzled. "I'll go down first thing."

Chapter Notes

When Captain Allen arrived in Mount Pisgah on 26 June with the request for volunteers, Wilford Woodruff sent him on to Council Bluffs. He also sent Thomas Grover ahead with word of what was happening. Thus when Allen arrived at the bluffs on 30 June, Brigham Young was already aware of what was happening and had met in council with the Twelve and decided it was best to accept the invitation. He met with the army officers at ten o'clock the next morning and immediately called for a meeting of the brethren to formally support the initiative.

Some of the reasons given here by Brigham Young for accepting the invitation for volunteers were given that day. Other reasons, expounded later, are also given here to help readers understand why President Young so quickly saw the advantage to the Saints in the U.S. president's offer. Immediately after the meeting, President Young said, he "walked out as recruiting Sergeant" and "took several names as volunteers." (See *MHBY*, pp. 202–6; Larry C. Porter, "Interrupted Exodus: Enlisting the Mormon Battalion as Iowa Volunteers," in Susan Easton Black and William G. Hartley, eds., *The Iowa Mormon Trail: Legacy of Faith and Courage* [Orem, Utah: Helix Publishing, 1997], pp. 141–42.)

Chapter Eight

Nathan left before breakfast, taking one of the horses down the bluffs. He reached the ferry site a little before half past seven. Wagons were already lined up for several hundred yards along the road, and he searched them carefully as he passed to see if President Young was in the line. He was not.

When he reached the ferry he reined in for a moment to watch. The flat-bottomed ferryboat was already halfway across the river, carrying its load of two wagons and teams and the families to whom they belonged. The spot they had chosen was not the narrowest spot on the swift-moving river, but the ground on both sides was mostly level and provided a staging ground for those waiting to load and those on the other side who were unloading. Ramps had been dug on both banks to allow the wagons to drive on and off the ferry easily. A heavy rope, made in their own ropewalk a few days before, angled across to the opposite landing located some distance downstream. This allowed the current to help move the loads across. Another rope angled across upstream. Nathan didn't have to ask what that was for. Even unloaded, the ferry was too heavy to buck the current and come back the same way it had gone across. So once it was unloaded, oxen would haul the flat-bottomed boat upstream to a point about a hundred yards above where he now sat. Launching it from there allowed the current to help carry the ferry back to its original launch site.

As he watched, the ferry bulled its way, with the help of several men, into the opposite bank, and immediately the front end was lowered and the wagons began to roll off. It was satisfying to see it working, and once again Nathan was amazed at Brigham's foresight and practicality. He looked around and saw Bishop George Miller, who had been put in charge of constructing a ferry and getting it operating. He leaned forward on his horse. "Bishop Miller."

The bishop was peering intently across the river, watching the unloading activities on the other side. He turned, and then, recognizing Nathan, waved.

"Has President Young gone across yet?"

There was a shake of his head. "No. We've taken some of his wagons across, but he's still at his camp."

"And where is that? I'm requested to have a meeting with him this morning."

Miller pointed toward a stand of cottonwoods a few rods away. "He's camped just beyond that grove," he called.

Nathan waved and reined his horse around.

"Thank you for coming. I was pleased to learn that Solomon and Jessica have returned."

"Yes. It was a pleasant surprise to see them."

"Are they settled in at your camp, then?"

"Yes."

"Good. I know that you have much to do, so I appreciate your taking time to come see me this morning. I'm going to try to get my family across the river; then we've decided that

Brother Heber, Brother Willard, and myself are going to go back to Mount Pisgah to talk with the Saints about volunteering for the battalion."

"Oh?" Now, that said something about how President Young felt about this latest opportunity. Or, he corrected himself, it may be that it said something about how well President Young understood the misgivings this call had created among the Latter-day Saints. "Is there anything I can do to help, President?"

He motioned to a stool. Then, as Nathan sank down onto it, Brigham leaned back, pulling at his lip thoughtfully. Finally, he leaned forward again. "I appreciate you and the others being among the first to volunteer yesterday, Nathan."

He shrugged and explained how they had already decided in a family council who would go west. "That made it easy," he concluded.

"I see." Again he was lost in thought for a moment, then seemed to make up his mind. "Nathan?"

"Yes, Brother Brigham?"

"In most cases I'm not inclined to interfere with an individual's decision or with that of a family." He frowned, his brows furrowing deeply. "But . . ."

When he didn't go on, Nathan finally couldn't stand it. "Yes, President?"

He let out his breath in a long sigh of weariness and frustration. "The coming of the army changes everything, Nathan. Everything."

Nathan waited as the Apostle sorted through what he wanted to say. "We are losing five hundred men, the very ones we would send with a vanguard company. Don't get me wrong. It's a good thing. There's no question but what the hand of the Lord is in it."

"Yes, sir. I can see that."

Brigham looked up. "Did you pass the ferry this morning?"

"Yes, I did. It seems to be operating very well."

"It is and I'm pleased. But it is so slow, Nathan. It's maddening. It takes almost half an hour to get two wagons across and the ferry back for its next load."

"I can believe that."

"Half an hour! That means no more than four wagons per hour. Our best estimates are that we have about two thousand wagons either here or somewhere on the trail behind us."

Nathan gave a low whistle. *Two thousand!*

"Even if we run the ferry day and night, that's less than fifty wagons a day. It's going to take us well into August just to get them across the river. Then we have the problem of getting hay for our stock, finding places where we can build whole communities for our people. You think about that for a minute. Twelve to fifteen thousand people and we have to find shelter and food for all of them through the winter."

He rubbed his eyes, shutting out momentarily the images which seemed to swim before them. "There's no way we can send a large company to the Rockies this season, Nathan. That's clear now. No way at all."

Nathan nodded slowly, not really surprised.

"So that changes everything. We have to be prepared to leave first thing in the spring. It was the interminable time it took us to get across Iowa that has put us in this position. Had we gotten here in April, or even May, we could have pushed on. But now it is too late."

"I think it's wise not to extend beyond our abilities," Nathan said, still not sure why the President was telling him all of this.

"Well, that brings us back to you and your family and what we need you to do."

"We stand ready to do whatever you ask of us, Brother Brigham."

"I know you do," he said heartily. "In that way you're just like your father. Benjamin was one of those rocks the Twelve could always depend on. And that's why I've been thinking a lot about it. We do need volunteers for the battalion, but we also have to think about here and now." He paused for a moment. "And next spring. It's not too early to begin making our plans for that now." He looked up. "I'd like to give you some counsel, Nathan."

"Yes, sir. I'm listening."

"Mind you, it's only counsel. You are free to do what you feel is best."

"I understand, President."

"After thinking carefully about it, and talking with Heber, I have this recommendation. I would like to ask that you and Joshua and Matthew withdraw your names from the army list."

"All right," Nathan said slowly, completely caught off guard.

"We need all of you to help here."

"Fine." He was thinking swiftly, trying to consider what that would mean. Lydia would be ecstatic. His mother—

"I want you and Matthew to go with the vanguard company that will leave first thing in the spring, but I want Joshua to stay here."

Nathan couldn't help it. His eyebrows shot up.

"With his teamster and freighting experience, Joshua will be important in bringing the main company across the plains next summer."

"He will be disappointed in that," Nathan said hesitantly. "He doesn't want to leave his family, but he saw this call to the army as a way to prove to the Lord that he is willing to do whatever he is asked."

Brigham smiled. "Bless him for that, but tell him *this* is what the Lord wants him to do."

"I will. What about the others?"

Brigham's shoulders lifted and fell. "I hate to say this, but I think your family needs to contribute someone to the army. A lot of people look up to the Steeds as an example."

"So Solomon and Derek?"

"No, just Derek. If both could go, that would be wonderful, but we need men to bring along the rest of the families, both those of the battalion and those of the lead company. If Solomon goes, that would leave only Joshua and the boys to bring your family on to the Rocky Mountains."

Brigham stood now and came over and laid a hand on Nathan's shoulder. "I'm sorry. I know that your family had this all worked out."

"We're here to do what you think is best, President."

"I know," he said softly, "and the Lord bless you for that."

"You're disappointed, aren't you?" Caroline tried to keep the note of accusation out of her voice, but it still crept in enough to be noticeable.

"This has nothing to do with the family, Caroline. You know that."

"I would think you'd be elated that you don't have to leave us. I am."

"You think I want to leave you?" Joshua exclaimed. "Do you think that's why I decided to volunteer for the army?"

"No." She reached out in the darkness and found his hand. "I know better than that. But if President Young wants you to stay, can't you be happy about that?"

"He doesn't have confidence in me. Not that I blame him. After all, I've only been a member for less than a month."

Now she understood and she was incredulous. "Joshua, that's not why he asked you to stay."

"Isn't it? And he's right. Who knows if six months from now I'll still be willing to be a Mormon?"

"*I* know," she said quietly.

He went right on as if she hadn't spoken. "Maybe I'd get out there on the road to California and say, 'This isn't worth it. I'm going home.' "

"Do you really think that's a possibility?"

He grunted, whatever that meant.

But she wouldn't let him get away with it. "*Do you?* Do you have questions about whether or not you believe?"

"I have a million questions."

"I'm not talking about questions involving *what* you believe, Joshua. I'm talking about questions concerning *if* you believe."

There was a long silence, then a quiet but firm, "No. I don't have those kinds of questions."

"You heard what Nathan said. The President needs you here

and for next summer. It's as important to the overall work as going with the army. Can't you just accept that?"

"I'd like to, but I still wonder."

"Not all soldiers go to the battlefront, Joshua."

There was silence for a time, then a soft chuckle. "How long do you think it will be before I learn not to try to argue with you?"

"Did I just hear a, 'Yes, Caroline, you are right, as usual'?"

He laughed aloud. "Yes, Caroline, you are right."

She poked him.

"As usual."

To his surprise she didn't laugh back at him. "Joshua, who is more important? the man with a sword in his hand, or the man who brings him food so he can continue to fight? the man who fires the cannon, or the man who brings him powder and cannonballs?"

He was silent for several seconds. Then she felt him relax a little in the darkness. "You think that's why Brigham wants me here? to carry powder and ball?"

"No. Powder and ball carriers have to go to the front lines. I think Brother Brigham needs somebody to cook for the troops."

Now the silence stretched long. She finally squeezed his hand. "There's not much glory in the cook tent, is there?"

He turned to her. "Do you think that's what is bothering me, Caroline? glory?"

"No, of course not. I think what is bothering you is that you think your Commander in Chief—and I'm talking about someone in addition to President Young—doesn't think you are worthy to carry His banner."

"And you think I am?"

"Yes, but more important, I think *He* thinks you are."

"I am going with you."

Derek stopped in the middle of removing his trousers, one leg poised in the air. "I beg your pardon?"

"I'm going to volunteer as a laundress, Derek."

His foot clunked to the ground. "No, Rebecca. Don't even think about it. I thought the whole idea was crazy when Jenny brought it up."

"If Matthew were going, I'd tell him to let Jenny go too, Derek. Think about it. It would be five less people for the family here to worry about. Our family is small enough that we can travel easily. Christopher is seven now. Little Benjamin just turned four."

"And Leah is just barely a year."

"She's almost sixteen months now, Derek. And she's such a good baby. She's handled this last three months without any problems. She hasn't even been sick once."

He blew out the lamp, then climbed into the bedroll beside her. "No, Rebecca," he said when he got settled. "It's too hard. It's too dangerous for a woman."

She leaned up and kissed him gently in the darkness. "We shall see," she said sweetly.

In Nathan and Lydia's tent, the two of them lay quietly. Lydia knew that Nathan was harboring some feelings of guilt that he would be allowed to stay with his family, while Derek was asked to leave. She also knew that having the call come directly and pointedly from Brother Brigham helped mitigate those feelings immensely. As for her, she was so filled with relief that it was hard to stop from being euphoric around Rebecca.

"Pa?"

Nathan turned his head. The tent was too dark for him to see the blanket that hung from a rope and separated their sleeping quarters from that of the children. "Yes, Josh?" he whispered.

"Is it settled, then?" he asked in a low voice. "You won't be going?"

"No, son. If President Young wants me to stay, then I'll stay."

Lydia smiled, guessing how all this talk of a vanguard company and volunteers for the army must have affected the children. If she was relieved, so must they be as well.

"I'm glad for Mama, Pa."

"I'm glad for all of us," Lydia said.

She heard Josh stir in his blankets and thought he was settling back down again. But when he spoke, it brought her up with a start.

"Pa, I want to volunteer."

"What?" they burst out together.

"I want to volunteer in your place, Pa. I want to go with Uncle Derek."

Lydia was up on one elbow, shaking her head fiercely at Nathan. It was too dark to see, so she grabbed his hand and placed it against her cheek, then shook her head vigorously again.

"You have to be sixteen, son," Nathan said, still a little dazed from what he had heard.

"Pa, I'll be sixteen in a little while, before the expedition ends."

"No, Josh!" Lydia said firmly. "I won't hear of it. You're not old enough."

"Pa?" It was plaintive and soft.

"Your mother's right, son. But thank you for even thinking about it."

This time they heard him lie back, and finally they did the same. No one said anything more, and in about five minutes Lydia listened to Nathan slip off to sleep. But she did not. For a long, long time, Lydia Steed lay awake in the darkness, staring up at the top of the tent, trying to push away the horrible feeling that had come over her.

Peter rolled over, kicking aside the light sheet. Through the tent's canvas he could already feel the warmth from the first rays of the morning sun that painted their tent now. He stretched, yawned, then lifted his head enough to look at his wife.

He shook his head. Her breathing was steady and deep, and there was no question but what she was in a very different world than he was. Her hair was splayed out on the pillow, as though she had deliberately arranged it that way to make herself look particularly alluring. For a moment, as he looked at her, he was tempted to reach across and kiss her, but then he gave in to his nobler self, which prodded him to let her sleep.

He yawned again, listening for any sounds outside the tent. After a moment, he heard the stamp of a horse's hoof, and then one low bellow from an ox that sounded farther away, but no human sounds as yet. Everyone was taking this rare opportunity to sleep in beyond sunrise. Last night the decision had been made to lay over here for the holiday. In the five days since they had left Fort Laramie, the temperature had turned hot, usually tipping beyond the one-hundred-degree mark each day. With that and the increased roughness of the road, they had averaged only fourteen or fifteen miles each day. The teams were in serious need of a rest.

Without being conscious of it, Peter's face pulled into a deep frown. Five days out from Fort Laramie and they were barely seventy-five miles farther west. They were in what was known as the Black Hills now. The North Platte River had turned to the northwest—occasionally almost due north—to skirt around the range that paralleled it on the south. The mountains were beautiful—the highest were still crowned with snow—but left many in the company filled with a quiet foreboding. Was this the kind of country that lay ahead of them?

He leaned forward, arms on his knees. Today was the Fourth of July. That was the main reason for their decision to lay over. The previous evening they had caught up with the pack train of William Bryant and Colonel Russell again and by mutual agreement decided they would celebrate Independence Day together before moving on. It was also important that they recruit their teams.

Peter did some mental figuring. They were still about twelve hundred miles from California. At fifteen miles per day—he shook his head. You couldn't travel every day. Both people and animals had to rest. Figure sixty miles per week, he decided. He drew with his finger, using his palm as a writing tablet to do the arithmetic. He shook his head, not believing his answer, then figured again. Now his mouth turned down distinctly. Twelve hundred miles at sixty miles a week was twenty weeks, or about five months. No cause for worry, he thought bitterly. That would only put them in the Sierra Nevada sometime in mid-December.

"My goodness, what is wrong, Peter?"

He turned, surprised to see Kathryn watching him. She hadn't stirred, but she was wide awake and looking at him curiously.

"The furrows in your forehead are deep enough to plant corn in. What is wrong?"

He lay back down, turning on his side to look at her. "Nothing. I was just thinking. How did you sleep?"

"Oh, no. Tell me what you were thinking and what you were writing on your palm."

He surrendered, knowing she wouldn't let it be until he told her. "You know me. I was just being gloomy."

She leaned her head in closer to him until their foreheads touched. "There really has been something bothering you lately, Peter. What is it?"

He considered that, not wanting to depress her but at the same time feeling a need to try and put it into words for his own sake. "I don't know, Kathryn. Ever since we arrived at Fort Laramie, I haven't been able to shake off this worry."

"Worry about what?"

"That's just it. That's what is so stupid. I don't know, at least not in specific terms." He shrugged, deciding not to share his calculations. "One thing is the spirit of the company. Like the drinking."

She frowned at that. She hated it even more than he did. It was as if the company had been wandering in a trackless desert, perishing of thirst, then unexpectedly had come upon a spring—only in this case the spring was Fort Laramie and the water was whiskey. And at a dollar a pint! The cost had made no difference to the travelers. With the holiday, everyone seemed to feel like drinking at the spring. By dark the previous night when she and Peter had tried to sleep, it had been impossible. A man passed by, ranting and raving, his mouth as foul as anything Kathryn had ever heard. In a nearby tent another man raged at his children because they refused to stop crying. There was hooting and hollering; drunken brawls; a knife fight when one man, still carrying a bottle in his hand, grabbed for his best friend's wife. His folly cost him a five-inch gash in his upper arm. About midnight someone tripped over a tent rope in the darkness and crashed into it, pulling it down on its inhabitants. Men of normal reserve and decency howled like savages. They made the most inane comments and thought themselves hilarious.

"But it's more than that too," he went on. "It's the bickering, fighting, racing ahead to see who can grab the best campsite or turn their stock out on the richest grass or pitch their tent nearest to the stream. There's no spirit of cooperation, no caring about others. How can the Lord bless our endeavors if that's how we act?"

Before she could answer, a rifle shot rang through the camp. "Happy birthday, America!" someone shouted. Then a pistol started firing one explosive round after another. Kathryn laughed. "Someone is starting the celebration a little early."

He smiled, then nodded. "Happy Independence Day, Kathryn McIntire."

"The same to you, Peter Ingalls. Do you think they'll let an Irish lass and an English lad join their American party?"

He made a face, looking fierce. "They'd better. I'd dare say we love America as much or more than anyone else in the group."

Chapter Notes

The Black Hills referred to in the journals of those who passed along the Oregon Trail are not the present-day Black Hills of South Dakota. They are a range of mountains that stretch from west of Fort Laramie all the way to present-day Casper, Wyoming. They likely got their name from the pine forests that cover the lower slopes and look quite black from a distance.

Other terms often found in the journals need some explanation. To "noon" meant to make a midday stop during which teams were rested and the emigrants usually ate a cold lunch. "Baiting" the teams meant to feed and water them. When teams were "recruited" it meant that they were allowed to rest and recuperate for a time.

Chapter Nine

Colonel William Russell and Edwin Bryant and the mule pack train were still traveling in proximity to their original company. The night before, they had come together and camped at the same site. Though Russell was no longer captain—ex-Governor Boggs was—many still looked on him as their leader. Therefore, Russell and Boggs decided to work together so as to give a united voice to all those present.

They called for an assembly at nine o'clock that morning. The various camps collected at a grove of trees a short distance upstream on La Prele Creek, or Beaver Creek, as some preferred to call it. Wagons were backed up to form a half circle beneath the trees; then the tailgates were lowered to provide makeshift tables. Almost as if by magic a feast appeared. There were baskets of bread, bricks of cheese, sliced ham, mutton, roast beef, boiled potatoes, fried carrots, broiled turnips, stewed tomatoes, boiled eggs, and fresh greens that someone had found along the creek. For being seven hundred miles into the wilderness it was a sumptuous spread. Sprinkled throughout were dozens of jugs of lemonade, milk, and tea that had been placed in the creek overnight to get them cold. As the women laid everything out, the children moved in with longing eyes, only to be waved away or, where necessary, slapped gently to ensure their patience. More than one husband had his hands slapped as well.

When the last of the people had gathered, Lilburn W. Boggs pushed to the front of the group and climbed up on a fallen log. He raised his hands and called for attention. When the group finally quieted he called out. In the hush of the grove his voice carried clearly.

"Ladies and gentlemen, today marks the seventieth anniversary of our country's independence. Though we are far from our native United States, our love of country has not dimmed, our patriotism has not waned. Therefore, by mutual agreement, we gather together to celebrate our independence from tyranny and oppression."

"Hear! Hear!" someone cried. Others applauded enthusiastically.

He turned to a small group of men who stood behind him. "Gentlemen!"

To Kathryn's surprise, they turned and walked a few feet away to where a long pole lay on the ground. Made from what looked like some form of aspen or birch tree, it was about fifteen feet long and had all its limbs neatly trimmed off. A hole had been dug, and the pole was dropped into it so that it stood vertically. There was a rope rigged to it, and then Kathryn understood. To everyone's delight, and to the accompaniment of much cheering, whistling, and clapping, an American flag was produced and run up the pole.

Now Colonel Russell gave a signal. Men all around the company lifted rifles and pistols. "Ready. Aim. *Fire!*"

With a tremendous roar, a hundred or so weapons blasted off into the air. In the distance a flock of crows burst skyward, cawing raucously at being disturbed.

"Again!" Russell bellowed. Again there was a tremendous blast of sound.

"All right," Boggs shouted. "Let's form a parade line. We don't have a Main Street, so let's go down around the wagons and the temporary stock corral and back." He bent down and lifted a crude drum. He had a knobbed tree limb for a drumstick. "We have a dog drum here"—he grinned wickedly—"contributed by Pete Peterson's mangy dog that chased his milk cow one time too often." The crowd roared with laughter. The dog had been an annoyance for the last two months.

Boggs gave it a few experimental thumps. "Okay, line up. Children first. Here we go."

What followed was pure chaos, but chaos bred of joy. Whooping and hollering, the children raced to get into position at the first of the line. Women and the older girls, many of them wearing Sunday dresses, lined up immediately behind the children. The men—weapons over their shoulders like soldiers marching to battle—brought up the rear.

Kathryn turned to Peter. "Come on, Peter. Let's go."

He gave her a quick look. The land was thick with sagebrush and not very level. It would be a challenge for crutches. "Are you sure? We can just wait here."

Suddenly her eyes were shining. The thrill of the moment and the sight of Old Glory, with its red and white stripes and twenty-eight white stars on a field of blue, had deeply stirred her. Memories of celebrations past with family and friends and far finer circumstances than they now enjoyed flooded her mind. "We're Americans now, Peter," she whispered fiercely. "And this is our birthday. You bet I'm sure."

Back at camp, shortly before noon, the Reeds and the Donners were putting things away. To their surprise, Edwin Bryant and William Russell came over to join them.

Russell was weaving a little and it was evident his celebration had been enthusiastic. "Well, Reed," he boomed, shaking the other's hand, "we're going to pack up and head out."

Reed nodded. "Heard that was the case. Good luck to you. I think we're going to lay over here for another day, recruit the teams and do some repairs. That means this will likely be the last we see you until we all reach California."

"I certainly hope so," Bryant said fervently. "We've delayed long enough. But now that Hiram Miller has agreed to accompany us, we're going to push ahead with all dispatch."

George Donner frowned in mock dismay. "You stole our journal keeper right out from under us, you know, not to say anything about one of my teamsters."

Bryant laughed. "I've seen Miller's journal." He nodded toward Reed. "Giving it to James here will be a definite improvement."

"We'll miss you," Margret Reed spoke up, a touch of sadness in her voice. "It has been a pleasure for us to get to know each of you."

Russell touched the brim of his hat. "And for us too, ma'am."

Reed stood up. "Stay here for one moment. I have something I want to show you." He turned and walked swiftly to the back of the big wagon. He went inside and they could hear him fumbling around for a moment. When he returned he was holding up a bottle of brandy. "Gentlemen, look what I have here," he crowed.

Kathryn shot Peter a look of dismay. He frowned. That had been their one comfort at Fort Laramie. Even the Donner brothers had bought a pint or two, but their drinking had been quiet and subdued. Reed had stayed away from it entirely as far as Peter knew.

Reed set the bottle down on the small table in front of the wagon. It was corked and had an expensive-looking label. "When we left Springfield, some of my gentlemen friends gave me this as a send-off present," he explained proudly. "They gave me specific instructions that it was not to be opened until the Fourth of July."

He turned to his daughters. "Virginia. Patty. Get some glasses, please."

Peter moved over to stand beside Kathryn and take her hand, but there was no way they could comfortably leave now.

In a moment glasses were produced. Reed uncorked the bottle with some flourish and splashed the liquor into them. Very solemnly now he handed them around to the men present. To Peter's surprise, Mr. Reed handed one to his wife. She smiled at him and took it without comment. Then suddenly Reed was holding out a glass toward Peter.

His eyes widened. "Uh, no, thank you, Mr. Reed."

Colonel Russell turned sharply. "What's the matter, boy? This is a celebration. We're about to make a toast."

"I . . . The Lord gave a revelation on not using alcohol, and Kathryn and I have committed ourselves to honor that."

Reed was watching him, his eyes showing open disappointment. The glass was still extended in invitation. "It's just a toast, Peter. No more."

"I . . . thank you, Mr. Reed, but I can't."

"Ingalls here is a Mormon," Bryant explained to his partner.

Russell, already showing that previous toasts had loosened his tongue and lowered his inhibitions, swore. "I don't care if he's the Augustus Caesar. This is a grand day, and one little toast isn't going to hurt him."

Margret Reed stepped in quickly. "It's all right, Peter. We have some lemonade for you and Kathryn and the children."

She poured quickly while the awkward silence stretched on. Then, when they were ready, Reed turned solemnly. "My friends and I promised each other that I would look to the east and drink to them, and they would look to the west and drink to us." He raised his glass high, pointing it toward the east. "To America."

"To America," they all joined in.

As Peter lowered his glass, he saw James F. Reed watching him. His eyes were dark and hooded, and Peter couldn't tell what thoughts lay behind them.

Joshua did not return to the bluffs until about three in the afternoon. He had gone down to the ferry to see how soon it would be the Steeds' turn to cross. There he had found John Taylor, and they ended up spending the next six hours helping the brethren find more efficient ways to get the wagons loaded and unloaded.

When he came back to camp, Savannah and Charles, with little Livvy in tow, were playing near the back of the wagon. When Savannah saw him approaching, she waved. "Hi, Papa."

"Hi, kids. Where's your mother?"

"She and Aunt Lydia went to visit Brother and Sister Hendricks."

"Oh. I'll go find her."

He didn't have to go far. James and Drusilla Hendricks were camped on Mosquito Creek a little farther upstream from where they were. But he had gone only about half the distance when he saw Caroline and Lydia approaching. He stopped and waited for them to reach him.

"Hello, dear," Caroline said. "When did you get back?"

"Just a few minutes ago."

He turned and they started walking back. "So how are Brother and Sister Hendricks?"

To his surprise, the two women exchanged a quick glance, and then Lydia looked away quickly. Something had passed between them, and it had been painful. He decided to let it lie.

"They're fine," Caroline finally said. "James can get around pretty well with crutches now, and that helps."

He nodded. James Hendricks had been shot in the back of the neck at the Battle of Crooked River back in the fall of 1838 and been paralyzed from the neck down. Over the intervening years he had gradually improved, but he was still far from being able to care for his family, especially out here on the trail. Drusilla had simply taken over, lifting him when necessary, though he was probably a hundred pounds heavier than she was, taking in laundry, knitting mittens and scarves, doing whatever it took to sustain the family. Joshua had come to have tremendous respect for her.

"Well, at least she's got that oldest boy," he said. "What is he, sixteen now?"

Again there was a silent exchange, only this time Joshua saw the stricken look on Lydia's face. She dropped her head. "I'd better see what my children are up to," she murmured, and with a little wave to Joshua, face still averted, she hurried away.

He looked at Caroline. "What did I say?"

She slipped an arm through his. "Nothing. Lydia's just having a hard time right now."

"Is everything all right?"

"Josh wants to enlist in the battalion."

He stopped, eyes widening a little. "He does?"

"Yes. Both Lydia and Nathan have told him he's too young, but it's like he's obsessed with the idea. He won't let it go." She took a quick breath. "Drusilla is having the same problem with her William. She and Lydia were having a good cry about it, actually."

"Oh." And he had to bring up the subject. That really helped. They started walking again. "But surely William won't go. I mean, he's all his mother has to help drive the team and get things done around the camp. No one would expect her to let him go."

"Drusilla is like Lydia. Both boys are too young, and both mothers are convinced that they shouldn't go. For Drusilla it's not just the fact that she needs William. Remember, she sent her man off to war once, and look what happened. James came back paralyzed. As she puts it, 'The burned child dreads the fire.' "

He didn't say anything more to that. What was there to say? They walked on. Then suddenly Caroline looked up at him and smiled. "By the way, happy Independence Day."

When all of the passengers aboard the *Brooklyn* gathered on deck, along with the majority of the crew, there was little room left for moving around. Fortunately for all, this morning was a clear, beautiful day, and the ship moved up and down smoothly on the long swells. After many weeks on the water, the people adjusted to that motion without conscious thought and had no problem keeping their balance. As much as possible, they were gathered near the bow, all facing forward.

The call from Captain Richardson for an assembly came as a surprise, and there was much interest as he climbed aboard a large chest near the bow where everyone could see him. Now he raised his hands, and the Saints fell silent.

"Friends and fellow shipmates," he began, "this is our fifth day out from the Sandwich Islands, and we are on our way to California."

"Hallelujah!" a man behind them shouted. That brought a ripple of laughter and considerable applause.

Richardson laughed too. "Yes, I agree. Hallelujah to that idea." He took a quick breath. "It was exactly five months ago today that we left New York Harbor and began our voyage. Since we left on February fourth, that means today is . . ." He let it hang in the air.

"Independence Day," they all called out.

"Yes, it is the Fourth of July, Independence Day. And while we are a long way from America, we are all still Americans. Therefore, while there is much to do, and while we cannot spend the day in celebration, neither can we simply let it pass unnoticed. I wanted us to take an opportunity to remember our heritage, to remember who we are and whence we came." He looked over the heads of the assembly to where the first mate and two other ship officers stood waiting. "Gentlemen, you may proceed."

The crowd of Saints and crew turned as one to face the opposite direction. With great solemnity the first mate walked to a small locker and opened it. He bent over, then straightened again. What he held in his hand was easily recognizable as Old Glory, even though it was folded into a neat triangle. He moved to the rigging and, with the help of the bosun, unfurled the flag. They attached it to the lanyard and then raised it in one continuous motion.

The people fell silent. Some put their hands over their hearts. Men removed their hats. Some of the women were weeping at the sight of it. Out to sea, when there was no one around, they did not fly the flag, as the salt water and sun were very hard on it. To see it suddenly run up the lanyard and hear it start snapping in the breeze was a stirring experience, and the group stood silently enjoying it. Alice moved closer to Will so that their shoulders touched.

Captain Richardson straightened to his full height and slowly saluted the flag. As he held that pose, suddenly a woman began to sing. It rang clear and sweet above the creaking of the ship and the snapping of the flag.

> Oh say, can you see, by the dawn's early light,
> What so proudly we hailed at the twilight's last gleaming,

For a moment, the assembly was silent, but then others quickly joined in with her.

> Whose broad stripes and bright stars, through the perilous fight,
> O'er the ramparts we watched, were so gallantly streaming?

Not all knew the words. There were a few who had recently emigrated from Europe. But those who did know the words sang them out with great enthusiasm. Many reached out and took one another's hands, united in this simple and yet profound moment of remembrance. Will had to stop for a moment, for his throat had so constricted that he couldn't get a sound out. He recovered enough to come back in on the last two lines. He threw his head back and, along with all the others, sang with full throat as they gazed up at the red, white, and blue cloth that crackled in the breeze above them.

Oh say, does that star-spangled banner yet wave
O'er the land of the free and the home of the brave?

Bringing a raft of logs that was the equivalent of fifty or sixty thousand board feet of lumber into shore was no easy task, especially when the current was running high and swift. But Jean Claude Dubuque was no ordinary lumberman and had brought in rafts that were much larger than this. Carl stood beside him, surveying the ropes and checking how the raft was snuggled into the shore. It was good. Jean Claude had done it again.

"You sure you have a place to stay?" he asked the Frenchman. "We've got plenty of room."

"No, no," Jean Claude replied. "I have a cousin who is expecting me."

Carl nodded, not asking the other two lumbermen who had come down with them about needing accommodations. They were from Wisconsin Territory and would sleep on the raft and make sure it was safe through the night. "Then we'll see you tomorrow."

"*Au revoir.*"

Carl suddenly stopped, smiling. "Do you know what day it is today, Jean Claude?"

"*Oui.*"

"Good." He glanced up at the afternoon sky. "We've probably missed all the celebrations, but at least we made it in time."

"Happy America Day, Carl," he said, lifting his hand.

"The same to you, Jean Claude." And with that, he hitched his shoulder bag a little higher and started up the grassy hillside. On top, as he knew he would, he found a path that headed south. In the distance he could see the gleaming white tower and walls of the Nauvoo Temple. Somehow it seemed just the right thing to welcome him home.

They had beached the raft about a mile north of town, and at first he followed the path along the river, thinking he would cut over to his house once he passed the stone quarry. Then, as the deserted quarry came into sight, he changed his mind. With the Fourth of July, there would be more people out and about, so Melissa would likely be at the store to handle the increased business. He swung over to Hyde Street, then headed south. He found himself smiling in anticipation of beholding Melissa's face when she saw him.

To his surprise, he passed no one as he walked briskly along. At one home there were two children playing in the backyard, and at another he saw a figure pass by a window, but the streets were deserted. His mood sobered a little as he realized how many more empty houses there were even since he had left three weeks before. The city was emptying out quickly.

As he rounded the corner of Knight Street and turned west, he stopped dead. For a moment, he thought he had not been paying attention and turned one street too soon. There was no store at the corner of the next block. He stared, recognizing the other houses on the street but not comprehending why there was nothing where the store should have been. And then he saw the pile of charred timbers and ashes where the Steed Family Dry Goods and General Store should have been. With a gasp of astonishment, he broke into a run.

Chapter Notes

Several diarists and contemporary letter writers, including Edwin Bryant and the Reeds' daughter Virginia, speak of the Fourth of July celebration held on Beaver Creek near present-day Douglas, Wyoming. The details given here—including the dog drum, the lemonade, and Mr. Reed's special bottle of brandy—are all drawn from those accounts. (See *Overland in 1846*, pp. 278, 427–28, 586; *What I Saw*, pp. 120–21; *Chronicles*, pp. 88–89.) Surprisingly, there was available at that time a lemon extract. The pioneers would mix it in water with sugar and vinegar or citric acid to make lemonade. (See Jacqueline Williams, *Wagon Wheel Kitchens: Food on the Oregon Trail* [Lawrence, Kans.: University Press of Kansas, 1993], pp. 90–91.)

In contrast, there is no known mention of the holiday by Latter-day Saints, either in Brigham Young's official history or in such journals as those of William Clayton and Wilford Woodruff.

Though it would not officially become the national anthem of the United States until 1931, by 1846 "The Star-Spangled Banner" had long been a favorite of Americans. During the War of 1812, Francis Scott Key, a lawyer, had gone to the British to negotiate for the release of a prisoner. The exchange was made, but the British warships had just begun an attack on Fort McHenry near Baltimore, and so they held Key on board a British vessel for a time so that he could not warn the Americans about the attack. Key watched anxiously as the poorly defended fort was bombarded for almost twenty-four hours. At dawn, when a break in the mists revealed Old Glory still flying proudly above the battered walls, Key was so stirred that he sat down and penned the first stanza of a poem inspired by what he saw. When he was returned to Baltimore, he wrote additional stanzas, and they were immediately printed as a handbill and distributed throughout the city. A few days later, an actor sang "The Star-Spangled Banner" in Baltimore, putting the words to a well-known English drinking song. The song became instantly popular and soon was felt to best epitomize the feelings of patriotism so many felt for America. (See *World Book Encyclopedia*, s.v. "The Star-Spangled Banner.")

Chapter Ten

Melissa spoke quietly, her voice flat and without emotion, as though she were telling him something that had happened to a total stranger. She finished, glanced up at him once, then looked down again. The children sat quietly around the sitting room, watching their father gravely. After a moment, he turned to young Carl. "I'm proud of you, son. Thank you for caring for your mother."

Melissa's head came up, and now he could tell she was close to tears. "If Carl hadn't come . . ." She couldn't finish and closed her eyes.

"If I'd have thought, Pa," young Carl said guiltily, "I would have stood guard at the store that night. We just didn't—"

"You did good, son. It's not your fault. I'm real proud."

"Thank you, Pa."

"Why don't you and David take the other children out and play for a time, Carl. I need to speak with your mother."

He nodded and they trooped out, almost relieved to escape

the pain in their parents' eyes. When the door shut, Carl went over and sat down beside his wife. "Are you sure you're all right, Melissa?"

She nodded.

"They didn't . . . ?"

There was a barely perceptible movement of her head. "No. Carl came just in time."

"Thank the Lord for that." He reached out and laid a hand on her arm. "It's all right, as long as you weren't hurt. We can rebuild the store."

Her head came up sharply. "With what, Carl? We don't have any money."

"We will, once we sell the lumber in St. Louis. If prices are good—and they say they are—I should end up with two or three thousand dollars."

To his surprise, she leaned forward eagerly. "Let's use it to buy a wagon and team."

He sat back slowly, withdrawing his hand from hers. "What?"

"I mean it, Carl. There's nothing left here for us. We haven't had an order for bricks for over two months now. The store is gone. There's more and more tension with our enemies. I don't want to stay here anymore."

"Look, Melissa, I know you are upset over this. I fully understand that, but—" Her look stopped him. "What?"

"Don't patronize me, Carl. This didn't happen last night. I was terribly upset after it happened—very upset—but that was almost three weeks ago, Carl. I've—"

He stood up, cutting her off in mid-sentence. "Look, Melissa, I'm very sorry about all this. I know it frightened you badly, but we can't settle this now. I have to be back with Jean Claude at first light. I'd like to spend some time with the children before I have to go to bed."

Her mouth pulled down. "I know. I'm sorry, Carl. The children are anxious to have some time with you."

"We'll talk about it when I get back from St. Louis."

She looked away. "All right."

He started toward the door.

"Carl?"

He stopped and turned his head.

"I believe it was the Lord who sent young Carl to help me."

His head moved slightly. "Whatever or whoever it was, I am very thankful that it turned out as it did."

She went on, half speaking to herself. "Young Carl was here watching the children. Suddenly he just had this strong feeling that things weren't all right. He even brought the shotgun. And that made all the difference."

He nodded slowly. That *was* unusual, he agreed.

"I think it was the Lord's way of blessing me for coming back to the Church."

He straightened slowly. So that was it? Well, no surprise there. "We'll talk when I get back," he said, keeping his voice level. He started for the door again.

"Carl?"

He sighed and turned back.

"I'm not willing to stay in Nauvoo any longer."

Though he tried to keep his face impassive, he felt himself stiffen and knew that she saw it. "And if I don't want to leave?" he asked slowly.

"I don't know." She bit her lower lip and he saw that it was trembling slightly. "When you get back, we have to talk."

"Kathryn?"

She looked up from the book she was reading. "Yes?"

"Would you like to go for a ride?"

She closed the book slowly. "A ride?"

"Yes. Mr. Bryant said there's a wonderful surprise if we follow the creek upstream about a mile and a half. Mr. Reed has given me permission to take one of the horses."

She was watching Peter closely now, the book forgotten. It was about two o'clock. The celebrations were done. The last of Mr. Reed's fine liquor was long since gone. Bryant and Russell and their party had packed their mules and left shortly after noon. The rest had determined to stay here at Beaver Creek for another day. There was good water and plenty of graze for the animals and more than one hangover to be slept off. The Reeds were in their commodious wagon. Peter had just returned from checking on the oxen. They had about another five or six hours until sundown. All of this went through her mind as she considered this unusual offer.

Her gaze was too penetrating for him to ignore. "I was just . . ." He sighed. "I would like to be alone for a while—to talk, to think . . . and to make some decisions."

She set the book back in her small trunk and got to her feet. "All right, Peter."

For a time, Peter was afraid there was no way through. To the south of the camp the first of the foothills rose quickly to the more imposing ridges of the Black Hills. Beaver Creek came out where two hills formed a narrow canyon. It was heavy with trees, willows, and other bushes, too thick to push through on a horse. But then he found a narrow trail—probably made by deer or elk—and guided the horse into it. They rode quietly, Kathryn holding on to him loosely, as he let the horse pick its own way.

The hills rose steeply on either side now, and it looked as though they were riding into a blind canyon. Then suddenly, after a few hundred yards, the canyon opened up into a small hollow, perhaps a hundred to a hundred and fifty yards wide at its broadest and maybe a quarter of a mile long. He reined in beneath a huge cottonwood tree.

"This is beautiful, Peter."

And that it was. It was as though they had ridden into a park that shut out the rest of the world. To their left the hills had become sharp cliffs that were fifty or sixty feet high. Most startling was their color. The rock was a brilliant reddish brown, a burnt umber that glowed warmly now in the afternoon sunlight. The color contrasted sharply with the foliage and grass that grew all around them. There was a hush, broken only by the soft murmuring of the creek and the slight stirring of the wind in the branches above them.

"Look," Peter said, touching her shoulder. He was pointing to their right now. Here the creek made a bend to the west.

As she turned, there was a quick intake of breath. "Oh, Peter!" she breathed.

A few yards away, the creek passed beneath a huge natural bridge cut through an abutment of stone that jutted out from the side of the mountain. Here the rock was more naturally colored, beige and yellow and brown. The arch of the natural bridge was perhaps fifteen or twenty feet high and a good thirty or forty feet wide, though the creek was only about half that width. Above the arch the stone was twenty or thirty feet thick, making the top of the bridge about fifty feet above their heads. It was a sight that took away the breath.

"Mr. Bryant said this was something worth seeing," Peter said quietly, not wanting to violate the stillness.

"It's the most marvelous thing I've ever seen," Kathryn whispered. "I can't believe it. It's so perfect, like someone made it."

"Someone did," he answered.

She smiled at him and nodded.

He turned and helped her slide off the horse, handed her the cane, then dismounted himself. He led the horse to a place on the bank of the creek where there was plenty of grass and where it could reach the water, then tied the reins to a branch. Then he took her hand and started toward the bridge.

"Can we sit right under it?" she asked, still a little awestruck at the sight that stood before them.

"Yes." He could see that there was a place directly beneath the arch, scoured out during times of flooding, that now was thick with grass. They moved there and sat down. Kathryn lay back on the grass and closed her eyes.

For some time they sat quietly, content to enjoy the setting. Peter flipped pebbles into the creek, noting the different pitches the plopping sounds made.

"So, are you going to tell me?" Kathryn asked.

"Tell you what?"

She opened her eyes. "You've made some kind of decision, haven't you?"

He hesitated for a moment, then nodded slowly.

"Was it the drinking?"

"Partly."

"You can't expect them to believe as we do, Peter. They've never heard of the Word of Wisdom. Even some of our own people still drink wine."

"I know that. That's not what disturbs me. It was . . . I don't know. Did you see the look Mr. Reed gave me when I refused to join in the toast?"

"Yes, I did."

"We're different from them, Kathryn. We're not part of what they believe and want. And it's not just the Reeds. It's everything. They're going to California on an adventure, to make their fortunes, to find free land. All we want is to find our family and a place where we can worship as we choose, free from having the mobs come in upon us."

"Yes," she agreed softly. "And that seems so strange to them, doesn't it?"

He nodded.

"So?"

He looked up at the mass of stone above their heads, studying the pattern in the rock. "So I've come to a conclusion. I want to talk to you about it, and see if we both think it's the right thing to do."

"All right."

She sat up and he scooted around so that he faced her. His eyes were deeply earnest, his face showing the depths of his concern. For several seconds he searched for the proper way to begin, then decided that with Kathryn it was best to just come right out with it.

"I would like to take you back to Fort Laramie, Kathryn."

One eyebrow lifted slightly, but other than that there was no immediate response. He rushed on. "The terrain is getting more difficult now. All the loose rocks beneath our feet make it more challenging for you to walk and get around."

"Go on."

"I had a chance to visit with Mr. Bordeaux, the man in charge of the fort. I was impressed that he was a gentleman and a decent man."

"I agree."

"So . . ." He took another breath. "So I would like to take you back there and leave you with Mr. Bordeaux until the rest of the family reaches Fort Laramie." Eager now, he let the words tumble out. "They can't be more than a week or two behind us. Maybe there will be word of them when we get back to the fort. If Mr. Reed will let us borrow one of the horses, I think I could take you there and catch back up to the Reeds and the others in five or six days. The layover here tomorrow will help."

He stopped, waiting for a moment, but her eyes were down and he couldn't read her feelings from her face, for it had showed no change.

"I can't just back out on our agreement with the Reeds." He spoke more slowly now. "They've been too good to us. And besides, we desperately need the money he's promised to pay us if we go all the way with him. So I'll go on to California with them; then I'll turn right around and come back to find you and the family."

His words slowed, then stopped. This time he waited for her to react. Finally, her head lifted and he saw that there were tears in her eyes. He reached out and took her hand. "I'm sorry, Kathryn, I just—"

She shook her head. "Will you answer me something honestly?"

"Yes."

"Does this make you feel better?"

"What do you mean?"

"You've been so bothered these past few days. When you think about taking me back and leaving me at Fort Laramie, how do you feel?"

For several moments he considered that, looking inward. Then he slowly nodded. "It's like a great weight has been lifted off my shoulders. I feel at peace."

"So do I, Peter." The tears welled up and spilled over. "I can't bear to think about you leaving me. But the moment you told me what you are thinking, it was like I was at peace too."

"You were?" The relief surged in like a cool breeze. "Really?"

"Yes, Peter. Because there's one other thing I've been worrying about that you haven't."

"What?"

"The road is getting rougher all the time now."

"Yes. It's going to be harder and harder to get around, I'm afraid."

"I'm not talking about it being difficult to walk when we are in camp."

He was puzzled. "Then what?"

"I'm afraid if I have to ride in that wagon every day when it is so jolting and bumpy that I might lose the baby."

It took a moment to register, and then his eyes widened.

She smiled now, even as the tears trickled down her cheeks. "Yes, Peter. Finally. We're going to have a baby."

He leaped to his feet. "Really? You're not just saying that?"

She wiped at the tears, laughing aloud now at his joy. "No, I'm not just saying that."

He pulled her to her feet and took her in his arms. He kissed her soundly, then did it again. "I can't believe it. You're sure?"

"Not absolutely, but pretty much." Now she sobered. "I didn't want to add another worry to you. I didn't know what I was going to do. I can tell that the constant pounding we've been getting these past few days is not good."

He let her go, his mind racing. "That will make it easier to explain this to the Reeds. They'll understand why you can't go on."

"I think so too. I'll miss the children desperately." Her voice caught. "And you. But now we've got someone else to worry about."

"This is wonderful. I am so pleased."

She nodded, touching her stomach. "Let's go right back and talk to the Reeds. If they agree, let's leave immediately."

When Peter and Kathryn returned from the natural bridge and asked for an audience with their employers, Margret Reed instantly saw the wisdom of Kathryn's going back to Fort Laramie, even though she was greatly disappointed to know she would lose the tutor and companion for her children. Mr. Reed magnanimously offered one of his horses for them to ride, then borrowed a mule from the Donners to carry Kathryn's things separately. There were copious tears as Kathryn bid farewell to the children. They left shortly after four p.m. on that Independence Day.

Constantly reassured by Kathryn that the rolling lope of the horse was not nearly as damaging as the jolting of the wagon, Peter pushed hard. They made about twelve miles before they stopped that first night. Fort Laramie was about seventy-five miles east of Beaver Creek. Originally Peter had hoped to average about twenty-five miles per day going east and thirty-five or more on the return, once he no longer had Kathryn's baggage and could switch between the horse and the mule. But in reality, in spite of her assurances, Kathryn tired quickly, and they came closer to making only twenty miles each day.

It was late in the afternoon of the fourth day when Peter reined in the horse and mule and paused for a moment to gaze on the sight before them. In the distance the tree-lined course of the Laramie River could be easily traced, and they could clearly see the adobe stockade with its open gate and dozens of people moving in and out of it. Around it on every side, in even more profusion than there had been when they were here the week before, wagons, Indian lodges, stock corrals, and white men's tents filled the plain. A hundred columns of smoke from cooking fires rose silently into the air.

Peter turned and looked at Kathryn, who managed a tired smile, and then they started down.

It was the next morning by the time Peter was able to go to the fort itself. When they had arrived yesterday afternoon, they had found a friendly wagoner who offered them a place to lay their bedrolls and also invited them for supper and breakfast. Then Peter had gone to find a place for his animals. That had proven more time-consuming than he first thought. It turned out that most of the animals at the fort were driven out some distance under the direction of armed guards to find better grazing. Then they were brought back in the corral for the night, where they were more secure. When he explained his purpose, the drovers agreed to let his animals join the herd for two bits, or twenty-five cents. Satisfied, he left them and walked back to their campsite, arriving just before dark.

As soon as they had finished breakfast this morning, Peter walked to the stockade. Inside, he had to wait for almost a quarter of an hour for James Bordeaux, the man in charge of the fort. But when he finally came over, he was smiling warmly and extended a hand. "Welcome, my young friend," he said. "How may I be of service to you?"

Descended from French ancestors but American born himself, Bordeaux was a stout man with a barrel chest and pockmarked face. His hair was black, cut short, and parted on one side.

Peter quickly explained who he was and the circumstances that had brought him back.

"Ah," Bordeaux said easily. "Yes, I remember. You were with Mr. Reed, right?"

"Yes. I am one of his teamsters."

"A fine gentleman, this Mr. Reed. We had a wonderful talk one night."

"Yes. He speaks very highly of you."

That seemed to please the trapper-turned-trader. He nodded, beaming. "Good, good."

"We didn't know this when we were here, but my wife is in the family way. It is of great concern for us. Our party is later than we should be, and we have to go all the way to California."

"I worry too," he said gravely. "The mountains of California are to be respected even more than an Indian war party on the trail." His eyes narrowed a little. "Are you thinking of turning back?" There was no mistaking the critical look in his expression.

"No. I have contracted with Mr. Reed to help him all the way to California. I intend to honor that contract."

"Good!" The faint look of condemnation had disappeared.

"But my wife and I are Latter-day Saints—Mormons, as we are often called—and I—"

"Ah," he said. "You are Mormons. Your people are coming too?"

"Yes. We thought they were ahead of us, but now we know they're coming behind." He took a quick breath, and plunged into the reason he had come. "Mr. Bordeaux, I've decided that it is not wise for my wife to keep going. I'm wondering if I could leave her here with you until our people come. It would be only two or three weeks."

Bordeaux was nodding. "I would be very pleased to help you out, Mr. Ingalls, but you have Mormons coming up the trail right now."

Peter's head came up with a sharp jerk. "What?"

"A rider came in from Fort Bernard late yesterday. He says there is a small group—fifteen or twenty wagons maybe—coming up the trail. They should reach Fort Bernard later today."

"Fort Bernard? That's the one downriver a ways?"

Bordeaux nodded. "About eight miles." He spat a stream of brown tobacco juice over the railing and into the dust of the courtyard. "John Baptiste Reshaw is trying to take away our business, but it will do him no good."

Peter wasn't interested in this local competition. "And he said it was a company of Mormons?"

"That's what he said. Before you leave your wife here to stay, best you go downstream and find out for yourself, don't you think?"

"Yes," Peter said, grateful now. "Thank you, Mr. Bordeaux. I shall do just that."

Fort Bernard was nothing like Fort Laramie in either size or activity. Only two sides of what was to eventually become a log quadrangle were completed, with small buildings attached to the inside of each wall. There were a few Indian lodges round about and half a dozen wagons camped between the river and the fort, but after Fort Laramie it seemed pitifully small, almost deserted. Peter dismounted at the largest of the buildings, went to the nearest door, and knocked.

"Come in," someone growled.

He pushed the door open and stepped inside. He stopped for a moment to let his eyes adjust to the gloom he found there. The room was about ten feet square, and both the walls and the floor were made of black mud. The roof was made of rough-hewn timbers covered with sod. There was a huge fireplace made from four flat stones laid on top of each other to form the firebox. A hole had been cut in the ceiling to allow the smoke to escape. In one corner there were several rifles stacked together. From nails driven through the mud daubing into the log walls hung various Indian paraphernalia—a pipe and tobacco pouch, what looked like some kind of medicine bag adorned with dyed porcupine quills, an Indian bow and otter-skin quiver. The only furniture in the room was a rough settee covered with buffalo robes on which lounged a tall Indian brave. In the light from the door Peter saw that his hair was plastered down against his temples with a thick vermillion paste. Beyond him, two or three mountain men sat cross-legged on the floor smoking pipes.

"I was looking for Mr. Reshaw," Peter said.

"Ain't here right now," one of the mountain men grunted.

"It's important that I see him immediately. Could you tell me where I might find him?"

Another of the heavily bearded men stirred. "Goshen Hole. Went down to trade some robes with an incoming emigrant company."

Peter swung to face him. "And where is that?"

"Downstream a few miles. Just follow the river."

"Thank you." He retreated, shutting the door behind him, then strode to his horse.

Chapter Eleven

The sun was nearing its zenith when Peter topped a small knoll and saw the white tops of wagons in the distance. He counted quickly. Nineteen. Bordeaux had said there were about twenty. They were not moving, which meant they were nooning. He had no doubt but what this was the company for which he was looking. With a surge of elation, he slapped his horse with the reins and sent it into a running lope.

At the sound of his horse, the camp came to a standstill and several people gathered at a spot near the lead wagon. He slowed as he approached them, feeling the euphoria dashed as quickly as it had come. He recognized no one. There was no Brigham Young. No Heber C. Kimball or John Taylor. He searched the faces quickly as he reined to a stop. Then came the most bitter disappointment of all. There was not one Steed family face in the crowd.

Two men stepped out in front of the gathering. The shorter of the two, Peter immediately guessed, was Reshaw. Though not tall, he had a slender, athletic build and appeared to be strong. He was a dark, swarthy-looking man with long black hair that was parted in the middle of his head and fell in thick curls over both shoulders. He was dressed in buckskins, and his frock was richly adorned with bead and quill work. Long fringes lined the seams of his sleeves and leggings.

The man beside him was an American and dressed for the trail. He was taller than Peter by an inch or two, probably over six feet, Peter guessed. He had a full head of hair and a thick dark beard. As he looked more closely, Peter was surprised. This was clearly the leader of the wagon company, and yet he was not much older than Peter was, perhaps no more than three or four years. Not only that, the man did seem familiar to him.

Peter swung down as the two men came forward. "Mornin'," the leader said, extending his hand. "John Brown here."

Peter took it and immediately liked the firmness of his grip. "Peter Ingalls," he answered.

Brown's eyes widened perceptibly. "Ingalls? But you're the Mormon. You're the one Mr. Clyman told us about."

Thoroughly astonished, Peter nodded. "Yes. You met Mr. Clyman?"

"We did. He camped with us at Ash Hollow. We asked him if there were any companies of Mormons on the trail ahead of us and he said no, but then he told us that he had met a Mormon couple with one of the California trains."

"That was my wife and I," Peter said eagerly. "So are you Latter-day Saints, then?"

"All but Mr. Reshaw here." He turned. "This is John Baptiste Reshaw. He and some other men run a fort a short way upriver."

Peter shook hands with the mountain man. "I was just at Fort Bernard an hour or so ago," he said. "Some of your companions told me where I could find you."

"Good. I was going downriver to do some trading when I met Mr. Brown. I think that has brought a change of plans for both of us." He turned to Brown. "I think this young man and his mount need a rest. Why don't you tarry here a little longer? I will go on to the fort and have things in readiness for when you arrive tonight."

Brown nodded, then smiled at Peter. "You look like getting out of that saddle for a time might be good for you."

"I left Beaver Creek five days ago."

"Whew!" Reshaw cried. "No wonder you are tired." He looked at Brown one last time. "Discuss what I have suggested. I am confident this is your best course of action. We shall decide tonight."

"Yes, sir. Thank you very much."

They watched as Reshaw walked toward the horses, and then Brown laid a hand on Peter's shoulders. "Come. We have just finished eating. There's still plenty left."

"Are you just an advance company, then?" Peter asked as they started for the nearest wagon, again searching the faces around him that smiled their welcome. "Where's Brother Brigham?"

John Brown's mouth pulled into a tight line and he was suddenly grim. "That's what we would like to know."

Brown watched Peter eat the thick slices of bread with cheese and drink down a small mug of warm milk. Only when Peter was nearly done did Brown straighten. "I think the easiest thing will be to start from the beginning and tell you the whole story. Though you haven't found your family, as you hoped, I think maybe we have a solution for your problem."

"I'm listening."

Brown leaned back against the wagon, pulling thoughtfully on his lip. "I joined the Church in Perry County, Illinois, in eighteen forty-one and shortly thereafter gathered to Nauvoo."

"That's why you look familiar to me."

He nodded. "I wasn't there for long. Brother Hyrum Smith ordained me an elder and I was called on a mission to the southern states."

"My brother and my brother-in-law were in the southern

states," Peter spoke up. "Derek Ingalls and Matthew Steed. They were in Arkansas."

He shook his head. "I went to Tennessee and Alabama, but mostly I labored in Mississippi. We had great success and organized several branches of the Church there. I was there for over two years, then returned to Nauvoo in the spring of eighteen forty-five."

Peter snapped his fingers. "You worked on the temple, didn't you?"

"Yes."

"That's where I've seen you."

"Probably so. Anyway, in January of this year, as everyone was preparing to leave Nauvoo, President Young called me to his office. He wanted me to return to Mississippi and organize a wagon company to go west. We were instructed to leave our families there and take only those families that were outfitted and ready to go. Instead of having us return to Nauvoo, which would have been way out of the way, Brother Brigham told us to go directly to Independence and then continue along the Oregon Trail until we caught up with him."

"That was our plan exactly," Peter said. "They left Nauvoo so much earlier than we did, we were afraid we would never catch up with them." He shook his head in disappointment. "I assume Mr. Clyman told you that there is no one out ahead of us."

"He did," Brown said. "We weren't able to leave Mississippi until the eighth of April, so we also assumed we would be far behind. Some were worried that we wouldn't catch them until we reached the Rocky Mountains, but I was optimistic. We are a small company and are making good time. I really thought we would overtake them, once we reached the Platte."

Peter was nodding vigorously. Brown could be telling his and Kathryn's own story.

"As we pressed on and found no sign of them, some of our number became reluctant to continue farther. After considerable discussion we determined that there was nothing to do but to move on and see what developed."

"It was Mr. Clyman who told us there were no Mormons ahead of us," Peter said quietly. "That's when we first knew for sure that something was wrong."

"And it was Mr. Clyman who gave us the same news. As you will appreciate, this threw our company into great disarray. Some wanted to turn back immediately and either return to Independence or find our people. Others wanted to press on. It was finally decided to move on to Fort Laramie and then perhaps wait there for our people." His eyes were dark and brooding. "Then, last night, we met Mr. Reshaw. He too confirmed that there were no Mormons out in front of us and told us that Fort Laramie is not a good place to winter over if that is what we are forced to do. He says it is bitterly cold there."

Peter grunted, picturing what Fort Laramie would look like in winter. "It's probably not the best place for a whole company."

Brown brightened a little. "But Mr. Reshaw has given us a possible solution, and it may be the solution for you and your wife as well."

"How is that?"

"Mr. Reshaw is leaving shortly to do some trading down south at Taos in Mexico. He claims that on the Arkansas River, at the eastern foot of the Rockies, there is a good place to winter over. It's called Fort Pueblo. The temperature is mild and they are raising corn there. He thinks the mountaineers who winter there would gladly trade surplus grain for our labors."

Peter was quiet, letting the implications of all that sink in.

"Once we get our people settled, those of us with families back in Mississippi could return there and bring them back out as well. Then come spring we'll hopefully know where our brethren are and join up with them then."

"So Kathryn could go with you?"

Brown nodded. "We would be most pleased to take her in and care for her until you can return from California."

Peter's shoulder's sagged a little. It was as if someone had just removed a heavy pack from them. Here was a far better solution than what he had previously been thinking. Kathryn would be with a company of Mormons. True, it was a small company—only about sixty people, he guessed—but that was a lot better than leaving her alone at Fort Laramie. He looked up. "That would be wonderful. Have you decided for sure that that's what you're going to do?"

There was a brief nod. "As you heard, Mr. Reshaw is expecting our decision tonight, but I don't think there is much question about it. We're of one mind in the matter already. We view this as an answer to prayer."

"As do I," Peter breathed softly. "As do I. I'll go for Kathryn right now."

In the pre-dawn darkness, Peter knelt down beside the bed of his wife, felt for her face in the darkness, then leaned over and kissed her gently. He tasted the salt of her tears and reached up and wiped them from her cheeks with his thumbs. "Good-bye, my love," he whispered.

"Good-bye, Peter. Godspeed."

He kissed her again, straightened, and was gone. Kathryn sat up and hugged her knees, blinking rapidly to stop more tears from coming. She listened intently, following the soft crunch of his footsteps in the grass until they died away. For several minutes there was silence; then she heard the muffled sound of hooves as he rode away. Then again came the silence—this time total, deafening, all-encompassing. Though she fought it hard, she could no longer hold it back. Her shoulders began to shake and a great sob was torn from her throat. She turned, throwing herself onto her pillow, and began to cry as she had not allowed herself to cry while he was still with her.

Peter had been so excited when he returned late in the afternoon yesterday to tell her of this new development. And it was wonderful news. When he took her to the camp of the Mississippi Saints, they had welcomed her as if she were one of their own. So in that sense, her worries were gone. And she wanted Peter to know that. So even though they both shed some tears and clung together for a very long time before finally going to sleep, she had held her emotions in check so that Peter would not be troubled more than he already was. But now her whole body shuddered and shook. It would be six or seven months at best, perhaps even a year. There was a chance that she would even have to have the baby without him. She buried her face in the pillow.

O dear God, put thy sheltering hand over my dear husband. Watch over him and keep him from harm's way. Only now do I fully realize the precious gift thou hast given me in this man. Help me to be strong, to be worthy of him, to be ready for that wonderful day when we shall be together again.

She rolled over onto her back, putting her arm across her eyes to help staunch the tears. Her other hand stole down to rest on her stomach. Gradually her body calmed and the shudders became mere tremors and then finally ceased altogether. She sighed, feeling the weariness now—they had barely slept three or four hours. She turned onto her side, trying to get more comfortable. As her hand fell across Peter's pillow, she felt something there. Surprised, she groped a little, then picked it up. It was an envelope. Instantly she knew what it was. The tears came forth again, but this time they were accompanied by a quiet smile.

Through the canvas she could discern the first light from the eastern sky. It would be full light in half an hour, but she couldn't wait for that. She went up on hands and knees and crawled to her trunk. In a moment she found a match and struck it on the side of the chest. In the flare of light she saw the candle and lit it. Moving closer to the candle, she opened the envelope and leaned toward the light. Her hands trembled slightly as she unfolded the single sheet. For a moment, tears blurred her vision as she recognized his neat and boldly dramatic scrawl. She blinked them back and began to read.

Separations

In the great, all-seeing providence of God,
Some things are made undivided
And indivisible—
The silver in the moonlight;
The heat within the fire;
The fruit within an apple's seed;
Laughter in a child's eyes.

Not the wisest of the wise,
Or the strongest of the strong,
Or the keenest of the keen,
Can separate what's made divinely one.

Long years ago, at Eden's wondrous gate,
Our God took two
And—miracle divine!—he made them one:
One in heart and mind and hand;
One in work and joy and pain;
One in spirit, life, and love.

In modern day,
The miracle has struck again.
Two hearts—
One from Ireland's emerald shores,
And one from England's teeming streets—
Became as one:
One in heart and mind and hand;
One in work and joy and pain;
One in spirit, life, and love.

No endless trail,
No boundless sky,
No dreary length of lonely days,
Can separate what's made divinely one.

My dearest Kathryn,

As you read these lines, I am riding ever-farther west. Do not think of this as taking me farther and farther from your side. Think of it as one great circle which brings me back to you. We are separated only by the miles. Every step I take shortens the distance and the time before we are rejoined. With that thought, I fly as if on the wings of lightning.

All my love,
Peter

Rebecca walked quietly beside her husband, content for the moment to leave him alone in his thoughts. She had a pretty good idea of what they were. This certainly would not be their first conversation on the matter. She also knew only too well how deeply stubborn Derek Ingalls could be when he set his mind to something. That was not all bad. He had shoveled coal in the boilers of the great cotton mills of Preston, England, in order to keep himself and Peter alive. That took some degree of iron will. She smiled inwardly. But the Steeds had some renown in the field of strong wills too. Since their last conversation she had begun to marshal her forces.

The Steed clan had not ferried over the Missouri River yet, but they were to do so in the next few days, and so they had moved their camp on Mosquito Creek down here to the river bottoms. Now she and Derek walked slowly along the riverbank about a quarter of a mile away from their wagons. When she had asked him if they could talk, his jaw had instantly set—he knew full well what the subject would be—but he nodded. Now they were here.

He nodded toward a dead log that had fallen near the water's edge. "Let's sit."

"All right." They moved over to it. He brushed it off and they sat down. For several moments, he stared at the muddy water. She waited. Her preparation had left her feeling really quite serene, and that pleased her.

"Look, Rebecca," he began, "I fully understand why you want to go on this march, and in some ways it would be wonderful, but . . ." He blew out his breath. "It's just not the wise thing to do."

"Why not?" she asked innocently.

"You know why not. We have three children. Leah's barely a year old."

She laughed softly. He had tried that one before on her. "She's sixteen months old, Derek, remember."

"Yes, like I said, barely a year. How can you think of taking her on a march of a thousand miles or more?"

She smiled sweetly. "I think we should have asked that question before we left Nauvoo."

"You know what I mean. I mean on a march with an army, going to war."

"Derek, this is not some idea that I cooked up on my own. It was the United States Army that said that each company could have four laundresses. Would they do that if they thought women were not capable of going along?"

"Single women, yes. I mean, not single but women without children." He was clearly exasperated by her calm reasoning, and his temper was rising a little. "Look at Melissa Burton and William Coray. They were just married a couple of weeks ago. This will be like a honeymoon to them. They don't have to worry about children."

"And what if she gets in a family way during the next year? Will the army send her home?"

"Of course not, but if she were that way now, I'll bet the army would say no."

"I think you make an excellent point," she said, nodding. "About newlyweds, I mean."

He gave her a suspicious look. "You do?"

"Yes. In fact, I just heard about another set of newlyweds who will be going too."

"Who is that?"

"Brother James Brown is going to marry Sister Mary McCree Black."

One eyebrow lifted slowly. "Do we know them?"

"I do. They plan to marry on the sixteenth, the day of mustering. Brother Brown has gotten permission to take his new bride along too."

"Well, that just goes to prove my point."

"*And*," she added innocently, "their two children. You see, Sister Black is a widow and Brother Brown is a widower, and they each have a child from their first marriages."

He grunted, irritated at himself for not seeing the trap. "So, two children. Are they older?"

"I don't know. But I did just happen to stop by the officer's tent yesterday afternoon and make a few inquiries."

"You what?" he exclaimed.

"The army officers that Captain Allen left here to help recruit, I asked them a few questions about the laundresses." Removing a slip of paper from the pocket of her dress, she rushed on before his fuming could be expressed in words. "Here is what I learned. Brother and Sister James Brown—this is James P. Brown, not the one marrying Mary Black—will be taking their *four* children. A Brother and Sister Button will be taking *four* children. You know Nelson Higgins. He and Sarah will be taking six children. *Six*, Derek!"

His mouth opened, then shut again. She went on, pretending not to notice. "So as not to flog a dead horse overly much, I'll just note that Brother and Sister Jefferson Hunt will be taking *seven* children, including two young twins, as will a family by the name of Shelton. *Seven*, Derek. That is more than twice the number of children that we have. In fact, with only three children, we shall be among the minority."

He scowled at her, and yet she was pleased to see that he was impressed. "And I specifically asked the lieutenant," she went on more gently now, "if my having three children gives the United States Army or any of its officers great concern. Even when I told him their ages, he assured me that it does not."

She folded the paper and returned it to her pocket, then crossed her hands and placed them in her lap.

He was eyeing a large mass of floating weeds going by in the current. He spoke without looking up. "Seven? You're not just fooling with me about that, Becca?"

"No, Derek. Right now there are two families who will have seven children with them on the march." Now she turned toward him. "I know that it's not going to be easy, Derek, but neither will staying here. You've heard how worried the leaders are about finding food and shelter for everyone. If we can get to Upper California with the army, that's five mouths our family doesn't have to worry about. That frees up a whole wagon for the others next spring. Think about that."

"I have," he sighed. "It's just that . . ." He shook his head. "You know I don't want to leave you, Becca. You do know that, don't you?"

"Of course." She took his hand. "And we don't want to have you leave us, either."

"I know. I just worry so about you."

"If we were staying in our home in Nauvoo while you go, it would be a different matter, Derek. But we're not. We're out here in the middle of nowhere. We don't have homes or enough food. We won't have until we reach the Rocky Mountains. So if we have to go anyway, I would rather it was with you."

He nodded somberly, but said nothing. For several minutes they sat together quietly, lost in their own thoughts. Finally he looked up. "They say President Young and the others are supposed to be back here tomorrow or the next day."

"Really?"

He nodded. "What if we asked him what he thinks?"

She felt her heart leap. "I think that is a good idea, Derek."

"If he says no, will you accept that?"

"Of course." She held her breath for a moment. "And if he says yes, will you accept *that?*"

There was no hesitation. "Yes, I will."

She threw her arms around him. "Thank you, Derek. That's all I ask. We'll let President Young decide."

Mary Ann Steed was cutting potatoes into thin slices and dropping them into the gurgling stew pot that hung over the fire. Lydia was dicing carrots by her side. Joshua and Nathan had managed to acquire some fresh vegetables at the trading post downriver, and tonight they were going to have a treat. Both stopped what they were doing to watch as Derek and Rebecca appeared from some trees and walked toward them.

"Well?" Lydia asked her mother-in-law, who was now more a mother to her almost than her own mother had been. "Did she convince him?"

Mary Ann nodded slowly and sadly. "Yes."

Lydia peered more closely to see what Mary Ann was seeing. "How can you tell?"

"Because it's right. The moment she first brought up the idea, I felt it was right." She sighed. "That doesn't make it any less frightening, and that's what Derek is struggling with. But it's right. Don't you feel it?"

Lydia started a little, then went back to work. "I suppose."

Mary Ann gave her a sharp look, but said nothing, and she too resumed her cutting. She knew that at that moment Lydia was not thinking of Derek and Rebecca at all. She was thinking of young Josh. His desire to volunteer for the Mormon Battalion would not be squelched, and it had become a source of major contention between mother and son—the first real problem that Lydia had ever had with him. So what if he was not yet sixteen? he countered every time she and Nathan fell back on that, their strongest argument. He had heard that they were taking a few men who were not eighteen yet for orderlies or to help care for the stock.

Derek let go of Rebecca's hand and went to get something from one of the wagons. Rebecca came straight to her mother and sister-in-law. She had kept her face without much expression until Derek turned away. Now it broke out in a huge smile.

"It worked," Mary Ann laughed.

"Yes!" She pulled the paper from her pocket and waved it triumphantly at them. "It was just what he needed. He's agreed that if Brother Brigham gives us his blessing, I can go."

"That's wonderful, Rebecca," Lydia said slowly. Her words and her expression were in direct contradiction to each other.

Rebecca slowly put the paper away and came to stand between them. "I know," she said softly. "Now the reality of leaving sets in." Her voice caught for a moment. "I can't bear to think about that."

"But you'll be with Derek," Mary Ann responded. "That will make it easier."

"Oh, yes." She looked sideways at Lydia. "If it were Nathan, wouldn't you do it?"

Lydia did not hesitate. "Of course. I would rather face whatever that march will mean with him than to be without him."

"That's what I told Derek. It's not that I want some great adventure. I just want our family to be together."

Mary Ann dropped the last of the potatoes in the pot and wiped her hands on her apron. She turned and gave Rebecca a quick hug, watching Lydia as she did so. "There are many roads to Zion," she said. "And for some reason, the Lord seems to think our family should take more than one." She stepped back and forced a smile. "But let's not forget that they all lead to the same place. That's all that matters. Someday, we'll all be together again."

Chapter Notes

The story of the group that came to be known as the "Mississippi Saints" is a little-known part of the great westward migrations of the Mormons. As Brigham Young's plans for going west had to be adjusted, what seemed to be a setback for the Mississippi Saints, who were out ahead of Brigham's group hoping to meet them on the trail, would prove to be one more evidence of the Lord's over-watching eye. (See "Pioneer Journeys," pp. 802–10; "Mississippi Saints Headed West in 1846," *Church News*, 13 July 1996, p. 4; Andrew Jenson, *Latter-day Saint Biographical Encyclopedia*, 4 vols. [1901–36; reprint, Salt Lake City: Western Epics, 1971], 1:511–12.)

Usually, little is said about the women who accompanied the Mormon Battalion. As part of the recruitment of the Mormons, the U.S. Army granted permission for each of the five companies to have four women designated as "laundresses." (In reality they also became cooks and seamstresses.) Only eighteen of the possible twenty such women have been identified, but it is known that thirty-one wives of battalion members and three additional women started the journey. Forty-four children also joined them. (See *MB*, pp. 28–33, which includes a roster of names.) All of the names used here by Rebecca are the names of actual people who accompanied the battalion.

Chapter Twelve

Melissa was deep in thought, trying to calculate how long it would be before she could realistically expect Carl's return from St. Louis. He had left on the fifth of July. Today was the eleventh. If it took four days for the raft of lumber to make it downriver—she decided to make it five to be sure—that meant that he and Jean Claude had arrived in St. Louis yesterday. She wasn't sure how long it would take to find a buyer, perhaps a day or two, and then two more days to return to Nauvoo, assuming they could get immediate passage on a steamboat bound upriver. Today was Saturday. So they could possibly be here by Tuesday, but almost certainly by Thursday or Friday, unless something had gone wrong. That would be the time—

"Mama. Look!" Sarah tugged at her mother's sleeve.

Melissa stopped, raising her head. Sarah, nearly eight now, had taken over pushing Mary Melissa in her pram, leaving Melissa free to let her thoughts roam. Now Sarah pointed up the street in the direction they were walking. There was a crowd collected there outside the post office, and even as she looked, Melissa saw other people hurrying to join it.

"What is it, Mama?"

"I don't know, Sarah. We shall go and see."

She stepped forward and took the baby carriage from her daughter. "Hold on, Mary Melissa. We're going to go faster now. Sarah, stay close by me, now." She strode out briskly, her curiosity piqued. With less than a thousand people left in Nauvoo, it was unusual to see large crowds of any kind anymore, especially in the afternoon when most of the men were still out in the fields working.

Before she reached the assembled crowd, Melissa sensed that something was seriously wrong. The faces of those she could see were showing dismay, and there was much talking and pointing. As she reached the edge of the crowd, she spoke to the nearest woman. "What is the matter?"

"I think someone has been hurt."

"Beaten, you mean," a man beside her said, his face grim.

"Beaten?" Melissa echoed.

But the man had pushed into the crowd so as to see better and didn't answer. She turned and looked around quickly. There was a large, open field across the street from the small store that served as post office and unofficial city hall now that the city was nearly abandoned. There were several children playing there together in the long grass. "Sarah, take Mary Melissa over there. You may get her out of the pram, but watch her closely."

"Yes, Mama."

Melissa didn't wait to see that she did as she was told. Sarah was quite responsible, and Melissa often left the baby in her care. Melissa circled around the back of the crowd to the far side, where there weren't quite so many people, then pushed her way in. She stopped as she neared the front of the crowd. Going up on tiptoe to see over the heads, she caught a glimpse of a strange thing. A man was leaning against the building, feet spread wide apart and hands propped up high on the wall so as to leave his body at an angle. She heard a cry of pain and saw his fingers dig into the wood. Surprised, she pushed in closer until she was near the front. Then she gasped. The man was stripped to the waist, and his back was a bloody mass of welts, cuts, bruises, and abrasions. Another man stood beside him with a cloth and a bucket of water. He dipped the cloth in the bucket and held it over the man's back, then gently squeezed it onto the wounds. She saw his body stiffen, heard him grunt, and saw the fingers clawing at the wall again. The water streamed down his back, turning bright red as it ran onto his trousers.

Melissa looked away, feeling her stomach lurch. Then she saw a second man. He was lying on a bench farther down the narrow porch of the store. A woman stood beside him, rubbing what looked like soft lard across a second lacerated back. He winced and shuddered each time her fingers moved across the battered flesh.

One hand came to Melissa's mouth. "What happened?" she exclaimed in a hoarse whisper.

A man she didn't know turned to look at her. "They were caught by a mob. There are more inside."

Her legs went weak, and for a moment she had to close her eyes and shut out the sight. "Who?" she managed to ask.

Another man in front of them turned. "That's more the outrage. They're not Mormons. They're new citizens."

Her first informant gave the other a sharp look. "When a man is whipped, it is an outrage whether he is a Mormon or not a Mormon."

"But," a third man joined in now, "it's the Mormons these so-called 'regulators' are after. But this time they didn't care who it was, they just—"

Just then someone came out of the store. It was James Wilson, one of the leaders of the new citizens committee. Melissa didn't know him well, but he had been to their house on a few occasions to meet with Carl, who was also an active member of the committee. They had finally stopped holding meetings there because of Melissa's feelings. She had little tolerance for these people who swept in behind the Mormon tragedy to buy up property for pennies on the dollar. Now they were finding, to their great dismay, that the anti-Mormons didn't much care which residents were Mormons and which were not; they wanted everybody out of Nauvoo.

Wilson raised his hands, and the crowd instantly quieted. He looked at the two battered men, then lifted his head. "Fellow citizens of Nauvoo. We have had a tragedy in our midst. You see the results of that tragedy in front of you. There are three more men inside who are just as badly wounded."

The crowd was shocked.

"From what we have learned, this is what happened. Five of our number—none of which were Latter-day Saints, by the way—hired out to help harvest wheat on the Davis farm up near Pontoosuc, which is about twelve miles north of here on the river. They worked all day yesterday without incident. But this morning, about nine o'clock, several bands of armed men suddenly appeared from different directions. In a moment they were surrounded. This was a group of the antis who have been stirring up trouble of late. One they call Old Whimp. Another was Frank Lofton."

The man who had been leaning against the wall straightened and turned slowly. "John McAuley from Pontoosuc was their leader," he said, grimacing even as he spoke.

Wilson motioned to someone at the front of the crowd, and Melissa saw a man writing the names down. Then Wilson straightened and went on. "Our men waved a white handkerchief as a sign of peace, but they came in and demanded these men's weapons."

Now the victim picked up the story. "Once they had our weapons they marched us to the nearest house, which belonged to a man named Rice. Here they held a quick council, then sent eight or ten men off to the woods." Now his voice became more strained, and it was clear that he was reliving it in his mind. "After a few minutes they all came back with hickory gads."

Melissa shuddered. Hickory was the wood of choice for making ox goads—or gads, as they were often called—because hickory was more like iron than wood. Usually a gad was three-quarters of an inch to an inch in diameter and four or five feet long. Again her stomach twisted as she sensed what was coming.

Now the man on the bench got to his feet and joined Wilson and the other man. He spoke, his voice low and filled with pain. "They called us out two by two. Me and John Richards were first. They marched us down to a ditch and made us kneel down in it, with our chests pushed up against the one bank. Then they each took turns." His eyes closed and he lowered his head. "The sentence was twenty lashes each."

"The man who whipped me," the first man broke back in, "had chosen the largest hickory gad of the bunch. He held it with both hands and swung it with all the force he could muster. He gave me my twenty lashes, then hit me once more for good measure." He hesitated, his eyes haunted and wide. "I think there's some damage. I can't move my shoulders without it hurting something awful."

The silence was total for several moments. Then James Wilson raised his head to look at the crowd. "This comes as no surprise. These so-called men, who are courageous only in bands of fifty or more, think this is the way to frighten us away. They want us to leave, particularly the Mormons. But I say that we are not going to leave. I say we get a warrant for the arrest of these men—McAuley, Old Whimp, Lofton, and whoever else was responsible—and bring them in for justice."

There was an instant and angry response from the crowd. Several men shouted out their support. "Go home," Wilson shouted. "Get your guns and horses, then report back here as soon as you can. The new citizens committee will deputize every man who is willing to let these bullies know that we will not stand for such lawlessness. We will not allow this . . ."

Melissa turned away, not wanting to hear any more, sickened by the sight of the bloodied men, unable to stand and listen to the call for escalation. As she walked quickly toward the field and her two girls, for the first time since Carl had left her to go to Wisconsin, Melissa was grateful that he was not there with her, for she knew that if he were here, he would be among the first to volunteer for the posse.

Most of Sunday morning was quiet. Melissa kept the children in the house. They read from the Book of Mormon, and then they acted out some of their favorite Bible stories. After lunch Melissa could not bear it any longer and sent young Carl to see what he could learn. He was back in less than half an hour. When she heard him come in the back door, she folded her sewing and put it in her lap. Carl came into the room. He looked a little flushed, and she supposed that he had run part of the way. "What did you learn, son?" she asked even as he entered.

"The posse rode out to Pontoosuc last night and arrested Mr. McAuley and another man and brought them back to the city."

"Did they meet resistance?"

He shook his head. She leaned back, letting some of the stiffness go out of her body. This was good. The mob had struck, but now they knew that the citizens of Nauvoo were prepared to defend themselves. It was the best way to prevent further depredations. Then she saw his face. "What, Carl?"

"They've got the two men in jail, Mama, and there weren't any problems with that—not last night, anyway."

She felt her heart constrict. "But?"

"There was a note delivered this afternoon to the committee."

"What kind of a note?"

"The mob in Pontoosuc have kidnaped five Mormons and are holding them hostage until the two leaders are returned to them."

She gave a low cry of dismay. "No!"

"Yes, Mama. Brother Phineas Young and his son. Brother Richard Ballantyne and two others that I do not know. The note was signed by the victims and addressed to the new citizens. It begged them to release the leaders in exchange for their freedom. Otherwise, their captors are promising to execute them."

For several moments Melissa sat motionless, chills shooting through every part of her body. Then she nodded slowly. "Carl, don't say anything to the other children, but I want you to go to the barn and get the two steamer trunks up in the loft."

"All right, Mama. What for?"

"We are going to start packing some things. When your father returns home, we're leaving Nauvoo."

For several seconds he stared at her, his eyes not comprehending, and then he nodded very slowly. "Yes, Mama," he said quietly. "I'll go at once."

When Captain Allen and his officers arrived at Mount Pisgah in late June with the news that they were there to recruit five hundred Mormon men into the army, they received a polite but cool reception. Such was not the case with Brigham Young. He immediately saw the broad advantages that would accompany the Saints' acceptance. Knowing that his people had good cause to distrust the federal government and that it would take some persuasion from the highest councils to change the people's minds, he left immediately for Mount Pisgah to help recruit for the army. He was successful. Once Brigham made it clear that he was in support of it, over sixty men volunteered and started west for Council Bluffs. Satisfied, Brigham turned west again too. The ranks of the battalion were starting to fill, but there was still much to do.

Brigham Young arrived back at the Missouri River late in the afternoon of Sunday, July twelfth. During his nine days' absence the ferry ran day and night, and there was now a sizeable encampment on the western side of the Missouri River. For miles up and down the eastern bluffs, however, the numbers had not diminished but were actually greater than when he had left. With the coming of summer and the drying of the roads across Iowa, massive numbers of people were on the move. Just between Mount Pisgah and Council Bluffs alone, a distance of about 120 miles, the eastbound party led by Brigham had counted 1,805 wagons—an average of one wagon about every hundred yards! There was hardly a time on the trail now that one could look in either direction and not see at least one wagon.

To no one's surprise, immediately after his arrival Brigham sent word up and down the camps on both sides of the river—the brethren were to assemble tomorrow at noon to hear their President who had just returned.

It seemed that there were only two choices that summer along the Missouri River—drenching rain or blistering sun, and either one came with swarms of voracious mosquitos. Those in the river bottoms began calling it the Misery River. To combat the blistering sun, Brigham Young had commanded that a bowery be built just below the bridge that spanned Mosquito Creek. Numerous holes were dug in the earth and filled with posts that extended about eight feet above the ground. A latticework of willow branches was laid across the top, then covered with leafy branches from the hundreds of trees along the river. It worked for either alternative that nature laid upon them—it was nearly waterproof when it rained, and it provided deep and welcome shelter from the sun.

When the Steeds awoke on that Monday morning, it was cloudy and cool. At eight it commenced to rain and quickly became heavy. But by ten the clouds were scudding eastward and the sun was shining brightly. By noon the heat was oppressive again. As Nathan, Joshua, Derek, Solomon, Matthew, and young Josh arrived—Nathan had finally agreed to let his son accompany them, even though Lydia strenuously objected—William Pitt's brass band began to play. In the month since the first arrivals here at Council Bluffs, enough band members had come so that Pitt had a nearly full contingent again. The marches were brisk and stirring, and many a foot was set to tapping. It set a proper mood for the assembly as they gathered beneath the bowery.

Nathan watched as the leaders of the Church gathered near the front of the bowery and shook hands with each other. There were now eleven of the Twelve in camp. Only Lyman Wight, who still refused to obey the call to bring his group back from Texas, was absent. There were also two men in uniform. The first was Captain Allen. The other was an officer named Colonel Thomas L. Kane. Kane was the son of a prominent jurist in Philadelphia whose family had great influence with the Polk White House. The Kanes were not members of the Church, but Thomas had been touched by the injustices done to the Mormons and became a staunch defender of their rights with the president. He had given invaluable help to Elder Jesse Little in Washington in getting an audience with the president of the United States. Now he had come west with Brother Little to assure the Mormons that this was not some deceptive trick by the government.

Brigham seemed in no hurry to begin the meeting but let the band play on for several minutes after the bowery was full and no more seemed to be coming. Finally at twenty minutes of one o'clock, the band stopped, a prayer was offered, and the meeting began. With characteristic directness, Brigham took to the podium first. Nathan was not surprised. During a brief greeting, Parley Pratt had told Nathan that even with the sixty-five or so men who had volunteered at Mount Pisgah, they had still barely filled two of the five required companies for the battalion. If that report had been given to Brigham—and Nathan was sure it had—then directness was what could be expected today.

"Brethren, I request your silence and your order so that we may begin."

When he had stood, the crowd had immediately quieted, but now it became perfectly still.

He looked around, letting his eyes sweep across the many faces. "As you know, I have just returned last evening from our encampment at Mount Pisgah. Things are well there and they send you greetings. Many of our brothers and sisters are on their way here, and we are pleased at their progress." He paused for a moment. "I would be glad to offer a great many ideas to you this day, but our time is limited, so I shall come straight to the point.

"The business to be laid before you today is the call from the War Department to furnish five hundred volunteers for the Army of the West to march to California." He paused again, but no one stirred, so he went on firmly.

"I know what many of you are thinking. You are concerned about your circumstances. Well, I am as well acquainted with the situation of every man in camp as they are themselves. But now the surrounding circumstances must recede from our minds. Let go of them. We may as well consider ourselves in good circumstances as in bad ones."

Now his eyes took on that fierceness that was typical of him when he felt strongly about something. "But says one, 'I will go if my family can be made comfortable.' " He frowned. "I told my brethren not to mention families today. I am aware it is desirable, were it our privilege, to have every man's presence in the camp to take care of his family and team and go along to the West. There are no more men here than what are badly needed. But these feelings must be dispensed with. We have to learn to control our feelings and act according to our best judgment.

"My experience has taught me that it is best to do the things that are necessary. I have learned to do the necessary thing independent of my feelings and at the expense of everything near and dear to me. Many of us have been called upon to forsake the society of friends, wives, and children, and you will all be brought into a situation to learn the same lesson."

Nathan saw Joshua give him a questioning look and knew his thoughts. Were Brigham's assignments to the Steed family about to change? Would Joshua be asked to leave the family after all?

"The blessings we are looking forward to receive," Brigham continued, "will only be attained through sacrifice. We want to raise volunteers. Are we willing to undergo hardships and privation to procure that which we desire? I say we can do it." The last sentence was punctuated with a hard slap on the podium that startled some of those near the front.

He shook his head wearily. "Some of you have said that you do not see the propriety of going and that the Twelve do not understand your 'peculiar circumstances.' There will be a time for preaching and answering those concerns, but we have not the time to reason together now. We want to conform to the requisition made upon us, and we will do nothing else, till we have accomplished this thing.

"If we want the privilege of going where we can worship God according to the dictates of our consciences, *we must raise the battalion.*" He pounded home each word with a stab of his finger. "I say that it is right. Who cares for sacrificing our comfort for a few years? I would rather have undertaken to raise two thousand men a year ago in twenty-four hours than raise one hundred in a week now. I know that you do not have your gardens planted and your farms growing. I know your circumstances. But we want the five hundred men. We can muster them now. We can do what other people cannot." He stopped, and now his eyes were blazing with passion. "Some of you are worried about going off to fight, but all the fighting that will be done will be among yourselves, I am afraid to say."

Then just as suddenly, the passion was gone. He spoke with intensity, but more calmly now and in a softer and milder tone. "Brethren, every man that enlists will have his name and the names of his wife and children inserted into a book, along with what directions you give concerning them. We will take care of them. We shall care for the families still coming from Nauvoo. Do you think we shall neglect your families if you enroll?"

Now there were many who were shaking their heads. As usual, Brigham's call had stirred and softened hearts. Brigham straightened to his full height. "Brethren, after we get through talking we shall call out the companies. And if there are not young men enough, we shall call out the old men." His glance pierced every man there assembled. "And," he thundered, "if there are not enough old men, we shall take the women!"

His voice dropped almost to a whisper. "I tell you, those of you who go on this expedition will never be sorry, but rather, you will be glad to all eternity. And those who are not here to go will be sorry they missed the opportunity to do what you will do."

The Steed women and children were waiting for them when they returned, and they gathered around to hear the report. Caroline asked the question that was most pressing on the minds of all of them. "Did President Young make any changes in what he wants our family to do?"

Joshua shook his head, unable to hide his disappointment. "No. Nathan and I asked him specifically. He only wants Derek to go."

"Did you ask him about me?" Rebecca asked quickly.

Derek shook his head, then grinned at the look of dismay that crossed her face. "I didn't have to."

"Why not?"

He straightened, striking a pose similar to Brigham's. "I tell you, brethren, when we call out the companies, if we do not have enough young men, we shall call the old men, and if we do not have enough old men, we shall call the women."

Rebecca clapped her hands. "He really said that?"

"He did," Derek said. "That was answer enough for me."

Christopher, now seven and their oldest, started marching around in a circle, swinging his arms. "I get to go in the army. I get to go in the army."

They all laughed except Lydia, who turned her face away. Young Josh saw it and went to her. "Mama?"

She turned.

"Did you hear that, Mama? President Young said he wants the young men first."

Lydia gave Nathan a sharp glance, an I-told-you-not-to-let-him-go glance, but then turned back to face the pleading eyes of her son. "You know what the letter says, Josh. Men eighteen to forty-five."

"But Mama, there are younger men going."

She swung around in surprise. "Is that true?" she demanded of Nathan and the others.

Nathan nodded slowly. "A fourteen-year-old drummer boy has been selected, and some of the officers will be allowed to take young men as orderlies."

"No."

"Mama!"

"*No*, Joshua. No! We've already talked about this." She was shaking her head emphatically all the time she was speaking. "No."

There was a long silence, but Josh was not defeated yet. "After President Young spoke, Elder Hyde talked to us too. Do you know what he said, Mama?"

"It doesn't matter, Josh. He wasn't speaking to you."

"He said, 'Let us rally to the standard and our children will reverence our names. It will inspire in them a gratitude which will last forever.' "

She didn't wait for him to finish, but began shaking her head again.

"Lydia—," Nathan began.

She whirled, furious now. "Nathan, don't you dare take his side in this. We've talked about it. The answer is no!" Then, bursting into tears, she spun around and ran toward their tent.

Shocked by the intensity of her outburst, the family looked awkwardly at one another. Finally, Mary Ann stood up. "I'll go to her, Nathan. But for now, I think any more talk of the battalion will have to wait."

Chapter Notes

By mid-July of 1846 the anti-Mormons around Nauvoo had lost patience. The Saints had promised to leave the city by spring. While most had, there were still a large number of the poor who seemed unable to leave. Also, new arrivals from Europe or from missions in the South and the East showed up almost daily. The antis had their own eyes set on expropriating the rich properties the Mormons would leave behind, so they did not welcome the non-Mormons who came in and bought out the Mormons. Tensions had been mounting through most of the summer, but on 11 July, open violence erupted as described here (see *MHBY*, pp. 230–32). Whether the men from Pontoosuc thought they were attacking Mormons or not is not clear, but this became the first in what quickly became an escalating battle for control of Nauvoo and Hancock County, Illinois.

After his return from Mount Pisgah, Brigham Young called for an assembly of the brethren and once again gave them a stirring call to volunteer. The address he gave on that occasion as presented here is taken almost verbatim from the transcript kept by Willard Richards and William Clayton. (See *MHBY*, pp. 234–38.)

Chapter Thirteen

Peter left Fort Bernard shortly after four a.m. on the morning of the ninth day of July. He rode hard the eight miles to Fort Laramie; bought some hardtack, pemmican, and venison jerky from Bordeaux; changed his saddle to the pack mule to give his horse a rest; then set out again before seven that morning. There was no way to gauge the miles. They passed in exhausting slowness. He rode well after sundown, until it became too dark to see and he was afraid he would lose the trail. He was up and off again before the sky was barely light enough to see, trading mounts, eating food and drinking from his leather water bottle as he rode. About three p.m. on the second day, he passed Beaver Creek and the campground where they had celebrated the Fourth of July. That was good. What had taken him and Kathryn almost four full days to do he had done in less than two.

At midafternoon of the third day he caught up with a small company of emigrants stopped at what was known as the "last crossing" of the Platte. Here the river turned south, not a direction the emigrants wanted to go. Also, from what they said, a few miles farther on the North Platte entered a narrow gorge that provided no possible road for the wagons. So here at the last crossing they left the river that had given them not only a clearly marked highway for almost six hundred miles but also water, wood, and game. From this point the trail struck off to the southwest, and about fifty miles farther on it would pick up the Sweetwater River, a tributary to the Platte.

Peter didn't stop to watch the emigrants' attempt to cross the river. Fortunately the high-water season—evidence of which was visible everywhere around him—was about over. But even then the current was swift, the channel deep, and the river still thirty or forty yards across. The emigrants would have welcomed his help, but time was too pressing. He found a spot on the opposite side of the river where the banks weren't too steep, and plunged in with his horse and mule.

With everything soaked through, Peter decided there was no point in camping for the night in a wet bedroll. There was a quarter moon and the air was so clear that he could easily follow the wagon tracks across the barren expanse of artemisia, or sagebrush, plain. Then, sometime after midnight, he learned that it is possible to fall asleep on a moving horse. He woke up just as he pitched headfirst off the saddle. Fortunately he caught himself in time to do little more than scrape his hands and bruise his pride. At that point he determined that, wet bedroll or not, it was time to camp.

Independence Rock, which from a distance had seemed little more than a large bump in the flat desert country, now looked like some gigantic loaf of bread half-buried in the flatness of the Sweetwater Valley. It was solid rock, one massive block of brown-gray granite that was easily a quarter of a mile long and two hundred feet high. Only a few low bushes grew from cracks and crevasses on its flank. Much of it rose precipitously from the flat ground around it, but nearer the center its slope was more gradual, and Peter saw in surprise tiny figures moving around on the top of it. He peered more closely and saw that they were people. That only added to the impression of sheer size and majesty. No wonder people spoke of Independence Rock as the most noted landmark west of Fort Laramie.

Peter stood up in his stirrups, reaching down to pat the sweaty neck of the mule. He lifted his hand and shaded his eyes against the lowering sun. Ahead, about a mile away, he could see a speckling of white—wagon covers, unless his eyes were deceiving him.

He sat down again, removed his hat, and wiped at his brow. It was the fourth day. If his calculations were correct, he had come almost a hundred and forty miles since Fort Bernard. That was close to thirty-five miles a day. He felt it too. His bottom had lost all feeling. The insides of his legs were chafed raw. His eyes burned and his face was flushed from too much sun. He rubbed at the thick stubble on his chin and felt the stickiness of the sweat beneath his armpits. Good thing Kathryn wasn't here to see him now, he thought.

Grinning, he slapped the mule affectionately on the rump. "Let's go, boy! We're almost home."

In the fading light of a spectacular sunset, the Reeds sat quietly around the campfire. Patty sat on one side of Peter, her arm through his. She was eight. Young James, who was five, sat on the other side, his shoulder pressed against Peter's. Thomas (or Tommy, as his mother called him), who was three, plopped squarely on Peter's lap. Mr. and Mrs. Reed sat across the fire, drinking coffee from tin cups. They smiled as they watched their children cling to Peter. He had always been good with them, and many nights he had joined Kathryn in teaching them their lessons. But everyone knew this response was partially to compensate for their loss of Kathryn.

Virginia sat beside her parents. She had turned thirteen last month and now liked to let everyone know she was an adult and no longer a child.

Peter had a tin cup as well, but it was filled with water from the river. He drank deeply, savoring it even though this was his third full cup. When he lowered it, Patty snatched it from his hand. "Would you like some more, Peter?"

"Yes, Patty. Thank you."

She ran to the bucket and brought it back sloshing over. He drank about half of it again, then took a deep breath. "Now, that is good."

"That's why they call this the Sweetwater River," James Reed said. "After that silty stuff from the Platte, this tastes pretty good."

"And after all the alkali springs we've had to drink from too," Mrs. Reed added, "it's wonderful."

"Yeah, I noticed," Peter said, pulling a face. A couple of the watering places had been downright foul.

"Did you see the big saleratus beds down the trail a little?" young James asked. "I got some of that for Mama."

"I did, James. I put a bit on my tongue. It tasted like it would make good baking soda."

"It does," Margret Reed agreed. "We baked bread with it, and it's as fine as any we could get back in Illinois."

"This is an amazing place," Peter said, letting his eyes lift toward the great mass of rock that loomed over them. It was now almost a pinkish rose in the sunset's light.

Reed turned. "Isn't it, though? Before we move out in the morning, we'll walk over to the rock. It's fascinating to see all the names that have been carved or painted here."

"Names?"

"Yes. Everyone seems to want to leave their mark. Some call this place the great 'register of the desert.' I found John C. Frémont's name and the cross that Captain Bonneville carved. It's something to see."

"I'd like to." Peter hesitated for a moment. "So we're moving out tomorrow?"

Reed nodded. "We've been here two days. It's time to get moving."

"Any sign of Mr. Bryant and Mr. Russell?"

"No. We heard they're four or five days ahead of us now. They are making good time."

"Did you know that Governor Boggs left us yesterday?" Mrs. Reed said.

Peter turned in surprise. "Really?"

"We decided to stay here an extra day and recruit our teams. He didn't want to."

Reed gave a short laugh. "He is so afraid that the Mormons are going to catch him that he wouldn't wait any longer. If we catch him again," he added with a droll smile, "let's not tell him that the only party of Mormons behind us have turned off for Pueblo."

They laughed at that, and Peter was gratified to find that the Reeds found Boggs as unsavory as he did.

James Reed turned more somber now. "I wasn't sure if you would come back, Peter. We're very glad to see you."

Peter's eyes widened slightly. "But I told you I would."

"I know, but things can change. Hiram Miller hired on to drive for the Donners, and as soon as Russell offered him a chance to join his pack train, all the promises were forgotten."

"Well, mine are not," Peter answered. "You and Mrs. Reed have been very good to Kathryn and me. Now that I know she's all right, I'll see it through to California."

"That's fair enough. And I'll pay you a bonus for doing so." He snapped his fingers suddenly. "That reminds me. Did you meet Mr. Bonney on the trail?"

"Mr. Bonney?"

"Yes. Wales B. Bonney. It would have been sometime today. He just left this morning going east."

"I did see one lone rider a couple of miles away, but I thought it was an Indian and steered clear. He's traveling all the way back to the States by himself?"

"Yes, can you believe it? But here's what I wanted to say,

Peter. He rode in here yesterday afternoon, and he was carrying a letter from Lansford Hastings. Hastings is out ahead of us on the trail. He gave a letter to Bonney to read to all the companies along the trail. He's forming up a train at Fort Bridger and will lead them across his shortcut route to California."

Peter remembered the solemn warning that James Clyman had given Mr. Reed about following Hastings's proposed new route around the south end of the Salt Lake Desert. Evidently his concern showed in his eyes, for Reed frowned.

"The letter was a great relief to those of us who are determined to take this shorter route, Peter. If he is there personally to lead us, that will make a great difference."

"Well," Peter said, finding it hard to resist his employer's enthusiasm, "that does make a difference."

"It's three or four hundred miles shorter," young James said sagely. "We must take it so we can get to California quicker."

"More quickly," Peter corrected him, without thinking.

"Yes, more quickly."

"Well, then," Peter said, talking to Mr. Reed now, "that is good news, isn't it?"

"Indeed."

Margret Reed abruptly stood up. "Come, children, you've not given Peter a moment's rest since he arrived. Let's find Eliza and get some supper started. I'll bet Peter is starving."

"Well," he admitted ruefully, "I *am* tired of soggy bread and wet pemmican."

"Pemmican?" Virginia cried. "Isn't that the Indian food?"

"Yes," Peter laughed.

"What is it like?"

"It's made from dried meat—which they pound into a powder—mixed with hot buffalo fat and dried berries or fruit."

"Ew!" Patty said, wrinkling her nose.

"Can I have some?" Virginia asked. "I want to taste it."

"All right, but it's all wet now. When I forded the river, the mule got everything soaked and it hasn't completely dried out yet."

"I don't care," Virginia replied.

"Me neither," said James. "I want some too."

Margret laughed happily. "Welcome back, Peter. You go teach my children about Indian food, and Eliza and I will fix you some good hot stew and fresh biscuits."

Lydia picked her way slowly through the cluster of wagons, stepping around cold fire pits, ducking beneath sheets and blankets hung up to air. She stopped as she saw a woman sitting beside a wagon a short distance ahead of her. It was Drusilla Hendricks. Drusilla was seated on a stool near the back of her wagon, mending an apron. In the wagon, Lydia could see James Hendricks reading a book. Two of the children were nearby, seated on the ground playing some kind of hand games. William and the other children were nowhere to be seen. That was good. Lydia raised a hand and called out a hello.

Drusilla looked up, then immediately set aside her sewing and got to her feet. "Lydia, what a nice surprise!"

"Good afternoon, Drusilla." She looked toward the wagon. "Hello, James. How are you doing today?"

He came up on one elbow. "Better, Sister Lydia. And you?"

"We're fine, thank you."

Drusilla came over and took Lydia's hands, clearly glad to see her. "I thought I heard that your family had crossed the river."

"We did. Nathan had to see Elder Taylor about something, so I came too."

"I'm so glad," she said. "Come and sit down."

Lydia hesitated, glancing first at James and then at the children. "Would you have time to go for a walk?"

A little surprised, Drusilla nevertheless nodded immediately. "Of course."

They moved slowly, heads down as they inquired after each other's family. Not until they were away from the edge of the easternmost camp did Lydia finally lapse into silence. Drusilla stopped, motioning to a spot where there was grass beneath the shade of a tree. "Shall we sit for a few moments?"

Lydia nodded, and they moved beneath the tree and settled into comfortable positions. Both were quiet for several moments, and then Drusilla gave Lydia a sidelong glance. "Are you ready to talk about it?"

"What?"

There was a faint smile. "Whatever it is you have on your mind."

That was enough. Lydia turned fully to face her. "Have you decided about William?"

Drusilla seemed not in the least surprised. "Yes. I am not going to let him go." It was said simply and without emotion, but there was no mistaking the forcefulness behind her eyes.

"Did you hear what Brother Brigham said the other day at the meeting?"

Drusilla didn't flinch. "I did. It didn't change my mind."

"Tell me why," Lydia entreated, almost eager now. "I don't disagree with you, but I'd like to know why."

Drusilla's eyes lowered, and she picked at the grass beside her skirt. "I suppose there are a lot of reasons. First and foremost, I have a husband who is crippled. He can get around the camp now with the help of his crutches or a cane, and for that we are very grateful. We know that is a bit of a miracle after his being paralyzed from the neck down. But he cannot drive a team. He cannot get water. He cannot chop firewood. My Billy is sixteen now. He's finally old enough that I have a man to help me again. How can I let him go?"

"I don't think anyone expects you to."

Her head came up. "Oh? Then why am I asked at every hand if he's going?"

"Who is asking you that?"

She shook her head. "Several. Part of it is because William keeps telling people that he wants to go."

Lydia nodded, thinking of Josh. "And what does James say to all of this?"

Drusilla's shoulders lifted and fell. She ripped off a handful of grass, then began to pick up one blade at a time and let it flutter into her lap. "I think James would let him go if it were up to him. But he knows how I feel about it and he knows how much I need a man around. So all he'll say is that unless I agree, William can't go."

"That makes it hard on you, doesn't it?"

She didn't seem to hear. There was a faraway look in her eyes now. "I haven't talked very often about that night, Lydia."

"What night?"

"October twenty-fifth, eighteen thirty-eight."

Lydia didn't have to ask anything more. That was the day a group of Mormon militia, riding out to rescue some of their brethren from a mob, had accidently stumbled upon the mob's encampment just at sunrise. In the ensuing battle James Hendricks had taken a ball in the back of the neck that left him paralyzed from the neck down. That night had begun for Drusilla Hendricks eight long years of sacrifice and suffering.

Drusilla sniffed softly and wiped at her cheek with the back of one hand. She still stared at her hands and did not look at Lydia. "I can't bear the thoughts of sending off another one of my men to face that. I can't."

"I don't think the Lord expects it of you. Not after all that has happened. Not after all you have done."

"I want to believe that, Lydia. But . . ." She finally looked up. "It's your son too, isn't it? Does Josh want to go?"

"Yes." It came out as barely a whisper. "He's as adamant about it as William."

"Don't let him go, Lydia," she said with sudden fierceness. "The army has called for our men, not our boys."

Lydia slid closer and put an arm around her, weeping softly now too. "I don't want to, Drusilla. I can't even think about it without starting to cry. And yet I don't want to be selfish. I want to do what's right."

Drusilla's mouth was set. "I don't think God would ask that of a mother," she said stubbornly. "I just don't."

Chapter Notes

Independence Rock supposedly got its name when some trappers working with William Henry Ashley's Rocky Mountain Fur Company camped at this spot at the eastern end of the Sweetwater Valley on 4 July 1825. Even though they were far from the United States, they wished to remember their American heritage and celebrated the holiday with various festivities. They ended by inscribing their names on the rock, along with the word *Independence*. Today, Independence Rock is a Wyoming state park about midway between Casper and Rawlins. Though many names inscribed on the rock have now faded away, many others are still visible, including some of Mormon pioneers who passed here later.

Lansford Hastings left California and headed east in the spring of 1846, along with others, including James Clyman, who was somewhat less than enthralled with what he saw as Hastings's naive enthusiasm for a new shortcut. Hastings's motives may have partly been economic, because he had invested in property in California and hoped to bring people into that area. He and Clyman parted company when they found Fort Bridger deserted. Feeling a need to get prepared for whoever would accept his leadership, Hastings stopped somewhere around South Pass and decided to return to Fort Bridger and organize a wagon train there. When Hastings arrived at the fort, Jim Bridger and his partner, Louis Vasquez, had returned.

When he met Wales B. Bonney, a man from Oregon who, incredibly, was traveling back east by himself, Hastings wrote a letter of invitation to the oncoming emigrants and asked Bonney to take it with him and read it out among the companies. Bonney arrived at Independence Rock shortly after the Donner-Reed company had camped there. His enthusiastic report on California, along with Hastings's letter, only further confirmed Reed's determination to take the new route. These details come from a letter written by Charles Stanton to his brother on 12 July 1846. It is from Stanton, who was traveling with the Donner-Reed group, that we also learn that Lilburn W. Boggs was still in great fear of the Mormons. (See *Overland in 1846*, pp. 614–15.)

Chapter Fourteen

Carl Rogers opened the door as quietly as he could and stepped inside. He removed his hat and vest and hung them on the pegs there, then bent down and removed his boots. There was a lamp on the table at the head of the stairs above him. It was turned to the lowest possible setting, but it still provided enough light for him to see. As he started down the hallway he stopped. In the parlor there was something large and dark on the floor. Curious, he went in to take a closer look. To his surprise he saw the two trunks which they kept in the loft of the barn. The lids were open, and as he bent down he could see that both trunks were nearly filled with various items. Perplexed, he straightened and looked around. He could see that there were other things piled on the chairs and on the sofas.

He frowned. What had possessed Melissa to start going through their things now? Normally this kind of sorting was done in the spring or during the long months of winter. But he was too tired to come to any logical conclusion. He moved quietly back into the hallway and up the stairs. He blew out the light, wondering how his wife had known he would be home tonight, then crept into their bedroom. He undressed quickly, then slid between the sheets beside her. Though he tried to do it without waking her, there was a soft murmur and her head turned.

"Carl?"

"Yes, Melissa. It's me. I didn't mean to wake you."

"Why didn't you come right home?" she murmured sleepily. "Someone told David you were on the six o'clock steamboat."

He was startled by that, just as he had been startled by the committee of new citizens waiting for him on the dock. It turned out that they weren't sure when he would arrive but were meeting every boat that landed at Nauvoo. He had gone straight to the home of James Wilson and gotten the report on the current crisis. "The new citizens committee met me and asked me to come to a meeting," he said softly. He said no more, hoping she was too sleepy to question him further.

It worked. There was a soft murmur, and then she was quiet again. Grateful that he didn't have to face a confrontation this night, he lay very still until he was sure she was soundly asleep, then turned onto his side. He felt like cursing, that was what he really wanted to do. Curse the anti-Mormons for seizing five of the new citizens and beating them without determining if they were Mormons. Curse the five Mormons who were foolish enough to go north past Pontoosuc the very next day when tensions were so high and allow themselves to be kidnapped. Curse the new citizens and their indignation. Let McAuley and Brattle go and get the five hostages released. The determination to show the antis that they wouldn't knuckle under to their bully tactics was only aggravating things further. And curse the timing of it all.

Things had not gone as well for him and Jean Claude in St. Louis as they hoped. The price of lumber was down. There was a glut on the market, partially because the long-sustained construction boom in Nauvoo and the surrounding settlements had been choked off as cleanly as a strangled goose. The big lumber rafts were no longer stopping at the bend in the river but went on down to St. Louis to sell the lumber off. So instead of coming home with three or four thousand dollars in his pocket, he had barely a thousand. That wasn't going to help him convince Melissa that everything was going to be all right. He remembered clearly her parting words before he left. She didn't want to stay in Nauvoo, which meant that she wanted them to go west and find her family. He had been dreading having to face her ever since he and Jean Claude had settled on a sale for less than half what they expected.

He turned over and buried his head in his pillow. Curse the whole situation of the Mormons and their enemies. Curse the state government for not doing one thing to intervene. If it weren't for that, Carl's life would be a lot simpler.

"Thanks for breakfast."

Melissa smiled at him. "You're welcome."

"It's good to be home."

"I'm so glad that you are home, Carl. We've missed you."

"I missed you the most, Daddy," Sarah said. That started an instant debate over the truthfulness of that statement.

"Children," Melissa broke in. "Don't make your father sorry to be home."

That shushed them for a moment, but when they saw their father wink at them they started to giggle again.

Carl turned to Melissa. "By the way, I saw the trunks in the parlor last night. Are you going through your things again?"

Melissa's head jerked around. The smiles instantly died. The older children glanced anxiously back and forth at their mother and father. The tension in the room was suddenly palpable. Melissa looked away. "Carl and David are going to take the children down to the river and watch the steamboats after breakfast. I thought we could talk then."

Carl felt himself go cold. This was worse than he suspected.

He pressed his lips together, and picked up the last of his bread. "All right," he said. "We'll talk then."

"Melissa, look, I know you're upset with all of this, but we are not going anywhere. Things are going to settle down again, once they get those men released." She watched him steadily but said nothing. Her emotionless expression and the flatness of her eyes irritated him a little. "Well, they are."

"Why don't you go tell that to Sister Young? It's her husband and son who have been held hostage for the past four days—assuming they are still alive. Why don't you go tell her that things will settle down? I'm sure that will comfort her to hear you say it."

"There's no call for sarcasm, Melissa. I know the situation is serious, but there is no direct threat to us."

"Carl, did you know that your son has been hiring out to cut wheat? Did you know that?"

He flinched a little.

"Yes. He went out with a party east of town. It could easily have been him with that group up at Pontoosuc." She was trembling now, fighting against letting her emotions take over. "If you had seen those men . . ." She shuddered. "It was horrible."

"I know, I know," he soothed. "And I'm not trying to say it wasn't. But that doesn't mean we are in imminent danger. More and more of the Mormons are leaving every day now. Once they're gone, then things will be all right."

There was a short, bitter laugh. "Have you forgotten so soon?"

"Forgotten what?"

"You say 'more and more of the Mormons' are leaving. *I* am a Mormon, Carl. And now it's not just in name only anymore. I am one of them. If anyone asks, I will tell them I am firm in my faith. I will no longer deny what I know to be true. So how do you plan to deal with that little embarrassment, Carl? Tell me that."

He *had* forgotten for the moment that complication. It was another thing that made him want to swear. Not that he cared a lot one way or another what she believed; but before, it didn't matter that much. Now, if she really insisted on going around waving the flag of faith, it could prove to be a challenge.

She watched him, shaking her head sadly.

He took a quick breath. "Once the main body of the Church has gone, things will be all right again. The antis are just angry because your people promised to leave by spring."

"Shall I tell you something else, Carl? It is more complicated than that."

"What?" he asked warily. "What is more complicated?"

"You have three sons who want to be Mormons too."

She sat back, watching the impact of her words on his face. Tears now welled up and filled her eyes. "I know what you think, but it's not true. I haven't tried to sway them while you were gone. They talked among themselves, and then Carl came and talked to me. They want to be baptized."

"No." It came out like a hammer blow on a piece of cold steel.

"They want to go west and join the rest of our family."

"*No!*" He jumped to his feet, pacing angrily now. "You didn't have to try and sway them. They'll do whatever they think you want them to do."

"That makes it easier for you, doesn't it? If it's my fault, then you don't have to face the fact that your sons might actually believe it's true."

"They're just boys, Melissa."

"Why is it that they're men when you expect them to work with you, and boys when it comes to what they believe?"

"I'm not going to argue with you. We've talked about this. I will not go west. There is nothing out there, Melissa. Nothing! I predict that within the year, Brigham Young is going to come slinking back looking for somewhere else to put his people. There's nothing for us anywhere else but here. So get that into your head, Melissa. We are staying here. I will see that you are safe."

"How much did you get for the lumber?"

It came from a totally unexpected direction and it took him back a step. "What?"

"Why haven't you been bursting to tell me the news from St. Louis, Carl?"

"I . . ." She had totally flustered him. "We did all right. Not as good as we hoped, but we have . . ." He hesitated for a split second, which he instantly knew gave him away. "We have about a thousand dollars."

There was a sad smile. "I guess it could have been worse."

That infuriated him. He kicked viciously at the nearest trunk, hitting it hard enough that the lid, which was propped against a chair, slammed down. "I did the best I could, Melissa! We didn't just stand around with our hands in our pockets, you know. There's too much lumber down there right now. We were lucky to get what we did!"

Her face was incredulous. "Is that what you think, Carl? That I'm disappointed in you? No! I know you're trying. But when are you going to see that we have nothing here anymore? Nothing! The store is a pile of ashes. The brickyard is all but closed. What are we going to do, Carl? You tell me. How are we going to survive?"

"I'll find something else. Once things settle down, business will pick up again. We'll rebuild the store. Sell the brickyard."

"All the time you're hiding the fact that your wife and sons are believing Mormons?"

"My sons are not Mormons!" he shouted. "And don't you forget it."

The tears spilled over now. "Carl, what's happening to us? Why can't we ever talk things through anymore?"

"I think you know the answer to that," he snapped. "Since you turned religious again, you don't listen anymore."

She stared at him, her eyes wide and filled with pain.

"I . . ." He started toward her, but then let his anger take the reins again. He clamped his mouth shut and looked away.

He heard her turn and walk slowly to the hallway. She stopped. He looked up. Her back was still to him.

"Perhaps the next time you choose to go off and leave us here alone, we won't wait to finish packing our things."

He stepped forward, fists clenched, mouth tight. "What are you saying? Are you telling me you're going to run out on me?"

"I'm telling you that I love you, Carl. I do. But I love my children too. I will not stand by and watch them be put in danger because you are too blind to see what is happening right before your very eyes."

"So you'd leave me?" he flung back at her.

Her chin dropped and now the tears flowed freely. "I don't know. Somehow I was hoping I wouldn't be forced to make that decision."

The morning of Thursday, the sixteenth of July, dawned bright and clear. By eight o'clock it was already promising to be a hot and humid day. Three things of great significance would take place on this day.

First, Brother Ezra T. Benson would be ordained and set apart as a member of the Quorum of the Twelve Apostles to take the place of John E. Page, who had fallen into apostasy.

Second, after hearing Wilford Woodruff's report of a leadership crisis in England, the Quorum determined that Reuben Hedlock and Thomas Ward, who had been left in charge there, be disfellowshipped for refusing to follow counsel. At the same time it was voted that Elders Orson Hyde, Parley P. Pratt, and John Taylor be sent to England to put the affairs of the Church there back in order.

Third, Companies A, B, C, and E of the newly formed Mormon Battalion gathered together on Redemption Hill, on the eastern bluffs above the Missouri River, and were officially mustered into the United States Army of the West.

The entire Steed clan crossed over on the ferry and walked up the eastern bluffs. The children were as excited as if this were a great holiday. The adults were considerably more subdued. By afternoon the day was sweltering, and they were all sweating by the time they reached the assembly area. That did little to diminish the euphoria the children were feeling. Emily and Rachel, the oldest of the female cousins, raced up to Mary Ann as they came in sight of the gathering out ahead of them. "Grandma, can we go find Uncle Derek and Aunt Rebecca?" they clamored.

She smiled and nodded. "Yes. Just don't get in the way."

"I'm going too," Luke hollered and took off after his sister. That was all it took. Half a dozen of the oldest cousins were off with a whoop. Lydia watched Josh carefully. He and Luke had been walking together—they were close to the same age—but Josh watched them go without stirring. She sighed. Once it was over, once they were actually gone, it would be easier, she thought. She wanted to reach out and touch him, reassure him that this was right, but she knew it wasn't the time.

In a moment, Mark appeared again, running and waving. He was accompanied by Christopher, Derek and Rebecca's oldest child. "They're up here!" Mark shouted. "Come on."

For a time it was little more than a pleasant and happy state of confusion on Redemption Hill. Men ran back and forth between their tents and their packs, grabbing last-minute items they had forgotten. Children raced everywhere, screeching and yelling just for the sheer joy of it. The officers and noncommissioned officers for each company, chosen from the ranks of the Saints themselves, shouted out orders, trying to get some control. They had little impact on anyone except those within a few feet of their voices.

At two o'clock the atmosphere suddenly changed. Several of the Twelve had arrived by then, including Brigham Young. A bugle sounded and everyone turned toward the sound. Mary Ann couldn't see who had blown it, but in the silence that followed she heard a bellowing voice. "We'll form into companies in a hollow square in ten minutes. Brethren, now is the time to say farewell to your families."

The clamor erupted again, but now any sense of celebration was gone. There were cries of disappointment and calls for the children to come together. The reality of separation was suddenly very much upon them. The crowd quickly separated into dozens of smaller groups to say good-bye to fathers and brothers, uncles and cousins—and, in some cases, mothers and sisters and aunts.

Mary Ann took a breath and moved forward to Rebecca. Till now her youngest daughter had been filled with excitement, talking animatedly about what lay ahead for her and her family. Her face was flushed and her eyes flashed happily. Then her mother stood before her. There had been promises all around not to cry, but no one remembered them now. The others held back as Mary Ann stepped forward slowly and faced Rebecca and Derek. For a moment no one moved; then Rebecca's shoulders began to shake and she threw herself into her mother's arms.

"Oh, Mama! How we shall miss you!"

"I know," Mary Ann soothed. "And we shall miss you." She looked at Derek, who was blinking quickly to stave the burning in his own eyes. "You take care of her and the children, now, do you hear me?"

"I will Mother Steed. I promise."

She went to him, hugged him fiercely, then turned to the children. As she took Christopher's hands, she tried to laugh through the tears, but it came out more like a sob. "Shame on you," she scolded. "You're not even sad to be leaving your grandmother, are you?"

Christopher had his father's build. At seven, he was already nearly as heavy as his mother. He also had Derek's even temper and mild disposition. He tried to smile, knowing that Mary Ann didn't mean it, but instead his lower lip started to tremble, his eyes filled, and he threw his arms around his grandmother and began to sob.

"It's all right," she said through a choked voice. "It's all right, Christopher. It will only be for a year."

Josh stood back as the family went one by one to make their farewells. Derek, watching him through it all, finally motioned him over. Josh was now two or three inches taller than his uncle, but Derek pulled his head down until their foreheads touched. "Josh?"

"Yes?"

"There are many ways and many places to serve God."

"I know."

"We have chosen one way, and I know you wish you were going, but it isn't the only way. It may not even be the best way."

"I keep telling myself that."

Derek nodded. "You're a good boy, Josh. The Lord will use you where you can do him the most good."

Josh nodded, unable to fully push aside the gloominess, then shook Derek's hand. "You take care, Uncle Derek."

"We will."

Behind them, listening and watching intently, Lydia began to cry again. Nathan too was watching and knew that his wife's tears weren't just for Derek and Rebecca now.

The bugle sounded again, this time running up and down the scales in the call for assembly. Amid the final cries, the last handshakes, the last hugs and kisses and tears, the four companies began to assemble.

"How come there's no Company D?" Luke asked his father.

Solomon shrugged. "They still haven't had enough people volunteer, is what I hear. Why it's Company D that's short and not Company E, I'm not sure."

In five minutes the four-hundred-plus men of the Mormon Battalion were lined up by companies, one to each side to form a hollow square. Now came the formalities. One by one the Twelve spoke briefly to the assembled men. There were good wishes, promises of doing the Lord's will, reassurances that their families would be cared for. Willard Richards caused the greatest stir when, after reminding them that they were serving not only their country but also their God, he said, "Brethren, I feel to say something to you. I know you are marching off to war, but I tell you, if you are faithful in keeping the commandments of God, not a man of you shall fall by an enemy." He stopped again as the impact of his words raced through the crowd. "Yea, there will not be as much blood spilled as there was at Carthage Jail, and as one who was there, I say that gives me great comfort."

Finally, President Young turned to where Lieutenant Colonel James Allen, recently promoted from captain, stood at stiff attention. "Colonel Allen," he said loudly. "I hereby present to you this Mormon battalion and commend them to you as good and faithful men."

Allen saluted smartly and stepped forward. He unrolled a paper in his hand and held it up high. "By virtue of the authority given me by Colonel Stephen W. Kearny, commander of the Army of the West, I hereby assume command of the Mormon Battalion, raised at this place for the service of the United States. We shall now march to Traders Point, where you will receive the first of your equipment. Thereafter, you will be held in readiness to march at the shortest notice, and as soon as the fifth company is filled, all will be ready for our departure."

He stopped. The silence across the field was total. Then Allen straightened and threw out his chest. "Companies! Ten-*hut!*" There was a snap of feet and the slap of hands against trousers as the men came to attention. "For-*ward . . . march!*"

Company A immediately began to move forward in a column of twos. The men in the other companies began marching in place, waiting for their turn to fall in behind. Though they were not in uniform and there were several who were out of step with each other, it was a stirring sight nevertheless. There were a few wives and mothers who were weeping, but for the most part all were smiling and waving.

Lydia turned to see how Josh was taking all of this. To her surprise, he was no longer standing behind her. Nathan saw her looking around and motioned with his head. She turned and looked, not sure what she was looking for. Then she saw a solitary figure walking slowly away from them up the knoll that was

"Colonel Allen, I Hereby Present to You . . ."

Redemption Hill. His head was down, his hands were thrust in his pockets, his back was turned.

Lydia finished nursing Tricia. "All right, my little ball of butter," she said, putting her on her shoulder and patting her back. "I think that's enough for now." She got two great burps from her, then wrapped her in her blanket and tucked her into her crib. She stood for a moment to be sure she was going to sleep, then went outside.

Josh was there by the wagon, working on something in a deep gloom. He didn't look up, and she decided there was no sense in saying anything to try and change things. Once the battalion was completely gone, it would get better. She heard the sounds of a horse coming on the run and turned. It was Nathan, coming back from across the river. He pulled up, not dismounting. "Lydia?"

"Yes?"

"There's something you need to see."

"What is it?"

"You've got to see it for yourself."

"Where?"

"At the bowery. Come. You can ride sidesaddle behind me." He didn't wait for an answer. "Josh. You watch the children."

"Yes, Pa."

Lydia moved tentatively toward the horse. Nathan reached down and grasped her forearm, then pulled her up smoothly.

"Tricia's asleep, Josh," she said. "The others are over at Aunt Jessica's."

"Yes, Mama." He waved as Lydia put her arms around Nathan and they rode away.

Chapter Notes

It was 16 July 1846, just a little more than two weeks after Captain James Allen rode into Council Bluffs, when the first mustering of the Mormon Battalion took place. Even after vigorous recruiting by Brigham Young and the Twelve, they were still about a hundred short of the five hundred requested by the army. It was while the Twelve were speaking to them that Elder Willard Richards made the remarkable prophecy about their safety. They were then marched about seven miles to the Indian trading post where they were issued the first of their provisions. (See *SW*, pp. 33–34.)

Chapter Fifteen

They were fortunate in that they had to wait for only about five minutes for the eastbound ferry. As usual, going back across the river the ferry was not crowded, and Nathan and Lydia dismounted and walked the horse directly on.

Once they were across, he pushed the horse into a steady trot, and in ten minutes they came up Mosquito Creek to where the bowery was. As it came into sight, Lydia could see that there was a table set up beneath its shade and two men in uniform were seated at it. In front of them a line of men snaked down the length of the bowery, leaving the last four or five men in the sun.

Nathan slowed the horse to a walk and spoke over his shoulder. "We may be too late. It's been more than half an hour."

"Too late for what?" Lydia said, seeing now where he was taking her.

"He was near the end of the line. I didn't think they'd be done that soon."

"Who would be done that soon?" she asked in exasperation.

But Nathan was peering now at the line of men, trying to see into the darker areas beneath the bowery. Then he was pointing. "There he is, Lydia. Third man back."

"There who is?" she started to say, but then her eyes followed his hand and she saw. Her jaw went slack and there was a soft gasp. It was William Hendricks, the oldest son of Drusilla and James Hendricks. And there was no question about what he was doing. He had a bedroll tied with a rope slung over one shoulder and a small battered suitcase in the other. He was watching intently as one of the lieutenants signed up the man at the table.

"But . . ." She looked away. It felt as though she had been struck violently in the stomach, and for a moment she thought she was going to gag.

Nathan started to swing down but she grabbed at his arm, digging her fingers into the flesh. "No, Nathan."

"Don't you want to talk to him?"

"No. I want to talk with Drusilla. Take me to Drusilla."

When Drusilla Hendricks looked up and saw them approaching on the horse, she didn't seem surprised. She removed her apron, put aside the flour she was mixing into dough, and came over to meet them. Neither woman spoke as Nathan helped Lydia down from the horse. Drusilla motioned toward the empty field where they had walked the last time Lydia had come, and they started away.

"I'll wait here," Nathan called.

Lydia, only then remembering that he was there, waved gratefully.

"What happened?" Lydia demanded the moment they were away from the wagons. The rawness of her emotions made her voice come out more sharply than she had intended.

Drusilla looked at her and Lydia saw that her eyes were swimming.

"You were so sure the other day," Lydia went on, more softly. "What happened?"

"This morning William was very depressed. The men had marched away and he was not one of them. He begged me to reconsider. I told him that I couldn't bear to lose him."

She looked away, and her voice sounded very far away as she continued. "I was starting to get breakfast. I went to the wagon for some flour. When I stepped up on the tongue to reach inside the wagon, the voice of the Lord whispered in my mind. It was just like a voice had spoken to me, only it was inside me, not outside."

"What did it say?"

" 'Drusilla,' it said, 'do you not want the greatest glory?' " She finally turned and looked directly at Lydia. "It came so clearly that I answered out loud in my natural voice, as if someone had actually spoken to me. 'Yes, I do,' I said. Then the voice said, 'Then how can you get it without making the greatest sacrifices?' "

"But you have made the greatest sacrifices," Lydia cried in dismay. "You let James go off to help rescue the brethren at Crooked River and he came back paralyzed. You didn't turn bitter about that. You stayed faithful. Through all those years when you had to support the family and care for James, you never complained. What more could anyone ask of you?"

Drusilla lifted a hand as though to speak, but Lydia rushed on, wanting to say all that she had been feeling since they had talked last. "And when the call came to go west, you of all people had every right to say no. You had no husband to drive your teams, no man to cut wood and care for your family. But you came anyway. Surely, of all people, you have made the greatest sacrifices."

Drusilla waited now until she was done, then smiled sadly. "When the voice asked me that question, 'How can you get it without making the greatest sacrifices,' all I could think of to say was, 'Lord, what lack I yet?' " She paused, and now the tears could no longer be contained. " 'Let your son go in the battalion,' came the answer."

At those terrible words, Lydia closed her eyes.

Drusilla watched her, waiting silently until she finally opened her eyes. "There was nothing more to be done," she said. "I was devastated. All that I had felt welled up in me and I wanted to shout out that I could not accept that. But I knew I had heard the voice of the Spirit. I went back and prepared breakfast, hardly knowing what I was doing. Then, as we were eating, William raised his eyes and looked me in the face, and in that instant I knew as surely as I have ever known anything that he would go. I told him that he had my permission and I was sorry that I had told him he couldn't go. Now it was too late, for the men had already marched away."

"And then came the announcement," Lydia said, her voice hollow and dead.

Drusilla was nodding. "Even as I was speaking to my Billy, a rider came tearing through the camp yelling that the roster was not full and that they needed more men. William shot to his feet and shouted that he was coming."

The tears were gone now, and she reached up and brushed at the wet streak on her cheek. Her eyes were somber but at peace. "I could not swallow another bite of breakfast, and as he gathered his things I couldn't help but think that I might never have my family together again. I have no picture of William, so I took one in my mind this morning. I looked at him until I knew I would never forget what he looked like. 'If I never see you again until the morning of the first resurrection,' I thought to myself, 'then at that moment, I shall know you as my child.' "

A sob escaped from Lydia, and a shudder shook her body. "Oh, Drusilla," was all she could manage to say.

"After breakfast, when William went to sign up," she went on evenly now, as though she were speaking only to herself, "I went out to milk the cows. I thought that perhaps they might give me some shelter. So there I knelt down and told the Lord that if he wanted my child in the battalion he could take him. I only asked that his life be spared. I felt that was all I could do."

Lydia looked away, and the silence stretched on for several moments.

"There's one more thing you ought to know," Drusilla finally said.

"What?"

She turned now to look at Lydia fully. "When I told the Lord he could have my son, the voice in my mind came to me one last time."

Lydia's chin lifted. "What did it say?"

Suddenly Drusilla's eyes were brimming with tears again, only this time they were tears of radiant joy. "The voice said as clearly as I am speaking to you now, 'Drusilla, my daughter, it shall be done unto you as it was unto Abraham when he offered Isaac on the altar.' "

By the time Nathan and Lydia crossed back over the river and reached camp, Tricia was awake again and starting to fuss. Josh and Emily were both caring for her. Elizabeth Mary was playing with the two younger boys behind the wagon.

As Nathan reined up, he half turned in the saddle. "Do you want me to tell him?" he asked quietly.

She shook her head. The tears were gone now and there was a cold emptiness inside her, but she had gotten her answer and she wasn't going to leave it to Nathan to carry it out. Nathan held one arm and helped her slide down to the ground, then dismounted as well. The three little ones had not spied their parents as yet, and Lydia wanted to keep it that way for now. She raised her hand and motioned for Josh to come over.

He did, but Emily thought she was being summoned too and followed right behind him.

"How did the baby do?" Lydia wanted to postpone the moment for as long as possible.

"Good," Josh said, looking at his baby sister. "She just woke up a few minutes ago."

"She's been fine, Mama," Emily added. "But I think she's hungry again."

"*Still*, I think, is a better word," Nathan smiled, taking the baby from Emily. Tricia was just over three months old now and smiled up at him as he began to coo to her. On the other side of the wagon, the flap to Mary Ann's tent opened and she stepped outside. When she saw them she too came over to join them.

Lydia was staring at the ground now, but feeling Nathan's eyes on her, she lifted her head and turned to Josh. "How long will it take you to pack?"

For a moment, it didn't register. He gave her a blank look.

She smiled faintly but it was filled with pain. "How long will it take you to pack your things, Josh?"

Mary Ann's eyes widened. She was just behind Josh, so that he couldn't see her face. She shot Nathan a questioning look. He nodded with the merest bob of his head and her eyes widened even more. Now she too turned to watch Lydia closely.

"Are we moving back across the river, Mama?" Emily asked eagerly. Solomon and Jessica were still on the eastern bank, which meant that Rachel and Emily were temporarily separated. A move back would be welcomed by her.

"No. I was just asking Josh," Lydia said softly. Then, to her son, who was still quite confused, she said, "You'll have to take everything you need until they issue you your equipment at Fort Leavenworth."

Now confusion was replaced by astonishment. He took a step forward, his mouth opening slightly. "Me? Do you mean . . . ?"

She nodded slowly.

His eyes became huge and his mouth fell wide open now. "In the battalion?"

"We stopped at the mustering table and signed you on. You'll be an orderly in D Company."

Emily squealed aloud and clapped her hands.

Josh gaped at his father, who smiled and nodded as well. He swung to his grandmother in disbelief. She was still watching Lydia carefully. "You're sure?" Mary Ann asked, speaking to Lydia and not to Josh.

"I'm sure," Lydia whispered.

For the third time that day—the fifth for Nathan—Lydia stood on the banks of the Missouri River waiting for the ferry to arrive. As the oxen dragged the ferry upstream from the unloading dock, Lydia shook her head. "I'm sorry, Nathan. I know I should be stronger, but I can't take any more today. If President Young has changed his mind—"

He turned from watching the ferry and pressed his fingers to her lips. "We don't know that he wants anything yet, Lydia. It's just a meeting he's called."

"Why a meeting now? What if he's heard about Josh and thinks you ought to go with him? Haven't we already given enough?"

Nathan was patient. "All Brother Allred said is that there would be a meeting for some of the brethren in the bowery this afternoon. He said nothing about the battalion." His words sounded hollow, even to himself.

Lydia nodded numbly and didn't say anything more.

They didn't speak any further as the ferry pulled up and they led the horse on. They didn't speak again while the ferry made its way across the river. On the ride up to the bowery Lydia clung to him tightly but still said nothing more. As they approached the low structure which was built to provide shelter from sun and rain, Nathan started to turn the horse toward where Solomon and Jessica were camped. But Lydia grabbed at his arm. "No, Nathan. I don't want to talk with anyone. I'll just wait for you there on that little knoll above the bowery."

He nodded and turned the horse toward the hillside. Careful not to let anything show on his face, he helped her down, handed her the bag of knitting, then bent down and kissed her forehead. "It'll be all right, Lydia. Please don't worry."

She nodded, not looking up.

It turned out to be an alternating rise and fall between sheer relief and renewed anxiety. Elder Heber C. Kimball began the meeting with the announcement that the necessary number of volunteers had been raised and would be leaving shortly to join the other companies at Traders Point downriver a few miles. That brought sheer relief. There was a call for men to help build a road on the west side of the river and an invitation for any who wished to join the Twelve in an exploration for a permanent settlement. Then suddenly the anxiety shot up again when Brigham Young stood and said, "Brethren, we need your help."

Nathan held his breath, watching intently.

"As you know," Brigham went on, "we gave our most solemn assurances that if our brethren heeded this call from the army, we would see that their families are cared for and watched over. This is an obligation that we cannot take lightly. One has only to look in any direction from this bowery and see the challenge that lies before us. The prairies are dotted with tents and wagons, and the hillsides are speckled with livestock. In many cases the owners of those tents and wagons and animals are no longer here. We made a covenant with those brethren." His voice suddenly thundered out. "*And that is a covenant we shall keep*."

Nathan felt himself relax. This was a matter of grave concern, but it was not a call for any brethren to leave their families.

The chief Apostle raised a hand as he emphasized his next words. "We have to care for the women and children of those men who have left us to march to Mexico. They must be provided for. They must be protected. *They must not be forgotten!*"

He paused. Every eye was on him. Every ear listened intently. "We of the Twelve have discussed this matter at length. We would now like to propose to you that we call out ninety of you men to serve as bishops to the families of those who are left behind."

Nathan leaned forward. Bishops? In Nauvoo there had been a few wards created, with bishops to govern them. But out here there was no city. And ninety? He blew out his breath. It was a stunning concept.

"As you know, the members of the battalion have volunteered to leave a portion of their wages behind with us to help us see our people through the winter. It is not much—only seven dollars a month for a private, but from five hundred men, that can still prove to be substantial. These bishops will be asked to take that money and apportion it out to the families. You will be responsible to see that the money is accounted for and properly distributed. Your calling is to be the shepherd to those who now have no fathers and husbands, to watch over them and see that they are not left as widows and orphans. We cannot have them crying to the Lord that they are being neglected. We simply cannot. We owe these brethren too much."

He held up a sheet of paper. "Here are the names of the men we have recommended. We shall post it for all to see. Those who find your names upon it shall receive further instructions about your new responsibility."

He turned and handed the sheet to Elder Kimball, who immediately picked up a small hammer and a nail. He walked to one of the outer posts that held the roof of the bowery and tacked up the paper. Brigham watched until he was done, then nodded in satisfaction. "There it is, brethren. Take a moment to see if your names are there. If they are, we shall meet with you after we return from finding a winter camp." He turned and called for a closing prayer and sat down.

Nathan was on the far side of the bowery from where the list hung, so he remained seated until the initial crush of men had lessened somewhat, then got up and walked to the post. There were still men four or five deep there, but he could see over their heads and began to read slowly. It said something about how rapidly the Church had grown these past few years that more than half the names on the list were ones that Nathan did not recognize. But there were many that he did, and most were no surprise to him. Priddy Meeks, William Draper, John Murdock, Levi W. Hancock, Abraham O. Smoot, Jesse C. Little (who had just returned from Washington, D.C.). These were good, solid men.

And then there it was. *Nathan Steed.* The two words jumped out at him as though written in gold. He felt a thrill of elation. Now he understood why his father had been so gratified with his call to be a missionary in Tennessee. Such a call was a witness that the Lord valued one's service, one's contribution. Nathan was deeply humbled to think that he had been viewed as worthy to serve.

He didn't look at the rest of the names. With a brief nod, as if to confirm to himself that he had found what he was looking for, he turned and strode out to where the horses were tied. He found his, swung up, and turned the horse toward the knoll which overlooked the bowery.

Lydia stood slowly as he rode up. She was searching his face carefully. He was sure that she would be able to read the joy there, but then he saw from her eyes that her worry was too consuming. Her mouth was drawn tight, her eyes pinched with anxiety.

He jumped down from the horse and walked to her swiftly.

"Nathan, before you tell me what happened, I want to say something."

He nodded, suspecting what was coming and feeling such a burst of love for this woman that for a moment he couldn't speak. "All right," he finally managed.

"I'll do whatever is asked of us," she whispered. "I'm better now."

"I know. I never thought otherwise."

Then, with joy spilling over into his voice, he took her in his arms and told her what Brigham Young wanted.

She looked a little confused. "A bishop? But what does that mean?"

"It means I'm staying right here with you for the winter," he answered.

Chapter Notes

The novel's depiction of events involving Drusilla Hendricks and her son William is based on Drusilla's own account of her family's experiences (see Drusilla Dorris Hendricks, "Historical Sketch of James Hendricks and Drusilla Dorris Hendricks," Archives Division, Church Historical Department, The Church of Jesus Christ of Latter-day Saints, Salt Lake City, Utah).

On the same day that the final company of the Mormon Battalion was raised, Brigham Young called for the selection of ninety bishops to help care for the families of those who were leaving with the army. Some of Brigham's words on that occasion as presented here come from William Draper's account of the meeting that day. (See *MHBY*, pp. 261–63; *SW*, pp. 35–36.)

Chapter Sixteen

To Mr. James Frazier Reed
From Mr. Edwin Bryant, recently removed from Louisville, Kentucky

July 17, 1846

My dear James,

I am writing this letter by lamplight from within the meager walls of a small stockade known as Fort Bridger, so named for its founder and co-owner Mr. Jim Bridger. We arrived here last night and pitched tents for the first time since leaving Fort Laramie. Through all of the intervening days, we have slept on the ground in the open, come rain, shine, or occasional frost.

There is a matter of utmost urgency that compels me to write this letter. I hope I can find someone going east so that you can receive this letter and be properly informed about the wisest course of action to pursue. But I shall speak of that in a moment. I thought perhaps it might be of some value to give a brief summary of our journey here since we last saw you at Beaver Creek. When we left you, there were twelve of us, along with thirty pack mules and ponies. I suspect that we are now ten or twelve days ahead of you. I think of you coming on more slowly and can picture roughly where you are day by day.

There are nine crossings of the Sweetwater altogether, and while we made our journey without undue hardship, we often thought of the difficulty the wagons would have in some places, especially the great sand hills near Three Crossings. I will be curious as to whether or not you recognize South Pass when you finally reach there. It is such a gentle incline and so broad in its width you hardly realize you have crossed the backbone of the continent. Not until we reached the spring just a mile or so west of the pass (appropriately named Pacific Spring because its waters run to the Pacific Ocean) were we sure we had crossed the Continental Divide. From there to here, as you will quickly see, is a series of hot, dry runs between the rivers—the Little Sandy, the Big Sandy, the Green, Ham's Fork, and finally Black's Fork, on which Bridger has built his fort. We calculate that Fort Bridger is 133 miles from the Pacific Spring. If our further calculations are correct, it was 983 miles from Independence, Missouri, to the Pacific Spring, or a total of 1,116 miles from our departure point to Fort Bridger.

Fort Bridger is a disappointment after Fort Laramie. It is really nothing more than a small trading post established by Mr. Bridger and his partner, Louis Vasquez, both experienced mountain men and fur traders. The only buildings are two or three miserable log cabins, rudely constructed, and bearing but a faint resemblance to habitable houses. There is a small stockade providing some protection from the Indians, but it is barely a hundred feet long on a side. It is, however, situated in a pleasant valley with good water and plenty of grass. The post is located about two miles south of where the Oregon Trail turns off to follow the Bear River to the Snake River and Fort Hall. There is a cutoff called the Greenwood Cutoff, which turns off between the Big and Little Sandy. You will know when you reach it. It is called the Parting of the Ways. This cutoff saves about fifty miles over coming to Fort Bridger, but includes 50 water-less miles that are very hard on stock. Thus, many trains come south to Fort Bridger, then turn north again.

And that brings me to the purpose of my letter. By now it is likely that you have met Mr. Wales B. Bonney and read the letter from Mr. Lansford Hastings. If so, you know that Mr. Hastings is urging all oncoming emigrants to come to Fort Bridger, where he will then guide them across a proposed new route to Upper California. Hastings is now here with us and is enthusiastically promoting his new route. He supposes he can save hundreds of miles over the Fort Hall route to California. My impressions, even after hearing him out, are unfavorable to the new route, especially for wagons and families. But a number of emigrant parties have been convinced by Mr. Hastings—who, I must admit, can be very persuasive—and have determined to adopt this route with Messrs. Hastings and Hudspeth as their guides. They are only waiting for other parties, including your own, I'm sure, to come up and join them.

Saturday, July 18

The press of preparations for our departure has prevented me from finishing my letter before now. This morning, our party determined to take the new route via the southern end of the great Salt Lake. Mr. Hastings will stay behind, waiting for additional companies to join him. Unfortunately, there is no one going east to take this letter to you. Therefore I have asked Mr. Vasquez to deliver it to you upon your arrival, which should be in a week or so now. My purpose in writing is this. Again I strongly encourage you not to take Mr. Hastings's proposed shortcut but to go on by way of Fort Hall as originally planned. I know you were of a mind otherwise, but I strongly discourage it.

But, you say, are you not yourselves taking the new way? Yes, but our situation is very much different from yours. We are mounted on mules and have no wagons and can make thirty-five to forty miles each day. Also, none of us have families with us. We can afford to hazard experiments and make explorations, whereas you cannot. I have great concerns about your crossing over the Sierra too late. Late yesterday afternoon, a rain shower came through here. The temperature dropped from 82 to 44 degrees in a quarter of an hour, and we can see fresh snow on the mountains. And this is still mid-July. I encourage you to take the safer, known route. This is my advice. I must go.

Your friend and fellow traveler,
Edwin Bryant

Melissa watched Carl wash his face in the basin of water, then dry it briskly. He folded the towel neatly and hung it back on the small rack fastened to the side of the dresser. She smiled faintly. Other women complained about how their husbands either tossed things into a corner or let them drop wherever they happened to be standing at the moment. But Melissa had no such complaints about Carl. He always liked things orderly. His socks were tucked neatly in one corner of the lower drawer. His shirts were folded carefully and sorted by color—the blues in one pile, the grays and whites in another. His boots—two pair—were lined up in one corner so that the heels were exactly on a line. Maybe that's why he had loved the brickyard so much. Bricks were neat and precise and exactly the same size every time.

Melissa sat in bed with two pillows propped up behind her. The book had been put away as the daylight had faded. She had heard him come in and so she had waited, her hands folded in her lap. There was still enough twilight outside to see, so she had not lit a lamp.

Carl hung his shirt on a peg—he had worn it only one day, and unless it was a particularly strenuous or grimy day, he always wore his shirts at least twice. As he moved toward the chair, he glanced in the mirror, took a moment to smooth an errant lock of hair, even though he would shortly be in bed and mess it up completely, then sat down and began to remove his boots. If he was aware of her watching him, he gave no sign. Off came the socks. He wrapped them together before tossing them in the wicker basket she kept beside the chair. It seemed effortless, almost as though he paid no mind to where they were set, but when he stepped back from putting these boots beside the other two pair, they were perfectly aligned with the others.

Suddenly there came a flash of insight. Strangely, she had not thought of it in this way before. Out on the trail, there wouldn't be much purpose in lining up boots in a perfect line. There wouldn't be a wicker basket for dirty socks or a dresser where he could keep his shirts arranged by color. It wasn't an obsession with him, just a strong preference for how he wanted things to be. But it *was* Carl. He wanted life orderly and everything in its proper place. He wanted to be able to rise while it was still dark and know which shirt he was getting without having to light a lamp. Trail life would hardly offer that. The whole experience was a plunge into uncertainty. It was the unexpected, the unplanned, and the unpredictable.

As he climbed into bed and pulled up the sheet, she wiggled down beneath the covers too, still lost in the surety of this discovery. It was something she wanted to think about. If she could find a way to get around that feeling of jumping into chaos, would he be more willing to consider going? Was there a way out there to preserve some of what he had now? At first look, it didn't seem so, but it was worthy of careful thought.

"I'll be leaving at five in the morning," he said suddenly, his face turned away from her.

She winced a little. This had once been a wonderful time for them. He would come to bed, she would be waiting, and they would lie there and talk, sometimes for as much as half an hour. Then he would come up on one elbow, kiss her gently, and wish her good night. But since his return from St. Louis this was the more common pattern—heavy silence while they got ready for bed, a brief sharing of essential information, then silence again.

"Fine. Are you taking all three of the boys?"

"Yes. I warned them. They'll be ready."

"I fixed a basket of food. It's in the icehouse."

"Thank you."

"Carl?"

There was a long pause; then, "I've got to be up early, Melissa. This is the first order of brick we've had in almost two months."

"I know. But will we ever talk about this, Carl? Will we ever sit down and try to come to some solution?"

"I've got to be up early," he said again.

Stung, she turned her head away from him. It had been a week since the beatings and the ensuing kidnapping of the five brethren who were members of the Church. The city was still in an uproar. Rumors flew anew almost every hour. The five men had been seen. They had escaped. They had been beaten. They had been executed. The tension in the city was still high, and people went around in considerable fear. Hardly anyone dared venture out of the city now. And through it all, Carl refused to even speak of it with her. He went to his meetings with the new citizens and returned in a shell of silence. He refused to answer questions or discuss the issue in any way. "It's going to be fine," was all he would say. "We're handling the situation."

She waited now, hoping for some sign of softening, longing for him to realize how he had hurt her and reach out his hand in apology. When it didn't come she felt the sorrow rise, and with it came a touch of anger. "Why is it that what I want, what I feel, what I think has no bearing on any of this? You won't even talk with me. Why, Carl? It didn't use to be this way between us."

There was no answer, but she could feel his stiffness beside her. She knew if she said one more thing, he would get up, take his trousers and shirt and boots, and go down and sleep on the sofa. That had happened now twice since his return, another change in their bedtime routine.

The despair and hopelessness were almost overwhelming. She felt the first of the tears start to sting behind her eyes, and that only made her the angrier. Why wasn't *he* crying? Why was *he* the one who was angry? Didn't he understand anything she was feeling?

Suddenly she pulled the sheet back and threw her legs over the side of the bed. She got up, reaching for her nightdress.

He turned. "What are you doing?"

"I'm going down to the store."

In the faint light she could see the incredulous look on his face. "What? There is no store. There's nothing there anymore."

"There is more for me there than there is here anymore," she said with great weariness. She moved to the door, opened it, then stepped through.

"Melissa?"

She paused.

"It's not safe for you to be out walking at night."

Her head came up. "If something happens," she said coldly, "I'll send for young Carl." And with that she closed the door and walked swiftly down the hall.

In the end, his final warning wouldn't leave her mind and she decided it wasn't safe to be out alone this late. She had already had one terrible experience with the new circumstances in Nauvoo. She wasn't looking for another. But neither could she stay in the house. Not after flinging that last shaft at him. So, let him worry about her. That would be nice for a change.

She stood for a moment on the porch, debating what to do. Then she had it. Kitty-corner across the street from their house was the small house where Benjamin and Mary Ann had first lived when they came to Nauvoo. It stood empty now. The family had deeded the house to Carl and Melissa before leaving. But there were too many larger and nicer homes; they hadn't had even one person interested in buying this one. Carl had padlocked both of the doors, but Melissa knew where the key to the back one was hidden. She walked swiftly across the street and through the gate. She found the key and let herself in.

The house smelled musty and close, still holding much of the heat from the day. She stopped. A prickling chill stole up her back. What if someone had broken in without their knowledge and was staying here? They hadn't checked the house for some time now. She gave a little shudder and nearly turned right around and went out again, but there was too much pride involved now. Steeling herself, she moved slowly into what had been her parent's bedroom. The dresser, chair, and armoire that had once been there were gone, taken to the store for sale, then lost in the fire; but the bed was still there, with its lumpy tick mattress. Gingerly, listening intently to make sure she was alone, she moved to the bed and sat down. The dust billowed up and she sneezed heartily. Holding one hand over her mouth and nose, she brushed off the mattress, then leaned back.

She was gratified five minutes later when she heard Carl's voice. "Melissa?"

She tiptoed to the front window and saw a dark figure step out into the street in front of their house.

"Melissa."

She nodded in satisfaction. He sounded worried. After a moment, he turned and started in the direction where the store had once been. She nearly burst from the house to call to him. He was worried. He had come looking for her. That softened her considerably. Then she remembered the curtness of his tone and his unbending attitude. With that, she went back to the bed and sat down again.

Carl returned after about a quarter of an hour. He called again before going in the house, but this time there was little hope in it. She didn't get up to see what he did. She heard their front door open and then close again, and then all was quiet.

There was no thought of sleep. Her mind was like the rapids in a fierce river—churning, roaring, tumbling wildly over the rocks. In Melissa's mind there were only two alternatives which now lay before her, and both were equally terrible to contemplate. Either she accepted Carl's decision and stayed here to see it through, or else she took the children and went to her family without him. Carl had closed every other door. He wouldn't consider returning to Kirtland to be with his brothers. Both of his parents were dead now, and his brothers wouldn't warmly welcome another family to support off the livery stable. Running the lumber operation was out of the question. Like the brickyard, there was no building boom to sustain the market. St. Louis. New Orleans. She had suggested them all, and he swatted each idea away as if it were an annoying insect.

Carl was sure that because he wasn't a Mormon they could escape any serious problems. But Melissa knew better. She knew what the mobs were like. Women and children engendered no mercy. Jessica, carrying Rachel in her arms, had been driven barefoot some twenty-five miles across a frozen prairie, leaving bloody footprints in the snow. Amanda Smith lost not only her husband at Haun's Mill but a ten-year-old son as well. Her seven-year-old lost a hip when another man jammed a rifle into the blacksmith shop where the boy was hiding and blew the hip away. Women were ravished to the point of death. Children were left to starve.

Why did Carl think these people would be any different? Yelrome had been burned to the ground within the last year. Edmund Durfee, an elderly, unarmed man, had been shot down by men too cowardly to face him. Some of the very men who now howled for action against the Mormons were the same ones who had painted their faces and stormed the stairs of Carthage Jail two years before. Ask Joseph Smith about mercy, she thought. Talk to Emma or Mary Fielding Smith about how much tolerance you could expect from Mormon-haters. Was she willing to stay by Carl's side when his bullheadedness put her and the children at that kind of risk? She didn't think so.

On the other hand, could she simply walk away from Carl? If he wouldn't bend, if he continued to adamantly refuse to consider going west—or anywhere else, for that matter—what would she do? They had shared the same bed now for fifteen years. She could not imagine life without him. Even in the consideration of it, the pain was so sharp that she had to cover her mouth to stop from crying out.

And there it was. So simple. So terrible. Lose Carl, or put her children at risk. Which part of her did she surrender—being a wife or being a mother? With that terrible dilemma weighing in upon her, she finally lay back and fell into a fitful sleep.

She awoke fully and realized she was perspiring. Her hair stuck to her forehead, and the mattress felt cold and clammy beneath her neck. She sat up slowly, brushing back the hair from her eyes. Her body was sluggish, showing the signs of deep exhaustion. She turned toward the window. It was still dark, and through it she could see stars. She guessed it was somewhere around three or four in the morning.

Quietly she slipped out of the house and padlocked the door again. Looking up and down the street to make sure she was alone, she darted quickly to her house and onto the porch. Now, moving with infinite care, she opened the door. Taking off her shoes, she tiptoed down the hall, stopping at the bottom of the stairs to see if there was any sound. There was not. She continued on into the kitchen and carefully rummaged through a drawer until she found a candle and a match. Making sure the kitchen door was shut, she lit the candle, then went to the shelf above the fireplace and got down her Bible. Carl would be up in an hour or two. There was no sense in waking him now.

Tired to a depth that she had not known before and unwilling to think anymore about what she had to do, she opened the book to the New Testament and began to read. There was no purpose in it other than to help her pass the time until she had to face him again.

She read idly in the Gospel of Matthew for a time but found herself looking up and staring at nothing. Finally, with a deep sigh, she set the book beside the candle and dropped to her knees. She closed her eyes, her thoughts still a jumble, and then finally she began.

"O Father, my dear Father in Heaven. I come to thee in the midst of the night—a night of darkness, a night of terror, a night of pain and indecision. I know not what to do, Father. I fear deeply for my children. I have seen what our enemies have done. I know that just because we are thy people doesn't mean there is always protection. I do not question that, O God. I trust in thy wisdom and thy mercy. But I fear for the safety of my children. Help Carl to see that we are in great danger."

There was a long silence; then, "I miss my family, Father. How I love them! How grateful I am that I was privileged to be born to such goodly parents! But I have my own family now, Father. I have Carl, and I know that he too is a blessing from thee. What do I do? I have wavered from the faith, but now I am determined to try to do thy will. What is thy will, O Lord? Must I leave Carl to find safety for my children? Must I put my children in danger in order to honor my vows with my husband? O Lord, my heart quakes at the very thought of either of these terrible choices. Bless me to be wise. Help me, Father. Help me to know what to do. In the name of Jesus Christ, amen."

She rose slowly and sat down again. For a long time she stared at nothing. The image of a headstone beneath an oak tree on the far side of the river came to her mind. "Papa, help me. Help me to know what to do."

There was no answer but the silence and the darkness. She reached for the book again and began to thumb idly, hoping that her eye would catch something that might be an answer. After ten minutes, she shut the book again, as deeply in turmoil as when she began. She set the book in her lap and bent down, putting her face in her hands.

Then a thought came to her. It came from a long time ago in her past. She remembered sitting around the fireplace one night back in Palmyra. They had been reading the Bible. Her head came up slowly. It had been something about women. She opened the book again, striving to remember. Was it something Jesus said? She slowly shook her head. She didn't think so. One of the Apostles, then. Peter, James, Paul. She began to think of them one by one. Peter maybe. Or was it Paul? Paul had written so much more. She began to flip through the pages, holding the book closer to the light now, feeling a sudden eagerness.

There was no way to know exactly what she was looking for, and so no way to know where to find it. But she saw that there were brief one- or two-line summaries at the head of each chapter. With that, she turned to the book of Acts and slowly began to read every summary. It took her over half an hour, and she had about decided that her memory was playing tricks with her. Then the words seemed to jump out at her.

It was the introduction to the third chapter of the First Epistle General of Peter: "Wives to honor their husbands. Obedience brings blessings."

Pleased and surprised, she leaned more closely to the candle and began to read to herself. "Likewise, ye wives, be in subjection to your own husbands."

She stopped, half frowning, half smiling. *Subjection* was not what she was looking for. Thus the frown. But the smile came from a memory that came stealing in as softly as a kitten's footsteps. She had been maybe sixteen or seventeen. They were gathered around the fire—it had been a winter's night, she thought. Her father had been reading in this very chapter. "I don't like that word," Melissa had blurted out. She could remember his annoyance. He had stopped reading and looked up. "What word?"

"*Subjection.*"

For a moment he had seemed confused. She rushed on. "Why should a woman have to do what the man says?" she demanded. "Why can't both have a say?"

A flash of irritation had darkened her father's face, but to her surprise it was her mother who spoke up. "Do you think *subjection* implies that you are inferior?" she asked.

"Well," Melissa had answered, "it sure sounds like it."

"Do you think your father views me as inferior to him?" Mary Ann persisted.

"No." That had come from several of them at once. There was no question about that. Benjamin Steed treated Mary Ann as if she were a queen in the home.

"Some men abuse their position as head of the home, and that is wrong," Mary Ann went on. "But the evil is in the abuse, not in the fact that he is the head and the wife is subject to him. There has to be a head, Melissa. That's all that Peter is saying here."

The remembrance brought a sharp pang—how she missed the sweet wisdom of her mother and the gentle love of her father! She sighed, then continued reading.

". . . that, if any obey not the word, they also may without the word be won by the conversation of the wives; while they behold your chaste conversation coupled with fear." She stopped and read that again, puzzled by the awkward language. "If any" had to refer to the husbands, she decided. Then her mouth rounded and there came out a soft, "Oh."

"If any obey not the word . . ." That had to mean husbands who didn't accept the gospel. She was almost startled by that. That was Carl! She stared, reading it again to make sure she was correct. Then the next concept hit her. "If any obey not the word, they also may *without the word* be won by the conversation of the wives."

"Conversation" was no difficulty to her. This was a word used in several places in the New Testament. As a child she had been taught that it was an old English word which did not mean "talking to one another" but rather "conduct, behavior, or the way a person acts."

She began to speak aloud now as she put it into her own words. "So if there are husbands who don't accept the gospel, they may be won *without the word*—" She stopped again. Without the gospel? That seemed strange. Then again, understanding flooded in. "Oh," she cried softly. "They can be won without preaching to them. The husband can be won—or changed—by how the wife lives or by her conduct."

Marveling at what was happening, she read the next verses. "While they behold your chaste conversation coupled with fear. Whose adorning let it not be that outward adorning of plaiting the hair, and of wearing of gold, or of putting on of apparel; but let it be the hidden man of the heart, in that which is not corruptible, even the ornament of a meek and quiet spirit, which is in the sight of God of great price. For after this manner in the old time the holy women also, who trusted in God, adorned themselves, being in subjection unto their own husbands: even as Sara obeyed Abraham, calling him lord: whose daughters ye are."

With a growing sense of wonder, she read the whole thing again, slowly and carefully. What was Peter saying? Not that the word, or the gospel, wasn't important, but that a woman could win a man in other ways—not the ways of the world, through outward beauty and adornment, but rather through being more like Christ, by following his example of patience and faith and meekness and obedience.

She was nodding now, feeling a rush of light and joy that pushed back the gloom which had so enveloped her this night. Melissa set the book down and for a long time sat quietly in the chair, lost in her thoughts. Then she read through the scripture one last time before she blew out the candle, got down on her knees, and once again began to speak softly to the Lord.

When she heard Carl get out of bed, she immediately ran up the stairs. When she opened the door, he was standing there waiting for her, looking a little unsure as to what he should do. She smiled and went to him, putting her arms around him.

"I'm sorry, Carl."

"No, I'm the one who's sorry. Where were you?"

"In Mama and Papa's house." She put her finger to his lips as he started to say something else. "It's all right. I got an answer."

"To what?"

"To what I should do."

"And?" he asked slowly.

"I'm not going to leave you, Carl. We're going to see this through together."

For a moment, he just stood there, not sure what to say.

Then finally his arms came around her and he put his face against her hair. "I couldn't bear it if you did leave."

"Neither could I," she whispered. Then she pulled back and looked at him, her eyes wide and beseeching. "But you have to promise me something, Carl."

"What?"

"You have to promise me that no matter what happens, you'll put the safety of our children first."

There was no hesitation. "And yours too."

She laid her head against his chest. "Yes."

"I promise," he murmured. "I promise that with all my heart."

Chapter Notes

Edwin Bryant's party reached Fort Bridger late on the night of 16 July. The Donners would not reach it until 27 July. Since their last visit with the main party on the Fourth of July at Beaver Creek, the pack mule party had gained eleven days on the wagon companies. On 18 July Bryant wrote in his journal: "We determined, this morning, to take the new route, via the south end of the great Salt Lake. . . . Although such was my own determination, I wrote several letters to my friends among the emigrant parties in the rear, advising them *not* to take this route, but to keep on the old trail, via Fort Hall." (*What I Saw*, p. 144.) We know from other sources that one of those letters was written to James F. Reed (see *Chronicles*, p. 108). There is no existing copy of that letter, and so the contents as written here are speculative. However, the details shared here by Bryant come from his journal account of this time. (See *What I Saw*, pp. x, xi, 133, 135, 142–44.)

The scripture Melissa reads is 1 Peter 3:1–6.

Chapter Seventeen

Peter walked steadily alongside the oxen. Even though it was past five o'clock in the afternoon, the sun was beating down with merciless power, baking everything living and dead underneath its powerful rays. Peter took off his hat and swiped at the gritty dust along the inside rim. Then he took out a bandanna and wiped his forehead. It came away dark and grimy.

"It's unbearable, isn't it?"

He turned and smiled up at Margret Reed and her oldest daughter, who were riding on the spring seats inside the wagon and who had the canvas sides of the wagon rolled up to let in at least some air. He could see dark rings around the rims of their bonnets and knew that they were as hot as he was. He smiled ruefully. "We didn't know how sweet the Valley of the Sweetwater really was, did we?"

Margret pulled a face. "Oh, what I'd give for an evening's bath in those wonderful waters!"

"At least we're going downhill now," Peter observed.

Ironically, it had taken them almost half a day to realize that fact. Two days before, they had camped at the last crossing of the Sweetwater. Not far from where they stopped, the Sweetwater turned north toward the Wind River mountain range, which was the source of its headwaters. They knew they were close to South Pass at that point, and a general excitement swept through the company at the thought of seeing that famous dividing point along the trail. There they would leave the Atlantic watershed and enter the Pacific. But to their great disappointment, they couldn't find it.

Yesterday they nooned in a gentle swale between two buttes, then about a mile farther on found a spring. Some thought it was Green Spring, or Pacific Spring, as it was also known, but others argued that since they hadn't crossed the divide, it couldn't be. They stopped at the spring for their evening meal, but decided to push on until they reached South Pass. After they had gone several miles, it was clear that the small creek spawned by the springs was headed west and was not going to circle around and join the Sweetwater. They also reached a place where they could see the land ahead for some miles, and it was all on a gentle downhill slope to the west. That's when they realized the gentle swale between the two buttes had been South Pass.

Now Patty, the Reed's eight-year-old daughter, poked her head out from beneath the roll of the wagon cover. "Will it be downhill all the way now, Peter?"

He laughed merrily. "I wish that were true, Patty. No, we've still got some high mountains to cross."

Another head appeared beside hers. It was young James. He was five but bright enough to be two or three years older than that. "But how, then, can the water reach the Pacific Ocean?" he asked.

Peter hadn't thought about that. "I don't know, James. Perhaps it goes around the mountains on one side or another."

"Then why don't we go around the mountains?" he shot right back. "Wouldn't that be easier?"

Margret laughed and tousled her son's hair. "Easier, yes, but not necessarily shorter. And if it's not shorter, then it may not be easier."

"Oh." And with that he was satisfied and pulled his head back inside.

Patty withdrew hers as well, and Peter turned back to watch the road ahead. Thinking they were not yet to South Pass, they had stayed on the road until long after dark the previous night, going on about thirteen miles beyond Pacific Spring. That had been a serious mistake. The only water was a few brackish pools in a dusty riverbed known as the Dry Sandy. To Peter's horror, Balley, one of Mr. Reed's best oxen, died a day after drinking that water. George, another of the better oxen, was now exhibiting similar symptoms. To lose two of the best oxen was not only a costly loss but a personal one to Peter, who had come to think of the oxen as friends.

They rose early this morning and pushed on, heading for the next substantial water source, which was the Little Sandy. The rest of the oxen were terribly thirsty and hungry and were wearing out quickly. Peter peered ahead, trying to see any sign of green in this vast expanse of sage and rock outcroppings. Ahead he saw a jackrabbit, startled out of its hiding place by one of the Donner wagons, race away in a breathtaking burst of speed, its huge ears marking its darting path through the sagebrush. Then he saw a small cloud of dust up ahead, off to the left of the main train, and after a moment could make out the dark figure of a man on horseback. He turned back to Mrs. Reed. "I think I see Mr. Reed coming."

She straightened, peering forward. "I think you're right, Peter."

The rider was coming at a steady lope, and it took only a minute or two to confirm that it was Mr. Reed on his mare. He slowed for a moment as he passed the lead Donner wagon, calling something to them, then spurred on to his own three wagons.

"We're almost there, Peter." He looked up at his wife. "Margret, the Little Sandy is only about two miles ahead."

"Wonderful. Is it really a river?"

He gave her a lopsided grin. "Well, if you're thinking in Illinois terms, no. If you're thinking in terms of where we camped last night, it's marvelous. It's a stream of clear water about three feet deep and forty or fifty feet wide."

"Really?" She clapped her hands in sheer anticipation.

Reed looked down at Peter. "There are several companies already there," he said. "Boggs and his party, the Campbell group, Dunbar and West. We'll have plenty of company."

"Is there enough grass?" Peter asked, always concerned about his oxen.

"Oh yes." He glanced at his wife, who had turned around to tell the children. He lowered his voice to a bare murmur. "The place where the routes separate is just a few miles beyond there. The Greenwood Cutoff leaves just west of the Little Sandy and heads for Fort Hall. We're having a meeting tonight to decide which way to go."

Peter nodded. "I don't think our stock could take a long, dry stretch right now, Mr. Reed. But even if we don't take the Greenwood Cutoff, we can still decide to go by way of Fort Hall once we reach Fort Bridger, can't we?"

"That's what I understand. Going that way is longer but has more water."

"Are you still of a mind to take the Hastings route, sir?"

Reed nodded emphatically. "Without a doubt, Peter. Without a doubt."

In the end it wasn't much of a debate. The minds of most of the emigrants were already made up one way or the other. James Reed was the most enthusiastic supporter of the Hastings Cutoff and kept hammering at the idea of saving three hundred to four hundred miles over the Fort Hall route. He had made a copy of the Hastings letter brought east by Bonney and quoted from it liberally. "Listen," he would say whenever it seemed appropriate, "the road around the Great Salt Lake is much nearer and better than the one via Fort Hall. Why extend the journey unnecessarily?"

But to those who had serious reservations about the new route and weren't sure that Hastings was a sure guide, his words carried little weight. After half an hour of vigorous discussion, the vote was taken. Ex-Governor Boggs would lead the group going north to the Big Sandy, where they would rest a day to recruit their stock, then make the long, dry run to the Bear River. Several other companies agreed to accompany him.

Others decided that they didn't want to risk the fifty-mile drive without water and determined to go to Fort Bridger. Then they would turn back north and head for Fort Hall. That was the more traditional Oregon Trail route.

On the other hand, James Reed, the two Donner brothers, Charles Stanton, Patrick Breen, the Murphys, and several of the German emigrants voted to try the new route. They would leave first thing in the morning and go straight for Fort Bridger to meet Hastings, who would then take them across his cutoff.

The two companies withdrew from each other to elect their new captains. Boggs was elected captain of those taking the Greenwood Cutoff. James F. Reed should have been chosen as leader of the group following Hastings. He was the natural choice; that was clear to everyone. But he was also the wealthiest member of the party, and with his lavishly equipped wagon and his thoroughbred mare, some resented him. He also made no secret of the fact that he was descended from Polish aristocracy. This too did not set well with good old-fashioned American democracy and those who mistrusted anything that smacked of being too European.

In the end George Donner was elected captain. It was a disappointment to Peter, but not unexpected. The younger of the two Donner brothers was sixty-two. Though he was also well-to-do, he was a farmer, not an aristocratic and wealthy businessman. Everyone called James Reed "Mr. Reed." Everyone called George Donner "Uncle George."

Peter's employer was disappointed too but took it in stride.

In reality, the Donners still depended heavily on his counsel, and he would take a leading role in the train's government. But from henceforth their little group would be called after its captain and would be known as the Donner Party.

As the meeting broke up and they started back for their wagons, the Reeds were together, walking a short distance behind the Donner group. Peter watched Tamsen Donner, wife of George Donner, carefully. She had sat back during both the meeting and the voting. There was considerable excitement in the air, with the division of routes soon to be upon them. People spoke in animated tones to each other and speculated on what this meant for their arrival date in California. But Tamsen Donner, a woman of unusual grace and learning, was strangely quiet and said little. Now she walked alone and said nothing.

Margret Reed noticed her and moved out ahead to slip an arm around her waist. "Well, Tamsen," she said brightly, "what do you think of our decision tonight?"

Tamsen turned to look at her. She was frowning deeply.

Margret smiled, though it seemed a little strained in the face of such gloom. "What? What is it, Tamsen?"

"I don't feel good about this," she muttered.

"Why not?" Margret Reed had been infused with the enthusiasm of her husband and this came as a complete surprise to her.

"How can we trust the statements of a man about whom we know nothing?"

"Hastings, you mean?"

There was a curt nod. "We've never even met the man. Who's to say that he is not some selfish adventurer who wants us to come this way for his own reasons?"

Now James Reed moved up beside them. "Tamsen, Tamsen," he soothed. "Mr. Hastings is a renowned explorer. He came across that route just this spring."

"What if he is a liar?" she shot back.

That so surprised Mr. Reed that he was nonplused.

Seeing his reaction, Mrs. Donner backed off a little. "Well, maybe not a liar. But how can you and my husband think for one moment of leaving a known road to trust in the statement of someone about whom you know nothing?"

"It's a four-hundred-mile savings, Tamsen," Reed said earnestly. "That's twenty days of wagon time. Twenty days! We can't just ignore that."

Mrs. Donner looked at him once, then looked away. Her whole body suggested resignation and surrender. "I don't feel good about it," she muttered again, then moved away from the Reeds to rejoin her husband.

It was midmorning when they reached the spot where the trail forked. The Donner Party had broken camp and started away first, and now they had no one out in front of them. Ahead of Peter a few dozen yards was a clear set of wagon tracks which turned to the right, angling off to the northwest across an endless sage-covered plain. Another set turned to the left, heading in a southwesterly direction. In the far distance, Peter thought he could see a smudge of green. That would be the Big Sandy, where both groups would camp for the night, though in different locations.

As he approached the fork, speaking softly to the oxen, he looked at the spot where the road joined. He was intrigued by it. At one point there was only one road. Then in what could be measured in inches, they began to diverge. In ten feet the tracks were separated by three or four feet. In fifty, they were two completely separate roads. In a mile they would no longer be in sight of each other. In a few days, they would be hundreds of miles apart.

It was a strange thought, and it occurred to him that in some ways life was like that. You came to a point where a decision had to be made. In many cases the choice seemed so inconsequential that you could barely tell the difference. But once the decision was made, you started off in a different direction. In a lifetime, one simple choice could bring you to widely separated destinations.

As his wagon reached the spot where the routes split, he popped the whip over the head of the lead oxen. "Haw, boys! Haw! Haw!" They swung their massive heads to the left. The wagon tongue creaked as it turned slowly in response to their pressure, and in a matter of moments they were on the left fork, moving on toward Fort Bridger. The road to the right lay empty and desolate, waiting for the companies coming behind.

About twenty minutes later, Peter peered to the north. Sure enough, there was a line of wagon tops crawling across the flat desert, slowly but surely moving farther and farther away from the company led by George Donner. The Boggs Party had reached and then taken the turnoff. Even as Peter watched, they seemed to be receding. No wonder they called it "the parting of the ways," he thought. Then he turned his face to the southwest and began to watch for any signs of the Big Sandy.

On the morning of July twenty-first a thunderstorm rolled in from the west, and it began to rain and rain hard. Umbrellas were brought out and coats were put on. The air was cold and the wind stiff. The children huddled in the two wagons while the adults went ahead with their preparations to depart. By nine o'clock, the rain slackened, but it was still a steady drizzle. By noon, which was so typical of the weather of late, the sky was clear and the temperature hot again.

Six days earlier, Captain (now Colonel) James Allen marched out with four companies of the Mormon Battalion. They went as far as Traders Point to get their initial supplies, then stopped to wait. A steamboat was supposed to meet them there and take them downriver to Fort Leavenworth, but it never showed up. It was just as well. He brought them back to the main camp, and the additional time had given them a chance to fill up the last company. Of the desired five hundred men, Colonel Allen now had four hundred and ninety-six. For the second time he made the announcement that the battalion was about to depart.

On the sixteenth, when the battalion had gathered and marched away, there had been great excitement in the air. Today, the finality of their departure had set in and the mood was very much different. This time there were no speeches. The officers and noncoms shouted and yelled and pulled their companies into line in a matter of minutes. Once in position, they shouted up to Colonel Allen, who stood with his sword out of its scabbard at parade rest. When the last officer called out that his company was ready, Allen snapped to attention. "Bat-tal-*yun!*" His voice floated over the bluffs and the camps that covered them as not another sound was heard. Four hundred and ninety-six men snapped to attention. "*For-ward! March!* Hup, two, three, four. Hup, two, three, four."

William Pitt, probably at the express command of Brigham Young, had brought his band together again. They were seated just behind where the colonel had stood. As the rhythmic stamp of feet began and Company A moved forward, Pitt brought down his baton. At march tempo, the band began to play "The Girl I Left Behind Me."

Tears came more profusely than the morning's rain, and they were not confined to those who waved good-bye. Many a man marched by with his head held high and his cheeks stained with tears as his wife and children called out their final farewells.

In five minutes they were gone. The band stopped and began packing away their instruments. The crowd began to dissipate. The Steeds stood silently. A few sniffles and sobs could still be heard, but for the most part they watched the disappearing columns in silence.

Emily was clinging to her mother, the reality of not seeing Josh for at least a year finally settling fully in upon her. Rachel stood nearby, also crying but not totally devastated. "At least," she managed to say through her sniffles, "he will be in the same company with Derek and Rebecca. It was very nice of Colonel Allen to let Derek and Rebecca change companies."

Lydia took a deep breath and then let it out in a long sigh. "Yes, thank heavens for that."

Mary Ann turned to face her family. "One more," she said simply.

"One more what?" Joshua asked.

"One more farewell," she said softly. "That's when Matthew and Nathan leave with the Pioneer Company in the spring." She managed a wan smile. "That will be as hard as this. But after that, it's going to be nothing but family reunions for the Steeds. And I can hardly wait."

Chapter Notes

The Donners, along with several other companies, reached the Little Sandy River (in what is now southwestern Wyoming near the town of Farson) at the same time. A council was called, and the companies decided to take different routes. Those who took the Greenwood Cutoff (or the Sublette Cutoff, as it was later called) faced a long drive of about fifty miles but a shorter route to Fort Hall, near present-day Pocatello, Idaho. The others, led by the Donners and the Reeds, chose to head for Fort Bridger, where Hastings had promised to wait for them to lead them across his new route to the south.

J. Quinn Thornton, one of the party who chose not to accompany the Donners, wrote in his journal for 19 July: "The Californians [i.e., those who chose the southern route] were generally much elated, and in fine spirits, with the prospect of a better and nearer road to the country of their destination. Mrs. George Donner was, however, an exception. She was gloomy, sad, and dispirited, in view of the fact, that her husband and others could think for a moment of leaving the old road, and confide in the statement of a man who of whom they knew nothing, but who was probably some selfish adventurer." (In *UE*, p. 22; see also *Overland in 1846*, p. 429; *Chronicles*, pp. 100–103.) Ironically, Tamsen Donner would be one of those who died in the Sierra when she refused to leave her dying husband after the rescue parties came (see *Chronicles*, pp. 298, 316, 318).

Though the sources usually list Jacob Donner as the older of the two Donner brothers (which is the way this series has depicted the situation), recent research indicates that it may have been the other way around (see Kristin Johnson, "The Jacob Donner Family," *New Light on the Donner Party*,

<http://www.metrogourmet.com/crossroads/KJR_JD.htm> [4 September 1998]).

After several delays, the Mormon Battalion marched away from Council Bluffs at noon on Tuesday, 21 July 1846. Henry Bigler perhaps summed up the feelings of all when he wrote: "It was a solemn time with us as we were leaving families and friends and near and dear relatives, not knowing how long we should be absent, and perhaps we might never see them again in this life." Zacheus Cheney observed: "It was a day of sadness, of mourning and of parting. The tears fell like rain." (See *SW*, pp. 44–45.)

Chapter Eighteen

The thirtieth of July was a hot, sultry day in Nauvoo, but Melissa Rogers didn't mind. For her, things were better than they had been in several months. On July twenty-fifth, after two full weeks of captivity and severe mistreatment, the five Latter-day Saints who had been taken hostage by the anti-Mormons were finally released and allowed to return home. That didn't completely end the tension that hung over the city, but it reduced it sharply, and life settled back into some kind of normalcy.

What had most significantly changed was the situation in the home of Carl and Melissa Rogers. After that night spent in her parents' home, her relationship with Carl had changed dramatically. Part of that came from her decision to accept his leadership and to trust in his judgment. Equally important, at least she suspected as much, was her absence from the house that night. After her scare at the store, it had really frightened Carl when he had not been able to find her. Since then he had been more loving and considerate of her feelings. He made a special effort to inform her of what went on at his new citizens committee meetings. And though she wasn't exactly sure what they were, she knew that he began to make some contingency plans in case more trouble erupted.

She found herself singing from time to time, and Carl had startled her two days ago when she heard him laughing and roughhousing with the children when he should have been putting them to bed. It was so unexpected and yet so welcome. Several times each day Melissa would close her eyes and thank her Heavenly Father for leading her to that scripture and helping her find her answer.

It was nearing five o'clock when the back door opened and she heard Carl's footsteps coming down the hall. She went to the door of the kitchen, wiping the flour from her hands against her apron. "Hi," she said, going up to kiss him. She could smell the odor of the harvest on him and she breathed deeply. It was as though she had stepped outside for a moment.

He kissed her back, pulling her into his arms and holding her tightly for a moment. "You smell like fresh bread," he said, burying his face in her hair.

"And you smell like fresh straw. Were you harvesting?"

"Yep. Young Carl and I helped Zebedee Franklin get in his wheat." He thumped his pocket. "Made four dollars."

"Good." She pulled away. "Come in. Supper won't be for an hour, but there's hot bread and honey."

"Now, that sounds good. Young Carl stopped to talk with one of his friends. He'll be along in time for supper." He followed her to the kitchen, but then stopped just inside the door. As she reached the table she looked around. He was holding a letter and waving it slightly back and forth. "This came today."

She started toward him. "What is it?"

He didn't answer, just held it out for her. Again she wiped her hands and took the envelope. When she opened it and withdrew the letter she recognized Joshua's handwriting immediately. "From Joshua? What does he say?"

Carl gave her a strange look. "Just read it."

She moved back to the table and sat down. She read quickly the first half of the page. "They're at the Missouri River now." She looked at the date. "This was written on the sixteenth, just two weeks ago now."

He nodded, but his expression said, "Keep reading." She did so. Suddenly her eyes widened. She laid the letter on the table and began to smooth the paper as she read. "Oh my," she breathed after a minute. She looked up at Carl, then continued to read swiftly.

"Can you believe it?" she said, half to herself. Then she looked up. "Did you read it, Carl?"

"Yes. A bit of a surprise, huh?"

"A bit?" she cried. "I am absolutely dumbfounded. Joshua baptized? I . . ." She shook her head and leaned back. "I can't believe what I'm reading. This is wonderful. Oh!" She started to reread it. When she was finished, she folded it slowly. Her eyes were moist and her voice was very soft. "I wish I could have been there. Oh, how I would have loved to see Caroline's eyes when he told her."

"I wish you could have been there too, Melissa," Carl said with equal softness. "I really do."

Her head came up in surprise. He had really meant it. The tears came as she looked at him. "Thank you, Carl." Then she took a deep breath. "Joshua Steed. Who would ever have guessed?"

Carl shook his head slowly. "Well, it wouldn't have been me, I can tell you that for sure."

Then, to her surprise, he reached in his back pocket and drew out another envelope. This was larger and of a darker brown paper.

She stared for a moment, then laughed. "You are full of surprises today, aren't you? Who is this one from?"

To her utter surprise, he was suddenly a little emotional.

She stood and came to him. "What, Carl? What is it?"

He held out the letter toward her. "This one is from Kathryn and Peter. They're all right, Melissa. Everything is all right with them."

James Reed called for a meeting with his teamsters right after supper on the evening of July thirtieth. They had arrived at Fort Bridger on the evening of the twenty-seventh and camped in a wide meadow near the fort. It was lush with green grass, and the pure, cold waters of Black's Fork ran through it. After the alkali dust and brackish water they had endured for several days, this was welcomed with great rejoicing. The excitement was high as they approached the area. At last they would meet the famous Lansford Hastings.

That excitement was quickly dashed. As soon as supper was over, Reed and the two Donner brothers rode the half mile to the fort to find Hastings and tell them they had arrived. To their grave dismay, Jim Bridger announced that Hastings had decided he could wait no longer and had started out with about sixty wagons a few days earlier. Hastings had left a message for any coming behind that he would mark the trail clearly and leave letters in prominent places to help guide them along the route. But he had not waited.

What a bitter disappointment that proved to be! Reed was furious. George Donner called it outright betrayal. For some in their party it was the last straw. Cursing the fact that they had been talked into coming this far instead of taking the Greenwood Cutoff, they decided to abandon the whole idea of a shortcut and join those who were taking the traditional route on the Oregon Trail.

Jim Bridger and Louis Vasquez did much to convince the others that Hastings's route was still the right way to go. They spoke in glowing terms of the easiness of the new way. Except for a forty-mile dry run across the Salt Desert, the trail crossed mostly level terrain where grass and water were abundant; and there were no canyons, just hard-packed soil that made it easy going for wagons.

Peter found that report a little too glowing and, like some others, started to have deep misgivings about the new route. But Jim Bridger's name was legendary, and he knew the West as few other men did. So when all the griping and muttering was done, all but a few decided they would stay with the Donners. They would lay over at Bridger's outpost for a few days for a badly needed rest for the teams and to repair and resupply; then they would start again. When they did they would follow the tracks the Hastings group had taken to the southwest.

Reed looked around the circle at his four teamsters and Baylis Williams, who was his all-around hired hand. "All right," he said, "we'll leave first thing in the morning. Let's get a report on how things are looking."

Baylis shot up a hand. The sun was down now, and there was heavy cloud cover, leaving the sky muted and gray. Baylis was an albino, and full daylight bothered him. He often stayed inside the wagon or the tents when they were camped. But once the light was reduced, as it was now, it was as if he were some nocturnal animal coming out of its lair. He was a completely different person. It was his assignment to oversee the restocking of their supplies. Reed nodded in his direction.

"I'm real pleased, Mr. Reed," he said. "As I told you yesterday, I'm very much surprised at how well stocked the fort here is. It doesn't look like much, but we've been able to either buy or trade for almost everything we need."

Milt Elliott, who was the lead teamster but who also helped Baylis with the acquisitions, nodded. "Prices are high." He pulled a face. "I saw someone give a ten-dollar pair of pants for a pint of whiskey this morning. But when you consider this is the last outpost between here and Sutter's Fort in California, that's to be expected."

Baylis nodded vigorously. "True. But we've taken in a good supply of wheat, flour, coffee, and sugar. I think we're about where we need to be."

Reed nodded in satisfaction. "Good. I'm a little surprised by what we've found here too. As you know, Mrs. Reed and myself and the Donners were invited to have dinner with Mr. Bridger and Mr. Vasquez last night. We ate off English stoneware with sterling silver forks and knives. Some of the things those men have in their quarters would feel perfectly right in some of the finest homes back east. They are a couple of fine and honest gentlemen, and their fort is a blessing for us."

Mrs. Reed smiled. "That Mr. Bridger, what a storyteller!"

Reed nodded vigorously. "He sure is. I guess that comes from all those long winters out here with nothing to do but talk to each other."

"Like what?" Peter asked. He was fascinated by these men who ran tiny islands of civilization in an ocean of nothingness. Bridger, Vasquez, Bordeaux, Reshaw—he found them all to be quite remarkable.

Reed chuckled openly now. "Well, for example, he tells me that there's a place to the south of here where there's a whole petrified forest—*peetrified*, as he calls it."

"What's *petrified?*" Baylis asked.

"It refers to wood that has turned to stone and rock," Reed answered. "I've seen some petrified wood before and it's quite remarkable. But anyway, according to Bridger, everything in this forest is 'peetrified'—peetrified wood, peetrified trees, peetrified birds singing peetrified songs." He laughed aloud as he remembered how they had all been suckered along until he added the part about the birds and their singing.

"Peetrified birds," Herron said, playing along. "Really?"

Reed laughed. "It's almost like Bridger and Vasquez try to outdo one another in the telling of these tall tales. Here's another one. Bridger claims that he's seen a glass mountain that provides a lens so powerful you can see elk grazing in a meadow twenty-five miles away through it, and that it's so clear that around the base it's littered with dead birds who were killed when they dashed themselves against its invisible cliffs."

Peter was laughing now too. "I'd say that qualifies as a tall tale."

"But here's my personal favorite," Reed went on, enjoying

himself greatly now. "Old Gabe—that's Bridger's nickname—says there's one place in the mountains where you have an eight-hour echo." He paused, waiting for them to take the bait.

"An eight-hour echo?" Elliott asked dubiously.

"Yes." Reed was grinning broadly now. "He says it is of great convenience. When you go to bed at night you just cup your hands and yell, 'It's time to get up,' and then the next morning the echo wakes you up at just the right time."

They all roared at that one.

"It's as good as any theater in Illinois," Mrs. Reed concluded. "We were thoroughly entertained for over an hour."

Reed's smile held for several seconds as he thought back on the previous night, but then he gradually sobered. "Well, enough of that. Let's get on with it. How is everything else?"

Milt Elliott nodded quickly. "All is in readiness. All the repairs have been completed on the wagons and harnessing. The women have the laundry done. They've also gathered herbs and berries and dried them, cleaned out the wagons and repacked them, and taken stock of our provisions. We've bagged some fresh meat and dried that as well. We bought two new oxen to replace the two we lost to bad water at the Dry Sandy."

"We lost on that one, Mr. Reed," Peter spoke up. "Balley and George were the two best we had. These new ones are a poor substitute."

Milt nodded. "Anyway, I think we're ready for whatever this cutoff has to offer."

That brought a lowering of Reed's brows. "I'm very surprised that Edwin Bryant didn't leave some word for me. He was here. I thought for sure he would leave me some word." Then he shrugged. "Well, be that as it may, it sounds like we're ready. Uncle George and I met together. As best we can count, we will have seventy-four people—twenty-seven men or older boys, twelve women, and thirty-five children ranging in age from an infant to fifteen years. We will have nineteen wagons total."

Milt Elliott, who also served as a kind of foreman for the Reeds, spoke when Mr. Reed had finished. "That's large enough to keep any Indians away but small enough that we're not eating one another's graze for the teams."

"Yes," Reed answered. "I'm pleased. I'll still have a word or two to say to Mr. Hastings when we catch him, but we're well prepared." He looked around the group. No one spoke. "All right, then," he concluded, "let's pack up everything we don't need for tonight. We'll leave at first light."

Rebecca Ingalls had guessed there would be times when she would ask herself if she had done the right thing by insisting on accompanying Derek on the Mormon Battalion's march. What she hadn't suspected was that those times would come frequently and within the first ten days of their departure. They had left Council Bluffs at noon on the twenty-first; now it was the evening of the thirtieth, and a miserable evening it was turning out to be.

About half an hour before—which would make it about eight-thirty—just as they were finally getting the children to sleep, a stiff wind from the west began to rustle the trees above their heads. It had the smell of rain in it, and immediately the men of the camp set about getting their shelters ready for a "blow." That was no easy task, for their shelters were not tents. They would not receive tents until they got to Fort Leavenworth. In the meantime, each night they built small willow lean-tos or conical shelters which they dubbed "wigwams" because of their resemblance, though in miniature, to the Indian lodges. On nights when the sky was clear, many just slept on the ground beneath the stars. But there had been clouds in the west even before sundown, and so most had prepared shelters. They were flimsy things and did little more than to provide some privacy and keep out the worst of the mosquitos.

The typical wigwam was usually only big enough to sleep one or two. Derek was obliged to make a larger one so that all five of them could sleep together. Josh made one just large enough for himself a short distance away, then always helped

Derek with the larger one. Both were becoming more adept at making them with each passing day.

Rebecca listened to the wind and felt the cool air flowing through the walls. That was good, but the fact that the wind was picking up was not. She could hear Derek and Josh and the other men moving around the camp, making sure everything was secure. Then came the splatter of the first raindrops against the west end of the wigwam. She groaned. *Not tonight!* She was desperately weary, and little Leah would be up in an hour or two wanting to eat. She knew the brush walls could withstand a light rain, but if it got heavy at all, and especially if it came slanting in on the wind, their so-called shelter would very quickly prove to be quite inadequate.

Ten days, and it already seemed like a month. The men were being driven hard, and morale was starting to collapse. The weather had been exceedingly hot, and the men were hoping that under those circumstances the marches would be moderated. Colonel Allen seemed to agree, but then his adjutant, a martinet by the name of George P. Dykes, argued that the men wished to do more than that. Dykes himself was a great walker and advocated that longer marches would get the men in shape more quickly.

Rebecca snorted in disgust. A great walker? That from a man who owned a horse and rode it more than half the time. But Dykes had convinced Colonel Allen, and so long marches became the order of the day. What really irritated the rest of the battalion was that Lieutenant Dykes was one of their own. The heat was enough to drain the strength from a healthy man, but for those who were suffering from ague, as many were, it was devastating. The heat wrung every drop of sweat from man and beast. The dust rose in choking clouds, and they had to keep their heads and faces covered in order to breathe. More and more men became ill, and only the administrations of the priesthood allowed them to continue on with the group.

Rebecca could not remember ever being so utterly exhausted as she was at the end of each day. She couldn't believe Derek. About half the time he carried either young Benjamin or the baby. Benji was four now and quite plucky, but after an hour or two he'd begin to lag and lose heart. Then Rebecca would have to take the baby and Benji would go up on his father's shoulders. Josh was also a great help. Sometimes he had to be up front with the officers to fulfill his duties as orderly, but whenever he was free to march with them, he helped with the children. Thankfully, Christopher still found the whole thing to be a wonderful adventure and marched ahead with enthusiasm.

Then had come the problem with the flour. There had been little flour for the army to purchase at Traders Point, but Colonel Allen had assured them they would make arrangements to purchase it en route. By the night of the twenty-fifth they had exhausted their supply and had been unable to find any more. Most of the camp went to bed fasting that night, though a few, like her and Derek, had some parched corn and made a meager meal of that.

They marched on for two more days—thirty-eight more miles—in that condition, weak with hunger, dizzy with the heat, on the verge of collapse from heat exhaustion. Finally they had come to the town of Oregon, Missouri, near where the Nodaway River emptied into the Missouri. Colonel Allen sent word that he had finally been able to procure some flour. Then, to everyone's dismay, when they went to get it, the Missourian who had brought it in his wagon refused to give it to them since he had learned that it was a company of Mormons he was supplying.

Colonel Allen was so furious when he learned what was happening, that he told the man he would either deliver the flour or be instantly arrested and put under guard. As the red-faced man grudgingly obeyed, the battalion let it be known what they thought of this non-Mormon officer who led them. The air had rung with shouts of "Good for the colonel" and "God bless the colonel."

The flour had helped immensely, but the road—

She broke off from her thoughts as Derek slipped into the lean-to and crawled up to lie beside her. She could smell the rain on his coat. "How is it?"

She could sense that he shook his head in the darkness. "I think we're in for it, Becca. It could be a long night."

As if to prove his point, a gust of wind rattled their wigwam and she felt a mist of water touch her face. She reached out and made sure the baby was completely covered. "I don't need a long night," she said wearily.

"I know."

They lay there for several minutes, listening to the rising storm. Above them the limbs of the trees began to creak. Flashes of lightning punctuated the darkness, followed by the ominous rumble of thunder. The makeshift walls of their shelter shook as a particularly violent gust hit it, and Derek reached out to hold it steady. "Whoa, there," he said softly, as if he were speaking to one of his horses. His voice showed a little anxiety, which only added to Rebecca's concerns.

"Will it hold?" Rebecca said nervously.

"Not if it gets much worse than this."

She moaned. Christopher stirred and raised his head. "Is it all right, Papa?"

"Yes, son. It will be all right."

But it wasn't all right. Lightning was cracking sharply now, and the night was filled with continuous flashes. The wind was gusting powerfully, rising to a shriek. "I don't like this," Rebecca said through gritted teeth, holding on to the branch framework as it shook and trembled.

Then over the sound of the wind there came another noise. It was a deep creaking sound, as if someone were pulling a nail out of a piece of wood with agonizing slowness.

"What's that?" Rebecca asked in alarm.

Derek's head was cocked to listen. For a moment it stopped; then they all jumped as there was a tremendous crash and the ground shook violently beneath them.

Ignoring Rebecca's cry, Derek shot through the small entryway into the night. He stood up, leaning into the fury of the wind. There was a flash of lightning and he saw Josh's shelter rip free and go tumbling away. Josh was struggling to put on his oilskin raincoat. He saw Derek and came to stand beside him. "What was that?" he called.

"I don't know," Derek shouted. He looked around. It was an eerie scene. The rising wind had whipped the dying coals of dozens of cooking fires into life again, and points of orange and red filled the darkness, spitting out long trails of sparks into the sky. That wouldn't last long, Derek thought, not once the rain started.

He turned in the direction of where the crash had sounded. He could see nothing. Then the lightning flashed again. He drew in his breath sharply. Not thirty feet away from where they stood, one of the towering hickory trees which surrounded their campground lay prone on the ground. He caught a momentary glimpse of the tangle of roots at one end.

He grabbed Josh's arm and spun him around. "Look," he shouted. "It took a tree down."

Even as Josh peered into the darkness, waiting for the next flash, they heard the deep creaking sound again. Derek whirled and darted back to his shelter. With one mighty jerk, he ripped the framework up and let the wind take it. "Rebecca. Get the baby. Josh, get Benji!"

He grabbed Christopher by the arm and jerked him up. There was a sharp crack overhead and a large branch crashed down just beyond them. "Hurry!" Derek shouted, helping Rebecca get to her feet.

Others were shouting now too, and he saw shadowy figures when the lightning flashed. They stumbled away from their campsite, leaning heavily into the wind. Josh yelled something. A shaft of lightning slashed downward, momentarily bathing everything in light brighter than midday. There was a glimpse of another tree toppling with sickening speed. It smashed into a neighboring tree, and both went down together as men screamed and jumped out of the way. Again the ground trembled noticeably under the impact.

Now the rain began, slicing in like hail, instantly drenching them. In moments what had been dry dirt became thick mud.

They stumbled and fell as they pushed their way through the darkness. Finally they were out in the open and far enough away that no tree could hit them if it fell.

"Here!" Derek shouted. He dropped to one knee, pulling Rebecca down beside him. Christopher followed and moved in close. Josh brought Benjamin in under his raincoat and moved in close as well. Turning their backs to the wind as much as possible, the six of them huddled together, drenched and miserable, shivering with both the cold and the fear. Benji was whimpering. The baby howled in protest, even though Rebecca tried to shelter her with her body.

Rebecca lowered her head and closed her eyes, her hair plastered to her face, the rain running in torrents down her body. And for the first time the doubts stole in. *What have I done?* she cried in her mind. *What have I done to my family?*

Chapter Notes

Though they were joined by others later, the number of people and wagons given here by James F. Reed is the actual count of the Donner Party as they left Fort Bridger (see *Chronicles*, p. 109). The total does not include Peter, who is, of course, a fictional character.

The tall stories from Jim Bridger recounted in the novel were actually part of the "repertoire" of this famous mountain man and are only a sampling of the folklore of the indomitable group of traders, trappers, and explorers from that era (see Bernard DeVoto, *Across the Wide Missouri* [Boston: Houghton Mifflin, 1947], p. 169).

The letter Edwin Bryant wrote and left with Louis Vasquez to give to James Reed (see pp. 203–6, 217, herein) was never delivered. When Reed finally met Bryant again in California, Bryant asked why Reed had ignored his warning. That was the first Reed knew of the Bryant letter. Reed later wrote, "Vasquez being interested in having the new route traveled, kept these letters" (as quoted in *Chronicles*, p. 108).

Most scholars believe that Bridger and Vasquez, who were characterized by more than one contemporary traveler as being honest and decent men, held these letters back with good intentions. The Greenwood Cutoff, which left the main trail at what is now called "The Parting of the Ways" near the Big Sandy, was becoming increasingly popular with emigrants. This bypassed Fort Bridger altogether, which would prove economically disastrous to Bridger's outpost. But there is some evidence that the partners really believed the Hastings route was a better trail that saved hundreds of miles.

The great storm that hit the Mormon Battalion on the night of 30 July tore down several large trees. Incredibly, no one was hurt. In the meadow where they had left their animals one ox was killed. Thomas Dunn, a battalion member, wrote of that night: "This appeared quite miraculous to us, but we considered we were in the hands of the Lord, for in his power, I trusted" (as quoted in *SW*, p. 64).

Chapter Nineteen

The fog was like a living thing. It swirled and moved around them in constant motion. Sometimes it would lift enough that they could see out a hundred yards or more across the water. Then it would close in again and they could scarcely make out the prow of the ship, a distance of no more than twenty-five or thirty feet. But the sun was up now, and from the gradually increasing brightness above her, Alice could tell that the fog was thinning and would burn off in another quarter of an hour or so.

There was a sharp jolt as the baby kicked out sharply. She winced, then placed a hand on her stomach, smiling. *Yes, child. We are almost there. Can you feel it too?*

She saw Will turn and give her a look of quick concern. He had evidently seen her jump. She gave him her most radiant smile. He smiled back, then looked forward again.

She was glad. If he had looked at her too closely, he might have seen into her heart, and for now she didn't want that.

What would he think of this woman who was his wife? At the moment she was euphoric to the point of giddiness, feeling as if someone had given her a very strong draught of wine. And why not? she decided in her own defense. Six months of sea life were about to come to an end. Half a year—the longest of her entire life—was now over. One hundred and eighty days of almost unbearable monotony. To only smile at this moment showed a remarkable amount of restraint. If she followed her natural inclination, she would be up on the bridge beside Captain Richardson shouting to everyone who would hear her: "It's over! At last it's over!"

She and Will were not alone on the deck. It was crowded, and she guessed that virtually every passenger who was able had come topside. She cocked an ear to see if she could still hear it, then felt a deep satisfaction. It was the sound of surf pounding against a shore. She lifted her head, glaring at the mists that surrounded her. *Be gone*, she commanded sternly. *You are ruining this for me*.

"It may just be an island."

Alice whirled to see who dared speak such blasphemy. "No," she said fiercely to the man who had spoken it to his wife. "There are no islands here." She turned to Will, who was staring at her in surprise. "Tell them, Will. There are no islands here."

"Well, the charts do show a small group called the Farallon Islands about twenty or twenty-five miles off the mainland." He rushed on when he saw the look Alice shot him. "But we passed them off the starboard side sometime during the night. No, what you hear is the mainland. I would guess from the sound that we're not much more than a mile offshore now."

Alice nodded in triumph at the puzzled brother and his wife, who weren't sure what they had done to generate such a passionate outburst. Alice ignored them, just as she ignored Will's questioning glance. *No islands. Not now.*

Captain Richardson had struck most of the sails, and they were moving forward very slowly. Two sailors stood at the prow with a sounding line—long ropes with knots every six feet, or every fathom, and a lead weight tied on one end. Another of the crew was high overhead in the crow's nest at the top of the tallest mast. Occasionally they could look up and see him; mostly he was shrouded in the mists. Every eye was fixed dead ahead. It was not a comfortable thing to bring a ship in this close to shore and not be able to see what lay in your path.

One of the sailors at the prow dropped the sounding line over the side again. The coiled rope unwound with a soft hiss until it finally was gone and snapped taut against the hawser to which it was tied. The sailor turned, cupped his hands around his mouth, and shouted back toward the bridge. "Still twenty fathoms or more, Cap'n."

"Aye," Richardson called back. "I want a sounding every minute."

"Aye, sir." The two sailors began reeling the dripping rope back in again, coiling it neatly as they did so. Alice peered forward. The fog was thinning noticeably now, looking like clouds of dust gusting before the wind. Suddenly there was a cry from above them, and every head jerked upward when it came.

"Land ho! Half a mile dead ahead off the port bow."

Alice swung her head to the left. There was a momentary glimpse of a high promontory of land and sharp cliffs that dropped to rock-strewn beaches. Much of the hillside was golden brown, but here and there clumps of low green bushes clung to the hillsides. And then it was gone again.

"I saw it," she cried, grasping Will's arm.

"Yes!" he answered.

Excitement swept the group. A stiffening breeze was blowing from behind them, the warmer air over the water rushing in to replace the cooler air over the land. It was sweeping the fog bank away in its rush to make landfall.

Then there was a collective gasp, followed by cries of joy. Off to the left of the ship, framed in perfect clarity by the surrounding mists, steep hillsides rose straight up out of the sea. They could see the white line of surf, rocky beaches, seabirds soaring over the heights, the thick green foliage which capped the upper reaches. What was most thrilling was that the landmass did not spread clear across their path. Directly in front of them it was clear water. The land came out into the sea, then stopped.

There were groans as another fog bank rolled back across their view. But the cloud was low enough that it didn't reach the top of the mast, and the man in the crow's nest could see over the top of it.

"Land ho!" the lookout cried again. "Another peninsula off the starboard bow, sir. Roughly the same distance as the first."

"Can you see if the land comes together?" the captain shouted.

"There are two points of land jutting into the sea, but nothing dead ahead, sir."

"Sounding line?"

"Still more than twenty fathoms, sir," came the reply.

Will nodded in satisfaction. The sounding line had only twenty knots on it, but that was more than enough. If it didn't hit bottom, that meant they had at least twenty fathoms, or a hundred and twenty feet, of water beneath the hull. Since the ship drew only between two and three fathoms when it was fully loaded, as it was now, there was no threat of beaching her yet.

The *Brooklyn* moved forward slowly, the sounding linesman crying out periodically, the lookout in the crow's nest reporting regularly. The breeze was strong enough now that it was whipping up the first of the whitecaps. The fog was clearing rapidly before it. Then suddenly it was clear, with only wisps of the fog before them. Directly ahead there was nothing but water. On both sides the land rose sharply out of the sea, but the distance between the two points was at least a mile.

Will gripped Alice's arms. "It's the Golden Gate, Alice. The entrance to San Francisco Bay. We're there."

Alice reached out and took Will's hand and squeezed it hard, beaming with joy. She went up on tiptoe and put her mouth to his ear. "You are a very fortunate man, Will Steed."

"I am?" he whispered back. "Why is that?"

"Do you know what day it is today?"

"The last day of July."

Entering San Francisco Bay

"That's right. Do you remember what I told you when we left the Sandwich Islands?"

He frowned, clearly stumped. Then suddenly the frown disappeared and he grinned broadly and nodded. "I do."

"That's right," she said happily. "I told you that you had July and then you'd better have me to California."

"Mr. Brannan! Come to the bridge immediately."

Will turned in surprise. It was Mr. Lombard, one of the officers. He was on the bridge beside Captain Richardson, who had a telescope to his eye, looking up toward the headlands that towered above them now on either side. They were still wreathed in wisps of clouds and mist. Above the excited chattering of the passengers, the officer's voice barely carried.

Lombard cupped his hands. "Mr. Samuel Brannan. Report to the captain immediately."

Will squinted a little. He had come to know the officers well, and there was just a hint of anxiety in Lombard's voice. "Stay here," he said to Alice. "I'll be right back."

She turned but he was already pushing through the crowd toward the back of the ship. He arrived at the ladder leading to the bridge just as Sam Brannan and one of his counselors did. Will stopped. He didn't want to assume he was wanted when he wasn't, but Brannan motioned for him to come along.

Now the noise had subdued somewhat. The passengers seemed to sense that something was afoot and were watching curiously. When the three Latter-day Saints reached the two naval officers, the captain motioned them to follow and they went to the back of the bridge where they were out of sight of most of the passengers.

"Mr. Brannan," said Captain Richardson, handing over the telescope, "take a look up on the point of that bluff."

Will's head snapped up. It took him only a second or two to see it, even without the spyglass. The edge of the cliff was lined with walls of stone. At regular intervals the tops of the walls were notched with square openings. At each opening Will could see the black snouts of cannon. This was a fort, and they were about to pass beneath a full battery of artillery.

Brannan put the glass to his eye, searched for a moment, then found it. He gasped softly.

"It has to be Mexican," Mr. Lombard said. "And they're looking right down our throats."

"I suggest you get all of your people below decks, Mr. Brannan," Richardson said, staring upward even as he spoke. "Just in case. We have no reason to expect that we'll be fired on, but we can't be sure." Then to his officer he began snapping out orders. "Mr. Lombard, alert the crew. Get the five-pounder ready for action. Rig the sails for fast running on my command."

The officer snapped out an "Aye" and was gone. Richardson turned back to Brannan. "We don't want to frighten your people, Mr. Brannan, but we need to move with dispatch."

Twenty minutes later the hold opened and someone came clattering down the ladder. "Mr. Brannan." It was the voice of Mr. Lombard.

There was instant quiet below decks. Sam Brannan stood and walked to the doorway which led into the passageway. Will stood and edged closer so he could hear.

"Yes?"

"The captain says your people are welcome to come back topside," the officer said. "We've passed the fort. Near as we can tell, it's deserted. There's no one there. We're into the bay now."

A great sigh of relief swept through the group as Brannan called back to Lombard, "Thank you. That is welcome news."

Once they had cleared the entrance to the bay, and with the fog gone, the captain raised more sail and the *Brooklyn* moved along briskly again. The passengers lined the rails all along both sides of the ship. For a time they kept looking back nervously, watching the fort they had passed, but they were beyond the range of her guns and soon the threat was forgotten. Now many of them were crying out, pointing to this or that sight in case someone had missed it.

Alice's own excitement—dashed so abruptly when they had to go back below decks—had quickly returned, and her eyes drank in everything eagerly. They had come through the narrow passage known as the Golden Gate, and now the water opened up into a huge bay, a great inland sea. Directly ahead and to their left a barren, rocky island thrust itself out of the bay, as though it were guarding the entrance. To the left, perhaps two miles farther on, another small island was wreathed in the last of the morning fog. Seabirds were everywhere, dipping, soaring, bobbing on the water, hopping awkwardly along the rocks. Across the bay the land came down to meet the water, forming the eastern shore. It was a bleak, treeless shore. Here there was little green to be seen. The summer sun had turned everything brown. It was nothing like Robinson Crusoe Island or Honolulu, but Alice didn't care. This was North America, the same continent from which they had left. More important, it was their final stop. The voyage was done.

A movement caught her eye, and she turned to see a line of soldier pelicans wing past them, barely skimming above the choppy water. She felt like shouting at them, telling them that Alice and Will Steed would soon be moving in to live with them.

"Sail ho!"

It was a cry from the man in the crow's nest again. Every head turned up to see which way he was pointing, then jerked around to look in that direction. It took almost a full minute more before the ship rounded the land enough for the rest to see what he had seen. Once again there was momentary panic. Once again they were roughly jerked back to the painful reality that they were entering a war zone.

"It's a man-o'-war!" the lookout cried. "Twenty guns."

There were cries of alarm, and several began running for the holds that led down to their quarters. Mothers yelled for children. Husbands moved to find their wives.

Will was peering ahead, looking at the cut of the sail and the shape of the hull. He felt Alice clutch anxiously at his arm, but didn't turn. The *Brooklyn* moved with agonizing slowness, and the other ship revealed itself very slowly. Finally, Will looked up. "I think it's a Yankee man-o'-war," he called up to the lookout. "Can you see a flag?"

On the bridge, Captain Richardson had the telescope to his eye and was peering at the other ship, which was now almost fully in sight. The man in the crow's nest also had a glass to his eye. He was leaning forward precariously, trying to see better. At his height, he had the better view.

"It's an American ship, sir. She's flying the Stars and Stripes."

A ragged cheer went up and there was applause from the passengers below.

Will felt Alice lean against him in relief. "I thought she looked like a Yankee ship," he said, trying not to show just how relieved he was himself.

"She's seen us, Cap'n. She's rigging for war."

Will leaped for the railing. Without a glass, he couldn't see much more than specks of movement, but then the sound of a bosun's whistle came to them faintly across the water. Instantly it was followed by the measured beat of a drum. Will felt his heart go cold. He had seen this enough times up close to know exactly what was happening. The watch on the American ship must have been deeply shocked to look up and suddenly see a ship rounding the entrance to the bay and bearing down on them. The bosun's whistle signaled the danger. The drum beat out the call to general quarters. Sailors would be racing for the stations. Guns were being loaded and trained on the approaching sails. Others would be racing to the magazine and would start wheeling out black powder and cannonballs.

"Call to quarters," Captain Richardson yelled, still looking through the telescope. Instantly Mr. Lombard began blowing their own whistle, calling all the crew to quarters.

Will leaped forward, racing toward the bridge. "Captain! Have the women line the rails. Have the men hold their children in their arms. They won't fire on us until they're sure who we are. Let's show them we're not hostile."

Richardson shoved the telescope into its case and turned toward his own ship. "Mr. Brannan," he bawled, "you heard Mr. Steed. Put the women alongside the railing. Get some children up there where they can be seen. Move! Move!"

The general scramble toward the hatch now reversed itself. Though nervous, the women moved swiftly to the railing. Men grabbed smaller children and put them up on their shoulders, then moved to stand behind the women. Soon the starboard railing, the one facing the oncoming ship, was lined with women and children.

"They're standing down, sir," cried the lookout. "They've seen us. It worked."

That brought another cheer from the people.

"Look, Will," Alice said, "there are more ships."

Will was already looking at the numerous masts that were coming into view behind the man-o'-war. He nodded. "That first one's a whaler. The next two look like hide droghers."

"Hide what?"

"Droghers. They're like barges, only rigged as cutters or schooners. There's a big trade in cattle hides out of this part of Mexico." He pulled a face. "Now, there is a sailing assignment I hope to never face. They say the smell is so strong, people know they're coming three days before they ever reach port." He was still looking at the little cove that was opening up to their view. "And there's a second whaler," he noted. Now they could see at least five or six ships anchored together, with the man-o'-war being the largest.

A cannon boomed and women screamed and dropped down, holding their ears.

"It's all right!" the captain shouted. "That's just the shore battery bidding us welcome."

"Bosun, fire one round of acknowledgment."

Three of the crew jumped to where their own small cannon was in readiness near the bow of the ship. In a moment, it roared an answering shot.

"Captain?" It was the lookout again. "They're launching a rowboat. I think they mean to come and say hello, sir."

"Fine, fine," Captain Richardson said. It was obvious that he was greatly relieved now, as were his passengers. "Mr. Lombard, prepare to receive visitors aboard."

Lombard nodded briskly. "Aye, Cap'n. Preparing to be boarded, sir."

As they watched the slow progress of the rowboat coming toward them, the *Brooklyn* continued to move toward the cove where the ships were anchored. Now the rocky headlands gave way to more rolling hillsides. These came down to the water to meet sandy beaches. There was suddenly the terrible stench of something dead.

"Ew," Alice said, pointing. "Look, Will."

Coming into sight was a long stretch of sandy beach. It was strewn with the bleached carcasses of slaughtered cattle that were white with swarms of seagulls. Farther back from the water were large stacks of dried cow hides, stiff as sheets of metal. Will wrinkled his nose. Did they do the slaughtering right on the beach? Incredibly, there were several people lounging on the beach, watching the approaching ship as though this were something that happened every day of the week.

"That must be Yerba Buena," he said to Alice. Just beyond the beach a few scrubby oak trees sprung out of a wiry-looking grass or vegetation. Farther back, low sand hills, or dunes, gave way to rising ground. There, in a totally random fashion, they could see a collection of buildings. The largest was an adobe building that looked like it had once been an army barracks. But all around it there were small wooden houses, lean-tos which faced away from the beach, and some ramshackle shanties that looked as though the slightest puff of wind would bring them crashing down. The finest-looking building was a newly constructed adobe building, also quite large. From past experience, Will guessed that that was probably the customshouse. Tax collectors always seemed to get the best accommodation. Next to the building another American flag snapped in the brisk breeze.

There was a loud thump as the rowboat from the American warship clunked alongside the *Brooklyn*. At Sam Brannan's urging, the Latter-day Saints moved forward in a group near the bow. There was considerable nervousness among them. It was a great relief to know that they had not landed in a country hostile to Americans. On the other hand, these were representatives of the United States of America, a country that had at least twice before refused to offer help or sanctuary to the beleaguered Mormons.

A rope ladder was tossed over the side, and in a moment a uniformed officer climbed aboard the *Brooklyn*. He was followed immediately by two others. Captain Richardson and Mr. Lombard stood at attention, waiting.

The lead officer—Will saw from the epaulets on his shoulders that he was a commander—came to attention and saluted Richardson sharply. "Sir. I am Commander John B. Montgomery, captain of the twenty-gun *Portsmouth*, a ship of the United States Navy." He turned and looked at the assembly of families who were gathered behind Richardson. "Ladies and gentlemen," he boomed loudly, "I have the honor to inform you that you are in the United States of America."

There was a moment of silence as those words sunk in, and then in one spontaneous burst of enthusiasm, someone's voice rang out. "Three cheers for America."

As one, hundreds of voices rang out with gladness. "Hip, hip, hurrah! Hip, hip, hurrah! Hip, hip, hurrah!"

"Derek."

It sounded far away, but he thought he recognized the voice. He tried to open his eyes, but it was as though someone had barred the shutters over the windows and there was no prying them open.

"Derek!" It was louder, sharper. And he thought he felt someone roughly shaking his shoulder. He wasn't sure, because the ague often shook his body as a bulldog shakes a rat. This new shaking was no rougher than that. He finally managed to crack one eye open and see the face before him. For a moment he wasn't sure if he knew who it was or not. The cheeks were deeply browned from the sun; the nose was peeled and had splotches of bright red. The lips were parched and cracked. A few strands of hair, bleached blond by the sun, poked from beneath a blue and white bonnet.

"It's me, Derek. It's Rebecca. We have to go. It's our turn for the ferry."

"Just rest a little." He closed his eyes again.

Now there was a younger voice, sharper and more piercing. "Pa. We have to go."

"Come on, Uncle Derek. Let me help you."

That roused him enough for reality to finally push its way in. He opened his eyes fully now. It was Rebecca. And there was Christopher, his eyes looking far too worried for a seven-year-old. Josh Steed, his nephew, stood beside his son, pulling on one of Derek's arms.

As he sat up, he saw they were beside the river. The muddy brown waters of the Missouri rolled past them in slow swirls. He tried to stand and nearly fell back again, but Josh stepped quickly behind him and helped him stand up.

It was no wonder that he and several others were sick. In addition to that one terrible storm, it had rained hard on other nights as well. They had spent several miserable, cold nights in wet bedding sleeping on the ground.

"Look, Derek," Rebecca said with a forced brightness. "That's Fort Leavenworth just across the river."

He turned his head a little and squinted against the afternoon sun. In the distance he could see a stockade wall with open gates. Inside, there were one or two large buildings, several small ones, and a cluster of white tents set up in neat rows. An American flag hung limp in the summer heat.

"We'll be there in a few minutes, Papa," Christopher said, taking his father's hand. "Then we can get some food and water."

"Come on," Rebecca said, urging him forward. He felt Josh start to gently push him from behind.

Now he saw that the ferry, already loaded with people he recognized, was just a few feet in front of them. Two men jumped off and hurried to them. "Come on, Brother Ingalls," one of them said. "We've waited five hours for our turn. Let's not miss it now."

When Derek awoke, his first awareness was of the sweltering heat. His body was bathed in perspiration. His eyes stung and burned from the sweat that ran into them. He reached up to wipe his brow with his arm, realizing as he did so that he had no shirt on.

He half rose, not sure where he was. All was whiteness. "Becca?"

Almost instantly a flap opened and Rebecca stepped inside the tent. She had a bowl of something in one hand. Her face showed concern, but on seeing him she immediately smiled. "Hi," she said softly.

He managed to get up to a sitting position, though he felt very weak. "Where are we?"

"We are in our own tent," she said happily. "U.S. Army issue."

"Tent?"

"Yes, we received them this afternoon when we arrived at Fort Leavenworth."

"We're there?"

She laughed. "No, we're here. And I must say that you picked a very good time to faint on me. Some of the brethren had to pitch our tent for me."

"I . . ." He looked around again, seeing now the canvas and the tent poles and understanding why it was so hot and why he had felt as if he were inside a cloud.

"They issued one tent for each mess of six men," Rebecca explained, moving over to sit beside him on the cot. "Since there are five of us, they let us have our own tent. Josh was assigned to the mess next to ours. I promised to help cook for them if they would help me with the tent and getting camp set up."

He let out his breath, feeling the shame. "I haven't been much good to you, have I?"

She waved that away, then brought up the bowl she had been holding. "I brought you something."

He looked down, squinting a little. It looked like milk at first, but then he saw it wasn't liquid but solid, more like the consistency of soft butter. Then as he looked more closely, he saw that some of it did seem to be melting. "What is it?"

She took a spoon from the pocket of her apron and scooped out a heaping pile of the white stuff. "It's ice cream." She shoved it toward him and he opened his mouth. What followed so surprised him that he gave a little cry, instantly followed by a sound of delight and pleasure.

"Isn't that wonderful?" she gushed, then gave him another spoonful.

"Absolute heaven," he answered as he savored the cool sweetness in his mouth. "Where ever did you get it?"

"The post commissary is selling it for a nickel a bowl. Christopher and Benji have already had two bowls each. I've had one too." There was momentary guilt. "I'm sorry. I know it's expensive, but I couldn't say no. Josh bought the boys their second bowl."

He took another bite, this time letting it melt slowly in his mouth so as to lengthen the pleasure. In Nauvoo, they would sometimes fill a bowl with ice shavings, then put another bowl inside of it and whip a mixture of milk, cream, and sugar until it partially froze. But that had never tasted anything like this.

"They have what they call an ice-cream machine," Rebecca explained. "They chop ice from the icehouse and pack it all around a metal can, then crank the machine until the mixture inside the can freezes. Isn't that wonderful?"

He took another bite, then closed his eyes with the sheer pleasure of it. "This is enough to make me a healthy man."

She laughed. "If that's the case, I'll go buy four more bowls."

Derek looked more closely at his wife, studying her face. Two hundred miles and more than ten days in the summer sun had taken their toll on Rebecca's normally clear and fair skin. But he couldn't remember her ever looking more lovely.

"How are you feeling?" she asked.

"Very weak, but better." He peered out the tent flap where he could see rows of additional tents. "Tell me what's happening."

"Well, we arrived here at Fort Leavenworth about five o'clock today. The army immediately issued us tents and some limited food supplies. They say they will issue the weapons and other equipment the day after tomorrow. They have authorized each mess to purchase a baggage wagon and four mules."

His eyebrows lifted. "Really?"

"Yes, isn't that good news?"

"Of course." Then, after another spoonful of ice cream, he asked, "How is Josh taking to all this?"

"Like a boy with a new drum. He's so excited. And to think he'll get his own musket. He's already strutting like a peacock."

He laughed. That was the wonder of the young. And the blessing of them. "What about General Kearny?"

"He left for Santa Fe a few days ago. There are only about seventy regulars left here." She wrinkled her nose in distaste. "There's a whole battalion of Missouri volunteers here as well."

"Missourians?" He frowned too. Mormons and Missourians didn't make for a good mix.

"Yes, and it looks like they're quite raucous." She straightened, remembering why she had come. "They have asked us to make a list for five days' rations. I was hoping you would be awake so you can tell me what to do."

He leaned forward and took her hands. "This isn't all that we expected, is it? Are you sure you still want to do this?"

There was no hesitation. Her head immediately began to bob. "It's been hard, Derek. Harder than I ever thought. But we're together. I wouldn't change that. Not in any way."

Chapter Notes

The first known white men to discover San Francisco Bay were Spaniards who arrived there in 1769. In 1776 they built a fort (the Presidio), which still occupies the site. Upper California officially became part of Mexico in 1820. In 1835 the Mexican governor appointed a British sailor to be captain of the port of San Francisco. He erected a tent near the beach at the base of what later became known as Telegraph Hill. Soon a ramshackle village grew up on the site. It was called *El Paraje de Yerba Buena* (The Place of the Good Herb). Though not in great numbers, more and more Americans began arriving in California.

A month before the *Brooklyn* arrived, the American settlers around San Francisco Bay declared their independence from Mexico in what came to be known as the Bear Flag Revolt. When the USS *Portsmouth* arrived in June, the ship's crew stood by to see what happened. Shortly thereafter they received different orders and seized Yerba Buena without any resistance. The fort on the bluffs had already been abandoned, and the cannons had been allowed to rust to the point where they were useless. The local general and most of the native residents fled southward, and the American flag was run up the pole beside the customshouse. (See "Voyage," pp. 64–65; *CS*, pp. 38–39.)

Many of the crew of the *Portsmouth* had heard about the Mormons, and there was considerable suspicion about them, but Brannan assured Commander Montgomery that they came in peace. Brannan also offered to put his men under Montgomery's command. This provided a welcome addition to Montgomery's meager forces, and he agreed that the Mormons could stay at Yerba Buena and unload their goods without any customs charges.

An interesting fact is that if the *Brooklyn* had not gone to the Sandwich (later Hawaiian) Islands first to discharge a load of cargo, they would have arrived at least a month earlier and found Yerba Buena still part of Mexico. Under those circumstances, customs charges of about twenty thousand dollars would have been required, and that would have greatly strained their ability to survive as a new colony.

The voyage of the *Brooklyn* thus came to an end after nearly six full months at sea. It was a historic voyage in many respects. Writers Richard O. Cowan and William E. Homer note: "As far as we have ascertained, the *Brooklyn* Saints were the first colony of home-seekers with women and children to sail around Cape Horn, the first group of Anglo settlers to come to California by water, and the first group of colonists to arrive after United States forces took California" (*CS*, p. 39). Yerba Buena also became the first city in what would become the western United States to be colonized by Mormons. The island they saw as they entered the bay is now Alcatraz Island.

Chapter Twenty

The *Brooklyn* sailed through the Golden Gate and into San Francisco Bay on the morning of July thirty-first. That was a Friday. Though a few of the men were allowed to go ashore that day, most of the passengers were asked to stay on board.

Saturday morning brought high tide, and the ship moved right in close to the beach. In an atmosphere more like that found at a country fair, the approximately two hundred and forty passengers lined up for their turn at the large rowboat that would take them to shore. With them went anything that was light enough to carry. Quickly the beach was filled with valises, large shoulder bags, boxes, crates, chickens in their pens. Even the two surviving milk cows, now both veteran seafarers, were soon on solid ground. Children shrieked as they ran up and down the beach, energized as much by the knowledge that this was the last stop as by the room to run.

As the tide began to recede, the *Brooklyn* had to back away and move a little farther west to another spot, but the unloading continued all through the day. By nightfall everyone but the crew was off the boat and looking for a place to bed down. The fog had come in again during the night, and the breeze was brisk and considerably chilling. Most of the passengers trooped a short distance up the hill to the *Casa Grande*, or "Grand House," to get out of the wind. The largest structure in Yerba Buena, the long adobe building that had previously been a barracks now served as post office for the tiny community. Its American owner was so pleased to have a whole shipload of his countrymen join the community that he offered sleeping space—room on the floor to roll out their blankets—to nine families. In typical fashion, Sam Brannan volunteered himself to take advantage of these accommodations. Commander Montgomery had turned the newest building, the Mexican customshouse, into a barracks for his men, but he had them move back to the *Portsmouth* and opened places for more families there. One or two other places were opened up by the locals, but the company of Saints was far too large for the little community and many ended up pitching tents on the beach or nearby.

Will and Alice—thanks more to Alice's advanced condition than Will's position as a leader—were given a place in the customshouse. Their tiny living spaces were divided by hanging blankets or similarly flimsy partitions across the room. But they had at least some small degree of privacy, something which they had seen little of on board ship. And even though the night grew quite cold, the thick adobe walls kept them comfortable without a fire. To her surprise, however, Alice had difficulty sleeping that first night, since there was no gentle rolling motion to lull her to sleep.

On Sunday morning Commander Montgomery sent an invitation to Sam Brannan asking if the Mormons wanted to join his men on board the *Portsmouth* for worship services. Pleased, and wanting to continue the favorable relationship they had with the genial ship's commander, Brannan agreed and they started rowing out to the naval vessel shortly before noon. It was a pleasant surprise. The commander had set up chairs under an awning on the quarterdeck, and they learned from some of the crew that Montgomery was a deeply religious man who read a printed Episcopalian sermon to his sailors each Sabbath.

The Saints were greatly amused by the curiosity they aroused, especially with regard to the women. Some of the navy men had heard enough about this strange sect—including the notion that the Mormons grew horns like the devil—that they watched with considerable interest as the first of the Saints came on board. One of the men was overheard to say, with obvious disappointment, "Derned if they don't look just like other women." But with that settled, it turned out to be a pleasant experience for Mormon and sailor alike. After the services, Commander Montgomery served lunch to all and then had his men conduct tours of his ship.

But that was yesterday. Today they had the task of unloading the heavier cargo on the ship. Though Will encouraged Alice to stay and sleep in, she insisted on being with him and came down to watch the operation. Once again, to their surprise, Commander Montgomery extended a warm hand of welcome. No sooner had they arrived at the landing sight and gotten the gangplank down than a detachment from the *Portsmouth* showed up with orders from the commander to help get the ship unloaded. They set to it with a will, the men of the navy and the men of the Mormons, and soon a great pile began to accumulate onshore.

Alice could scarcely believe it as she watched the cargo come out—and she thought she had known roughly what they had brought with them. To the sailors it was unbelievable. Agricultural tools of every conceivable type were piled in one place. Mechanical and manufacturing devices formed a huge stack a short distance higher up on the beach. There were groceries, dry goods, hardware, lamps, a five-ton printing press—which really astounded the sailors. Not sure what to do with it, Brannan finally secured a place on the second floor of an old gristmill. Alice had to close her eyes as Will and about ten others wrestled the monster up the rickety outside stairs and secured it in its place.

By one o'clock the task was done, and the crew of the *Brooklyn* raised the sails and began backing her away from the beach. The men from the naval ship stood around in easy camaraderie and watched until she was heading for her anchorage, which was not far from their own ship. Then they shook hands all around, and with many calls of thanks ringing in their ears they returned to the *Portsmouth*. One by one, the members of the company moved off. Finally Will and Alice stood alone on the beach. Tonight there would be guards posted to watch their goods, but for now the beach was theirs.

Will's eyes were on the *Brooklyn*, now almost a mile away from them. "It seems strange, doesn't it?"

Alice turned to look at her husband. "What?"

"After almost six months she's no longer our home."

"Does it make you sad?"

"In a way. You know me and the sea."

"Yes." She took his hand.

Now he looked down at her. "And how does it make you feel to know you'll not ever spend another night on board her."

She managed to keep her face expressionless. "I have mixed emotions," she admitted.

He looked a little surprised. "Really?"

"Yes. I'm torn between deep joy and pure elation," she said dryly.

Joshua Steed sat astride his horse just off to the side of the muddy road, watching the scene before him. And it was a scene to behold. Below him, winding lazily for as far as the eye could see in either direction, was the Missouri River valley. A hundred different shades of green met the eye—the green of the cottonwood trees, the paler foliage of Russian olives, the almost black-green of the underbrush, the upper prairies already turning yellow in the summer sun, and the beautiful emerald green of small grassy meadows along the bottoms. And through it all ran the meandering brown line of the Missouri River.

But what drew Joshua's eye was the scene that had been imposed upon this once pristine landscape. Two months before, when they arrived at Council Bluffs, which was almost directly across from him now, there had been the Indian trading post at Traders Point, a few scattered Indian villages, and nothing more. Now everywhere the eye fell—on the opposite bluffs, along the heights where he now was, lining the river bottoms, along the creeks, in the trees and meadows—there were wagons and teams, tents, makeshift willow shelters, droves of cattle, roads and pathways that had not been there just a few weeks before. Across the river, well more than a mile away, he could see that Redemption Hill and Mosquito Creek, two of the more visible landmarks, were lined almost solid with splotches of white from wagons and tents. On this side of the river, not far from where he sat, he could see the Cold Spring Camp, where Brigham Young and other leaders were now staying. They were clustered around the springs that gushed pure and wonderfully cold water in seemingly inexhaustible amounts.

He shook his head in wonder and discouragement. The latest estimate he had heard was that almost ten thousand Latter-day Saints were along the Missouri now, with another one or two thousand expected to arrive before snow came. How could they do it? How could they possibly care for that many people? And once spring came, however would they get them to the Rocky Mountains?

Just then he heard the sound of horses and wagons and turned. Heber C. Kimball and his company were coming toward him on the road that led to Cold Spring Camp. That surprised Joshua a little. First, he had expected Brigham Young to be at the head. Second, he had thought this was to be just an exploration party. Heber had his full company with several wagons and all of his people. Then Joshua had a third surprise. Nathan was riding just behind Brother Kimball. At the sight of Joshua, Heber and Nathan both spurred their horses and rode up to join him.

"Good morning, Joshua," Heber called. "Looks like you're ready to go."

He smiled and nodded. "I thought Brother Brigham was going with us to scout a location for our winter settlement," he said.

"He was, but he's been ill since yesterday. He'll try to follow us a little later in the day. Also, one of his oxen fell in a creek and broke its neck. He's been getting the meat distributed around the camp."

"I heard that," Nathan said. "There's always something, isn't there?"

Heber nodded and reined around. "Well, brethren. Brother Woodruff left yesterday to see if he could find us a place, so I suggest we do the same."

As they wheeled their horses around, Joshua moved over to Nathan. "I didn't know you were going with us."

"I'm not. I'm headed to the other side," Nathan answered. "I'm a bishop, remember? I promised I would help some of my families come across the river today."

Joshua nodded. That made better sense.

Heber had heard Nathan and was nodding. "And that's the very kind of thing we hoped you bishops would do. Keep up the good work."

"It's proving to be a fulfilling, though challenging, assignment," Nathan answered.

Heber nodded, then clucked to his horse. "Well, let's be off. Tell everyone that as soon as we find a place, we'll send word back."

"Come in, please."

Nathan lifted the tent flap and stepped inside. Sarah Rich, wife of Charles C. Rich, was there to greet him, holding out her hand and smiling warmly at him.

"Good morning, Bishop Steed."

"Good morning, Sister Rich. How are you feeling today?"

"Much better. I'm up and about, as you can see."

"And the babe?"

"Doing fine. We're both doing fine."

"Good." He moved a little so that he could see the man lying on the bedroll in one corner. "And how are you, Charles?"

"I am better too, thanks to my angel wife."

"Is it the ague?"

"Probably." He managed a laugh. "I guess misery doesn't really care what the cause is, does it?"

"Well put," Nathan chuckled. He looked at Sarah. "I just came by to see how you are faring. We are taking some of the families across the river today, but I thought it might be better to wait a day or two until Charles and you are both feeling stronger."

"I think that would be wise. There will be—"

There was a rap on the tent flap and Sarah turned around. "Yes, come in."

The flap lifted and a woman stepped inside. She let the flap drop again, surprised to see that there was someone else with the Riches. Nathan did not recognize her, but saw that she was distraught. Her eyes were red and swollen and lined with dark circles beneath them. Her face was pale; her hands trembled a little as she wrung them together.

"Oh, I'm sorry," she stammered. "I didn't realize you had company."

"That's all right, Sister Brookstone. This is Nathan Steed. He is our bishop."

She nodded and smiled faintly. It was gone as quickly as it had come. "I tried to find our bishop, but I don't know where he is."

Charles Rich went up on one elbow. "What is it, Sister Brookstone? Is something wrong?"

She stared at him for a moment, then put her hands to her face and began to weep. "My children are so hungry. We ate the last crust of bread yesterday. I have no money, no goods to trade. What am I going to do?"

Sarah stepped closer to Nathan. "Her husband was one of those who went with the battalion," she whispered.

Sister Brookstone struggled for a moment; then she straightened a little. "I'm sorry. I know that you and Sister Rich have little of your own. I don't know why I came to you. I—"

"Who is your bishop, Sister Brookstone?" Nathan asked.

"William Draper."

"I know where he is camped. I shall take word to him immediately. In the meantime, if there is something I can do to help, I'll—"

Charles Rich pulled himself into a sitting position. "Sarah. Let Sister Brookstone have some of our flour."

Sarah swung around in surprise.

He nodded. "We have about twenty pounds. Give it all to her."

"But . . ."

Nathan was staring too. There was hardly any flour to be found. People were carefully husbanding what little they had until more could be purchased. And Nathan knew that even if there was flour to be had, the Riches had no money with which to purchase it. Charles's announcement had stunned them all, including Sister Brookstone.

"Let us trust in the Lord to provide for us," Charles said softly.

Sarah immediately nodded, turned, and went to a box in one corner. She opened the lid and brought out a sack that was two-thirds empty. Without hesitation she came to Sister Brookstone. "Here. Give your children some bread."

"But . . . ," came the astonished reply, "but what will your children eat?"

"The Lord will provide," Sarah said, echoing her husband's words. She smiled and pressed the sack of flour into the woman's hands. "It's all right."

Tears began to flow again, but this time they were tears of relief, of gratitude, of great joy. "Thank you, Brother and Sister Rich. God bless you for your generous hearts."

"God bless you, dear sister," Charles Rich said.

She turned and almost plunged out of the tent in her eagerness to return to her family. Sarah moved over and sat down beside her husband, and he took her hand. "Thank you," he murmured softly.

Nathan stepped forward. "I shall locate Bishop Draper and tell him about Sister Brookstone. I shall also see if I can find some flour for you."

Charles looked up. His eyes were calm and at peace. "Brother Steed, I know that the Lord will open up a way for us to live. Do not feel uneasy on our account. There will be a way opened up for us to have a loaf of bread in our home."

Nathan was deeply touched by such simple faith. "Perhaps I can be the instrument in helping that come to pass," he said. He shook both of their hands, not trusting himself to speak further, and left the tent. For a moment he stood there, then bowed his head. "O Lord, if it be thy will, let the faith of this family be fulfilled. Help me to find them some bread."

It was past eight o'clock when Nathan finally waved goodbye to his last family and watched the ferry start across the river. He watched them go, too weary to move for a few moments. It would be dark soon, and he felt every hour of the day weighing in upon him. His feet ached; his back was sore; he had a rope burn from grabbing at a chest that had started to topple and a blackened nail where his thumb had been crushed by another box.

He sighed, strongly tempted to tie his horse and then lie down in the grass and rest until the ferry returned and could take him across. But he resisted and swung back up again. Deeply discouraged, he turned the horse and started back toward the bluffs, headed for the campsite of the Rich family. Worse than the weariness was knowing that he had not kept his promise. He had found no flour for them. Tomorrow, on the west side of the river, he hoped to have better luck. If nothing else, his family would share their meager supply. But tonight he had nothing.

He hesitated for a moment, seeing the shadows move against the tent canvas. He could hear the murmur of children's voices. He shook his head, dreading what he was about to do, then rapped softly on the tent pole.

"Bishop Steed," Sarah Rich said in surprise when she saw who it was. "I didn't expect you so late. Come in."

"No, I just wanted to report that—" He stopped. Through the open flap he saw the children seated by their father at a low table. There were cups and plates. But the thing which had stopped Nathan short was the sight of two nicely browned loaves of bread, one of which was half gone. There were also pieces of bread on the plates.

Sarah Rich turned, not sure what had caught his eye. Then she smiled. "Yes, Bishop. Our table has bread on it. Come in. You need to hear what has happened."

Charles Rich got to his feet slowly and shook hands with Nathan. He still looked quite weak and somewhat drawn, but his color was good and he was smiling. "Surprised?"

"I most certainly am. What happened? I haven't been able to find any extra flour."

Sarah shooed one of the children off a stool and motioned for Nathan to sit down. He did so slowly, still unable to take his eyes off the bread. He wanted to reach out and touch it to make sure it was real.

Sarah began. "As you might guess, I was greatly concerned when Mr. Rich asked me to give all the flour that we had to Sister Brookstone."

"*I* was concerned too," Nathan said. "I've worried about you all day."

"Well, I decided I needed to have the same faith as my husband," she went on. "So throughout the day I prayed that the Lord would open a way for us to live. Then about an hour or so ago now, I saw some wagons coming toward us. It was Brother

Sidwell and Elder Ezra T. Benson. They were just starting on their journey east for their missions."

"Yes." Nathan was aware that Brother Benson, the newest Apostle, had been called to preside over a mission in the East somewhere.

"Well, we have known Brother Sidwell for a long time, and so he asked if he might stay the night with us. Elder Benson was staying with another family. We of course agreed, though I had no knowledge of how I might offer him any food."

She stopped, and Nathan saw in the lamplight that her eyes were glistening. She took a deep breath. "We had said nothing to him about our situation. We were simply visiting when suddenly he turned to Mr. Rich and said, 'The Spirit tells me you are out of money, and whispers that I am to help thee.' " She smiled for a moment. "I remember that he spoke like a Quaker and used the word *thee*." She stopped again, then with a catch in her voice added, "And then he handed us fifty dollars."

"Fifty dollars!" Nathan exclaimed.

Charles nodded. "It was a miracle, of course. I turned to Sarah and said, 'Now, you see, the Lord has opened up a way for us to get flour.' "

Sarah came in again. "We were overcome with thanks. Brother Sidwell has gone to visit with another family. I wish he were here to tell this himself. But anyway, he then asked about our situation and we explained what had happened. He then went immediately to his wagon and got some bread. 'We have enough for your needs tonight,' he said. 'But more important, we have learned that there is a wagonload of flour due by here either tonight or in the morning. We shall ask them to stop so you can purchase the breadstuffs you need for your family.' "

One hand came to her mouth and she touched her lower lip, very emotional now. "So you see, we simply had to trust in the Lord."

Josh Steed stood as tall as possible and kept his shoulders

pulled back. He didn't mind the good-natured ribbing he took from his fellow soldiers about his youthfulness, but he sure didn't want the paymaster to have any reason to question his right to his clothing allowance. Gratefully, he had matured early. His whiskers weren't thick, but they were noticeable. He was almost as tall as his father now, nearing six feet, and he had inherited his grandfather's broad shoulders and lean waist. His dark hair was thick and bushy, which also helped.

"Next?" The paymaster was a young lieutenant with a neatly pressed uniform and well-polished boots. Beside him sat a sergeant. Everything about the noncommissioned officer looked dusty. He had large watery eyes, a nose that revealed too many mugs of rum, and a huge drooping mustache that looked as though it would be sucked into his mouth each time he spoke.

"Name?" asked the sergeant.

"Joshua Benjamin Steed, Company D, sir."

"Don't call me sir," he barked. "I'm not an officer. I work for my wages."

The lieutenant didn't even blink. He had probably heard it a thousand times before.

"Forty-two dollars," the lieutenant said, after finding Josh's name. He turned the book around. "Can you sign for yourself, son?"

"Yes, sir." He took the pen from its holder and quickly signed his name.

The lieutenant shook his head. "Every one," he said, half to himself.

"Begging your pardon, sir?"

He looked up at Josh. "So far, every one of you Mormons has been able to sign the payroll. Only about one in three of the Missouri companies can do that."

Josh nodded as he held out his hand and the lieutenant counted out the forty-two dollars. Josh didn't like the Missourians and stayed away from them. They were a rough-looking lot. About every third or fourth word was a cuss word. Most smoked or chewed tobacco, and many used their money to stoke up on liquor at the store. The day before, one of them had buried a hatchet in his comrade's head during a drunken brawl. The one was now in the brig, the other in the infirmary with no guarantee that he would live.

"Next table," bawled the sergeant. "There you'll get your equipment. Muskets are being issued by the sutler at the store."

"The sutler?" Josh echoed tentatively.

The sergeant pointed. "The storekeeper. It's that building there."

Josh nodded and walked swiftly to the next line.

One hour later, Josh Steed had gained about thirty pounds in weight. The rifle, a flintlock musket, was huge, weighing between twelve and fifteen pounds. The barrel was long and had a large bore. The powder magazine was designed to hold enough black powder to shoot a one-ounce ball a full mile. With the rifle he was given a cartridge belt hooked to a leather strap designed to be worn over the left shoulder. The bayonet and its scabbard were attached to a similar belt that went over his right shoulder. One of the men told him that the Mexicans called such an outfit a *bandolier*. He was surprised at how much comfort the solid weapon gave him as he hefted it onto his shoulder.

They were also issued a wide white belt of thick leather upon which was fastened a canteen that held three pints of water. The belt, which they received strict orders to keep clean, was the only "uniform" that everyone got. Each man got a bedroll, a knapsack in which to carry his clothes and other necessaries, and a small cotton haversack that could carry a day or two of rations. The knapsack went on the front, the bedroll went on the back, and the haversack was tied to the belt. When fully "dressed," the man was covered from neck to waist and also carried the musket in his hands.

He checked everything once more to make sure he had put it on as the others around him had, then turned to go and join Derek and some others who waited near the fort store.

"Soldier!"

He snapped around at the crisp command. Another lieutenant was eyeing him up and down. "Yes, sir?"

"Do you have everything you're supposed to have?"

Josh checked quickly, doing a mental check as well. "I think so, sir."

The man walked around him slowly, then nodded. "Very well. Carry on."

"Yes, sir." As the officer walked away, Josh threw back his shoulders proudly. The man had called him soldier. Not son. Not boy. *Soldier!* Grinning widely, he strode with sure and confident steps over to join the rest of his brethren in the Mormon Battalion.

"Uncle Derek! Aunt Rebecca!"

Derek looked up in surprise. Rebecca turned from where she was reading a Bible story to Christopher and Benjamin by the light of the fire.

Josh ran up to them. He had come from the direction of the main parade ground.

"What is it, Josh?" Rebecca asked.

"We have visitors."

"Visitors?" Derek echoed. "Here?"

"Yes. Three of the Apostles and Elder Jesse Little."

Derek stood quickly. "Which Apostles?"

"Elders Parley Pratt, Orson Hyde, and John Taylor."

"But," Rebecca said, closing the Bible now, "I thought they were going to England."

"They are," he said right back. "But they are going by way of St. Louis, so they stopped here to see how we are faring." He paused for breath. "There's going to be a meeting."

Parley Pratt was near tears. He held up the bag that was now stuffed full of money, the money that represented a substantial portion of the battalion members' forty-two-dollar clothing allowance. "Brethren and sisters, I don't need to tell you what this will mean to your families and to the Church. While Elders Taylor and Hyde have been addressing you, I have counted the contributions you have made. I hold here five thousand eight hundred and sixty dollars."

That brought cries of amazement and several low whistles. That was a staggering sum.

In a low and husky voice he went on. "We have determined that Elders Taylor and Hyde will continue to Europe in company with Elder Little, who is going back to preside over the Eastern States Mission. I shall, however, take this money to President Young at Council Bluffs. May the Lord bless you for your generosity and consecration. May he protect you as you now prepare to march to Mexico to fight for your country. God bless you, brothers and sisters. It is an honor to be numbered among such men and women as you."

Chapter Notes

As shown here, the Mormon emigrants who arrived at Yerba Buena were welcomed warmly and treated fairly both by the military commander, Commander Montgomery, and by the locals in the small village that was there (see "Voyage," pp. 64–66; *SW*, pp. 71, 73, 75–76).

Though there was still some discussion about whether to send anyone west that season, by the first part of August 1846, Brigham Young had largely made up his mind that the Saints would have to winter on the Missouri River. Accordingly, on 5 August he and several of the Twelve set out in company with others to scout for a suitable place for their winter encampment (see *MHBY*, pp. 295–96). With the enlistment of the battalion, they now had permission to settle on Omaha Indian lands.

The author took some liberties with the account of Charles C. Rich and his family. In her autobiography Sarah Rich does not give the name of the sister they helped, so "Brookstone" was supplied by the author. Also, the incident took place at Mount Pisgah and not at Council Bluffs, but other than that—along with the addition of Nathan in the scene—it happened at this period of time as described here. (See *SW*, pp. 78–79.)

The details of the outfitting of the Mormon Battalion when they arrived at Fort Leavenworth, which is about thirty miles northwest of present-day Kansas City, come from the journals and histories of those who were there (see *MB*, pp. 35–40; *CHMB*, pp. 134–37).

The nearly six thousand dollars that Parley P. Pratt took back to Brigham Young would have, by itself, justified answering the call of the government for Mormon volunteers. That infusion of cash would prove to be an enormous boon to the Church, which was desperately poor at this time and facing the challenge of caring for a large population during the coming winter.

Chapter Twenty-One

The animals were nervous, and Peter stayed right beside them, talking to them quietly. Virginia Reed came up beside him. "What's the matter with them, Peter?"

"I'm not sure. I think the echo in the canyon is spooking them a little."

Virginia cocked her head slightly. She needn't have bothered. The sound was everywhere evident, bouncing off the great vermillion cliffs above them as though they were all confined in a barrel. "It does sound strange," she agreed.

"In my opinion, the oxen think they hear other oxen somewhere off in the distance and it's making them nervous. They can't see what's making the noise and they don't like it."

"But it's so beautiful."

"Spectacular," Peter agreed, tipping his head back to look at the towering masses around them. They were now six days west of Fort Bridger. This morning they had dropped down from the Bear River into a wide and gentle canyon. The going had been relatively easy, though nothing like the "level trail with hard soil and plenty of grass" that Bridger and Vasquez had promised. But then about noon the canyon began to narrow and deepen. By three the scenery changed dramatically. Along the north wall of the canyon, great outcroppings of brilliant red stone, rising four or five hundred vertical feet, jutted out at regular intervals. They were crowned with cedar trees and oak brush and provided a view that stunned the senses.

Then had come the surprise. As they neared its mouth, the canyon closed in to where it was only about two hundred yards across. That is when they first noticed the echo. Nineteen wagons creaked and groaned down the sage-covered track. Men shouted back and forth to one another. Cattle bellowed, horses whinnied, and oxen lowed. And the towering walls of stone threw it all right back at them.

"Listen," Peter said. He strode out ahead of the animals a few paces so as not to startle them. Then he cupped his hands, tipped his head back, and shouted, "Hey!"

There was an instant response. "Hey-hey-hey!"

That brought the rest of the family to the front of the wagon. "What is it, Peter?" Margret Reed asked.

Five-year-old James thrust his head beneath his mother's arm. "Did you see something, Peter? Did you?"

Peter laughed. "No, I was just showing Virginia the echo here. Listen." He did it again, and again got the same result.

"Oh, boy!" James cried. "Can I do it?"

"Sure."

He moved to the front of the wagon where the canvas cover was pulled back. "Hey, what are you doing?"

The echo came back as an unintelligible rumble.

"Use short words, James. It works better."

He thought for a moment, then tipped his head back again. "James!"

The boy's voice was higher and clearer than Peter's, and the effect was even more noticeable. Back it came. "Ja-ja-james."

The other children clapped their hands in delight.

Ten minutes later when James Reed rode toward them from the mouth of the canyon, they were still trying out the echo, and half the rest of the train were doing it as well.

Reed pulled up, smiling as he watched his children making themselves hoarse.

Peter, back at the head of the oxen now, looked up. "What did you find, Mr. Reed?"

"Good news. The Weber River is just beyond where the canyon opens up. It's a pretty good stream—three or four rods across at least. And plenty of good feed."

"Wonderful," Peter answered. They had been following a small creek all the way down the canyon—everyone was calling it Red Canyon, but in Peter's mind it had become Echo Canyon—but they crossed the stream several times, and the water was now muddy and foul.

"Where do you want to camp, then?" Peter asked.

Reed shrugged. "We'll follow the river and see what looks good. We've still got another two or three hours of daylight."

When they emerged from the canyon, they entered a gently sloping valley that opened up rapidly until it was more than a mile wide. They were following the river now, staying a quarter of a mile or so away from it so as to avoid the tangled underbrush along the bottoms. Mr. Reed was riding ahead again, only this time just a little out in front of the lead wagon. Suddenly he spurred ahead, racing right up to the bank of the river. He bent way over in the saddle, and when he straightened Peter saw that he was holding something white in his hand.

For almost a minute Reed sat motionless on his horse. Then with a jerk he reined Glaucus around and came back to them at a hard lope. As he reached George Donner's first wagon, he waved a piece of paper. "It's a letter from Lansford Hastings."

They swung their nineteen wagons into a circle so that

everyone was close enough to hear. Reed stood by Glaucus, impatiently waiting for the last wagon to pull in. As soon as it did so, he straightened, holding up the letter. "I found this wedged in a stick at the ford. It was put there in such a way that it could not be missed."

"Hastings?" Jacob Donner asked.

"Yes. Written by his hand two days ago."

"Are we only that far behind them?" Lewis Keseberg, one of the Germans, asked.

"No, a little more than that," Reed answered. "Hastings rode back to leave the note for us, so they're probably three or four days out in front of us."

"What does it say?" Tamsen Donner inquired. "Read it to us."

Reed nodded, gripping the paper with both hands to steady it against the breeze that was blowing down the canyon now. " 'To the trailing companies. From Lansford W. Hastings, company guide. I am leaving this note for anyone still coming behind us. You will observe that we took the route down Weber Canyon, following the river. This was against my recommendation, as I had heard that the Weber is a difficult route for wagons. I wanted to cut a road over the Wasatch Mountains and thus into the Utah River valley. An associate convinced our company to take the shorter route in my absence. It proved to be the wildest and most dangerous place we have yet encountered. If you look northwestward from the spot where you received this note, you will see that Weber Canyon closes in again. Just beyond that, the road becomes almost impassable. We have taken wagons where no wagons were ever intended to go. The only route is through the river bottom, which is filled with boulders and choked with undergrowth. We lost one wagon and all of its oxen when we tried to bypass the river on a steep side hill and could not hold it.' "

Reed stopped. "He doesn't say if anyone was killed. Let's hope not." He read again. " 'Though we are now through two bad stretches and are once again in a broad valley, we see again where the canyon becomes little more than a tunnel before it opens onto the Salt Lake. Therefore, heed carefully my counsel. Do not attempt this passage. There is a better way. Send a messenger ahead to catch our company. Upon hearing from you, I will come back and guide you across the better road, which bypasses the Weber route altogether and provides a shorter route to the Salt Lake Valley. Do not risk losing your teams or equipment by attempting to follow us. Yours sincerely, L. W. Hastings, Esquire.' "

James Reed lowered the paper and looked around. The faces that he saw were grave, the eyes lined with worry. They were already dangerously late in the season. It was the sixth day of August, and there were still about seven or eight hundred miles to go before California. If they halted another three or four days, it was pushing the limits badly. On the other hand, what choice did they have? The canyon ahead was impassable. Fort Bridger and the proven Oregon Trail were five days behind them. Waiting for Hastings required less time than that.

"Well?" Reed finally asked.

"What do you think?" Uncle George asked soberly.

Reed considered that. Though George Donner was formally captain of the train, James Reed was by far the more dynamic leader and everyone naturally looked to him. He took a deep breath, then let it out in frustration. "I don't see a choice. Let's make camp here, and tomorrow I'll take a couple of men and we'll try to catch Hastings and bring him back to help us."

John Baptiste Richard—or Reshaw, as he pronounced it—stopped his wagon at the top of a slight rise and motioned for the others to pull up alongside him. They did so one by one, glad for the respite from the dusty trail.

The Crow family wagon in which Kathryn was riding was one of the last in the small train, so by the time they reached the front, most of the people were standing in a cluster pointing toward the south and talking with great animation. John Brown walked over as the Crows reached the point where they had topped the rise and could see the prairie out ahead of them.

"We thought you might like to see this," the wagon captain said with a smile.

"Mother? Children?" Brother Crow said. "Come take a look. Kathryn, you get on the wagon seat so you can see better."

Sister Crow, who had been keeping company with Kathryn, climbed out of the back of the wagon. Kathryn moved to the front and slid through the opening in the canvas onto the wagon seat. She didn't need anyone to point out what they were looking at. About three or four miles away, stretching across their whole field of view, a long, winding strip of green stood out in sharp contrast to the relentless brown of the prairie.

"Is that it, Papa?" one of the children asked.

John Brown answered for him. "That is the Arkansas River."

"The Arkansas River?" someone exclaimed. "We're that far?"

Brown laughed. "Well, it is the Arkansas, but we're a long way upstream from the state of Arkansas. If you look just a little left of straight ahead you can see Fort Pueblo."

Kathryn peered forward, shielding her eyes from the sun. Then she saw it. "Yes," she cried at the same time that Sister Crow did. "I see it."

Kathryn bent down and began helping the younger children pick it out.

Reshaw walked up, his teeth showing white against his swarthy skin. "That is it, no?" he said happily. "Fort Pueblo. The green squares by the river are fields of corn. The darker greens are fields of squash and pumpkin." He laughed aloud, rubbing his hands. "I told you I would bring you to Pueblo. And here we are."

"You have kept your word, Mr. Reshaw," John Brown said gratefully. "You have done as you said you would. And for that, we are in your debt."

For the last several days, anyone who was associated with Brigham Young, even in the slightest way, was aware of the urgency he felt about finding a place for a permanent encampment. Wilford Woodruff had ridden north first, in company with Colonel Thomas Kane, who was proving to be such a loyal friend to the Saints. Then Joshua had left with Heber C. Kimball's full company. Later that same afternoon Brigham finally started. Like Heber, he brought his company and their wagons with him.

Now they all converged on the same spot about a full day's ride upriver from Cold Spring Camp. It was a pleasant spot up on the bluffs about three miles from the river. It was eight-thirty on the morning of the third day of their exploration. All of the adults who were present had gathered in the center of the wagon circle at the request of President Young. Three others of the Twelve were also there—Heber Kimball, Willard Richards, and Wilford Woodruff. As was often the case, Elder Kimball called the group to order and then, after prayer, turned the meeting over to Brigham Young.

"All right, we need your counsel. Brother Calkins, tell them what you found."

Luman Calkins stood up, hat in his hand. "President, as you suggested, I followed that Indian trail another twelve miles upriver from here. I didn't find anything that had sufficient timber to start a settlement." He looked around. "I saw nothing to equal what we have here." He sat down again.

Brigham nodded. "We are getting similar reports from other scouts. I think we have hit upon the best location right where we are. We're close to the river bottoms, where there is timber and there is water nearby. How many of you would be in favor of stopping here?"

There were one or two who didn't raise their hands, but most of them came up immediately. Joshua was one of those who raised a hand without hesitation. They hadn't seen anything better on the way up, not for a large encampment, which was what Brigham had in mind. To Joshua, it seemed like an easy decision.

"Then I propose," President Young continued, "that a city be built somewhere near this location, up here on the bluffs, preferably near a spring. My feeling is that all those who are going to winter on the west side of the Missouri River should stay together and form a city. I want this community to be organized as a family. If the brethren wish to hear preaching, then they must stay at the headquarters. If we are organized as a family, as a compact body, we can build in a systematic order. In addition to houses for our people, I want a council house and a school built. We will need to build pens for our cattle. Before we can even begin construction on homes, we must cut enough grass for the cattle for the winter. And I would propose that a municipal council be called to govern the city."

He stopped for a moment and looked around. Joshua was a little dazed. In typical fashion, Brigham had thought well in advance of most of the rest of them.

When he was satisfied that there were no serious objections to his plan, Brigham continued. "I think we need to do the same thing for those who stay on the eastern side—gather into one settlement for the same reasons and for the same purpose. We already have Father Isaac Morley appointed to direct a high council on that side of the river and to watch out for the needs of the poor among us. I propose that Alpheus Cutler, who first discovered this place, be placed at the head of the high council on this side of the river." He lifted a paper and read off eleven other names. "Those men will serve as the council here. All in favor."

This time every hand came up.

"Good. We shall call it Cutler's Park. I should like us now to divide into smaller groups, with a member of the council taking each group. Let us explore the region hereabouts to determine exactly the best location for our city."

Peter watched Margret Reed as she stood at the edge of the wagon circle and looked northwestward. The sun had just gone behind the mountains now, and the ridge tops were silhouetted sharply against the brighter sky. He didn't have to ask what she was looking at. Four days earlier, on the morning of the seventh, her husband and two other men had ridden toward the spot where she now looked. There the mountain wall split into a sharp V. There the Weber River entered the passage that Lansford Hastings had characterized as the wildest and most dangerous that he and his company had ever encountered.

Nor was she the only one looking. Every day, all through the day, heads throughout the camp lifted and searched the valley to the west of them. James Reed had said he would return with Hastings as quickly as possible. No one had supposed that that would be four days or more. Peter didn't like it either. He couldn't bring himself to think through what the implications might be if Reed and the two men who had ridden with him had been caught by Indians or were somehow lost in this wild and desolate wilderness. But then he would remind himself that Reed was one of the most competent and confident men he had ever known. He couldn't bring himself to believe that Reed had let something happen. It was more likely that it had simply taken them longer to catch up with Hastings than they had first believed.

"Rider coming in."

That shout brought everyone to instant attention. It was Baylis Williams, one of Reed's hired men, who had shouted. To Peter's surprise, Baylis was not looking westward but southwest. About a mile south of where they were camped on the Weber River, the valley began to give way to gently sloping hills. Beyond that, they quickly became ridge after ridge of towering mountains, a sight which daunted everyone in the camp. But as he squinted in the direction that Williams was pointing, Peter saw a tiny black speck working its way down one of the ridges. It was a man on a horse.

George Donner ran swiftly to his wagon, rummaged in a chest, and brought out a telescope. By the time he reached the edge of the wagon circle, most of the company had gathered around him, watching anxiously as he brought the glass up to his eye. Margret Reed stood next to him, her body tight with tension.

There was a low grunt; then Donner slowly lowered the glass and looked at Margret. "It's James," he said.

She clapped her hands together and gave a little cry of joy. But George Donner did not share it. "He's all alone," he said ominously. "Where are Pike and Stanton?"

"And Hastings?" Jacob Donner exclaimed. "Where's Hastings?"

The other of the two brothers shook his head slowly. "And why is he coming from that direction instead of up Weber Canyon?"

He looked tired, Peter thought. Or maybe it was discouragement. That was a rare thing for James Reed, but Peter was sure that part of the weariness was the deep sense of betrayal he was feeling.

Reed looked around at the circle of faces. "Where are Stanton and Pike?" he said in sudden surprise.

"That's what we were wondering," George Donner said.

Reed blew out his breath, another sign of his growing frustration. "They must be lost. We'll send someone out in the morning. They can't be that far away."

"What about Mr. Hastings?" Milt Elliott asked. "Why isn't he with you?"

Reed's shoulders sagged a little and he passed one hand before his eyes. "He's not coming."

"*What?*" Milt Elliott, Lewis Keseberg, George and Jacob Donner, Margret Reed, Peter Ingalls, and half a dozen others all said it as one.

"Let me start at the beginning and tell you everything. We have some important decisions to make."

"Hastings is not coming?" Tamsen Donner said in a plaintive voice. "But he said he would pilot us through."

"Let James tell us," her husband said, though there was clearly anger in his eyes.

"First, after passing through Weber Canyon, I can tell you that there is no question but what if we attempt that route, many of our wagons shall be destroyed. Just a few miles from where we are now, the route becomes virtually impassable. I cannot believe they took sixty-six wagons through there. Then again a few miles farther on, at the mouth of the canyon, it is extremely difficult. We barely made it through with our horses."

"So what are we to do?" one of the Donner bullwhackers called out.

"I'll come to that in a minute," Reed answered. "We finally caught up with Hastings and his company camped on the south end of the Great Salt Lake near a place we called Black Rock. Hastings didn't seem too surprised to see us, as he had all confidence that we would find his letter. When I asked him to return with us and show us the other route that he proposed, he agreed to do so.

"As you remember, all along Mr. Hastings proposed a different route over the mountains. He told me again that had he been able to prevail upon his company to follow his advice, they would have taken that route themselves and not lost a wagon and team." He looked at Margret, who watched every nuance of his expression with growing concern. "Anyway, we started out the next morning. I traded my horse for a fresh mount the company gave me. Stanton's and Pike's horses were too tired to go on, and there were no more to be spared by the lead company; so they decided to rest for a day, then retrace the route we took. That's why I was surprised when they weren't back yet. But I'm not overly concerned. I think we can easily find them."

"So if Hastings came back with you, where is he?" Keseberg's voice was angry and demanding.

"He rode back with me partway, then decided that it was farther than he had remembered. He said that he couldn't abandon the larger party as they prepare to cross the Salt Desert."

"So he abandons us instead?" Baylis Williams half snarled.

Reed ignored that. "He rode with me to the top of a mountain and from there pointed out his proposed route." He looked down at his hands. "Then he left me and returned to his company."

"And did you find this new route?" George Donner asked quietly. The news had greatly depressed the group now, and they were all very much subdued.

"After descending from that mountain, I came across an Indian trail. Using that as my guide, I blazed a trail where I think a road can be made. I have marked trees all along the way."

"So, is it a good road?" Jacob Donner asked.

For several seconds, Reed did not answer. Then his head came up. "There is no road. It will take much clearing and digging to make one, but I think it can be done."

No one spoke as they let that sink in. Finally, someone—and Peter couldn't tell who it was—said, "Is there any other choice?"

They already knew the answer to that. They could turn back and take the old Oregon road, or they could take their chances in Weber Canyon—neither of which was a choice at all. All around the circle, heads wagged back and forth slowly.

Finally George Donner got to his feet. "As captain, I propose that we agree to work faithfully to make this road, if Mr. Reed will show us the way. If there are any other alternatives, let's discuss them now. Otherwise, I would like a vote."

No one spoke.

"All right, then. All in favor of taking this new road over the mountains."

Every hand around the circle slowly came up.

For the first time since his return, James Reed managed a wan smile. "Thank you. It will not be easy, but I believe this is the best way to go."

Chapter Notes

The Mississippi Saints reached Fort Pueblo on the Arkansas River (in present-day Colorado) on 7 August 1846, not quite a month after turning south from Fort Laramie. It was just three days later that word came that the main body of the Saints was encamped for the winter on the Missouri River, confirming the wisdom of the Mississippi Saints' decision not to continue on west that season. (See "Pioneer Journeys," pp. 807–8.)

For the first two months after reaching the Missouri River, Brigham Young was heavily occupied in seeing to the needs of his people and recruiting for the Mormon Battalion. Once the battalion left, he turned his focus to preparing his people for the winter. On 1 August a firm decision was finally made that no one would be sent to the Rocky Mountains that season. A few days later, an exploration party found a site on the west side of the Missouri River some distance north of the Cold Spring Camp. Named Cutler's Park for Alpheus Cutler, the location was designated as the site for the Saints' winter home. Later, a better site was found closer to the river, and that became Winter Quarters. (See *SW*, pp. 69–82.)

When the Donners left what is now known as Echo Canyon (near the junction of Interstates 80 and 84 at the town of Echo in northern Utah) and came to the first crossing of the Weber River (present-day Henefer), they found a note written by Lansford Hastings. The actual letter no longer exists, so its exact contents are not known, but several contemporaries describe the general message. The description of the difficult passage through the narrow spots of Weber Canyon (near present-day Croydon and Devil's Slide on I-84) comes from the journal of Heinrich Lienhard, who was traveling with the advance company. (See *Chronicles*, pp. 116–19.)

James Reed returned to his company on the evening of 10 August, four days after leaving to go find Lansford Hastings. Most of the details given in this chapter come from Reed's later account of events, as well as from other contemporaries. (See *UE*, pp. 24–27, 186–88; *Overland in 1846*, p. 262.)

Many writers have tried to make Lansford Hastings the villain in the Donner tragedy. For example, one author wrote of Hastings's refusal to return with Reed: "By this time, it would seem that Hastings was losing what little judgment he ever had, and possibly his nerve had broken" (George Stewart, as cited in *Chronicles*, p. 118).

While there is little question that Hastings was a naive and overzealous promoter and that his failure to keep his word contributed greatly to the eventual disaster, it is only fair to balance that against the factors that must have weighed on his mind. He was leading a large group (the Harlan-Young

Company) that was already giving him difficulty (they refused to follow his counsel about Weber Canyon). That group was about to embark on the Salt Desert crossing (now known as the Salt Flats of western Utah), the most difficult stretch of the entire cutoff. The Harlan-Young Party was also about triple the size of the Donner Party. If he delayed them long enough for the Donners to catch up, it would put them at risk. And there was no way he could offer his services to both companies. He had to choose which group to lead, and he chose the larger group, which was already in the lead and had no one out ahead of them to break trail.

Chapter Twenty-Two

James Reed looked grim as he rode up to the first of his three wagons. Peter and the other two drivers got to their feet. Margret Reed, on hearing the horse, came to the flap of the wagon to see what was happening. Virginia Reed, their thirteen-year-old daughter, who was standing beside Peter, started to smile and wave, but the sight of her father's face froze both the smile and the lifting hand.

Reed glanced at his wife, shook his head, then turned to his teamsters. "We're going up and over."

"What?" Milt Elliott erupted, his face twisting.

"No!" Peter cried. "We'll never make it."

"The decision has been made," Reed said through tight lips. "We've been outvoted."

"But you said it's no more than half a mile more down the creekbed and we're out of the canyon."

Reed swung down from Glaucus and came forward a few steps. "Perhaps not even that." His voice was lifeless and flat, his eyes showing the weariness they all felt.

"Then let's cut our way through," Milt said. "If we're that close—"

Baylis Williams, who rarely said anything in councils such as this, surprised them all. "I'm not chopping one more bunch of willows or moving one more boulder," he said bitterly. "I've had enough of that for a lifetime."

"But it will kill the teams," Peter exclaimed. He turned and pointed at the steep ridge that loomed high above them. "Look at that incline. You can't take wagons over that."

"We'll hook up as many teams to each wagon as we need to," Reed answered. "All of them, if need be."

"They can't do it, I tell you," Peter countered. "They're already near exhaustion after these past twelve days of coming through the mountains."

James Reed swung around, his eyes blazing. "Are you deaf, Peter?" he roared. "I said we're going over the top. If you can't accept that, I'll find someone else to drive."

Peter would not have been more stunned if Reed had jerked out his pistol and fired it at him. He rocked back in astonishment. Milt Elliott's mouth was open as he gaped at his employer. Williams was aghast. James Reed never lost his temper. Now his jaw was clenched and the veins along it stood out. His nostrils flared as his chest rose and fell. His eyes were like two black glowing points of fire, daring anyone to disagree with him. Margret Reed was as deeply shocked as any of them. "James—," she started.

He whirled, swearing. "Woman! This is not your affair. I suggest you stick with things that are."

Her face instantly drained of color. Then, as tears sprang to her eyes, she turned quickly and stepped back inside the wagon.

Reed glared at his three drivers. "Make up your mind, Peter. What will it be?"

"I . . ." Peter stammered. "You know I'll do whatever you say, Mr. Reed. I was—" He stopped. "I'll do whatever you say."

The others nodded quickly as he swung on them.

"Then unhook the teams. We'll take Uncle George's wagons

over first." With that, he pulled on Glaucus's reins and walked past them, ignoring the utter astonishment he left in his wake.

Peter stood quietly beside the two yoke of oxen for which he was responsible. They were now yoked ahead of George Donner's own three yoke. Milt Elliott was yoking up two more to the front of Peter's teams. Baylis Williams waited beyond Milt with one additional yoke beyond that. They had decided to take one of Donner's supply wagons first. It was not fully loaded, and they had decided it would be a good test to see how the oxen fared. But eight yoke? This was madness!

Peter turned his head and looked at the path the scouts had chosen. The ridge rose steeply for about three hundred feet before it crested. What an unfortunate accident of nature! They had entered this canyon two days before and been working their way down by following the creek. This was the route that Lansford Hastings had shown James Reed some two weeks ago. Even though they were moving downhill now, it had been tough going through the underbrush, which was too thick for even a bear to go through. Then last night, when they finally could see that they were nearing the mouth of the canyon, they had rounded a bend in the creek and found this. Just where the canyon should have opened up onto the valley, a high ridge jutted out from the left canyon wall to dam the canyon's mouth.

It was heartbreaking. They were so close to being out of the mountains. The valley was just over the ridge or, if they chose the other option, less than a mile farther downstream. It seemed like such an obvious choice, but Peter understood what had led the group to choose this route, even though he bitterly disagreed with the decision. The past twelve days had broken the spirit of the company. They had so exhausted themselves in cutting a road over the mountains, that now the thought of even one more half mile of hacking and chopping and shoveling was unbearable. They couldn't—or wouldn't—do any more. They would leave it to the animals instead.

If they had been a company the size of the one Hastings was leading, which had more than a hundred men and sixty wagons, it would not have been so desperately difficult. But the Donners had only twenty-seven able-bodied men and boys who were capable of the kind of work required. Two days into the mountains they had been joined by the Graves family. The Graveses—consisting of three men, one older boy, three adult women, and six younger children—were from Illinois. They had been with a larger company which had two men killed in a vicious attack by the Pawnees. At Fort Bridger they had been told that the Donners were not too far ahead of them and decided to push ahead and join with them. It was a welcome addition. That brought the company's working force to thirty-one men and the number of wagons to twenty-two. But it still wasn't enough for the task at hand.

The creek bottoms were a wild tangle of willow thickets, wild rose and service berry bushes, cottonwood, box elder, and alder trees. In most cases even a man and a horse couldn't make their way through unimpeded. Therefore, there was no choice but to hack a road through it yard by man-killing yard. The sun beat down upon them, only slightly tempered by the higher elevations. Mosquitos swarmed thickly enough to form a shadow. They were under constant attack from large brown flies whose bite stung like that of a horsefly. They chopped and slashed; dragged brush and trees; attacked side hills or creek banks with shovels to make them passable for wagons. Their arms and faces were a mass of scratches and cuts. Their legs were scraped and bruised. Even those with the toughest of hands quickly raised huge blisters that had to be doctored every night. One day they worked from first light until dusk and barely made two miles. In another eight-mile stretch, they crossed a creek thirteen times, either digging down the banks or creating makeshift bridges with logs and brush. Going up the mountains required double teaming the wagons, and then they would have to lock the wheels and chain up the animals behind the wagons to take them down the other side. Twelve days and they had barely come thirty miles as the crow flies.

That was why the company voted to go up and over the ridge. It was criminal, a major mistake, in Peter's mind, but it was also perfectly understandable. Yet it worried Peter to the point that he felt ill. It was not just the teams, though that made him a little sick as well. It was what was happening to the company. They had lost their heart, abandoned reason. They couldn't see that today, but they would tomorrow.

Peter blew out his breath. When they left Fort Bridger they had estimated it would take them seven weeks to reach Sutter's Fort in California. That required averaging a hundred miles a week, an ambitious schedule but not an impossible one. But here they were, three weeks into the seven, and they had barely come a hundred and twenty-five miles. It was the last week of August, and they still had six hundred miles to go!

He heard a footstep and turned. James Reed was coming toward him. Peter straightened. He suspected that his employer had been making peace with his wife. After tying Glaucus to the back of the wagon, Reed had immediately gone inside their commodious wagon and Peter had heard the soft murmur of voices.

Reed came up alongside Peter and stopped, watching Baylis Williams starting to hook up the last yoke of oxen. "Eight yoke," he said softly and with open bitterness, "sixteen animals, and I'm still not sure it will be enough."

Peter nodded. "This is one of the more lightly loaded wagons. I don't think eight yoke will be enough to take yours up, Mr. Reed."

"If we have to put on every team, we'll do it."

Peter nodded again, not about to contradict him anymore.

The silence was awkward and heavy for a moment; then Reed cleared his throat. "Peter, I want to apologize for what happened earlier. I—"

"No need," Peter broke in quickly. "It is I who should apologize. It's not my place to question the vote of the company or your orders, Mr. Reed."

Reed went on quickly. "I tried to reason with the rest of the men, but they rode right over my protests."

Peter waited, troubled by the despair and hurt he saw in Reed's face.

"They're saying it's my fault, Peter."

His head came up quickly. "What's your fault, sir?"

Reed looked away. "Choosing to take this cutoff."

"But," Peter exclaimed, "they all voted to follow Mr. Hastings's new route. You didn't make them do that."

There was a sad smile. "No, but I was such an enthusiastic supporter of the idea, they're saying I convinced them against their will."

"Balderdash, Mr. Reed. Those who didn't want to take this way went with Mr. Boggs and company. No one forced anyone to come with you."

"They're also saying we should have taken Weber Canyon."

"But . . ." Peter stopped, seeing that Reed wasn't listening.

Reed rubbed at his eyes with the heels of his hands. "It would have been difficult, but I think we could have gone through Weber Canyon in four or five days."

Peter didn't know what to say to that. Reed's despondency was nearly as alarming as his anger.

"It will be all right," Peter said, not with a great deal of conviction. "It will be a hard pull up, but then we'll be out of the mountains. We'll rest the teams for a day or two, then be on with it. We'll make much better time across the flatlands."

Reed nodded absently, almost as if he hadn't heard. "Well, the die is cast. We've been outvoted, Peter, and there's nothing to do now but make the best of it."

"Here, Peter." Virginia Reed handed him the pewter cup filled with water. He lifted his head and blinked several times. She was standing in the sun, which was now low in the sky, and for a moment he wasn't sure who she was. He squinted in order to clear the burning from where the sweat had run into his eyes.

He swiped at his forehead with his bandanna, but it was already sopping wet and did little to relieve him. He took the cup and lifted it to his mouth. It was warm and tepid. He drained it in three eager gulps. She filled it again. He drained it again. A third time she filled it and the third time he drank it as though he were a dying man. With the fourth one he removed his hat and dumped it over the top of his head.

"Thank you," he breathed. He handed back the cup.

"Are you all right, Peter?" Virginia asked anxiously.

He peered at her. Had she noticed that his head was swimming with the heat and he was having troubling focusing his eyes? Had she seen the trembling in his legs? They had been up and down the ridge how many times now? six? eight? And then he remembered. There was only one wagon left—Mr. Reed's family wagon—which meant they had made twenty-one trips up the ridge. No wonder his legs felt like butter left out in the sun. No wonder his lungs burned and his hands were raw inside his gloves. No wonder he was dizzy. He managed a crooked smile. "I'm fine, Virginia."

"Just one more," she said, touching his arm. "Then you can rest."

He took a deep breath and let it out with a great *whoosh*. "Yeah," he said. Unfortunately, that one more was the "pioneer palace car," as Virginia had dubbed it. Reed's family wagon was not much larger than a normal wagon, but with its two-layered design, its built-in stove, its side steps, and all of the other things which made it so comfortable, it was one of the heaviest. He looked around. Everywhere he saw men near the brink of collapse just as he was. They sat with their heads on their arms, breathing deeply. Three were laid out on the ground, hats over their eyes, snatching even a moment's sleep. Others leaned heavily against the wagons. They let their wives and daughters wipe their heads with wet towels. They drank in desperation. They stared woodenly at nothing.

If the men were a sorry sight, to look at the teams was to view something tragic. It made Peter want to cry. Some of the young boys had brought buckets of water for them. They had to force the oxen's noses into them in order to get them to drink. The animals stood with feet spread wide, swaying slightly, heads down to where their noses almost touched the ground. Even the lowing had stopped. They were too exhausted to protest what was being asked of them. Their withers were dark with sweat. Drool dripped from their mouths as their tongues lolled out and hung limply. Into Peter's mind came the image of the great bull buffalo that James Reed had shot some weeks before. When the bull had reached a certain point, the legs could hold him no more and he collapsed in a heap. It looked to Peter as though several of the animals were at that point now, just waiting for their legs to buckle so that they could rest at last.

He walked over to the animals for which he was responsible. He moved among them, speaking softly, rubbing his hand beneath where the great yokes sat across their necks, scratching them behind the ears, patting them on the shoulder, all the while praising them for their magnificent effort.

There was a shout from below. At the edge of the hill James Reed and George Donner shouted something back. They turned. "All right, boys," Reed shouted. "Let's bring up the last one and then we can rest."

Wincing at the stiffness in his body, Peter leaned down and picked up the chain. "One more time up the hill, boys. That's all. You have my word on it."

James Reed stepped back, made one last check of the line, then raised his hand. "On my mark." He held it high for a moment, then dropped it quickly. "Go!"

"Ho, boys!" Peter shouted. "Go! Go!" He snapped the whip above their heads, making it split the air like a firecracker going off. They lunged into their yokes as one animal. Up and down the line of fourteen yoke of oxen the teamsters were shouting and whips were cracking.

"Push! Push!" George Donner shouted to the men on the

wagon. They leaned into it, grunting and straining. Some grabbed at the spokes of the wheels and tried to pull them forward. Oxen bellowed. Hooves tore into the black dirt, already pulverized into soft loam by previous efforts. There was a creaking sound, and Peter saw that the wagon had begun to move.

"Go, boys!" he screamed. "Lean into it." The first twenty yards was level ground. They had to have the wagon rolling by the time they started up the hill or they wouldn't make it.

Up ahead, five or six yokes forward, an ox went down. The teamster ran to it, screaming hoarsely, beating at its back with the butt of his whip. It was being dragged along, knees plowing furrows in the dirt. If he didn't get it up, it would be severely injured and the wagon would stop on the slope. Peter darted forward. Other teamsters ran to help.

"Get him up! Get him up!" the teamster shouted. Peter jabbed at its rump with his ox goad. Another man reached in and yanked the chain away from its knees. Two men grabbed the end of the yoke and lifted mightily. Finally, eyes rolling wildly, nostrils flaring, the animal got to its feet—half dragged, half on its own effort. No one waited for thanks. Each teamster ran back to his place to urge on his own animals.

Two-thirds of the way up, the line of beasts faltered and the wagon slowed. Reed screamed at the teamsters. "Don't stop! We'll never hold it."

"Ho! Ho!" Peter yelled into the ears of his animals. If the wagon rolled backwards it would take the teams with it. That was extremely dangerous. All up and down the line, panic broke loose. Teamsters became madmen, whipping and lashing at their teams. The men on the wagon threw their weight into it, eyes bulging, veins standing out on their heads and arms, sweat pouring in rivulets down their faces.

In all the time since they had left Springfield, Illinois—some four months now—Peter had never once laid his whip on the backs of his animals. But as he turned to see how the wagon was coming, Brindle, the wheel ox on the far side of the yoke, stumbled and went down on one knee. It bawled wildly as the yoke bit into its neck and began to drag it forward.

"Up, Brindle!" Peter screamed. "Go! Go!"

The animal was trying but without success. Blindly, barely realizing what he was doing, Peter stepped back and let the whip fly. It caught the animal on the back, just behind the shoulders. He saw the tip of the whip crack sharply, drawing blood. With one startled bawl, Brindle leaped forward, finding his footing again.

Shouting, screaming, yelling, begging, Peter laid the whip across their backs now, not popping them with the tip, but letting them feel the full fury of the lash. He started to run. The wagon was rolling faster now. Several men, leaning hard into the wagon, went down. But Peter didn't see them. He felt his own legs buckling beneath him and screamed at himself not to stop.

And then they were over the top. The teams came to a stop, quivering and bawling frantically. Peter turned, peering through the sweat to make sure the wagon had really come over the crest. At their feet lay the wide expanse of the Great Salt Lake Valley. But he didn't see that. Dimly he was aware of James Reed stumbling toward him, but he didn't care for that either. He turned and fell on the shoulders of the nearest ox. He laid his head against the wet flank, mindful of the bloody welts. He felt the tears start to come. "I'm sorry," he whispered. "I'm so sorry."

Wednesday, August 26, 1846
Twenty Wells, on the Great Salt Lake Desert

My dearest Kathryn—

I am writing this letter in my journal. I do so because we go alone now, and we make our own road. There is no hope of seeing anyone who can take a letter back to you. I have debated long about writing this to you, but if something should ever happen to me, I wanted you to know that I was thinking about you at the last. If the Lord sees fit to reunite us, I shall tear this page out so that your eyes shall never see it.

A great sense of gloom has settled in upon me. This is far more than what I felt while you were still with me. It is like a deepening darkness closing in all around. The spirit of our little company grows more and more out of harmony with God each passing day. How can we, who claim to be followers of the Master, act in this manner and still claim the favor of heaven?

I am so glad that you are no longer here. It would make you heartsick to endure what is now commonplace. Tempers flare at the slightest provocation. Bickering has replaced brotherhood. Contention has overcome cooperation. Selfishness overrides service. We seem to curse God in the day when things are at their harshest, then wonder why he does not hear our cries at night around the fires.

All my love to you, dear Kathryn. By now I suppose you are feeling the first stirrings of life. I pray for our unborn child and for you every day. Oh, how I wish I could be there when the baby comes! Be safe. I pray earnestly each morning and night that we shall some day be reunited, but it is mostly without hope now. I have detailed, and shall continue to detail, the events of our journey, and that will help you understand why I write as I do. If you are reading this without me, then know that I never forgot you nor ceased to love you.

Forever bound together,
Peter

Wednesday, August 26, 1846
Twenty Wells, on the Great Salt Lake Desert

It has been four days since we came out of the Wasatch Mountains. We have moved slowly, resting our teams after the terrible last pull to get out of the canyon. They have improved somewhat, but we dare not take the time to recruit them as they need to be. We had a further delay when an axletree on one of Mr. Reed's wagons broke. We had to ride fifteen miles for timber and then work all night to cut a new one.

The specter of winter in the Sierra stalks us like wolves following a wounded deer. We must press on or face the prospect of wintering this side of the mountains. Since we are already low on supplies and have some six or seven hundred miles left to go, that is not a possibility that we can accept.

The travel is much better now. The blue expanse of the Great Salt Lake has been on our right since we came into the valley. Here we have found several wells that have been a great blessing. The water is good and cold. These are not springs, but deep holes. We plumbed some with 70 feet of rope and could not hit bottom. They do not overflow, but when we drink water out of them, they immediately fill again.

I must say that I am greatly cheered by the aspects of the valley in which we now find ourselves. If this is where Brigham Young means to come with our people, it will be a pleasant home. The valley is wide—I'd guess about twenty miles—and perhaps thirty miles long. It is ringed on both east and west by beautiful mountains. There are many creeks which come down from the mountains to provide water. The soil seems rich and able to take crops if given water. The Great Salt Lake is like some great inland sea and sparkles a deep blue in the sunlight. The water is stronger than any brine you can imagine. Amazingly, one cannot sink in its waters. One night we camped just a few rods from the water, so after supper we went for a "swim." It seems incredible, but when I sat down in the water, I bobbed like a piece of fat in a bucket of buttermilk. I did make the mistake of getting some of the water in my eyes, and it burned terribly. It certainly is not drinkable. But the valley of the Great Salt Lake is a beautiful place. It would make a wonderful home for our people.

We had our first death in our company since Mrs. Keyes died. A man by the name of Luke Halloran died of consumption with his head in Tamsen Donner's lap. Gave him a decent burial.

We approach that point where Mr. Hastings says we have a hard forty-mile drive without water. Taking in wood, water, and grass to help us make that run.

Friday, August 28, 1846—Hope Wells

Bad news. Today we found a board with scraps of paper tacked to it. From the pieces of handwriting, it looked like another letter from Mr. Hastings. Unfortunately, it had been pecked to pieces by birds. Tamsen Donner—may that woman ever be praised—was not satisfied to let it go. We all searched and gathered up the pieces from the ground. She placed the board on her lap and fitted the pieces back together with great care as we all watched in fascination. It was a letter from Hastings, but not good. What they had been able to salvage read: "2 days — 2 nights — hard driving — cross desert — reach water."

This terse message brings a great pall upon us. Two days and two nights? This has to be greater than forty miles. And we cannot possibly carry enough food and water to care for our oxen on a drive of that distance. Even if we only wet towels and bathe the animal's tongues, I fear we will not make it. Once again Mr. Hastings is proving to be an unreliable guide.

Kathryn Ingalls stood back. At times like this she felt keenly that she was not part of this group, even though in every other way they had accepted her as one of their own. But now it was time for farewells. Their little company was settling in on the south side of the river across from Fort Pueblo. It was the first of September. Fall would quickly be upon them. There could be no delay.

The six men who had come without their families went down the line, shaking hands and hugging the women and children. John Brown, their company captain, was in the lead. With him went Brothers Crosby, Thomas, Holladay, Lay, Smithson, and Bankhead. The eighth man who would be leaving with them stood back, like Kathryn. He was Mister Wales Bonney, a non-Mormon who had only recently come to Pueblo. Incredibly, he had come from Oregon, traveling the two-thousand-mile trail totally alone. He was brave, he was experienced, and he knew the way to Independence. He would serve as a guide to the seven Mormons.

Kathryn felt a stirring in her stomach and for a moment wondered if the baby sensed her dismay. Then she chided herself for being so . . . well, like Jenny. It would be like Jenny to wonder such things.

She smiled, knowing even as she thought it what had taken her thoughts in that direction. Brother Brown was carrying a long letter Kathryn had written to the family that he would mail at Independence. In that letter were two full sheets just for Jenny. There was no way to write to Peter now, but next to him, she was closer to her sister than anyone else in the world. And with the letter, she had been thinking a lot about Jenny lately.

There were still fourteen families here, she reminded herself. It was not as if they were being left alone without men. And yet for a company as small as this Mississippi company, the loss of seven able-bodied workers and hunters was not to be taken lightly.

The men were finished with their farewells now, and John Brown climbed up into his saddle. As the others followed suit, he looked around. "Farewell, dear brothers and sisters. We shall return with our families as soon as possible."

"How long?" someone called out.

He frowned. "We expect that it will take us about a month to reach Mississippi, then a week or two to prepare for departure, and about a month back. We should return sometime in November."

Brother Crow, who would become the leader with Brother Brown's departure, spoke up. "If something changes, you go to Council Bluffs and come with the main group. We'll leave here as soon as the weather turns good in the spring and wait at Laramie for whoever comes first."

Brown nodded, then turned to his men to see if there was anything else. When they shook their heads, he raised his hand again in a last farewell, then turned and spurred his horse forward. The others fell in behind him and splashed across the river.

The little company stood there silently until the eight men

could no longer be seen; then they went quietly back to the work of building a settlement that would see them through the winter.

Chapter Notes

Today, not far inside Emigration Canyon, on the south side of the highway, a simple monument marks the site of Donner Hill. It was here that the members of the Donner Party chose to go up and over the ridge instead of continuing to cut a road along the creek. It is difficult for the mind to comprehend taking wagons and teams up that steep and treacherous slope. It seems odd that after cutting a road through thirty miles of difficult mountainous terrain, the last half mile or so should deter the Donner Party enough that they chose to go up and over the ridge. The only hint as to why they did so seems to be that by this time they were so mentally and physically exhausted that the ridge seemed a better option. The interchange between Peter and Mr. Reed is the author's creation. There is no evidence that Reed opposed the ridge route. In fact, he doesn't even mention the incident in his journal. It is from his stepdaughter, Virginia, and other emigrants that we learn of the difficult ascent. (See *UE*, pp. 24–28, 142–43, 186–88; *Chronicles*, pp. 120–31; *WFFB*, pp. 217–20.)

There are bitter ironies in the events of the Donner Party at this point in their journey to California. One of those ironies has to do with Lansford Hastings's counsel that the better route to the Valley lay through the Wasatch Mountains rather than through Weber Canyon. Had his own group (the Harlan-Young Party) accepted that counsel and turned south at what is now Henefer, Utah, things would have turned out very differently for the Donners. With a larger number of able-bodied men, the Harlan-Young Party could much more easily have cut a road up and over the Wasatch Mountains. If Hastings's group had chosen to go that way, the Donners would not have delayed four days while Reed went looking for Hastings, and also they would have been following a prepared road over the Wasatch instead of having to cut a new one. In those circumstances, they would easily have caught up with Hastings and accompanied the larger party safely to California.

A second irony is their decision to tackle Donner Hill. In July 1847 the Mormon pioneers, following the road cut by the Donners the year before, reached that same spot. When they saw where the Donner group went, they explored the creek route. They had a great many more working men than the

Donner Party did, and that influenced their decision, but they chose the creek route. In a mere four hours they cut their way through and avoided Donner Hill altogether.

But upon such small things do monumental happenings swing.

For all of its ironies, the combination of circumstances in the Hastings-Donner tableau proved to be a great blessing to the Mormon emigration a year later. When the Mormons reached Henefer, they turned south and followed the road made by the Donners. Though much of it had grown over again and much work still had to be done, the Saints covered the distance from Henefer to the mouth of Emigration Canyon in five days. It had taken the Donners *twelve days* to travel that same distance, not counting the four-day layover at Henefer. This time savings allowed the Pioneer Company to arrive in the Valley in time to plant some crops which would help see them through the winter.

When John Brown and the other brethren who were leading the Mississippi Saints west learned that Brigham Young was wintering in Iowa and Nebraska, they decided to return to Mississippi for their families. They left Pueblo on 1 September and reached Mississippi on 20 October. Shortly after their return they received an epistle from the Twelve asking that they again leave their families in Mississippi for one more year and organize a small company of men who could go west with the Pioneer Company in the spring of 1847. They did so, leaving Mississippi in January and arriving at Winter Quarters just a few days before the vanguard company left. (See "Pioneer Journeys," pp. 808–9.)

Chapter Twenty-Three

Private Joshua Benjamin Steed stood with hooded eyes, listening to the complaints being voiced all around him, but saying nothing.

"Why is it that only the officers get to vote?" one man demanded.

"Because they don't think we enlisted men have any say in what happens to us," another growled, "even though we're the ones who are most affected by it."

"Brethren, brethren," one of the older sergeants soothed, "in the army it is always the officers who make the decision. That's just the way it is."

"But this isn't just the army," shot back the first. "This is also the Church. I thought we were supposed to be brothers and treat each other with Christian charity."

Josh moved away, not wanting to hear any more. This wasn't his breakfast mess, but he had stopped to warm himself by their fire as he came in from guard duty and, at their invitation, stayed to eat with them. Now he wished he had just gone on to eat with his own mess.

Carping had become a way of life among many in the battalion, but for the past five days it had grown particularly bad. Before they had ever left Council Bluffs, Brigham Young and others of the Twelve had admonished them to live the gospel while they were serving their country. Marvelous promises were made to them if they would only remember that they were followers of Christ and exemplify his life in their own lives. But too often those admonitions were forgotten. It was not uncommon to hear profanity, usually among the younger men of the battalion. There was grumbling and backbiting. Some of the men spent what seemed to Josh like a lot of time playing cards or dominoes. But most common was the murmuring.

He smiled to himself. "Mur-mur-mur-mur," he said softly. That cheered him up a little. He remembered his mother's teachings about the spiritual dangers of murmuring. She had taught them how it got its name—because the word mimicked the sound people made when they were muttering under their breath. In the family they had developed a little game. When anyone started grumbling without real cause, someone would smile sweetly and say, "Mur-mur-mur-mur." That was enough. Soon they would all be laughing and not complaining. His smile broadened as he thought how the men he was marching with would respond to that kind of reminder. A good way to get your head thumped, he decided.

Especially now that Lieutenant Smith and Doctor Sanderson had arrived.

The battalion had been deeply shocked when word came from Fort Leavenworth that Lieutenant Colonel James Allen had never recovered and was dead. The men had come to respect him, and he had come to respect them. His death was a significant loss. Then three days later Lieutenant Andrew Jackson Smith rode into the camp. Lieutenant Smith was a graduate of West Point and a regular officer in the U.S. Army. He went straight to Captain Hunt and, though Hunt outranked him, announced that he would like to take over the leadership of the battalion. Hunt had already assumed command at the news of the colonel's death; but Smith pointed out that when it came to requisitioning supplies, or getting money from the paymaster, or winning other concessions from the army, a regular officer, no matter what his rank, would fare much better than a Mormon volunteer. Hunt finally agreed to put it to the other Mormon officers. To everyone's surprise, all but four voted for Lieutenant Smith.

The enlisted men were furious that they hadn't been consulted. Grudgingly they decided to sit back and see how their new commander did before passing judgment. That's what was stuck in everyone's craw now. In a matter of days Smith had proven to be an unbearable tyrant with a deep prejudice against these "Mormon volunteers." It was hard to tell, when he spoke that phrase, which word was the more distasteful to him.

To make matters worse, Smith had brought a new military physician with him. Doctor George Sanderson was a Missourian, and rumors quickly spread that if Smith despised the Mormons, Sanderson hated them. He immediately ordered the men to come to him for an examination before they could be put on the sick roll. With many still in various stages of sickness from their stay in the Missouri River valley, that quickly became a cause for concern.

Josh caught himself, and shook his head. Now he was doing it. Not really complaining, but worrying about things and letting them upset him. He set his jaw and strode forward with determination to be different. Yesterday they had entered Comanche territory. That was plenty enough to worry about. The hostility of the Comanches toward the whites was known all up and down the Santa Fe Trail, and tension was high in the camp. For the first time last night, as he stood guard duty, Josh had felt a little prickling of fear, and he had had no trouble staying awake.

He looked up and saw that their tent was down and already packed on the wagon. He could see Christopher and Benji standing beside the wagon, but there was no sign of Derek and Rebecca. He blew out his breath. That was not a good sign.

When he came around the back of the wagon, the two boys ran to him happily. "Hi, Josh."

"Good morning, Benji. Mornin', Christopher. Where are your mother and father?"

Sergeant Tom Williams straightened from checking the harnessing on the mules. "They're in the wagon. You're uncle isn't going to be doing any walking today."

"He's down again?"

Williams nodded his head.

Josh frowned. If the shakes were back, it would mean another miserable bout for Derek.

Williams was grim. "We got more sick than we can handle."

"Thank you for taking them into your wagon."

Williams grunted softly. He was a taciturn man, but Josh had come to respect him greatly. At Fort Leavenworth he had used his own money to purchase a wagon and team to help carry some of the company's knapsacks and spare the men. Now it had become another hospital wagon as well, much to the blessing of those who were sick.

Josh went to the back of the wagon and lifted the flap. Rebecca looked up. "Good morning," she said.

"Hi," he answered softly. Derek's eyes were closed and he didn't stir. "How's the patient?"

She just shook her head.

"I'll take Christopher with me today," Josh said. "I saw the Buttons family just now. They said they'll keep Benji if you'd like."

"That would be wonderful," Rebecca sighed.

There was a noise behind them. Josh turned and saw Lieutenant Smith, Doctor Sanderson, and Lieutenant Dykes, the battalion adjutant, approaching the line of wagons. One look at their faces and Josh could tell they were not happy. They stopped two wagons back. Their voices carried clearly.

"What is going on here?" Lieutenant Smith demanded. The driver came to attention, a little flustered by the anger in the officer's voice. "We're preparing to move out, sir."

"What are all these men doing in your wagon?" Sanderson demanded.

"They're sick, sir. Too sick to walk."

The lieutenant swung around and jerked up the wagon's cover. "You there!" he snapped. "Are you sick?"

There was a muffled reply.

"Why didn't you report to Doctor Sanderson? He's got medicine. If you're too sick to march, why didn't you report to the doctor?"

The driver, a man by the name of Owens, started to speak, but the lieutenant ignored him. He was slapping one hand against the side of his trousers, his anger building visibly. "I won't have this," he shouted. "No one rides in the wagons unless they're on sick report."

Then, as the stunned onlookers watched, he stepped to the back of the wagon, grabbed the man by his boots, and dragged him out. The sick man stumbled and went down on his knees. "Out! Out!" the officer was screaming. He grabbed another man and dragged him out, letting him fall to the ground with a crash. "If you're not on the sick report, you're not sick enough to ride."

Several men came running up, shocked by what they were seeing. Nathaniel Jones, a sergeant with Company D, darted in, blocking the lieutenant from grabbing any more of the men. "Sir," he said sharply, "let me explain. These men mean no disrespect, sir, but we have religious scruples against taking army medicines. Since that's what Doctor Sanderson administers, they didn't want to report, sir."

Lieutenant Smith looked confused for a moment. He turned to his adjutant. "Is that true, Lieutenant Dykes?"

George P. Dykes was one of the Mormon officers, but he had quickly fallen into disfavor with the men because his position of authority had gone straight to his head and he had become a little martinet, demanding that he be treated like a regular army officer.

Lieutenant Dykes instantly shook his head. "There's nothing in our religion which forbids the taking of medicine."

Brother Owens broke in. "Sir, before we left, you know that President Young—" He looked at Smith. "Brigham Young, our leader, whom we view as a prophet, counseled us that if we got sick, we were to live by faith and to let the doctors' medicines alone. We were to use only healing herbs and mild food. He promised that if we would heed this counsel, we would prosper."

"Ridiculous!" Doctor Sanderson roared. "These men are sick. Calomel and arsenic is exactly what they need. Live by faith, indeed."

Dykes did not meet Owens's eyes. "There is nothing in our religion that forbids the use of medicine," he said stubbornly.

Lieutenant Smith spun on his heel and walked swiftly toward where Josh and Sergeant Williams were standing watching all of this. Without a word to either of them, Smith stepped to the back of the wagon and dropped the tailgate. As he reached in to grab Derek by the feet, Williams jumped in between the two men. "Stop! Leave these people alone."

Williams was a good hand span taller than the lieutenant and had squared his shoulders. The lieutenant was dumbfounded. "Get out of my way, soldier!"

"You'll not be dragging these people out of my wagon, sir," Williams said calmly.

Smith fell back a step, eyes blazing. Then he fumbled at his scabbard and whipped out his sword. Now his eyes were narrow and like two pieces of blue ice. "Step out of my way, soldier, or I'll run you through. There'll be no more people riding in this wagon."

Williams had his bullwhip coiled and tied to his waist. With one swift movement he had it in his hand and gripped the thick handle like a club. Other than that, he did not move. "Lieutenant," he said, his voice low and filled with menace, "you take one more step, and I'll strike you to the ground. This wagon is my private property. I purchased it out of my own funds at Fort Leavenworth, and I will haul in it who and what I choose."

The defiance caught Smith totally by surprise. He stood there, eyes bulging as they stared at the whip, mouth working but no words coming out.

"These are my brethren, Lieutenant. We have been counseled not to take your doctor's medicine, and I will never leave one of them lying on the ground as long as my team can pull them."

Neither the officers nor the doctor spoke. Sanderson and Dykes watched their commander to see what he would do. After several interminable seconds, Lieutenant Smith, his face nearly purple, slid his sword back into its scabbard and turned away. As he and his party withdrew, Josh clearly heard the lieutenant's question. "Who is that man?"

"Sergeant Thomas S. Williams, sir, Company D," Dykes answered. Smith said no more but kept on walking, his back stiff and his head high.

"Stop this wagon, Sergeant."

Thomas Williams looked up at Lieutenant Smith and Doctor Sanderson, who had ridden up on horses. Williams pulled up on the reins and brought his team to a halt. As they dismounted, Williams jumped down quickly and moved with them to the back of the wagon. Josh was marching with his company a few yards away. He broke ranks and trotted over, worried that another confrontation was about to take place.

"Open the flap, Sergeant."

Williams hesitated. "There won't be any dragging of these people out of the wagon," he said; then, at the officer's look, he pulled back the flap and let down the tailgate.

Lieutenant Smith stepped forward and peered inside. Josh arrived just then, and the lieutenant swung on him. "What are you doing here, Private?" he demanded.

"This is my aunt and uncle," Josh explained, pointing to Derek and Rebecca.

Lieutenant Smith assessed the situation quickly. There were six people in the wagon, all but two lying on beds. Rebecca was propped up against a flour sack holding the baby. She was serving as nurse to the sick. Derek was on his back, his arm over his eyes, moaning softly. Albert Dunham, a private from Company B, was also seated. His arms were folded across his knees, and his head was down upon them. He hadn't even lifted his head to see what was going on. Smith leaned in and poked him sharply. "You there. Get out of the wagon."

With a groan, Dunham slid forward and got down. His face was pale, his eyes watery, his limbs trembling slightly.

"What is the matter with you, soldier?" Smith barked.

"Ague, I think, sir."

"Have you taken any medicine for this illness?"

"Yes, sir."

"By whose orders?"

"Doctor McIntire, Lieutenant." Doctor William McIntire had been assigned by Brigham Young and approved by Colonel Allen to serve as assistant surgeon to the battalion. With the arrival of Doctor Sanderson, Lieutenant Smith had issued an order that McIntire could not minister to his fellow Mormons without the express approval of the chief surgeon, Doctor Sanderson.

Doctor Sanderson seized on that like a bird on a beetle. "Ha!" he cried. "I told you so."

Smith looked at the surgeon. "And Doctor McIntire did this without your permission, Doctor?"

"He certainly did. In spite of your orders, Lieutenant."

By now several other men had gathered around, and the lieutenant was aware of the grim resentment in their faces. Livid now, he whirled on Dunham. "It is expressly forbidden to take treatment from anyone other than Doctor Sanderson, soldier. You have disobeyed a direct order."

"Sir—," Sergeant Williams began, but Smith was in a rage now and cut him off sharply.

"I will not have my orders disobeyed," he screamed. "Do you hear me? I am in command of this battalion now. My orders must be followed." He turned on the men gathered around him. "Are you listening to me? If I hear of one more man who takes medicine from Doctor McIntire without Doctor Sanderson's permission, I will take that man and cut his throat."

The men gaped at him, not sure that they had heard him correctly. Captain Jefferson Hunt, the senior Mormon officer, stepped forward. "Lieutenant, what—"

Smith spun around and grabbed Private Dunham by his shirt, jerking him up to stand straight. The lieutenant's face was mottled with red splotches and his voice was shrill, almost hysterical. "And you, Private, if I hear of you taking any more medicine without my permission, I shall personally tie a rope around your neck and drag you behind this wagon. Do you understand me?"

Dunham gulped, looking very frightened. "Yes," he murmured.

"*Do you understand me?*" Smith screamed.

"Yes, sir!" Dunham cried loudly.

Smith let go of Dunham's shirt, and Dunham slumped and almost fell. The officer's hands were trembling. He stepped back, glancing sideways at Doctor Sanderson. "All right, Doctor," he said, as if nothing untoward had happened. "We have some sick men here. I suggest that you give them some medicine so that we can continue."

With a gleeful look, Sanderson stepped forward. He had a black bag and quickly withdrew two large bottles, one containing a white powder, the other containing something dark brown. He also withdrew a large spoon, and Josh saw that it was rusty and tarnished. Josh turned toward the wagon. Derek was awake now, as were the others, watching anxiously. Rebecca clutched Leah to her breast, her eyes wide and frightened.

"Now," Sanderson said, "you first." He was looking at Derek.

"I'm fine. I don't want any medicine."

"You want to be left here on the prairie?" Lieutenant Smith yelled. "I swear to you that any man that doesn't take his medicine as the doctor prescribes will be dumped where he is and we'll go on without him."

Sanderson had filled the spoon with calomel powder. Now from the other bottle he dropped on several dabs of molasses. Muttering curses under his breath about the stupid Mormons and wanting to see every one of them in hell, he held it out for Derek. Derek started to turn away, then saw Josh nodding at him. Surrendering, he opened his mouth, and the doctor shoved the rusty spoon into it. Derek gagged, gasping for breath. Quick as a flash, the doctor had another bottle out and poured a thin, dark liquid into the spoon. Again he held it out. "A little arsenic is good for the soul," he chuckled wickedly. He thrust it out, and Derek took it down. Again he choked and sputtered as the bitter liquid hit his throat.

Mumbling curses in a steady litany, Doctor Sanderson treated each of the men in the wagon exactly as he had Derek, using the same spoon without even bothering to wipe it off. When he finished, he looked at Rebecca.

"She's not sick," Josh blurted. "She's just tending to those who are."

Doctor Sanderson glared at Josh, clearly irritated, but then, without a word, turned again to his bag. In a moment he had two smaller bottles. He poured from both into the spoon. "You look ill, young lady. Here's some bitters of bayberry bark and some tincture of camomile flowers."

Rebecca opened her mouth and took it without protest. It was terribly bitter and she pulled a horrible face.

"What about the baby?"

Rebecca clutched her tightly, turning her away from the doctor. "The baby's fine."

Sanderson looked dubious, but then turned to the commanding officer. "All right, Lieutenant. With your help, I think we can treat the rest of the men now."

They retrieved their horses and led them away, heading back to the next wagon. As soon as they were out of earshot, Sergeant Williams stepped forward and shut the wagon's tailgate. "There is as corrupt a sample of a Missourian as any of those who shed the blood of the Saints while we were among them," he said quietly.

Carl Rogers was furious. He leaped to his feet and leaned over the table, his ruddy complexion beet red now. It was a meeting of the new citizens committee in Nauvoo, but some Mormons had also been invited because of the importance of what was happening. Carl banged his fist against the table. "You call this a treaty?" he shouted. He slammed the papers down and pounded his fist on them. "This isn't a treaty. This is a sellout."

"Now, Rogers," Major James R. Parker said, his own face reddening, "settle down and let me explain."

"Let you explain what?" Carl shouted. "How you've made a deal with the devil?"

Abner Colfax leaned forward. "Carl, getting angry isn't going to solve anything."

Carl spun around on his fellow committee member. "So what is, Abner? Major Parker was called by the governor to help us, to maintain the peace. He is the state's authority in Hancock County." He swung back to Parker. "What happened to your proclamation that everyone was to return to their homes? What happened to your promise to raise volunteers to help us protect our homes and families? Tell me that, Mr. Parker."

Now Richard Steele jumped up. "Carl is right," he cried. "The state is supposed to be helping us, not giving in to the mobs."

Parker was a big man, balding and with a sallow complexion, but he was a decent man in a difficult spot. He took a deep breath, fighting for control. "Colonel Singleton, the leader of the posse from Carthage, and I tried to work out an agreement that was fair to both sides. They have warrants for the arrest of many of the men in the city."

"Posse?" Carl exploded. "Mob, you mean. Singleton is not an officer of the state. Why are you negotiating with him?"

The major leaned forward over the table, thrusting his face right up against Carl's. "Because posse or mob, he is in command of over seven hundred men, Mr. Rogers. Most of them are members of the Carthage Greys. Do I need to remind you about the Carthage Greys?"

That stopped Carl. No, he didn't need to be reminded of that. It was primarily the Carthage Greys who had painted their faces black and stormed the jail in Carthage, leaving Joseph and Hyrum Smith dead and John Taylor severely wounded. They were virulent Mormon-haters and had no qualms about expressing that hatred through violence. The Carthage Greys had also teamed up with the citizens of Warsaw and Green Plains in the attack on Yelrome and the cold-blooded murder of Edmund Durfee. And now they were the number-one factor behind the call for more "wolf hunts," the cry for extermination of the Mormons, and the demand for the expulsion of the last of the Saints from Nauvoo.

"But that's why Governor Ford has given you authority to raise volunteers," Steele said, jumping in at Carl's hesitation.

Carl picked up the papers and shook them in Parker's face. "These are not acceptable conditions. Sixty days for the Mormons to get out of the city. In the meantime, a force of twenty-five members of the mob—or posse," he said sarcastically, "—to be stationed in the city, with the citizens of Nauvoo paying for half their board. The Mormons are to surrender their arms. What kind of conditions are those?"

"The arms would be returned to them as soon as they left the state," Parker broke in, but it came out lamely and even he knew it.

Daniel H. Wells, one of the few Mormons who were in attendance at this meeting of the new citizens committee, spoke for the first time. "The last time the Mormons surrendered their weapons, Major Parker," he said grimly, "it led to the fall of Far West in Missouri. It was all that the mobs were waiting for. Once they knew we couldn't defend ourselves, they sacked the city, shot down innocent people, ravished our women. We will not agree to that again."

Carl turned to his fellow committee members. "I say that we do not agree to any of this." He flung the papers down again. "I don't care if you have signed the agreement, Major Parker. This is not acceptable."

"Then there will be war," Parker said ominously.

Richard Steele stood up beside Carl. "Then let there be war," he declared.

Carl made sure the windows were covered before he lit the lamp, and even then he kept the wick low. In the dim light he moved to the back of the shed, where normally he would lay out the rows of bricks after they had been fired in the kiln. He moved several boxes that had been stacked across one end, and looked around once more to be sure he was alone. Then he stepped through the small opening into the makeshift room he had created with his temporary wall. He stood there for almost a full minute, letting his eyes move up and down the wagon that he had hidden there and the boxes, barrels, and sacks with which it was slowly filling up. He wished again that it was a smaller, lighter wagon. This was meant for hauling bricks. It was heavy and long. A team could pull it, but it really would take two yoke of oxen to keep it moving over long distances. But at the moment, finding a wagon and two yoke of oxen in Nauvoo was virtually impossible.

He moved around the wagon, taking mental inventory of what he had gathered so far. It seemed woefully small for a family of seven people. And some of the staples—sugar, flour, salt—were still not where he wanted them to be. But it was a start, and it had taken a good share of the thousand dollars he had gotten from the lumber sale. He still worked on supplementing his little secret every day. That took some doing, for with the brickyard shut down now, Melissa was far more aware of his activities during the day than she had been before. He was doing this for her and the children, in keeping with his promise to her, but he didn't want her knowing about it. At least not yet. He still had hopes that they would never have to use it.

He sighed, moving back out into the main part of the shed. After tonight's meeting, his hopes were waning. That brought his mouth into a tight line. "Sixty days," he muttered as he started moving the boxes back across the opening he had made. "Surrender our weapons. What kind of fools do they think we are?"

When he was finished he stepped back and surveyed his work again. To the casual eye, it looked now as if the whole end of the shed were being used for storing junk. But as he looked more closely, he could see that there was a large space behind the boxes. Enough to hide a wagon. He went to work again, moving several stacks of bricks over in front of the boxes and piling more boxes on top so that the space behind was not as obvious.

Finally, after more than an hour's work, he blew out the lamp and left the shed, carefully locking the door behind him.

Melissa was still up, sitting in the living room sorting the laundry she had brought in from the clothesline earlier that day. She looked up as he entered. "Hi."

He nodded and went over and kissed her on the forehead.

"The meeting went long," she said.

It wasn't a direct question, and Carl understood it for what it was—a probe for a report. He decided there was no point in trying to hide it from her. Word would be out in the city by morning anyway. "Major Parker signed an agreement with the mob in Carthage."

"And?"

He shrugged. "It wasn't acceptable. They asked for too much and gave too little."

"So what does that mean, Carl?"

He avoided her eyes. "We don't know yet. Parker has to take it back tomorrow and tell them it was rejected." He turned and looked toward the stairs. "How's Mary Melissa?"

Melissa shook her head slowly. "Maybe a little better, but not good yet by any means."

"Did her fever break?"

"No. I gave her a sponge bath, and that seems to have brought it down a little. She is sleeping for a change."

"Good."

Melissa folded and then smoothed a pillowcase in her lap. "Sarah is starting in too, I think."

He turned back toward her. "No, with the shakes?"

"Yes. I'm afraid so. She said she was really cold tonight. The rest of us were sweating."

"Were you able to find any quinine?"

"Mary Fielding Smith brought me about a quarter of a pint. Don't ask me where she found it."

"She's an angel, isn't she?"

That surprised Melissa a little, but she immediately nodded. "Yes, she is. In spite of all she has to worry about, she always finds time to help others."

"I'll go by and thank her tomorrow," Carl said.

That surprised Melissa even more. Carl was politely friendly with some of the Mormons still left in town, but he didn't go out of his way to associate with them. "That would be nice, Carl." She took a quick breath, and then added, "She plans to leave in a few days."

He moved to a chair and sat down. "I thought they didn't have an outfit."

"Joseph Fielding sold his farm."

"Ah. And how much did he get?"

Melissa bit her lip. This was indicative of what was happening in Nauvoo right now. "Two hundred dollars. Or that's what the buyer said he was giving him. In actuality, he got a wagon, two horses—one of which proved to be so balky that Joseph had to trade him for a yoke of small young oxen—a coat, some cloth, and four and a half dollars in cash."

He exhaled wearily. "What a tragedy."

"Twenty acres of cultivated land, fruit trees, a garden, a brick home, an excellent well—all of that for a wagon, two horses, a few bolts of cloth, and four and a half dollars in cash."

"He was lucky to get a wagon," Carl said, thinking of his own unsuccessful attempts to trade his brick wagon for something else.

Melissa only nodded. Mary had confided in her that after considerable wrangling in the probate court, she had finally gotten a settlement of seven hundred dollars on Hyrum Smith's extensive properties. She had used all of that to purchase her own wagons and teams. In addition to her own family, she had Mercy Thompson and her child, and was caring for the children of Samuel Smith, whose widow, Levira, was seriously ill.

Carl came out of his thoughts and looked at his wife. She looked very tired and seemed quite discouraged. Then, as he looked more closely, he thought he detected a flush in her face. He stood up and reached out to touch her forehead. It was quite warm to the touch.

"You're not starting in with this too, are you?" he asked in sudden alarm.

She shook her head. "No, it's just hot in here."

He felt his own forehead. The flesh was cool. He felt her again, then took the clothes from her lap. Fever was often one of the first signs of a coming onslaught of ague. "Come on, Melissa. You're going to bed."

"I'm all right."

"I know. But it's late. Let's go to bed."

She got to her feet, taking his hand and holding it. "Bed does sound good."

Then, as they started toward the stairs, she stopped. "Carl?"

He stopped too and turned to look at her. "What?"

"You haven't forgotten your promise, have you? about putting the safety of the children first?"

He wasn't sure if he winced or not. "No, Melissa. I haven't forgotten my promise."

Chapter Notes

On 29 August, Lieutenant Andrew Jackson Smith, a career military officer, joined the Mormon Battalion and proposed that he take command. For the reasons listed here, the majority of the Mormon officers finally voted to accept him. Five days later, the men learned what kind of officer had taken over when Lieutenant Smith became furious at the refusal of the sick to report to the doctor and be put on the sick list. (See *MB*, pp. 48–49; *CHMB*, pp. 143–46.)

Though it seems incredible to modern readers that men could be so harshly treated, the details of the lieutenant's threats and Doctor Sanderson's treatment of the sick, even down to the rusty spoon, come from the accounts of those who had to suffer these things (see *MB*, pp. 50–51; *CHMB*, pp. 147–51). One needs to remember that in the army, discipline and the use of authority were often harsh and unjust. Also, battalion members were hundreds of miles from any higher authority to which they might appeal. It is a testimony to the faithful nature of the Saints that they submitted to such treatment without open mutiny.

As summer ended and fall approached, the patience of the anti-Mormons in Illinois was wearing thin. Brigham Young had promised that the Saints would leave Nauvoo in the spring of 1846. The great majority of the Saints had complied with that agreement, but there were still several hundred of the poor and the sick left behind, and things began to fester again. On 21 August 1846, Governor Thomas Ford ordered Major James R. Parker, a member of the Illinois militia, and ten other men to go to Nauvoo and maintain the peace. But the antis far outnumbered this token show of force. Parker sent a proclamation asking all the citizens of Hancock County to return to their homes. When his men took the proclamation to Carthage, they were violently assaulted, then sent back with a message that the constable's posse that was assembling near Carthage did not recognize Parker's authority and would not disperse. Clearly intimidated, Parker finally signed an agreement with the posse's commander on 3 September setting forth the conditions outlined in this chapter. The citizens of Nauvoo flatly rejected the proposal, and this set up the events that followed. (See *SW*, pp. 114–42.)

Chapter Twenty-Four

Sunday, Sept. 6, 1846 — Pilot Peak

We have been through hell and have lived to tell about it.

I shall be brief, as I am thoroughly exhausted and must sleep. We began our journey across the Salt Desert one week ago. What was originally promised to be 40 miles turned out to be 80. The crossing was unbelievably harsh. Great wastelands of salt beds constitute this desert. It is as flat as a tabletop and as white as if it were new-fallen snow. There is not a single blade of grass or any living thing to be seen. The late summer sun beats down with merciless fury and reflects back into our faces as if we were traversing on the face of a mirror. For long stretches, the salt-soil is so compacted that even oxen and loaded wagons barely leave a mark upon it. In other places, a shallow depression has collected water beneath the crust and turned the hardpan into mush. The wagons broke through and mud as thick as bookbinders' glue clung to wheels, feet, hooves, and everything else it touched. Should outer darkness ever become too crowded, God could banish

Satan and his minions here and it would be sufficient punishment for them.

As soon as we entered the desert, our company broke into segments as every family sought to fend for themselves. William Eddy forged ahead. We (the Reeds) and the Donners brought up the rear. We have the heavier wagons and our animals quickly fell behind. After plodding on for a day and a night and into part of the next day, our water gave out. Pilot Peak, green and shimmering in the distance, seemed no closer after thirty hours than when we started. The company prevailed upon Mr. Reed to ride ahead and bring back water. He left us reluctantly, instructing us to unhitch the cattle and drive them on when they could pull the wagons no farther. After a time, even the Donners pulled ahead, and we were left seemingly alone in the bleakness that was everywhere around us.

By the morning of the fourth day, when Mr. Reed still had not returned, there was nothing to do but to unyoke the oxen and drive them forward. Milt Elliott and the other teamsters took them all. I stayed back with the wagons and the family. Mr. Reed returned just at sunup on the fifth day, telling us that he had passed Milt and instructed him to return for us quickly once the oxen were watered. We waited all that day and finally determined that we could stay stationary no longer. We left the wagons and began to walk. That night we caught up with the Donners and slept for a time with them. Mr. Reed and I went ahead to find the teams, leaving the family with the Donners.

When we finally reached the base of Pilot Peak and the springs that are there, we learned that disaster had struck. When Mr. Reed passed Milt and the teamsters bringing the cattle in, he warned them to keep them on the road, for once they smelled water they would bolt for it. But while they were going along, one of their horses gave out and they stopped to try and get it going again. They weren't paying attention to the cattle. The cattle caught smell of the water, which was some distance away, and started for it. Milt, who certainly knows better, was not concerned, for he supposed they would stay on the road which led to the springs and to the camp. When they finally started again, the oxen were nowhere to be seen. They continued on to camp, assuming the cattle would be there. They were not.

Thirty-eight cattle were lost, including nine yoke of Mr. Reed's oxen. Nine yoke! We have spent two days looking for them, but to no avail. This is disastrous beyond belief. In one stroke of bad luck—or better, of pure carelessness—Mr. Reed has gone from being the richest man in our party to being nearly destitute. He now has only two oxen left. Mr. Graves, Mr. Pike, and Mr. Breen have kindly consented to loan oxen to Mr. Reed, but even then he had to divide his food supplies up among the rest of the company and abandon two of the wagons. We cached much valuable material in the desert. Mr. Reed says we will come back for it next season. I have no such hope.

My feelings of impending tragedy only deepen with each day. Oh, my beloved Kathryn, shall I ever see you again?

The wagons were lined up along the fence in front of the house. Children were playing around them and waved happily, but Melissa could see no adults. She stopped, not wanting to intrude, looking toward the house, feeling the warmth of the loaf of bread beneath her arm. After a moment, the door opened and Joseph Fielding came out carrying a pile of bedding.

As he came down the steps, he caught sight of her and smiled. "Hello, Melissa."

"Good afternoon, Brother Joseph."

"Mary and Mercy are inside. Go on in."

"Thank you." As she opened the gate for him and then stepped through herself, she looked toward the wagons. "Are you nearly loaded?"

He nodded, lifting the bedding up and tossing it inside the nearest one. "When you are leaving almost everything behind, it doesn't take too long to pack."

"Yes," Melissa said sadly, then turned and went up the walk.

The door was still half-opened, so she pushed it a little farther open and called inside. "Hello."

Almost immediately Mary Fielding Smith appeared. She had a dust rag in her hand and a scarf around her forehead. "Oh, Melissa. What a pleasant surprise!"

Melissa held out the loaf of bread wrapped in a dish towel. "Here's something for the children."

Mary took it and pressed it to her face, breathing deeply. "Mmm, it smells wonderful. Thank you. Come in and sit for a minute."

"I know you're about ready to leave."

"It doesn't take long," she said wistfully. "Not when you're leaving almost everything behind."

"That's what Joseph said too."

Mary turned and looked around. "Look at this. It's a completely furnished house. There are dishes in the cupboards and blankets on the beds. There are even some clothes left in the wardrobes. The trees in back are loaded with peaches that will be ripe in a few more days. All of that, and we're going to simply close the door and drive away."

Melissa watched the sorrow in Mary's eyes. This was a graceful, cultured, educated woman. Even after these many years, she still spoke with a noticeable English accent. Melissa could still remember when she had first seen Mary Fielding. Mary and her sister Mercy had come to Kirtland from Toronto, in Upper Canada, in company with Joseph Fielding and John and Leonora Taylor. Rebecca and the tall, graceful English girl struck up an immediate and deep friendship, though Mary was some years Rebecca's senior. It was a friendship that had endured for over nine years, and through it all the family had grown close to Mary. Melissa felt a great loss to know that it was over now.

"I suppose Emma hasn't changed her mind about not going with you."

There was a quick shake of her head. "Emma's leaving but not with us. She's going upriver to Fulton, Illinois, to stay with the Marks family."

"Oh," Melissa said. That wasn't a surprise. From the time of Joseph's death, Emma had made it clear that she was not going to follow Brigham Young anywhere.

The door opened and Joseph Fielding came back inside. He glanced at the two of them, then quietly went into the next room and began to gather up more things.

"What about Mother Smith?" Melissa asked.

There were instant tears in Mary's eyes. "I took the children and we went and said good-bye to her this afternoon." She stopped, brushing at her eyes. "It was very difficult. She's so old and feeble now. We both knew that we'll never see each other again."

Tears welled up in Melissa's eyes too, and her throat constricted so tightly that she could barely speak. "I don't think the two of us shall ever see each other again either," she whispered.

Mary set the bread down on a chair and opened her arms. Melissa stepped into them, weeping openly. "Nonsense," Mary said. "Someday you're going to be reunited with your family." She smiled brightly. "And where they are, that's where we will be."

"I don't think so," Melissa sniffed. "I don't think I'll ever see them again either." Her shoulders began to shake as the utter loneliness took over.

To her surprise, Joseph Fielding was suddenly standing at the entrance to the room. "Melissa?"

She wiped at her eyes with her handkerchief, then turned. "Yes?"

"You must leave Nauvoo. Time is running out."

"I feel that too," she exclaimed, "but I can't convince Carl."

"I will talk to him."

She shook her head. "It won't do any good."

He glanced at his sister, then went on. "Have you heard the news today?"

Melissa's chin lifted. "What?"

"Major Parker has withdrawn. He says he can't do anything."

Both women were surprised at that declaration.

"Governor Ford appointed another man to take his place—Major Flood, the commander of the militia in Adams County. But Flood is afraid of angering the non-Mormons and refuses to intervene."

Melissa's hand came to her mouth. "What are we going to do?"

"Oh, the governor finally appointed a Major Clifford to take charge of things here." The very tone of his voice indicated how effective he thought that would be. He took a quick breath, not sure how much to say, and yet knowing this was far too serious to leave Melissa unprepared. "There's now a mob of about seven hundred armed men camped a few miles out of town on the Nauvoo-Carthage Road. Reportedly they have three or four cannons. Major Clifford is calling for men to take positions along the high ground just east of the temple."

Melissa fell back a step, her eyes wide with shock. "Does Carl know this?"

"I don't know. If he's been in the meetings, yes. I just heard it from Daniel Wells, who was on his way to join our defense group."

Mercy Thompson, Mary's sister, came running lightly down the stairs with a box in her arms. "I'm ready, Joseph," she called. Then she stopped when she saw Melissa with Mary. "Oh, I'm sorry." Then, seeing their faces, she came forward anxiously. "What's wrong?"

"We have to hurry, Mercy," Joseph said. He turned and spoke gently to Mary. "If we don't leave soon, we'll not get across the Mississippi tonight. We have to go."

Then he turned to Melissa and took one hand. "I will try to find Carl and talk to him if you want me to, Melissa."

Sick to her stomach, she considered that, her mind racing. From outside she heard the children laughing, and that made up her mind. "No, Joseph. You get your family across the river. I'll find Carl." She reached in the pocket of her dress, pulled out a letter, and thrust it into Mary's hand. "When you see my family, will you give them this?"

Mary nodded, then kissed Melissa on the cheek. "Hurry," she said. "If you come across the river, you can travel with us."

"Thank you." Melissa gave Mercy a quick kiss, shook Joseph Fielding's hand, and walked swiftly out the door.

When she was still half a block away from her home, Melissa saw Carl exit their house, then turn down the street toward her. She called and waved. At the sound of her voice, he broke into a trot toward her. As he ran up, he spoke before she could.

"There you are. Thank heavens."

"I was saying good-bye to Mary and Mercy," she said. "Didn't young Carl tell you that?"

"Yes. I was coming to get you." He grasped her hands. "We're leaving, Melissa. We've got to pack some things."

She gaped at him, not believing her ears. "Do you mean that?"

"Yes! Things are falling apart here. The mob is camped about—"

She cut him off. "I know. Joseph told me. Oh, Carl. I'm so glad you're safe."

He took her by the arm and started walking swiftly toward their house. "We've got to hurry. I want to be out of the city before dark."

"Joseph said that he thinks we can still take the ferry across the river tonight. We could travel with them and—" She stopped speaking at the curt shake of his head. "What?"

"We're not going that way. We're going east. I've got some friends in Peoria who will watch you and the children until I can come back."

She stopped, jerking free of his grasp. "Come back?"

"Yes, Melissa. I can't leave our house and the brickyard. I can't expect the men here to defend our property. I have to come back and help them."

"I don't care about the house, Carl. I don't care about the brickyard. I just want us safe. I want to go west."

"No." He tried to take her arm again, but she spun away. Exasperated, he barked at her. "Melissa, we don't have time for this."

"Why can't we go with our people, Carl? I want to be with my family."

He stepped to her and took her gently but firmly by the shoulders. "Listen," he said, "if we go west, there's nothing. They don't even have homes yet. You read their last letter. They're living in tents and wagons and dugouts in the riverbank."

"I don't care," she cried.

He shook her gently. "Think, Melissa. Our daughter is very ill. Sarah is sick now too. You're still not completely better. What is there if we go west? Nothing. In Peoria there will be doctors and medicines. We can rent a house."

She had started a retort, but his words cut her off. She hadn't thought it through that far.

"Winter's coming, Melissa. We have to think of the children."

"I—"

He pulled her to him. "I know you want to find your family, but we have to think of *our* family first."

She laid her head against his chest. She thought of her two-year-old daughter, who was so weak and listless now that Melissa stayed by her side every moment when she was awake. "Is Mary Melissa still sleeping?"

He nodded. "Carl's with her. I've already set the other children to packing." He stopped for a moment, then smiled faintly. "I have a wagon, Melissa."

Her head jerked around.

"Hidden in the shed at the brickyard. It's already stocked with some food and supplies. Not a lot, but enough to get us to Peoria."

She wasn't sure if he was telling her the truth. "Why didn't you tell me?"

"I didn't want you worrying."

She threw up her hands. "That's exactly why you should have told me."

He kissed her softly. "Go. Help the children. I'll get the horses and bring the wagon."

She finally nodded, then kissed him back. "Thank you, Carl."

"Go," he said again, giving her a little shove. "I'll hurry."

The first thing that caught Carl's eye as he came around the shed was the two or three loose bricks that lay on the ground in front of the double doors. One of the bricks had been dragged across the ground, leaving a reddish brown skid mark. Then he saw the bright slash of splintered wood on the small door that allowed entry without opening up the big wagon doors. He leaped forward, his heart suddenly plummeting.

Whoever had taken a crowbar to the hasp and the padlock had carefully put them back in place so that from a distance it looked as though the door were still locked. With a cry of dismay, Carl tossed them aside, jerked open the door, and darted inside. One look was all it took. The false wall that he had so carefully constructed of boxes and brick was scattered in great heaps up and down both sides of the shed. Whoever had done it—sometime during the night, he guessed—had left just enough room to back a team of horses up to the wagon and then take it out through the doors. He turned and leaned against the wall, his head against his arms. He felt sick. Who? Who had known? Was it some Mormon so desperate for escape that he had eliminated Carl's family's chance? Was it river scum who somehow had known it was here?

He shook his head. Whoever it was, they had effectively nullified all of his careful preparations, wiped out nearly a thousand-dollar expenditure, and effectively condemned Carl Rogers and his family to one option. Now there was no choice but to stay.

"Melissa, I tried. I thought—"

She put a finger to his lips. "I know, Carl. Thank you. I know you tried to keep your promise."

He turned and got his rifle down from its place above the fireplace.

"Do you have to leave?" she asked quietly.

He nodded grimly. "The only way I can keep you and the children safe now is to go out on the defense line with the others and help keep those men out of the city." He looked at young Carl. "Son, I'm leaving you the shotgun."

"Yes, Pa."

He turned back to Melissa. "That's just a precaution. I won't leave you alone. If they start to break through, I'll come here first and get you."

"I know."

"Stay in the house. Don't let the children out."

"We'll be all right."

He laid a hand on her cheek, anguish filling his eyes. "I love you, Melissa Steed Rogers."

"And I love you, Carl," she whispered. "Be safe."

"I will."

Joshua Steed straightened, arching his back in an attempt to stretch out the muscles a little. "I am definitely getting too old for this," he muttered to no one in particular.

Nathan groaned and got to his feet, dropping the sickle and letting it lie where it fell. He followed Joshua's example, stretching like a cat. They were down by the Missouri, in one of the flat areas the river had scoured out sometime long ago and which now provided a lush green meadow with grass that grew past their thighs.

Matthew, on his knees in the meadow hay, making long, smooth cuts with his sickle, grinned over at Solomon. "Hey, old man," he said, "how come you're still down here working while those young bucks are standing around moaning?"

Solomon laughed. The four of them had started out together

in a rough line about six feet apart so that they overlapped one another. Now his six-foot swath was out ahead of the other three by at least ten feet.

"Because he's cheating," Joshua growled.

Solomon straightened, hands on his knees. "How do you figure I'm cheating?"

Joshua shook his head. "I don't know. But you must be. Look how fast you're going."

Nathan went to the bucket of water and filled the dipper, then drained it quickly. "So what is your secret, Solomon?" he asked as he wiped his mouth with his sleeve.

Solomon answered with a sly smile. "I'd say about ten acres. In Mount Pisgah I contracted with some families to cut hay for their stock in exchange for food. It turned out to be about ten acres." He smiled demurely. "I got to be pretty fast at it by the time I was done."

Now Joshua groaned aloud. "No wonder we can't keep up with you."

Solomon stood up. "Why don't we all take a break and rest for a while?"

"Let me ask all of you a question," Joshua said from beneath his hat. "You're the expert Mormons here." There was a moment's silence. The four of them were lying side by side in the shade of an elderberry bush. Joshua came up on one elbow. He wasn't smiling now. "How do you tell the difference between a prompting by the Holy Ghost and your own feelings?"

Nathan turned his head in surprise. Solomon and Matthew turned now too. "That's no easy question," Matthew said. "I've wondered that many times."

"As have I," Solomon responded.

Nathan gave his older brother an appraising look. Joshua was asking questions all the time, but usually it was about a verse of scripture or about something Brigham or one of the other brethren had said at worship services. "Can you give us an example of what you mean?"

Joshua lay back down in the grass and pulled his hat down again. "I can give you the actual problem I'm struggling with."

"All right," Nathan said.

"For about the past week I've not been able to get Carl and Melissa out of my mind," he said.

That sobered them all. "I've been worrying a lot about them too," Solomon said. "The reports coming out of Nauvoo are not good."

"That's just it," Joshua said. "Maybe that's all this is. I've heard those reports, and there is cause for worry. So is that all it is? Am I just worrying about them as any normal person would do? Or is it something more?"

Solomon and Matthew both looked to Nathan, willing to let him take this one.

"Tell me a little more," Nathan responded. "You say they've been on your mind a lot. Like what?"

"Well," Joshua growled, "for one thing, I've been thinking about taking a good length of hickory wood and knocking Carl alongside the head. What's the matter with him? Why can't he see that it's foolish to stay there?"

"Because he doesn't see things the way we do," Matthew volunteered. There was an impish smile. "We once had another person in the family like that too, but he's not with us anymore."

Joshua gave him a slow grin. "Wouldn't be anyone I know, would it?" Then he went on. "But seriously, I just keep thinking that maybe we need to go get them."

Nathan nodded slowly. Matthew, on the other hand, was shaking his head. "You read Melissa's last letter. Carl won't come out here with us."

"I know. And as much as I'd like to force him to see the light, just like Nathan did me—"

"What?" Nathan cried in feigned offense. "I didn't force you to do anything."

"But you did, little brother," Joshua said softly. "You took me along and asked the Lord to open my eyes. What if we went back and tried that with Carl?"

They were all silent for a time, considering that. Then Nathan leaned forward, probing Joshua's eyes. "How do you feel about all this? Are you inclined to think it's just worry, or do you think it's something more?"

"I'm not experienced in these things," Joshua said, throwing up his hands. "That's why I'm asking you."

"I know," Nathan persisted, "but when it's all said and done, what do you feel about it?"

For a long time, Joshua sat silently, staring out across the fields. Then he looked at Nathan. "I think it's more than worry," he said slowly.

Nathan nodded. "Then I think we'd better call a family council tonight and talk about it."

When they returned to camp just before sunset, there was already a family council of sorts under way. As the four men approached, they saw the whole family gathered around the cooking fire. At the sight of their fathers, Emily and Rachel both jumped up and went running to them. "We got a letter from Kathryn," Emily bubbled as she reached Nathan.

"We got a letter from Melissa," Rachel called to Solomon.

"Two letters?" Joshua asked in surprise.

"Well," Rachel explained, "actually Kathryn's letter went to Nauvoo; then Melissa wrote her own letter to go with it and sent them both on to us."

"Girls, girls," Jessica called. "Let your fathers come in and get some dinner. Then we can tell them all about it."

It was almost ten p.m. and time for lights out when Nathan stepped outside the tent to uncrick his back and saw Joshua sitting by the dying fire. He moved over and sat down beside him on the log. "We got another long day tomorrow. Aren't you tired?"

"I am."

Nathan waited, sensing that something was troubling Joshua. When his brother didn't speak, Nathan decided to make conversation. "That's wonderful news from Kathryn, don't you think? We've worried about them all this time. Now they're halfway across the plains, while we sit here and wait."

"They're probably to California by now," Joshua observed. "It was the end of June when she wrote. That's more than two months ago."

"True. Makes you kind of envious, doesn't it?"

"More than kind of."

"And Melissa's letter was sure positive. It sounds like she and Carl have worked out this whole problem of what to do."

"Maybe," Joshua said somewhat hesitantly.

"What do you mean, maybe?"

"Oh, there's no question that Melissa has come to terms with Carl's unwillingness to bring her here to join us."

"Yes," Nathan said, sensing there was more.

"Remember our conversation today?"

"I do."

"When you asked me how I felt and I told you I thought it was more than worry?"

"Yes, what about it?"

"I was so sure that I finally understood. Then in a matter of hours we come back here and there's a letter waiting and the whole problem is solved. Carl has promised to get the family out of there if things get too bad."

"And that makes you think you were wrong?"

"No," he said shortly, "it doesn't make me *think* I was wrong; it proves I was wrong. So much for learning how to recognize the voice of the Spirit."

"Joshua, that's one of the hardest things there is about living the gospel. The Spirit doesn't shout at us or pound us on the shoulder. The scriptures say the voice of the Lord is still and small and it whispers. It takes time to learn how to recognize it."

"Yeah," he said glumly. "And it takes a lot more time with some than with others."

When Nathan came out of his tent, sickle in hand, he was surprised to see that his mother was still sitting by the breakfast fire. He changed direction and went over to sit beside her. "You all right?" he asked, searching her face.

She nodded. "I'm just thinking." She glanced at the sickle in his hand. "How much hay do you think you cut yesterday?"

"A couple of tons, I would guess."

"That's good."

He nodded. "Two or three more days like that and we should have enough to see us through the winter. Then we can start on building our cabins."

"Did you hear that President Young has changed his mind about Cutler's Park?"

Nathan raised one eyebrow. "He has?"

"That's what Sister Kimball told me yesterday. The Twelve are afraid this isn't quite right for the main settlement."

"Hmm," Nathan said.

"They're going out in a couple of days to scout for a better place. Vilate says President Young wants something a little closer to the river."

"Well, there are plenty of good places around here. We're lucky that there is so much grass. We've got a lot of cattle to feed."

"Yes." She fell silent, looking steadily into the fire.

She seemed pensive, and Nathan sensed that there was something bothering her. "Are you sure you're all right, Mama?"

She looked up, her eyes meeting his. "What did you think of Melissa's letter yesterday?"

He hadn't expected that question, but answered immediately. "I was very pleased. It sounded much more positive than the one before that."

"Yes, it did, didn't it?"

He peered at her more closely. "You don't sound convinced."

Her shoulders lifted and fell. "It *was* more positive. Since she told us about the store being burned I've been worried sick. So yes, this was encouraging."

"But?" he prompted.

She shook her head slowly, her mouth pulling down. "I don't know what it is, Nathan, but I've not been able to get Melissa off my mind these last few days."

He pulled back a little, staring at her.

"I know that everything sounded fine, but I just have this feeling." She stopped at his look. "What?"

Turning, Nathan cupped his hands. "Joshua?" He waited for a moment, then called again. "Joshua, can you come out here for a second?"

The flap to Joshua and Caroline's tent opened, and Joshua stepped out. He blinked for a moment at the brightness of the early-morning sun and then, seeing the two of them, came over. "What?" he asked.

"Tell him, Mama. Tell him what you just told me."

Looking a little puzzled, she did so. As she spoke, Joshua gave Nathan a sharp look, then slowly sat down. When she was finished, he spoke to Nathan. "So it's not just me?"

"No," Nathan said slowly. He blew out his breath in disgust. "And here I tried to talk you out of it. So much for my being the so-called expert in these things."

"What things?" Mary Ann asked, thoroughly confused by their conversation.

"Tell her, Joshua."

Joshua did so, going through the conversations of the previous day. When he was finished, Mary Ann was nodding slowly. "So what do we do?"

Without thinking, they both turned to Nathan. Ever since Benjamin's death, that seemed like the natural thing to do. He met their gaze for several long seconds, then spoke. "Today is Thursday. I figure we have two more days of cutting hay, maybe two and a half. We have to do that before the weather turns on us. So, let's get that done as quickly as we can. Then we'll go talk to President Young and tell him what's going on."

Chapter Notes

The details of the Donner Party's laborious trek along the Hastings Cutoff come from the various journal entries and later reminiscences of those who took that ill-fated journey in 1846. Most important of these would be the journal and later writings of James F. Reed himself and the writings of his stepdaughter, Virginia. Frank Mullen Jr. (see *Chronicles*, pp. 132–65) gives an excellent summary of what took place during this leg of the journey. George R. Stewart gives a more dramatic telling, but his historical facts are occasionally incorrect (see *OBH*, pp. 40–58). Copies of the original documents can be found, with excellent footnotes, in *UE*, *Overland in 1846*, and *WFFB*.

Chapter Twenty-Five

Rogers?"

"Here, sir." Carl stood up.

Colonel Johnson, leader of the Nauvoo forces, waved him forward. As Carl reached him, he motioned to another man. "Do you know Bill Anderson, Rogers?"

"Yes, sir, I do."

"Hello, Carl," Anderson said as he joined them.

"I understand you're a pretty good shot with a rifle," Johnson said.

"Fair, sir," Carl admitted.

Anderson smiled. "I'll take fair, Colonel."

Johnson was grim. Their forward observers had already spotted the mob coming up the road from Carthage. The estimated count was very sobering—seven or eight hundred armed men and that many or more who came to back them up. They were now less than five miles out of town. The bluffing and sputtering were over. This was for real.

"Bill here is forming a company called the 'Spartan Band.' There'll be thirty men. We have fifteen repeating rifles which can shoot up to eight shots before they need reloading. This group will be our primary strike force—mobile, deadly, hitting from ambush. Bill says he'd like you in it."

"I don't have a repeating rifle."

Anderson waved his hand. "Give your weapon to someone else. You'll be using one of ours."

"I'd be honored, sir," Carl said to the colonel.

He nodded curtly, then turned away and began barking commands to another group. The defenders were divided into three companies—three others besides the Spartan Band—who were now digging in along a line about half a mile from the old Hyrum Smith farm on the Nauvoo-Carthage Road. William Anderson motioned to where a group of men were standing separate from the others. They started walking toward them.

"Do you know who the Spartans were?" Anderson asked.

Carl shook his head. "Romans, I think."

"Actually, they were Greeks. They were considered to be the fiercest of the Greek warriors." He paused for a moment before he went on. "They had a saying that their mothers used whenever they sent their sons off to war."

"What was that?"

" 'With your shield or on it.' "

Carl looked puzzled, and Anderson smiled thinly. "The Spartan shield was long enough to protect most of the body. If a man was wounded or killed, the shield was also used as a stretcher."

Nodding slowly, Carl began to understand. "So . . ."

"So retreat, or flight with the shield, was not an option. You came back either carrying your shield or carried on it." There was a short laugh. "I don't expect we'll be quite that grim, but we thought the Spartans offered a good model for us."

Carl felt his stomach knot up a little as the implications of all that sank in, but he kept his face impassive. "It will be a privilege to be part of your group, Bill."

"What are they doing?" someone whispered.

Carl lifted his head a little, peering through the bushes that hid their place of ambush. About five hundred yards ahead of them, just beyond the house where Hyrum and Mary Smith had once lived, he could see that the column of men had stopped. They were running around, obviously doing something, but the foliage was too thick for Carl and the others to see exactly what.

"Steady, boys," Bill Anderson called back. "Don't let them know we're here."

Carl jumped as there was a sudden explosion and a huge puff of smoke. These were instantly followed by a whistling sound overhead; then after a moment came a solid *whumph* from somewhere behind them.

"Cannons!" someone yelled, and immediately everyone hugged the ground. There was a second blast, and then a third. Carl raised his head again. Blue smoke from three separate sources billowed upward. After a moment, a cannon roared again, only this time the smoke came from another spot. "They've got four artillery pieces," Carl called to Anderson.

Anderson waved a hand. "That was the report."

Boom! Boom! The other cannons roared again, and the whistling filled the air. Again the men instinctively ducked, but the artillery was not aimed at them. It was shooting toward the city. There was another *whumph*, followed almost instantly by a loud crash.

Carl winced. That ball had found a target, probably a house or a barn.

"They're not advancing," someone cried. "I think they're going to bombard the city for a time."

"Let's go get 'em," someone else called out.

Anderson raised up to a crouch. "No. There's too much open space between us and them. Just stay put, men. We'll get our chance."

With the sound of the first cannon, Melissa jerked around so sharply that she woke up Mary Melissa. The small dark eyes fluttered open and she started to whimper.

"It's all right, honey," Melissa soothed. "Mama's right here."

After a moment her eyes closed again and she relaxed against Melissa's body. Melissa raised her finger to her lips as the other children came running up the stairs and into the bedroom.

"What was that?" David demanded, his eyes wide.

Before she could answer, two more explosions echoed over the city.

"What is it, Mama?" Caleb whispered, coming to stand beside her and hold her arm.

"It's cannon fire," young Carl said. "They've got cannons. Ten-pounders, I'd say, from the sound of it."

"What shall we do, Mama?" Caleb wailed, clearly terrified.

"They're not that close, Caleb," Carl said confidently. "They can't hurt us."

Melissa looked at him in amazement. He was so calm. And her son's courage was a steadying influence for all of them. She reached out with one hand and touched Caleb's face. "If they get close, we'll go down in the root cellar. But Carl's right. We're in no danger right now."

On the bed across the room, Sarah stirred, and then sat up, rubbing at her eyes. Melissa was relieved to see that much of the flush had gone out of her face. At almost eight, Sarah was handling the fever and shakes much better than two-year-old Mary Melissa, but she was still not well yet. "What is it, Mama?" she asked sleepily.

David, who was twelve now and two years younger than Carl, went quickly and sat down beside her. "It's nothing to worry about, Sarah. I'm right here."

"Get her a drink, David." Melissa said. She flinched as another explosion sounded, and then another.

"Do you think they're shooting at Papa?" Caleb asked anxiously. Though he was ten, he was the most sensitive and tenderhearted of the three boys, and his eyes were wide as he stared out the window toward the sound.

The same terrible thought had already hit Melissa, but she shook her head. "No, Caleb. Papa will be safe."

Carl took a step forward. "I'm going to go find out what's happening."

"No!" Melissa blurted.

"I won't go anywhere near the fighting, Mama. But we need to know what's happening."

He was right, of course, but the fear was a bitter taste in her mouth.

"I promise, Mama. I'll be careful. The mob hasn't even come into the city yet."

She nodded finally. "Half an hour, Carl. No more. Promise?"

"I promise."

David stood up. "Can I go?"

"No," Carl and Melissa said together. David sank back down in disappointment.

Melissa turned back to her oldest son. "Promise me you won't take any chances, Carl. Not one."

He nodded. "I promise, Mama."

A runner came darting toward where the Spartan Band lay concealed in the woodlot near the Nauvoo-Carthage Road. He ran in a crouch, the natural reaction to the bombardment, even though the cannonballs were whistling high above his head.

"Captain Anderson! Captain Anderson!" he called as he entered the trees.

"Over here."

"Colonel Johnson wants you to fall back."

"What? Why? We're in a perfect position when the mob starts to advance."

Carl, who was just ten or fifteen feet away from his

commander, noted that Bill Anderson didn't say "if" they advanced but "when."

"We're bringing up five cannon of our own, sir. And we're going to start giving answering fire in about quarter of an hour."

Anderson and the men around him were dumbfounded. "We have cannon?"

"They've taken some steamboat shafts they had down at the foundry and converted them into crude cannons, Captain. They're bringing them up now."

"Wonderful!"

"The problem is, sir, no one knows how accurate they're going to be. We're not even sure they're going to work yet. Colonel Johnson can't guarantee that the cannonballs won't fall short and drop on you."

Anderson nodded, then looked around at his men. "I think we're willing to take that risk rather than give up our position." All around him the members of the Spartan Band were nodding vigorously. "Tell Colonel Johnson that if we see we're in danger, we'll fall back."

The man looked dubious. "Are you sure, sir?"

"We're sure. You tell them to start their answering fire as soon as possible."

"Here they come!" William Anderson called in a hoarse whisper. "Shooters on the line. Backup line, have your cartridges ready to reload and take the second volley."

Carl Rogers wiggled his arms, digging his elbows deeper into the soft earth so that they were firm and solidly set. He moved the rifle slightly to the left, finding the first rider on horseback in his sights. Then he decided that everyone else would take that target as well, and so he moved the muzzle more to the left, picking out one of the men who was following behind.

"Steady," Anderson called out softly. "Let them come in range first."

The men on the road were coming slowly, cautiously, looking

around in every direction. Three men were out ahead, acting as scouts. The horses drawing the cannon had now come into view, and Carl decided the men there were more critical targets and readjusted yet a third time.

"Steady."

Carl squeezed the trigger softly, taking up the fraction of an inch in slack. He had never fired one of these new repeating rifles, but he had been told they recoiled less than some of the muskets and long rifles he was used to shooting.

"Steady," Anderson called again in a low whisper. "Let them get in range."

The main body was down to about a hundred and fifty yards now, but the scouts were just fifty or sixty yards away, coming slowly on their horses. One of the scouts had a spyglass and was scanning the landscape ahead of him. He turned toward Carl and the others, then pulled his horse up, standing in his stirrups, looking directly at them.

"Uh-oh," Anderson said.

Suddenly the scout shouted and started waving his hands frantically, pointing in their direction.

"Fire!" Anderson shouted.

Fifteen repeating rifles blasted out in a ragged volley. One of the scouts was knocked violently off his horse and hit the ground. Carl cursed as the man in his sights didn't drop. He had pulled the muzzle up slightly, anticipating the recoil, and missed cleanly. He levered another round into the chamber and swung the muzzle. He saw that two men were down in the dust of the road. The column was in wild panic as men dove for cover or turned and ran. A man ducked behind one of the artillery pieces. Carl squeezed off a shot and saw a puff of dust and smoke as the round hit the barrel of the cannon. The man yelped and took off running at full speed.

"Fire! Fire! Take your aim, boys!" Anderson was on his feet, urging them on.

Now puffs of smoke were exploding all up and down the line, and Carl realized the mob was returning fire. He heard a ball whip through the leaves above him and all at once he understood they were vulnerable. Fire. Move the muzzle a few inches. Find target. Fire again. This time the man he had in his sights stumbled and his rifle went flying. Another target, this time a man on a horse. Fire. He missed.

Suddenly he became aware that the man behind him was pounding on his shoulder. "You're out of bullets," he shouted. Only then did Carl realize that his last pull had brought him only a loud click. He rolled away, letting the man take his place.

At first it sounded like the popping of firecrackers. After the constant boom of the cannons, the light-arms fire seemed harmless, but Melissa knew better and felt a clutch of fear. She glanced at the clock. It had been one hour and a half since young Carl had gone. "Where is he?" she muttered to herself. "He promised me half an hour."

She looked down at her two daughters. Sarah was awake and was lying beside Caleb, who was reading her a story. She seemed to be feeling much better. Mary Melissa was another matter. She was asleep in the trundle bed, but it was not a deep sleep. Her hands would twitch involuntarily, or she would moan softly from time to time. From the flush of her face, Melissa could tell without touching her that the fever was still ravaging her.

David was at the window, staring eastward up toward the temple. He could see the smoke rolling slowly toward the river. He had watched the men and teams take up five cannon in wagons, and so when deeper booms sounded, he told his mother that they came from their own weapons. Suddenly he jerked forward. "Here comes Carl," he cried over his shoulder.

She went quickly to the window and felt a great shudder of relief as she recognized Carl's figure running down Mulholland Street toward them. "Caleb, watch the baby," she said. Then she raced out of the bedroom and down the stairs, with David hard on her heels.

The moment Carl stepped through the door, Melissa grabbed him by the shoulders and shook him, more roughly than she intended. "Where have you been? You promised you wouldn't be more than half an hour."

"I know, Mama. But we don't have enough ammunition. The captain asked us to pick up some of the enemy's cannonballs so they can use those. It seemed pretty important, Mama."

"You promised you wouldn't go where there was danger."

"I didn't, Mama. We just took the cannonballs to a wagon, and then they took them up the hill." He decided not to tell her how a cannonball had hit a barn just a few rods away from him and blown out the whole end of it.

"I told you—"

He cut in quickly. "Mama, they want us to leave."

Her eyes widened. "Who wants us to leave?"

"The commanders of the forces defending Nauvoo. They say the cannonballs are falling right in the city now. They can't promise the women and children that they'll be safe. They want everyone who can to go across the river and wait there."

She looked blank for a second as she tried to consider what that meant for them. "I can't, Carl. Mary Melissa is too ill and—"

"I know, Mama. But the cannons are starting to hit some of the houses. We're all right for now because we're on the west side of the city, but if the mob gets any closer . . ." He didn't finish that sentence. He didn't have to.

Desperate, she turned toward the stairs. "I can't take Mary. If she's out in the cold tonight . . ." She turned away, feeling the burning of the first tears. *Oh, dear Lord. What shall I do? Help me!*

And in that instant her mind was suddenly calm. She turned back to her two oldest sons. "David, you know the boxes we started to pack yesterday?"

"Yes, Mama."

"Get what you'll need for a few days. Take whatever food you can find. And blankets and warm clothing. The nights are getting cold now. You won't be able to carry a lot."

"Yes, Mama."

"Carl, I want you to run back to where you were. Find someone who can take a message to Papa. Tell him that all of you have gone across the river but that I'm still here with Mary Melissa."

"Mama, I—"

"Carl, I know you want to stay and protect me, but I need you with the children. Find Mary Fielding Smith and her family. They just went over last night, so they should be there somewhere. Tell her what's happened and that we'll get there as soon as possible."

"I will, Mama. I'll take care of them."

She reached out and touched his face, the tears trickling down her cheeks now. "I know you will, Carl. I'm so glad I've got you."

"What about Sarah?" David asked.

"Sarah goes too. She's a little better now. But be sure and keep her warm tonight. Don't let go of her. Not for one minute."

They both nodded.

"Go, Carl. Then come back as quickly as you can."

By Saturday morning the sheer weight of numbers was proving to be decisive. The little band of defenders, numbering no more than one hundred and fifty, was making it costly for the larger force to advance, but advancing they were.

The three companies of the defenders had retreated down Temple Hill and taken up positions along the defensive wall they had thrown up along Mulholland Street. The Spartan Band retreated as well; then they quick-marched through the West Grove, a thick stand of trees where Joseph Smith had so often preached to his people, and took up their positions in a cornfield that gave them a commanding view of Mulholland where it came past the temple and dropped down the bluffs. They hoped that their enemies saw this as a rout and would come after them.

They had only half an hour to wait. They could hear the opposing forces coming before they saw them. Somewhere just beyond the temple, cannon were booming constantly, and Carl could hear the screech of the cannonballs passing overhead. The mob forces had received another wagonload of ammunition from Quincy during the night and were making Nauvoo pay for it dearly.

Carl forced himself not to think of Melissa and Mary Melissa each time there was a loud explosion behind him and he knew one of the balls had found another mark. A few minutes earlier, as they were coming up the hill, he had looked back and seen the large puffs of dust appear where the cannonballs fell into one of the fields. He didn't have to look hard to see that they were falling beyond Granger Street. That meant Steed Row was now within range of the guns.

"Here they come!" someone hissed, and Carl leaned forward, peering through the green stalks of corn.

They were marching four abreast, with their officers in the lead. A man on a horse just behind the officers carried a banner on a pole—a banner for the Carthage Greys, Carl suspected. Though they were not in uniform, they had every other appearance of an army on the march, and had they not been the enemy, it might have been a stirring sight. He smiled. It had worked. They were coming on as if they had conquered the city and were now ready to claim their spoils.

"Cannon ready?"

He turned. The Spartan Band had been given one of the steamboat-shaft cannons. That was an important concession because one of the five homemade cannons had stopped working after only three shots, and another one was being repaired. But William Anderson's band was out front and would be the first to meet the oncoming enemy, and so Colonel Johnson had sent one up to them. It was now placed in front of the men, hidden behind only one row of corn. William Anderson stood behind it, eyeing down the barrel, then leaning over to judge the angle. They had no way to aim it accurately. Even the cannonballs they had collected from the bombardment didn't fit snugly. There was a quarter-inch space all around as they put the ball

The Battle of Nauvoo

into the muzzle. That would significantly lessen its velocity and distance. Their chance of hitting what they were shooting at was remote if not impossible. But they had learned something in these last two days, as Colonel Johnson put it: Accuracy was no more critical than effect.

The man with the small torch stood beside Anderson, waiting for the command. Anderson, satisfied with the position of the gun, was now staring at the column as row after row of men came over the top of the hill. "Look at those cocky fools," he muttered. Then he looked at the man beside him. He hesitated only another second or two, then dropped his arm. "Fire!"

With a roar that shook the ground, the cannon belched smoke and flame ten feet out from the muzzle. Off to the left of the column, a spurt of earth and bushes flew into the air. They had shot wide by almost three rods. But it was all right. If it had hit the column directly, it couldn't have created greater pandemonium. The officers wheeled their horses around and dug their spurs into their flanks. Men were screaming and running hard back toward the top of the bluffs. Carl and the others leaped to their feet and began firing as fast as they could pump shells into the chambers. Johnson was right, he thought joyously. Their accuracy was nothing to brag about, but the effect was terrific.

Carl trotted steadily down Mulholland Street, past Partridge and Hyde and Main Streets, then turned south on Granger. He had only a few minutes. William Anderson was reluctant to let him go once the firing stopped, because they all knew that the mob forces would regroup and come again. Only when Carl showed him the message he had received, that Melissa was alone with a very sick child, did Anderson agree to let him go.

Now Carl threw open the gate and ran up the walk and into the house, searching for any signs of damage. "Melissa!"

"Up here!" There was a muffled cry of joy.

By the time he started up the stairs, she had burst out of the bedroom and was waiting for him. She threw herself into his arms, nearly knocking them both down the stairs. "Oh, Carl, you're safe!"

"I'm fine," he said, holding her tightly. "How's Mary Melissa?"

She stepped back into the bedroom, taking his hand. "Not good. I've used the last of the quinine. Nothing seems to help."

"What about the rest of the children?"

"Across the river safely," she reported with gladness. "One of the ferryman's boys brought a message from Mary Smith. They're all safely with her."

"Good. We've got to get you across, Melissa. I don't know how much longer we can hold them off."

"I don't dare move her, Carl. She's so sick. If the balls start landing close, we can go down in the cellar."

He hesitated, not liking it but not seeing any choice. "Promise?" he said. "Even if they're anywhere close?"

"Promise," she said.

Suddenly the crackle of rifle fire could be heard to the east of them. He looked up in alarm. "They're coming back, Melissa. I've got to go."

"I know. Thank you for coming, Carl. I've been so worried."

"I'll be back as soon as I can."

She followed him out to the head of the stairs. "I'll be praying for you,"

He gave her a strange look. "And I'll be praying for you and the children," he said. Then he was gone.

Melissa listened to his footsteps through the house and then she heard the door shut. She went back into the bedroom and sank slowly to her knees at Mary Melissa's bedside. She bowed her head and began to pray in earnest.

To Nathan's surprise, when they returned to camp from cutting hay on Friday evening, there was a message waiting for him from Brigham Young. There was to be a high council meeting at six the following morning. Nathan wasn't sure why he was invited, but decided perhaps some of the bishops were wanted as well. When he told Joshua about the meeting, Joshua decided he would go too. He wasn't invited to the meeting, but he would wait for Nathan and then afterwards they could talk to the President. As it turned out, that proved to be unnecessary.

"Brethren, we have two items of business to discuss this morning. The first has to do with a new site for our primary settlement."

Nathan looked around. There were about twenty men gathered around Brigham's wagons. There were a few members of the Twelve and the men of the high council for Cutler's Park—those he had expected. But there were three or four others, including himself. He was the only bishop. He wasn't sure why. It had surprised him when Brigham saw Joshua and insisted that he come to the meeting as well.

"Yesterday," President Young went on, "I went out with the Twelve. We have found a place more suitable for our winter settlement. It is a beautiful piece of flatland near the river, with some prairie hills directly behind it. We began a survey and have laid out Main Street. The survey will continue over the next week, and the lots will be divided out and assigned. We have decided to call our new city Winter Quarters."

There were nods and a few murmurs of approval.

"We shall call on our people to move there immediately and begin building homes. It is now the twelfth day of September, and we cannot delay further without serious consequences."

He stopped for a moment to let them know that that was all he would say on the subject. The lightness in his tone disappeared now. "There is a second matter. We have received additional dispatches from Nauvoo. Conditions there are not good."

Nathan and Joshua exchanged surprised glances.

"The enemies of the Church grow more bold. Some of our number were kidnapped and held hostage for several days. The call for another 'wolf hunt' is being issued by the likes of Thomas

Sharp and the Carthage Greys." He sighed deeply. "We have seen these conditions before, and they do not bode well for our people."

Joshua leaned over. "Maybe we won't have to ask him what to do," he whispered.

Nathan nodded.

"As you all know," Brigham continued, "our brethren and sisters who still remain in Nauvoo are the poor and the sick and the helpless. They do not have the strength or the means to come on here by themselves. They must have help."

He reached down and picked up a piece of paper from the table beside him. "Last night I directed that certain individuals in Nauvoo be sent for and helped to come here or to Garden Grove or Mount Pisgah."

He began to read the names one by one. Nathan recognized some of them. Thomas Bullock had served as a clerk for the Twelve. Addison Everett had worked with them on the temple. Thomas Stiles was an elderly gentleman who often came in the store and visited with Lydia and Caroline. Truman O. Angell had helped on the design and construction of the Nauvoo Temple and was Brigham's brother-in-law. When Brigham read the name Mary Smith, Nathan assumed that was Mary Fielding Smith, and that startled him a little. In a letter that had come more than a month ago, Melissa had mentioned that the long-time family friend would be leaving Nauvoo very soon. They had watched for her and waited for word of her, but nothing had come. That she was on Brigham's list implied she might still be back in the city or somewhere along the way.

Brigham laid the paper down again. "There are others, of course. All will almost certainly need our help. Some of you here have families still there." He looked directly at Joshua and Nathan. "So we are asking for teamsters who will volunteer to take wagons back for these people."

Nathan nudged Joshua's arm, smiling at him. "I think from now on," he whispered, "I'll ask you how to recognize the Spirit."

Joshua only smiled, seeming pleased.

Brigham went on. "So far, we have the following volunteers." He picked up a second piece of paper and began to read. When he was through, Nathan and Joshua put up their hands as well. Brigham nodded knowingly. "And," he added, "Nathan and Joshua Steed. Brother Orville M. Allen will serve as foreman of the company, and Pliny Fisher will serve as his counselor. We shall prepare a letter of instructions for you to carry with you. You have three hundred and twenty-five miles to go. We would like you to begin preparations for departure as soon as possible. Any questions?"

He looked around. No one raised a hand. He nodded curtly and the meeting was dismissed.

Chapter Notes

On 11 September 1846, Brigham Young and those of the Twelve who were with him selected a new site for their permanent settlement on the west side of the Missouri River, a settlement which was to be called Winter Quarters. It was a little north and west of Cutler's Park, which had been selected previously. A week later another slight adjustment was made that placed the settlement a bit closer to the river, the site being in what is now called Florence, Nebraska. (See *SW*, pp. 155–58; *MHBY*, pp. 377–78.) There were also sufficient numbers still on the east side of the river that a settlement in Council Bluffs was also planned.

Though the Saints gathered at the Missouri had no way of knowing that a battle had already erupted in Nauvoo, Brigham Young was greatly concerned about the "poor Saints" still there. On 11 September he designated specific names of people either in Nauvoo or along the way that he wanted brought out, and the next morning in a high council meeting he called ten volunteers to go back and get them.

Chapter Twenty-Six

The Arkansas River was a true curiosity to Rebecca Ingalls. It was a wide streambed of mostly dry sand with only occasional pools of water. In other places, where there was no water, they could dig down a foot or two and have water bubble up. In many places the men speared fish with their bayonets in the shallow pools, and occasionally found live fish buried in the wet sand. It was a wonder, and Rebecca was pleased to be camped beside it. There had been more than one night in the last month when they had camped without water. Even if they had to dig for it, there was plenty here to be had.

"More grits?" Rebecca asked.

Derek grinned, setting his now empty plate aside and rubbing his stomach. "If I eat one more spoonful, I'll get me a tummy ache, and then I'll be riding in Doctor Sanderson's 'black wagon' tomorrow." He pulled a face. "As good as your cooking is, Becca, nothing is worth that."

She nodded, pleased to have Derek sitting up again and

making jokes. He had frightened her terribly. For the next three mornings after Doctor Sanderson—or Doctor Death, as everyone was now calling him—had decided Derek was sick, he forced him to ride in the official sick wagon, dubbed the "black wagon" by the men, and to take his "treatment." The prescription was always the same: calomel powder mixed with molasses, followed by a dose of arsenic—all given with that terrible rusty spoon. And each day Derek grew progressively worse. There was no choice. If he didn't submit to treatment, he could not be put on the sick list. If he wasn't on the sick list, there was no riding in the wagons. On the fourth morning, he had motioned her close. "Take me as far as you can today," he whispered. "Then if I die, dig a hole and put me in it."

Frantic, she had sought out Josh, who had immediately gone for Tom Williams. The big sergeant listened, nodded once, then turned and walked away. Half an hour later, as they were starting breakfast, he was back, rolling a large pork barrel along with him. He also carried a small bottle of liquid in his pocket. "Sister Ingalls," he said, "one more day of treatment, and your husband will no longer be with us. Yet we can't risk having the good doctor find out that Brother Ingalls is still sick and not being treated. So I have a suggestion."

"What?"

"He's already experiencing discomfort," Williams went on. "What I am about to propose won't change that, but it will change the form it takes."

Rebecca and Josh were listening intently. "We are willing to try anything to escape the doctor's poison," Rebecca said.

The sergeant held up a small bottle. "I was able to purchase some quinine this morning from those trappers that came in last night from Bent's Fort. This will do better for the ague than any calomel and arsenic." He turned and thumped the barrel. "It will be cramped, but it's a place to hide."

It was such a unique idea that Rebecca had clapped her hands and laughed aloud. Josh just stared, then slowly began to nod.

It had worked perfectly. When it was time for the battalion to roll out, they gave Derek his blanket and put him inside the barrel, which was now inside the wagon. He had to sit with his knees jammed up against his face and his head bent down a little, but he fit. Several times during the day, making sure that the wagon flap was closed and that neither Lieutenant Smith nor Doctor Sanderson was nearby, Rebecca would pry off the lid and give Derek quinine and water. Once they reached camp and had the tents pitched, Josh and Sergeant Williams would lift Derek out and carry him to his bed. Josh answered for him at roll call each morning.

The change was immediate and dramatic. By the end of the first day, he was coherent again. By the third morning, he got himself into and out of the barrel. After five days in hiding, the barrel was returned and Derek began to walk alongside the wagon for short distances, riding on the wagon seat beside Sergeant Williams only when he had to. The last three days, he had started marching with the men again. Whenever Sanderson rode by, Derek had made a point of calling out to him so that the doctor could see for himself that Derek was better.

"It's so good to see you eating again, Derek," Rebecca commented.

"It feels so good to be up once more." He grinned. "And out of that barrel."

"Thank heavens for that barrel," she said fervently.

"Yes. If it weren't—"

There was a shout and they both turned their heads. Josh was running toward them with the two Ingalls boys racing along at his side.

Derek and Rebecca both stood. For a moment there was concern, but then they saw that the three were excited but not frightened. As the three of them rushed up, Christopher spurted ahead. "Mama. Papa. There are Mormons in camp."

"Mormons?" Derek said with a smile. "We're all Mormons, son."

"No, new Mormons."

Derek gave Josh a questioning look. He smiled. "You know that group of government teamsters that rode in this evening?"

"Yes."

"Well, we just found out there are seven Latter-day Saints traveling with them. There's to be a meeting at Captain Hunt's tent in just a few minutes."

Captain Jefferson Hunt looked around, letting the last of the people settle down on the ground in front of his tent. When the last ones sat down, he stood up. "Brothers and sisters, we have a surprise for you." He turned and motioned to where seven men stood together in a small circle. "Brother Brown, why don't you come forward. You can explain your situation better than I can." As one of the seven stepped forward, Hunt turned back to the assembled Saints. "Let me introduce Brother John Brown, originally from Illinois but lately from Mississippi."

Brown was a lean man with a sharp face and an angular nose. His beard was thick and bushy. His face was tanned deeply by the sun. His eyes were dark, and sparkled with energy. "Brothers and sisters," he began in a deep, pleasant voice, "my name is John Brown. Like you, I am a member of The Church of Jesus Christ of Latter-day Saints."

The people looked at each other in surprise. A Mormon out here in the middle of nowhere?

"My brethren and I are on our way back to Mississippi to get our families. This spring, under the direction of Brother Brigham Young, I was asked to put together a company of our people and head west. President Young suggested that we not detour up to Nauvoo but rather go straight to Independence and then westward along the Oregon Trail until we caught up with the main body of the Saints. This we did. Then in early July, at a place called Ash Hollow, we met some trappers going east, back to the States. They had come from Oregon. You can imagine our dismay when we asked them how far behind our people we were and they told us that there was no group of Mormons out ahead of us."

He paused, his mouth pulling down with the memory of that day. "We didn't know what to do. We talked about wintering at Fort Laramie, but then a trapper by the name of Reshaw told us about a settlement on the Arkansas River called Fort Pueblo. He said it was of a reasonable climate and that we could buy corn there.

"After much discussion, we decided to wait out the winter there. Next spring, when President Young and our people start west, we'll go back up to Fort Laramie and meet them, then continue on west with them to our final destination."

One of the men raised his hand. "Where is this Pueblo from here?"

"On past Bent's Fort. We left there on the first of September. Today is what? the twelfth?"

Several nodded.

"So Pueblo is twelve days from here, probably a little more if you're traveling with wagons. By the way, is there anyone here by the name of Steed or Ingalls?"

Derek and Josh both started, then raised their hands. "I'm Derek Ingalls. This is my nephew Joshua Steed."

Brown seemed a little surprised, then smiled. "Know a couple by the name of Peter and Kathryn Ingalls?"

Derek leaped to his feet. "Yes. Peter's my brother."

Brother Brown seemed pleased. "Well, you'll be interested to know that we met them near Fort Laramie." He quickly told them how Peter had sought them out and asked if they would take Kathryn with them, then rode on west with the emigrant company. When Brown finished, he smiled. "Did you know that Kathryn is in a family way?"

Rebecca cried out. "Really?"

"In about four more months, I think. She was a delight to us. She has already started a small school for our children."

Captain Hunt spoke up. "Originally our plan was to go to Bent's Fort, but now that General Kearny has captured Santa Fe, our orders are to march directly there. Otherwise, you might have been able to work out a way to see her."

Rebecca stood now, smiling happily. "Brother Brown, I'm sure there are going to be a lot of invitations for supper tonight, but we would be most pleased if you would come and sup with us. I've still got a pot of stew on the fire and a pan of grits just waiting for someone with a big enough hunger."

John Brown inclined his head, smiling back at her. "My brethren can accept those other invitations. I would be pleased to join with you. I suspect we have a lot to talk about."

Only five of the ten teamsters who had volunteered to go to Nauvoo to rescue the poor Saints were ready by Monday morning, but Brigham didn't want them to delay further. The rest would follow when they could.

As Joshua checked the yoke on his oxen and the chains which were fastened to the wagon tongue, Caroline watched him silently. When he finished, he patted the horses' noses, then came over to where she was. "I don't want to leave you," he said.

She stepped up to him and laid her head against his chest. "If it were under other circumstances, I wouldn't want you to either. But I think we both know that this is what the Lord wants."

He nodded. "Evidently. I don't know if we can convince Carl to come with us, but at least we'll be there to help them if they need us."

"I'm so proud of you," Caroline said, looking up at him.

He seemed a little surprised. "Why?"

"For being close to the Spirit." There was a teasing smile. "This is the same man who once threatened to leave me if I joined the Church."

"I never said that."

"Close to it," she retorted.

He shook his head, then pulled her close again. "I said a lot of foolish things back then, but I was never crazy enough to say I would leave you."

"No," she murmured. And that was true. They had experienced

rocky times because of their differing views about the Church, but there had never been any question about his loving her.

"Well, the rest of the family is over there wondering what we're doing. I'd better go."

He tapped the near ox on the shoulder. "Go, boy," he urged. They moved forward to where Nathan had his wagon ready and the rest of the family was waiting.

As Joshua's wagon pulled in behind Nathan's, Solomon and Matthew came over. "Looks like you're ready," Matthew said, with some longing in his voice.

"We are," Joshua answered.

"Are you sure all four of us shouldn't be going?"

Joshua laid his hand on his youngest brother's shoulder. "No, I'm not, Matthew. But I know this. It will probably take us a month or more for the round-trip. If we wait until mid or late October to start building our cabins, that will not bode well for us. And you're the carpenter, remember? It's not that we don't want you along, it's just that you are needed here."

Matthew held up his hands. "I know, I know. I was just grousing a little."

"I understand. We'll tell Melissa why you didn't come."

"You just bring them back with you," Solomon said.

Nathan nodded slowly. "We're certainly going to try, but I don't have high hopes. Not with Carl feeling as he does."

"Ready," Joshua said.

"Then let's roll them out. The others are probably at the ferry by now."

"Rebecca. I need to ask you a question."

She turned onto her side so that she faced him. They spoke softly so as not to wake the children. "What?"

"Lieutenant Smith has decided to send a detachment of men to Pueblo."

"He has?" That rocked her. Rumors had been rife in camp for the past two days that their martinet commanding officer wanted to get rid of some of the sick men and, more important, the women and children.

"He's assigned Captain Higgins to take command of the detachment. There will be ten of the sickest men sent along with several of the wives and children. He's calling it the family detachment."

"Colonel Allen promised that we wouldn't be split up."

He sighed. "I know. Levi Hancock explained that to Lieutenant Smith, but it got him nowhere. Colonel Allen is dead. The original plan was for us to meet up with General Kearny at Bent's Fort, so Kearny ordered all of our supplies to go there. Now that he's conquered Santa Fe and we're going straight there, we have to bypass Bent's Fort, which means we are short on rations."

"Are you one of the sick they plan to send?" she asked quietly.

"No."

"Then I'm not going either."

"Rebecca, Kathryn is at Pueblo. It would be safe there."

"I'm not going, Derek. Not without you."

"Listen, Rebecca. It could become very difficult traveling now."

"Are you going to Pueblo?" she asked again.

"Rebecca, you have—"

"Then it's settled." She reached out and touched his mouth with her fingertips, letting him know that it really was settled.

By Tuesday, the fifteenth of September, the "Battle of Nauvoo" was over. A committee of citizens from Quincy had come to the city, just as they had during the hostilities of 1845, and negotiated with both sides to see if they could find a way to peace.

Triumphant, Thomas Brockman, the commander of the opposing forces, set down his demands for an end to the conflict. It was more an ultimatum than a proposal. The "posse," as he insisted on calling his forces, still had numerous arrest warrants for various Nauvoo citizens, Mormon and non-Mormon alike. Those warrants would be set aside and there would be no destruction of either persons or property, on the conditions that the citizens surrender their arms and that all Mormons, with the exception of a committee of five men and their families who were authorized to dispose of properties, be out of the city within five days.

By that time, Colonel Johnson, who had fallen critically ill during the battle, had turned the command over to William Cutler and Daniel H. Wells. Though many of the citizens were furious with the harsh demands and wanted to fight on, Wells urged them to accept the offer. They were heavily outnumbered, he pointed out. Sooner or later they would be defeated and have to give up anyway. If they did it now, lives could be spared.

But it was William Cutler who finally convinced them. He stood slowly after Wells had finished and looked around. "Brethren," he said in a dejected tone, "it is reasonable that we leave Nauvoo. Not only for the reasons Brother Wells has so clearly stated, but also because the time has come for us to depart. God has called upon us to go, and most of our brethren and sisters have already done so. If we refuse to follow his command, then perhaps he will let the mob loose on us so that we are at last driven out. Not that they will get any glory for it. Someday they will have to suffer for the wrongs they have committed against God's people. Let us go. I hope the day is coming when we shall no longer have to suffer from the mobs as we have done here."

Carl Rogers, thoroughly shattered by the knowledge of how desperately wrong he had been in refusing to leave, lifted his hand and asked for an amendment. He wanted a guarantee that the sick and the helpless would be protected. When that was agreed to, he raised his hand in favor when the vote was called.

The next morning there were some brief skirmishes, but shortly after noon both sides agreed to sign the treaty. Hostilities were to cease immediately. The Saints would begin preparations for their final departure. The following day the forces under the command of Thomas Brockman would be allowed to enter the city uncontested.

When word came to the Spartan Band that the treaty had been signed, Carl Rogers surrendered his rifle to one of the members of the Quincy committee, then immediately turned around and started for his home.

Melissa stopped rocking and looked at Carl. He saw her, but went right on folding up Mary Melissa's bedding into a tight bundle. "We can't do this, Carl," she finally said.

"I don't think we have a choice."

"Carl, you can see how sick she is. If we try to move her—"

His head snapped up. "Melissa!" The sharpness of his tone stopped her. "I've got some money hidden," he said more softly now. "Once we get across the Mississippi, we'll go downriver to Keokuk. Then we can buy tickets to St. Louis."

"What happened to Peoria?" she said. She hadn't meant to sound bitter, but it had an edge to it when it came out. She saw him visibly flinch and was instantly sorry. "I'm sorry, Carl. I didn't mean that. I know you tried to get us out."

"But I didn't, did I?"

"I'm sorry, Carl. I'm just so worried about Mary Melissa."

"As I am, but I am also worried about that mob, Melissa. Maybe they'll honor the conditions of the treaty, but Brockman is a barbarian. And he leads a whole battalion of savages. We have got to be ready to move immediately if they decide not to honor their word."

"I know," Melissa said meekly, looking down at her sleeping daughter. For several days she had been flushed and hot. Now she was pale and listless, refusing to eat or drink anything. To Melissa, that was even more frightening. The only time she slept now was when Melissa rocked her in her arms.

Suddenly Carl cocked his head, listening.

"What?" Melissa asked.

He didn't answer, but got up and went to the window and opened it. Now it came clearly to them, and it sent instant chills up and down both of their backs. Across the tops of the houses, looking up Mulholland, Carl saw the enemy that he had fought so bitterly for the last week marching triumphantly down Mulholland Street toward them. But there was no kind of order. The men were like a thousand banshees, yelling, whooping, hollering, shrieking, firing off their weapons into the air. It was the most horrible sound Melissa had ever heard, and she pulled the baby closer to her instinctively.

"Here they come," Carl said tightly, and then he shut the window again and returned to his packing with renewed determination. After almost a full minute, he looked up. "That settles it, Melissa. We're going, and we're going now."

Melissa didn't say anything. She just nodded and kept on rocking the baby, singing to her softly now.

When they reached the ferry landing at the end of Parley Street, the riverbank was jammed with people. There were only a few who had wagons or carts. The rest were people with nothing but what they carried on their backs. Some had small handcarts. One or two had a child's wagon piled high with bundles. The lack of wagons was a blessing in a way. That meant the ferry could take that many more people on each trip. Even then, Carl's heart sank when he saw the number waiting. It would take until long after dark to get them all across.

He strode down the line and went up to the ferryman. "Look," he said, "I can see that you have a very difficult challenge here, but I've got a little baby that is desperately ill. Is there any way we can get her across before it gets dark and turns cold?"

The captain of the flatboat straightened slowly. He looked very tired. "Do you know how many other sick people there are here? And most of them are women and children too."

Carl didn't fight him. "I can see that. We're not asking to be first. Just to get across before dark."

The man sighed, then pointed to a group on the other side of the landing. "Bring 'em up here," he said. "If the baby's as sick as you say, we'll see what we can do."

"Thank you."

By five-thirty, Carl was getting worried. The air had already noticeably cooled, and Melissa had a blanket over Mary Melissa's face. For the past two hours Carl had been calculating the time it took for each trip of the ferry—about twenty-five minutes for the trip over, fifteen to come back across. There were still more than a hundred people, and most of them had been there before him and Melissa. At forty to forty-five people per load, it would probably be an hour, possibly an hour and a half, before it would be their turn. He looked up at the sky. They had maybe another hour before sundown. It was going to be very close.

He turned as there was a stir behind them. What he saw made his blood run chill. Down Parley Street a group of some fifteen or sixteen militiamen was approaching. A few were on horseback. Most swaggered along with rifles over their shoulders. Carl shrank back, pulling Melissa with him deeper into the crowd. "Don't look," he cautioned. "Just keep your eyes on the ferry."

Word went quickly down the line about what was happening. The men had come to search for contraband weapons, or at least that was the ostensible reason. In reality they had come to add one last shot of misery with which to afflict the escaping refugees. They ripped wagons apart piece by piece, throwing everything into the dust and leaving it for the owners to repack. They shouted at the men, leered at the women, mocked the little children. They crowed about their great victory, promised to thoroughly desecrate the temple, and vowed to kill any Mormons who were left in the city by the following day.

No one contradicted them. Most would not even meet their gaze, which only caused them to roar with laughter.

Suddenly four of them split off from the rest and came walking to where the group stood next to the ferry dock. At the moment, the ferry was about halfway across the river, coming back for another load.

"And what have we here?" the first man sneered, looking with contempt on the miserable group that stood before him.

The ferryman's assistant—perhaps his son—spoke up. "These are the sickest and the weakest. We're taking them across first."

"You a Mormon?" another one demanded, speaking to the boy.

"Nope," came the easy reply. "We're just making money off them."

The man laughed, pleased by the boy's pluck. Then he turned to the people. "They don't look that sick to me."

"They look like Mormons," another one exclaimed. "That's pretty sick, ain't it?"

They guffawed.

"Don't look at them," Carl whispered to Melissa. "Keep your head down."

"You there!" the first man said, jabbing his finger at an elderly man. "You a Mormon?"

"Yes, sir," the man said, his voice trembling. Carl peered between the heads of the people, careful to watch if any of the men turned in his direction. The elderly man was shrunken and bent. He looked to be in his seventies, maybe older.

"It's Brother Stiles," Melissa whispered. "He used to come in the store all the time."

"Why you running with yo' tail between yo' legs?" the man from Carthage said insolently.

"I was told I had to leave," the old man replied, looking very frightened.

The man who seemed to be the leader of this band of four turned to his companions. "Now, who do you think might do a cruel thing like that?"

They hooted. "Probably them Mormons," one of them exclaimed. "I hear the Mormons are driving out their own people down here."

The others roared at the joke. "I've got an idea," the leader said, brightening suddenly. "We're not sure this man is a Mormon or not. What say we baptize him, just to be sure?"

"No," Stiles began, half stuttering in terror. "I am a Mormon."

In one swift movement the leader swung his rifle off his shoulder, unclipped the bayonet, and stuck it into its place next to the muzzle. He stuck the bayonet point within an inch of the old man's chest. "You ready to be baptized a Mormon, old man?" he cawed, half giggling to himself at his own joke.

"No, oh please. No."

"Go," the leader shouted, angry now. He prodded him with the tip of the blade, pushing him toward the water's edge. "Mormons believe in baptism by immersion, you know."

Three additional militiamen, seeing what was happening, broke off and came to join in the fun. They were all shouting, encouraging their leader on.

The old man was begging now, but each time he stopped moving, the sharp point of the bayonet pushed him on again. When he reached the water he stopped, trembling visibly. One of the other men stepped to him and lifted a foot. Carl jerked forward, but Melissa caught his arm. "No, Carl!" she hissed. "You can't."

Carl stopped, torn. The man kicked out and Thomas Stiles was shoved hard. His feet hit the water and he tripped. He fell headlong into the river, sending up a great splash. He came up on all fours, spluttering. The leader, laughing merrily, stepped into the river beside him and planted a foot on the old man's back. He lifted both arms, holding his rifle high above his head. "I hereby baptize this man—" He bent down. "What's your name, old man?"

"Thomas Stiles," the man gasped.

"I hereby baptize Thomas Stiles in the name of Mr. Thomas

Sharp, one of our esteemed leaders and one of the best of all the Mormon-haters." With that, he shoved down hard, pushing Stiles under the water again.

"That's enough!" Carl shouted, breaking free from Melissa's grasp and pushing through the crowd.

All of the men spun around, lifting their rifles. Carl walked past them and into the river. He took Stiles by the arm and helped him up. "Are you all right?" he asked.

The old man nodded, wiping at his dripping face. Carl helped him out of the river and gave him a gentle shove back toward the group.

The baptizer stood for a moment, too shocked to believe what he had just seen. But as Carl started out of the water, the bayonet swung up and pressed against his shirt. "Not so fast, mister."

"Leave him alone," Carl said evenly. "Can't you see he's old and sick?"

The man was incredulous. "Am I hearing this correctly? You're telling me what to do?"

Carl tried to go past him but the bayonet pressed firmly now.

"Tell me who you are, Mister Crusader."

Carl looked up, aware that he was on very dangerous ground now, but still quite calm. "My name is Carl Rogers."

"You a Mormon?" one of the others demanded.

He shook his head. "No, and I don't ever plan to be."

"Well, well," the leader said, peering at him more closely now. "Is that a fact? So why are you down here waiting for a ferry?"

"I have a very sick child."

"Aw," one of the men said with mock gravity. "Now, ain't that too bad?"

Suddenly an eighth man came striding up. As Carl looked up, his heart dropped. This was Ronald Granville. He had once been a member of the new citizens committee but had broken off his tie to that group when they refused to surrender to the anti-Mormon demands for surrender. "Do you know who this is?" he asked the leader.

"Yeah," the other one sneered. "He is the big and brave Mr. Carl Rogers."

"He's also a member of the new citizens committee," Granville said. "And if I'm not mistaken, he was one of the Spartan Band."

At that moment Carl knew he was in serious trouble. Word was already out in the city that the mob was looking for those non-Mormons who had fought against them. But the Spartan Band had caused the mob the most trouble and were the most hated by them.

"That right, Rogers?" the leader said ominously.

"Of course it's right," Granville shouted. "This man probably killed some of our men."

Moving too fast for Carl to respond, the leader of the men flipped his rifle around and slammed the butt hard into Carl's side. He screamed in pain, stumbling backward. Two more men waded in, rifle butts flying. Carl threw up his arms to protect his face and turned his back. He felt something snap as there was a terrible blow to his side. He went down, trying to reach out and break his fall. By then he was in the river and went under face first. It was such a shock that he gasped and took in a lungful of muddy water. He came up, gasping and choking and spitting out water.

Somewhere far off he heard a woman's scream. He stumbled to his feet and went down again as another rifle butt struck him, sending searing pain through his body.

"Leave him alone!"

Through the haze that filled his brain and seemed to block his vision, Carl saw Melissa, the baby in one arm, throw herself at the back of the soldier, flailing at him with her free fist. With a roar, the man swung around, grabbed her hand, and yanked it hard, pulling her in the direction of Carl. Totally unprepared for that, Melissa shot forward, stumbled once, and then went down. The baby flew out of her arms.

There were several screams and two women raced to the water. One grabbed the baby just as it started to sink. The other helped pull Melissa to her feet.

"Let her go," the leader roared, starting to raise his rifle. "If she wants to be with her husband, then leave her be."

"No!" another voice shouted. "You leave 'em alone."

The leader turned in surprise. It was the boy on the ferry dock.

"Stay out of this, boy."

Then a deeper voice boomed out from behind them. "I'd say *you'd* better stay out of it, mister."

They whirled. The ferry was now about twenty or thirty yards offshore. The ferryman stood with his feet planted and a double-barreled twelve-gauge shotgun held firmly in both hands. It was pointed straight at the militiaman's chest. "I'd say you boys have had about enough fun for one day."

"This ain't your affair," another one of the men growled, but he stood very still.

"And this ain't part of your treaty," the ferry operator snapped. "What kind of animals are you, throwing old men and babies into the water? Now, get out of here." He lifted the shotgun and blasted off one of the barrels. The men jumped and started backing away hastily. "Git!" he shouted, "or you'll be growing a new crop of hair on your chest."

They turned and ran.

As the boy and his father pulled the ferryboat into the dock, a man and two women rushed down and took Carl by the arms. As they lifted him up he screamed out in pain. They stopped and others rushed in to help. They lifted him gently as he bit down on his lip to stop from screaming again. A few feet away, Melissa took the baby from one of the women who had helped her out of the river. "Is she all right?" Melissa cried.

"Yes. But her clothes are wet." The flatboat bumped up against the dock and the ferryman hopped out. "Get aboard," he barked. "Your husband is in great danger. They're arresting all the non-Mormons who fought against them."

"My baby," Melissa said.

"We'll find her dry clothes once we're under way," he replied more gently now. "We've got to hurry." He stepped to those who were holding Carl. "Easy, now," he said. "Get him onto the ferry."

Chapter Notes

The story of hiding a man in a barrel to escape Doctor Sanderson's treatment actually happened to Sergeant Luther Tuttle of Company D (see *MB*, pp. 51–52).

John Brown and six other men from the Mississippi company left Fort Pueblo on the first day of September and headed east to get their families. They caught up with a group of forty government teamsters going to the States. They were traveling with that group when they met the Mormon Battalion on 12 September near where the Cimarron Cutoff turned off the Santa Fe Trail. (See "Pioneer Journeys, p. 808; *MB*, p. 53.)

The details of the Battle of Nauvoo as they unfolded during the first half of September 1846 are summarized in several excellent sources (see, for example, *Church History in the Fulness of Times* [Salt Lake City: The Church of Jesus Christ of Latter-day Saints, 1989], pp. 317–19; *SW*, pp. 138–71; "Battle of Nauvoo Was the Final Chapter in the Expulsion from the Beloved City," *Church News*, 14 September 1996, pp. 11–12). Sadly, a day or two before the treaty was signed William Anderson, captain of the Spartan Band, was killed when he was shot from ambush. Even more tragic, his fifteen-year-old son was killed the same day. These were two of the three fatalities that occurred among the defenders during the battle. (See *SW*, p. 160.) It is not known exactly how many of the mob forces were killed.

Once the treaty was signed, in a pattern typical of other confrontations the Saints had had with mobs, the anti-Mormons largely ignored the conditions of the treaty. The "posse" immediately began to ransack the town, including the wagons and belongings of those waiting to cross the river. Thomas Stiles, an elderly man, was "baptized" as depicted here. Ironically, Thomas Sharp, the editor of the *Warsaw Signal*, was the name used in baptizing Stiles. It was Sharp who, more than any other man, was responsible for stirring up anti-Mormon sentiment to the point that it led to the Martyrdom. (See *SW*, p. 174.)

Edwin Woolley, who was in Nauvoo at the time of its surrender, wrote: "Nauvoo is now like Babylon of old, a sink of iniquity, a place of foul spirits, and a gathering place for the damned. All that beauty, all the grandeur and all the loveliness that once was there has fled, it has gone and gone forever. Desolation and the cries of the damned are the only sounds that you hear, even in the hours of the night that should be still and quiet." (Quoted in *SW*, p. 182.)

Chapter Twenty-Seven

By mid-September, Yerba Buena had taken on a considerably different look. The hills that rose upwards from the west shore of San Francisco Bay were still largely untouched by any settlement, except for the very north end not far from the entrance of the Golden Gate.

As the small whaling boat that they were on passed Yerba Buena Island out in the middle of the bay and turned its nose directly toward the village of Yerba Buena on the far shore, Will Steed stood up, steadying himself against the single mast. When they had sailed into the bay on July thirty-first, there had been the Presidio (or the deserted fort on the bluffs), the new customshouse, and the old barracks. Scattered around those main buildings were a few small houses, some thrown-together shacks, and some willow-and-stick shelters. And that was it. Now at least two dozen homes were either newly completed or under construction. The hillside was still dotted with the white squares of tents, but a good many of the Saints who had come in on the

Brooklyn had now found permanent shelter for the winter.

"Beautiful sight, isn't it?"

Will turned. Sam Brannan had come over to join him.

"I've only seen one to equal it, and that's Hong Kong Harbor in China. But San Francisco Bay matches it." Will had expected that when they came out of the Sacramento River and reached the bay that it would be shrouded in fog, but instead it was perfectly clear. A stiff breeze off the ocean had polished the sky to an unbelievable brightness. The bay was a deep blue dotted with whitecaps, and all of it framed by surrounding hills of green.

"We've got to convince Brother Brigham that this is the place for his Saints."

Will turned in surprise. There had never been any plan to make California the final stopping place when they had left. When did this notion come into Brannan's mind?

The leader of their colony saw the look and rushed on. "I don't mean here in the bay area necessarily, though this is a wonderful place for growth too. But you saw the San Joaquin Valley, Will. It's a site to rival Kirtland or Nauvoo." He gave Will a strange look. "I even wonder if it might not be the sight for the New Jerusalem." He rushed on before Will could answer. "You could settle ten thousand people here and do very well."

"But . . . ," Will began. And then he stopped. The site they had explored had been breathtaking. It was near where the Stanislaus River joined the San Joaquin River. There a broad natural valley lay at the base of the Sierra foothills. The land was almost perfectly level for as far as the eye could see looking north and south, and the few locals living there claimed that the soil was rich and very deep. They saw elk, antelope, deer, and signs of bear. There were thousands of geese and ducks along the rivers. And the climate was like that of southern Italy or some parts of Asia where Will had been. He didn't think for a moment that the New Jerusalem would be built in California, but he did have to admit that if you were looking for a site for the Holy City, you might give serious consideration to the place they had seen.

Brannan went on. "I tell you, San Francisco Bay is going to become a great seaport someday. California is going to become the new center of the nation. And those of us who are here at the beginning stand to prosper greatly as it does so."

At that, Will nodded. As a sailor he had instantly seen the potential of this wonderful natural bay, with its narrow gate and coastal mountains that protected it from Pacific storms. In fact, he was so impressed with its potential that the first kernel of an idea was starting to form in his own mind. And yet he couldn't help but remind Sam Brannan of something else. "I thought Brother Brigham's plan was to find a place in the Rocky Mountains, in what they call the Great Basin."

Brannan snorted in disgust. "That's because he hasn't seen California. The potential here is tremendous, Will. Can't you feel that?"

"Yes, I can," he said, and he meant it. But that didn't mean he thought—

"What did you think of New Hope?" Brannan cut in again.

"New Hope?" Will asked.

"Oh, that's right. I haven't told you. That's what I plan to call our new settlement up there. New Hope. Don't you like that?"

Will smiled, nodding. Sam Brannan should have been a promoter, and Will didn't necessarily mean that in a negative way. Brannan was always thinking, always dreaming, always looking to the future and seeing what might be done. "I think that is an appropriate name, considering who and where we are."

"And you won't join us?" Brannan said in disappointment.

Will shook his head. "I'm not a farmer, Brother Brannan. I'm a sailor, and if not that, probably a merchant."

"Well," the leader of their colony boomed right back, "there's a place for that as well."

"I think so too."

There was a narrowing of his brows. "Remember the covenant, though. You'll still be part of that, even if you don't go to New Hope with us."

"I remember," Will said. After they had left Honolulu, Brannan had gathered all of the adults in their group and proposed that they form a communal compact. All would work for the common good for the first three years. And Sam Brannan, of course, would serve as president of the group. Some had been irritated by that, fearing that it put Brannan in the position of governor and possible dictator, but eventually they had signed the compact, seeing the wisdom in pooling their labors for a time.

"So tell me what you're thinking, Will. Have you got any plans?"

Will hedged a little. "Well, first thing is to get the baby here safely. Then Alice and I need to sit down and really talk about what we want to do."

"Isn't much employment in Yerba Buena yet," Brannan said, pushing a little. "Taking in laundry from the sailors, doing odd jobs for the naval officers from time to time, unloading an occasional ship. By spring maybe, but not now."

Will didn't rise to the bait. "I know. That's one of our concerns too. That's why we need to talk."

"So," Alice asked, "are you thinking of going upriver once the baby's here?"

Will sighed. They were speaking in low voices. They were still living in the customshouse, which had been converted into living quarters by hanging blankets and putting up thin partitions made from packing crates. "I think so. I wish I could have taken you with me, Alice. It's beautiful country."

"I wish I could have gone." She smiled and reached out and took his hand. "But I'm glad I didn't. I thought the baby was coming three nights ago."

"Really?" His eyes lit up at the thought that it might finally be the time.

"Really," she laughed. "But I just told this boy he had to wait for his papa."

"There's no question in your mind, is there? It's going to be a boy."

She laughed softly again. "Of course."

"I won't be disappointed if it's a girl," he said.

"Nor will I, but it's not."

Will nodded, his thoughts already back to the other question. "Captain John Sutter is looking for men to help him build a gristmill near the fort. Once that's done he wants to build a sawmill about forty miles upriver. Several of our people have agreed to hire on with him."

She seemed a little surprised. "And is that what you'd like to do?"

He shook his head slowly. "Not permanently." He was lost in thought now. "Sam Brannan bought an old whaling boat while we were on the San Joaquin River, and we converted it into a small sailing boat. We sailed it all the way here—down the San Joaquin to the Sacramento River, then all the way to San Francisco Bay. We could have taken a much larger vessel if we chose to. The river is that big."

Now she began to understand. "So you're thinking . . ." She was priming the pump a little.

"Captain Sutter needs supplies. Right now he brings in his own, but he doesn't like to do it. He'd be happy to pay someone else."

"Did you actually get to meet Sutter?" Alice asked.

"Yes. We stopped at his fort for a day." Now he looked a little sheepish. "I talked to him about possible employment."

"You did?"

"Alice, if I could work for him during the winter, I might be able to earn enough to buy my own boat. Then I could take supplies upriver from Yerba Buena and bring their farm products back down here. They're growing a lot of wheat and corn. And if Brother Brannan gets New Hope up and going, they'll need supplies and have farm products to ship out too. I think we could make a wonderful living."

"For as long as we're here," she said softly.

That startled him a little. For a moment he had totally forgotten that they were only waiting for word from Brigham Young as to where to go. "Yes," he amended, "for as long as we're here."

Alice felt bad that she had deflated his excitement. "The famous Sutter's Fort that we've all heard about, what was it like?"

He shrugged. "A typical fort, I guess. It's pretty big, though. I'd say it's about the size of a city block back in Nauvoo. It has high adobe walls which are whitewashed so you can see it from a great distance. It sits near the American River, just a short distance before it merges with the Sacramento. Inside, built right into the walls, there are shops, barracks, granaries, stables, and so forth. In the center is a large, open courtyard for the animals."

"Were there any women?"

He nodded. "Quite a few Spanish and Indians, not many whites yet. All around the fort Sutter has farmland, and he hires some of the local Indians—Miwoks, they call them—as well as some of the Spanish families who didn't flee when the Americans took over."

"I'd like to see it."

He leaned forward, taking both of her hands. "If you think all of this is a good idea, we can leave as soon as you and the baby are strong enough."

"Once you get the boat, would you live down here or up there?"

He responded without hesitation, for he had thought a lot about that on the way back down. "Up there. Probably near Sutter's Fort. I like it much better than here."

"Good. Having been raised in St. Louis, I don't think I'm going to get used to this ocean climate very soon. I'm always cold." She squeezed his hands. "I like the idea, Will. I don't think you'll be happy farming."

At that he frowned.

"What?"

"And what am I going to sail in the middle of the Great Salt Lake Valley?"

By the last week in September, Winter Quarters had already begun to take shape as a city. As Mary Ann walked along the streets—some churned into obvious roads by the wagons and carts, others still only marked off by stakes hammered into the ground—she was amazed at how quickly the settlement was developing. Cabins already filled many lots. They were simple and small—crude, the less generous might say—and many still needed chinking and their sod roofs put on. But it was nevertheless remarkable. It had been just two weeks ago that the Twelve had selected the site.

And what a beautiful site it was, she thought. It was on the second bluff from the river, on an area that was mostly flat and that was about fifty or sixty feet above the level of the Missouri. That was good. When the spring runoff came, there would be no need to move to higher ground. The trees along the river were turning yellow and orange now, and some of the shrubs were a brilliant red. The site was about a mile long and perhaps half a mile across at its widest spot. It was shaped a little like a gourd, narrow at the top—the north—then widening at the south, or the fat part of the gourd. At each end there were small brooks of clean, cold water, saving them having to go to the river for their daily needs.

She was headed for the northern creek now, where Matthew was working on the gristmill Brigham had ordered built there. She hurried along, feeling the dampness in the air and suspecting that it would rain before long.

Matthew was on a ladder, helping to put up the framework for the eastern wall. When he turned to get some more nails, he saw her coming towards him. A little surprised, he immediately climbed down and went to greet her. "Hello, Mama."

"Hello, son." She looked up, shading her eyes as she examined what would prove to be one of the larger buildings in their new city. "It's coming along nicely."

"Yes. We're making good progress." He gave her a sharp look. "Is everything all right?"

Her eyes dropped, and after a moment she shook her head. "There's news from Nauvoo."

"Oh!" He took her by the arm and they started to walk slowly.

"Brother Daniel Wells and William Cutler arrived in a light buggy last night."

"But—" He stopped, trying to remember if he was correct. "I thought the last report said they were in charge of the resistance there."

"They were," she said in a low voice. "Nauvoo has surrendered."

He stopped, struck hard by that.

"A battle raged for several days. The mob forces had artillery and outnumbered our people by about ten to one."

"Nauvoo is gone?" He was having trouble accepting the harshness of that.

"It's in the hands of our enemies. They're looting everything. They've turned the temple into a pigsty." She bit her lip and looked away. "All of our people have been driven out."

"What about Melissa?" he cried. "Is there any word about her and Carl?"

"I don't know," she answered, her voice hollow. "Brother Cutler and Brother Wells are meeting with the Twelve now, giving them a full report. I haven't had a chance to talk with them."

"When?" Matthew demanded, his mind racing now. "When did all this happen?"

"I'm not sure. The treaty giving up the city was signed on the sixteenth. I guess almost everyone was gone by that time or the next day."

He felt sick. Nathan and Joshua had left with the first five wagons on the fourteenth, almost two weeks ago. But if all of this happened about that same time, that did not bode well. Wells and Cutler had made the journey across Iowa in less than two weeks. The heavier wagons could take half again that long, more if the roads were bad.

"Where are our people, did they say?"

"They're in a camp at Montrose, on the west side of the river."

"Then all we can do now is pray," Matthew said solemnly.

Will awoke with a start, coming up on one elbow. Then he realized that it was Alice who was touching him in the darkness. "What?" he said, remembering the night when she had felt something run across her sheets and they had spent the next half hour, along with several of their neighbors, trying to either catch the mouse or rat or drive it out of the customshouse.

"I think it's time," she said.

He thought for a moment. Time for what? to get up? But it was still pitch-black. He was fighting to come out of the fog. He had been so far under and it was like clawing his way back up.

"Will," she said more firmly. "It's time."

Suddenly he sat straight up. "*That* time?" he blurted, fully awake now.

"Yes, Will. You'd better send for the midwife."

He threw back the covers and swung out of the low bed. In moments he had his pants on and was groping for his boots. "Are you all right?"

"I'm fine, Will."

He pulled his shirt on over his head and shoved the tail inside his belt. "I'll hurry," he called as he darted out into the hallway and out the door.

Smiling, she lay back down again. In a moment, the smile disappeared as the next contraction began to build.

It was nearly noon when the girl came running around the back of the customshouse. Will was there puttering on a bench he was making, trying to keep his hands and his head occupied. As soon as he saw her, he leaped up. "Has it come?"

"I don't know. Mama just said to fetch you."

Will raced around the building and went in. The three women who had assisted Alice were still inside when he entered. "Has the baby come?"

The midwife smiled and nodded. "Yes, Will. It's come."

"How is Alice? Is she all right?"

The smile broadened. "It always pleases me to hear that question first," she said to one of the others. "Yes, Alice is fine. Very tired right now, but fine."

"And the baby?" he rushed on. "What is it?"

She looked surprised by the question, then laughed. "But that's not my place to say."

He bolted past them and ran down the hall to his and Alice's room. He hesitated for just a moment, then pushed inside. Alice was sitting up, propped up with a pillow against the wall, with a tiny bundle nestled under one arm. He went to her, his eyes wide with wonder. "Are you all right?"

"I'm fine."

"And the baby?"

"She's fine."

Will stopped. "She? It's a girl?"

Alice watched him closely for any signs of disappointment, then laughed and shook her head. "No, Will, *he's* fine. Come see your son."

"Brethren!" Brigham Young's voice boomed out over the assembly of men waiting under the bowery. Almost instantly the low buzz of voices died and it became quiet.

"Brethren, as you know, three days ago two of our brethren arrived from Nauvoo. They did not bring good news."

Many heads nodded but there was no sound. By now, the news that Daniel Wells and William Cutler brought had spread up and down both sides of the river. And when the call for the meeting came, everyone guessed what it was for.

Matthew looked at Solomon, who only nodded.

"There is much that we could say. In a way it is no surprise to us. For some time now I have been concerned that there was a good deal of suffering among the Saints in Nauvoo, as there has been among us. There are some now languishing in the poor camp in Montrose who did not come because they had neither the means nor the strength. But there are others who should have left long ago but had not the faith to do so. But let us not forget, even now, that the Lord God, who has fed us all the day long, still cares for us. And when the Saints have been chastened enough it will cease."

He stopped and looked around at the men, several hundred strong. His face showed deep lines of weariness, and his shoulders seemed even more stooped than usual. But his voice showed no weakening as it suddenly rose in volume.

"I have never believed the Lord would suffer a general massacre of this people by a mob. If ten thousand men were to come against us, and no other way was open for our deliverance, the earth would swallow them up. As you know, some of our brethren have already started back to help our brethren and sisters, and thanks be to God for that fact. But even ten wagons will not be sufficient to take all who need to come."

He blew out his breath, as though he were reluctant to say what now had to be said. "I know that we are desperately short of manpower here. We have already sent off five hundred of our best men to war. We have already sent ten more east to help our people. I know that we have homes to build, and hay to cut, and meat to salt and dry so that we can see the winter through. I know that there are very few of us whom we can spare."

Now he straightened visibly, and his one hand began to move, giving emphasis to his words. "But what does that matter, brethren? Our brethren and sisters—the poor, the sick, the widows and the orphans, the weak, the destitute—are lying on the west bank of the Mississippi River, waiting for teams and wagons to come and remove them."

Not a sound could be heard beneath the covering over their heads. Every eye was riveted on their leader.

"I would ask that you take your minds back almost a year now.

We were privileged to begin the sacred work of the temple. We were privileged to endow many of you with power and administer the sacred ordinances to you. You made covenants there, my brethren. Sacred covenants. And many of you went into the temple with me and together we raised our hands in a solemn covenant that when the time came for us to leave Nauvoo we would not leave our poor brethren and sisters behind. Just as we did when we were driven from Far West, we solemnly vowed that any who wanted to come, regardless of their means or ability, would be brought. Do you remember that covenant, brethren?"

Now there were several murmurs of assent throughout the group. Matthew was nodding, as was Solomon. Both had been there in the temple and raised their right hands up to sustain Brigham's call. The silence fell again as Brigham surveyed the crowd, his brows lowered and his jaw set. The next came out as a roar of affirmation.

"*Now* is the time for our labor, brethren! Let the fire of the covenant, which you made in the house of the Lord, burn in your hearts like flame unquenchable, till you, either by yourselves or by those whom you delegate, have searched out every man to rise up with his team and go straightway and bring a load of the poor from Nauvoo. We must bring them here or somewhere in the immediate country where they can get work and find shelter for the winter."

He smacked his fist against the table. "*This is a day of action and not of argument*."

As Matthew and Solomon walked back toward their camp, they both were silent. Matthew wasn't sure what Solomon was thinking, but Brigham's words had stirred him deeply. *The fire of the covenant*. He had not thought of it in that way before, but now it did consume him like flame unquenchable.

He looked at Solomon. "What do you think?"

Solomon seemed surprised. "Is there any question about what we must do?"

Matthew nodded slowly. "Even though we don't have the houses completed yet?"

"Those people don't have anything, Matthew. Do we have any choice?"

"No," Matthew answered, pleased that Solomon was one in thought with him. "Let's go tell the family. If possible, I'd like to be on our way first thing in the morning."

Derek walked slowly, letting the others go out ahead. It was just after noon and the sun beat down upon him, making him a little dizzy. Josh was talking earnestly with Sergeant Williams and didn't notice that Derek had fallen behind. Then suddenly Josh stopped, his head turning as he searched for his uncle. When he saw him, he immediately came back to join him.

"Are you all right?"

Derek nodded. "Just tired."

Josh reached up and put his hand on Derek's forehead. The hand felt wonderfully cool to Derek.

Josh gave him a sharp look as he withdrew his hand. "Your fever is starting in again."

It was tempting to deny it, but Derek knew there wasn't much point in it. If this was the typical pattern of fever, chills, and violent shakes, they would know for certain in a few hours.

"Oh, Derek," Josh murmured. "Not again."

"That's what I say." He looked around. "Not a word to anyone until I'm sure, all right?"

Josh pursed his lips, but finally nodded. Up ahead, the column had stopped, probably in response to the small group of riders that had come in from the west a few minutes before. Lieutenant Smith had brought the battalion to a halt, but it was strung out for more than half a mile and Company D was near the tail end. Finally they reached the main body and moved up to join the others.

Lieutenant Smith was pacing up and down beside his horse. The other officers were directly in front of him. Doctor

Sanderson and Lieutenant Dykes were off to one side and slightly behind him. "Men, we've just had a communication from General Kearny."

That was no surprise. As they drew close, Josh had seen that the riders were a group of dragoons. They had to be from Kearny's regiment, which was out ahead of them.

"General Kearny," Smith went on, "is not waiting for us in Santa Fe. He left there on the twenty-fifth of last month."

Derek and Josh looked at each other. General Kearny was obviously an impatient man. He couldn't seem to wait for them anywhere.

"He says we are moving much too slow," the officer went on, clearly not pleased. "He needs us in Santa Fe by the tenth of the month."

That brought instant cries of dismay. Today was October second. They had calculated that Santa Fe was still about two weeks ahead of them.

Smith let the noise die again, then held the letter up in the air, waving it at them angrily. "General Kearny has said that if we are not in Santa Fe on the tenth, he will discharge the battalion and find someone who can give him the help he needs."

Now the surprise and disbelief turned to shock. Discharged? in the middle of Mexico? after only two and a half months of service?

"Men, I am not about to have my command disobey a direct order from our commanding general. We will be in Santa Fe by the tenth of October. Are there any questions?"

Several hands shot up. Smith ignored them. "Good. We will immediately begin our line of march. We will not stop to rest the teams. We will not have supper until we have reached the Red River." He looked around, daring anyone to cross him. When no one spoke, he flicked his hand in the direction of the officers. "See to it. Get those men moving immediately."

Josh Steed gave a low sound of sheer pleasure as he dropped

his other boot and began to massage the bottom of his feet. "Oh my," he groaned, "that feels good."

Derek, who was already lying down with his feet propped up on his knapsack, opened his eyes. "Funny how the simple pleasures change, isn't it?"

"How far did we come today, Papa?" Christopher asked.

"Twenty-seven miles, according to Captain Hunt."

Rebecca hauled herself up wearily, stretching as she held her back. "I know what my back feels like after that far in a wagon. I can't imagine how sore your feet must be."

Josh reached down and peeled of his socks, then continued to knead the muscles with his fingertips.

"Josh?"

"Yes, Benji?"

"You got a big sore."

He turned his foot enough so that he could see the bottom. Sure enough, there on the ball of his foot was a blister nearly half an inch across. "I know, Benji. I can feel it."

"We can't keep up this pace for the next seven days," Derek said. "Command or no command, we're not going to make Santa Fe by the tenth."

"Not unless we can teach mules how to fly," Rebecca agreed.

"Some of the men think Kearny's bluffing," said Josh. "He won't really discharge us. How can he get replacements out here?"

"He can't," Derek said shortly. "But Lieutenant Dykes says you always take Kearny seriously. He says he is a good officer but tougher than a blacksmith's anvil."

Rebecca hooted softly. "Well, maybe if we were that tough, we could make it." Then, softening a little, she looked at Derek. "If we have another march tomorrow like the one we've had today, I think we'd all better go to bed now."

They were up at dawn and on the road before breakfast. There was surprisingly little grumbling, perhaps because they were still exhausted from the previous day. They had gone about six miles when Lieutenant Smith called for a halt near the bank of a creek. While the women began getting a cold breakfast, Smith called for a meeting with all of his officers.

Ten minutes later Derek, Rebecca, and Josh looked up as Sergeant Thomas Williams approached their wagon. "What's the word, Tom?" Derek asked.

"Thought you'd better know. Lieutenant Smith has decided that there is no way that we can make Santa Fe in eight days. He's going to split the company."

"What!" Derek blurted. Josh had also jerked up at that announcement.

"He wants fifty of the strongest men from each company, along with the best teams and wagons, to make a forced march to Santa Fe. The rest will be put under command of Lieutenant Oman and come along as best they can."

"No!" Derek exclaimed. "President Young said that we were to stay together."

"This is not right," Josh said quietly. That surprised them all. Josh was always the last one to criticize, even when there was more than ample cause.

"Well," Williams said reluctantly, "right or not, Josh, you and I have been assigned to go with the advance group." He held up his hand quickly to cut off Josh's protest. "You should know that our officers agree this is the best course of action. We can't risk being discharged."

Josh was deeply disturbed. "So we just leave Derek and Rebecca and the children?"

"We're going," Derek said, trying to stand. He had to close his eyes as a wave of dizziness hit him.

"Sorry, Derek," Williams said sadly. "The determination has already been made. We have no choice but to trust the judgment of our officers." Then there was a rueful smile. "There is one consolation."

"What?" Rebecca asked. She wasn't as upset as Josh and Derek, as long as her family would stay together.

"Doctor Death will be going with the advance group. You'd think he would be required to stay behind with the sick, but with his usual loving care, he's decided he should go ahead."

That stopped Derek. He squinted a little at Williams. "He has?"

Josh groaned. "He'll be with us?"

Williams nodded.

Derek sat back. "Maybe staying in the second group is not so bad after all."

Chapter Notes

John Augustus Sutter, a Swiss pioneer, led a group of white settlers to Mexico in 1839. They settled on the American River about two miles upstream from where it joined the Sacramento River. In return for an oath of loyalty to Mexico, Sutter was given a land grant of fifty thousand acres. He established a fort there and began to farm. He called it New Helvetia, Helvetia being the Latin name for Switzerland, but it quickly came to be known widely as Sutter's Fort. It became the western terminus for the California Trail and an important trading center for the region.

The description of Winter Quarters in late September of 1846 comes from the journal of Hosea Stout (see *SW*, p. 188). The gristmill built by Brigham Young still stands near the river in Florence, Nebraska.

The speech given here by Brigham Young calling his people to go forth and help save the poor Saints back in Montrose is actually part of speeches given on two successive days, 27 and 28 September, one in Winter Quarters and one on the east side of the Missouri River in Council Bluffs. They are combined here for purposes of the novel, but except for a few transitional phrases to help it flow better, these words are the very ones used by Brigham Young to stir his people to action. (See Richard E. Bennett, " 'Dadda, I Wish We Were Out of This Country': The Nauvoo Poor Camps in Iowa, Fall 1846," in Susan Easton Black and William G. Hartley, eds., *The Iowa Mormon Trail: Legacy of Faith and Courage* [Orem, Utah: Helix Publishing, 1997], pp. 162–63.)

On 3 October the Mormon Battalion split into two groups in order to comply with General Kearny's order to reach Santa Fe by 10 October.

Doctor Sanderson went with the advance party, which led Sergeant Daniel Tyler to later write: "The sorrow which they [those in the second group] felt at the loss of friends through having the Battalion divided, was in a great measure compensated by the relief they experienced at being rid of the Doctor's drugs and cursing for a few days. There was a noticeable improvement, too, in most of those who were sick after the Doctor left, so that when they arrived in Santa Fe many of them were convalescent." (*CHMB*, p. 163.)

Chapter Twenty-Eight

Saturday, October 3 — On the California Trail

I have not written for some time, so I shall try to summarize. After crossing the dreaded Salt Desert, we took inventory of our provisions and got confirmation of that which we already feared. We do not have sufficient supplies to see us to California. With no trading posts between here and Sutter's Fort, things are grim. We had no choice but to send two men on ahead to purchase supplies and bring them back to us. Charles Stanton, from New York, is a bachelor traveling with the Jacob Donner family. William McCutchen, who has a wife and baby girl, joined us at Fort Bridger. They are from Missouri.

We camped at Pilot Peak springs for a time to rest the teams but could wait no longer. There was snow on the higher mountain peaks and dread drove us onward.

By the twenty-second day of September, we finally made our way around a high range of mountains called the Rubys. Very discouraging. Too high to cross, so we went south around them, then traveled back to almost the same point but on the other side. Took nine days and well over a hundred miles to go 30 miles directly west.

By then our company had become hopelessly fractured. We no longer travel as one group, but each smaller party makes its way as best it can in the day. The Germans—Keseberg, Wolfinger, Spitzer, etc.—stay together. The Breens, who are Irish, stay to themselves. We and the Donners, who are viewed as the rich of the company, mostly stay together. The tedium and the strain tell on tempers, and contention is as common as the dust. We camp together at night but there is not much mingling. The Salt Desert left us broken in more ways than one.

Bitterness against Mr. Reed grows. Lansford Hastings is not here to take the blame, so many put it upon Mr. Reed. Our alienation from others in the party grows noticeably each day. Part of this now festers from months ago when Mr. Reed confronted Keseberg, a haughty German, about mistreating his wife. Keseberg, a man with a great temper, still seethes over what he saw as his humiliation.

Seeing more signs of Indians. Shoshannees, or something like that. Uncle George (Donner) lost two horses several days ago. Assume Indians stole them.

Six days ago we rejoined the California Trail. Mr. Reed totaled up the mileage from his journal. He calculates that instead of saving three hundred miles as Mr. Hastings promised, in actuality we have likely come an extra one hundred twenty-five miles. Someone suggested we rename the route "Hastings's Long Trip." Though we are now on the California Trail, there are no wagons in sight. We are alone, so far as we know. Notes and sign boards left by parties ahead confirm that this was a terrible mistake. At the Weber River, we were just four days behind Hastings and his group. Now we are at least eighteen days behind them. Some of us now remember—not without pain—Tamsen Donner's deep melancholy when we chose this new route. Standing guard each night on livestock. Have lost two oxen and several horses to Indians. We have none to spare! Making better time. Company still split. Donners are now about a day in the lead. The heavy family wagon so artfully constructed back in Illinois now slows us considerably, since we have insufficient oxen. My thoughts are constantly of Kathryn and the baby. It is now just three months from coming into the world. Oh, how I wish I could be there when it comes!

It was not that steep a hill. Compared to what they had come over in the Wasatch, especially that last killer ridge that had nearly broken their teams, this was barely more than a long rise. They had seen worse coming across the desert. But that had been a long time ago and when their teams were stronger. This hill, long and with deep sand, had stopped them again. Along the river it was too marshy. Fording the river to go around the hill wasn't an option either. Their teams, down in number and almost utterly wasted, simply could not pull them alone. So once again the fragmented, straggling company known as the Donner Party had to stop and double team in order to get their wagons up and over the top.

Peter shook his head grimly. Why did he still refer to it as the Donner Party? George Donner was the elected captain, that was true enough, but after the loss on the Salt Desert the Donners had the strongest teams, and in the last few days they and their party had gradually pulled ahead of their companions. Judging from the signs they left behind, they were now at least a day ahead of the others, more likely two. That was too bad, for at times like this, the Reeds and their fellow travelers desperately needed the extra oxen.

But that was wishful thinking and won them nothing. Peter sighed and walked back to James Reed's wagon. Milt Elliott was just finishing the yoking up of the extra team borrowed from one of the Graveses' wagons. "You want me to take this one up?" Peter asked.

Reed's lead teamster shook his head. He and Peter were the only Reed drivers still with the family. With most of Reed's oxen lost and two wagons abandoned, Reed had sent the others on with the Donners, who had more provisions. "You took the last one. I'll take this one," Elliott answered.

"All right." Peter moved past him around to the back of the wagon. Pushing at the back of this heavy wagon wouldn't give the oxen much help, but it was something to do and perhaps it helped enough to give the animals some relief, even though small.

Once in place, he turned and looked up the hill, then shook his head. The wagon that had started ahead of them was now stopped about halfway up. John Snyder, a teamster for the Graves family, was now blocking the trail.

"Milt," Peter called. "Look."

Elliott turned, then swore. "Come on, Snyder," he yelled. "Keep it going."

Peter heard the sound of a horse and turned. Mr. Reed approached, riding his mare. During the noon stop he had gone out on a brief hunting trip. Peter saw that he had bagged nothing. Reed surveyed the situation quickly, then swung down and tied Glaucus on the back of the wagon. Peter couldn't help but notice the difference in the once proud thoroughbred. Its ribs could be easily counted. Its coat was dull and dirty. The spirit was largely gone.

Reed came over to stand beside Peter, peering up the hill. "What's going on?"

Peter shrugged. "We took Pike's wagon over first and now we've got his team. Mr. Graves was going to send his teams back for his last wagon, but Snyder said this one was lighter and he could make it without the extra help."

Reed snorted. "What was he thinking? That sand is like adding on a thousand pounds."

"Well, as you can see, he was wrong. Looks like he's stuck now and is going to have to wait for the extra teams anyway. So, here we sit."

Margret Reed had been standing with the children on the other side of the wagon to get some relief from the sun. She came around now to see what they were talking about. Reed squinted up at the wagon that was ahead of them, then made up his mind. "Milt," he called irritably, "we're not waiting any longer for that fool. Let's go." Then he cupped his hand and shouted. "Move out of the way, Snyder, we're coming up."

Peter was a little surprised. There was no love lost between Franklin Graves and his family and James Frazier Reed. Graves was now openly blaming Reed for convincing them to take the Hastings Cutoff, even though the Graves party hadn't been at Fort Bridger when the decision had been made and only joined the Donner group when they were two or three days into the Wasatch Mountains. But John Snyder and Reed had quickly struck up a friendship, and it had been Snyder who had convinced Graves to lend a yoke of oxen to Reed after his were lost in the Salt Desert. So Reed's anger at the teamster was a little unusual.

Up the hill, Snyder was standing by his team. He spun around and shouted back. "There's no room. Wait your turn. We'll be out of here in a few minutes."

"Only a fool would think you could pull that hill without help," Reed shouted back. "Now, move over." To Elliott he snapped. "All right, let's go." He stepped over beside Peter and prepared to help push. "Margret, you take the children and stand back."

As she did so, Milt gave Peter a startled look. The road up the hill was pretty narrow, and it wouldn't take much to tip their wagon if they got too far to the side. Reed saw that look and swore. "Are you deaf, Milt? I said let's go."

Elliott had still not fully recovered from the shame of being the one who had lost the oxen, and so without another word he turned and lifted his whip. It popped over the lead yoke. "Ho, boys! Let's go!"

The animals hit their yoke and the heavy wagon began to move. Snyder, seeing what was happening, started waving his arms and yelling at them, but they couldn't distinguish his words over the sounds of the wagon and team.

The wagon slowed as the large wheels sank into the sand.

"Don't stop! Don't stop!" Reed shouted at Elliott. "We'll never get them going again."

Peter looked around the wagon and saw that they were closing on John Snyder. Snyder was waving furiously now, screaming for them to stop.

"There's not enough room," Peter yelled at Mr. Reed. "He's not moving."

Reed leaped around Peter to see for himself. He let fly with an expletive, running forward, shouting furiously. "Give way. We're coming through."

Now Snyder's voice carried over the noise of the wagon. "You bullheaded idiot! Wait your turn." Then when he saw they were still coming on and that he would be trapped between the oncoming oxen and his wagon, he darted forward, grabbing at the yoke of his oxen, yelling at them to move. They hit their yokes, but it was like trying to pull a barn. Nothing happened. No longer pushing Reed's wagon but running alongside and urging the animals, Peter saw that Snyder, in a fury, was beating at the heads of his oxen with the butt of his whip to try and get them to move.

Suddenly Peter was angry. That was no way to treat your animals. Snyder was punishing them for his own stupidity. Peter shouted and started to run forward.

Milt Elliott, trotting alongside the oxen on their left side, saw that when the wagons came together he was going to be caught in the same squeeze that Snyder had scrambled away to avoid. He hurried around the front of the oxen to the off side, screaming profanities at Snyder. Peter darted forward, swinging around so that he could pass around the other side of Snyder's wagon and stop the teamster from beating the oxen.

All three men—Reed, Elliott, and Peter—reached Snyder's wagon at the same moment. They didn't have to look back. On its current course Reed's family wagon was going to collide with Snyder's. "Watch out, Milt!" Peter shouted.

But Milt Elliott had already seen what was coming. "Gee! Gee!" he screamed, giving the oxen the command to turn to the right.

"Not too far!" Reed shouted, running up to grab the yoke of the lead oxen and stop them from turning too sharply. "We'll go over the side."

Peter's attempt to stop Snyder was forgotten. He dropped back behind Reed's wagon to size up the space between it and Snyder's. The Reed wagon was turning, but it was going to be close. "More," he yelled.

But Elliott's commands now created another problem. Snyder's lashing fury had driven his oxen into a frenzy. They couldn't move forward, but they couldn't stand still under the beating. When they heard Elliott's cries to turn right, they responded as well. The off ox jerked to the right just as Reed's lead yoke came up alongside. There was a loud bawl of protest as the two teams collided and tangled up in a mass of kicking, struggling animals. Yoke locked against yoke, feet fought for the same ground, and one ox nearly stumbled.

"Get out of there," Snyder snarled at Reed. "Pull back. Pull back." Then he leaped sideways and began raining blows on the heads of the Reed team, shouting, cursing, slashing downward with his whip again and again.

Stunned at the ferocity of the teamster's attack, Reed rushed forward, grabbing at Snyder's arm. "What are you doing?" he yelled. "Let them alone. Let us through."

The teams, hopelessly entangled now, came to a stop and the Reed wagon sank down in the sand. Snyder jerked free from the older man's grasp and stepped back, raising his whip. "Get back, Reed. Wait your turn."

Reed took a step toward him, fists clenched, eyes blazing. "You miserable fool. Now you've stopped us. If you can't make it, then get out of the way for those who can."

The hand holding the whip rose high above Snyder's head. His face was flushed and his mouth working. "I'll teach you who can make it and who can't."

Elliott and Peter started forward at the same moment. "Stop, John!" Elliott shouted.

But James Reed was not a man lacking in courage. With a

blur, his hand dropped, then swung up again. In it was the large hunting knife he kept in a scabbard at his side. "Put down the whip, John," he exclaimed.

"No, James." It was Margret Reed, and it came out as a strangled cry of pure terror.

For one long second Snyder stared at the naked blade in astonishment; then with lightning speed he lunged forward, bringing his hand downward. The butt handle of a bullwhip was usually made of a solid piece of hardwood, like oak or ash, or was made of a softer wood hollowed out so that melted lead could be poured into it. Either way it was heavy and more like a club than a handle. Reed was so startled, he didn't even have time to step back. The butt caught him just above the left temple. He staggered back, blood gushing from a four-inch wound.

"No!" Margret Reed hurled herself forward as Snyder raised his hand to strike again. She threw herself between her husband and his assailant. Snyder was in a black fury and barely perceived who had jumped in front of him. Down came the whip again, the butt hitting Mrs. Reed alongside the head and knocking her sprawling. Reed stared in stupefied shock. He had one hand to his head, trying to staunch the bleeding. Snyder moved in, swinging hard, and struck him twice more. The second blow knocked Reed to his knees.

Then the rage swept over James Reed as well. With a cry of pure animal instinct, he leaped upward, diving at Snyder, the blade of the great knife flashing in the sun. His aim was true and the knife struck Snyder in the left breast, just below the collarbone.

There was a startled, strangled "Oh!" and Snyder fell back against one of the oxen, clutching at the wound. The whip slipped from his fingers and fell to the sand. He turned, staggering away for several steps; then he sank to his knees, staring at Reed in total disbelief.

Reed flung the knife away and took a step forward. "John?" He seemed as dazed as Snyder.

The rest of the party, who were at the top of the hill, had

started running toward the two wagons as soon as they saw what was happening. They arrived just in time to see the final blow. Patrick Breen, the Irishman, ran to Snyder and dropped to his knees, reaching out to steady him. Snyder gazed into the Irishman's face, totally bewildered. "Uncle Patrick," he said, struggling now to speak. "I am dead."

His head slowly dropped to his chest. After a moment, his eyes closed. Breen laid him down gently in the sand and took his hand. There was not a sound. No one moved. And then finally, there was a final gasp—the death rattle, as many called it—and a momentary shudder, and then the teamster's body rolled against the big Irishman.

Breen looked up, his eyes filled with tears and with shock. "He's gone," he said, his voice sounding very much like Snyder's just a few moments before.

Lewis Keseberg was a big man, and very German. In his early thirties, he was blond, handsome, and highly educated. He often bragged that he spoke three languages fluently. He had come from Germany only two years before and spoke with a heavy accent. He never spoke of why he had come to America and then almost immediately decided to embark on a journey such as this. Many speculated that there was something in his past that he wanted to escape.

He was not well liked. He was loud, brash, eccentric, opinionated. Worse for a company that when traveling together was like a tiny village community, there had been strong suspicions that he beat his wife. A wagon cover offers little privacy. One night it had become so bad that James Reed had publicly rebuked him and threatened him physically if it happened again. He made Keseberg walk at the rear of the company for several days.

That had started a festering bitterness in Keseberg against the aristocratic Reed. And now finally, James Reed had done something that provided a chance to get even.

After the tragedy, the Graves family took Snyder's body up the hill, and then they quickly made camp. The Reeds followed, placing their wagon some thirty or forty yards away. William Eddy chose to camp with the Reeds, making a clear statement where he stood in this matter.

The Eddy family was not part of the Reed-Donner group. A carriage maker in his late twenties, Bill Eddy was married and had two small children. He too was from Illinois, and so he had naturally drawn closer to the Reeds and the Donners than to the others. But he was not one of them, and everyone knew that. They also knew of his expertise with a firearm and that of all the company he had the greatest skills as a frontiersman. He had some rudimentary tracking skills, was an excellent hunter, and seemed able to fix about anything that got broken. His skills had served the company well many times, and he was greatly respected by all. It was therefore of great significance that he chose to bring his family with the Reeds now. The Donners were not there, of course, being a day or two ahead of the rest.

Margret Reed, injured herself, was still in a state of shock, so plucky Virginia took scissors to her father and snipped away the hair from the three cuts, then bathed and bandaged them. That afternoon the Graveses held a funeral for John Snyder. Reed, totally shattered by what he had done, went over to Franklin Graves and tried to explain what had happened. He offered wood for a coffin. He was coldly rebuffed.

As the evening wore on, it was clear, even though the two groups were camped some distance from each other, that the Graves family was building an emotional head of steam and wanted vengeance. The Reeds and the Eddys stayed close to their wagons, trying not to listen to the angry shouts and the wailing of the women. Reed seemed far away, so distraught that he barely noted what was going on around him. Then, on the still night air, the harsh voice of Lewis Keseberg sounded clearly.

"Vhere is de justice?" he cried. "A man is dead. A good man. An honest man. Vhere is his murderer? He sits by his fire drinking coffee as though nothink had happened."

James Reed shot to his feet, but Margret grabbed his hand and pulled him down again. "No, James," she said softly. William Eddy had also jumped up to block his way. He sat down when Reed sank back again.

"Vhere is dis reech man who is too good to drive his own vagons? Where is dis man who is so qvick to condemn others?" He swung around and, in what looked very much like a staged maneuver, grabbed an ox yoke and held it up high. "You know what vee do vith murderers in my country? Vee hang them so dey cannot kill again."

In other circumstances it would have sounded so bizarre and so ridiculous that it would have brought smiles or open guffaws. No one laughed now. Beside Reed, Margret gasped and clutched at his arm. Eddy, looking grim, stood and went to the wagon. When he came back, he had his rifle and was loading it. Milt Elliott nodded and did the same.

Peter felt like he was going to throw up. He had been no more than five feet from John Snyder when he saw the blade plunge into his body and the horrified look which crossed his face. The image was burned in his mind and against the back of his eyelids, so that every time he closed his eyes the scene unfolded again. He glanced at Reed. He wasn't looking at anyone. But then Peter saw that Reed had sometime in the last hour strapped his pistol on. Elliott jerked his head at Peter, his eyes demanding.

Peter's mind was racing even as his stomach churned. Would it come to that? he wondered. Would they take up arms against each other now? But he already knew the answer. Out on the plains there were only two things that provided justice—the will of the majority and sheer firepower. Near Independence Rock one of the men in the Oregon company had killed another man. A quick trial had been held. Some argued for leniency because the man had a wife and children. The company agreed that leniency was needed, so they promised to care for the family and promptly hanged the man from a wagon tongue while his wife looked on.

What was frightening was that with the Donners being a day or so ahead of them, James Reed did not have a majority. His other hired men were with the Donners as well. Besides his family, he had only Peter and Milt Elliott. Eddy's siding with them helped, but those in this camp who would stand for James Reed were in a distinct minority.

With a sigh, Peter stood up, went to his bedroll, and found the pistol that James Reed had given him back in Illinois. He came back and sat down beside the fire, feeling more ill than he had before.

Keseberg was still on his feet, but all they heard now was the angry muttering of his audience. Then the German spun around, still holding the yoke high above his head. He strode to his wagon and in a quick movement lashed the yoke to the wagon tongue. Then he lifted the tongue until it stuck straight up in the air. "Dere!" he cried. "Dere is our gallows. Now, vhere is de murderer?"

James Reed got to his feet again, only this time slowly, with great weariness. Margret tried to hold him down, but he shook her off. He looked at Elliott, then William Eddy, then Peter. "There's no running from it. We have to face it."

They nodded, knowing the inevitability of it as well as he. What had happened today had torn the whole fabric of their company. Something had to be done, if not to mend it, then to stop it from ripping further. They were too far from civilization and in too desperate a strait to hope it would heal itself.

Mrs. Reed stood up, but her husband turned to her and took her by the shoulders, gently, tenderly. "It will be all right, Mother," he said softly. "You stay here with the children."

She sat back down slowly, then put her face in her hands and began to cry.

As they crossed the creek, Keseberg saw them and cut off his harangue in midsentence. Everyone turned and a great silence fell over the camp. Several of them were armed as well, Peter saw. If they couldn't settle this reasonably . . . He shuddered, not wanting to finish his thoughts on the matter.

"Sit down, Keseberg," Reed said flatly.

The man reared back, starting to sputter, but then Patrick Breen turned on him too. "Sit down, Lewis."

And then it began. No formal meeting was called. No one asked for order. James Reed simply and with deep sorrow told in his own words what had happened. Faces went grim and eyes turned angry, but no one spoke. As soon as Reed sat down, Franklin Graves leaped to his feet. This was not a case of self-defense, he cried. Reed had been too impatient to wait his turn. When Snyder had tried to reason with him, Reed had pulled his knife in a fit of temper and stabbed him. Only then did Snyder hit Reed with the butt of his whip.

Breen motioned to Milt Elliott, noting that he had been the closest to the event. Milt completely contradicted Graves. Mid-way through, as he told them how Snyder, in a rage, had struck Mrs. Reed, John Breen, Patrick's fourteen-year-old son, leaped up, his voice so filled with anger that he could barely speak. "That is not true," he shouted. "You are the one who started all this. John Snyder was a gentleman. He would never strike a woman."

Breen, who made little bones about the fact that he stood squarely against Reed on this, had nevertheless become the acknowledged judge, or at least the adjudicator. He waved his son down and turned to Peter. Peter confirmed all that Milt Elliott said and what James Reed had testified. It was not enough. Keseberg said he had seen it clearly from the top of the hill and that Reed had struck first. Others angrily blamed Elliott for not waiting his turn.

It raged on like that for a quarter of an hour. Finally Breen raised his hands. The group fell silent. When he spoke, his Irish accent was as distinctive as Keseberg's German one, and yet so much softer. "Shall we call for a vote?" he asked. "The question at hand is whether James Frazier Reed is guilty of murder and should be hanged."

There were murmurs from the larger group, and several cried out for a vote.

William Eddy, rifle held easily in the crook of his arm, raised his hand. "I say that a vote is not the answer in this case. Those who are unfriendly to Mr. Reed—and I am speaking of your feelings before what happened today—outnumber those of us who take his side. If the full company were together, a vote might be appropriate."

"Vote! Vote!" Keseberg cried. "Hang him."

Reed swung around, baring his neck. "If that's what you want," he said hotly. "Come on, gentlemen. Here I am."

No one moved, and Keseberg fell back a step in the face of Reed's daring anger.

Eddy turned back to Patrick Breen. "We believe that Mr. Reed is totally innocent of the charge of murder. What happened today was a tragedy, a tragedy caused by hot tempers and difficult circumstances. If you vote to hang Mr. Reed, know that Mr. Elliott, Mr. Ingalls, Mr. Reed, and myself shall defend him to the death."

There were gasps and quick indrawn breaths. He was defying the law of the majority.

Eddy went on calmly. "We cannot—" He stopped, waiting for every eye to turn to him. "We *cannot* afford any more deaths in this company. We shall need every man if we are to reach California before winter comes. Therefore, I suggest that we put this matter aside for now. Let it rest until we get to California. Then we shall have a formal trial and justice will be done."

"No!" A couple of the Graves men had jumped up to stand beside Keseberg. "We will not travel with a murderer. Hang him!"

Eddy watched them for several seconds, then raised his hand again. "Feelings clearly run deep on this matter." He glanced quickly at Reed, who stood with his head down, staring at the ground. "Therefore I suggest a compromise." He hesitated, and finally Reed's head came up. "I suggest that Mr. Reed be banished from the company."

"What?" Reed cried, his face draining of color.

"I see no other way," Eddy said softly, meeting his eyes directly.

"I will not leave my family," Reed cried hoarsely. "This is not right."

Eddy turned to him. His voice was sad. "You have our word that we shall care for your family and bring them on, Mr. Reed. If we don't do this, there will be further bloodshed." He was pleading now. "Do you think you will be safe if you stay? Every day you will have to watch your back. At night you won't dare sleep. This is the only way."

Others cried out in protest as Reed and Eddy stared at each other for a long moment; then finally Reed's head dropped again. But then it nodded silently.

Breen called for silence. "The sentence of banishment is acceptable," he said finally, "but on these conditions. Mr. Reed is to have no weapon, no food, no horse."

Peter whirled. "What? That is the equivalent of a death sentence," he cried. "We are hundreds of miles from civilization."

"It is that, or he shall hang. And if we cannot agree, then we shall stand to our weapons," Breen said evenly.

Peter started to speak again, but William Eddy reached out and grabbed his arm. "It's all right, Peter." He peered into his eyes and Peter saw pleading there. "Let them have it," his eyes said.

Peter clamped his mouth shut and stepped back again. Eddy looked around the circle one last time, letting his eyes stop on Patrick Breen. "Agreed," he said.

Without another word, Reed and his companions turned and walked back to their camp.

"I'm going with you, Mr. Reed."

James Reed didn't look up, but just shook his head. "No."

"I'm not asking, Mr. Reed," Peter said quietly.

Now his employer's head came up sharply and there was fire in his eyes. "What did you say?"

"I hired on to go with you to California," Peter answered, perfectly calm. "And that's what I'm going to do. No one will know I'm gone until it is too late." As Reed started to speak again, he rushed on. "Mr. Eddy and Milt are needed here with your family, Mr. Reed. You know that they are better qualified to care for them than I am."

Milt Elliott was staring at Peter, and then he slowly nodded. "Yes," he said thoughtfully. "That is an answer. We know that George and Jacob are just a day or two ahead of us and will help you. But the Indians here are not friendly. A day or two is all they would need to kill a solitary man."

"Did you say you're not asking for my permission?" Reed asked Peter, ignoring his other teamster. His voice was cool and distant.

Peter didn't flinch. "That's what I said."

"I'm not even sure I'm going yet," Reed said bitterly, giving Eddy a baleful glance.

Mrs. Reed, who had sat quietly through all this, her eyes red and swollen, now looked up. "James?"

He turned to her.

"I want you to go." That took him aback. She rushed on. "If you stay, there will be great trouble. But even if you do, what then? Do you want to be here as you watch your wife and children slowly starve to death?"

"But, Margret—"

Her voice was strong now, hard with determination. "No, you listen to me, James. Mr. Stanton and Mr. McCutchen rode on ahead for supplies. There has been no sign of them. Perhaps something has befallen them. If you go, you can ride ahead to California and get help and supplies. It is a way that you can save us."

Eddy broke in eagerly. "She's right, Mr. Reed. It could be our only hope."

"And I want Peter to go with you," Margret Reed said evenly. "I don't want you out there alone." Now she looked directly at her husband. This woman might be devastated by what was happening, but this was not a woman who was broken. Her eyes held his, daring him to disagree. "You don't say one more word. You just do it."

William Eddy was nodding. "When you catch up with the Donners, in addition to supplies I'd ask for Walt Herron or Baylis to go with you too. Three of you will stand a much better chance."

Through all of that, Reed's eyes had never left Peter's face. "You're a little cheeky, aren't you, boy?"

Peter, surprised at the sudden use of a good old English phrase, smiled. "Yes, sir. I suppose I am."

Then Reed's mouth softened and his eyes relaxed. "Thank you, Peter. I would be honored to have you along. Why don't you leave before first light and I'll meet you down the trail a mile or two."

"And I'll be there too," Virginia Reed spoke up, startling all of them.

"What?" both her father and her mother said at the same time. Virginia had changed too in these months since they had left Springfield, Peter thought. She had been a young girl—pleasant, cheerful, but also spoiled and pampered. She was still pleasant and cheerful, but the trail didn't pamper anyone, not even a thirteen-year-old.

"I will saddle Glaucus and ride out early in the morning. I will have your rifle and that brace of pistols, Papa, and enough food to help you reach Uncle George."

"No, Virginia," her father said. He was trying to be firm, but her courage had touched him deeply and he was close to tears. "I won't risk your getting hurt."

"No one will suspect *me*, Papa. And poor Glaucus. She is just skin and bones. She won't be any use to us."

"Virginia, I—"

Milt Elliott stepped forward. "I'll go out with her, Mr. Reed. We'll be careful."

Reed was still clearly hesitant.

Virginia Reed glanced at Peter and then very soberly said, "I'm not asking, Papa."

Chapter Notes

Later the eyewitness accounts of the fight between James Reed and his friend John Snyder would differ significantly. Some would say that Reed struck first with his knife and that Snyder then used his whip to defend himself. Others claimed that Mrs. Reed was never struck, that Snyder was too much a gentleman to hit a woman. But even those hostile to Reed would admit that Snyder in his rage had struck Margret Reed and that's when Reed went after Snyder with his knife. There is no way to know exactly what did happen. The account presented in the novel follows what many researchers believe to be the most likely chain of events. (See *Chronicles*, pp. 168–69; *OBH*, pp. 63–65.)

Unquestionably, a major factor lay not in either Snyder or Reed but in the weeks of exhausting, spirit-breaking frustration that pushed otherwise normal men to near madness. In those conditions, men went to lengths where they otherwise would never have gone. The irony is that this confrontation occurred between two men who were friends, even though there were deep feelings among other members of the group. When Reed spoke of the experiences of the Donner Party even many years later, he never referred to the killing, suggesting that he was haunted by what had happened for the rest of his life.

Later that same day the company debated what to do with James Reed. Lewis Keseberg demanded that Reed be hanged from a wagon tongue. Others testified to his innocence. We don't know who acted as mediator in the subsequent "trial." Franklin Graves and Patrick Breen seemed to be the natural leaders of the larger group, but since Snyder was a Graves teamster, Franklin Graves probably would not have been chosen to settle the matter.

The compromise sentence of banishment, suggested by William Eddy, was really the only practical solution. Emotions were simply too deep for the group to exonerate Reed or to wait until they reached some outpost of civilization. (See *OBH*, pp. 65–66; *Chronicles*, p. 169; *UE*, pp. 36–37, 275–77.)

In the end, as Reed left camp the next morning, someone met him and gave him his weapons, probably his horse, and some food. Some say it was Milt Elliott and William Eddy, but Virginia later wrote that she did it in company with Elliott. (See *UE*, p. 277.)

An episode that would occur 150 years later shows how deeply the feelings over this incident ran. At a 1996 Donner Party sesquicentennial commemoration (held in connection with an annual event called California Trail Days), a descendant of Franklin Ward Graves, who had hired Snyder as a teamster, would confront a descendant of James F. Reed and say that Reed was a coward who killed a good man for only the slightest of reasons. As writer Frank Mullen Jr. notes, so deep were the feelings which resulted from this brief flash of anger that "after fifteen decades, the anger will still burn." (See *Chronicles*, p. 168.)

Chapter Twenty-Nine

The Orville Allen rescue company, with which Joshua and Nathan Steed were traveling, passed wagons going west all along the trail across Iowa. As they reached the eastern part of the territory, some of those wagons began to be those belonging to the first of the refugees from the Battle of Nauvoo. But they were few and had enough supplies to get them to the next settlement, so the seven wagons went on, headed for the main camp at Montrose. It was late in the afternoon of October seventh when they pulled up at the top of the crest of a long, gentle rise. Allen signaled for the others to stop. They did so, pulling out of their single file line to park abreast of each other.

Nathan had seen this sight before, but it was still a stunning panorama. The sweeping bend of the Mississippi River was clearly visible. On the far side of the great river, cradled in the elbow made by the bend, Nauvoo lay bathed in the late afternoon sunlight. Over all, the temple shone like a white beacon. Closer, directly below them on this side of the river, they could see the buildings of Montrose. Just to the north of the town they could also see the signs of the poor camp. There were wagon tops, tents, and a few cattle grazing in a field.

Joshua instinctively leaned forward, searching Nauvoo for any signs of the battle that had raged there a few weeks before. There was nothing. It shouldn't have surprised him. They were three or four miles from the city at this point, much too far to see any details. But from the terrible reports they had heard along the road, Joshua had expected to see something that was immediately noticeable.

"What do you think?" Nathan said. "Can we make it across the river tonight?"

Joshua turned and glanced back at the sun, then nodded. "If we hurry."

Orville Allen turned. "Brethren, you've heard the reports. There is great danger for any of our people going to the city. The mob is stopping anyone coming across the river, and if they're Mormon, they're treating them very badly."

Joshua looked at Nathan, then at their foreman. "We've got to find out about our sister, Orville."

"I understand, but maybe she's in the poor camp here in Montrose."

Nathan shook his head. "You don't know our brother-in-law. He's not a member and he was bound and determined not to leave the city."

"Yes, I know. But we need you, brethren. We need these wagons."

"Oh, we won't take the wagons across. We'll just slip over and see what we can learn."

"We'll see," the foreman finally said. "Let's go down and see what we have waiting for us down there first. Maybe there'll be word of your sister." He snapped the reins and his team started forward. The other wagons pulled in behind him and started down the hill.

"Maybe," Joshua agreed, speaking to no one. Then to Nathan he muttered, "But if there isn't, we're going across."

What they found at Montrose was shocking beyond anything they had expected. This was more than just tragedy. This was tragedy and poverty and misery and suffering all rolled up and bound tightly together. There was barely even a welcome, as though rising up and waving in welcome were more than the people had energy to do. They sat in their tents or in their brush lean-tos, or in many cases on blankets laid out on the wet and muddy ground, and stared out at the newcomers.

Maybe they didn't know these wagons had come from the west, Nathan thought, as he tried not to stare at the gaunt and haunted faces. Maybe they thought they were just additional stragglers coming in who would be more mouths to feed and more people to shelter. Whatever it was, they weren't creating nearly the stir that he had expected their arrival would trigger. A few people got up and began to follow them along curiously, but most just stared at them as the wagons rumbled by.

It was as if they had driven into a charnel house or a cemetery where the dead had not yet been buried. Men sat on stools or on the ground, heads down, staring vacantly at nothing. Those who did look up had blank eyes and lifeless faces. Mothers stood with half-naked waifs clinging to filthy, torn skirts. Children held out hands to pitifully small fires. Even though it had been a beautiful, sunny day, now the sun was almost down and the air already had a nip to it. They were still a few days away from frost, Nathan guessed, but not many.

Every kind of shelter imaginable passed before them—one wagon looked like it had eight or ten people crammed inside it. There were a few tents, but many had long tears in them or sagged dangerously. Everywhere in between there were lean-to shelters made of woven willows lashed to stick frameworks and open on one side to the weather. Some had taken blankets and tied them to four stakes driven into the ground, providing a shelter barely high enough for a person to crawl under in order to sleep. These were usually open on all four sides.

Most appalling were the dozens of places where a few bundles, maybe a battered valise, and some loose clothing sat beside blankets spread on the ground. These had nothing but open sky—whether clear or stormy—as their roof.

And everywhere the smell assaulted the nostrils. It was a terrible combination of smoky fires, musty bedding, moldy food, rotting leather, sickness and disease. And death. Nathan had to look away as he saw a group of forms laid out in a row beneath blankets. One was small and covered with a baby blanket. A few feet away, a woman sat in one of the lean-tos, nursing a baby that had nothing but a thin cotton shift on. It would pull free from its mother's breast at intervals to wail piteously.

As they came into the main part of camp, it opened into a large circle. Allen raised one hand and motioned for the wagons to circle. As they started to do so, Joshua brought his wagon up alongside Nathan's. "I can't believe this," he said softly.

"Worse than I ever imagined," Nathan answered, his voice almost a whisper.

"We don't have enough food to feed this many."

"Not nearly enough."

"I had no idea," Joshua murmured to himself. "No idea it would be this bad."

By the time they pulled their wagons in a circle and dismounted, the first of the curious began to arrive. Orville Allen wasn't willing to wait. He stood up on the wheel of his wagon and shouted out across the camp. "Brothers and sisters, we have come from Council Bluffs. We are sent here by the Twelve to help you."

It was as though he had poured the waters of life onto the camp. There were startled cries, and people stood slowly and began to move toward them. Nathan could hear the shouts being tossed from tent to tent and shelter to shelter as the excitement spread. In three or four minutes, they had a couple of hundred people gathering in around them.

"Brothers and sisters, may I have your attention."

They quickly quieted.

"It is true. We have come from Brother Brigham. We have some food and clothing to distribute." He raised his voice as a ragged cheer went up. "More important, we have come to take you across Iowa so that you can join with the rest of the Saints."

"But there are only seven of you," a man shouted from near the back of the crowd.

"Yes," Allen said brightly. "But more are on their way. Your brothers and sisters have not forgotten you."

Right in front of Nathan a woman with a small child in her arms began to sob. The child looked up at its mother, startled by her sudden breakdown, then started to wail also.

"We were sent to bring as many of you as we can, and we shall do it. We shall take you to Council Bluffs. We do not promise you plenty. We cannot even promise you all warm homes. But we promise you that you shall be free from the violence of the mobs. We promise you—" He had to stop as his voice suddenly started to tremble. "We promise you," he went on, more softly now, "freedom from tyranny. Freedom from danger. Freedom from oppression."

For a moment it looked as if he wanted to say more, but then he shook his head. "I'd like to meet with the leaders of the camp so that we can begin making plans for the distribution of food," he concluded, then hopped down from his perch.

"Nathan Steed?"

It was a woman's voice, calling from behind him. Nathan turned to see who had spoken. At first he could see no one; then near the back of the crowd he saw someone waving her arm. "Nathan, it's me. Mary."

And then as a woman pushed her way forward, the crowd backing up enough to let her through, Joshua grabbed Nathan's arm, gripping it tightly. "It's Mary Fielding Smith," he said.

Not waiting for her to come to them, both brothers strode quickly toward her. At the front edge of the crowd she finally burst through. "Nathan? Can it really be you?"

"Yes, Mary. And you're here? Melissa told us in one of her letters that she thought you would be leaving sometime in late June or early July. We've been waiting for word of you."

She took both of his hands and squeezed them tightly, her face infused with joy. "We thought we were leaving sooner. But my brother had difficulty selling the farm. Obviously we didn't make it."

Joshua looked around. "This is pretty bad. How are you and your family doing?"

"Wonderful compared to others." She shook her head. "It has been terrible. So much hunger. So many who are sick. We've even had several babies born."

"Oh, no," Nathan said in dismay.

"Yes. In one case it was raining and the only place they had for the woman was under a blanket, so the sisters stood around and caught the rainwater in pans while the midwife brought the baby forth."

That deeply sobered both of the brothers. "Is there any word of Melissa?" Nathan asked. "Are she and the children safe?"

A radiant smile broke out. "They are now."

Joshua jerked forward. "What about Carl? Are they still on Steed Row? We need to find them."

The smile only broadened, and now her eyes were filled with both pain and joy. "Come with me. There's something I want you to see."

It was clear that the Fieldings were much better off than some of the Saints who had been driven out of Nauvoo. Mary's clothing was reasonably clean, and she didn't have that pall of malnutrition as so many of the others had. As she threaded her way through the camp, it became obvious she was headed toward where several wagons stood close together to form a hollow square.

She called out and waved as she approached. A man stood up and waved back. Nathan saw that it was Joseph Fielding,

Mary's older brother. When they came up, Joseph's eyes widened and his mouth formed an O, but Mary put her finger to her lips. She stepped in between Joshua and Nathan, taking each of them by the hand. Then she led them around the back of one of the wagons. A woman was standing there with her back to them, bent over an overturned washtub, sorting something on it.

"Melissa?"

"Yes?" She straightened and turned. The momentary surprise at seeing two strangers with Mary registered on her face; then suddenly her eyes flew open and she gasped.

"Do you recognize these two brethren?" Mary said, with a twinkle in her eyes.

Whatever it was that Melissa had in her hands crashed to the ground as she threw her hands to her face, not believing what she was seeing. Without a word, Nathan opened his arms and went to her, with Joshua right behind him.

Joshua knelt down beside the makeshift cot in the small tent. He reached out and took Carl's hand, holding it against his chest. "How bad is it, Carl?"

He shook his head. "Three broken ribs," he said in a strained whisper. "Maybe four." He had to stop and catch his breath, and both Nathan and Joshua heard the wheezing rattle in his throat.

Nathan looked at Joseph Fielding. He nodded. "One of them punctured his lung. That's the one we're worried about. The others seem to be healing—slowly, but healing."

Joshua turned back and laid his hand against Carl's cheek. "It's all right, Carl. Nathan and I are here. It will be all right."

Nathan stood and turned to Melissa. "What about the children? Are they all right?"

It was as if he had loosed the floodgates. Her face crumpled and tears instantly filled her eyes. She turned away, her body shuddering with sobs.

Stunned, Nathan looked at Mary Smith. She took a deep breath as she put an arm around Melissa and drew her close to her. "Mary Melissa was very sick when they were driven out. She got thrown in the water." She began to rub Melissa's back. "She died two days after they came across."

"Oh, Melissa," Nathan cried, stepping to her and taking her from Mary. "Oh, my beloved Melissa, I'm so sorry."

"It's my fault."

It came out as a hoarse croak. Nathan and Joshua turned to Carl in surprise. He was weeping. "I should have listened."

Melissa pulled clear, wiping at her tears with her apron, and went to Carl, dropping to her knees beside him. "No, Carl. You did all that you could."

He shook his head. Then he looked up at Joshua. "Have you come to take us west?"

Joshua couldn't hide his surprise. "Are you willing to go west, Carl?"

"You ask Melissa," he said. "You ask Melissa. Whatever she wants to do, that's what we'll do."

Melissa dropped her head against her shoulders, sobbing heavily now. "I want to be with my family, Carl."

He reached out a hand, moving it slowly and gingerly, and laid it on her head. He stroked her hair for a moment, then looked up at Joshua and Nathan again. "You heard her," he said. "Take us to the family."

"That's what we've come for," Nathan responded softly.

Suddenly Carl half raised his head. "I don't want to be a Mormon," he managed to gasp.

Joshua grinned. "That's what I once said too, Carl." Then instantly he sobered. "There won't be anyone in this family, or anywhere else, that will make you a Mormon against your will, Carl."

He lay back, wheezing heavily now. "I just wanted you to know before you decided."

Nathan leaned forward. "Carl," he said gently, "our love for you and our respect for you have nothing to do with what you choose to believe. You just rest now. We're here, and we're taking you home."

In the end, there were only forty-two out of the nearly three to four hundred people in the Montrose camp who volunteered to leave for Council Bluffs with the seven wagons brought by Orville Allen. After a full day of preaching and persuading and, in a few cases, downright begging, they had convinced barely ten percent of the total number in the camp of the poor that they should start west immediately. In many cases there were good reasons—too ill to travel, husbands or fathers away trying to find food—but in most cases it came down to a simple lack of heart.

And Nathan was not about to fault them for that. What they had been through was enough to break even the strongest of men, and if they wanted to wait for something a little more certain than the seven-wagon rescue group, then he understood. But the Allen group couldn't wait with them. It had taken them almost a month to come from the Missouri. If it took that long going back, it would be the first of November before they reached the Missouri River. That meant snow and freezing temperatures. The rescue company had brought food, clothing, and bedding, but they had used up some food just getting here. They would leave all but a few essentials with the poor Saints and hope they could find places along the trail to purchase or work for more. Forty-two people wasn't many to take back, but if the rescue wagons didn't get rolling, there would be forty-two more people consuming what little food there was. So within thirty-six hours after their arrival, they were ready to start back.

Nathan looked down the line of wagons. Going back it wouldn't be just seven of them. They had added twenty more wagons now, along with sixteen oxen and four horses to pull them. But, he thought, six of those forty-two people were his own family. That alone justified their coming.

Joshua went around to the back of his wagon and pulled open the canvas flap. They had made a bed in Joshua's wagon for Carl. Melissa would stay with him to care for him. The three boys and Sarah would sleep in Nathan's wagon. "You about ready in there?"

Melissa's head appeared. "We are."

From Nathan's wagon, young Carl waved. "We're ready too."

"Good," Nathan said, then turned to see if Orville Allen was about ready to give the signal. Suddenly he leaned forward, staring at the western sky. "What's that?"

Joshua turned. "What?" And then he too saw it. A dark cloud had appeared just above the prairie to the west of them. Only it was not a cloud. It was blacker, and moving rapidly.

"Look at the birds!" someone up the line shouted, pointing in the same direction.

And birds they were. It was a huge flock of whatever they were and coming directly toward them.

"There are hundreds of them," Melissa said in awe. But they just kept coming and coming in an endless stream from below the horizon.

"Not hundreds," Nathan cried. "Thousands! What are they?"

All up and down the wagon line, people were shouting and pointing now. In the camp, people came running from their tents and shelters, then stopped dead, struck with astonishment.

Now the first of the birds were approaching the lead wagon. The whir of their wings was like the sound of a huge hive of bees stirred up to anger. Joshua recognized that distinctive whir almost instantly. "They're quail," he cried.

As if a flock that huge were not surprising enough, as the first few birds approached the front of the train, suddenly they began to drop out of the sky. In moments, it was as though a great hailstorm had swept over them, only the hail was black and round and about the size of small loaves of bread. Some continued to fly over them, but most tumbled out of the sky in unbelievable numbers. A bird hit Nathan's wagon cover and bounced off, plunging to the ground, where it fluttered helplessly. Three more hit Joshua's wagon. Melissa yelped and ducked as one sailed through the opening and crashed into Carl's bed. One bounced off of Nathan's shoulder and dropped to the ground. It sat there motionless, looking dazed. He reached down, thinking it would fly. It didn't move, and in a moment he held the warm body in his hands and could feel the incredibly fast pulse beneath his fingertips.

"I got one! I got one!"

Nathan turned. Three birds had lit on the back of Nathan's oxen. Carl's boys, who had jumped out of the wagon at the first cries, were trying to catch them. Two flew away, but the third didn't move as David reached out and took him.

Now there were quail everywhere and people going after them in a frenzy. This was meat. This was food! To a camp on the verge of starvation, it was incredible. Food was falling from the sky.

"They're too exhausted to fly," Joshua shouted, ducking his head as another bounced off the top of his wagon and fell to the ground.

There was a shriek from Nathan's wagon. He turned and ran around to the back. Sarah, Melissa's eight-year-old, sat on her bed with a look of total astonishment on her face. A quail was sitting on her lap, motionless except for its head, which bobbed up and down and turned this way and that.

Nathan walked away from the wagon, taking care where he stepped. The ground was covered with them now. Not all just sat where they landed. A few ran away, but others walked calmly amid the running figures. If one did try to take flight again, it would rise up to about the height of the wagon cover, circle around two or three times, then drop again to the ground. It was absolutely amazing. They were flying into tents, landing on tables, perching on the back of animals, crashing into everything. Small children were scooping them up and running to show their parents. On a wagon tongue there were half a dozen perched like roosting chickens. Four stood on an overturned washtub. One man had an armful and was weeping joyously as he ran to show his family.

"Catch them," Orville Allen was shouting. "Catch as many as you can."

It took nearly half an hour before they were gone. Many were caught by the astonished Saints. The remainder rested for several minutes, then flew off again, headed for the river. Barely had the people begun to recover when another shout went up. As they turned, the sound was heard again. Another flock, easily as large as the first, appeared. Once again they barely reached the camp when they began to fall from the sky. Now the people were ready for them. One man grabbed some chicken wire and quickly fashioned a makeshift trap. In five minutes he had snared a dozen birds. Men grabbed birds as quickly as they could catch them. They would wring their necks, hand them to a waiting child or wife, then go after another.

Nathan and Joshua worked out a system with the three boys. The boys would catch the quail and run them to their uncles, who would then kill the birds and hand them to Melissa, who filled one bag, and then a second.

The second flock did not stay as long. After three or four minutes they rose again as a body and whirred away. Now the people turned to the west, waiting expectantly. They were not disappointed. Within minutes a third flock appeared.

The pattern went on until noon, when Orville Allen came running down the line of wagons, calling for everyone's attention. When they turned to him he raised his hands. "Leave them alone," he cried. "We have all we can eat." As the people looked at him in surprise, he went on, reasoning with them. "Though we are driven by our enemies," he cried, "the Lord has not forgotten his people. His eyes are continually upon us for good. Let us not show ingratitude by taking more than we have need."

At once the killing stopped. Parents called to children; men straightened from their chase. Though there were quail flying all around them, they had enough.

"Brethren and sisters, I would suggest that the first thing that you do is go to your wagons, go to your tents, go wherever you want to go and drop to your knees and thank your merciful God.

Then set to work to make use of God's bounteous gift. Clean the birds. Cook them however you can. Boil them, smoke them, salt or dry the meat. Do whatever it takes to preserve the meat for days to come."

As Allen spoke to them, a thought that had been on Nathan's mind all morning came back to him. He stepped quickly to the back of his wagon and reached past Sarah to his small valise. In a moment he stepped back. As the captain finished, Nathan waved his arm. "Captain Allen, can I read something to the congregation?"

Allen saw the Bible in Nathan's hand and nodded in approval. "Come over here, Nathan, where all can hear you."

As he stepped away from his wagon, Nathan thumbed quickly through the first part of the Bible. When he found the sixteenth chapter of Exodus, he stopped and turned around. A great hush now fell over the crowd. He lifted the book and began to read in a loud voice: " 'And the Lord spake unto Moses, saying, I have heard the murmurings of the children of Israel: speak unto them, saying, At even ye shall eat flesh.' " He paused, letting his eyes skip a line or two; then he went on with great solemnity. " 'And it came to pass, that at even the quails came up, and covered the camp.' "

He closed the book and lowered it to his side. The silence stretched on for several seconds before he spoke. "Brethren and sisters, in days of old, God watched over the children of Israel. He worked mighty miracles in their behalf. Today, we who are part of the modern house of Israel have seen God work a mighty miracle in our behalf. Let us never forget what we have seen here this day."

Off to Nathan's left, a voice spoke one word: "Amen!"

As one, the people bowed their heads and answered, "Amen."

"Bat-*tal-yun*. *Halt!*"

It took several seconds, but eventually the meandering

double line of men came to a stop. Private Josh Steed raised his head and peered through the rain. Lieutenant Smith had turned his horse to face his men and had one arm held high, as if he would stop them by the sheer force of his body. Josh wiped the water from his eyes. It was raining hard and many were soaked, even through their rain slickers. But in spite of all that, a ripple of excitement went up and down the line.

Even through the rain they could see the first buildings of Santa Fe—low, flat-roofed houses made of *adobe*, as the Mexicans called it. Around them, cedar trees covered the hillsides and made a most pleasant setting for the town.

"All right, men, listen up," Smith shouted. "We've done what some thought we could not do. Today is Friday, October the ninth. That is one day ahead of when we were commanded to report to Santa Fe."

A ragged cheer went up and several waved their arms.

"We are now a day ahead of Colonel Price's calvary company."

Now the cheer roared out. Colonel Sterling Price's group were all Missouri volunteers, and there had been some gentle competition between them and the Mormons. Not only did they have horses, but they had left Fort Leavenworth two days ahead of the Mormon Battalion.

"You've done yourself proud," the lieutenant went on. "And now we're going to march into the town like the soldiers that you are." He raised up in his stirrups, then whipped out his sword and held it up high. "Battalion! Fix bayonets."

There was the rattle of metal as men fumbled inside their slickers for their bayonets and attached them to their muskets. The officers all drew their swords and held them vertically in front of them. Josh looked at Sergeant Williams and grinned. "We're pretty shabby-looking soldiers, I'd say." And that was true. They had no uniforms except for their white belts and bandoliers. Many of them, including Josh, had worn holes through the shoulders of their shirts where they carried their muskets. Their boots were scuffed and many had worn through the soles.

Their hair was long and shaggy, their beards untrimmed.

Williams smiled back at him. "True enough, but we're here. Eight hundred sixty miles from Fort Leavenworth, and we did it in less than two months. And we've come a thousand from when we left our families. We may look shabby, but I'm proud to be a part of this."

"Me too," Josh said earnestly. In spite of all the hardships—the storms, the collapsed shelters, the long, hard marches, the days without water, the "tender mercies" of Doctor Sanderson—at this moment it was thrilling to think that he was part of the Mormon Battalion.

Lieutenant Smith waited for the men to finish attaching their bayonets, then spoke again. "All right. We'll go in columns of four. Keep your eyes to the front. Colonel Doniphan is in command here and is waiting for us. I want to go in like soldiers."

"Alexander Doniphan from Missouri?" someone called out.

"Yes, I believe that's where he's from."

A murmur of excitement broke out up and down the ranks. Josh turned to his companion. "Who is that?"

"Well," Williams replied, obviously pleased, "if it is the same Doniphan, he is a great friend of the Mormons. He was the one who saved the Prophet Joseph Smith's life during the Mormon War of eighteen thirty-eight when he refused to carry out an order to have Joseph and Hyrum executed. He will be a blessing to us."

"Bat-tal-*yun!* Ten-*shun!*" The men straightened quickly, moving into four columns, checking to make sure they were dressed into neat lines. Smith swung his horse around to face toward the town and went up in the stirrups again. "For-*wurd*"—he stabbed the air with his sword—"*march!*"

To Josh's surprise, in spite of the heavy rain, what looked like the whole town turned out to see them. Men, women, children, donkeys, and dogs all lined the street as they entered the town. Umbrellas, ponchos, thin boards, and even some large bowls were used to ward off the rain. Most were Spanish-looking, with jet-black hair, large dark eyes, and olive skin. The children were the most friendly, waving and shouting out "*Buenos días, señores. Bienvenidos!*" The adults were more reserved, and Josh could discern two distinctly different reactions in their faces. Some seemed glad to see them. Others were sullen and resentful. Then he reminded himself that they were at war with Mexico and that these people were the conquered and the Mormon Battalion was part of the group that had conquered them. Santa Fe had fallen to General Kearny without a serious struggle; nevertheless, an occupying army was in their town.

And then Josh's eye was drawn upward. There on the roofs of the adobe houses on both sides of the streets were uniformed men with rifles held at attention. It was the men from Colonel Doniphan's regiment come to welcome the Mormons, and there must have been at least a hundred of them.

From somewhere up ahead, and he couldn't distinguish exactly where, he heard a man's voice shout out. "*Red-dee!*"

The men on the roofs all stiffened to attention.

"Shoul-*der arms!*" The command floated across the stillness broken only by the sloshing of the men's marching feet.

With impressive precision the men above them snapped the rifles up to their shoulders, barrels pointed at the sky.

"Red-*dee*. Take your *aim. Fire!*"

A hundred rifles exploded as one. The muzzles belched fire and smoke, and several of the children screamed joyfully and clapped their hands over their ears. Almost instantly Josh smelled the acrid odor of black powder burning.

"Fire at will!"

Gleefully, almost like children themselves, the men on the rooftops began blasting away at the sky in an unrestrained welcome to the arriving troops.

Josh turned and looked at Sergeant Williams, his face split with a huge grin. "I think we're here," he called over the noise.

Williams was more sobered by their welcome. "Welcome to the war with Mexico," he answered. "Let's hope this is as bad as it gets."

Chapter Notes

On 9 October 1846 one of the most remarkable miracles in the history of the Church occurred at Montrose, Iowa, across the river from the now all-but-deserted city of Nauvoo (see *SW*, pp. 213–14). The details found in this chapter are not exaggerated in any way and come from the eyewitness accounts of those who were there. A few months later, after hearing what had happened, the Council of the Twelve wrote the following in a letter to the missionaries in England: "Tell ye this to the nations of the Earth! Tell it to the Kings and nobles and the great ones—tell ye this to those who believe [in] that God who fed the Children of Israel in the wilderness in the days of Moses, that they may know there is a God in the last days, and that his people are as dear to him now as they were in those days, and that he will feed them when the house of the oppressor is unbearable, and he is acknowledged God of the whole Earth and every knee bows and every tongue confesses, that Jesus is the Christ." (As cited in *SW*, p. 214.)

Chapter Thirty

The second division of the Mormon Battalion marched into Santa Fe late in the afternoon of the twelfth of October, three days behind the advance company. This time there was no formal welcome from Colonel Doniphan's regiment, but many of the battalion members met them about a mile east of town and escorted them in.

Josh was very pleased to see that though Derek looked a little peaked, he was sitting up beside Rebecca on the wagon seat and was driving the team. Josh ran over to join them as soon as he saw their wagon. "Welcome to Santa Fe," he called up happily. "Is everything all right?"

"We're very tired, but we're fine."

"How's Derek doing?" he asked Rebecca.

"Holding on," she answered.

"Thanks to not having Doctor Death treating me, I'm doing all right," Derek corrected her. "I'm still a little weak, but I'm—"

"That's too bad. I was going to take you two out on the town tonight."

"Out on the town?" Rebecca repeated, smiling at his enthusiasm.

"Oh, yes. Santa Fe is wonderful. I want you to try some of the Mexican food." He got a wicked look. "Like their pepper pie."

Derek hooted. "Why do I sense a trap in that remark?"

Josh grinned. "It was a real experience. I wouldn't want you to miss it." Then he brightened. "That reminds me. We have a new battalion commander."

They both looked surprised. "What happened to Lieutenant Smith?" Derek asked.

"The army doesn't feel like he's a senior enough officer." He flashed a broken smile. "I knew you'd be heartbroken at that news."

"So who will take command?" Rebecca asked.

"His name is Philip St. George Cooke. He's a lieutenant colonel." Josh was speaking in a rush now. "He's the one who captured Santa Fe without any incident. Because of that, General Kearny has great confidence in him. Kearny put Cooke in charge." He chortled with glee. "I wish I could have seen Lieutenant Smith's face. They say he was absolutely dumbfounded."

"I would give a month's wages for that sight," Derek agreed.

"Another express came in this afternoon from General Kearny confirming the change. The men who have served with him say that Colonel Cooke is a strict disciplinarian but fair and well respected by his men."

"That would be a nice change," Rebecca said with a droll smile.

A head suddenly popped out from the wagon cover between Derek and Rebecca. It was Benjamin. "Josh!" he cried.

Instantly another head appeared. "Josh!" Christopher pushed past his brother until he was half onto the wagon seat.

"Hello, boys," Josh said, reaching up to grasp Christopher's hand. "I've missed you."

"Can we walk with you, Josh?" Christopher asked. He looked at his mother. "Can we, Mama? Please."

"We're less than a mile from town," Josh said.

Rebecca nodded and the two heads disappeared. There was a happy squeal from inside the wagon. Josh went around to the back in time to catch four-year-old Benji and set him down on the ground, then give a hand to Christopher. They strode forward again until they were walking alongside their parents.

"You'll love it here, Rebecca. The people bring in all kinds of things to trade. You can buy just about anything—apples, peaches, pears, pine nuts, grapes, carrots, potatoes, bread, corn, melons, onions. Oh, you should see the onions. They're as big as saucers. They eat them raw, like turnips, and they're really quite sweet to the taste."

He turned to the boys. "And you've got to try the pine nuts. They're about this big"—he showed them with his fingers—"and in a hard shell, which you crack with your teeth. They're delicious."

"You sound like a representative for the town fathers," Rebecca said, laughing.

Now the smile died as Josh looked up at his aunt and uncle. "There's some news that's not so good."

"What's that?" Derek asked.

"In the express that came from General Kearny today, Colonel Cooke got his orders. He's to get sixty days' rations for us, and then we're to follow the general's trail to the Pacific. Then we'll probably go by boat up to Monterey."

"What's so bad about that?" Derek replied. "I didn't expect to stay here very long."

Josh looked away. "Colonel Cooke met with all of the officers today. He says that the march ahead is going to be a very difficult one."

Rebecca's face fell. "No, Josh. Don't tell me."

"Yes. While he was complimentary of what we have done thus far, he has a lot of concerns. Our clothing is tattered and worn. Our mules are utterly broken down." He glanced quickly at Rebecca and away. "He says it was a mistake to let families enroll with the battalion. We're at war out here. It's no place for women and children."

"But Colonel Allen promised," Rebecca cried. "He promised."

"It's the sick too," Josh went on. "Colonel Cooke says we have too many that are old, too many that are too weak to make the kind of march that lies ahead of us. He's proposing that another detachment be sent back to Pueblo."

Rebecca was staring forward, her lips pressed into a thin line. "I won't go, Derek. I won't leave you."

"The lieutenant colonel says the sick detachment will spend the winter at Pueblo with the first detachment and then will be taken, at government expense, west in the spring."

"I won't," Rebecca said again. "I'm sorry, but I won't."

Josh looked only at Derek. "Our officers have agreed that this is the best thing to do."

"Did they even ask the men?" Derek cried.

"No. We were not consulted."

"Figures," he muttered.

Now Josh couldn't meet the look of either of them. "The decision is final. They've already started making up the roster."

Rebecca was outraged. "I'll go talk to this Colonel Cooke. I'll—"

There was a deep sigh. "All of your family is on the list to go to Pueblo, Aunt Rebecca," he said quietly. "Including you, Derek."

Once Peter and James Reed left their camp, they had made good time, pressing forward sometimes until after dark. Had Glaucus been her old self, Peter would have been hard-pressed to keep up, but the horse was almost as exhausted as the men and made no better time than a walking man. They took turns riding her, trying to conserve their strength.

The two of them caught up with the Donner group on the second day. Reed sadly told his longtime friends about the tragedy. He told them he had accepted the banishment to avoid further trouble and also to go ahead for food. There had been no word from Stanton and McCutchen as yet, so no one thought to question that. A shortage of food was on everyone's mind. After a brief discussion it was determined that Walt Herron would go with them. The Donners also offered them food for a week, but Reed refused. Those staying behind needed it more desperately than those going ahead. The three of them finally agreed to accept enough for three days, planning to stretch that out over six or eight days by supplementing it through hunting. They also decided that they would not take any more horses. There again, those still coming on with wagons had a more desperate need than the three going on ahead.

After eating breakfast with the Donners, the three men moved on.

On the fifth day—the third day after leaving the Donners—Reed, Herron, and Peter came to what were known as "The Sinks," where Mary's River simply disappeared in the desert vastness. They decided to go day and night across the "Fortymile Desert" and made it in about twenty-eight hours, stopping only once to sleep for a couple of hours. When they reached the Truckee River, they left letters for Reed's family to let them know he was all right, shot a couple of geese, and pressed on. The geese were a welcome treat but a bad omen. They were Canadian geese and were part of the large numbers that were headed south.

At Truckee Meadows, they let Glaucus graze for half a day while they rested at the base of the Sierra Nevada. When they started again, they followed the track of the companies that had gone before them, but clearly no one had been on it for a week or more. By then their food was gone and there were no more geese to be found. There was plenty of water to drink, but nothing to eat. They debated about stopping long enough to hunt for game, but James Reed was driven with a great urgency to return to his family. If they stopped to hunt, there was no guarantee they would be successful. If they weren't, it would delay them further and make their food situation all the more critical.

The Sierra Nevada was a great mountain wall looming before them, often shrouded with dark clouds, showing brilliant white crowns when it was clear. It was mid-October, and neither the clouds nor the snow were encouraging. No one rode Glaucus now. Reed held her reins and she followed along, as painfully slow as the men. Now, two days after starting to climb, they were within an estimated five or six miles of the pass. The trail had become steeper and they plodded onward, heads down and too exhausted to speak.

Peter was thinking of Kathryn, focusing on the trail only enough to keep his feet moving forward one step at a time. That was no surprise. Kathryn was constantly on his mind of late. As usual, whenever he thought of her now, a great sense of gratitude welled up inside him. When he thought about what it would have meant to have her still with them—hacking their way across the Wasatch, stumbling through the hell of the Salt Desert, now with him gone on ahead—it made him shudder.

"Look!" James Reed leaped forward and dropped to one knee. He fumbled in the pine needles and dried grass. Then he held up his hand triumphantly.

Peter leaned forward, staring. It looked like he held a small pebble. Walt Herron moved over beside Reed. "What is it?"

"A bean!" He waved it back and forth like a flag.

"A bean?" Herron said stupidly.

"Yes. If there's one, there may be others. It evidently dropped out of one of the wagons."

Had they been able to see themselves, and had the circumstances been different, they might have laughed aloud. Three grown men moved slowly along the wagon track, scouring the ground with their eyes as though they were looking for gold. Each time they found a bean, there was a glad shout and great rejoicing.

They found seven in all, and then there were no more. Some careful wife had evidently seen the beans leaking out of the sack and fixed the problem. When it was evident that their "bounty" had ended, they solemnly divided them up. Herron—who was doing the worst on no food, or at least who made the most noise about it—got three. Peter and Mr. Reed each took two. They washed them down with water from the river, now a tumbling stream, then moved on again, more disheartened than ever.

Two hours later it was Peter who saw their next startling sight. "Wagons!" He virtually screamed it at his companions.

"Where?" Herron exclaimed.

"There. Through the trees." Ahead of them about fifty or sixty yards, the wagon track took a sharp bend to the left. Beyond that, through the pine trees, they could see splashes of white and portions of wagon wheels.

"It is!" Reed cried. He raised his hand and began shouting. "Hey! Halloo the wagons!" It came out not much more than a hoarse croak.

They broke into a stumbling run, but as they came around the bend and saw the three wagons in full view, they slowed to a halt. There were no horses, no oxen, no life of any kind.

"They're abandoned," Peter exclaimed bitterly.

They stared for several seconds, the disappointment so sharp as to make them twist in pain. Then Reed started forward. "Maybe they left some food."

They tore into the wagons like madmen. Whoever had decided that they couldn't make it over the pass with these wagons had left considerable goods behind—books, cooking utensils, tools, toys, blankets, bolts of cloth. But to no one's surprise, they found not one scrap of food—not a forgotten crust of bread, not a rusting tin of sardines, not a barrel that hadn't been completely emptied before it was tossed aside.

After fifteen exhausting, bitterly disappointing minutes, they came back together, heads down, panting heavily. "Nothing!" Reed whispered. "Not so much as a whiff."

Peter and Herron nodded, too weary to confirm that they had had no better success.

Suddenly Reed leaned forward. The other two raised their heads to see what he was staring at. To their surprise, he went to the second wagon. A bucket hung from the side. Peter had seen it earlier and checked it, but it was the bucket for the grease they used to lubricate the axles and the hubs. He had gone on, looking for better things. Reed took it off its hook and peered into it. There was a grunt, more of interest than of triumph. Curious, Peter moved over to see what he'd found. Herron stayed slumped on the wagon tongue.

"What is it?" Peter asked.

"Axle grease," Reed said, wrinkling his nose. He had a wooden spatula and scooped up some of the dark brown mixture. Then suddenly he began to scrape in earnest, wiping the grease against the wagon wheel. "Look!" he cried again, holding up the bucket.

Peter leaned over, putting his face right next to it. He saw a white streak in the bottom in sharp contrast against the dark grease. Then the smell hit him. It was so awful that he recoiled as though he had seen a rattlesnake in the bucket.

"What?" Herron called. "What is it?"

"It's tallow," Reed said, holding the bucket away from his own face. "Probably hog tallow, judging from the smell. They didn't mix it in very well when they made the grease."

"And rancid as a dead carcass," Peter said, backing up a step.

Herron leaped up, hollering something unintelligible. He came hobbling over and peered into the bucket. He pulled a face, but he didn't pull away. "Sure it's rancid," he agreed, "but it's food."

"You can't eat that," Peter cried in disgust.

Herron whirled on him. "You got any other suggestions?"

Reed blanched. "Walt, that's not edible."

"Give me a bite."

"Walt!"

"I'm not going to die on this mountain. Give me a bite. If we can keep going for just another couple of days, we can make it." When Reed just stared at him as if he had finally gone mad, Herron slapped the bucket. "Give me a bite."

Reluctantly, Reed took the spatula and scraped out a glob about the size of a walnut. Herron stared at it for a moment, took a deep breath, then opened his mouth. Gingerly, Reed held the spatula up to Herron's mouth.

Herron gulped it down without chewing it. He nearly gagged for a moment, but then he swallowed hard and the impulse passed. "Another one," he demanded.

Peter turned away. Even four or five feet away, the smell tied his stomach in knots.

He heard the spatula scrape the bucket. He looked around in time to see James Reed take a small bite of the stuff. Reed, however, made the mistake of biting down on it once and nearly threw it back up before he managed to swallow it.

"Give me another bite," Herron said.

Reed was still struggling to keep his down, but he scraped up another small ball of the stuff. Herron gulped it down again without hesitation. "More!"

Reed shook his head. "No, Walt. Any more and it will kill you."

Suddenly Reed doubled over and groaned in pain. The bucket and paddle dropped from his hand. He turned and ran, nearly smacking into one of the wagons, then stumbled on, groping his way like a blind man.

Peter started after him as the violent retching began. "Are you all right, Mr. Reed?"

"I can't see," came the strangled reply. He fell to his knees, retching violently now but waving Peter back. "Leave me be," he gasped.

"Oh mercy!" Herron cried. "He's dying. Don't die on us, Mr. Reed. Don't leave us."

Thoroughly disgusted, Peter didn't look at the other teamster. He hovered back a few feet as Reed, down on his hands and knees now, fought the dry heaves. "He's not going to die," Peter finally said in order to shut Herron up. "He's just sicker than any man I've ever seen before." He peered at Herron. "How are you feeling?"

Herron touched his stomach briefly. "A little queasy, but all right, I guess."

Peter shook his head, amazed that the man was not laid out flat on the ground.

Finally, after what seemed like forever, James Reed slowly straightened. His face was white, his hands trembling. "I think we'd best get started," he said in a voice not much louder than a whisper. "There's a storm coming and we've got to get over the pass. Peter? Can you see to Glaucus for me for a while?"

It was late in the afternoon of October seventeenth when they went over Truckee Pass. It was snowing, and the new snow was falling on six or eight inches that were already on the ground. But once over the rugged, granite notch, they quickly dropped out of the snow again. By dark they were back in rain. The ground snow became patchy, then disappeared altogether. Crossing the pass had given them almost as much of a boost as if they had found food in the wagons. Part of it was that they were going downhill now. More important, they had crossed the last major barrier to their destination. They weren't to civilization yet, but they could almost smell it, and that was a powerful stimulant. It was the twelfth day since leaving the company.

The next day they were following the wagon track, half stumbling, only partially aware of their surroundings. The track was snaking its way down a pine-covered ridge. The trees were thick and only gave occasional glimpses of other forested mountainsides. Then suddenly the ridge dropped more steeply and a grand vista of a narrow valley opened up below them.

Peter stopped, struck by the sudden beauty that lay before them. Reed and Herron lumbered on, too tired to care about scenery. Just as Peter started again, something caught his eye. At first he thought it was patches of snow in the trees by the riverbank, but they hadn't been high enough for snow since early morning. He leaned forward, squinting. The patches came into focus, looking very much like half a dozen wagons or more. He rubbed at his eyes. Then he gasped. A tiny dark figure came out of the trees and passed directly in front of one of the wagons, silhouetted momentarily by the canvas cover.

"Mr. Reed," Peter cried. It came out as a harsh, indistinguishable croak. He broke into a run, and catching up with his employer, he grabbed his arm. "Mr. Reed. Look! Wagons!"

Reed pulled up and Herron did as well. They stared in the direction he was pointing. "Abandoned?" Herron said, still not seeing them.

"No!" Peter exclaimed. "Look, there's people. See the smoke? We found them!"

No one bothered to wonder who "them" was. Reed started jumping up and down, waving his arms. "Halloo the wagons!" Peter and Herron joined in, shouting at the top of their lungs. Below, no one stirred. The three men were so weak they were hardly making themselves heard twenty rods away.

"Come on," Reed called to the others, breaking into a stumbling run. "We've found them. We've found them."

"Them" turned out to be the party led by Samuel Young, the Young of the Harlan-Young Party that Lansford Hastings had guided across his cutoff. The rest had gone on, but Young decided to rest his teams at the head of the Bear River before going on to Sutter's Fort. Young was stunned to learn that these three filthy, starving men had come from a whole company that was still somewhere back on the Truckee River.

To the further amazement of Reed, Herron, and Peter Ingalls, they had no sooner arrived in camp and been swarmed by the emigrants than a man stepped forward to greet them. It was Charles Stanton, the man who, with Bill McCutchen, had left the Donner Party more than a month before to ride for supplies.

Sam Young wouldn't let Stanton talk to them until he had the three arrivals seated around the fire sipping strained beef broth, warning them about eating too much too fast. But once they were settled, Reed was too anxious to wait any longer. He turned to Stanton. "Where is McCutchen?"

"By the time we reached Sutter's Fort, he took real sick. I had to leave him there."

"You're traveling alone?" Peter said in astonishment.

Stanton shook his head quickly, then pointed to where two Indians stood off by themselves. "Mr. Sutter lent me two of these Indian boys. Miwoks, they're called. They're two of Sutter's *vaqueros*, or herders. They're Christians and very good men." He smiled at them and they lifted a hand briefly to acknowledge they had heard his compliment.

"But you have supplies?" Reed asked eagerly.

"Yes. Flour, sugar, some jerked beef, beans. Seven mules' worth."

"Thank the Lord," Reed said, sagging back.

"Captain John Sutter furnished them," Stanton said quietly. "I had nothing but your letter promising to pay him, but he accepted it." Then his mouth turned down. "Seven mules' worth? It will help but it won't be nearly enough to sustain them."

"It will be a start. They've got plenty of cattle to live on if need be, but the flour and other things are critical. We're going for more."

Stanton seemed surprised. "You're not going back with me?"

A quick look passed between Peter and James Reed, and Peter knew that the banishment had instantly come to Reed's mind. Then Reed turned to Stanton. "No. If we go with you, we'll only consume more of your supplies. They're going to need more, much more. That's why we came ahead."

And, Peter thought, when they returned with additional badly needed supplies, perhaps there would be some softening on the part of the Graves family and Lewis Keseberg and the others who so hated James Reed. If not, they would have mules and supplies and would simply take the Reed family and come on alone.

"I'll be leaving at first light to start over the pass," Stanton said, accepting that. Then he turned to Mr. Young. "Finding these people here was a blessing for me as well. It gave us a chance for a good night's sleep without worrying about getting an arrow in our backs."

"You have to hurry, Charles," Reed urged him. "We had snow coming over the pass."

"So did we," Young said.

"I will," the bachelor replied. "But you come on back as quickly as you can get Sutter to outfit you. He's a good man. He'll help you."

On October eighteenth, the second detachment of the Mormon Battalion marched northward out of Santa Fe. There were eighty-six men, twenty women, and all of the remaining children, which were numbered somewhere around forty.

Tears were streaming down Rebecca's cheeks. She reached up and caressed Josh's face tenderly. "Dear Josh, how we will miss you!"

Josh was on the verge of tears too and could only nod. He had already said his good-byes to the little boys, and they had been ushered away by another family.

"We promised your mother that we would take care of you, Josh, and now look at us."

"I'll be all right, Aunt Rebecca. I promise. At least Derek is going with you."

"You'll be in our prayers every day," Rebecca promised.

"And you will be in mine." He turned as Sergeant Williams gave the command for the detachment to form up. He took Rebecca's hands and squeezed them hard. "Give Kathryn my love."

"We will. That is the only bright spot in all of this. We will get to see her and be there when the baby is born."

Josh leaned forward, kissed Rebecca on the cheek, then stepped back. Derek stuck out his hand and Josh gripped it hard for several seconds.

"You forgive me for the pepper pie?" Josh said gruffly.

"Never!" Derek growled.

Josh laughed, and then with one last small wave of his hand, he turned and walked swiftly away.

Chapter Notes

It is from Reed's own accounts, one of which was written some years later, that we learn of his ordeal after being banished by the company. The details as given here are accurate, with the exception of the addition of Peter, of course. Reed and Herron found five beans—not seven. Walt Herron had three and Reed had two. Herron took two bites of the rancid tallow and Reed took one. Reed became so violently ill that Herron thought he would die. (See *Overland in 1846*, pp. 290–91; *UE*, pp. 191–92.)

Though the dating through this particular time period for the trek of the Donner Party has several difficulties, we know that the group led by Samuel Young (of the Harlan-Young Party) may have been the last of the emigrant companies to go over Truckee Pass in 1846. They crossed on 16 October. (See *Chronicles*, p. 178.) This means that James Reed and Charles Stanton, coming from different directions, met up with the Young Party on 18 or 19 October.

In his later account Reed clearly states that both he and Stanton left the "next morning" after they met in the wagon company camped on Bear River. This would mean that Stanton probably crossed the pass going east around 21 or 22 October. This is significant because it shows that the pass was still open at that time.

It is tempting to put all of the blame for the Donner tragedy on the long delays they experienced while crossing the Wasatch Mountains and on their having subsequently lost thirty-eight head of cattle while crossing the salt flats of western Utah. There is no question about the costliness of those two events. But there were other, more tragic contributing factors. Contention within the camp became so severe after they left Pilot Peak, the wagon train broke up into individual fragments, sometimes traveling together, sometimes spread out by as much as two days' separation. This fragmentation was a major contributing factor in the death of John Snyder and the banishment of James Reed.

The disunity would cost them dearly after Reed left. The Paiutes, an Indian tribe that the emigrants held in great contempt and which they often called Diggers, had been harshly treated by the companies crossing the California Trail earlier that season. One report even claimed that some whites used the Indians for target practice. Some natives were killed. By the time the Donners came along, the Paiutes were in an ugly mood and looking for revenge. While they were not a large party, the Donners could have easily handled the Indians had they stayed together. Strung out as they were, however, they became easy prey. Stock was stolen or shot. Some of their people were ambushed, though no one was seriously hurt.

The Snyder killing was not the only symptom of the deep problems in the company. After Reed left, an old man fell behind and didn't show up when they camped. William Eddy wanted to go find him, but no one would give him a horse, so the man was left to die. When Wolfinger, one of the German emigrants, had to abandon a wagon, he asked the company to wait while he cached his goods. They refused. Two companions stayed with him but later came back under suspicious circumstances, saying he had been killed by Indians. One of those later admitted that they had murdered Wolfinger for his money.

Still strung out in a long line, the group was continually harassed by the Paiutes. A band snuck in and stole all of Franklin Graves's horses. The next day they killed or drove off eighteen head of oxen and cattle. A short time later, attacking from ambush, the Indians killed twenty-one more cattle. This loss of teams was disastrous and slowed the company considerably. It would delay them at least another week, and probably closer to ten days. Ten days sooner would have put them over Truckee Pass around 22 October, a time when we know (because of Charles Stanton) that the pass was still open.

By the time the main part of the group reached Truckee (now Donner) Lake, which is five or six miles below the pass, it was raining. In their naivete they waited, hoping the rain would pack down the snow that had fallen previously and make it easier to cross. But when the next day dawned clear, they could see their mistake. Rain at the lake had been snow at the pass.

Even though panic dogged them now, they still could not overcome the antipathy that also dogged them. On 3 November they moved ahead through three feet of snow past the lake. By the time they approached the pass itself, the snow was almost waist deep and they could see they had to abandon the wagons. But even here the contention continued. An extensive debate ensued about what to take with them. One wanted to drag a crate of tobacco; another argued for a bale of calico.

After two or three miles Stanton and his two Indian helpers pressed ahead to break trail, while the others collapsed in exhaustion. Pushing through snow up to their chests, the three men finally reached the summit and gazed down upon the western slopes of the Sierra. They rushed back to the group and found them camped beside a dead pine tree they had set ablaze. Stanton could say nothing that would convince them to go farther. They turned around and went back to Donner Lake to wait for better weather. (See *Chronicles*, pp. 186–92.)

The details given in this chapter about Santa Fe, the food there, the decision to change commanding officers, and the sending off of a second sick detachment are all recorded by those who were there during this time of the Mormon Battalion's experience (see *CHMB*, pp. 163–68; *MB*, pp. 65–71; *SW*, pp. 216–32).

In the end, the enlisted men did have their voices heard about who should go in the second detachment, at least to some degree. When Lieutenant Colonel Philip St. George Cooke took roster he found that he had 486 men. Sixty of those were too sick for service. In spite of the fact that some of the women and children had been sent to Pueblo with the first "family detachment," there were still twenty-five women and almost double that many children in the battalion. Cooke, appalled at what this would mean for a march across hostile territory, decreed that a second detachment be sent back to Pueblo.

Many were furious. They appealed to the lieutenant colonel, reminding him of the solemn promises made to the battalion by Colonel Allen before they enlisted. Cooke was sympathetic but adamant. The men went over his head and appealed directly to Colonel Alexander Doniphan. After listening carefully, Doniphan wisely ruled in favor of both sides. Colonel Cooke was right. Reality had to be faced. On the other hand, the army had to honor its commitments. He ruled that some of the husbands, sick or not, would be sent back with their wives and families. Five women, wives of the officers and sergeants, were allowed to continue with the battalion on the condition that they would be transported and provisioned at their own expense. (See *MB*, pp. 68–71.)

Chapter Thirty-One

On board an oceangoing ship, one learns to do many things. One of those is basic carpentry work. When Will had sailed to China, the crew included a ship's carpenter, but the old man almost always enlisted one of the sailors to help him, and through that, Will learned some fundamental skills. But a gristmill took a lot more than fundamental skills, and so when Will had been sent by Captain John Sutter to help with its construction, he had come basically as a laborer. And that was fine with him. He couldn't work on the construction of the waterwheel or build the huge gears that turned the millstones, but he could nail up planks on an outside wall just as well as the next man.

But John Sutter hadn't hired him because of his carpentry skills. Two weeks after Jared Will Steed was born, Will and Alice sailed up the Sacramento River on Sam Brannan's new boat called the *Comet*. Will had sought out Sutter and made him a proposal. If he would give Will work and help him find a place to house his family for the winter, Will offered to invest his wages and go into partnership with Sutter to freight goods up and down between the San Joaquin Valley and San Francisco Bay.

Sutter was a little dubious at first. He was not sure that a twenty-two-year-old "kid" could deliver on such grand promises, but Sutter was already learning that the Mormons were good, dependable workers and didn't run off every time a new load of liquor was brought to the fort. Liking Will's confidence, Sutter invited him and Alice for dinner. While they ate he plied the young couple with dozens of questions, drawing out the story of how Will had gone looking for his pa's killers and was shanghaied into becoming a sailor. He learned of the voyage to China and about Will's partnership with his father in a freighting outfit.

Convinced now that Will was capable of doing what he set his mind to do, Sutter drew up a contract as soon as the meal was finished. For half partnership in a freighting business, he offered Will the following: employment for the winter; a small one-room cabin not far from the fort; an extension of credit so that Will could purchase a boat even if he didn't have enough money from his earnings come spring; and a guarantee for at least one shipment of goods to San Francisco Bay.

Deeply grateful for Sutter's generosity and trust, the next day Will cleaned out the cabin and moved Alice and Jared and their meager belongings into it. The following morning he walked the short distance upriver and started work on the new gristmill. He had come up every day since—excepting Sundays, of course—for the last two and half weeks. In another few days most of the outer building would be done. There might be another day or two of work helping build the millrace, but after that he would have to leave Alice for a time. Forty miles upriver, close to the vast forests of timber that covered the western slopes of the Sierra, Sutter was also planning to build a sawmill. With the rush of emigrants to California, the cry for good lumber was already far outpacing the supply. It would be a profitable venture.

Will hammered in the last of the thick nails they had brought up from the blacksmith's shop, then stepped back to survey his work. He turned as he heard a voice calling his name. Coming up the path from the fort he saw Samuel, one of Sutter's many Indians. About eleven, Samuel served as messenger and all-around errand boy for Sutter. Like many of the other Miwoks around the fort, Samuel was a Christian who spoke mostly Spanish and his own native tongue. Like most of the Indians, he was cheerful and unfailingly helpful.

"Mr. Weell. Mr. Weell," he called, his head turning back and forth as he searched.

Will smiled. Samuel and many of the others called him "Weell Stid." They called Alice "Aleece."

"Here, Samuel," he called, waving. "I'm over here."

"Weell! Weell!" he cried, breaking into a run. "Come queek. Aleece says come queek."

Will let the hammer drop from his grasp. "What is it, Samuel? What's wrong?"

The boy's shoulders lifted and fell and his face was a mask of inscrutability.

"Is she sick?"

He shrugged again. "Aleece says come queek."

Will yelled to one of the other workers that he would be back shortly, then turned and ran. Samuel fell in beside him, trotting along easily.

Will ran up to the cabin and threw the door open. "Alice? What's the mat—" He stopped so abruptly that his feet skidded a little on the dirt floor. "Peter?" he gasped.

"Hello, Will."

He took a step forward, gaping. "Peter Ingalls?" He was completely dumbfounded.

There was a hollow laugh. "Yes, it's me. Or at least about eighty percent of me."

"What happened to you?" Will stepped up to him, his eyes searching the gaunt face, the deep-set eyes ringed with dark circles, the tattered, filthy clothing, the ragged beard.

"It's a long story, Will. I've just come over the mountains."

"What?" Will exclaimed. "But they said the last of the companies had come across more than a week ago."

Peter shook his head. Then, looking around, he moved to a box and sat down. He looked at Will. "I can't believe it. When we arrived here at the fort about an hour ago, I asked Mr. Sutter if he knew anything about the ship *Brooklyn* and Mormon emigrants. Imagine my shock when he said you and Alice were right here." He managed a wan smile.

Alice leaned forward anxiously. "Can I get you some food, Peter?"

He shook his head again. "No, we've had food these last few days. I'm just still a little weak. We went over a week with nothing but water and a couple of beans."

"But where's Kathryn?" Will said, moving over and pulling out a stool to face him.

Peter rubbed his hand across his eyes, looking suddenly very tired. "She's with a group of Saints in a place called Pueblo, somewhere in the eastern foothills of the Rocky Mountains."

"She's not with the family?"

Peter shook his head. "I forget. You and Alice left so early. You don't know anything." He took a quick breath. "Kathryn and I left the family early this year and hired on with a company from Springfield, Illinois, that was employing men to help them go to California. We thought that would be a good way to spare the family two more mouths to feed. We just assumed we'd catch up with our people somewhere on the trail. But Brigham Young didn't come west."

Now both Will and Alice cried aloud. "What?"

"That's right. They're still back on the Missouri River; at least that's what we were told. We never saw them. I happened to find another group of our people from Mississippi who had also hoped to catch Brother Brigham. They decided to winter at Pueblo, so I sent Kathryn with them. But the group I was with—the Donner Party—they're still on the other side of the mountains."

Will gave a low whistle. "Have they got a place to stay? Everyone says the passes are closed by now."

Peter shook his head, his eyes troubled. "Me and Mr. Reed—he's the man who hired me—came ahead to get supplies. We're leaving as soon as possible to go back and help them."

Will was reeling. "But—"

"I know, Will, but we have no choice. We've got to try." He stopped, looking haunted. "It's been terrible, Will. Mr. Reed is talking with Mr. Sutter. He's promised to help. We need men, Will."

Will glanced quickly at Alice, who nodded silently after only a moment's hesitation.

"I'll go, Peter. I'll talk to Mr. Sutter this afternoon about it."

Peter closed his eyes and leaned back. "Thank you," he whispered.

The day after the arrival of James Reed and Peter Ingalls at Sutter's Fort, a light rain started to fall. The next morning there was snow on the mountains. Captain John Sutter was grim. It was the earliest he had seen snow down that low.

It took them three days to put everything together. Sutter gave them bags of flour and a quarter of beef, several horses and a mule. He also gave them a letter of introduction to Mr. Cordway, who lived near Johnson's Ranch, about twenty-five miles up the Bear River.

By the time they left Johnson's Ranch, they were well equipped—thirty horses, a mule, two Indian drovers to help them. There were only four white men—Reed and Peter, Will Steed and William McCutchen. McCutchen had been left behind by Charles Stanton because of illness. Now he was well enough to go, but it was Walt Herron who was too ill to return. The reason for the dearth of others was not that no one cared, but rather that almost all of the white adult males in this part of Upper California had already been enlisted in the war with Mexico.

They moved up the Bear River making good time, though they were worried about how often the mountains ahead of them disappeared behind heavy clouds. As they approached the head of the river, which was where their serious climbing would begin, the clouds descended and a heavy rain mixed with sleet began to fall. By morning the sleet had turned to snow and there was nearly eighteen inches on the ground. They pressed forward in light but steady snowfall all that next day, and by the time they reached the head of the valley, they were pushing through close to two feet of snow. A deepening dread weighed in on all of them as they pitched their tent. Snow was still falling steadily and covered everything with a white shroud.

They made slow progress the following day. The snow continued unabated, and soon the horses were battling for every yard. The lead horses would stop for a moment to get their breath, then rear up on their hind legs and leap forward, breasting the snow. But as soon as they came down again, they would sink in the powdery fluff until only their heads, necks, and the tops of their backs were visible. By nightfall, after making less than ten miles, they camped again. As they huddled around their miserable little fire, they talked about leaving the horses and carrying what they could on their backs.

No one spoke of the question that was on everyone's mind. Had the emigrant group made it over the pass? How far ahead of them were they now? five miles? ten? James Reed and William McCutchen sipped their coffee and stared out into the snowy night. For them, this was much more than just making a noble effort. Their families were somewhere out ahead of them, waiting.

Will jerked his head up as he felt Peter roll away from him. When they had gone to bed, the sky was still overcast and showed no stars, but with all the snow it was as though there were a soft moon out. Now the whiteness permeated the canvas of their tent enough that Will could see Peter in silhouette. He was sitting up, his head cocked to one side.

Will reached out and touched him. "What's the matter?" he whispered.

"Listen!"

There was the sound of muffled hoofbeats.

The four of them were sleeping in one tent. The two Indians had made their bed in the snow, refusing shelter. Reed and McCutchen were both sitting up now. A horse whinnied. Another made that curious ruffling sound that horses made when they blew out breath. There was no question about what they were hearing. It was horses on the move.

"They're taking the horses," Reed shouted. In a second the tent was a scramble of men grabbing for trousers, boots, and coats.

They might have saved themselves the trouble. By the time they were dressed and ducked out of the tent into the night, about half the horses were gone, back down the trail that they had so painfully broken during the day. McCutchen swore and immediately began to saddle his horse.

"You won't catch them," Reed said, muttering angrily.

"Maybe they'll stop once they reach the valley," McCutchen growled. He slapped his rifle into the scabbard. "If they do, I think I can persuade them to come back."

"You'll get lost," Peter said.

"Not in this snow. There's only one trail to follow."

He swung up and, without looking back, started down the trail.

It had been light only about half an hour when Bill McCutchen appeared on the trail below their camp. His breath and that of his horse made great clouds as they rode up to the tent. He shook his head curtly, then dismounted. "They stopped in the valley, but only long enough to get the horses in a line again. They're long gone."

The tent was down and packed away, but they had a small fire going with a coffeepot in the coals. Reed poured a cup of coffee and handed it across the fire. "Our horses can't go any farther in this. Maybe it's just as well. Now that we've lost half the herd, we've got more than we can possibly carry anyway."

McCutchen grunted, but said nothing.

"Even with packs, we'll be quite a bit lighter than the horses. Hopefully the snow will hold our weight."

McCutchen turned, eyeing over the top of his cup the deep snow around them. Then he nodded. "I'm ready. Let's get going."

They went no more than a hundred yards before they had to admit defeat. The snow was chest deep, and it was so light and powdery that it didn't hold them at all. It was like wading through deep water, only water didn't resist you the way this did. And no water was as cold.

Reed, who was breaking trail, stopped, his chest heaving. He backed up a step, then leaned over, hands on his knees, gasping heavily.

"We can't do it," Peter said in despair. "There's no way we can go on."

"We have to," McCutchen cried. "My wife and daughter are waiting for me." Cursing steadily, he pushed around Reed and took the point, thrusting his body forward with great leaps. He went maybe ten feet, then had to stop, like Reed, gasping for every breath.

Reed slowly straightened. Despair haunted his eyes. "We're too late. Sutter said if the pass closes now, there'll be no getting over it until February or March."

Now Will spoke up. "I don't want to discourage you, Mr. Reed, but Mr. Sutter called me over to his home before we left there. He told me he didn't think there was a chance we'd make it, not with the storm."

"He said that?" McCutchen cried. "Why didn't he tell us that?"

"First, because he knew you wouldn't believe him. Not with it being your families and all. Second, because it was important to try. The storm might have blown over and we could have made it."

"Well, it didn't," Peter said shortly. "And now we've proven him right."

"But," Will went on earnestly, "he said that if we didn't make it, that doesn't mean all is lost. He was quite optimistic, in fact."

"Why?"

"Because Mr. Reed told him that your group has almost fifty head of oxen and cattle, plus a few horses and mules. They also have more than a dozen dogs."

"Yes," James Reed said. "That's right. He quizzed me at length about that."

"So, how many people are there?" Will continued.

"Around eighty-five, more or less," McCutchen answered.

"I know they're low on other supplies," Will went on, repeating the observations John Sutter had made, "but with that many cattle, they're not going to starve."

Reed considered that, brightening a little. "That's almost half a beef per person, not counting the horses, mules, and dogs."

"And a good many of those eighty-five or so people are children. They won't eat half that much. Remember, you said Stanton took seven pack mules to them. He must have made it over the pass, or we would have heard from him by now. With what he brought, plus all the stock, they can see it through the winter." Will forced a smile. "That's how Mr. Sutter sees it."

After several moments, Reed began to nod. "There's some good reasoning in that way of thinking," he admitted.

Peter jumped on that. "Better to save our strength, and then come February or March we'll mount a real rescue effort. It won't do your families any good if we all perish here in the snow."

James Reed looked at William McCutchen and then at Peter. For the moment, Will was excluded. And that was all right. He was the outsider here. He didn't have family waiting, and he hadn't come across the mountains to find help. He stepped back, letting them have their moment together.

"What do you think?" Reed said.

McCutchen was staring at his gloved hands, his face twisted with dark emotion. Peter seemed far, far away. Reed waited. Finally, McCutchen looked up. "I told my Amanda that I would do everything possible to come back for them." He turned and looked at the wall of chest-deep snow that had finally stopped him. "This is not possible."

Reed's head bobbed once. "I told Margret that I would either come back for her or die trying."

"I think," Peter said slowly, realizing with sharp pain what the implications of his words might be for Margret Reed and the Reed children. "I think Mrs. Reed would rather have us come back for them than have us die trying."

For several more seconds they stood there, the three of them, snow-covered and cold, breath coming in clouds of steam, eyes staring balefully up at the leaden sky above them. Then finally James Frazier Reed turned around and faced back the way they had come. "All right," he said in a tortured voice. "Until spring, then."

Kathryn Ingalls straightened wearily, pushing at her back to relieve the ache there. She felt her stomach push against the tightness of her dress and chided herself again for not working on that new, larger skirt she had been sewing for almost two weeks. But then, Kathryn did not like sewing. She much preferred teaching the children. Perhaps she could trade one of the mothers some extra tutoring for the sewing she needed.

She moved among the children's seats—a ragtag collection of stools, benches, sagging chairs, and wooden boxes—picking up the papers that had been dropped in haste when she lifted the little handbell and signaled the end of the day.

She had sixteen pupils now, including four from the trappers' families at Fort Pueblo and the new one she had picked up when the sick detachment from the Mormon Battalion arrived. It was a good thing that they had moved into this little one-room log cabin, which also served as Kathryn's home. It was mid-November now, and Pikes Peak, glittering and majestic sentinel of the plains, was crowned with snow. The brilliant yellows and reds of fall had long since disappeared. Even the days were getting uncomfortably cold now, and she was grateful that they were not still trying to meet out under the trees where she had started their first class.

Outside, there was a sudden commotion. She stopped, looking out the window. She couldn't see anything and moved to the door. As she opened it, she saw people running and pointing toward the south. One of her students came darting by.

"What is it, Sarah?" she called.

The girl barely stopped. "Another company from the Mormon Battalion is coming in," she shouted over her shoulder.

Another company? Kathryn looked doubtful. The arrival of the one detachment early last month had come as a wonderful and incredible shock to the group of Saints at Pueblo and had been a wonderful addition to their little settlement. She could scarcely believe there would be a second one. She reached behind the door, grabbed her shawl and her cane, and wrapped the shawl around her shoulders. Even if it wasn't the battalion, the arrival of anyone new out here was exciting enough to warrant an investigation. And if it was, perhaps . . .

She shook her head, not daring to hope. The first group had brought a long letter from Derek and Rebecca. She had been stunned. Josh and Derek in the battalion was surprise enough, but to learn that Rebecca and the children were with them as well was a real shock. She hurried on, not daring to hope, but unable not to.

As she came out of the trees, she was surprised to see a whole line of people coming up the trail toward their settlement. This wasn't a small group. There were several wagons, numerous men on horseback, and quite a few walking alongside the wagons. A man shot out of the trees behind her, spurring his horse to go out and meet them. People were pouring out of their cabins now as the word spread rapidly. Off to her right she saw that even those at the fort had heard the news and were coming across the shallow river to see who it was.

When she reached the back of the crowd, she stopped. By some unspoken signal, those of the Mississippi Saints held back, letting those who had been with the battalion race forward to meet their comrades. As Kathryn watched them fall on each other, she finally had to accept the fact that it was true. It *was* a battalion detachment. Over a hundred people, came back the report, with several children. That was wonderful news. She might have to ask for a larger room for her school.

She searched the nearest faces of the new arrivals as they came up to the crowd. Then suddenly her eyes widened. She closed her eyes once to clear her vision, then leaned forward, peering at the third wagon in the line. "Rebecca?" It came out as an incredulous whisper.

She started forward, half-dazed, unable to believe what her eyes were seeing. Rebecca had a baby in her arms. Then she saw Derek walking alongside the wagon. She broke into a hobbling run, waving one arm high in the air. "Rebecca! Derek!"

They too had been scanning the waiting crowd anxiously, and when they heard her cry, Derek stared for a moment, then started waving wildly as well. "Kathryn!"

Now she could see a strapping young boy on the wagon seat beside Rebecca and another, younger one walking with Derek. It must be Christopher and Benjamin. She shouted again, pushing through the crowd.

Rebecca thrust the baby and the reins into Christopher's hands and leaped down from the wagon. She took Derek by one hand and Benji with the other and they started running now too.

Derek stopped just before he reached Kathryn, not wanting to knock her off balance, but she didn't stop. She dropped her cane and threw herself into his arms. They met with such force that Kathryn nearly bowled Derek right over. "Derek? Is it really you?"

"It is," he laughed. "Yes."

She turned and fell into Rebecca's arms, who was laughing and crying all at once. "I can't believe my eyes," Kathryn said. "You two here?" She finally pulled back. "But how? How come you are here?"

"That is a very long story," Derek answered happily, "but I am pleased to say that we have all winter to explain it to you."

Chapter Notes

Immediately upon reaching Sutter's Fort, James Reed began to mount an effort to take supplies back to the emigrants who had driven him out. But it was too late. The same series of storms that closed the pass to the Donner Party blocked the route of the rescue team. Reed later wrote that it was Sutter's argument that the emigrant group had enough cattle to survive that convinced the rescuers to wait until spring to try further. (See *UE*, pp. 193–95; *OBH*, pp. 102–4.)

What none of them could know, of course, was that after James Reed had left the wagon company, the Paiute Indians had ravaged the Donner Party's herds. Collectively they had lost around fifty animals. The other thing they had no way of knowing was that these farmer-emigrants were not savvy enough to mark with long poles those places where their cattle died or were butchered. When the snows came, many of the animals were buried and could not be found again.

Because of his experience as an officer in the Black Hawk War back in Illinois, when James Reed first arrived at Sutter's Fort he was asked to lead a company of men in the war with Mexico. Because of his need to return for his family, he declined. When he and McCutchen returned after their aborted rescue effort, Reed immediately accepted the invitation. There were probably two reasons for this. First, it would occupy his time until spring. Second, it would win him the acceptance of the locals, on whom he would have to depend for help when spring finally came.

In January, when the war ended, Reed returned to Yerba Buena and began working to put together a rescue party to make another attempt to cross the Sierra. He was engaged in that effort in late January when seven emaciated figures—out of seventeen who had started out on snowshoes—stumbled out of the mountains and reached Johnson's Ranch with the horrible news of what had happened to the Donner Party. (See *UE*, pp. 195–97.)

The second detachment of the Mormon Battalion, which left Santa Fe on 18 October, arrived in Pueblo on 17 November. With the Mississippi Saints and the first and second detachments, the number of Latter-day Saints in Pueblo swelled to more than two hundred.

Chapter Thirty-Two

Once the second detachment of the sick and the women and children were gone, Lieutenant Colonel Philip St. George Cooke began two things in earnest. The first was highly unpopular. Colonel Cooke immediately began to impose military discipline on the battalion. Guns were not to be fired in camp or out on the trail without the express order of one of the officers. Those caught sleeping on guard duty would be executed, standard procedure in a battle zone during wartime. Orders were issued and punishments inflicted immediately when they were disobeyed. One man was lowered in rank when he was late for roll call. Another man was tied to a wagon wheel overnight for trying to purchase extra food from the quartermaster. The men were to carry their own knapsacks and equipment and not load them in the baggage wagons. From the Mormon point of view, Cooke was being unnecessarily harsh. Many in the battalion saw his actions as just another extension of Lieutenant Smith's dictatorial manner.

But Josh Steed did not agree. He could see that from a soldier's point of view, especially a soldier like Colonel Cooke who had been trained at West Point, the battalion was in hopeless disarray. Men obeyed or disobeyed orders depending on whether or not they agreed with them. Privates often openly quarreled with officers. Cooke was tough, but he was fair. It was no more than Josh had expected an army commander would be, particularly when they were supposedly marching to war. There was a lot of grumbling, but gradually the men began to shape up into a much more orderly outfit, and Cooke began to earn their grudging admiration.

The second thing Colonel Cooke did was push the battalion to make a serious effort to follow General Kearny's orders and march to California with as much dispatch as possible. He bought a few new mules or traded off the worst of the current lot for better ones. He ordered packsaddles for the mules so that the wagons wouldn't be so heavily loaded. Mess groups were enlarged from six to ten, which significantly reduced the amount of cooking utensils needed. In addition, he ordered all skillets and ovens to be left behind. Each mess was allowed only one kettle.

From Santa Fe they turned south, following the route of the Rio Grande. Much of the road was deep sand, and the animals had great difficulty in pulling the wagons. The men were ordered to help push and pull. Some of the poorest animals began to die, and in many cases their hooves were split and bleeding. At a few settlements along the way they were able to purchase supplies and additional animals; often, however, they were met with quiet hostility by the Mexican inhabitants.

They reached Albuquerque in the Mexican province of New Mexico on the twenty-fourth of October, five days after leaving Santa Fe. There the natives were a little more friendly, and they were able to trade off thirty broken-down mules for fifteen good ones. Without stopping for more than one night, they pushed on, still going mostly south. Now the weather became their enemy. Cold, heavy rains left many men sick and the roads a nightmare. Even on clear days the men suffered as they sweated and baked in the day and froze at night. Influenza became commonplace, and even Colonel Cooke was stricken for a time.

On the third of November they experienced their first death since leaving Santa Fe. Private James Hampton of Company A had left his family in Illinois because they did not want to join the Church and go west. Now he was wrapped in a blanket and buried in a solitary grave and they would not see him again in this life.

They marched seventeen days—two hundred and twenty miles—without stopping for more than one night to rest. Now, even for the young and healthy like Josh Steed, the days became a mindless blur. One lowered the head and plodded on, trying not to think beyond the next step. Often men fell behind and would come into camp long after dark. Many of those seventeen days were spent pushing and pulling the wagons through deep sand or mud. As many as twenty men would have to help with each wagon. The mules became so exhausted that they no longer had to be staked out at night; they simply did not stray from where they were freed. The men, nearly in the same shape as the animals, begged Colonel Cooke to abandon the wagons and let them carry the supplies on their backs.

Seeing that they couldn't keep up as they were, Colonel Cooke took yet another group of the sick and one of the five women who had been allowed to continue with them and sent them back to Pueblo. Between the three detachments, the deaths, and one desertion, they had lost one hundred sixty-two men, twenty-nine women, and forty-three children. The battalion's strength, originally at four hundred and ninety-six, was now at three hundred thirty-five, just two-thirds of full strength.

Again, many of the men complained bitterly at the further separation of their group. Josh would have no part of it. If they continued dragging the sick with them, the deaths would only multiply. And by sending that many men back, in one stroke Colonel Cooke had extended his rations for another eight days. Fortunately, Josh's health was still excellent, and for the third time he survived the cut.

A little even to his own surprise, he was pleased. He did not enjoy what was happening. Every day was one long, sustained misery. But he had come this far, and now the desire to see it through, to go all the way to California, was like a voice in his head driving him on.

On the day the third sick detachment turned back, Colonel Cooke finally agreed that most of the wagons had to be abandoned. Supplies and equipment were moved to the packsaddles. There weren't enough mules to go around, and so packs were put on the backs of the oxen. Accustomed to a yoke and not a pack, they kicked and bellowed, whirled and fought, reared and bolted. But eventually they were brought to bear. More equipment was abandoned. Tent poles were left behind. From now on the men would use their muskets to shore up their tents. And whatever wouldn't fit on the backs of the mules and the oxen went on the backs of men. There was no complaint. There would be no more pushing and pulling the accursed wagons.

On November thirteenth, almost a full month after leaving Santa Fe, they finally left the Rio Grande and turned southwest for California. Now all of the hardships and sufferings and sacrifices of the previous months seemed but prelude. They jumped off into the desert, where water sources were separated by many miles. Often the only water, if there was water at all, was stagnant, insect-infested pools found in depressions in the rocks, or, in one case, in the footprints of buffalo (the buffalo dung had to be strained out before the water could be drunk).

Surprisingly, though the usual grumbling took place, the serious complaining and disgruntlement largely disappeared, and a sense of pride began to develop. In spite of the murderous terrain, in spite of the threat from hostile Indians and Mexican troops, in spite of short rations, filthy water, devastating thirst, blistering heat, numbing cold, blinding rain, raw blisters, and all-around misery, the men were enduring. The men had come to respect their commanding officer, who suffered equally with them, and he had come to respect these Mormons who seemed to have an infinite capacity to endure suffering. One man who had run out of ink was so determined to keep his journal current that he would poke himself in the arm each night, then make the entry in his own blood. The others quickly dubbed it the "blood journal."

There was one day when it seemed as though there would be trouble again between Cooke and the men. When the guides could no longer find a route westward, a distress fire was built, and soon some Apaches and Mexicans came to see what it was. They reported that there was a good road that led into Sonora, which was deep into Mexico. Running short on rations and ordered by Kearny to find a wagon route to California, Cooke finally called the Mormon officers together and told them he was going to take that route. They objected strenuously. Marching deeper into Mexico only enhanced the danger. But Cooke could not be swayed.

The officers were so upset, that night they asked the men to pray that Cooke would change his mind. That took little urging. The men were greatly dismayed with the decision and feared that there would be clashes with Mexican regulars. They were isolated and with no chance of being resupplied. It seemed madness to go directly toward the enemy.

Never in all his young life had Josh Steed felt such a dark feeling. He had made up his mind to be loyal to Colonel Cooke as his commanding officer, and he didn't often agree with the complaining spirit of the men. But this time he did. Every time he thought about marching farther southward, the darkness seemed to swell within him. That night, he knelt on his bedroll and prayed with more fervency than he could remember having ever prayed before.

The next day, completely adamant in the face of the men's feelings to the contrary, Colonel Cooke started them southward. Then, after just two miles, the battalion reached a small knoll. Cooke, out front on his horse, reined in. Ahead as far as he could see, the trail stretched to the southeast, not to the southwest as he had been told. He swung around, suddenly determined.

"Gentlemen, this is not my course." He glanced back at the trail behind him. "I was ordered to go to California." He swore. "And that I will do or I will die in the attempt!"

He jabbed his finger at the bugler. "Blow the right!" he commanded.

Behind him, the long string of men were watching the scene up at the front with curiosity and some misgivings. But when the notes of the bugle sounded, a cheer went up and down the line. One of the men near the colonel who had heard what he said could not contain himself. "God bless the colonel," he shouted.

Colonel Cooke spun around, his eyes narrowed, searching for the man who had said it. Then his face relaxed. There was a faint smile and a brief nod of satisfaction. "Thank you. To the right, gentlemen," he said. "Let's go to California."

Private Josh Steed wiped his razor against his pant leg as he peered into the tiny square mirror he had propped up against his knapsack. "Why do you suppose there are only bulls and not any cows or calves?"

Sergeant Luther T. Tuttle was methodically packing his knapsack. He didn't look up. "My guess is that the Indians have killed the cows and calves because the meat is so much more tender."

Josh grunted, pulling a face. "That makes sense. I may as well have eaten my belt as the piece of meat I got last night."

"I thought we *were* eating our belts," Tuttle said dryly.

Josh laughed, then walked to his knapsack and stored his shaving gear. "How many cattle must there have been originally?" he wondered aloud.

Tuttle straightened. "Probably hundreds, if not thousands. Remember, it's been fifteen years since the Apaches drove the Mexicans out of San Bernardino. It was a large ranch, and fifteen years is a long time."

Nodding, Josh dropped to his knees and began to gather up the rest of his gear. On the last day of November they crossed the

Guadalupe Mountains and began their descent into a broad, pleasant valley. To their great surprise, they began seeing wild cattle in significant numbers. On the second of December they reached a deserted Mexican town known as Rancho San Bernardino. Now the wild cattle were everywhere. They were told that fifteen years earlier there had been a huge cattle ranch here, but eventually the Apaches drove the Mexicans out and scattered their cattle. No one had ever come back to gather them in.

It was a welcome treat for the battalion after more than three weeks of hard marching. They had crossed uncharted territory, making their own way and creating the wagon road that General Kearny wanted to California. They had been on shortened rations, and game had become scarce. When something was killed their appetites were so ravenous that they ate head, feet, hide, tripe, and everything else that was possibly edible. At the ranch the hunters killed over twenty of the wild cattle—most of which were bulls—and they had taken a day to build frames of mesquite and dry the meat. Once they marched on, they constantly saw signs of the wild bulls but rarely cows or calves. Even now, more than a week later, they were still seeing the bulls on a regular basis.

"That's why that meat those Indians sold us was so good, wasn't it?" Josh asked. A short time after the battalion left the ranch, several Indians had ridden into camp with about two hundred pounds of very fat and juicy meat.

Tuttle grunted. "I wouldn't be surprised if the Indians have rounded up the cows and calves and have got them corralled somewhere."

"Probably," Josh agreed. "I hope they come selling some more."

Just then they heard the bugler sound assembly. Tuttle shouldered his knapsack and picked up his musket. "We'd better go. Don't want to miss roll call."

Josh grinned. "If we're late, they can bust you to private. But what can they do to me?"

The sergeant growled something which he didn't understand. Josh laughed and shouldered his pack as well. Together they started to where the rest of the men were lining up.

The battalion left the San Pedro River shortly after departing camp and wound their way through some low hills for a couple of hours, then dropped down to the river again. The drovers took the cattle ahead of the main column so that they could water at the river while the men came up to join them. As they were approaching the river bottoms, suddenly rifle shots rang out. Startled, Josh swung his musket off his shoulder, looking around wildly. There was another shot, then another. Sergeant Tuttle had his rifle at the ready now too and bawled at the men to stay alert. Cries of "Ambush" and "We're under attack" ran up and down the line. Men scrambled for protection as they readied their weapons. Josh found himself behind a large rock, his mouth suddenly dry and his heart pounding.

After a minute or two, one of the officers came riding down the line. "It's all right," he called. "Some wild bulls got in with our cattle and the drovers had to shoot them."

Sheepishly the men got to their feet again, laughing and talking in relief.

"We'll take an hour's break at the river," the officer said. He gave the men a mocking look. "Keep your weapons handy, men. You never know what's going to jump out at you." Then he rode away, laughing uproariously to himself.

Josh sat beside the river—not really much more than a wide creek at this time of year—holding his stomach. After some of the water they had been forced to drink over the last several weeks, this was delicious and he had drunk until his belly hurt. Across the stream, the drovers were skinning and cleaning the bulls they had shot earlier. Every now and then the air would stir slightly and he would smell the ripe odor of blood and death. But he could live with that. There would be fresh meat tonight. It would be tougher than saddle leather, but it would be fresh.

He turned to where Sergeant Tuttle and the rest of his platoon were lying side by side, hats over their eyes to protect them from the sun. Now, that wasn't a bad idea, he thought. They still had half an hour before the call to move again would sound. Josh had learned that in the army you grabbed sleep whenever and wherever you could. With a soft moan of pleasure, he lay down in the soft sand and closed his eyes.

Three minutes later, just as his mouth was sagging in that final relaxation before sleep, there was a bellow from somewhere behind him. He opened his eyes. It was deeper than that of an ox. Then there was a scream and a rifle shot. He sat bolt upright, looking around in confusion.

The riverbed itself was wide and mostly sand, with the stream being only a few feet wide, but all along the banks there were thick stands of underbrush—willows, manzanita, some mesquite and other desert brushes. As he leaped to his feet, a dark shape burst out of the undergrowth about fifty yards from where he and the others were standing. It was a huge bull, black as a coal bin, with massive horns that curved to wicked-looking tips. It whirled to the right, hooves kicking sand outward. Directly in front of it was one of the few wagons the battalion still had with them. With a bellow that rumbled like thunder, the beast lowered its head and charged. Men yelled and exploded in panic. There was a tremendous crash as the bull hit the wagon at full charge. One horn went through the wood sideboard as if it were paper. The wagon rocked violently; then, as the bull lunged forward, twisting with its massive neck, the wagon lifted and slowly tipped over, spilling sacks and boxes out as it hit the ground.

"Watch out!" It was Sergeant Tuttle. Josh whirled around. Three bulls burst out of the trees right behind them. "They can smell the blood," Tuttle shouted, throwing his musket up to his shoulder. He fired and a puff of smoke rolled outward from the barrel. There was a grunt and the lead bull went down, its muzzle plowing a track in the riverbed. The other two swerved, one to the right and one to the left, the latter coming directly toward Josh. He fumbled for his rifle, which was still tangled in its sling from when he had lain down with it. He freed it and snapped off a shot. The bull, no more than ten feet away, jumped and flashed past him.

Now the noise of rifle shots, screams, bellows, and cries was everywhere. A horrible sound split the air. Josh whirled, reloading even as his eyes took in what was happening. The bull that had overturned the wagon now turned on the mule team. The overturning wagon had caught the mules in the traces and they were down, all tangled up with one another. The bull stood over the nearest mule, its head down and one horn buried almost to its full length in the mule's belly. With astonishing speed, the bull withdrew, its horn showing bright red, then lunged again and gored the mule a second time. Another horrible shriek was torn from the fatally wounded animal.

Beside Josh a man dropped to one knee, took aim, and fired. The bull leaped sideways, then fell to its knees, bellowing wildly. Finally it rolled over, almost landing on the mule that it had just killed.

Josh swung around. Bulls were coming out of the underbrush too quickly to count now. Eight! Ten! A dozen! The air was filled with dust, and it was difficult to see clearly in all directions. But one thing was evident. This was not just a stampede. Tuttle was right. These were animals infuriated by the smell of the blood of their own kind. They were thundering masses of destruction, bent on charging and destroying anything that moved.

Josh saw a younger bull whirl in full stride as it caught sight of Amos Cox, one of Josh's fellow privates in Company D. Cox was running as hard as he could in the soft sand, trying to reach the protection of a wagon. It was incredible to Josh that the huge bull could move so quickly. Josh yelled, but Cox either didn't hear or was so intent on escape that it didn't register. He was fast—sheer terror adding greatly to his speed—but he wasn't fast enough. In four or five great leaps the beast reached Cox. Again there was that terrible sweep of horns, the massive upthrust of the shaggy head. Cox screamed as he went flying over the bull's back. There was a flash of red on the horn and Josh knew that his friend had been gored.

The bull swung around, spraying dirt and dust and gouging great furrows with its hooves. It had its victim down and was ready to finish what it had started. There wasn't time to think. There wasn't time to aim. Josh raised the rifle and fired as the animal started slowly forward. It flinched heavily; then, bawling like a steamboat's whistle, it turned and ran back into the brush.

Josh dropped to one knee again, frantically groping for a cartridge. There was another scream. Just ten yards away a bull had a man pinned up against a wagon. Fortunately the man was between the horns. He was yelling and screaming and beating on the animal's head. Another man ran up and fired point-blank into the bull's head. It went down. The man went down as well, writhing on the ground in agony.

"Josh! Behind you!"

Again Josh whipped around at Tuttle's cry. Another bull burst from the thicket and was headed straight for him. For one split second, Josh froze. He was still loading the musket and had no chance for a shot. He saw the crazed eyes and the nostrils flaring like bellows. Out of the corner of his eye he saw the puff of smoke from Tuttle's rifle, and he heard the explosion; but Tuttle missed and the bull came on, puffing and snorting. For one instant Josh thought about Amos Cox trying to outrun the beast; then his instincts took over. He fell on his musket, throwing his arms over his head. He felt the ground tremble and heard the pounding hooves bearing down on him. Then for a moment they stopped and he felt something graze his shoulder and dirt rain down on him. There was a great thud, and then the pounding of hooves moved away from him. The animal, losing its moving target, had jumped over what was now no more than a log and raced on, looking for something else to destroy.

As Josh turned his head to see what had happened, three

men shot the animal at the same time. It ran another ten yards, sloshing into the river, then finally went down with a tremendous splash.

"Whoo-ee!" Tuttle said, running up and helping Josh to his feet. "That was close."

"You're telling me?" Josh gasped, still not sure that he was all right. Not wanting to make the same mistake again, he started jamming another cartridge in the musket as he tried to recover his breath.

There was a shout from behind them, and they both spun around. Downstream a few rods, Colonel Cooke was riding his white mule, racing up and down, shouting commands. Yet another bull had exploded out of the underbrush. It was enormous, the largest yet, and was as black as the inside of a hog's belly. It trotted forward, swinging its head back and forth, puffing like a railroad engine. Colonel Cooke instantly pulled his mule to a halt so as not to draw attention to himself. Then suddenly a man came running out in front of him.

Someone yelled for the man to hold still, but he trotted onward another eight or ten paces. Seeing the movement, the bull roared, lowered its head, and leaped forward. It headed straight for the moving figure. As Josh peered more closely he recognized Corporal Lafayette Frost of A Company. The corporal stopped, planted his feet, then calmly raised his rifle and took aim.

The bull had come out of the brush about a hundred yards from Colonel Cooke. Now with blinding speed it had cut that distance by half. Everyone froze at the sight of this single man standing calmly as he waited for the animal's charge.

"Load your weapon, Corporal!" Colonel Cooke shouted, thinking that the soldier had obeyed orders and was marching with his weapon unloaded. Frost didn't move. He stood there as cool and unruffled as if he were watching a pheasant come out of the weeds instead of twelve hundred pounds of raging fury. Frost waved an arm, as though he didn't want the bull to lose sight of him.

Cooke swore, thinking the corporal was so terrified that he had lost his senses. "Run, you fool!" he screamed.

Corporal Frost moved only enough to lower his head and sight down the barrel. The huge beast was down to thirty yards and was closing with breathtaking swiftness.

"Run!" someone else shouted.

Frost stood his ground. Then, just as it was certain that the bull was on him, Frost fired. He must have hit it squarely between the eyes, for the bull dropped as if someone had cut its legs out from under it. It slammed into the ground in a great cloud of dust. For a moment, Josh couldn't see what had happened, and then the dust slowly dissipated. Corporal Frost stood where he had been before, the only discernible change being that his rifle was lowered now. Barely six paces directly in front of him the bull was in its last death struggle, the legs jerking spasmodically.

Chapter Notes

Whole novels and books could be written—and have been—about the incredible march of the Mormon Battalion. The details given in this chapter all come from the various journals but are only a small portion of what these Latter-day Saints experienced on their way to California (see *MB*, pp. 70–85; *CHMB*, pp. 165–207; *SW*, pp. 232–93).

On 3 December 1846 the Mormon Battalion reached Rancho San Bernardino (not the same as the current San Bernardino in California but located just below the present Mexican-U.S. border near the state line dividing Arizona and New Mexico). Before they reached the deserted ranch, they began seeing hundreds of wild cattle, mostly bulls. Eight days later as they were marching along the San Pedro River, dozens of wild bulls suddenly shot out of the brush and attacked men, animals, and wagons. One mule was killed, a wagon was tipped over, and three men were injured. A bull ran Amos Cox down and gored him in his leg. Witnesses say he was tossed ten feet into the air, completely over the bull's back. Albert Smith was hit by a bull but managed to stay between its horns. He was badly bruised and suffered three broken ribs. One lieutenant, while frantically trying to reload, dropped two cartridges into the chamber of his rifle. One exploded, taking off the upper joint of his thumb. Levi Fifield was charged by a bull, but he dropped to the ground. The bull jumped over him and ran on, leaving him very frightened but without injury. It is not known how many bulls were actually killed in what came to be known as "The Battle of the Bulls." Two men counted nine carcasses in one spot. Some said at least twenty were killed and two or three times that many wounded. (See *MB*, pp. 94–95; *CHMB*, pp. 219–21.)

Colonel Cooke himself would later say, according to battalion member William Coray, that the march of the Mormon Battalion "had not a parallel in the world" (cited in *MB*, p. 121). This is an exaggeration born of Cooke's personal enthusiasm, but there is no question but what in U.S. annals it is one of the longest infantry marches in history, if not the longest.

Chapter Thirty-Three

In Winter Quarters, Christmas Day 1846 began with a rousing boom. John Scott, who was in charge of the Church's three small cannons, took them up on the bluff and fired off each one just as the sun rose over Winter Quarters. Many people were already up by then, and they poured out of their houses to see what was happening. When they realized it was because of Christmas, there were cheerful cries of "Happy Christmas," "Merry Christmas," and "Christmas Gift" all up and down the street.

Nathan stepped back inside the house as Lydia appeared from behind the blanket that separated their sleeping area from the children's. She was in her nightdress and looked very sleepy. He smiled. For Lydia, rising was always a slow process. He went to her and took her in his arms. "Happy Christmas, Lydia."

She pried one eye open wider. "Was that what that was?"

He nodded, chuckling.

Emily peeked out from behind the blanket that partitioned off their "bedroom." "Happy Christmas, Papa."

"Christmas Gift," he answered.

Nathan left immediately after breakfast. He stopped for a moment in front of their hut and took a deep breath. It was going to be a beautiful day. The sun was rising in a perfectly clear sky. There had been a hard freeze during the night and his breath came out in large puffs of silvery white, but it would warm up soon enough. "Good," he said aloud. "A beautiful day to celebrate the birth of the Savior."

He was out this morning because he wanted to ensure that all of the families in his ward would have a good Christmas. In some cases that would be a matter of just stopping in to wish them a good Christmas and to let them know he was thinking of them. In other cases it would not be so simple. There were women whose husbands were with the Mormon Battalion or on missions. For all intents and purposes these women were widows and needed special attention. Then there was Mary Northrop, whose husband, Amos, was near death. Nathan was on his way to the gristmill to make sure that the family had something to eat, and he would try to bring them some comfort and see if he could do anything for Amos's suffering.

It was a holiday, and it might be saluted with a volley from the cannons, and there would be Christmas suppers tonight—meager but festive—but it was still a workday. There was simply too much to be done to have it be otherwise. Even though it was not yet eight o'clock, everywhere he looked there was a bustle of activity. Men and boys were laying a sod square on the ground, the first foundations of another home. Young girls sat on benches in front of homes or wagons spinning flax into thread or tending younger brothers and sisters. Boys moved back and forth carrying baskets filled with a variety of clothing or goods. He passed women who stood before kettles hung over fires in their yards, starting to do the day's laundry. He saw Sister Stone, another ward member, coming back from the creek, staggering under the load of two buckets of water hanging from a yoke on her shoulder. He walked quickly to her, took it from her, and carried it the last way to the wagon that served as "home" to her, her husband, and three children.

She touched his arm as he set the buckets down. "Thank you so much, Bishop Steed." She spoke with a lilting English accent.

"Happy Christmas, Sister Stone."

"Christmas Gift, Bishop. God bless."

He walked on, amazed once again at the bustle around him. Men were chopping wood, repairing chimneys, shoveling dirt and grass up on top of their houses to make roofs. Behind a log cabin, a man had what looked like a yearling heifer strung up on a block and tackle and was skinning it out. Nathan passed one open-ended sod building where five or six men were working on building or repairing a wagon. That was a sober reminder that all of this was temporary. Come spring, they would be moving west, and preparations for that day were never set aside for very long.

As he rounded the corner, he saw the nearly completed Winger cabin. Without being aware of it, he frowned. There were the others in his ward who presented a different kind of challenge than widows or families who lived in tents and wagons. John Winger was one of those. The Winger family had come west with the Orville Allen rescue group that Nathan and Joshua had accompanied. But instead of staying at Mount Pisgah, as the refugees had been counseled to do, Brother Winger insisted on coming on. Brigham had not been pleased, but he assigned them to Nathan's ward and asked him to work with them.

He blew out his breath in mild exasperation. It was Sister Winger and their two children who suffered because of her husband's laziness. All the way across Iowa Territory, John Winger had been a source of constant irritation to everyone. His cattle were constantly lost because he simply turned them loose. And unfortunately there were others like him. On more than one day the company had been forced to lay over while they spent the day rounding up stray cattle.

Brother Winger had been an eye-opener for Nathan. Some

of those they had found in the poor camp on the west bank of the Mississippi were poor because of the terrible circumstances which had befallen them. Carl Rogers was a good example of that. With the store burned, the brickyard gone, their house abandoned, Carl and Melissa were absolutely destitute. But Carl was a hardworking man. Even though he was still weak and hurting from his punctured lung, he was up helping the family in whatever way he could. Joseph Fielding and his two sisters were another example. Poor, yes, but down and out, definitely not.

But Brother Winger? On their arrival here, Nathan had gotten a group of men together and raised them a log cabin. Even though he himself and several of the other men had only sod huts, they had cut the logs and erected a one-room cabin for the Wingers. And what did John Winger do while they were doing that? He stood back with his thumbs in his belt and watched them work. Since they had finished the main structure Brother Winger had done nothing more to find shutters for the windows—Nathan could see that the same thin blanket was all that kept them from the cold—or to make it more comfortable for his family.

He sighed, loudly enough that a passing woman looked at him in surprise. Embarrassed, Nathan smiled and waved. "Merry Christmas."

"Christmas Gift," she murmured back, still looking at him strangely.

At the gristmill he would get a sack of cornmeal for Sister Winger and the children. They were the ones who suffered. And so, irritated at John Winger or not, Bishop Nathan Steed was on his way to make sure they had food and got at least some kind of cheer on Christmas Day.

He thought with longing on those first days as bishop when he had been given just three or four families to care for. Now the wards were made up by city block and each block had twenty lots. In his block there were twenty-eight families. His own family, for example, occupied three lots, but with the addition of

Carl and Melissa there were five separate family units living on those three lots. On the lots of several others were wagons or tents with families living in them until they could build more permanent shelters.

As he walked along, he thought of some of the others, and that pushed away his gloomy mood. It was Christmas, and though there were challenges in carrying out his calling as bishop, there was also great joy. For the most part, his families were faithful and cheerfully endured very difficult circumstances. They shared their resources in a manner that was most gratifying. Even in death they showed remarkable strength. In the few weeks since they had formed his ward, he had already lost five people—an elderly man, a mother who left her husband with four children to watch over, and three young children. And now it looked like Amos Northrop would be next. Those losses had really been hard, but for the most part, his people wept for a time, then threw back their shoulders and went on with life.

With that, he picked up his step, smiling happily now as he passed others and called out a holiday greeting to them.

By ten o'clock, the sun was warm enough that the women put on only light shawls. The ground was thawing and the challenge was to stay out of the mud. They left the older children in charge of the younger ones and set out. Mary Ann, Lydia, Caroline, Jenny, Jessica, and Melissa all walked together, chattering happily.

"What a beautiful morning!" Melissa exclaimed, throwing back her head and closing her eyes against the bright sun.

Mary Ann laughed, then spontaneously hugged her older daughter. "And how good it is that you are here with us to enjoy it!" she said.

"Oh, yes," the others said. "We're so glad you're here, Melissa."

There were sudden tears in her eyes. "When those men

started beating on Carl back in Nauvoo, I thought the world had come to an end. Now, knowing that it changed his mind about our coming west, I'm almost glad—" She stopped, blushing furiously as she realized what she was about to say. "Oh dear," she cried. "Don't tell Carl I said that."

The others laughed. "We promise," Lydia said, reaching out to touch her arm. "And we're glad that whatever it was the brought it about, you and Carl are here with us now."

"I was surprised," Jenny said, "that Carl didn't object any more than he did to young Carl and David and Caleb being baptized."

"Me too," Melissa said happily. "Sarah wants to be baptized also, but Carl says she has to wait until she's ten and old enough to make up her own mind."

"That's all right," Mary Ann said. "Carl is a good man, Melissa. We all know that."

She nodded in quiet pleasure. "I know."

Jessica broke in. "Look, there's Sister Richards."

They turned to see where she was pointing. Then Caroline smiled. "You mean the *Sisters* Richards."

And so it was. Mary Richards, wife of Samuel W. Richards, lived in a tent near the center of the city. Her sister-in-law Jane Richards, wife of Franklin D. Richards, lived nearby in one of the cabins that the Steed women were just now passing. Franklin and Samuel Richards were brothers and had been called to serve together as missionaries in England.

Mary looked up, saw them coming, and waved. The six women turned off the street and walked over to where the other two women were standing. They had a fire going beneath a kettle of steaming water and piles of laundry waiting for their turn in the large tin washtub beside the fire.

"Good morning, Mary," Mary Ann said. The others all greeted the two sisters-in-law as well. "Surely you're not doing laundry on Christmas Day," Caroline said, teasing them.

Mary Richards, who was a woman Caroline very much admired, pulled a face. "Jane and I decided that it was better to spend Christmas over a washtub than to sit and mope over our husbands being gone to England."

They all nodded solemnly at that. Would that more of the women had the attitude of these two sisters-in-law! Throughout the encampments, which stretched now for ten or twelve miles up and down both sides of the Missouri River, there was a significant number of women without husbands. Some of those were widows, and they had it the worst. Others, like these two or Louisa Pratt, whose husband, Addison, was in the Sandwich Islands, were left alone when their husbands were called to serve the Lord. Then there were the several hundred battalion members' wives who now were on their own with their families. Finally, a significant number of men had left the settlements and gone to Missouri to find work and earn enough to care for their families.

The Steed women stayed with Jane and Mary for a quarter of an hour, then moved on. To a casual observer, it might have looked as though they had no purpose other than taking a walk together. But Lydia had taken Nathan's calling as bishop as seriously as he had, and often went from home to home to let the people know they were cared for. Today she would stop at the Newel K. Whitney store and bishops' storehouse for supplies for some of the ward families. Mary Ann also wanted to trade some salt and sugar they had for a few potatoes they could use in their Christmas dinner.

That was optimistic. Scurvy—or "blackleg" or "black canker," as most of them called it—was rampant in the camps now that winter had fully come. The Saints knew the cause. A lack of fresh leafy green vegetables in their diet directly influenced the prevalence of the sickness. Potatoes were one of the things that seemed to help, but potatoes were in very high demand. If they were able to get one potato for every two people, it would be a fortunate day. Fresh fish also seemed to help. When they returned home, they would send the older boys down to the Missouri River—now shallow and sluggish, a full twenty feet below what it had been when they arrived in the summer—to see what they could catch.

Melissa looked around as they walked. "In some ways, this reminds me of when we first went to Nauvoo," she said.

The others turned their heads to see what she was referring to, then nodded almost immediately. It was quite astonishing, Caroline thought, to see what had been accomplished in just the last few months. The site for Winter Quarters had not even been selected until mid-September. Now Nathan told her that in a census taken by the bishops they counted over three thousand people just in this settlement alone. And there were an estimated nine or ten thousand more altogether. Logs, straw, bricks, slabs of sod, lumber, and stone were scattered on virtually every lot, showing the great activity going on in construction. Hundreds of homes, mostly simple cabins or sod huts, were now done, but many others were under construction. Smoke from hundreds of stone or sod-brick chimneys rose in straight lines in the still morning air and gave off pleasant aromas. Wagons lined the streets and were parked in many of the yards. Some of these were newly arrived and still waited for unloading. Most were being used as homes until something better could be found.

"Tell me," Lydia suddenly said.

Caroline turned in surprise.

"You were somewhere deep in thought," Lydia said. "Tell me what you were thinking."

She smiled somewhat sadly. "In a way this is starting to feel like home, and yet . . . it's not going to be our home for very long."

Jenny hooted. "And you're sad about that?" she asked. "You're going to miss our house that leaks mud whenever it rains and where the chimney won't draw and we all nearly choke to death every time we cook a meal?"

Caroline chuckled, glad for the reminder. "Now that you say that," she said, "maybe I was a little hasty."

"I'm going to miss the dirt floors," Jessica said. "How will little Solomon get his pantaloons black as coal if we have wooden floors again?"

"How about the parched corn?" Melissa said, jumping in

with what had suddenly become a game. "How will you ever be able to do without parched corn?"

"I think I could adjust to that," Caroline said dryly.

Mary Ann watched her daughter and daughters-in-law for a moment, enjoying their warm sisterhood, and then said, "Let me ask you a question. When you think about the time when we reach the Rocky Mountains and finally have a permanent home, to what do you most look forward?"

That stopped them for a moment, and they looked at each other as they thought about it. Finally, Jenny spoke first. "I want a large, bright kitchen."

"With a pump right in the sink so I don't have to go outside in the winter to draw water," Melissa added.

"I don't care if it's a large house," Lydia said dreamily, "but I picture a white picket fence all around with flowers everywhere."

Jessica nodded at that. "Oh, don't flowers sound wonderful right now? And a big oak tree with a swing for the children."

"Savannah would love that," Caroline agreed. "And a piano." Now there was a deep wistfulness in her eyes. "Oh, I hope someday we can have a piano again."

Lydia came in now. "How about an orchard with apples and peaches, so every spring we'll have pink and white blossoms? I loved that when I was a girl."

"As long as there is plenty of food for the children," Melissa said, suddenly sober, "I'll be happy."

That brought a murmur of assent from all of them. Then Lydia turned to Mary Ann. "What about you, Mother Steed? What would you like to have?"

Mary Ann was thoughtful for a moment, but then spoke softly. "First of all, I want my family all around me. I want us to build another Steed Row."

"Oh, yes," several of them cried. "All together."

"And I want the mobs gone. I want to sit on the porch and watch my grandchildren play and know that they are safe from our enemies."

Now they were all silent, struck deeply by what that would mean. Melissa, who had experienced the viciousness of the mob most recently, nodded slowly. "I don't want my children to ever have to see their father threatened again."

"Amen," Lydia said softly. "I'll trade that for ten apple orchards."

They fell silent, each occupied by her own thoughts. Mary Ann watched them, then smiled warmly. "But that *is* what we are going to get," she said with assurance. "On this Christmas Day as we remember the birth of our Savior, let's remember that too. He watches over us. He knows our needs. He is our Savior and Redeemer. Though we have suffered much—and are still suffering—he will lead us to a new home in the wilderness. Of that I am sure."

"Christmas Gift," Jessica said quietly.

"Happy Christmas," they all responded back.

Kathryn Ingalls pushed open the heavy wooden shutters about halfway and immediately felt the rush of cold. There was no window glass to block the winter air. Even if glass had been available at the fort—which it was not—it would be horribly expensive. Since the Latter-day Saints from the Mormon Battalion and the Mississippi company planned to abandon the cabins they had built come spring, window glass was not even considered. Instead, they made heavy wooden shutters to cover the openings, then stuffed blankets or sacks in front of them to hold out the cold.

As she looked north across the Arkansas River, Fort Pueblo looked almost like a painting. It sat framed against the leaden sky and was partially obscured by the light snow that had been falling most of the day. It seemed like an appropriate picture for a Christmas Day. Then, as they almost inevitably did, her thoughts turned to Peter. Was this what Sutter's Fort looked like? What was Christmas like in California? Would the Reeds and the Donners and Peter stay near the fort during the winter, as she and Derek and Rebecca were doing, or would Mr. Reed use all of his money to construct another fancy home like their one in Illinois?

She felt the baby stir within her, and for some reason, coming just at that time, it brought tears to her eyes. Peter would be leaving to come back to her in the spring, but it would be well into the summer—perhaps even fall—before they met again. It would be another six months at the least, perhaps as many as nine or ten. By then their baby would be crawling, maybe even taking its first step or two, and Peter would not even have seen it yet.

Rebecca, who was sitting at their makeshift table feeding Leah some oatmeal mush and goat's milk, had been watching Kathryn since she had first stood and gone to the window. Now, seeing the tears, she motioned to Derek to come and take over. Derek was on their bedroll in the corner. He had been telling Christopher and Benji the story of Christ's birth, but they had both fallen asleep now. When he saw Rebecca waving at him, he got up and came over to her.

Without a word, she handed Derek the spoon, then got up and went over to stand beside Kathryn. "Kind of a gray day, isn't it?" she said.

Realizing she had been caught, Kathryn quickly wiped at her eyes and nodded. "They say it doesn't snow in California." She sniffed a little. "If I find out that Peter spent all winter just lying around in the sunshine doing nothing, I'm going to be very angry with him."

Rebecca laughed. "So will I. That sounds downright criminal right now, doesn't it?" She touched Kathryn softly. "You really miss him, don't you?"

"Yes."

"Did you and Peter talk about what to name the baby? You're not going to have to wait until you see him to decide on a name, are you?"

"Oh, no. We didn't settle on anything, but we talked about it."

"And?"

"If it's a boy, we thought about Alexander." She flushed a little. "Sounds a little grand, doesn't it?"

Derek looked up now. "For Alexander the Great?"

"Yes," she said, pleased that he had guessed. "Peter said that Alexander wandered over half of Europe and Asia, and by the time we reach our new home this baby will have covered a good part of North America."

"And if it's a girl?" Rebecca asked.

"Nicole."

"Oh, that's pretty."

"It's French," Kathryn explained. "We don't know anyone with that name, but we both like it." Suddenly she shivered. "It's getting cold. We'd better shut the window."

Rebecca laid a hand on her shoulder. "We don't know where Peter is this Christmas, Kathryn, but I know this for sure. He's thinking of you."

Kathryn could only nod. Then she reached out and brought the heavy shutters closed.

At Sutter's Fort in Upper California, the rain had ranged from a light mist to a heavy downpour for over a week, never once clearing enough for the sun to be seen. Peter was standing at one of the windows, looking out through the thick glass at the continuing drizzle. The fields, which had been golden with wheat or green with corn, squash, and melons just a few weeks before, were great lakes of standing water.

"But no snow," Peter said, half to himself.

Will looked up from the table in surprise. "What?"

Peter turned. "I said, there's still no snow. Here it is Christmas Day. We've had rain for more than a week now and not a snowflake. No frost. No ice. No blizzards. Maybe there really is something to be said for California."

"Beats Nauvoo, doesn't it?" Will said.

Jared, now about three months old, was lying contentedly in

his father's arms but watched him carefully as he spoke. Alice had taken the umbrella and run the quarter mile to the fort to see if she could get some vegetables for their Christmas supper.

Peter turned back, noting how thick the gray of the sky looked. "So how soon is Sutter going to want us to go upriver and start cutting lumber for his mill?"

Will shrugged. "Last I talked to him, he was thinking maybe right after the first of the year."

"So that will please Alice if we don't have to leave for another week." Sutter wanted to build a sawmill about forty-five miles up the American River to prepare building materials for the influx of emigrants that would come next season. He had already contracted with Will, because of his experience in the pineries of Wisconsin, to help, and Peter would go along as laborer.

"Yes. She is already dreading our being gone for two months or more."

Finally Peter turned away. Though he had not spoken her name to Will as yet this day, his mind was really on Kathryn, not the rain, not John Sutter, and not cutting timber. And the longer he looked out the windows, the more agonizing was the pain of missing her. "Do you think Alice will be much longer?"

"Another few minutes is all."

He turned and started for the door. "I'll go get some more firewood so that it will be ready for Alice when she gets back."

Chapter Notes

The first Christmas at Winter Quarters was largely a workday, though the Saints were aware of the holiday. In the evening small parties were held in celebration, but for the most part, except for the cannon fire and the Christmas greetings shared by all, it was pretty much a normal day for that time.

(See David R. Crockett, "Christmas in Winter Quarters," *Church News*, 21 December 1996, pp. 11, 14.) Though it is not certain how the expression "Christmas Gift" came about, it is found in the journals. It was probably a reminder that each person had received the gift of Christ in his or her life.

There are reports of those who were unwilling to work and who basically depended on the Church to care for them, and there are some entries showing frustration with them. But the John Winger mentioned here is a fictitious name.

Chapter Thirty-Four

Rebecca finished tucking in the quilt around Kathryn's feet. "Are you ready?"

She nodded. Though pale and weary, she was smiling happily.

Rebecca nodded at Derek, who then turned and pulled back the blanket that separated Kathryn's "room" from the main part of the cabin. "All right, children. But be soft and quiet."

Christopher, Benjamin, and Leah—seven and a half, four and a half, and almost two, respectively—marched in, trying to peer around their father to where Kathryn was on the makeshift bed. When they saw her they slowed, eyes wide with concern. She laughed. "It's all right. Come forward and see your new little cousin." She pulled back the blanket from the baby's face as they came up to stand beside her.

"Ohh," Christopher said in awe. "She's cute, Aunt Kathryn."

Rebecca lifted Leah up so that she could see better. Her eyes were large and filled with wonder. Benji was up on tiptoes, peeking at the tiny red face. "Is it a girl, Aunt Kathryn?" he whispered.

"Yes, Benji. Children, I'd like you to meet Nicole Ingalls. Nicole, these are your cousins—Benjamin, Christopher, and Leah Rebecca." Solemnly she reached down and took the baby's hand, then lifted it to make it look as though she were waving to them. "She is very pleased to meet you."

"Look how teeny her fingers are," Benji exclaimed.

"Face red," Leah said with some concern.

Kathryn laughed, stroking the smoothness of the cheek with the back of her finger. "Her face is red, Leah, but she had to work so hard to get here."

"So it's Nicole for sure?" Derek asked.

"Or is it Nicole Kathryn?" Rebecca ventured.

"No, I think just Nicole. Nicole Kathryn Ingalls is a pretty big name for such a little girl." She looked at Benjamin. "Don't you think so, Benji?"

"I like Nicole," he said gravely.

"All right, children," Rebecca said, starting to shoo them back toward the blanket that partitioned the room. "Kathryn needs to rest now. We'll see the baby some more in a little while."

"Thank you," Kathryn said as they moved back out into the main part of the cabin.

They waved and let the blanket drop again. For a long time, Kathryn looked down at the rounded face, the soft lashes, and the thin dark fuzz that covered the head. Then she looked toward the window. "It's a girl, Peter," she whispered. "I'm going to call her Nicole."

Josh Steed marched along with a cheerful heart. In some people's minds, there was no justification for cheer of any kind. It was January twenty-seventh, 1847. That meant it had been more than six months since their enlistment and here they were still marching westward, not yet at their destination. But they were getting close. And they were out of the desert and into beautiful Upper California now. Those two facts cheered Josh immensely. He had made it. He, Joshua Benjamin Steed, oldest son of Nathan and Lydia McBride Steed, had done it. Though he was one of the youngest members of the battalion, he had seen it through.

He chuckled to himself. To look at him, one couldn't be sure whether he had made it or not. He was a sorry-looking sight, that he knew. His clothes were tattered and worn almost completely off his back. They had lost any color they had once had. His hair was long and shaggy, and he now had a respectable beard. He had long since given up shaving, something that he missed. He looked forward to shaving off the beard as quickly as possible. His face was deep brown, his nose peeled and sunburned, his lips cracked and prone to bleed if he forgot and smiled too broadly. He had no shoes. They had long since worn out and been discarded, and now, like many others in the battalion, he wore "ox hide slippers," as they called them. When an ox died or was killed, they would take a knife and cut a strip of hide off from each of the four legs just above the knee joint. The hide had a natural curl to it, and when sewn together and worn for a couple of days it shaped itself to the foot and provided an ankle-high boot. It was never comfortable, but it beat going barefoot or wrapping one's feet in rags.

To be sure, the few months since they had left Santa Fe had been incredibly difficult. They had faced blistering heat, freezing cold, bitter winds, snow, sandstorms, crazed bulls, sullen Mexicans, filthy water, no water at all, reduced rations, no rations in some cases. They had marched a total of two thousand miles and cut a wagon road across a trackless, hostile desert for the last four hundred miles of that. In some cases they had actually cut through mountain passes with picks and shovels to make a way for the wagons.

But all of that was behind them now. For the past several days, everywhere was green. Spring had come to California, even though back in Nauvoo the Mississippi was likely frozen over and there would be snow on the ground. The gently rolling hills were covered with grass and wild oats that were a foot high. They marched through valleys where thousands of wild cattle, ducks, geese, deer, and other animals roamed freely. The air was delightfully cool and the sun's rays welcome. About noon of this day they had passed a beautiful Spanish mission on a slight rise that made it stand out like a beacon and reminded Josh of the Nauvoo Temple. Even its name was beautiful—Mission San Luis Rey. His spirits had lifted so much now that he felt like whistling.

And as if all of that weren't enough, two nights before, as they were making camp, a rider came in with a message from General Kearny. They were not to march to Los Angeles. They were to go directly to San Diego, which was no more than fifty miles away. The war with Mexico was over in this part of California. There would be no calls to battle, no mustering for war. It was stunning news for the men. Brigham Young had been right. They had not been called upon to fight. The Battle of the Bulls was the only "combat" they would see.

He lifted his head as he heard a commotion up ahead of him. A cluster of men had stopped and were pointing. Others were hurrying up to see. He saw Sergeant Luther Tuttle waving for him to come up. Curious, he broke into a trot and ran to join the others.

He stopped, transfixed. They were on a hilltop and the ground fell away before them. About two miles ahead of them the emerald hills gradually ended, and there, for as far as the eye could see, deep blue water, as beautiful as anything Josh had ever seen, stretched away to the horizon.

"There it is, boys," Colonel Cooke said from his mount. "The Pacific Ocean. That's what we've been waiting for."

There were no cheers, no applause. Everyone just stood there, staring at the beautiful sight before them, moved as much by the knowledge of what it meant as by the sight itself.

Josh looked away, suddenly filled with emotion. "Dear God," he said beneath his breath, "I thank thee. I thank thee for bringing us here safely. In the name of Jesus, amen."

By the first of February, 1847, the Saints along the Missouri River had largely changed from a community on the move to a residential one. Though from its very inception, the plan was to make the settlement a temporary one, the Saints fell to work with their usual industry and determination to make the best of what was an otherwise difficult situation. The first order of business had been to prepare winter hay for the vast hordes of cattle the Mormons owned, their only real wealth of any kind. They had an estimated ten thousand head. Just south of Winter Quarters a huge stockade was built, where a large part of the herd was kept. An even greater herd was taken north a few miles into the lowlands, where there were lots of rushes on which the cattle did well. In addition, the Saints cut an estimated fifteen hundred to two thousand tons of meadow hay and stacked it for the winter.

Once that was taken care of, Brigham Young, with his vast ingenuity and his enormous organizational skills, set the people to work building settlements. Winter Quarters was started on the west side of the Missouri River on the border between Omaha and Otoe tribal lands. On the eastern side of the river, near Council Bluffs, another major settlement was also under way. It was the largest settlement on the Iowa side. The population of these two centers quickly swelled until they both neared a peak of about four thousand each. But there were more than twelve thousand Latter-day Saints up and down the Missouri, and dozens of lesser settlements had sprung up everywhere. Still others waited out the winter at the way stations of Garden Grove and Mount Pisgah in the newly formed state of Iowa.

Winter Quarters became a well-laid-out city with some thirty-eight city blocks. Except for those right along the bluffs, each block had twenty lots. The people were instructed to build their homes at the front of the lot on the streets and use the rest of the space for gardens. This provided a feeling of openness and encouraged a sense of community, as neighbors could easily associate with each other. There were not to be more than five wells per city block. Outhouses had to be put at the very back of the property and dug no more than eight feet deep.

Most of the houses were small and crudely built, made either of logs or sod bricks. There was virtually no access to shingles, and so roofs were covered with a loose base of rafters and planking, then covered with sod. There were some innovations. Willard Richards built an octagon-shaped house with a square office on the front of it for conducting Church business. A large Council House was immediately begun in Winter Quarters, and a log tabernacle was started across the river at Miller's Hollow in Council Bluffs. These were to provide meeting facilities for larger groups. Thousands were still without adequate shelter as winter finally began to loosen its hold on the Great Plains. Hundreds of wagons were used throughout the winter as family dwellings. Others dug holes in the riverbank and lived there in miserable squalor.

In those conditions, it was not surprising that death was no stranger along the "Misery River," as many called it. The combination of exhaustion, constant exposure to the elements, inadequate diet, and unsanitary living conditions made for difficult living. By February, the known death toll since the Saints' arrival was approaching a thousand, but this was only what was known. Some families did not report deaths, especially of children, but would simply bury deceased loved ones nearby and mourn in silence. The smaller, outlying settlements didn't keep good records or report the numbers of their losses to the Church authorities.

Chills and fever were usually listed as the most frequent cause of death, with black canker, or scurvy, as the next most frequent. The ratio of deaths from each of these two dreaded sicknesses changed as winter came on. Once the first frost came, ague dropped off sharply, but with the coming of winter, the Saints no longer had access to the fresh berries, wild fruits, and edible greens that had been abundant along the river bottoms. Blackleg quickly set in as salted meat and parched corn became the primary diet for most families. So called because the disease hit first in the ankles and then quickly turned the legs black, blackleg, or black canker, was extremely painful and often fatal.

Children constituted the largest number of victims, with more than half of the total deaths coming among children ten and under. Many a family stood before open graves as their little ones were laid to rest. Some were especially hard hit. The Utley family lost a seven-year-old, a nine-year-old, a fourteen-year-old, a sixteen-year-old, and their mother all within a two-month period. Stillman Pond left Nauvoo while he and most of his family were gravely ill. He was so sick that he drove the last one hundred and fifty miles lying down in the wagon, holding the reins up and over the driver's seat and looking through a knothole. By spring he had lost not only his wife, Maria, but eight children as well.

But in spite of the grimness of their existence, the Latter-day Saints developed a remarkable sense of community and for the most part endured their circumstances cheerfully. Mingled with the tears for the sick and the dead were the squeals of happy children, the laughter of young people enjoying a dance, the soft murmur of those who were courting, the singing of choirs, the chatter of women gathered around a quilting frame or some other project. Schools sprung up everywhere, though for the most part they were held out-of-doors under small boweries and were therefore dependent upon the weather.

Especially popular with both youth and young adults were the singing and dancing schools. When Brigham Young received a revelation from the Lord on the fourteenth of January, 1847, among other instructions came these: "If thou art merry, praise the Lord with singing, with music, with dancing, and with a prayer of praise and thanksgiving." It was counsel that many of the Saints were already practicing. By the end of 1846, Stephen Goddard's singing school had become so popular that Winter Quarters could boast of a large choir that frequently performed and offered concerts. Hiram Gates taught various dance steps to individuals of both sexes and of all ages. Square dances, cotillions, reels, and rounds were among the dances that he taught.

There was a dance nearly every evening in the Council House. These were called the "promiscuous universal dances," meaning that dancers exchanged partners with those they knew well, they refrained from any alcohol, and the bishops or other Church leaders were there as chaperones.

Not all agreed that this was a good thing. Alpheus Cutler questioned the propriety of having dances carried on in the camp while others were languishing on their beds of sickness. And when more and more "Gentiles" started coming upriver from the trading post, Elder Wilford Woodruff wondered what it would look like when the angels of heaven recorded that the Saints spent more of their time fiddling and dancing than they spent in prayer and praise to their God.

Perhaps it was so, but the most widely attended activity in all the settlements was Sunday worship services. There were the usual large convocations in the Council House, or out-of-doors when the weather was mild, but these were more like conferences and were not held on a regular basis. A new development began to emerge from the organization of wards in the two largest centers—Council Bluffs and Winter Quarters. Each Sunday, the smaller, more intimate ward groups would meet both Sunday morning and evening in someone's home, or outside when the weather permitted. The Saints prayed, sang, exhorted one another, and as they partook of the sacrament covenanted to remember the Savior. Led by the bishop and his two counselors, these meetings were used to conduct ward business, including the receiving of updates on who was in need of temporal help, finding out who was sick, and other practical matters. Other ordinances, such as the blessing of children or the confirmation of older children after they were baptized, also began to take place in the ward setting.

With so many of the men off to work, on missions, or with the battalion, a heavy load fell on the women of the settlements. The Relief Society had stopped functioning as a formal organization after Joseph's death. When Emma Smith strongly opposed Brigham Young's leadership and refused to go west with the

Saints, the Twelve were concerned that as president of the Relief Society she might use the meetings to sow discord among the sisters. So the organization was discontinued. But that was only the formal organization. The women continued to function much as they had before in terms of the compassionate service they rendered to others.

The sheer demands of survival and of running a household required many varied activities—spinning wool, churning butter and cheese, sewing and mending clothing, tending a garden, caring for the children, finding food and preparing meals, doing the laundry, milking the cows, hunting for stray animals, giving birth to children or, in too many cases, burying them. Through all of that, the women found time to build sisterhood. Often they would band together to perform their duties. The need to survive only seemed to strengthen the bonds which bound them. As sickness and death became more commonplace, it was largely women who became the physicians and nurses to those in need. Often, women fresh from their own tragedies could be found walking up the street to take a neighbor a warm loaf of bread or an extra set of mittens for the little ones.

That was not to say that all was perfect harmony among the Latter-day Saints. Human nature being what it is, it was inevitable that there would be tension and disagreements. There were, as there would be in any large group, the lazy and the industrious, the slothful and the careful, the whiners and the stoics, the sour and the sweet, the disgruntled and the satisfied.

When Parley P. Pratt returned from Fort Leavenworth with more than five thousand dollars contributed by the battalion members from their clothing allowance, Brigham gave about a fourth of the money directly to the battalion families, then used the rest to purchase badly needed provisions for the whole community. Some of the battalion wives complained. Some even wrote their husbands and told them not to give any more of their salaries, since it wasn't coming directly to them.

With his usual acerbic response to what he saw as lack of faith, Brigham noted that the battalion members had received about twenty-two thousand dollars from their clothing allowance, and yet had sent back only about six thousand of that. Rather than writing letters grumbling against the Twelve, he suggested, perhaps the wives should say something to their dear husbands who had kept back about seventeen thousand dollars to spend on themselves.

These, however, were the exceptions, the minority. For the majority of the Saints, there was a remarkable sense of community, a willingness to put everything into the common pot—assets and liabilities, sufferings and successes—to be shared equally. So with joy and gladness, misery and complaints, love and heartbreak, sickness and song, dancing and murmuring, the Saints slowly moved through the winter of 1846–47, waiting for the weather to break, signaling that it was time at long last for the Saints to depart for the Rocky Mountains.

In spite of a horrendous administrative load and problems that would have crushed ten lesser men, Brigham Young never lost sight of the fact that Winter Quarters was but a momentary respite in the great gathering of Israel to their new home. Virtually every council meeting spent at least some time on one topic—when would they start west and what needed to happen before that time came? There were a thousand questions to answer. What day should they leave? How many would go? What kind of men were needed? How long would it take? How many wagons? How many teams to pull them? Should they be oxen or horses or mules? Could they make it in time to plant sufficient crops to help sustain a group through a Rocky Mountain winter? What organization should be used to govern? Which was the best route? Were there places to resupply along the way?

Though the location was pretty firm, the Brethren grasped at every opportunity to learn more about where they were going. They obtained copies of John C. Frémont's maps made from his survey of 1845. There were trappers and mountain men coming downriver from the west continually. These were welcomed and questioned carefully. Several offered to guide the Mormons, but the Church did not have the hundreds of dollars they demanded for their services.

Gradually a plan began to develop. They would leave as early in the spring as possible, taking one company of nothing but able-bodied men who could race across the plains without being delayed by women and children. They would plant crops and hopefully get enough of a harvest in to see those that followed through the first winter. This was the vanguard company that Brigham had been contemplating for some time. In addition to the teamsters, hunters, and scouts that any wagon train needed, they would take carpenters, glaziers, blacksmiths, fence builders, architects, farmers, millwrights, wheelwrights, coopers, tanners, and those skilled in a dozen other occupations who would be critical to the establishment of a large settlement. They would follow Frémont's route up the Platte and North Platte Rivers to Fort Laramie—about six hundred miles to the west—and then make the jump across to the Sweetwater River, following it another hundred miles to South Pass. Then the Green River and the Bear and the Weber would become their directors. This was not a route of convenience but a route that never strayed far from water. It didn't matter if it meant a longer way around. When they weren't following the rivers, they would be jumping from creek to creek or spring to spring.

After hundreds of hours of investigation, inquiry, and discussion, Brigham began to firm things up. On January fourteenth, 1847, he received what came to be known, from its opening line, as "The Word and Will of the Lord," the first formal written revelation given since the Prophet Joseph had died. That day, Brigham wrote the revelation down and shared it with the Twelve. The following day, they decided to take it before the councils of the Church for ratification. Three days later it had been accepted as scripture and viewed as binding upon the Church members.

"The Word and Will of the Lord concerning the Camp of Israel in their journeyings to the West." Thus began the revelation. What followed were specific instructions about organizing the trains into companies of hundreds, fifties, and tens—instructions so detailed that they included counsel on dealing with widows and orphans, guidance regarding what kind of men were needed on a "pioneer" company, and the names of company captains. It even gave such intimate counsel as what to do about borrowing from one's neighbor or how to respond when one found something that had been lost in the companies. But for all of their specificity, those instructions were put into the broader context of spiritual covenants. "Let . . . those who journey with them, be organized into companies," the revelation went on, "with a covenant and promise to keep all the commandments and statutes of the Lord our God." A few lines later, that thought was reemphasized. "And this shall be our covenant—that we will walk in all the ordinances of the Lord."

The revelation was the impetus needed to fully launch the plan for moving west in the spring. As March came, Brigham Young funneled more and more effort and resources into the task of preparation. As had happened in Nauvoo in the fall and winter of 1845, Winter Quarters became one vast workshop. Wagon shops rang to the sound of the saw and the hammer. Wheelwrights undertook the skilled labor of constructing hundreds upon hundreds of wheels. Tents were repaired. New canvas was purchased and tents and wagon covers made. Food was prepared, tools collected, equipment gathered, clothes packed, men for the advance company selected.

In "The Word and Will of the Lord," God had called upon his people to gather to the West. Now the Missouri River valley was filled with the sound of twelve thousand people determined to honor their covenants and comply with the Lord's wishes that they do just that.

Chapter Notes

The Mormon Battalion caught their first glimpse of the Pacific Ocean on Tuesday, 27 January 1847. Some say it was midday; others describe the sun as just setting. Two days later they arrived at San Diego and completed their march from Council Bluffs, which had begun on 21 July 1846. (See *MB*, pp. 117–18; *CHMB*, pp. 252–53; *SW*, pp. 414–15.)

The details of life in and around Winter Quarters during the winter of 1846–47 come from several important sources (see Richard E. Bennett, *Mormons at the Missouri, 1846–1852: "And Should We Die . . ."* [Norman: University of Oklahoma Press, 1987], pp. 68–198; *SW*, pp. 259–422; *MHBY*, pp. 435–507).

One brief entry in Brigham Young's manuscript history gives a glimpse of what some of the women endured during that winter. Under date of 7 January 1847, it is noted: "Cynthia, wife of Geo. P. Dykes, was delivered of a daughter. She was formerly James Durfee's wife; *this is her tenth daughter and twentieth child*." (*MHBY*, p. 500; emphasis added.) This is the same George Dykes who was adjutant to the Mormon Battalion, so her husband was not with Cynthia at the time of this birth.

Chapter Thirty-Five

By mid-February, the snow in the lower elevations of the western side of the Sierra was starting to melt, and the American River was a raging torrent in many places. So for the last two days, the team of workmen John Sutter had sent upriver nearly fifty miles from his fort had to leave the logs waiting on the banks of the creeks. They would wait for the water to subside a little before taking them into the river and floating them down to the site for a sawmill that they had chosen. It didn't make a lot of difference whether they sat here or down at the site. The important thing was to let them start drying so that when it came time to cut them into planking they would not shrink and curl.

Yesterday they had cut enough to provide about two days' worth of work, and today they were trimming off the limbs and sawing the pine trunks into eight-, twelve-, or sixteen-foot lengths. It was not as hard as bringing down the trees, but it was still hard enough work that it left the men pouring sweat.

About halfway through the cut on a particularly thick log, Will and Peter, who were working the saw together, stopped to rest. Will removed his hat and wiped at his face with a rag. He watched Peter move to the creek and go down on his belly to drink deeply. "Think we can finish in another week?"

Peter rolled over onto his back. "I hope so."

Will was ready to get back to his family. In the six weeks since they had first come up here they had made only one brief trip back down to the fort for supplies. All of them were anxious to finish the job and return downriver. He sighed, stood up, and walked to the saw. "Let's get to it, Peter, or we'll be here another month."

Twenty minutes later, while both of them were seated on the log sharpening the saw with files, someone called out from above them. "Rider coming in." Both Peter and Will turned to look. Coming from the north, or downstream, a single rider leading a packhorse was coming steadily toward them. He had his animals at a walk, obviously headed for their camp.

Will laid the file and saw down. "More supplies, I suppose. Let's go see what the news is from the fort."

There was mail—Will had two letters from Alice—and supplies enough to keep them going for another week. To no one's surprise, Sutter wanted a detailed report on their progress. When the foreman was done giving it to the messenger, the messenger turned to Peter. "Mr. Ingalls?"

"Yes?"

"Mr. Sutter wants me to convey some news to you."

"Oh?"

"It's not good. About a month ago, seven people stumbled out of the mountains and were found by Indians not far above Johnson's Ranch."

It wasn't just Peter who was surprised by that. "Out of the mountains?" one of them said. "In the winter?"

"People from where?" Peter asked, still not sure what this had to do with him.

"They were from a wagon company called the Donner Party."

Peter nearly staggered backwards. "The Donners?"

"Yes. There's a whole bunch of them stranded up near Truckee Lake, just the other side of the Truckee Pass. It's about five miles—"

Peter waved his hand impatiently. "I know where that is; I came that way last fall. What happened?"

"They are in a starving condition," the man went on, quite somber now. "They sent a group ahead on snowshoes to let people know there's a whole party stranded up there." He looked away. "Seventeen started out with that little group on snowshoes. Two turned back. Only seven of the remaining fifteen survived and made it to Johnson's Ranch. They said they were in pretty bad shape."

Peter was deeply shocked. "Do you know any of their names?"

"Not for sure. A man wrote a letter to Mr. Sutter from Johnson's Ranch asking for help. His name was Edie or Eddy or something like that."

"William Eddy?" Peter looked at Will, his face ashen. "He's the one who saved Mr. Reed from being hanged." Then he turned back to the rider. "But they couldn't be starving. They had fifty head of cattle or more. We tried to get to them last fall and couldn't make it through."

"Evidently the Indians got their cattle coming along Mary's River and the Truckee." His eyes dropped and he looked away. "The reports are that those who snowshoed out were eating each other."

It didn't register. "You mean eating each other's supplies?" Will asked, a little bewildered.

"No, sir. The report is that they started eating their own dead in order to survive."

All of the men were staring at the messenger in total shock. "You mean . . . cannibalism?" the foreman asked in a hoarse whisper.

The man nodded grimly. "It was the only way the seven who survived made it out. But the letter Mr. Sutter got said even conditions in the high camps were more desperate than anyone could imagine." He looked back at Peter. "Mr. Sutter has sent word downriver to Mr. Reed. He's supposedly back in Yerba Buena after serving in the war against Mexico. One small rescue party has already started toward the pass. Mr. Sutter expects that once Reed hears the news, he will mount another."

"He will," Peter said, still trying to comprehend what he was hearing. "Nothing will stop him now."

"Mr. Sutter thought you would like to know," the messenger said.

Peter turned away, his knees suddenly weak. What about Margret Reed? Virginia? Tommy? Patty? He passed a hand before his eyes, then turned to Will. "You were there," he said in anguish. "We only turned back because we were sure they had so many cattle."

Will nodded, not knowing what to say.

"I'm going," Peter suddenly said. "I'm going with them."

The man was nodding. "Mr. Sutter said he figured both you and Mr. Steed would likely want to help. You have his permission to ride back with me tomorrow, if you're of a mind to."

Peter looked at Will, who immediately nodded. "We'll go, Peter. Of course we'll go."

Peter sat by the window in the cabin that belonged to Will and Alice, staring out at the rain. Behind him, Alice worked quietly on a piece of deerskin, softening it to the point where she could make herself a dress. Thankfully, she understood his mood, and left him alone.

Thanks to the rain and the terrible roads, it had taken Peter and Will two days to come back down the river to Sutter's Fort. To Peter's great disappointment, by then James Reed had already come and gone on. Not that Peter had expected that James Reed should wait for him. As Sutter put it, once Reed got word of the terrible situation his family was facing in the mountains, "the fire was on him." In Yerba Buena he had raised thirteen hundred dollars for supplies and a substantial number of men and started up the Sacramento River. With the rains, he was not making good time either, and it had taken them several days to come the eighty miles up the Sacramento River to the fort. They stopped at Sutter's place only long enough to get the supplies which had been shipped up by boat and to get a few more horses, and then he moved on to Johnson's Ranch. But if Will and Sutter could find some horses, Peter was sure that he and Will had a good chance of catching them. They would not be slowed by pack animals—if they could get started today.

If. That was the big word. The problem was that Sutter had already outfitted the first rescue party, which had gone on ahead of Reed. Then he had helped to outfit Reed's group. There was no longer available even one horse that was good enough to undertake a trip to the high country. So Will and John Sutter went out among the Indians to see if they could find two more good horses that could be spared. Peter stayed behind to get things ready.

And he also fretted. Today was the twenty-second day of February. Reed had left the fort on the nineteenth. Every hour they delayed meant they were falling that much farther behind—and another hour of suffering for the party.

All seven of the surviving snowshoe party were recovering at Johnson's Ranch, and the news that was coming out from them had shaken Peter deeply. There were no fifty head of cattle. The Indians had run them off or killed them. The few remaining head died in the snow, and the emigrants had not been experienced enough to mark with long poles the places where they fell. It was hard to fault them for that. These people were from Illinois, where three feet of snow was almost unthinkable. At the lake, it was at least twenty feet deep on the level.

He shuddered, his mind unable to even contemplate that such a thing could be real. Thank heavens William Eddy and others had been wise enough to know that no one was coming back for them. No one in California knew that they had come on to the mountains. If they hadn't made the snowshoes and come out . . .

He shook his head. He had now read the letter William Eddy wrote from Johnson's Ranch to Sutter's Fort. What he said was impossible to fathom. The little group had left the camp in mid-December, but it was not until January seventeenth, a staggering thirty-three days later, that they stumbled out of the mountains. And by then ten of the seventeen had turned back or died. Strangely, all of the five women who had started out made it.

His mouth tightened in anger as he peered out into the steady rain. Once William Eddy's letter reached Sutter's Fort, it had taken thirteen days to pull together the first rescue party. Thirteen days! And then, even though Captain Kern, the commander of the military attachment at Sutter's Fort, offered three dollars a day wages, they were able to find only seven men who would accept the challenge. Three dollars a day was three times the wages Sutter was paying his workers.

Peter got to his feet abruptly and began to pace. Where were Sutter and Will? Suddenly his head jerked up.

Alice, seeing the abrupt movement, spoke for the first time. "What is it, Peter?"

"I just remembered something." His eyes were wide and haunted.

"What?"

"When we made the decision to take the shortcut"—there was a bark of bitter laughter—"or, better, the so-called shortcut, we were at a place called the Parting of the Ways. Tamsen Donner, the wife of George Donner, didn't like it. I had forgotten that."

"Didn't like what?" Alice asked, shaken a little by the expression on Peter's face.

"She didn't like the decision to take the Hastings route. As we went back to our wagons, she was very depressed. When Mrs. Reed tried to cheer her, she wouldn't be comforted."

"Why?"

"She said it was a terrible mistake to listen to a man whom we knew nothing about and leave the old, proven road." He stared at her, his eyes wide with the memory. "She knew," he said softly. "Somehow she knew that this was a terrible mistake."

Alice stood and went to stand beside him, laying a hand on his arm. "So did you, Peter. Those dark feelings you had. You knew too. Think what it would mean now if Kathryn were still with them."

He nodded slowly. That was indeed the one bright thought in this deepening tragedy. Kathryn was not with them. And thanks be to God for that.

Will Steed and John Sutter finally returned about two o'clock that afternoon. At the first sound of their horses, Peter was out in the rain, without coat or hat, to see how they had fared. They had found two sturdy horses and a few pounds of dried beef that would get them to Johnson's Ranch.

The moment Sutter left and they were back inside the house, Peter spoke to Will. "How far have you ridden today?"

"Not that far. Fifteen miles perhaps."

"You need to rest. I'm going to start. You come as soon as you can."

Will shook his head. "Let me gather a few things and we'll go."

"Are you sure you don't need to rest?" Peter said with obvious relief.

"Yes."

"All right. Then let's go."

The day after Peter and Will left Sutter's Fort and swam their horses across the muddy American River, the rain finally stopped, but it was overcast and cool and there was little improvement in the roads. The lowlands of California were nearly impassable during the latter part of February. It took them two and a half days to cover the forty miles to Johnson's Ranch. There they learned that Reed had stopped for two days while the second rescue group slaughtered some cattle and dried the meat. They had also gotten two hundred pounds of flour from the Indians. Determined to catch them, Peter and Will slept at the ranch only four or five hours; then, with two additional packhorses loaded with food, they pressed on.

As they moved up the Bear River valley, they quickly ran into snow. First it was a foot deep, then two, then three. So they altered their pattern of travel. They began to sleep during the day, then travel at night when it froze enough to form a hard crust. It wasn't easy going, but it was easier. They took comfort in the fact that Reed was breaking a trail in the snow that had fallen since the first rescue party had come this way, which meant he had to be making slower progress than Will and Peter were.

On the first day of March, they were approaching the head of Bear Valley. It was near here, four months before, that Peter had looked down from a ridge top and seen the wagons of the Samuel Young party. For Peter, Mr. Reed, and Walt Herron, it meant they were out of the mountains and safe at last. For Peter and Will now, it meant they were about to embark on the most difficult part of the journey. Night travel would be too dangerous in the high country. Reluctantly they decided they should let their animals rest for a day before making the assault on the pass. For the first time in several nights, they pitched their tent and went to sleep while it was dark.

They were just finishing breakfast the next morning, when Peter straightened slowly, staring toward the mountains. "Am I seeing things," he said to Will, "or is that smoke?"

Will looked up. "Where?"

"Straight ahead, near the upper end of the valley. I can't see it now, because the snow is behind it, but—" The wind shifted and blew the smoke in front of the deeper green of the trees. "There! Do you see it?"

"I see it!" Will cried. "It *is* smoke." Now they could see that there were two or three separate columns of smoke. "It's got to be them."

Without another word, they both turned and quickly began breaking camp.

As they drew within a mile of the smoke, the camp came into view. To their surprise, it was quite small. There were only a few horses and mules and no more than three or four tents.

"That can't be Mr. Reed," Peter said in sudden disappointment.

"I'm thinking the same thing," Will responded. "He's got a score of men and half again that many horses."

Peter shook his head, puzzled. It couldn't be Mr. Reed's rescue group, and yet who else would be this far out from the nearest settlement?

About half a mile out, the two incoming riders were spotted by the camp. Three men began to halloo and wave their arms. Peter and Will shouted and waved back. Then after a moment the men started toward them, walking swiftly on the still-frozen snow. As they drew to within about a hundred yards of each other, Peter leaned forward in the saddle, staring.

"I think that's Daniel and John Rhoads," he said in amazement.

"Who?"

"The Rhoads brothers," Peter said eagerly. "They were with our party when we first left Independence last spring. Their family split off from us and went on ahead. Remember, I told you that we knew about two Latter-day Saints who came west last season—Sister Murphy, and the other was Thomas Rhoads? Well, these are Rhoads's two sons." He went up in the stirrups, cupping his hand to his mouth. "Daniel Rhoads, is that you?"

The lead man stopped for a moment, peering forward. "It is. Who might you be?"

"Peter Ingalls, one of James Reed's bullwhackers."

There was a cry of surprise, and then the men broke into a run. Peter and Will urged their horses forward as well.

As they reached the two men, Peter swung down. The two brothers stopped, a look of astonishment on their faces. "Peter Ingalls?" Dan Rhoads cried. "But what are you doing here?"

"That's what we were going to ask you," Peter exclaimed. "I'd heard your father had settled on the Consumnes River. That's a long way from here."

"We were with the first rescue party that went out to find the Donner group," Dan replied.

Suddenly Peter understood. Of course. The Rhoads boys would be among the first to volunteer to go on a rescue mission. That was how that family was. But then, at another thought, he frowned. "And you've come only this far?"

John Rhoads shook his head. "No, no, we're on our way back again. We're taking out some of the people we found."

Peter stiffened. "You have people from the Donner group? Here? Now?"

"Yes," Dan answered. He shook his head, his dark eyes deeply troubled. "We started with twenty-three, but we had to send two of the children back. Then three more didn't make it. There was an Englishman—"

"John Denton?"

"Yes. And we lost two children, a Keseberg girl who was about three, then a ten-year-old boy yesterday. A boy named Hook."

Peter had to swallow hard. How many names that he knew would be added to the list of the dead before this was over? "What about Levinah Murphy? She is a Latter-day Saint too, you know. Is she with you?"

Daniel shook his head. "No. She wasn't strong enough." He looked away. "Her son Landrum was dead by the time we got there. You remember her daughter Harriet Pike, don't you?"

"Yes. She made it out with the snowshoe party, didn't she?"

"Right. Well," Daniel went on, his voice very low, "John here promised to bring Harriet's two little daughters out. Sadly, her baby daughter, Catherine, died the day after we arrived at the camp."

"And the other one? Did you make it with her?" Peter asked.

John nodded, but it was Daniel again who spoke. "Naomi is three. John strapped her in a blanket on his back and carried her out."

Peter felt his eyes burning. He had watched Sister Murphy's grandchildren playing around the wagons on more than one occasion.

John peered at Peter more closely. "But how come you aren't back there with them?" Then he snapped his fingers. "That's right, you came ahead with Mr. Reed."

"Yes. And speaking of Mr. Reed, have you seen him? He was leading a second relief party. He should have been this far by now."

"Yes," John answered. "We met him two days ago. You can imagine his joy to see his wife and some of his children, but—"

Peter jerked forward. "You have Mrs. Reed with you?" Peter cried.

"We do," Dan Rhoads answered, "and two of the children. Unfortunately, it was the two other Reed children that we had to send back. They were too weak to come with us. So Reed and the others have gone on to find them and the rest of the people up there."

"So all of the Reeds are safe?" Peter said, suddenly weak with relief.

"We hope so," John answered. "The two who went back, Patty and Tommy, were pretty weak, but Reed should have reached them by now. And he's got food."

Will looked more closely at the two men. "Is it as bad as the reports say?" he asked softly.

Both men dropped their eyes. Dan shook his head slowly. "It was pretty bad. When we finally reached the camp at Truckee Lake, it was like we had walked onto a battlefield. There were corpses lying out in the open. They had no way to bury them. At first we thought we were too late. There was not a living soul to be seen. But when we called out, suddenly heads started popping up like prairie dogs from what we thought were just snowdrifts. We hadn't even realized there were cabins there."

"It was like our voices were Gabriel's horn," John added, "and the dead started coming out of their graves. Suddenly these skeletons started appearing everywhere around us."

Dan Rhoads's eyes were shining. "When one woman saw us, she said, 'Are you from California, or are you from heaven?' "

John went on now, his voice very quiet. "They are in ghastly shape, Peter. They've had nothing to live on except for a few rotten hides for several weeks."

Peter could only nod. He wanted to ask for names of those who were still alive, but there would be time for that later. "I'd like to see Mrs. Reed and the children. Then Will and I will press on and try to catch Mr. Reed."

Dan Rhoads considered that for a moment, then shook his head. "Maybe you ought to reconsider moving on farther. Mr. Reed has quite a few men with him, including a couple of mountain men. But there's only half a dozen of us. We could use your help and what food you have to get these people back to Johnson's Ranch."

When he saw Peter's reaction to that, he went on. "I think Mr. Reed would appreciate knowing that his wife and children were being helped to safety. He will bring the other two children with him."

Peter changed his mind at that. "All right," he agreed. "I'd like to see Mrs. Reed if I can."

"All right," Dan Rhoads said slowly, "but you'll have to steel yourself. You can't let her see the shock in your eyes." He took a quick breath. "And you will be shocked."

"It's that bad?" Peter said in a near whisper.

"You may not recognize her at first," came the answer.

When they reached camp, there was no need to ask which were the rescuers and which were the rescued, and that was not because Peter immediately knew his former companions. Though he had traveled with them for months, now he barely recognized them. Their cheeks were hollow and their eyes deeply sunken. They looked like walking skeletons. Their clothes were filthy and in rags and barely hung on their emaciated bodies. But it was the eyes that were unrecognizable. They were empty, lifeless, haunted. As he moved among them, touching their outstretched hands, he could scarcely stop from crying aloud in horror.

Here was Doris Wolfinger, now a widow at nineteen years of age. It was her husband, if the reports William Eddy had sent were true, who had been murdered by two of his companions for the gold he carried. She stood beside four of the Donner children and Noah James, one of the Donners' teamsters. Philippine Keseberg, wife of the arrogant and obnoxious Lewis Keseberg, didn't respond at all as Peter took her hand. She simply stared through him as if he weren't there. She had lost an infant at the camp. She had lost her second child, a toddler, as they came down from the mountains.

Eliza Williams managed a wan smile when she recognized him, but Peter didn't have the courage to ask about her brother, Baylis. Was he dead or just too weak to come out? There were two of the Murphy children, two of Patrick Breen's, and three-year-old Naomi Pike, the child John Rhoads had carried on his back and whose mother had come out with the Forlorn Hope party. She was anxiously awaiting word of her family at Johnson's Ranch.

"I thought William Eddy was with your group," Peter said to John Rhoads.

"He was, but we sent him to Johnson's Ranch for more horses and food. I'm surprised you didn't see him."

"We camped during the day and traveled at night."

"Oh," Dan said, then shook his head. "Both his wife and baby daughter are dead," he went on in barely a whisper. "He doesn't know that yet."

Then Peter saw Virginia Reed. She had stepped out of one of the tents and was squinting against the brighter light, trying to see what was causing the commotion. He stifled a gasp. At thirteen, Virginia had been turning into a young woman when Peter had last seen her. Now she looked like a stooped little girl. Suddenly her eyes widened. She took a step forward. Peter broke into a run, calling her name. Now he couldn't hold back the tears as he reached her and swept her up. Her long dark hair was matted and tangled. Her lips looked like cracked leather left too long in the sun. Virginia had been so clean, well groomed, and full of energy that to see her so dirty, unkempt, and weak was a shock.

"Peter?"

"Yes, Virginia, it's me. I'm here."

She threw her arms around him and began to sob. "Oh, Peter."

He stroked her hair, holding her tight. "It's all right, Virginia. I'm here."

"Did you see Papa?" she asked, seeming a little confused. "We saw Papa."

"I know. They told me."

"Mama fainted when she heard Papa was coming. But I ran to him and hugged him. I was so glad to see him."

"Your father said he would come for you, Virginia. He promised, remember?"

Suddenly she looked wounded. "But why did it take so long, Peter?"

"We tried last fall, but the snow stopped us. We thought you had food."

Great tears pushed over the eyelids and started down her cheeks. "Milt's dead, Peter."

He felt a deep stab of pain. "He is?" he whispered. Milt Elliott, Reed's lead teamster, had been almost like an older brother to the children, but he had been especially close to Virginia.

She nodded, her mouth twisting with horror. "Mama and I dragged him out of the cabin after he died," she said. "We buried him in the snow. He was such a faithful friend. We commenced burying him at his feet. I patted the pure white snow softly over him until I reached his face. Then I started to cry."

She was crying hard now, and Peter had to steady her.

"Poor Milt!" she sobbed. "It was so hard to cover his face and to know that our best friend was gone."

"I know, Virginia," Peter said, holding her as her body shuddered against him. "I know." No one should have to face such a terrible thing, he thought, but especially not an adolescent girl. "It's all right now. We've come to take you to where it's safe and there is plenty of food." He took her hand. "Come on, I want to see your mother and James."

Wiping at the tears with the back of her hand, she nodded, then led him to the tent. Will hung back, but Peter motioned him to follow.

When they stepped inside the tent, the light was subdued, but Peter was still shocked at the sight of Margret Reed. "Look, Mama," Virginia exclaimed. "Look, James, it's Peter."

Margret Reed raised her head slowly. Then, when she recognized him, there was a strangled cry of joy.

He went to her and dropped to one knee, pulling her up and against his shoulder. "Oh, Mrs. Reed. I'm so sorry. I'm so sorry."

James leaned forward and there was what should have been a smile but looked more like a horrible grimace. "I told Mama you would come, Peter," he said. "I told her."

Now tears were streaming down Peter's checks. Behind him, Will stifled a sob.

"Yes, James," Peter said, reaching out to take his hand. "We're here now. It's all right."

After Peter and Will took Margret Reed and her two children to Johnson's Ranch, almost a full two weeks passed before the second rescue group led by James Reed returned from the mountains. For a full day after that, Will and Peter did not see James Reed. That was not a surprise, and no one was of a mind to interrupt the reunion of this family who had come so close to tragedy. With Reed's safe return, Will and Peter prepared to return to Sutter's Fort.

They were nearly finished packing on the morning of March seventeenth, when there was a soft knock at the door of the cabin where they were staying.

Will got up and went to the door. When he opened it he stepped back. It was James Reed. Peter stood immediately and went to greet him. "Come in," he said.

Reed removed his hat and stepped inside. He looked around. "I heard that you were going."

Peter nodded. "We promised Mr. Sutter we'd get back as soon as we could."

"Yes." He took a deep breath, then let it out slowly, clearly suffering. "Peter, I . . ."

Peter broke in quickly. "There's no need to say anything, Mr. Reed. I am just glad that we could do something. I'm sorry that we didn't hear soon enough to go in with you."

He waved that aside. "What you did was more important," he said gruffly. Reed started twisting his hat in his hand. "Peter, I've sent a letter back to Illinois to have my funds transferred out here to California, but until they come—"

Now Peter cut him off. "Mr. Reed, you've lost everything. Don't fret about it. If it weren't for you, Kathryn and I could have been up there in the mountains."

Reed stepped forward and gripped his shoulders. "Listen, Peter, while I was fighting in the war with Mexico I was given a large land grant down near Pueblo de San Jose. I signed documents in the names of those of our party so that there would be land for them when they finally got here. I have land for you." His words came out in a rush in his eagerness now. "Go find Kathryn. Bring her out here. We'll help you get started."

Peter glanced at Will, who was listening to all of this but for now chose to stay out of it. Then he turned back. "Thank you, but our place is with our people."

What Reed said next came as a total surprise. "Did you know that Sam Brannan is planning to leave as early as possible and go east to find your Brigham Young so that he can persuade him to come to California?"

"Brannan told you that?" Will asked slowly, his mind racing.

"Yes. Before I left Yerba Buena. He said he plans to leave around the first of April." He turned back to Peter. "Will you at least consider our offer if your people decide to come here?"

"Yes, of course," Peter said.

Reed stepped back a little, in full control of himself again. "Good-bye, Peter. I can never repay you for what you've done."

"Good-bye, Mr. Reed. Thank you for all you did for us."

For a moment it looked as if Reed might say something else, but then he put on his hat, gave one last little wave, and walked out the door.

Chapter Notes

When the seven surviving members of the snowshoe party—what later was labeled the Forlorn Hope party (see *UE*, p. 49)—staggered out of the mountains and reached Johnson's Ranch on 17 January 1847, that was the first that anyone realized that the group of emigrants stranded in the mountains were in such desperate circumstances. Due to the war with Mexico and also to the small number of Americans who were in California at that time, there were not a lot of available men. However, it is still somewhat shocking to see how little response there was to the call for rescuers. Eventually, the men had to be promised five times normal wages so that they would continue. (See *Chronicles*, pp. 258–89; *UE*, pp. 195–97.)

The first rescue party reached Truckee (now Donner) Lake on 19 February, more than two months after the Forlorn Hope party left in search of help. In that rescue party were two Latter-day Saints, Daniel and John Rhoads. When the two brothers learned of the fate of the Donner Party, they vowed they would help bring them out or die trying. (See *Chronicles*, pp. 260–96.) It was Daniel who later told of the woman who asked if they were from California or from heaven (see *Overland in 1846*, p. 328). The vivid description of Gabriel blowing his horn and raising the near dead from their snowy tombs was that of historian George R. Stewart (probably inspired by a later statement by Lewis Keseberg) but is given expression in the novel by John as well (see *OBH*, p. 191).

James Reed's second rescue party met the descending first rescuers and those they were bringing out on 28 February. After a joyous but brief reunion with his wife and two children, Reed pressed on to find his other two children, who had been sent back. He brought both out safely. The Reeds were one of only two families who came through the tragedy without any loss of life. The other was Patrick Breen's family. Of the eighty-two members of the Donner group that took the Hastings Cutoff, only forty-seven survived. (See *UE*, pp. 294–98, and *Chronicles*, pp. 352–61, for complete rosters of the Donner Party, information regarding who survived, and a description of what happened to the survivors later.)

Reed did secure land by signing documents for some of his group, evidently with the understanding of the authorities that they were stranded but would be coming on later (see *Chronicles*, p. 217). This and his own previous wealth helped Reed and his family become prominent in northern California's early history. Sister Levinah Murphy, the only known Latter-day Saint with the Donner Party, died at Donner Lake. Marysville, California, was named after Mary Murphy, her daughter.

Lansford Hastings, whose book and whose promises of guide service led the Donners to take the cutoff that would thereafter bear Hastings's name, would never take any blame for what happened. All that was needed, he said, was better roads and more water in the desert.

Virginia Reed's description of the burial of Milt Elliott comes from her own account written later. Virginia claimed throughout her life that the Reeds were the only family which did not eat human flesh, though the Breens also denied being part of that. In a letter written to her cousin in May of 1847, Virginia also gave this now famous counsel about coming west: "Never take no cutofs and hury along as fast as you can" (in *WFFB*, p. 238).

Chapter Thirty-Six

"It's a simple matter, Josh," Sergeant Luther Tuttle said in conclusion. "When the elephants fight, the mice get trampled."

For a moment, Private Josh Steed was puzzled by that expression; then understanding came. "And we're the mice?"

"The foot soldier always is," Tuttle muttered, more in resignation than anger.

Josh considered that, then nodded. Sergeant Luther Tuttle had a lot of savvy about things, including the "military mind," a phrase that he dryly noted was a contradiction in terms. It was nearing sundown and they were off duty for the night. The four other men they shared the tent with had decided to go to town and look around. Tuttle was on call as backup to the duty sergeant and couldn't leave. Josh had gone into Pueblo de Los Angeles once and had not found it at all to his liking and turned down the invitation to join the others.

Los Angeles was much larger than San Diego—about five

thousand people, Josh had been told—and was inhabited mostly by Mexicans and Indians, who were accepting of their American conquerors but not appreciative. Around the town there were rich farms and vineyards, but the city itself seemed quite dilapidated. *Cantinas*—Mexican grog shops—and gambling houses abounded, and there were always girls trying to become friendly.

He sighed, longing for the cool isolation of Mission San Luis Rey. He would have been content to finish out their tour of duty right there. Or San Diego would have been an acceptable second choice. But they had been in San Luis Rey for barely six weeks when the elephants began to bellow.

After seeing the Pacific Ocean for the first time on January twenty-seventh, at a spot not far from the deserted Mission San Luis Rey, the battalion marched down to the beach below the mission and camped near the water. It had been a new experience to hear the constant roar of the surf. Some of the men complained that they couldn't sleep with the unexpected noise, but Josh found it strangely soothing. The next day they marched on to San Diego and took up camp near the mission there, which was about four miles from the port.

When General Kearny learned that the battalion was nearing San Diego, he came down from Los Angeles to meet them. Thus, on the twenty-eighth of January, Lieutenant Colonel Philip St. George Cooke proudly reported to his commanding officer that the battalion had fulfilled their orders and cut a wagon road through from the Santa Fe Trail to the Pacific Ocean. They had brought five government wagons and three private ones across a trackless desert, a feat of enormous magnitude. Kearny had been greatly pleased and praised the men, which pleased them immensely. Even more pleasing to the men was the news that the Mexican forces in the southern portions of Upper California had surrendered and that no further conflict was anticipated. The war with Mexico was not over yet, but the fighting in this area seemed to be.

Kearny only stayed a short time, then prepared to leave by ship for Monterey. Before doing so, however, he ordered Colonel

Cooke to take the battalion back to Mission San Luis Rey because he was worried that hostilities might break out again. So after only two days in San Diego, they took up their march once more and returned the forty miles to the deserted mission. That was fine with Josh. California was in full spring now, and the hills around Mission San Luis Rey were verdant and beautiful. Whenever he was off duty he would go for long walks, finding a place where he could see the ocean and then sitting for long periods of time, enjoying the solitude.

When the order came on March fourteenth to move the battalion north to Los Angeles, it came as a sharp disappointment to Josh Steed. Part of that was because the battalion was to be split once again. Company B would be going to San Diego; the other four companies would march to Los Angeles. As they finally started north on the nineteenth of March, they began to learn what Sergeant Tuttle meant by the "battle of the elephants."

General Kearny brought with him a letter from Washington appointing him governor of California once the war was won. But Lieutenant Colonel John C. Frémont, who had come to California on an exploring expedition for the U.S. Army in 1845, had a large contingent of soldiers called the "California Volunteers." It was Frémont who accepted the Mexican surrender at Los Angeles, and therefore Commodore Stockton, the senior naval officer in California, made him the governor. Kearny was furious.

With the Mormon Battalion and his First Dragoons, Kearny commanded over two thousand men who were totally loyal to him, and that finally convinced Stockton to accept his commission. But Frémont flatly refused, saying that since his troops had done most of the fighting—a fact that Kearny bitterly disputed—he had every right to be the governor. Even though Kearny was a general and Frémont only a lieutenant colonel, Frémont refused to budge. That was what had brought the order for the battalion to march to Los Angeles so that Kearny would have some muscle to back him up.

They arrived at Los Angeles shortly after noon on Tuesday, March twenty-third. For two hours Kearny kept the battalion standing at attention, and it looked for a while as though they might have to go to war with their own countrymen. There were a lot of Missourians in Frémont's unit, and old resentments started to smoulder again. Finally, and wisely, the two forces backed away from a confrontation, and Kearny had Cooke bivouac the Mormons some distance from town.

Today it had nearly erupted again when Colonel Cooke went to Frémont's volunteers and asked for the two artillery pieces that had been brought by Kearny's forces. The captain in charge told Colonel Cooke that he was acting under direct orders from Frémont and would not surrender the weapons.

Cooke had come back to his troops in a black fury. "Treason!" he cried. "Mutiny! A *colonel* refuses to obey a *general's* orders? This is an outrage! Kearny's dragoons brought those cannon across the desert. He brought them up here and used them to help Frémont win the war, and now they refuse to give them over to me?"

He had muttered all the way back to their camp, then left the men in order to go in and file an official protest and report of Frémont's insubordination.

"What do you think will happen, Luther?" Josh asked his companion. "What if Frémont won't back down?"

Luther pursed his lips. "It's hard to say. I think you'll see Kearny call for a court-martial. But you know who Frémont is married to, don't you?"

Josh shook his head.

"Jessie Benton."

Josh looked blank.

"Jessie Benton, daughter of Senator Thomas Hart Benton from Missouri, only one of the most powerful men in the United States Congress."

"Oh," Josh said meekly. The name did sound familiar to him.

"Frémont knows he's got some powerful backing in Washington too. He's not totally defenseless. But in the meantime, as long as the elephants insist on dancing, we'll just stay out of the field. I think we can do that for twelve more weeks, don't you?"

Lydia slipped her arm through Nathan's and squeezed it affectionately. He turned and looked down at her. "What?"

"Nothing. I'm just happy."

"Good. Anything in particular?"

She threw one arm out, breathing in deeply. "Well, for one thing, it's April. Winter is finally over. Look at the cottonwood trees. You can see they're starting into bud. And there, along the river, that is green grass, I do believe."

He chuckled. "I'm not sure. It's been a long time since we've seen any of that."

"I know. Isn't it wonderful?"

He nodded, pleased at her happiness. When he had mentioned he was going down to the wagon shop to help, Lydia had surprised him and insisted on coming with him. He expected that the sight of the nearly finished wagons would make her despondent. Now he wasn't so sure. The departure of the Pioneer Company was no more than a few days away and the time for their separation was imminent. But instead of feeling sorrow, she was filled with joy and anticipation.

She was watching him and guessed at his thoughts. "Yes, I know we're soon to be apart, but it's not the same now. We'll be only a few weeks behind you. I can stand that. It just feels so good to know that after all these months we're finally leaving."

"Doesn't it?" he agreed heartily. "It seems like we've been waiting all of our lives to get started. Now it's finally here." He slipped his arm around her and pulled her in against his shoulder. Then suddenly he bent down and kissed her. It took her totally by surprise and she pulled away in embarrassment. "Nathan! Someone will see us."

"And if they do, what are they going to say? that Bishop Steed loves his wife?" He kissed her again.

Laughing, she only half resisted. "And I love you," she whispered.

As they rounded the corner, they could see the crudely built wagon shop up ahead of them. It wasn't much, really, just an overhead covering made of interwoven willows and tree branches to keep out the worst of the weather. But it was large enough to hold two wagons beneath its shelter, and today both of them were already there. Crossing the plains of Iowa had pretty well destroyed the two older of the Steed wagons. The others would be fine, but here were their replacements.

Both wagons were up on blocks with no wheels. Carl and Solomon had taken those to the blacksmith's yesterday to have the tires set—the steel rims put on hot so that they bound into the wood when they cooled. Today they would go from the blacksmith's to the wheelwright to make sure each wheel was properly "dished," or made concave like a saucer. That shape made it so the weight and movement of the wagon would push the spokes in more tightly rather than pull them apart. Matthew was a skilled carpenter, but dishing was a skill beyond him.

As they drew closer, to their surprise just about the entire family was there. Derek and Solomon were working on the bows—the thin, flat, and flexible lengths of ash and hickory that would hold the wagon covers up in their unique shape. Joshua was pounding on something with a hammer. Matthew, Carl, and two of the cousins, Luke Griffith and young Carl Rogers, were sawing a long board, working the two-man saw in pairs and spelling each other off. But what was really unexpected was that most of the women and children were there too.

Lydia laughed aloud. "No wonder we couldn't find anyone home. They're all here."

"I think spring and the excitement of leaving are affecting everyone," Nathan said.

"I should have just told Emily to bring the other children down here. Maybe I'll go back and get her."

"I will in a minute," Nathan answered. "But first, let's go see what's going on."

Mary Ann saw them and waved. She and Melissa were working on sewing a wagon cover, or perhaps it was a tent. Mary Ann was saying something, and Melissa was laughing to the point where she had to stop sewing or risk pricking her finger. Mary Ann smiled as Nathan and Lydia approached. "Hello, sleepyheads," she said.

Joshua raised his head. "No wonder you asked if we could do some plowing today," he growled. "Didn't want us to disturb your slumber, eh?"

They all laughed when they saw Nathan's expression. Fortunately, it was Lydia who came to his defense. "*I* was sleeping in," she admitted, "but Nathan has already been to the mill and gotten some flour for Sister Bagley."

"Good for you, Bishop," Matthew said heartily.

Lydia sat down to join the women and children, and Nathan walked over to examine the work the men were doing. "Looks like the new wagons are about done," he noted. "Good. Brother Allred wanted to know if he could bring his wagon down and have us take a look at the reach. He's a little worried that it's not strong enough." The reach was that beam that ran down the center of the wagon beneath the wagon box and held the two axles together. If the reach broke, a wagon wasn't likely to go much of anywhere.

"Wheels will be finished in an hour or so," Carl said. "Then I think we'll be done."

Nathan nodded, pleased again at how naturally Carl had returned to the family. He never spoke of what happened at Nauvoo, and no one ever brought it up, but it had clearly shaken his faith in his fellowmen. Though he would have nothing to do with the religious side of their lives, he was openly complimentary about how the Mormons stuck together and took care of their own.

No, Nathan corrected himself, it was not religion that he had nothing to do with; it was the Church. Carl joined them every night for family prayer, and Melissa told them that he read the Bible each night to the children. If Melissa and the children read from the Book of Mormon or the Doctrine and Covenants, he would excuse himself; but if it was the Bible, he fully participated.

Nathan walked to his brother-in-law and punched him lightly on the shoulder. "You must have gotten up before dawn to get that much plowing done," he teased.

Carl looked at Joshua and smiled. "Solomon and I thought the ground was still a little too wet, so we thought we'd spend one more day here," he said easily. "Actually, Joshua wasn't there to give us his opinion. I think he slept in."

Joshua howled in protest. "That was to be our little secret, Carl, remember?"

"*You* slept in?" Nathan said incredulously.

Frowning, Joshua ignored Nathan and looked directly at Carl. "How would you like me to break a few more ribs for you there, sonny?"

The women and children had stopped to follow this conversation and laughed at that rejoinder.

Carl just smiled and tapped his son on the shoulder, stepping in to take over on the two-man saw. Nathan watched with satisfaction. Carl moved without pain now, something that had taken more than three months for him to finally accomplish. If he overdid it, one could still hear a slight wheeze in his breath from the punctured lung, but other than that, the effects of the beating were gone now. Matthew started to take over the other end of the saw from Luke, but Nathan moved quickly and did so instead. "I'll take it for a while," he said.

It was just before noon and the women were starting to put their sewing and mending away to prepare for the midday meal, when a tall man with a heavy beard approached the Steed family wagon shop. Solomon had returned with the wheels, and all of the men were working to get them on the axle hubs. It was the sound of the women suddenly lapsing into silence that caused the men to look up.

The man was obviously coming to them and not just passing by. Nathan set down the wooden mallet and, wiping his hands on his trousers, moved around the wagon. "Howdy," he said. "Can we help you find someone?"

"I'm looking for the Steeds' wagon shop. Would this be it?"

"It would," Nathan said, stepping forward and sticking out his hand. "I'm Nathan Steed." All the others had stopped now and were watching.

"Brother John Brown," the man said. His voice was pleasant and his handshake firm.

"Pleased to meet you," Nathan said. "Can we help you?"

There was a slow smile as he turned and surveyed the women. "One of you sisters wouldn't be Jennifer McIntire Steed, would you?"

Jenny had come over to stand by Matthew. There was a little exclamation of surprise and then she raised her hand. "I'm Jenny Steed."

"When was the last time you heard from your sister, Kathryn?"

That so took her by surprise that she just stared at the man. Matthew answered for her. "We got a letter from her a few months back."

"Do you know Kathryn?" Jenny said, recovering now.

"And where was she at that point?" Brown asked, ignoring the question and addressing Matthew. "I mean when she wrote that letter?"

"A little beyond Fort Laramie," Matthew said again.

"So she was still with Peter?"

"You *do* know them!" Jenny cried. "Have you seen them?"

"Yes, I do know them," Brown said with pleasure, "especially Kathryn. But I did get to spend one day with Peter."

Mary Ann stepped forward. "One day? What do you mean? Peter and Kathryn are traveling together with a company going to California."

Brown nodded slowly. Then a smile stole out from beneath the bushy beard. "And you wouldn't be the mother of Rebecca Steed Ingalls, would you?"

Mary Ann gasped. "You saw Rebecca?"

"And Derek and the children," he laughed. He looked around until his eyes stopped on Lydia. "And you must be Josh's mother. He looks very much like you."

Sudden tears sprang to Lydia's eyes as they flew open wide in astonishment. "You met our Josh?"

Brown chuckled, fully enjoying his role. He took out two letters from his pocket. "Why don't we sit a spell and I'll tell you the whole story. Then I have some mail for you."

Brown told it quickly, about the Mississippi Saints and how Peter had left Kathryn with them. Then he told them how after he left Kathryn at Pueblo he had started east and met the battalion on the Santa Fe Trail and met Derek, Rebecca, and Josh.

When he was finally finished, Joshua leaned forward. "So have you brought your families back with you now from Mississippi?"

"No," he said with a touch of regret. "That was our plan when we returned, but then I wrote President Young and told him all that had happened."

"Yes," Solomon broke in, "President Young told us about a group of Mississippi Saints who were wintering in Pueblo."

"Well, President Young wrote back and asked if we would leave our families one more season and bring a few of the best-outfitted men to join the vanguard company this spring. We have seven wagons and about a dozen of us, including two of our black servants that we thought might be of help as we go west. Unfortunately, another servant died on the way here and another died just yesterday." He frowned. "Traveling in this cold weather was just too much for them."

"We've heard that Derek and Rebecca and the children were part of the second sick detachment that also went to Pueblo,"

Mary Ann explained, "but we don't have confirmation of that."

"Really?" Brown said. "I hadn't heard that."

"So you're going with us?" Matthew said, pleased. "Nathan and I have been assigned by President Young to go ahead with the Pioneer Company as well. Then our families will come with the next companies."

"Yes, I know. President Young told me."

"So do you plan to go down to Pueblo and get your people?" Nathan asked.

Again Brown shook his head. "When we left Pueblo last September, Brother Robert Crow—whose family, incidentally, were the ones who took Kathryn in—said he would bring a few people up this spring and wait for us at Fort Laramie."

"Wonderful," Nathan said. "That means we'll see Kathryn for sure, and maybe even Derek and Rebecca much sooner than we thought."

Mary Ann stepped forward. "We would be honored if you would sup with us tonight, Brother Brown. We would love to hear all that you have to tell us."

He inclined his head, smiling. "That was exactly what Derek and Rebecca said that night when we chanced upon their camp and I told them about Kathryn."

Chapter Notes

When the Mormon Battalion reached California, the hostilities with Mexico were all but over and the Mormons did not have to fight. Instead, the battalion members became pawns in the struggle for power between General Kearny and Colonel Frémont. After a bitter dispute, Kearny and Frémont agreed to return to Fort Leavenworth, where Frémont could be put on trial. At a court-martial hearing Frémont was found guilty of insubordination for failure to obey a ranking officer, but President Polk overturned the ruling and Frémont escaped any punishment. He did, however, retire from the army after that. (See CS, pp. 87–91; *World Book Encyclopedia,* s.v. "Frémont, John C.")

John Brown, who had led the Mississippi Saints west in 1846, came to Winter Quarters with a few well-outfitted men "just a few days" before the Pioneer Company left (see "Pioneer Journeys," p. 810).

It is a little-known fact that there were blacks in the original Pioneer Company. One of them, Green Flake, joined the Church upon reaching Salt Lake. (See Hal Knight and Stanley B. Kimball, *111 Days to Zion* [Salt Lake City: Big Moon Traders, 1997], p. 127.)

Chapter Thirty-Seven

"Papa?"

Nathan pushed the sack of beans forward until it fit snugly in the space between the barrel of salted pork and a large can of sugar. Done, he turned to look at his daughter and her cousin. "What?"

Emily Steed, oldest daughter and second child of Nathan and Lydia, would be fifteen in another few months. She was fully a woman now and, if anything, was going to be even more beautiful than her mother. Her dark hair was full and fell halfway down her back, where it curled naturally at the ends. Her eyes were dark and could alternate between flashes of impudent humor and scorching anger if she felt she had been wronged.

Rachel Garrett, daughter of Jessica Garrett and now adopted by her stepfather, Solomon Garrett, was about six months older than her cousin, and in many ways more mature. Sober, reflective, more inclined to listen than to talk, she had also become a lovely young woman, though not as striking as Emily. Her hair too was long, but was soft brown and perfectly straight.

They were not alike in any way, Nathan thought. Emily was filled with energy and daring, taking life impetuously and dramatically. Even the slightest turn of events could leave her exulting joyously or weeping copious tears. Rachel was more deliberate, thoughtful without being fearful, conservative and yet open to new experiences. She was a perfect companion for Emily, and Nathan had offered thanks to the heavens for their friendship on more than one occasion. It constantly amazed both Nathan and Lydia how close these two had grown. Even to say that they were like sisters was an understatement, for many sisters did not share the bond that was between these two.

Emily was looking at him curiously, and he realized that she had asked him something. "I'm sorry, Em, what did you say?"

"You said that Rachel and I couldn't go with you because Brother Brigham wasn't letting anyone but men go with the Pioneer Company."

"Yes, I did."

"That's not true, is it? Yesterday at conference, April Fowler told Rachel and me that President Young has now decided to let women go."

"Well, yes and no."

"Papa!" Emily said in exasperation.

"All right, let me put it this way. Brother Brigham did not change his mind about not letting women go with the first company. He agreed to let Harriet Young go because Lorenzo Young won't leave her here with her asthma, and Lorenzo is such a skilled farmer that President Young wants him to go. So he did agree to let Harriet go."

"But—"

He went right on, knowing what was coming. "And President Young didn't think it was proper to have one woman traveling alone with all those men, so he is going to take his wife Clara, who also happens to be Harriet's daughter by a previous marriage, and Heber's Norwegian wife, whatever her name is."

"Ha!" Emily cried triumphantly. "See? I told you."

Nathan just smiled. "There will be no other exceptions."

Joshua and Matthew came out of their sod hut carrying more sacks of flour. Emily paid them no mind but pressed on. "And what about the children?"

"There are no children," Nathan said flatly.

Matthew tossed the bag up onto the tailgate, then shook his head. "Guess again, Nathan. Harriet Young refuses to leave her two children behind with anyone else."

"You're serious?" Joshua asked. He thought Matthew might just be playing along to prod Emily's sense of tragedy.

"I'm serious," Matthew said cheerfully. "One hundred forty-four men, three women, two children."

"Oh, Papa, won't you just ask President Young? Please. Rachel and I are fifteen now."

"Rachel is fifteen," Nathan said with a smile. "You won't be until July."

"We could cook and help drive the teams and do the laundry."

Nathan took Matthew's sack of flour and put it with the other two. Then he hopped down from the wagon and put his arms around her. "Look, Emmy, Brother Brigham didn't change his mind. It is just that circumstances left him little choice."

Rachel broke in. "It doesn't seem fair just because Sister Young refused to stay home." It was said calmly and without malice. It would be as close to a protest as Rachel would ever get.

"Why don't *you* refuse to go unless President Young lets me and Rachel come?"

Both Matthew and Joshua turned away in amusement, but Nathan had to hold in his smile as Emily searched his face. How she loved tragedy, especially when she felt that she was at the center of it!

"I think you know the answer to that, Emmy. But I can tell you this. Where you and Rachel are really needed is with the family. You two are so wonderful with the children, your mothers can't do without you."

Emily looked at Rachel, who shrugged, seeming to accept it. Then, realizing that she had lost, which she had totally expected in the first place, Emily also gave up. "Let's go help get the rest of the stuff, Rachel. We're certainly not being treated seriously here."

Now Nathan did smile as she turned and flounced away. Matthew and Joshua came over, chuckling as well. "It's a good thing she didn't know about the cow," Matthew drawled.

That was too much. Joshua threw up his hands. "Brigham has agreed to take a milk cow?"

Matthew nodded. "This morning when I was down watering our teams, I saw this milk cow standing behind Lorenzo's wagon. I guess Brother Brigham saw my look. 'Don't ask,' he said with great weariness. 'Just don't ask.' I found out later that after all of that with the women and children, Lorenzo came with his milk cow this morning. Brigham's patience snapped and he flatly said that no one was going to bring a milk cow along on a vanguard-company trek. But Lorenzo vowed that if she slowed them down for even one hour, they would abandon her on the prairie. I guess at that point Brigham just threw up his hands and walked away."

"You're going with a whole bloomin' menagerie," Joshua growled. "It's just as well I'm staying back to bring along the rest of the family."

"And by the way, I saw William Clayton, who has taken a tally. We won't have the full one hundred and forty-four men. Someone is too sick and won't be going. But there will be seventy-two wagons, ninety-three horses, fifty-two mules, sixty-six oxen, nineteen beef cattle, seventeen dogs, and a few chickens."

"And one very fast-walking milk cow," Nathan said, straight-faced.

Joshua just shook his head. "Come on," he muttered. "Let's get you loaded and on your way."

Heber C. Kimball left Winter Quarters on the afternoon of Monday, April fifth, with six wagons. He was the first to go. But he went only about four miles and then camped. The following day was the sixth of April, the seventeenth anniversary of the organization of the Church. Brigham called for what would be the last general conference of the Church for a time, and so most of Heber's group came back for the meetings. It was so like Heber to be the first to leave, Joshua thought. A man of enormous, almost inexhaustible energy, he was a driving force that could not be discouraged. Brigham Young had wanted to be on the road as early as March, but there were just too many preparations to be made. When it became obvious that early April would be the actual starting date, Brigham determined to hold the conference and then leave the next day.

Heber, totally organized and prepared in advance of that schedule, decided to move out even for a few miles to show the Saints that the time for the exodus had finally arrived. After yesterday's meetings were over, his group had returned to their camp and were probably on their way again first thing this morning.

Matthew and Nathan could have been ready early enough to go with the Kimballs, but it was one thing for a member of the Twelve to lead out and another for someone like themselves. So they decided they would wait for Brigham and follow after him. They would not be the only group on the move with Brigham's company. Elder Wilford Woodruff and his group of eight wagons left shortly before noon. Elder Orson Pratt followed shortly thereafter. When Nathan had gone with Carl and Solomon to fetch their team, they saw Elder Willard Richards in the final stages of packing as well. But it was not until word had come that Brigham's group had finally started to roll that Nathan gave the signal. The wagon was packed, the team harnessed and waiting for a driver.

Though there were a few tears in Winter Quarters this day, for the most part the atmosphere was more like that of a festival than that of a funeral. At long last the waiting was over. Even for those who were not departing with the Pioneer Company, this signaled a new beginning. Eight or nine additional companies were making preparations to follow closely behind, and the

Steeds would become part of one of them. By late May or early June they would follow in the footsteps of the vanguard group. And for those who couldn't leave this year, Brigham had promised to return to Winter Quarters before winter and lead them back next season.

So as the Steed family gathered for their final good-byes to Nathan and Matthew, the mood was one of excitement and anticipation rather than sorrow and disappointment. When the final moment came, Lydia and Jenny clung to their husbands fiercely and their eyes were glistening, but they were still smiling.

Mary Ann stood back this time, content to know that all the threads that had been rolled out in so many directions were now starting to be gathered in by the weaver and soon there would be a tightly woven Steed tapestry again.

After one final, lingering kiss, Matthew stepped back, waved to them all, and climbed up onto the wagon seat. Nathan took little Tricia for the last time and held her close, then handed her to Lydia and got up beside Matthew. They lifted their hands in one last farewell, and then Matthew popped the reins. "H'yah," he called softly. "Get up there, boys!"

"Good-bye," Nathan called as the wagon began to roll. "See you in a month or two."

There were cries of farewell and much enthusiastic waving as the wagon moved to Main Street and then turned north and disappeared from sight. For several moments, the family, now silent, stood watching the point where the wagon had last been.

After a moment, Joshua moved over to stand beside Caroline. He took her hand and held it lightly.

"It's hard to have to stay behind, isn't it?" she murmured, looking up at him.

He looked surprised, then nodded. "A little. But we've got our work cut out for us too. It's not like I'm not feeling needed."

"I'm glad," she said, slipping her arm through his. "Because in just a few weeks that's going to be us up on that wagon seat, and then you are going to feel very needed."

"Do you remember what Brigham said at worship services about a month ago?" Nathan asked his youngest brother.

Matthew, who was standing on the north bank of the Loup Fork River, sizing up the crossing they would have to make, turned. "What was that?"

"He said that he could just as easily find satisfaction in sawing up his house, grinding it for Indian meal, and eating it as he could find satisfaction in leading this many people across the plains to the mountains."

Matthew laughed shortly. "I do remember that. And I think we're about to prove him right."

They both turned to watch the scouts moving up and down the riverbank looking for a suitable place to attempt to ford. It was ironic. Though they had left on the seventh of April, they went only twenty miles northwest to the Elkhorn River before they stopped for a time. Brigham and others of the Twelve made several trips back to Winter Quarters before everything was finally in readiness, and on the sixteenth of April they moved out. Now just one week later they had run into their first major obstacle. The Loup Fork of the Platte River ran mostly east and west at this point, almost paralleling the Platte, which was about twenty miles to the south. In late summer, Nathan guessed, this would be barely enough to wet the teams' hooves, but now it was nearly three hundred yards across and in places waist deep and moving quickly. The problem the scouts were finding was that the silty bottom was like quicksand. If they let their horses stop even for a moment they would begin to sink into the mud. They had already come four miles farther upstream than they planned trying to find a ford.

"Here comes Brother Brigham," Matthew noted.

Nathan jumped down from the wagon and walked up to where Matthew was standing. Most of the wagons pulled up alongside each other on the low bluffs overlooking the river. Below them, a few rods from where they stood, four wagons had gone down to the river's edge. They would be the first to cross. Brigham stood with several other men, and Nathan guessed the debate now going on was whether they would have to unload their goods first and ferry them across in the "Revenue Cutter."

Nathan shifted his gaze a little. The nearest wagon—or rather, wagon-boat—was Luke Johnson's. As he looked at the odd-looking vehicle, Nathan once again was impressed with Brigham Young's organizational skills and his great foresight. The "Revenue Cutter," as it had been nicknamed, was a flat-bottom boat with a blunt nose and a square back. Made of a wooden frame over which thick hides had been stretched tightly, the boat looked ungainly and crudely made. But it floated like a cork in the trial runs they had made with it on the Missouri. Remarkably, it could carry as much as fifteen to eighteen hundred pounds of goods without sinking more than a foot in the water. In order to carry it across a thousand miles of wilderness, a wagon had been stripped of its box and the Revenue Cutter substituted in its place. It was clearly recognizable among the other wagons. Not only did it have the odd-shaped "wagon box," but it did not have a cover or bows. Brother Luke Johnson had been given the assignment to drive the cutter as his wagon.

Now the scouts came riding back to where the wagons were waiting. Nathan, Matthew, and the other men moved closer until they were just above the group where Brigham was. After listening to the reports, Brigham turned. "It looks like there's no better place. Luke, you want to try it?"

Luke Johnson nodded and climbed up onto the wagon seat. "Just take it right across there," Brigham said. At this point, the river was split into two streams by a long sandbar about midstream. For at least a hundred yards or more, the water was no more than a foot or so deep. But around the sandbar there were two main channels. Here the current was swifter and the water looked like it might be as much as four or five feet deep.

Johnson snapped the reins and his team started forward. The Revenue Cutter still had its full load of goods packed in it. As they hit the water, Johnson whistled sharply at his team, urging them forward more quickly. "Get up there, team!" he shouted. They leaped forward into a run, kicking up great sprays of water.

It was all right until he reached the main channel. Then suddenly the water was up to the hubs of the wheels. The wagon started to slow. "He's sinking," Matthew cried.

That he was. The wagon had slowed considerably, though the horses were fighting hard to keep it moving. The wheels were bringing up black silt now, which left a dark stain in the clear water. Johnson was shouting at his team, urging them on. They were up to their bellies now and fighting for footing. He was almost to a standstill when they reached the sandbar and the footing beneath them became firmer. They shot forward, the wagon jerking around sharply behind them.

"Don't stop! Don't stop!" Brigham was shouting.

The wagon-boat careened as it passed over the sandbar, the wheels throwing sand in a fine spray, then hit the water again. The stream on the other side of the sandbar was narrower and deeper, and here the current was at its swiftest. In just a few feet, the horses were up to their chests and the water was over the front wheels and pushing at the bottom of the Revenue Cutter. The back end of the wagon started to swing around. The horses slowed, then stopped, wheezing and jerking their heads. In one quick motion Luke wrapped the reins around the brake lever, then jumped into the water. It nearly swept him away, and he had to grab at the harnessing to catch himself. He pushed forward to reach the heads of his horses, then took them by the bridle. "Come on, boys!" he urged. "Don't stop on me now. Giddyap. Come on. Go! Go!"

His effort paid off. Fighting and lunging in great leaps, the horses began to move again. They crossed ten more feet and then the bottom began to rise again. It was only to the animal's knees, and that gave them enough strength to lunge for the bank. In a moment, wagon-boat and team were across. Luke Johnson let go of his team and doubled over, hands on his knees, gasping for air. Then he finally straightened. He was soaked to his chest. "You can do it," he shouted, "but whatever you do, don't stop."

Brigham nodded and turned. "All right, who's next?"

Orson Pratt had decided that taking a loaded wagon across the soft bottom was the problem. Without waiting for instructions, he unloaded half his wagon. It didn't matter. He didn't even make the sandbar. Those watching plunged into the river to help him. A dozen men threw their weight against the box, lifting and pushing at the same time. They unloaded the remainder of the wagon at the sandbar, and the men carried the items across. But as Elder Pratt took his team into the second channel, they foundered in the deep water and one of the horses went down in the traces. It could have been dangerous. A horse struggling to free itself can deliver a deadly kick, but it was too tangled to kick out any way but forward. In a moment the men had the harnessing undone and both horses were free from the wagon. They finally had to tie a rope to the stalled wagon and pull it out by hand.

Norton Jacob was convinced that his oxen had greater strength than the horses and wanted to try crossing with his wagon fully loaded. It stopped twenty yards short of the bar. Luke Johnson and others unloaded the Revenue Cutter and they began to ferry Norton's goods across to the other side.

By the time they got their fifth or sixth wagon across, Brigham called for a halt. They were going to have to build a raft. At this rate they would lose two or three days making a linear distance of three hundred yards.

In the end, they did not build the rafts. The following morning, as they started work on cutting down the trees, the scouts went out to see if they might find a better place for the crossing. About a mile upstream they found a place where they felt they could take the wagons across if they lightened the loads some and double and triple teamed the wagons.

They worked in teams. One team would unload about half of

each wagon and carry it down to the water where the Revenue Cutter waited. A second team rowed it across the river and unloaded it, then returned for the next load. A third team worked on taking the extra teams and hitching them to each wagon. It was hard labor for all of them, but it was working. With the extra teams, the wagons were making it across without the help of men in the water.

To their pleased astonishment, with the passing of each wagon, the sand in the river bottom began to pack together. By noon they were passing easily with the extra teams. By two they were no longer unloading the wagons. They still had to double team but they were taking them across fully loaded. By four o'clock they were done.

Nathan and Matthew's was one of the last wagons to go, and so they had not been forced to unload their supplies. As they reached the other side and began unhitching the extra team of mules Brigham had lent them, Wilford Woodruff sidled up to them. "Well," he said with a droll smile, "all Israel went over today. Not over the mighty Jordan, but across the Loup Fork of the Platte River. And we did so without harm to man or beast."

"If you ask me," Nathan said without expression, "I think I'd prefer the Jordan."

Chapter Notes

Four principal sources have been used by the author for the information about the original Pioneer Company as they crossed the continent from Winter Quarters to the Salt Lake Valley. The four sources are described below:

1. *Day by Day with the Utah Pioneers—1847* was a series of articles published in the *Salt Lake Tribune* in 1897, the fiftieth anniversary of the journey of the Pioneer Company. It is a day-by-day account of the trek west written by Andrew Jenson, who was at that time the Church historian. It contains a detailed account of each day, along with biographies and pictures of those who came with the Pioneer Company.

2. Hal Knight and Stanley B. Kimball produced a book called *111 Days to Zion*. This too is a day-by-day account of the trek west. While this draws on the Jenson source for some of its information, it has additional material and some excellent maps showing the campsites for each day. A reprint edition of this book was published in 1997 by Big Moon Traders, Salt Lake City.

3. William Clayton's journal is an invaluable source of information on the crossing, though it is written from the point of view of his own experience. George D. Smith has provided an edited version of Clayton's journals in *An Intimate Chronicle: The Journals of William Clayton* (Salt Lake City: Signature Books, 1995). The entries are by date and therefore easy to find. However, Smith has cut a great deal of material in order to have a one-volume edition. The pioneer-trek portion of William Clayton's journal can be found in full on the *Infobase Library* available from Bookcraft on CD-ROM or at <http://www.ldsworld.com> on the Internet.

4. Wilford Woodruff was a meticulous and careful journal keeper. His journals have been published in several volumes by Signature Books, with volume 3 covering 1847 and the trek west. Portions of Wilford Woodruff's journal appear in Matthias F. Cowley, *Wilford Woodruff: History of His Life and Labors* (Salt Lake City: Bookcraft, 1964), and this book is also found on the *Infobase Library*.

Hereafter, rather than tediously document all of the details used in the novel in each chapter, reference citations will be given only for significant items from other sources. Each of the four sources above uses a day-by-day format, so that the interested reader can easily check the details for any particular date.

The trip across the plains is generally said to have taken 111 days (from 5 April, when Heber C. Kimball first began to move, until 24 July, when Brigham Young's carriage finally entered the Valley).

To the casual reader, it may seem as though the start of the Pioneer Company was somewhat disorganized. However, from the beginning the plan was that the various elements of the company would make their way separately to the Elkhorn River, about twenty miles west of Winter Quarters, and assemble there. Heber C. Kimball was the first, leaving on the fifth of April. As depicted here in the novel, four other members of the Twelve, including Brigham Young, left on the seventh, the day after general conference.

They didn't move either very far or very fast at first. On the eighth of April, word reached Brigham Young that Parley P. Pratt had just arrived at Winter Quarters from his mission in England. Anxious to talk with his fellow Apostle, Brigham returned to Winter Quarters, then rejoined his company on the eleventh. They had barely finished ferrying their wagons across the Elkhorn River when another letter came to the camp. Now it was John Taylor who had returned from Great Britain. In addition to bringing a substantial sum of badly needed cash from the British Saints, Elder Taylor also carried about five hundred dollars' worth of scientific and surveying instruments—two barometers, two sextants, two artificial horizons, a circle of reflection, and a telescope. Those would prove to be of critical value in laying out a trail for others to follow and for surveying new cities and towns in the Great Basin. So while some of the camp moved slowly westward and others stayed in place, Brigham returned again to Winter Quarters. With him went seven of the Apostles. After getting the funds and the instruments and holding a warm reunion with their brethren, the Twelve left Elders Parley P. Pratt and John Taylor in charge of organizing the companies that were to follow as soon as possible. On April fifteenth, the Apostles rejoined their company on the Platte River, about forty-six miles west of Winter Quarters, and prepared to formally depart the next day. (See Leonard J. Arrington, *Brigham Young: American Moses* [New York: Alfred A. Knopf, 1985], pp. 130–32.)

Originally there was to be 144 in the original Pioneer Company, a number symbolizing that this was the camp of Israel—there being twelve men chosen to represent each of the twelve tribes of Israel. Three dropped out because of sickness, and two—Thomas Bullock and William Clayton—were added at the last minute, leaving the final total at 148 people with the three women and two children.

The Luke Johnson mentioned here was one of the original Twelve Apostles chosen in 1835, but had left the Church during the Kirtland apostasy. He came to Nauvoo seeking fellowship and was rebaptized in 1846. Thereafter he remained faithful for the rest of his life. He was not restored to the apostleship.

Lorenzo Dow Young's milk cow went the full distance to the Salt Lake Valley, providing the Pioneer Company with greatly appreciated milk and cheese.

Chapter Thirty-Eight

Alice Samuelson Steed rose to her full height, which was barely more than five foot two inches, and waved her hands. "All right, you two, that's enough."

Both Will and Peter looked up in amazement. They had been so engrossed in their argument, they had totally forgotten that they were not alone. To see Alice standing before them with her eyes locking theirs in challenge came as a bit of a shock.

"What?" Will said, not sure what it was that she had said.

"I said that's enough." She moved between them. "Sam Brannan is going to come back here and want an answer and you two will still be fighting over who gets to go with him."

They looked at each other sheepishly, knowing she was right.

"All right," she said, coming to a decision. "I'll be the judge here. Peter, you go first. You give all the reasons why you think it should be you who goes east with him. Will won't say a word until you're done." She glared at her husband. "Will you?"

He shook his head meekly.

"Then when you're done, Peter, William here can have his turn. And you will listen until he is finished. Understood?"

"Yes, Alice," Peter said with equal humility.

She moved back to her chair, trying not to smile. "Okay, Peter, you may begin."

"All right," he said, leaning forward. "First, we know for sure that there is no way that Sam Brannan is going to agree to let Alice and Jared go with you. Which means you have to leave a wife and child behind. I don't. That's the most important reason. Second, my wife and the child I have never seen are waiting for me somewhere at a place called Fort Pueblo on the east side of the Rockies. I promised that I would come for them as soon as possible."

He was trying hard not to sound triumphant. He knew he had the strongest case, and he was pretty sure Alice would agree with him. "Third, if we were going by ship, I would have to defer to you, Will. But we're not. We're going overland. And which of the two of us has just come all the way across the continent by wagon? Tell me that, please."

Will started to mutter something, but Alice held up her hand. "Not yet." She turned to Peter. "Is that all?"

He looked sober. "We could say something about having the better-looking of the two of us go, but that would just be rubbing salt into the wound."

"Ha!" Will cried.

"I'm afraid I would rule against you on that one," Alice laughed merrily. "You're very nice-looking, Peter, but my Will—oh, goodness, he is so handsome."

"*Now* can I speak?" Will cried in exasperation.

"Yes, dear," Alice answered sweetly.

He turned to Peter. "Granted, you've made some strong points, but let me note the following. I have driven many a wagon with my father in the freight business. Maybe I haven't crossed the plains, but I'm not inexperienced."

"Can you drive three yoke of oxen at the same time?" Peter shot back.

"Peter," Alice warned.

"Sorry," he murmured.

"Next," Will went on, as though he hadn't been interrupted, "yes, I will have to leave Alice and the baby here, but if Brother Brannan's right, then the Saints may end up here. Then she won't have to go anywhere. As far as my leaving her alone, you'll be here to make sure she's cared for." He took a quick breath. "And as for meeting your Kathryn and your new baby, I understand how you feel. But remember, my family is coming across the plains too. I haven't seen my father and mother in over a year now. Savannah and the other children—they are my brothers and sisters. I am as anxious to see them as you are to see Kathryn."

Again Peter stirred, but said nothing when he saw Alice's look.

"Finally," Will went on, "I know Samuel Brannan well. You have met him only once. We have lived with him and dealt with him for over a year now. I know how he thinks and acts, and that's important. He can be very frustrating at times."

He stopped, and Peter leaned forward. Alice looked at the two of them. "Are you finished, Will?" she asked.

He nodded, and Peter jumped right in. "I know Brannan now too, so that's no great advantage for you."

Away they went again, and Alice jumped to her feet a second time. They sputtered out like candles in a rainstorm. When they were silent, she spoke quietly but forcefully. "I would like to rule on what I've heard," she said.

They both nodded, watching her expectantly.

"You both make strong arguments, but . . ." She turned to her husband and her eyes softened. "But I'm afraid that I'm going to rule in favor of Peter."

"*Alice,*" Will cried. "I—"

She cut him off quickly. "I know that you think it's because I don't want you to leave me, Will. And that's true, of course. But that's not enough. There's one reason stronger than all the rest. That's why Peter has to go."

"What?" Will asked, already seeing that he was going to lose this one.

"Kathryn and the baby," she answered quietly. "That outweighs everything else. If it were me out there, Will, I would want it to be you that came for me."

Sam Brannan had somehow secured the services of Charles C. Smith, an experienced mountain man and trail guide, and that was a great comfort to Peter. As they checked their saddle girths and the lashings on their pack mules one last time, he remembered what John Sutter had said the night before. "This is pure, unvarnished folly," he had exclaimed in his heavy Swiss accent.

"Now, John," Brannan replied, trying to smooth things out. "Charles here knows what he's doing."

Sutter just harrumphed at that. "First of all, it's madness for three men to travel alone. Yes, yes, I know it's the end of April, but even the Indians are saying they've never seen the snow deeper in the Sierra. It'll take you two months just to get over Truckee Pass."

"We're counting on the warmer weather and the rain to help pack the snow more solid," Smith had drawled lazily. "Some of them up in Bear Valley are reporting that a horse can pretty well stay on top of the snow now, especially at night."

Sutter ignored that. "You'll never make it, Brannan. Give it another month."

Peter didn't say anything through all of that. He had been in that snow twice now, and he had deep misgivings. But he also trusted Charlie Smith.

None of that changed Sutter's mind, but it was not like him to pout about it. This morning as they prepared to leave, Sutter had come out to wish them farewell and Godspeed. He also brought a sack with almost twenty-five pounds of dried beef to send with them.

Brannan looked around, then at his two companions. "Are you ready?"

"I was ready three days ago," Smith drawled amiably.

"Ready," Peter answered.

Will stepped forward and gripped Peter's hand. "You take care now, you hear?" he said softly.

"When I see your parents, I'll tell them you wanted to come."

"Thanks. It's okay, Peter. Alice is right. It's you who should be going."

Peter went to Alice and took the baby. He kissed him quickly, even as Jared struggled to be free of the attention. "Good-bye, my little friend," Peter said. Then he gave Alice a big hug. She threw her arms around him and hugged him back tightly.

"That's for all the family," she said, near tears. "And especially for Kathryn."

"I'll give it to her," he promised. Then he stepped back and mounted his horse. Smith was already up. Brannan shook hands with Will and Alice, then with Sutter one last time. Then he too mounted up, and with a jaunty wave he nudged his horse and it started for the gate.

Peter thought he had been exhausted before. The night he and the Reeds had come across the Salt Desert they had gone over thirty miles on no more than three or four hours of sleep. But that had been a child's task compared to what they were undergoing now. They had ridden the twenty-five miles to Johnson's Ranch, rested for less than an hour, and pushed on, making an estimated forty miles before they stopped. When they camped at Mule Springs at the head of Bear Valley that first night, it was clear and cold. By morning the temperature dropped and a light rain started. Charlie Smith looked up towards the mountains, which were hidden in the gray clouds. "This will be snow on top," he said darkly.

That did it. Aside from the risk of being trapped themselves, Brannan did not want to be delayed further. Peter had not yet figured out exactly what urgency was driving the leader of the

Brooklyn, but whatever it was, it was driving him hard. They set out immediately. Within an hour they were in snow five or six feet deep, but Charlie was right. The weeks of warmer weather mixed with rain had packed the snow in a denser mass than the deep powder Peter and James Reed had tried to bull through. The crust was not hard enough to carry the weight of a horse and rider, but a horse alone could stand in most places without breaking through. So they tied their horses in a string and moved ahead on foot.

It was the twenty-seventh of April. In the valleys below them, spring had come two months before. But here winter still had the mountain locked in its grip. They made the pass at about five o'clock that night. As they stood amid the rocky crags, looking down on the lake below them—still partially covered with ice—Peter felt sick to his stomach. From the descriptions given by the survivors and the rescue party, he knew exactly where the camp had been. He was looking at the site. There below him was the place of death and suffering, and it made him sick to think again of those he had known who had died there.

Brannan was watching him closely. After a moment he touched Peter's arm. "Come on," he said. "We won't stay long."

Charlie Smith looked at the sky. Snowflakes were floating gently down upon them. "It's all down from here," he said with satisfaction. "I think we beat the main storm."

When they reached the meadows near the east end of the lake, the snow was only three or four feet deep, and there were bare patches of ground around the trees and where the sun shone in its strength. Brannan stopped the horses for a rest. "I'm going to go take a look," he said. "Do you want to come, Peter?"

Peter immediately shook his head. "I'll stay here with the horses."

Brannan nodded and handed him the rope; then he and Charlie set off at a brisk walk and disappeared into the trees. They were gone only about fifteen minutes. When they reappeared, Peter watched them closely for any reaction. Both were shaken. Brannan looked a little gray, but that might have just been the fading light.

"Unbelievable!" Brannan muttered, then said nothing more. Charlie Smith kept looking back in the direction from which they had come and shaking his head. They took their horses to the creek and let them drink. As they waited for the animals to get their fill, Charlie suddenly gave a short, triumphant laugh. "Don't you wish old John Sutter were here?"

"Why?" Brannan asked.

"He said it would take us two months to get over the pass."

The other two nodded. This was only their second day since leaving the fort, and they had come all the way from Bear Valley in just over fourteen hours.

"I know we're tired," their guide continued, "but I think we need to keep going, all night if necessary, and get out of the mountains."

"Agreed," Brannan said.

Smith laughed again. "If you figure another eight to ten hours to get down, that means we will have crossed the pass in under thirty hours. I'd like to rub Sutter's nose in that a little."

With a nod, Peter and Brannan fell into line behind him. As they started eastward again, Peter did not turn and look back, not even once.

Kathryn Ingalls stopped for a moment, leaning heavily on her cane, and looked back into the room. It was empty now except for the plain wooden table and three stools that Derek couldn't fit into the wagon. For a moment, there was a twinge of sadness. Last spring when she and Peter had started out with the Reed family from Springfield, Illinois, who could have guessed that by fall she would be teaching school on the Arkansas River at a little place in the middle of nowhere called Fort Pueblo? But she was glad. Here she had taught as many as twenty-one pupils. Some spoke with the deep twang of Mississippi; others chattered away in Spanish. Some were fair skinned and blue-eyed. Others had eyes as black as a beetle's belly and either the olive skin of the Mexicans or the copper skin that spoke of white fathers and Indian mothers.

Here also she had given birth to little Nicole. Here they had spent a lonely Christmas far from their families. Here she had spent many an hour on her knees praying for Peter's safety. Now they were leaving and would never see it again.

The little cabin wouldn't stay empty for long. There were only seventeen of them heading north this early. The rest of the nearly two hundred and fifty people here now would wait for this lead group to send word back if they had found the Latter-day Saints before they came on. So one of the families from Mississippi would move in here before they had been gone an hour. At Fort Pueblo, housing was too limited for a dwelling to sit empty for very long.

She turned as Rebecca came into the cabin to stand beside her. "Is Nicole still asleep?" Kathryn asked.

"Yes. Christopher is watching both her and Leah." Rebecca looked more closely at her sister-in-law. "Does it make you sad to leave?" she asked.

Kathryn instantly shook her head. "No. We were happy here, but I am so ready to leave."

Rebecca slipped her arm around Kathryn's waist and squeezed her. "Me too. In fact, I am so excited, I barely slept a wink last night."

"A wink?" Kathryn asked in mock surprise. "That would be a very long time compared to how long I slept."

Rebecca laughed.

They stood in silence for a time, and then Kathryn straightened. "If we're so happy to be leaving, how come we're still standing here?"

"Good question," Rebecca said, taking her arm. "I think everyone's ready. Let's go."

They came outside to where the five wagons were waiting. The last one was theirs, one Derek had gotten in trade for working most of the winter for one of the traders at Fort Pueblo.

Robert and Elizabeth Crow and their extended family would have the three lead wagons. George Therlkill, a son-in-law of the Crows, had one for him and some of his own immediate family, and the Ingallses had one for their three adults and four children.

As the women came up, Derek was talking with Brother Crow. He stopped and smiled. "Are you ready?"

"More ready than I have ever been for anything else in my life," Kathryn said eagerly.

Robert Crow laughed softly. "We feel exactly the same, Kathryn. So let's mount up and get this party on the road."

It was their twenty-fifth day out of Johnson's Ranch, and their twenty-third since coming out of the Sierra. Once again the endless monotony of the landscape left Peter feeling depressed and despondent. He had been especially melancholy since they had passed the sandy hill where he and Milt Elliott and James Reed had tried to take Reed's wagon up and around John Snyder's wagon. The memory of that instantaneous flash of anger that left John Snyder dead came back as vividly as if it were happening again. Against his will, his eyes searched the ground for the dark stain where John Snyder had fallen, but thankfully, there was nothing now in the sand but the eroded marks of the wagon tracks.

They moved steadily eastward, making twenty to thirty miles on some days, but dropping the average to more like twenty when they had to stop to hunt or to rest their animals. When he saw the dark line that was the Ruby Mountains and watched it grow close enough to beckon them with its pine-covered slopes and snowcapped peaks, Peter began to watch more carefully the trail they were following. Finally, about two o'clock on this, their twenty-fifth day, he saw what he was looking for. It was faint, and had he not been watching they might have passed it by.

"There it is," he said quietly, reining in his horse.

Sam Brannan and Charlie Smith pulled up as well. Charlie stood in his stirrups, squinting against the harsh glare of the sun off the desert floor. Then he grunted and sat down again. "I see it."

Brannan nodded. "I don't understand. Why were you coming up from the south at this point?"

"Well," Peter responded, "that was one more little surprise that Lansford Hastings hadn't warned us about." He pointed toward the wall of the Ruby Mountains that stood directly east of them. "The Great Salt Desert is about straight east from here, but when we reached the other side of the Ruby Mountains there, there was no way for wagons over the mountains."

"That's for sure," Smith grunted.

"So we turned south and went all the way around them." He shook his head, his eyes dark with the memory. "It took us ten days. *Ten days!* Do you realize what that ten days would have meant to them in the Sierra?"

Charlie was looking at the high mountains, whose top third was still snow covered. "I can see why you didn't want to take wagons over that," he noted, "but we could make it fine with horses and mules."

"No," Peter said, more sharply than he had intended.

Brannan shook his head too. "Peter's right, Charlie. The Hastings Cutoff is not for us. We'll stick to the known trail."

Peter was a little chagrined that he had reacted so strongly. "See how faint the tracks are here? Well, there are some places where we barely left any track at all. I'm not sure I could find the way."

The man who was the most experienced of the three of them finally nodded. "You're right. We need to resupply at Fort Hall anyway."

"There's nowhere else between here and Fort Bridger to do it," Brannan said.

"Nothing," Peter murmured, "except one stretch of trail that even the devils in hell would stay away from."

Chapter Notes

Sam Brannan, Charles C. Smith, and an "unnamed young man" left Sutter's Fort on 26 April 1847 and headed east to find Brigham Young and the Saints. Whether Smith was a Latter-day Saint or not is not known, though it is recorded that he had been in Nauvoo previously. Later Brannan wrote: "We crossed the Snowy Mountains of California, a distance of 40 miles, . . . in one day and two hours, a thing that has never been done before in less than three days. We traveled on foot and drove our animals before us, the snow from twenty to one hundred feet deep." (Quoted in *CS*, p. 87.)

By the time the last of the Donner group were rescued, those left in the mountain camps had also been forced to begin eating their dead. Brannan's party did stop at the camp beside the lake where most of the Donner Party had perished, and found skulls and bones scattered about in every direction. Thus, though newspaper accounts of the Donner tragedy had been sent east previously, Brannan was the first known white man to bring an eyewitness account of the tragedy out of California.

As shown here, Brannan's small party elected not to take the Hastings Cutoff through the Salt Lake Valley. Instead, they took the California Trail, which joined the Hastings route about twenty-five miles west of the Ruby Mountains. The California Trail went northeastward through present-day Nevada to join the Oregon Trail at the Snake River.

The exact date is not known that a small group of Saints from Pueblo left for Fort Laramie to intercept the main body of the Saints. It is known that they had been at Fort Laramie about two weeks when the Pioneer Company arrived there on 1 June, so the assumption is that the Pueblo group left sometime around the first of May, as depicted here.

Chapter Thirty-Nine

Matthew and Nathan Steed sat in the back of their wagon while the rain drummed softly on the canvas above them. Nathan was writing, though Matthew couldn't tell if it was in his journal or if he was writing a letter to Lydia and the children. He sighed, knowing that he should be writing too but not feeling like making the effort. And besides, they had only one pen and ink bottle.

The problem was that Matthew was just plain bored. Today was . . . he had to stop and think for a moment. It was the twenty-ninth of May, which meant it was almost two months now since they had left Winter Quarters. For the most part, each of those almost sixty days had been much the same. That was bad enough, but this was the second day that the rain had been heavy enough that they couldn't move forward. Here it was half past nine and they were still sitting in place.

That really frustrated him. They were now within fifty miles of Fort Laramie, just two or three days' journey from here.

Everyone was looking forward with great anticipation to that milestone on their journey. Since they had left the Elkhorn more than six weeks ago they had not passed a single community, not a village, not a farm, not a way station of any kind. Fort Laramie couldn't be much of a splash of civilization this far from nowhere, but after what they had seen in the last month and a half, it couldn't be anything less than wonderful.

He turned his head. "Letter or journal?"

Nathan looked up. "Letter."

Matthew grunted, not surprised. They had started to meet up with people moving east now. Near Ash Hollow a trapper had ridden across the river and volunteered to take mail east, but he was in a hurry and couldn't wait. Matthew had finished a letter and sent it with him. Nathan had planned to get one done, but hadn't and so missed the opportunity. At Fort Laramie they would almost certainly find someone to take mail east for them.

"How many miles did William Clayton say we've come?" Nathan asked, looking up.

"Well, at Scotts Bluff, which was two days ago, it was almost an even five hundred miles from Winter Quarters."

"So what now do you think? About five hundred and a quarter?"

Matthew hooted. "Are you kidding? At the rate we're moving, I'll bet we've not come fifteen miles since Scotts Bluff."

Nathan nodded absently and returned to his writing.

Matthew lay back and closed his eyes. Five hundred miles. In some ways it seemed like a thousand, as if they had been traveling in this wagon from the time of his birth. The whole experience had been huge stretches of tedious monotony broken only by an occasional burst of interest. And even new things had a way of turning monotonous as well.

He thought of the first day they had seen buffalo. The whole camp was in a high state of excitement. That had been the first of May. He remembered the date because they ended up calling it their "May Day hunt." The hunt went on for almost three hours as the wagons moved along slowly, stopping to watch the hunters when the action was close enough to see. That night the whole camp had exulted over the opportunity to have fresh meat and to taste buffalo for the first time.

But in a few days buffalo had become so commonplace that one hardly glanced up at the sight of them anymore. There were whole days when the prairie on both sides of the river was black with buffalo. William Clayton, ever the one to count things, one day estimated that there were at least fifty thousand head in view.

As he let his mind go back, he was suddenly struck by the irony of the things which stood out in his memory. Their very insignificance was proof of how deeply the tedium was affecting them all. He thought of anthills which sparkled with brightly colored Indian beads. Evidently, after Indians had camped in the vicinity, the ants found the colored "pebbles" fascinating and carried them to their hills. When they were first sighted, grown men would call for their companions to come and see this unique phenomenon. But after a week, that too became commonplace and they barely glanced at them as they passed.

There was the day that Brigham Young lost his telescope as they rode hard to stop some cattle from mingling with the buffalo. Brigham was not a happy man after that. The glass had cost forty dollars and was a favorite of his. The man who should have been watching the cattle got a tongue-lashing, and for the rest of that night the company got a taste of a very grumpy President Young. The next day it was decided that there was not much sense in moving on with their president in such a mood, so a search party went back. Finally, late in the day the glass was found—miraculously undamaged by the buffalo that had passed all around it—and the mood of the camp and Brother Brigham cheered considerably.

There was the day the "roadometer" was put into service. William Clayton had been charged by Brigham Young to keep an accurate record of the trail so that they could provide help to those companies that would be coming after them. Mileage covered each day was an important part of that record. At first

Clayton tied a red bandanna to a spoke on a wagon wheel and counted the number of revolutions. He had calculated that exactly 360 revolutions made one mile. That was both dizzying and tedious. So one night Clayton took his problem to the man who was considered to be the most learned in the group, Elder Orson Pratt. Intrigued with the idea of creating a mechanical device to do the counting, Pratt designed a series of wooden cogs that attached to the axle and automatically counted the rotations of the wheel. Appleton Harmon, a skilled mechanic, made it, and to everyone's amazement it worked. They called it the "roadometer." William Clayton was as pleased as if he had just received word of the birth of a new child. That's what monotony did to you.

Somewhere off to his left, Matthew heard a burst of laughter and a man's howl of protest. Another card game or perhaps some dominoes, he thought. That too was evidence of the mental state of the men. Any kind of diversion was welcomed in their attempts to beat the tedium.

"How tall do you think Chimney Rock was?" Nathan said, again interrupting his thoughts.

Matthew half rolled over so that he could look at his brother. "From the base, or just the chimney itself?" Now, there had been a break in the routine, he thought. After five hundred miles of prairie where a tree or two along the river were considered as stunning scenery, Chimney Rock had been a source of great excitement.

"From the base. Well, both."

Matthew screwed up his mouth, trying to remember. "Brother Pratt took some sightings on it, I remember."

"Does two hundred sixty feet for the shaft sound right?"

"Yeah, I think that's about it. And it was like four hundred and fifty feet above the level plain if you counted everything."

"Yeah, thanks."

Matthew sighed and rolled to his knees. He crawled to the end of the wagon and peeked out the crack in the canvas. He groaned. The rain was lightening up, but the ground was still covered with large puddles.

Nathan looked up. "What?"

"Nothing." He came back and lay down again and closed his eyes.

Nathan stopped writing, laying the pen down. He picked up the paper and blew on it to dry the ink. Then he carefully folded it and put pen, ink, and letter back in his trunk. When he finished he turned to Matthew. "And what have you been thinking about so hard?" he asked.

Matthew was a little startled. He hadn't thought Nathan was paying any attention to anything but the letter. "Boredom."

It came out with such disgust that Nathan chuckled. "Reaching Fort Laramie will help."

"And just how do we do that when we sit here waiting for this blasted rain to stop?"

Nathan ignored the outburst. "They say once we leave Laramie, we're out of prairie country. That will help. The endless prairie is part of it, I think."

"I don't know," Matthew drawled lazily, "I like getting up in the morning and being able to see three days in advance."

Nathan laughed, then stretched out beside his brother on their mattress. "They tell me that one of the best cures for boredom is a quick nap."

"Hmm," Matthew said dryly. "Maybe that's a theory we ought to test."

Shortly after ten o'clock the bugle sounded across the camp, giving the signal to hitch up the teams. Matthew leaped up immediately and opened the flap on their wagon. The sky was still overcast, but it was considerably lighter than before and the rain had stopped. He kicked Nathan on the bottom of his boot.

"I'm awake," he growled. "Don't you be worrying about me."

Matthew sat down and began pulling on his own boots. "I hate this waiting."

Not until twelve o'clock were they finally ready to move out. By that point Matthew was ready to scream. Two hours to hitch the teams, pack the rest of their gear, and gather in the stock. Two hours! How did Brigham stand it? This must drive him to distraction. By now, had Matthew been in charge, he would have gone after several of the brethren with a bullwhip to see if he couldn't spark a little life into them.

He turned as a shout sounded over the camp. It was Heber C. Kimball. "Brethren, we'd like you to gather your teams around the boat, please."

Matthew gave Nathan a questioning look, but Nathan just shrugged. He was up on the wagon seat. Matthew was standing beside the team. The "boat" was Luke Johnson's wagon, the Revenue Cutter. Since it had no top, it made a good stand from which the leaders could address the company. Matthew groaned. Not another delay! With a sigh borne of deep pain, he took the bridle of the near horse and clucked to him softly. "Okay, boys, let's move."

To gather seventy-two wagons and teams tightly around one point was not an easy thing and it took some jockeying. As they finally got into place, Brigham Young climbed up into the leather boat. "Brethren," he said in a loud voice, "we'd like the captains of tens to lead out your respective companies and get all of your men together." He motioned to Luke Johnson to drive ahead. "We'll gather over there."

This time Matthew's questioning glance at Nathan was filled with curiosity. There was some order of march, usually based around the companies of ten, but they had never lined up all the companies before departing in quite this way before.

Nathan shook his head, equally puzzled. "Something's up."

Matthew and Nathan had been assigned to John Brown's company of ten, the thirteenth ten. Nathan looked around, then spied Brother Brown moving forward. He clucked to the team and got their own wagon moving in that direction. It took another five or six minutes to get everyone in position.

Finally, when they were all aligned by companies, Brigham Young got up in the boat a second time. The camp quickly fell quiet.

"Brother Bullock?"

Thomas Bullock, the camp historian, raised his hand. "Here, President."

"Brother Bullock, I'd like you to take a roll of the camp, please."

Now everyone looked at each other in surprise. This definitely was not the usual procedure. Bullock nodded, evidently already having been warned, and climbed up into the boat with the chief Apostle. He had some sheets of paper. He held them up and began to call out names. "First Ten. Wilford Woodruff, captain."

"Present," Elder Woodruff called out.

"Jacob Burnham."

"Here."

One by one he quickly moved through the fourteen companies of tens. But with one hundred and forty-eight names, it took almost ten minutes. When he was finished he glanced quickly through his sheets. "We are missing four, President. Joseph Hancock and Andrew Gibbons, who are reported to be out hunting, and Elijah Newman and Nathaniel Fairbanks."

"Brother Newman is sick and confined to his wagon," someone called out.

"The same with Brother Fairbanks," said another.

"Good," Brigham Young said. "Thank you, Brother Bullock."

As Bullock jumped down again, Brigham let his eyes sweep over the assembly. No one made a sound and every eye was on their leader. They could tell from his demeanor that something significant was about to happen.

"Brethren," he began, his voice clear and firm, "as you remember, last Sunday I told you that I had not felt much like preaching to you on this mission. This morning I am going to change that. I feel like preaching to you now."

The men looked at each other in surprise. It was not the Sabbath. It was now half past noon on a day when they had already been delayed four or more hours.

Now his face darkened and his eyebrows lowered noticeably. "And this is what I shall take for my text. I am no longer willing to pursue our journey with this company in the spirit that we now possess. I am about to revolt against it."

That hit the men like a bucketful of cold water. Men turned to look at each other in shock and surprise. Nathan and Matthew stood together beside their team. They looked at each other, and Nathan just shook his head. Brother Brigham was clearly upset.

"I want you brethren to understand and comprehend the principles of eternal life and to watch the spirits. Be wide awake and not overcome by the adversary. You can see the fruits of the Spirit, but you cannot see the Spirit itself. With the natural eye you behold it not. But you can see the results of yielding to the evil spirit and what it brings. You do not see that spirit either, nor its operations, only by the spirit that is in you."

He stopped, shaking his head as though he were having difficulty with this. "Nobody has told me what has been going on in the camp, but I have known it all the while. I have been watching its movement, its influence, its effects, and I know the result if it is not stopped."

Now there were looks of embarrassment, or men dropped their heads and stared at the ground.

"I want you to understand that we are beyond the power of the Gentiles. We are beyond their reach. We are beyond their power. We are beyond their grasp. So what has the devil to work upon now?" His voice rose sharply. "Well, I shall tell you. He will work upon the spirits of the men in this camp, and if you do not open your hearts so that the Spirit of God can enter your hearts and teach you the right way, you are a ruined people."

Whoo-ee! Matthew was reeling a little. This wasn't just strong language; these words were smoking.

"Do you hear, me, brethren? I know that you will be

destroyed and that without remedy. I tell you with all soberness that unless there is a change and a different course of conduct, a different spirit to what is now in this camp, *I go no further!*"

His words died away. There was not a sound except for the stamping of horses' hooves and the soft jingle of harnessing.

"I am in no hurry to move farther," Brigham went on, more mildly now. "Give me the man of prayer, give me the man of faith, give me the man of meditation, a sober-minded man, and I would far rather go amongst the savages, with six or eight such men, than to trust myself with the whole of this camp with the spirit they now possess.

"Brethren, we are the Camp of Israel. If this camp was composed of men who had newly received the gospel, men who had not received the priesthood, men who had not been through the ordinances of the temple and who had not had years of experience, enough to have learned the influence of the spirits and the difference between a good and an evil spirit, I should feel like preaching to them and watching over them, and teaching them all the time, day by day. But here are the elders of Israel, men who have had years of experience, men who have had the priesthood for years. Have they got faith enough to rise up and stop a mean, low, groveling, covetous, quarrelsome spirit? No, they have not, nor would they try to stop it unless I rise up in the power of God and put it down."

One hand came up and rubbed for a moment at his eyes. When he straightened again, his mouth was tight and his eyes narrow. "The brethren say they want a little exercise to pass away the time, but if you can't tire yourselves enough with a day's journey without dancing every night, then I say, start carrying your guns on your shoulders when you walk. Carry your wood to camp instead of lounging around or staying in your wagons, increasing the load until your teams are tired to death and ready to drop into the earth. Help your teams over the mud holes and bad places instead of lounging in your wagons and that will give you exercise enough without dancing."

Matthew felt his face burning. Had Brigham known that he

and Nathan had spent the morning "lounging" in their wagon so as to get out of the rain?

"Well, and what if it's not dancing?" Brigham roared, really angry now. "What will they do? They will play cards. They will play checkers. They will play dominoes. And if they had the privilege and were where they could get whiskey, they would be drunk half the time, and in one week they would quarrel, get to high words and draw their knives to kill each other. This is what such a course of things would lead to. Don't you know it? Yes, if we do not correct it, this is exactly what such a course of things would lead to."

He stopped again, his chest rising and falling as his eyes challenged one man after another. No one would meet the twin points of glowing fire. Every eye dropped and looked away.

"You never read of gambling, playing cards, checkers, dominoes, and the like in the scriptures. You do read of men praising the Lord in the dance, but who ever read of praising the Lord in a game of cards? If a man had sense enough to play a game at cards, or dance a little, without wanting to keep it up all the time, and then quit it and think no more of it, he would do well enough. But you want to keep it up till midnight and every night and all the time. You don't know how to control yourselves."

Matthew and Nathan were close enough to the Revenue Cutter that Matthew could see the weariness on their leader's face. As he stopped, it settled in upon him and his shoulders seemed to sag a little.

"I am one of the last to ask my brethren to enter into solemn covenants, but if you will not enter into a covenant to put away this iniquity and turn to the Lord and serve him and acknowledge and honor his name, then I want you to take your wagons and retreat back, for we shall go no further under such a state of things. If we don't repent and quit our wickedness we will have more hindrances than we have had, and worse storms to encounter."

He fell silent for a time, and seemed to be lost deep in

thought. A very humbled group of men watched his every move. Finally, he looked up again.

"I want you brethren to be ready for meeting tomorrow at the time appointed, instead of rambling off and hiding in your wagons to play cards. I think it will be good for us to have a fast meeting tomorrow and a prayer meeting to humble ourselves and turn to the Lord. If we do this, he will forgive us."

He looked down and motioned to Brother Bullock to come up beside him again. "I should like your help in taking a count," he said.

Bullock scrambled up beside President Young. When he was in place, Brigham turned back to the group. "I should like all the high priests to step forth in a line in front of the wagon." He motioned with his hands where he wanted them as the men started to move forward. "Line up right here. Then all of you who are bishops, you come step in front of the high priests."

A little surprised, men began to respond to his instructions. Nathan, being a bishop, walked over to stand in front of the assembling line of high priests. President Young turned to Thomas Bullock.

"Fifteen high priests, four bishops," Bullock said to the unasked question.

"Good. Next I want the seventies to line up behind the high priests, then the elders to form a line in the rear of the wagon."

Now many of the company began to move. Matthew, being an elder, moved quickly to his place.

"The members of the Twelve should come up here right below me."

Once they were in line, Bullock counted quickly. "They are seventy-eight seventies, eight elders, and eight members of the Quorum of the Twelve, counting yourself, President."

"Thank you." He looked directly down at his brethren in the Quorum. "Are you brethren who are called to the holy apostleship willing to covenant to turn to the Lord with all your hearts, to repent of all your follies, to cease from all your evils, and serve

God according to his laws? If you are so willing, manifest it by holding up your right hands."

With great solemnity, each of the eight, including Brigham, raised his hand. He then put the same question to the high priests and bishops, then to the seventies, then to the elders, and lastly to all the other brethren who were not in one of the lines.

Without hesitation, every hand was raised to the square. Now Brigham's face softened and his eyes looked down on them with deep affection. "Bless you, my brethren. I have spoken boldly to you because of who we are and what we are about. This work is so important and Satan will do whatever he can to thwart it. I pray to God that he will enable us to fulfill our covenants."

He paused once more, then decided that was enough. "Thank you. I shall now withdraw to give opportunity for others to speak if they feel like it."

Heber C. Kimball was up immediately. "Brethren," he said in great solemnity, "I agree with all that President Young has said to us today." He looked around, his dark eyes challenging. "I receive it as the word of the Lord to me, and I believe it is the word of the Lord to the camp, if you will receive it."

Most were nodding.

"All who are willing to accept this as the word of the Lord to them, please show by raising your right hand."

Matthew looked around, awed and touched by the sight of every hand in the air.

On the North Platte River

Sunday, May 30, 1847

My dearest Lydia,

Tomorrow or the next day, we shall hopefully reach Fort Laramie, where we can leave mail for you or find someone who is willing to carry it eastward. I have written much over the past several days, but I have thrown it all away. All that I had written earlier was trivial and no longer in keeping with my new feelings.

Today is a new day for the company and for me. Yesterday, Pres. Young called the company together and chastised us dearly. I will tell you all the details when we see each other again, but what it came down to was that he was greatly displeased with the spirit in the camp. And rightly so. We were no longer worthy of the title, The Camp of Israel. Pres. Y. put us under covenant to be more obedient and charitable. I raised my hand in solemn affirmation of my willingness to keep that covenant, not only for this moment when we are out here by ourselves, but also for when we are reunited. I have promised my God that I shall be a better father, a better husband, a better follower of Jesus Christ.

We set this Sabbath day apart as a day of fasting and prayer. This morning, I watched Elder Woodruff go down to the river. There he bathed himself all over, shaved, and put on new clothing. I felt impressed to do the same to show that I am willing to become a new person. I have not seen the brethren this still and sober on a Sunday since we started from Winter Quarters. There is no jesting, nor laughing, nor nonsense. All appear to feel to remember their covenant, which makes things look far more pleasant than they have done heretofore. Matthew and I read several chapters in the Bible and the Book of Mormon together this morning, which added to the sweetness of the day.

The camp had a prayer meeting this morning. We were given a chance to express ourselves about what happened yesterday. There were many confessions of sin and expressions of determination to do better in the future. At eleven, we held a sacrament meeting, the first in some time. It was good to remember the tokens of our Lord's flesh and blood and that he gave himself a ransom for our sins. I've always known that, but today it took on special significance.

In the afternoon, Pres. Y. and the other apostles and leaders went a short distance from camp and there met together in most solemn prayer. Brother Clayton told us it was a most sacred occasion and another reflection of the covenant the company has made to bring themselves in harmony with the Lord's will. We did not eat until they returned, as we were fasting for the Lord's Spirit.

Oh, how I wish you were at my side so I could tell you all that is in my heart. My love for you and the family grows ever more dear as the days pass away and our separation continues. Give my best to all, especially to Mother. Tell her that thus far we have not found the trail too difficult. Pres. Y's careful preparations are reaping much fruit now.

All my love,
Nathan

The first day of June dawned bright and clear and beautiful. The feeling that had prevailed in the camp since President Young's call to repentance was still clearly evident. The brethren were in good spirits. Cheerful calls floated back and forth, and a feeling of peace and camaraderie was everywhere evident. The three women were out and about, and Ellen, Heber C. Kimball's wife, was singing a Norwegian song which carried clearly on the morning air. Nathan had heard that Norway had beautiful mountains, and maybe that was what had inspired her, for off to the west, probably at a distance of some forty or fifty miles, they could see the dark line of a mountain range. One prominent point higher than all the others was thought to be Laramie Peak, which was reputed to be some ten thousand feet high. These were serious mountains now and were the first harbinger of what was yet to come.

There was also a distinct feeling of anticipation in the air. Unless there was some unexpected delay, before the day was done they should reach Fort Laramie. It was odd, Nathan thought. In some ways it was like when he had returned home from his mission to Canada or when he returned to Kirtland after the trek to Missouri with Zion's Camp. He found the same sense of excitement, the same anxiousness, even though it wasn't home to which they were coming. Indeed, it was a place no one had ever before visited.

He turned as Matthew climbed down out of the wagon, then sat down on the wagon tongue to pull on his boots. "Well, little brother, this is a glorious morning."

Once his boots were on, Matthew leaned back and breathed deeply. "Isn't it, though?" He stood up, stretching. "Want me to get the horses this morning?"

"I think the cooks about have breakfast ready. Let's eat first; then we'll both go get them."

Matthew patted his stomach. "I'm ready. I could eat my way through about ten pounds of bacon and johnnycake."

Chuckling, Nathan stood to stand beside his brother. "Do I sense a bit of excitement over the prospects of reaching Fort Laramie today?"

"You do indeed," Matthew admitted cheerfully. "After five hundred miles of magnificent scenery—and not a tree to spoil the view—I am ready for a change. Let it be no more than a few sticks thrown together and a couple of lopsided wigwams, I shall greet it with open arms and a warm heart."

Nathan shook his head, amused by this sudden eloquence. "I think we'd better get you something to eat."

At the sound of footsteps, Derek set the ax down and turned to see who it was. George Therlkill did the same. They and two other men from their group were down in the trees along the Laramie River cutting a wagonload of firewood to take back to their camp. They could see a single figure coming toward them on a horse, but through the trees they couldn't make out who it was. Archibald Little and Lewis Myers, who had been cutting down a large dead cottonwood, came over to join them. "It think it's Robert," Myers said.

And so it was. Robert Crow, the leader of their little company, waved as he saw them and slowed his horse as he entered the trees and threaded his way toward them.

"Brethren," he said even before he reached them, "there's good news."

"What?" Derek asked.

"Word of a substantial wagon company coming upriver just reached the fort."

They all straightened at that, but George Therlkill was a little dubious. George was Brother Crow's son-in-law and seemed more comfortable challenging him. "No idea who they are yet?"

"No, the rider just said it's sixty or seventy wagons."

"Oh," Little said. "That's a good sign."

"It could be just another company of Oregon or California emigrants," Therlkill persisted. "Let's not get our hopes up until we know."

"After two weeks of just sitting here," Derek said dryly, "I'm willing to get my hopes up for just about anything."

They nodded in agreement as they chuckled. "I think you'd better load up what wood you've cut now," Bob Crow suggested, "and let's take it back to camp. Then we'll go and check out this new company just to be sure."

Something in his eyes piqued Derek's curiosity. "Do you know something we don't, Brother Bob?"

A wide grin spread across Crow's face. "Yep." He had all of their attention now.

"What?"

"This company is different in one way from all the others that have come in so far."

"In what way?" Myers asked eagerly.

"This one is coming along the north side of the river, not the south like all the others."

Chapter Notes

The incidents and details recalled here by Matthew occurred between 26 April and 29 May and can be read about in the journals.

On 29 May 1847, at a spot a few miles west of Scotts Bluff, near present-day Henry, Nebraska, Brigham Young assembled the men and severely chastised them for the spirit that had taken over the camp. William Clayton recorded the details of that day, including an extensive copy of Brigham's speech, less than half of which is included here.

After the meeting concluded at one-thirty p.m., Brigham Young quietly gave the order to move out. It was a completely different camp that did so. That night, William Clayton wrote in his journal: "It seemed as though we were just commencing on this important mission, and all realizing the responsibility resting upon us to conduct ourselves in such a manner that the journey may be an everlasting blessing to us, instead of an everlasting disgrace. No loud laughter was heard, no swearing, no quarreling, no profane language, no hard speeches to man or beast, and it truly seemed as though the cloud had burst and we had emerged into a new element, a new atmosphere, and a new society."

Chapter Forty

The Pioneer Company moved forward slowly throughout the day, nooning across the river from the burned-out ruins of a fort. John Brown, with some sadness, explained that this was Fort Bernard, located downriver a few miles from Fort Laramie and run by a trader and mountain man named John Baptiste Richard—or Reshaw, as it was pronounced in French. It had been Reshaw who had volunteered to take the Mississippi Saints to Pueblo. He had left his fort with only two of its walls completed and gone south with the Mormons. While they were in Pueblo, word came that once Reshaw left, someone set fire to his half-completed fort and neatly eliminated the competition it presented to Fort Laramie.

As they prepared to start again, Brigham decided to lead a small party ahead to scout for a campsite. He asked Luke Johnson to bring the Revenue Cutter in case they had to cross the river. John Brown, greatly excited at the possibility of seeing some of the people he had left nine months before, went ahead with them.

About three o'clock a cry went up. The first wagons had come up another small hill, and from there, about four miles to the southwest on the opposite side of the river, could be seen the clear outline of a stockade. Fort Laramie was in sight at last. The excitement went down the line of wagons like a dandelion seed whipped by the wind.

As they topped the gentle hill, Nathan reined up and Matthew stood up in the wagon seat so that he could see better. "Yes sirree," he exclaimed ecstatically. "It's a fort, all right. And bigger than I thought it would be." He sat down again, grinning. "I think we're going to get a little taste of civilization again, Nathan."

Nathan slapped him on the shoulder. "Well, I'm ready enough, that's for sure."

Fort Laramie was situated on a level plain about a mile south of the North Platte River and just a few hundred yards west of the Laramie River, or Laramie Fork, as the locals called it. The fort itself stood at the north end of the plain, which left everything to the south of the fort open for camping—Indians along the river, whites more to the west. Robert Crow and the group from Pueblo had arrived at Fort Laramie two weeks before. Wanting to stay clear of the Missouri emigrant companies, they camped to the southwest of the fort about half a mile where no one else would bother them.

When the Mississippi group heard Robert Crow's report, everyone wanted to go out and meet the incoming company, but Brother Crow finally ruled that just a few of the men should go and make sure who it was. The North Platte was at the height of the spring runoff and was a good quarter of a mile wide now. The swift current carried a lot of debris, including logs that could stave in a wagon or knock a horse off its feet. It wasn't as if they could wade across to say hello when the company came.

Five of them went, walking past the fort, moving northeastward toward the spot where the North Platte and the Laramie

Rivers came together. Just west of that confluence, on the north side of the river, there was a large flat area with plenty of grass that would make a good place to camp. They decided to wait across from there and see what happened. It was nearing four o'clock and the sun was still high.

As they came through a small stand of trees and reached the edge of the water, Robert Crow suddenly started. "Look," he exclaimed. "There are some riders over there."

There were two men on horseback and two others on foot leading their horses.

"Can you tell who they are?" George Therlkill asked.

"Not for sure." A quarter of a mile made it difficult to recognize any features.

"I think that one is Brigham Young," Derek said, squinting at the one on the ground striding around, his head moving back and forth as he surveyed their potential campsite.

"Do you think so?" Archibald Little asked. "Which one?"

Derek suddenly realized that these men were natives of Mississippi. They did not know Brigham Young. "The one on the left, the one with his hat off."

They were all peering intently now at the four men.

Suddenly one of the men on horseback started to wave. "They've seen us," Derek said.

Lewis Myers took off his hat and began to wave it wildly. "Hello!" he shouted.

"That could be Heber Kimball with him," Derek said, feeling his heart start to beat a little faster. "I think it could be them."

"Hello! Ahoy there across the river!" They all started to shout now.

They heard a shout come floating back, but there was a fairly stiff breeze blowing and it was impossible to make out the words. They shouted again and an answering call came back, but again they could not make out the words.

"This must be their scouts," Bob Crow said.

Just then George grabbed his father-in-law's arm. "Look, there's a wagon."

They all swung back. Sure enough, from behind a slight rise a wagon pulled by two horses appeared. It was accompanied by two other men on horses. Derek immediately noticed that the wagon did not have the usual canvas cover. To his greater surprise, no other wagons followed behind it. As they watched curiously, the wagon pulled right down to the water's edge, then swung around. In a moment whoever was driving it started backing the wagon into the river. Now the men on horseback dismounted and those on the ground gathered around it. When they stepped back, there was a boat in the water and nothing but the base of a wagon left on shore.

Robert Crow slapped his leg in delight. "It's a boat. They've got their own boat."

It was about half past four when finally Nathan couldn't stand it any longer. The three wagons in front of him were pulled by oxen and moved ahead much too slowly to satisfy him. "H'yah," he called softly, pushing the horses into an easy trot and pulling around.

"Good," Matthew said. "I was about to get out and crawl past them."

In another three hundred yards, Nathan and Matthew came up over a small rise. There before them lay the swollen North Platte River and beyond that Fort Laramie. Nathan pulled up. Directly below them there was a large meadow right next to the river. They could see several men standing around in a group and Luke Johnson's wagon, which no longer had the boat on it.

"Look," Matthew said, noting the same thing. "They've got the Revenue Cutter in the river. And look! There are some men on the other side."

Nathan was looking, but something seemed odd. He counted quickly. Four men, including Brigham, had ridden ahead to scout. Luke Johnson and John Brown had taken the Revenue Cutter, and Port Rockwell and another man had accompanied them. That meant eight had come ahead. But there were twelve men down by the river now and three more on the far side. "They've met someone," he exclaimed. "I'll bet they brought them across in the cutter."

This time when he snapped the reins and shouted at the horses, they lunged ahead, jerking the wagon into a bouncing run. They came down the hill, making enough noise to startle every animal and bird within five miles. The men at the river all turned to look. Matthew saw Brigham raise his hand and point in their direction, saying something to the others. No sooner had he done so than one of the men broke away and started running hard toward them.

As the distance between them and the running figure closed to less than fifty yards, Matthew leaped to his feet. Hanging on frantically with one hand, he pounded Nathan's shoulder with the other. "It's Derek! It's Derek!"

"Whoa! Whoa!" Nathan pulled back with all his strength and brought the team to a sliding halt in a cloud of dust and a rattle of stones. Before the wagon had stopped rolling, Matthew leaped off, nearly stumbled, then caught himself and started running. Nathan flung the reins around the brake lever and vaulted over the side. As he sprinted forward, Matthew and Derek collided like runaway ore cars. Down they went, rolling around and around as they pounded each other. Nathan dove into the middle of it, shouting and laughing and yelling.

They finally pulled apart and got to their feet, brushing off the dirt from themselves and each other. "I can't believe this," Matthew exclaimed. "What are you doing here?"

"You didn't get our letter?"

"We got the letter you sent from Fort Leavenworth, but that was all."

Nathan broke in. "We heard there was another sick detachment sent to Pueblo and that you and Rebecca might be part of it, but we never learned for sure." Suddenly he straightened. "Is Josh with you?"

Derek's face fell. "No. He stayed with the battalion. Rebecca and I were sent back. And guess who we found?"

"Kathryn," Matthew said. "Yes, Brother Brown told us all about that. So is she with you now?"

"Waiting anxiously across the river."

"Well, then," Matthew cried, "let's go."

It was nearly full dark when Derek stepped inside the tent, startling both Rebecca and Kathryn. Rebecca got quickly to her feet, but Kathryn had Nicole in her arms and could only look up.

"Derek!" Rebecca said. "I didn't hear you coming."

He went forward and kissed her lightly. "Hi."

She jabbed at him. "Hi! That's all you've got to say? What took you so long? Tell us! Was it a Mormon company?"

He nodded gravely.

"It was?" Kathryn cried. "Really?"

"Yes, really!" he said, grinning now. "Brother Brigham said to give you both his regards."

Rebecca clapped her hands together. "Brother Brigham? Really? Oh, Derek. That's wonderful."

"What about the family?" Kathryn demanded.

Christopher and Benjamin were up now too, clamoring to know what was happening.

Derek shook his head. "This is the vanguard company. There are only three women in the whole company. More companies are coming, but they're still a few weeks behind them. Brother Brigham says our family will be with those later companies."

"Wonderful," Kathryn said, but she was clearly disappointed.

"So," Rebecca said, her mind racing now, "what does that mean for us? Are we going to wait here for the family?"

Derek seemed not to hear. It was as though he had just thought of something. "Hold it," he said. "I've got to get something. I brought a little surprise for you." And without a word he turned and left the tent again.

Rebecca gave Kathryn a puzzled look.

Then the tent flap opened again and Nathan and Matthew

stepped inside. Rebecca gasped. Kathryn jerked forward sharply enough that Nicole awoke with a start and started to cry.

"Surprise!" Derek said happily as he came in behind them.

Nathan held Leah on one leg and Benji on the other. Matthew had Nicole in his arms, and Christopher stood behind his uncles, one hand on each of their shoulders. Kathryn just kept shaking her head. "I can't really believe I'm sitting here with you two again."

"It has been a long time," Matthew said. "How long since you and Peter left us in Nauvoo to go to Springfield?"

Her mouth pursed in thought. "Let's see, we went to Springfield in January, so it's been almost a year and half since we've seen any of you."

"And it's been almost a year for us," Derek said. "You can imagine how surprised and pleased we were when we found that Kathryn was in Pueblo and then we ended up there too."

"That was a great blessing for both of you," Nathan said. "Any word at all from Peter, Kathryn?"

She shook her head, her eyes suddenly sad. "None."

"I'll bet he's on his way east already," Matthew said.

"Uncle Matthew?"

"What, Leah?"

"I love you."

He bent over, pulling her close. "I love you too, Leah. You've grown up on me. You're so big now."

"Do you have a wagon, Uncle Nathan?" Benji asked. "We have our own wagon now."

"Yes, we do. How would you like to bring your wagon and come with us?"

He nodded gravely, then looked at his father. "Can we do that, Papa?"

"We'll have to see what President Young says, but I think that's the plan."

"There's only one thing that could make all this better,"

Rebecca said wistfully, "and that would be if Mother and the rest of the family were here as well."

They all nodded at that.

"How long before we get to see Grandma?" Christopher asked.

"About a month," Matthew answered. "Maybe a little longer."

Derek stood. "Well, children, it's way past your bedtime now."

There was a cry of dismay from all three of them, but Derek was unmoved. "There'll be time enough to visit tomorrow. President Young is going to talk to Mr. Bordeaux and see if he will rent his flatboat to us to bring the wagons across the river. Maybe we can all go down and watch."

That pacified the children a little, and Leah and Benji slid down from Matthew's lap.

"How about if we said our family prayer together right here?" Derek suggested. "I think we have a lot to thank the Lord for tonight, don't you?"

Though the Mormons had traveled alone on the north side of the Platte and the North Platte Rivers, at Fort Laramie that was no longer an option. The terrain along the north of the river was too rough for wagons, and so even though it meant joining the numerous other companies on the Oregon Trail, there was no choice. The day after their arrival across from Fort Laramie, Brigham Young contracted with James Bordeaux, the trader who ran the post, for the use of his flatboat. For fifteen dollars they could ferry their entire company over. They began ferrying the first wagons across on the third of June, 1847.

That took almost two full days, but they made good use of the time while the wagons were brought over. A blacksmith shop was set up near the fort and coal purchased from Bordeaux to fire it. Many a wagon tire had been loosened by six hundred miles of prairie and these were set again. Tools and harnessing were also repaired. After much discussion it was determined to send someone for the Pueblo Saints. Rather than send Brother Crow or any of his people back again, Brigham picked four men, with Elder Amasa Lyman as their captain. They would go south and guide the nearly two hundred fifty Latter-day Saints who were still at Pueblo back up to Fort Laramie; then they would follow the Pioneer Company to their final destination. They left Fort Laramie headed south on the afternoon of June third.

At noon on the fourth day of June, the Pioneer Company lined up their wagons to the west of the fort. Brother Crow brought his little company and joined their five wagons to the seventy-two of the main company. With the four guides gone, the Pueblo group brought the total number of the company up to one hundred and sixty-one. For the three women of the company, the addition was most significant. Where before there had been only one woman to every fifty men, now that ratio dropped to about one woman to every seventeen men. And Harriet Young's two children now had companions on the journey.

For the first few days, Kathryn became the unofficial guide for the company, being the only one who had been west of Fort Laramie. She pointed out where the Reeds and the Donners had camped the year before. On the fourth day out, she took Nathan, Matthew, Derek, and Rebecca up Beaver Creek and showed them the natural bridge where she and Peter had decided that she should not continue on further.

Two things were significantly different once they left Fort Laramie. The first was in the nature of the road. The prairie was about a hundred miles behind them now. The North Platte flowed from northwest to southeast, skirting the base of a substantial range of mountains known as the Black Hills. While this made for more timber, grass, water, and game, the deep, soft soil of the Great Plains gave way to flint-hard rock that chewed into the hooves of the oxen and wore out leather soles quickly.

The second change was that they now shared the trail. There were several other emigrant parties moving westward. Most of these were smaller parties—half a dozen to maybe twenty wagons—but several were from Missouri. When those emigrants learned that there were Mormons close by, tension filled the air. The rumors that the Mormons had come out to slaughter any emigrants, and especially Missourians, was still going up and down the river. With about a hundred and fifty men, the Mormons far outnumbered the Missourians, and the non-Mormons well knew it. But Brigham wisely kept apart from them as much as possible, and no clashes resulted.

That did not mean, however, that there wasn't considerable competition for the best grazing and watering sites. Often one company would rise and leave without breakfast so as to get the jump on others.

William Clayton still took very seriously his charge to keep a careful record of the trail and continually left "signposts" for the following companies. One was a buffalo skull on which he left a notation of date and distance. On another board he noted the mileage and the date, then said, "All well." On the twelfth of June, just before five o'clock in the afternoon, an advance group of the Pioneer Company reached what was known as "the last crossing of the Platte." As they reached this significant point, William Clayton put up another of his trail markers: "Fort John, 124 miles. Winter Quarters, 655 and 1/4 miles."

Matthew was driving. Kathryn and her baby were on the wagon seat beside him. Rebecca, who had been in the back feeding Leah, was now on her knees on a blanket, looking out from between them. Nathan, Derek, and the two boys were walking alongside. As they came over a slight elevation, they saw the river below them and the flats near the river dotted with white wagon tops. Matthew reined in. "There she is," he said.

"What, Papa?" Benjamin cried. "What is it?"

"That's the North Platte River again, son," Derek said, hoisting him up on his shoulders. "That's where we're going to camp tonight. See those wagons off to the left? Those are the men who went ahead of us."

"Look," Nathan exclaimed, "there's the cutter taking some-one across."

Even from a distance, they could easily spot the Revenue Cutter. The boat was midway across the river. Two men were rowing what looked like a full load of goods across to the far side.

Matthew turned and looked at a second group of wagons clustered in a circle about a quarter of a mile away from their group. "And those must be the Missouri companies."

Derek frowned. "I hope there's no trouble. We normally don't have to camp quite that close to them."

Their attention was drawn away from the river when Heber C. Kimball came riding toward them on his horse. When the Steeds stopped to look, several other wagons in the company also pulled up alongside of them. Others were now coming up behind them. Elder Kimball stopped a few yards away. He turned in his saddle to point. "Brethren, you can see where the advance group has made camp. It's a good site. Brother Brigham wants us all to camp there."

"Have we already started to ferry our stuff across?" Nathan asked. "I see the cutter's already working."

"No. Actually we are ferrying goods for the Missouri companies."

"What?" Matthew exclaimed in surprise. There were also several other cries of dismay.

Heber turned again to look toward the river. The cutter was now reaching the far bank, and there were men there waiting who immediately began to unload it. "There's no way to take a loaded wagon across that river. It's too dangerous. So we carry across their loads; then they try to swim their wagons across. And without much success, I might add."

"Why would we want to take their goods across?" Kathryn asked, still quite surprised by that news.

Heber gave a short laugh. "Because they're paying one dollar and fifty cents a load for us to do it. Since yesterday we've already earned thirty-four dollars, to be paid in flour at two dollars fifty cents a hundred weight."

Nathan gave a low whistle. "Two dollars fifty cents per hundred is Nauvoo prices. At Fort Laramie, flour was selling for ten dollars a hundred weight."

"Exactly," Heber said, smiling. "As Brother Woodruff said just before I left camp, 'It is as much a miracle to see our supplies replenished in the midst of the Black Hills as it was for the Israelites to find manna in the wilderness.'" Then he sobered. "The Lord continues to bless us, and may his name be praised for that."

"That's wonderful," Rebecca said, feeling a great surge of rejoicing. She and Kathryn had used the last of their flour three days before. If there was a new supply, that would be a great blessing to them.

"So far, we've taken in about thirteen hundred pounds of flour," Heber went on, "along with some bacon and a few pounds of cornmeal. We'll distribute that throughout the camp tomorrow." Now the smile wreathed his whole face again. "I would say that the Revenue Cutter has earned its name. And more than that. When our men came up yesterday afternoon, they said the Missourians were friendly but wary. All of them had bowie knives and pistols in their belts to let us know they were prepared for any trouble. Then late yesterday afternoon one of their men decided to swim across the river by himself. The fool kept his clothes on, thinking he'd be all right. When he got about halfway across, he started floundering, screaming and yelling that he couldn't make it. Fortunately our men had seen him and took out after him in the cutter. They got there just in time to save his life."

"Oh, that's good," Christopher said, who had been listening to all this intently.

"More than good, son," Heber said. "Next thing we knew, the knives and the pistols had disappeared and the Missourians invited some of our boys over for a hot supper prepared by their cooks. So the boat has paid rich dividends in other ways as well."

He picked up the reins and prepared to go. "Well, come on down. We need to get camp set up as soon as possible. As you know, it's the Sabbath tomorrow, but how much a day of rest it will be remains to be seen."

Sunday or no Sunday, the challenge of getting across the river weighed heavily on Brigham Young's mind. Well over a hundred yards wide, filled with limbs and logs big enough to stave in a horse, the North Platte during the spring runoff was enough to give anyone a chill just looking at it. This was not going to be a simple crossing, and yet every day spent here was one less day for growing crops when they reached their final destination. After the morning worship services, Brigham called for a meeting with the Twelve and the various captains. There was no debate about whether to unload the wagons and ferry their goods across on the Revenue Cutter. The question was how to get the wagons across even if they were empty. After what the Missourians had experienced, the Twelve were understandably nervous about trying to swim them across. Two courses of action were decided upon. First, a group of men would take wagons south the eight or ten miles to the mountains—the Black Hills—to cut long poles. These would be used to lash the wagons together in sets of twos or fours so that they would not roll over in the current. A second team, under Howard Egan's direction, was given the assignment to start cutting timber along the river and build a raft large enough to carry a wagon. To no one's surprise, Matthew was assigned to that team because of his carpentry skills. Derek and Nathan were asked to take their wagons with the group that went to cut poles. By afternoon of that day, both teams were hard at work fulfilling their assignments. The work of finding a way across the flood-swollen river had begun.

Chapter Notes

On the first day of June, 1847, advance scouts, including Brigham Young and Heber C. Kimball, reached a spot across the North Platte River from Fort

Laramie. As they were deciding on a campsite, they saw some men across the river approaching from the southwest, the direction of the fort. Brigham sent the Revenue Cutter across for them, where they discovered they were part of the Mississippi Saints who had wintered in Pueblo. They had been waiting at Fort Laramie for about two weeks by then.

Though the most common name for the trading post near the confluence of the North Platte and the Laramie Rivers was Fort Laramie, officially at this time it was named Fort John, presumably for John Sarpy, who had built it (see LeRoy R. Hafen and Francis Marion Young, *Fort Laramie and the Pageant of the West, 1834–1890* [1938; reprint, Lincoln: University of Nebraska Press, 1984], p. 70). William Clayton consistently referred to it as Fort John; in other journals it is called Fort Laramie.

The Black Hills mentioned often in trail journals were not the current Black Hills of South Dakota. Rather, this was the name given to the range of mountains that parallel the North Platte River in what is now eastern Wyoming. Heavily forested, they appear black from a distance, which probably generated the name.

Chapter Forty-One

The men of the Pioneer Company began the task of crossing the river at four a.m. on Monday morning. Since the Steeds had women and children with them, Derek stayed behind to help the family with a fire and breakfast. Matthew and Nathan went to the river where the first division of the company was to meet. They were not surprised to see that Brigham Young already had one of his wagons there and was unloading it.

Even as they set to work transferring the President's goods to the Revenue Cutter, more wagons got into line. Two of these also belonged to Brigham; others were from Heber C. Kimball's second division. They formed a "bucket brigade," and the goods were handed from man to man, quickly filling the cutter to its capacity. It could hold from fifteen to eighteen hundred pounds, which was about the equivalent of a fully loaded wagon. For the first trip they left enough room to take three other men across in addition to the rower. They would serve as the unloading crew on the other side. They also carried a coil of rope which they strung out as they went across. This would be tied to the raft to help pull it across the current.

As the boat pushed off, Brigham turned to the men. "Let's have some from the second division unload the wagons," he said. "The rest of you come help with the raft."

The raft Howard Egan and his team had hastily built the day before was just a rod or so from where the unloading was taking place. It was not surprising that the raft was fairly crude—two logs set about eight feet apart, then a base of thick branches lashed onto them to serve as a platform. Working quickly in the lightening darkness, they pushed the raft into the water, unhitched the team from the now unloaded wagon, and rolled it onto the raft. To be sure it didn't roll off during the crossing, the wagon had to be secured with ropes. The only way to do that was to take them from the wagon and tie them to the two base logs. But that could only be done if someone was in the water, so Nathan took one side and Matthew the other.

"Whoo-ee!" Matthew exclaimed as the icy water embraced his legs. "Now, there's how to wake up in a hurry." Gasping, he moved to the far end of the raft. The water was now up to his waist. Nathan was taking quick in-and-out breaths as he waded out on the other side.

"Here, let me give you a hand."

Matthew was not at all surprised to see that it was Brigham Young who waded in beside him. Brigham was not one to expect others to do what he wasn't willing to do himself. On the far side, Heber Kimball went in to help Nathan. That was no surprise either.

"I've been meaning to tell you something, Brother Steed," Brigham said as the man above handed them the end of a rope and they started to secure it.

Matthew snatched it, fed it through one of the cracks between the poles, then sunk down to his neck in order to reach under the log and grab the end of it. As he came up, gasping for breath, Brigham took the rope and cinched it tight. "What is that, Brother Brigham?" Matthew said between clenched teeth.

"I've been meaning to talk to you about your personal hygiene. I think it's time you took a bath."

"Thank you," Matthew said as they tied the knot and then tested it to make sure it was taut. His teeth were rattling like musket fire now. "I'll take that under advisement."

Brigham laughed as they moved to the back of the raft and secured the second rope. In a moment, with help from those on shore, they shoved the raft into the river. The two men riding with the wagon had long poles and began to push the raft into the current. On the far side two more men began hauling on the rope to help bring it across.

After two hours' work, it became painfully clear that this wasn't going to do. The transfer of the goods was going well. Using the Revenue Cutter, the goods from the wagons were being moved across the river in good time. But the rafting was terribly slow. The current was just too powerful. They took a second rope across to use for pulling the raft over, but even then, once the current caught the raft, it was like trying to hold in a team of runaway mules. They had to either let the current take it or risk breaking the ropes. When they finally got a wagon across, they were generally a quarter to a half mile downriver from where they started. Then once they got that wagon off, they had to manhandle the raft back upstream far enough that they could send it back across, again angling with the current so that it would reach the loading point on the south bank. That took just over an hour per wagon.

Shortly after eight o'clock Brigham called for a halt. Most of the men were soaked to their necks, and though the sun had come out, they were still deeply chilled. "Any suggestions, brethren?" he asked. "This clearly is not the answer. We'll be five or six days at this rate."

Zebedee Coltrin, who was in Stephen Goddard's company of ten, raised his hand. "We've got the poles now. Let's try lashing two wagons together with the poles for floats, then raft them across."

John Pack, who was in Nathan's company, spoke up. "My wagon's got some iron in it—tools and sheet iron for blacksmithing. We didn't want to risk poking a hole in the cutter by taking it across that way. But the weight might serve as ballast and hold the wagon from rolling too easily."

Brigham nodded. "It's worth a try. Bring your wagon beside this one here."

They worked swiftly, securing four of the long poles to the two wagons—one on the outside of each, and two together between them. Back into the water Nathan and Matthew went, helping guide the wagons as other men pushed them far enough out into the river that they began to float.

For a time it looked like Coltrin's idea was going to work. The two wagons drifted quickly downstream but the men with the ropes pulled the wagons steadily across toward them. Then, just as they reached the opposite bank, the front wheels struck the river bottom and stopped short. Unfortunately the backs of the two wagons were still in the full current. There was a sharp crack as the river took the wagons. Ropes began to pop and the two inside poles snapped like twigs. As the men watched in horror, the river lifted the first wagon and rolled it onto the second, snapping the bows and dumping all of John Pack's iron into the river.

"All right," Brigham said grimly, "let's see if this is any better."

The men in the river came out, hugging themselves to get warm, as the men on shore pushed the wagons farther into the water.

This time they had four wagons lashed together, hoping that the broader base would prove more stable. It was almost noon now, and they still had only five or six wagons on the north side. To their dismay, a stiff breeze had sprung up, blowing directly from the southwest. With their high canvas covers, the wagons were just like sailboats. Between the current and the wind, the men lost what little control they had.

Halfway across, the upstream wagon started to roll. It was as if there were no ropes, no poles, no other wagons. It simply lifted up, like a child climbing out of a washtub without permission. The bows started to snap, sounding like pistol shots, and then the wagon rolled onto its side, two wheels twisting slowly above the water. With six men pulling on the ropes from the far side, they finally dragged the four wagons up onto the far bank. Two of the wagons were damaged—not terribly, but sufficient that the idea of lashing four wagons together was abandoned.

"All right," Howard Egan said. "The problem is, the wagons are empty. There's no weight to hold them down."

Matthew thought about reminding him of the iron and tools in one of those they had sent across, but said nothing.

"Let's take only one wagon but send a man with it. He can stand on the one side and let his weight keep it from rolling."

Brigham pursed his lips thoughtfully as he considered that. Several were shaking their heads, but they were running out of options. "All right," he finally said. "You want to try it?"

"Yes."

They rolled Egan's wagon down to the river, secured the ropes from the far side, removed the wagon tongue, then pushed the wagon into the water. Egan stood on the wagon seat, steadying himself by holding on to the front bow. As the wagon reached the depth where the wagon box began to float, Egan grinned jauntily. "Okay, let her rip."

Brigham was shaking his head. "Be careful, Howard."

Matthew didn't like what he saw either. The wind was blowing strongly now and whipping at the canvas. With a quick movement, he ripped off his shirt and plunged into the water. "I'll go with you," he shouted, reaching out and grabbing the edge of the tailgate with one hand. He tossed his dripping shirt into the wagon, then got a firm grip on the tailgate with both hands, edging to the side where the current struck it to add his weight to Egan's. At its deepest point, the channel was about six feet deep. Supposedly, except in a spot or two, a man could touch bottom most of the way across. But in this current, that didn't mean a lot, so Matthew simply floated, letting the wagon pull him across.

When the current took them, the back end of the wagon began to swing around. "Pull! Pull!" Egan shouted to the men with the ropes on the far side.

"Tell them to keep the nose into the current," Matthew called. "If the current takes her broadside, she'll roll." The wagon bed was already starting to tip ominously.

But Howard Egan was too occupied to be telling anyone anything. As he felt the wagon bed lifted by the current, he moved to the far left of the wagon seat, standing up now and balancing himself by grasping the front bow through the canvas. "I've got it!" he shouted.

For a moment Matthew thought his weight would do it, but as he lifted his head to see better, he saw water squirting into the wagon box through cracks between the planks. The water was already four or five inches deep and rising quickly. Matthew could feel the wagon settling deeper into the river. "The box is filling up, Howard," he shouted. "We can't hold it."

There was a momentary glimpse of Egan's head as he leaned down and peered into the wagon; then through the canvas Matthew saw his shadow moving upward. Egan climbed onto the edge of the box itself, moving back toward the center of the wagon. The shadow spread-eagled, as though Egan would hold the wagon down by sheer force of will.

Matthew pulled himself to that same side of the wagon box, hoisting himself up half out of the water, trying to hold it down. But the river and the wind both had it now, and the two men were no match for them. The box tipped sharply, dropping the right side, the side away from the current, low enough that it plunged below the water's surface. Water gushed in, and in an instant the box was totally filled with muddy water.

"Jump, Howard!" Matthew screamed as he pushed away before the wagon took him down with it. He was stunned by the power of the current against his body and began to stroke hard to combat it. He turned his head in time to watch the wagon slowly start to roll completely over. Dimly he was aware of the shouts of the men on the shore, but they were as helpless as Matthew was. Howard Egan leaped out and away, but at that same moment the wagon jerked sharply and the front wheel shot up out of the water. Egan's foot slipped as he pushed off, arms flailing. He bounced off the wheel with a sharp cry, then hit the water with a huge splash.

"Howard!" Kicking hard, Matthew swam toward the spot where Egan had gone under. He swung away as a wagon wheel suddenly rose out of the water right beside him. The wagon was still rolling and was completely upside down now. As Matthew looked around frantically, Howard Egan's head suddenly shot out of the water. He was spluttering and gasping as he wiped at his eyes. He saw Matthew immediately. "I'm all right! I'm all right!" he cried. "I hit my leg on the wheel, but I'm all right."

Matthew came up beside him and grabbed a handful of shirt. They both began to swim for the far shore, angling farther downstream than where several men, including Nathan, were running hard trying to catch up with them. They let the current work for them, angling across it toward a spot where the bank was fairly low. When they reached shallow water, they dragged themselves to the bank. Matthew saw that Howard limped heavily as he tried to stand. They bent over, chests heaving, sucking in huge gulps of air. Matthew turned to look at Egan. "I don't think this old river likes us much," he gasped between breaths. "Not one little bit."

"Savannah?"

A head of dark red hair poked through the door. "Yes, Mama?"

"You know the plaque that was on our piano that Papa brought back from Nauvoo? Have you seen it?"

"It's in the trunk, Mama. Remember? I helped you pack it."

Caroline threw up her hands in despair. "Oh, that's right. Thanks, dear."

"You're welcome, Mama."

"Are your father and Solomon back yet with the teams?"

"Yes, Mama. Our team is already harnessed. Now they're hitching up the oxen. They're just about ready."

"Oh, dear. I'm not nearly ready. What about Mother Steed? Does she have all of her stuff out yet? You and Charles help her get all her things into the wagon."

At that, Savannah came through the door and into the sod hut. She was giving her mother a reproachful look, which nearly made Caroline smile. Savannah had turned ten in March, and in the last few months her hair was starting to darken. Instead of the more startling red that it had once been, it was turning auburn, much like Caroline's. It was going to be her finest feature, Caroline suspected. Savannah had also started to shoot up these past few months. She was now up to Caroline's chin. In another year or two she would pass her in height. With these changes, something even more welcome had happened. She and Savannah had become the best of friends. The relationship Caroline had once had with Olivia was again developing between her and Savannah. Savannah might be only ten, but she was two or three years beyond that in maturity and a wonderful companion for her mother.

"Grandma's all packed, Mama," Savannah said patiently. "Jessica and Solomon are all packed. Jenny is bringing out two more boxes and then she says she's done. Carl's got his team already harnessed and all of their family is already out there." She hesitated for a moment. "What's left for us, Mama?" she asked gently. "I thought we were ready too."

"I haven't swept out the cupboard. The mattresses should be turned. I still need to—" She stopped, and inexplicably started to cry.

Savannah seemed not too surprised. "It's all right, Mama. We don't have to do everything. Sister Starr said she would clean up things. After all, we're giving her the house for nothing."

Caroline sniffed back the tears, angry with herself for being so foolish. "I know, but I can't leave a filthy house."

Savannah took her by the arm. "It's not filthy. We cleaned it all yesterday." She peered up at her. "Do you not want to leave, Mama?"

Caroline lifted the hem of her apron and wiped at her eyes. "That's not it. I'm excited to go. I can hardly wait to leave. It's just that—" She looked around, feeling the tears threatening again.

"You're just tired, Mama." Savannah came over to touch her arm. "Livvy has kept you up for three nights. That's all it is."

Caroline had to smile in spite of herself. It was as if she were hearing herself speak. "Yes," she said, cheered just by having Savannah here beside her. "I'm sure that's part of it." Livvy, now three, had started in with what Caroline was afraid was going to be the measles a week ago. It had turned out to be only a high fever and cough, but it left her with a serious case of crankiness. She had kept the family up three different nights now with her fitful sleeping. "Is Charles watching her?" Caroline asked.

"Actually, she fell asleep while Papa and I were packing in the tools. One minute she was awake, then when we looked again she was curled up in a ball, sound asleep."

That didn't seem fair, thought Caroline. Sleep sounded so good right now.

"Caroline?" It was Joshua's voice from outside.

"I think Papa's ready, Mama," Savannah said, moving toward the door. She leaned out. "Coming, Papa." Then she went back and took her mother's hand. "Let's just go, Mama."

"I . . ." She looked around one last time. "Yes," she said, suddenly determined. "Let's just go."

Outside, the five Steed wagons took up most of the block, and the family swarmed around them like ants at a sugar-water picnic. As she and Savannah came out of the hut and Savannah pulled the door shut, Joshua glanced up at his wife. He stopped what he was doing, looked at her more closely, then came over as she reached the wagon. "Are you all right?" he asked softly.

"I am now," she said brightly. "I was just having a few final misgivings, I think."

He nodded gravely. "Me too." He turned and surveyed the family. "When I see how many of us there are, I've got all kinds of misgivings."

"Nonsense," she said. "There are only twenty-nine of us to worry about."

He choked a little on that. "I know, but there are only three men. Six women, twenty children, and only three men. You don't think that's a little overwhelming?"

It was just what Caroline needed. She forgot her own concerns, touched by Joshua's worry. "Well, you can't count Emily and Rachel or the four oldest boys as children, Joshua. They're old enough to be of great help."

He nodded. That was surely true. Emily and Rachel, both fifteen now—or soon to be in Emily's case—were mature young women. In addition to taking a major role in caring for the children, they were excellent cooks and for the past three weeks had been practicing cooking over an open fire in the yard behind Jessica's house. Young Carl, the oldest of the male cousins who were with the family now, was also fifteen; and in exactly four months from today Jessica's Luke would turn fifteen as well. Each of these would be treated as men in the coming months.

They had apportioned out their manpower carefully. Carl would drive the wagon with his own family, while his son Carl drove Lydia and her children. Luke would drive Jenny and her two children and Mary Ann. Solomon and Joshua would both have their own families. Jessica's Mark and Melissa's David, both nearly thirteen, had responsibility for the livestock and getting firewood each night. The younger children each had their own chores as well. Caroline was right. They would do just fine.

Joshua moved over to where his mother stood beside Jenny, holding two-year-old Emmeline, Matthew's youngest, by the hand. "Are you ready, Mother?"

"More than ready, Joshua."

"Shall we call everyone together and have a prayer before we begin?"

Mary Ann looked at him in surprise. "You don't have to ask me, Joshua. You're the patriarch of the clan now, and I don't mean just in age. We are all looking to you to lead us."

"I'm not sure I'm comfortable with that," he said slowly.

"That's why you'll be wonderful." She smiled up at him. "Humility is nice in a patriarch."

He laughed, then bent down and kissed her on the cheek. "You really are something, aren't you?"

To his surprise, her eyes were suddenly glistening. "I am, Joshua. And do you know why?" She flung her arms out to include all of the family. "Because of this. It's my family that really makes me something. And to have you stand at the head, in place of your father"—her voice broke—"doing what he would be doing if he were here, makes me more proud than I can put into words."

He put his arms around her and held her tightly. "Thank you, Mama," he whispered.

Then, clearing his throat, he stepped back. "Can I have your attention?"

Parents turned and then began shushing their children. He waved them forward. "Let's all gather around Grandma Steed."

With a little thrill of excitement running through the group, they quickly started to come in closer. As they waited for the others, Caleb, who was Carl and Melissa's third child and now about eleven, touched Joshua's arm. "Why do we have to go to the Elkhorn to meet everyone, Uncle Joshua? Why can't we just meet here?"

Savannah, who was Caleb's age, answered for her father. "Because a city isn't a good place for a wagon train to gather, Caleb. You need water and lots of grass and room for the wagons."

"That's right," Joshua confirmed. "There are going to be a lot of wagons coming together, Caleb. We need a big place to collect them."

"What's the Elkhorn?" Betsy Jo, Jenny's five-year-old, asked.

"That's a river," Sarah Rogers said, proud to have the answer. She was eight and Melissa's oldest daughter.

"How far is it, Uncle Joshua?" Jenny said in a little girl's voice.

The children giggled wildly at that. Jenny smiled down on them. Of all the aunts, she was the favorite, for she was always playing children's games with them.

"About twenty miles, little Jenny," Joshua answered back in a squeaky voice. "That's about one day's ride from here."

The children were delighted and squealed with laughter. By then, they had all gathered around, and Joshua sobered. "Is everyone ready?" he asked.

One by one they nodded their heads.

He took a deep breath. "Then let's have a prayer and we shall depart." He looked around and his eyes fell on Carl and Melissa. "Melissa, will you say our family prayer for us?"

Surprised, but pleased, she nodded.

Joshua quickly went on. "Before you do, however, I just want to say one word."

As everyone quieted, he kept looking at the two of them. "For all of us, I want Carl and Melissa to know how happy we are that they are with us here today."

"Hear! Hear!" Solomon called out.

"Amen," Lydia exclaimed.

"We are so pleased that we are not leaving you behind," Joshua finished.

Melissa was taken aback and smiled shyly. "Thank you."

"Thank you," Carl said as well. "It only took three broken ribs and a couple of knocks on the skull to get Melissa to change her mind about coming—" He stopped as the family hooted him down on that; then he got more serious. "It only took three broken ribs and a couple of knocks on the head for me to get to this point," he said again, "but I want you all to know, this is where we ought to be." He turned to Melissa and took her hand. "I know that now."

"Thank you," she murmured, her eyes filling as she looked at him.

"I know someone who was once that hardheaded and stubborn too," Joshua said.

"What do you mean, *once was?*" Caroline asked sweetly.

Both children and adults clapped and cheered at that. Joshua just laughed, then turned to his mother. "Is there anything you want to say, Mama, before Melissa prays?"

Mary Ann nodded and stepped forward. She couldn't meet anyone's eyes directly, for the affection there would have brought the tears again. So she stared out at the western sky and spoke softly. "Do you remember what I said a while back? about no more partings?"

Several nodded.

"Well, that time has finally come. We start this morning on the journey that will bring all of us back together. We leave many friends behind today in Winter Quarters. They are good friends and we shall miss them, but our place is not here any longer. Our family is waiting for us out there somewhere. So let there be no tears on this day. Let there be only smiles of joy, for the time for reunion has come."

"Amen," Joshua said quietly. Then he motioned to Melissa. As she stepped forward, the men took off their hats, and all bowed their heads.

Chapter Notes

All of the journals speak about the difficulty the Pioneer Company had getting across the North Platte River at the last crossing. At the very time they were struggling to find a way to take their wagons across, the various families and groups that would come to be called the "Big Company" were preparing to depart Winter Quarters and follow in the footsteps of the Pioneer Company.

Eventually the Big Company would consist of nine different companies made up of about five hundred seventy-five wagons and over fifteen hundred people. The first of these groups left Winter Quarters around the fourteenth of June and assembled at the Elkhorn River, about twenty miles to the west, before forming into wagon companies and starting the trek west, the first company leaving on the eighteenth.

Chapter Forty-Two

By the fifteenth of June, their fourth day at the last crossing of the North Platte River, the Pioneer Company still had only half of their wagons on the north side of the river. The men were exhausted, many of them having spent long hours up to their armpits in the icy water. The river was coming down from the heights of the mountains and was still bitterly cold. So after four days of backbreaking work, they had half their number across, several wagons had sustained minor damage, Howard Egan had a badly bruised leg, and one of Robert Crow's horses had got tangled in a lariat and drowned while swimming across.

All of that was on Matthew Steed's mind as he walked toward Brigham Young's tent. At the rate they were getting the wagons across, they could be here for several more days. Reaching the tent, Matthew hesitated for a moment, then rapped lightly on the pole.

"Come in."

He pulled back the flap and stepped inside, where Brigham, George A. Smith, Willard Richards, and Heber C. Kimball were seated. Brigham stood immediately and came to him. "Matthew, thank you for coming."

"You're welcome. I'm happy to be of service," he answered. He suspected that this might have something to do with the river crossing. Word in the camp was that Howard Egan had the assignment to make a much larger raft.

"Sit down, Matthew." The President pointed to a stool, then sat down himself. As was his style, he jumped in without preamble. "We have an assignment for you, Matthew."

"All right."

"I'm sending Howard to cut some bigger trees."

"I heard that," Matthew said. "Would you like me to go with him?"

"Yes. We're going to build a larger ferry."

Matthew's eyes widened a little.

"Another company of emigrants came by today and paid us to take them across the river."

"I saw that. That's good. We can use all the flour we can get."

"That's what started me to thinking," Brigham said, musing now. "This crossing is a terrible thing at high water. And yet there's no way around it. Everyone has to do it. You've seen what it takes out of both man and beast."

"That I have," Matthew agreed.

"We're sending a second group upriver to find timber good enough to make some planking. With that and what we already have, we can make a substantial ferry, something large enough to take two wagons across or a wagon with its team."

"Very good," Matthew agreed.

"We've got a lot of people coming behind us," Heber said now. "Five or six hundred wagons in all likelihood. We've got to be thinking about them as well."

Matthew had already discussed that with Nathan and Derek. The thought of having Joshua and Solomon make that crossing with all the women and children was pretty sobering.

Finally, Brigham smiled. "How would you like to be the first to see your family again?"

Totally taken aback, Matthew leaned forward. "You want me to go back?"

They all laughed. "No, nothing quite that dramatic," Heber smiled.

"We're going to leave a group of men here to run a ferry service across the river," Brigham came in again, this time completely serious. "At least through the high-water season. You've heard the reports. They say there are a thousand wagons between here and Fort Laramie and who knows how many more behind them on the Oregon Trail. Even if half of those used our service, the income would be a rich blessing to our people. And our own following companies are not only going to need to get across the river; by the time they reach here they'll need their supplies replenished too. Imagine what a blessing it will be to them to get here and find not only that we have our own ferry but that foodstuffs are available as well."

Matthew was excited. It was a brilliant solution to several problems all at the same time. "And you'd like me to stay?"

Brigham nodded slowly. "Yes. We've asked Thomas Grover to serve as captain."

Heber chuckled and Brigham shot him a warning look. It only made Heber laugh out loud. Everyone in the camp knew about the confrontation between Brigham Young and Thomas Grover. Grover was an experienced boatman, and when they had started work on one of the smaller rafts, Grover had told Brigham that he was going about it all wrong. Brigham was a highly skilled carpenter in his own right and didn't take the unsolicited advice favorably. Grover backed down a little, muttering, just loud enough for the President to hear, something like, "I've forgotten more about water than you'll ever know."

When it came time to launch the raft, Grover was standing by, predicting that it would never float. Tight-lipped and angry, Brigham ignored the salty-tongued builder and launched it anyway. When it promptly sank, a humbled Brother Brigham sighed painfully, turned to Grover, and said, "All right, Brother Thomas, what is your plan?"

It was still a bit of a tender spot with the chief Apostle, and Heber was the only one who dared goad his friend about it a little.

"Thomas Grover will be the captain," Brigham said again, ignoring the gibe. "We've also picked Luke Johnson, Edmund Ellsworth, and Appleton Harmon, among others."

Matthew was pleased. Those were all good men. "All right. I'll be happy to stay."

"Good. I'll explain what we're doing to Nathan. Now that he has Derek to help, we think your family will be fine. We appreciate your willingness to serve."

Caroline nudged Joshua. He had his head bent down, cleaning his pistol. He looked up at her. She gestured with her head. "I think that's Elder Pratt and Elder Taylor coming."

Joshua turned, then hastily set the weapon down when he saw that she was right. Mary Ann was across the fire from them and turned too.

"It's Elder Taylor," he heard Rachel say in surprise.

Solomon was getting something out of the wagon. He looked, then called softly to Jessica. She poked her head out of the tent to see, then came out to join Solomon. Jenny heard the call and also came out to see. She walked over and sat beside Mary Ann.

"Carl?" Joshua called.

Carl was currying his team, which were staked out behind his wagon. He stepped to where he could see Joshua.

"We've got company."

Carl looked at the two men walking toward them and seemed a little puzzled, obviously not recognizing who they were, but put the currycomb down.

"Get Melissa and Lydia, will you, Carl?" Joshua said.

"Who's the third person?" Caroline asked her husband, as Carl went toward the tents.

Joshua turned back. "I don't know."

"That's Daniel Spencer," Mary Ann said.

By the time the three men arrived at their little circle of wagons and tents, most of the family had come out to see who it was. Parley P. Pratt started around one side of the family and John Taylor took the other, shaking hands, inquiring after them, asking each of the children their names. Brother Taylor was particularly warm when he came to Carl and Melissa. Brother Spencer stood back, watching the two Apostles greet the family.

Finally, Parley Pratt reached Joshua. "Good to see you, Joshua. Any word from Nathan and Matthew?"

"Yes. Both Lydia and Jenny got letters a week or so ago. They're doing fine. They were only about two hundred miles out when they wrote, however."

Elder Taylor came up now too. "We had a recent communiqué from President Young," he said. "They had just passed Chimney Rock at that point."

Elder Pratt turned and motioned the third man forward. "Some of you know Brother Daniel Spencer, I'm sure. Let me introduce the rest of you."

Spencer shook hands as Parley introduced him around. They made room for the three men on a low wooden bench they had brought for use around the campfire at night. When they were settled they chatted for a few minutes. Then, in a lull in the conversation, Elder Pratt turned to Joshua. "We understand that your family is equipped and ready to go."

"We think so," he answered. "No one ever has all that they'd like to have, but we're better off than many."

"Good. That's what we like to hear." He glanced at Elder Taylor, who took it from there.

"As you can see," Elder Taylor explained, "we have about three hundred wagons here at the Elkhorn now. Many of those are ready to go, but many others are still waiting for additional teams or supplies to come from Winter Quarters. Elder Pratt and I are going to stay until we have the full complement of those who can go this year."

"How long do you think that will be?" Carl spoke up.

"Another week."

Joshua pulled a face. When they had arrived three days before, they had been disappointed to learn that no one was actually ready to depart yet.

"No more than that, we hope," Elder Taylor said. "It's already the seventeenth of June. We wait much longer and we could be facing some nasty weather in the Rockies."

"We've talked about that too," Solomon said. "It's getting late in the season."

Parley Pratt came in again. "Brother Spencer here is one of our captains of hundreds. He's got a group about ready to go. We decided tonight that he should leave immediately and not wait for the rest of us."

Joshua and Carl exchanged glances. If anything, Carl was more impatient to leave than Joshua was. Joshua looked at Brother Spencer. "Is your company full?"

"That depends," the man answered with a smile.

"On what?" Carl asked.

"On whether your family can be ready to leave in the morning."

"In the morning?" Caroline exclaimed. It was not said in dismay but in pleased surprise.

Spencer nodded. "If you can join us, we'd love to have you. If not, we'll look for someone else."

"You're the first we've asked," Elder Taylor added.

Joshua looked around the circle at his family. "What do you think?"

Solomon didn't hesitate. "We'll have to do some work tonight, but we can be ready."

Carl turned to Melissa, who was smiling. She nodded; then he did the same. "Let's go."

Lydia and Jenny were likewise nodding.

Joshua turned to his mother. "Absolutely," she said before he could ask.

Suppressing a grin of pleasure, Joshua turned to Daniel

Spencer. "Well, Captain," he said, "looks like you just got yourself a passel of Steeds with whom to travel."

The new raft Howard Egan's crew made under the direction of Thomas Grover was huge. They had cut down two cottonwood trees that were a good two and a half feet in diameter and close to twenty-five feet long. They were then hewn to a point at each end and hollowed out to form two rough "canoes." These provided the floating base for the ferry. On top of that, fastened both by lashing and by nails the blacksmiths had made, they laid a platform of planking. A large oar was constructed at each end. They had learned that oars provided the best means of controlling an ungainly craft in the swift river.

While the building team put the raft together, another team set to work building five wharves on both sides of the river where the wagons could be loaded straight on and off the raft without delay. Five were needed because they couldn't always judge where the current would take them. The blacksmiths also forged out oarlocks and the ironwork necessary to hold them in place. All the while, the men not assigned to the construction crews continued carrying their wagons and goods across the river.

On Friday, the eighteenth of June, the new raft was finally done. Ironically, by that time all the Mormon wagons had been ferried across and were on the north side of the river waiting to continue westward. The company had come up the south side of the North Platte since Fort Laramie, but here the river took a sharp bend to the south and they could follow it no longer. From here they would strike out across a fifty-mile stretch of country where there were only a few creeks and springs. Then they would pick up the Sweetwater River, which would become their next guiding water source.

All of the Mormons were across, but the ferry was not going to sit idle. Two companies of Missouri emigrants were waiting to be carried across, and another large company arrived just as the raft was about to be launched. Word was already spreading up and down the river that the Mormons were putting a ferry into service that eliminated the hazards of crossing the North Platte. People were coming up to see for themselves rather than risk a dangerous crossing.

At one forty-five p.m., the first wagon from one of the Missouri companies was taken across. When it reached the other side and docked at one of the wharves with no difficulty, a cheer went up from the assembled Latter-day Saints. As the cheering died, Brigham turned to Thomas Grover. "I think you have yourself a ferry, Brother Grover. We shall leave it in your capable hands. The Lord bless you."

"Mama, Benji keeps hitting me."

"Do not. You keep getting in my way."

Rebecca poked her head out of the wagon to look at the two of them. "All right, children, that's enough. Leah and Nicole are asleep. Don't wake them."

Kathryn was riding on the wagon seat beside Nathan, who was driving. Derek had borrowed one of Robert Crow's horses and was riding ahead with the scouts. "Boys," she said softly, "there's plenty of room out here. Don't walk so close to each other."

That worked for almost thirty seconds. Then Benjamin picked up a pebble, made sure none of the adults were watching, and flipped it at his brother. His aim was true. It hit Christopher on the back of the head.

"Benji!" He swung around and took a swipe at Benjamin.

Nathan handed the reins to Kathryn. "Can you drive for a while?" he asked. She nodded and he jumped down, moving to walk between the two boys. "All right, young men, we have to be a little more quiet now."

From the front wagon flap Rebecca appeared again. She had been fighting a fever and headache all day—a malady that was starting to occur with increasing frequency in the company—

and had been trying to sleep in the jolting wagon along with Leah and Kathryn's baby. Her patience had about reached its end. "I said that's enough, Benji," she snapped.

"He looked at me mean, Mama," Benji wailed.

"I did not," Christopher retorted. "You hit me."

"Boys, boys!" Nathan said, taking Christopher and moving them farther apart.

"They're just bored," Kathryn said, remembering her classroom in Pueblo. Boredom was the quickest way to start problems in a group of children. And she too was bored beyond endurance. It had been ten days since they left the last crossing of the North Platte. The challenge of getting across the river had occupied the hearts and minds and hands of virtually every camp member for a week. Then just like that, the old monotony had slipped back in to ride with them again. Kathryn felt like flipping rocks at someone too. "I've got an idea," she said. "Let's play a game."

"What?" both boys said at once, squinting up at her in the afternoon sun.

"Uh . . ." Her mind was racing. "How about 'Guess What It Is'?"

"Is that really a game?" Christopher asked skeptically. He was eight now and much more savvy about parental tricks than his brother.

At five, Benjamin was more trusting. "How do you play it, Kathryn?"

Nathan was watching her, knowing that she was improvising on the fly. "Yes, Kathryn," he said innocently, "how do you play it?"

Kathryn turned to Rebecca. "You go back to sleep. They'll be fine."

Rebecca nodded gratefully and disappeared again. Kathryn turned to the boys. "Well, someone thinks of something and describes it with a sentence or two; then the others have to guess what it is."

"Can we think of anything?" Christopher asked.

"Well, I suppose that's pretty broad. How about if it has to be something we've seen or done since we ferried across the river?"

"Like the desert?" Benji asked.

Kathryn laughed. "We've seen enough of that, haven't we? But yes, you could say, 'I'm thinking of something that's very big and very dry and doesn't have any trees.' "

Christopher raised his hand and waved it. "I've got something."

"Let me start it, to show you how it works. Then whoever guesses right gets to go next, all right?"

Nathan smiled. It couldn't last forever, but for the moment her idea was working. The two boys were totally attentive and their battle was forgotten.

"I'm thinking of something that is very large, much taller than a wagon. It's hard, it's brown, and from a distance it looks like a loaf of bread that is buried in the ground. Guess what it is."

The two boys looked at each other, anxious to be first but clearly puzzled.

"It's very large," she said helpfully, "and a lot of people wrote their names on it."

Christopher's hand shot up. "Independence Rock."

"That's right, Christopher. Good. It's your turn now."

"I knew what it was," Benji pouted. "I just couldn't remember the name."

"It'll be your turn in a minute," Nathan soothed.

"I'm thinking," Christopher started, "of something that was very small. You could hold it in your hand if you wanted. It was ugly and it hopped. Guess what it is."

"The toad with horns!" Benji burst out, jumping up and down.

"That was too easy," Christopher said in disappointment. Three days ago the boys had discovered the strange-looking creature beneath some sagebrush. They had wanted to bring it along with them, but Rebecca had refused, afraid that it might be poisonous.

"I'm thinking," Benji began. "I'm thinking . . ." He looked

around, and then his face lit up. "I'm thinking of something that's white and brown and moves all the time. Guess what it is."

Nathan had watched his eyes and smiled. "Would it be our wagon?"

"Yes!" It didn't matter that it was an easy guess; Benji was pleased that he knew how to play the game.

"All right, what I'm thinking about," Nathan said, "was very, very tall. It was made of rock and had water going through the middle of it."

Christopher nudged him. "You're supposed to say, 'Guess what it is.' "

"Oh. Guess what it is."

The boys looked puzzled, so Nathan went on. "Actually it had very 'sweet water' in it."

"Oh, I know," Kathryn said. "Devil's Gate."

"That's right."

Christopher turned to his uncle. "It had sweet water in it?"

Nathan laughed. "Don't you remember Devil's Gate, just west of Independence Rock a few miles? Your father and I took you over to see it."

"Where the really high cliffs were?" he asked.

"Yes. It was that narrow cleft in the mountains."

"And what is the name of the river that goes through Devil's Gate?" Kathryn asked, smiling.

"Oh!" Christopher said in surprise. "The Sweetwater River. I get it."

"Kathryn's turn," Benji said.

She thought for a moment. "I'm thinking of something that is so big you can't see it. Guess what it is."

The three of them looked at each other, thinking hard. "So big that you can't see it?" Nathan finally said. "How could that be?"

Kathryn smiled sweetly. "It just is." She waited for almost a full minute as they talked among themselves. Then Nathan looked up and shrugged. "We give up."

"It's South Pass," she chortled. "Don't you remember, Christopher? Just yesterday morning we came over it, but we weren't even sure that we had crossed it because it is so wide and so gentle a rise that it doesn't seem like a pass at all."

"All right," Nathan agreed. "That was a good one." There had been some excitement in the company the day before at the thoughts of crossing the Continental Divide. Orson Pratt and others rode ahead to pinpoint it. But when it came down to saying where the exact spot was where the water would flow to the Pacific instead of to the Atlantic, no one could do it with certainty. A short time later they had come to Pacific Spring and everyone had wanted to take their first drink of "Pacific water," but at the actual pass no one could actually say, "This is the exact spot where the continent divides."

Nathan turned to Derek's two sons. "And do you remember how high Elder Pratt said South Pass was?"

Instantly Benji's hand shot up. "Seven thousand eighty-five feet."

"That's right," Nathan answered, not surprised. Christopher was the one who could tell you every piece of a horse's harnessing or every part of the wagon. But Benji was the one who was always counting and tabulating things. He loved numbers.

"All right," Kathryn said, "since no one guessed mine, I get another turn." She thought quickly. "We passed it this morning. It is very important to every traveler on the Oregon Trail. You have to make a choice there. Guess what it is."

Christopher started dancing up and down. "I know, I know. It's the Parting of the Ways. That's where we could have gone to Oregon if we wanted."

"Good, Christopher," she answered. "It's your turn."

Chapter Notes

After spending six days at the "last crossing," the longest delay they had seen up to that point, the Latter-day Saints of the Pioneer Company finally left the North Platte River. What came to be known as "the Mormon Ferry" was put into operation at a site near the present-day site of Fort Caspar in Casper, Wyoming. Nine men were assigned to remain behind to man it. Later, as the water levels began to drop, the Latter-day Saints moved the ferry downstream several miles.

Back at the Elkhorn River, twenty miles west of Winter Quarters, Elders Parley P. Pratt and John Taylor were gathering the people who would come west with the Big Company. Daniel Spencer's company was the first to leave, rolling out on 18 June, the same day that the Pioneer Company was launching their "Mormon Ferry" about seven hundred and fifty miles to the west.

The Pioneer Company crossed South Pass on 27 June 1847, the third anniversary of the martyrdom of Joseph and Hyrum Smith. It is not known exactly where Orson Pratt was when he took the barometric reading on South Pass and concluded it was 7,085 feet high. Today it is marked on the maps as 7,550 feet in elevation. William Clayton indicated that South Pass was two hundred seventy-eight and a half miles from Fort John (Fort Laramie), which would make it a total of eight hundred twenty-one and three-quarters miles from Winter Quarters.

Chapter Forty-Three

The Pioneer Company of the Latter-day Saints reached the Little Sandy River about four-fifteen on the afternoon of June twenty-eighth. They were about twenty-five miles west of South Pass and moving across a vast expanse of sagebrush desert broken here and there only by a few dry hills. Off to the north the towering, snowcapped Wind River Mountains continually drew the eye, but there wasn't much else, besides the great herds of antelope, that caught one's attention.

Actually the Little Sandy was more like a substantial creek than a river, in the eastern sense; but out here any water was a welcome sight, and Nathan wasn't surprised that it was labeled a river. It was about three rods wide but only two feet deep, though the current moved along quite rapidly. The water was filled with silt from the sandy nature of the soil in the area, but the bottom was solid and presented no substantial problems for the wagons. In half an hour they were all across and on their way again.

They had gone only about a mile, however, when four riders and three packhorses appeared in the distance. Brigham immediately signaled for the train to come to a halt. One rider was not a surprise. Elder George A. Smith had ridden ahead to scout the way. But he had gone alone.

Nathan was staring forward. "I'll go see what's going on," he said.

Derek, who was taking his turn at driving, handed the reins to his wife and climbed down from the wagon. "Hold them here," he said. "We'll be back in a few minutes."

They reached the lead wagons about the same time that Elder Smith trotted up and swung down. The other three men slid off their horses. Two stayed where they were; the third stepped forward with Elder Smith. One look told Nathan that these were mountain men—trappers and traders of some kind. The one coming up with the Apostle was not a particularly big man. He was maybe five foot ten and weighed no more than one hundred sixty or seventy pounds. He wore a fringed buckskin shirt, trousers made of tanned deerskin, and knee-high boots made of soft leather, probably calfskin. His hat was dusty and battered, showing many days of sun and rain. He wore a heavy beard and mustache that nearly hid his mouth, but his eyes were like two black marbles set in deep brown cheeks. They were pleasant and alert. His nose had a pinkish hue, suggesting more than one night cuddled up with a bottle. His face was so weathered from being out-of-doors that it was hard to assess his age, but Nathan guessed he was around forty, maybe a little older. The other two looked much the same as this one did, perhaps a bit shabbier. All in all, they presented a fascinating and arresting sight.

"President Young," George A. Smith said, walking up to Brother Brigham, "may I present Mr. Jim Bridger."

A ripple of surprise and excitement went through the men who had come forward. Jim Bridger was one of the most famous names in the West. They were even now on the way to his fort. Could this really be him?

Brigham stepped forward and gripped his hand. "A pleasure to meet you, Mr. Bridger. My name is Brigham Young."

"I've heard of you, Mr. Young," Bridger said, shaking his hand. "A group came through a few days back saying there was a large company of Mormons on their way."

"There is," Brigham said, "and we're just the first. In fact, we were looking forward to stopping at your fort. We hoped to have a chance to talk with you about our possible destination."

"Well," Bridger said, "me and my men here are on our way to Fort Laramie to do some trading. But I'll tell you what. If you're willing to turn off the road here and camp for the night, we'd be pleased to stay with you and answer whatever questions you might have."

"I'm sure you know Moses Harris," Brigham began.

"Old Black Harris?" Jim Bridger exclaimed. "That's what we all call him. Sure do. What's that sidewinder up to nowadays?"

They were in a small grove of trees near the Little Sandy. It was about seven-thirty, but the sun had not gone down yet and the shade still felt good. Brigham and the other members of the Twelve had asked for the meeting with the mountain man, but soon many others in the company gathered around to listen. Nathan and Derek stood together a little behind Bridger and his two men.

"We met Harris at Pacific Spring," Heber Kimball explained. "He's waiting there for some of the emigrant companies to guide them on to Oregon."

"That old horse thief," Bridger laughed. "And he'll probably charge them two hundred dollars to do it too, even though the road is as plain as a wart on a purty woman's nose."

There was an appreciate chuckle around the circle. Harris had offered to guide the Mormons for a hefty fee and Brigham had politely declined. Brigham went on. "Mr. Harris was not very encouraging in his reports. He said he's well acquainted with the Bear River valley and the Valley of the Salt Lake, but he said the regions around the Salt Lake are not favorable to settlement. Would you agree with that?"

"Did he try to talk you into going up to Cache Valley?"

"As a matter of fact, he did," Brigham answered.

"Thought so. That's a favorite place of his. He's hoping to attract settlers up there so he can set up a fort and make some money for himself."

The mountain man leaned back, thoughtful now. It seemed evident to Nathan that Bridger had been nipping at a bottle ever since they had camped. He was relaxed and affable, but his speech sometimes slurred just a bit. "As for the Valley of the Great Salt Lake, you'd be better off going to the Utah Lake. It's about a day's ride further south."

"Harris mentioned that too," George A. Smith said. "He said there's more timber there."

"Along the creeks," Bridger said, "but not by the lake itself. But it's good soil around there. Been there forty or fifty times myself," he added. "Lots of wild cherries and berries. Never seen no grapes there, but plenty of other stuff. Further south, the Indians grow corn, wheat, and pumpkins as good as any you could find in Old Kentuck." He was rambling, warming to the subject.

"I understand the Hastings Cutoff runs just south of the Great Salt Lake," Brigham came in. "How far is the lake from your fort, would you say?"

"Not sure exactly. Two- or three-day ride. Been there fifty times at least."

"Hastings said it was a hundred miles. Does that sound about right?"

Bridger looked at his companions. They nodded. "'Bout that, I guess. Better watch out for them Utah Indians. Mean bunch down there. If they can catch a man alone, they'll abuse him real bad." He leaned forward, realizing he sounded discouraging. "Won't bother an armed group like this, though. You'll be fine."

"Are you saying that the valley around the Salt Lake is all right for settlement?" Brigham persisted.

"Ain't as bad as Harris told you," he agreed. "He's just trying to take you to Cache Valley." He looked around at the men. "We call it that because a lot of us use it to cache our furs and hide them from the Indians until we can take 'em out for trading. It's cold there, though."

"In Cache Valley?" Willard Richards asked. Bridger was jumping from topic to topic like a bird on a limb.

"No. Well, it's really cold there too, but I meant the Valley of the Salt Lake. It's cold there. You'll get frost 'bout every month of the year. Probably can't grow corn."

The members of the Twelve looked at each other with some dismay. It was obvious now that Bridger was just a touch drunk. How much that was affecting his memory was hard to tell.

"Actually," Heber said, "we're looking pretty seriously at stopping in the Salt Lake Valley. But you don't think that's wise?"

Bridger had turned and was looking at some of the men listening to his report. "Been in these parts since '22," he said expansively. "Barely eighteen when I come. Hired on with Colonel William Ashley to come west and get furs. Been here ever since. Twenty-eight years now."

"Twenty-five," one of his men corrected.

"That's what I said," he shot back.

"Mr. Bridger," Brigham broke in, "we thank you for your information. This has been most helpful."

"Harris doesn't know what he's saying," the mountain man said. "The Valley of the Salt Lake is all right. 'Cepting for the frost. Not sure if you can grow corn there. Utah Lake valley would be better. Further south is better yet."

"We'll take that under consideration." Brigham stood. "Thank you again."

The next morning as Derek went down to get the team and bring them back to the wagon, he saw Jim Bridger and his two men saddling up their horses. Their packhorses were already loaded. Brigham Young and Heber C. Kimball were there with them, along with a few other men. Curious, Derek moved over closer to hear what was going on.

As he got there, Brigham was handing the trapper a piece of paper. "This is a pass for our ferry at the last crossing of the Platte," he explained. "This will get you and your horses free passage across the river."

"Much obliged." Bridger folded it and stuck it in some pocket inside his coat. "You've got plenty of water between here and the Green River, except for one stretch of about twenty miles. But even then there's grass for your animals. You'll be all right." There was no liquor in the man now, Derek could tell. He spoke quickly and with confidence. His eyes were clear and probing. "And as for the Great Salt Lake Valley, except for the cold, it would be a good place to bring your people."

"The Lord can temper the weather, Mr. Bridger," Brigham said easily.

There was a derisive laugh. "The Lord hain't done that very often for us, has he, boys?"

They laughed, shaking their heads.

"More 'n one man been frostbit by the Lord, Mr. Young."

Brigham laughed now too, not in the least offended. "Well, unless the Lord changes his mind, I think we'll be settling on the Valley as our final stopping place."

"Tell you what, Mr. Young," Bridger said, his eyes glittering with amusement. "I'll give you one thousand dollars for the first bushel of corn you grow in that valley."

"Tell you what, Mr. Bridger," Brigham shot right back, "you start saving your money, because I'll deliver that bushel personally to you."

About noon of the second day they crested a low ridge, and there about a quarter of a mile ahead, cutting its sinuous way through the barren bleakness, was a ribbon of dark green. Those were the trees and willows, but here and there they could see open patches of water that were at least three or four rods wide.

"Is that the Green River, Papa?"

"Yes, Christopher," Derek answered. "That's the Green."

"Hmm," Nathan said. "It's wider than I thought. Pretty impressive for out here, I'd say."

"It's strange," Kathryn said. "There's not a living thing taller than a gopher, then suddenly you come upon a river like that making its way through the whole of it."

"It's not hard to see where it got its name, is it?" Rebecca said.

Nathan shook his head. Even from this distance there was a distinctly green cast to the water.

"Do we have to cross it, Papa?" Benji asked.

"Oh, yes. We're going west. It's running almost straight south."

Kathryn eyed it warily. "It looks deep."

Nathan had thought the same thing. The floodplain wasn't as wide as the North Platte's, but the main channel looked deeper, and the current was at least as swift as what they had seen at the ferry site on the North Platte.

Brigham Young, standing a few feet away, turned at Kathryn's comment. "I think we're going to have to build another ferry," he said for all to hear. He was quite serious now. "We'll noon down beneath the trees and start work immediately. I think we'd better build a raft for each division. We don't want to spend forever getting across."

Charlie Smith was in the lead. In the heat, they didn't have to do much else other than point their horses' noses up the trail, then just let them go. Across this expanse, the two tracks made by the hundreds of wagons that had passed through here were clear enough to follow even in the dark.

Peter had learned a lesson once about falling asleep in the saddle, and it was a painful one. On this trip Charlie Smith had taught him a trick. You slouched down low, tied the reins around the saddle horn loose enough to give the horse its head, then wrapped the end of the reins around your hand. If you started to slip sideways in either direction, the reins would tug on your hand and wake you up. It wasn't a perfect solution, but for the long, interminable stretches in this unbearable heat, it allowed Peter to doze fitfully.

He shifted his weight slightly, noting that Sam Brannan's head was down too. Charlie had his hat pulled low over his eyes, but he was alert, watching for any sign of Indians. And that was good. In another hour Peter would take his turn at point, and there would be no dozing off then. He closed his eyes, letting the rocking motion of the horse start to lull him off to sleep again.

"There she is," Charlie suddenly called.

Both Peter and Brannan came awake immediately, straightening in their saddles.

"There what is?" Brannan asked, looking around in some confusion.

"The Green River."

Undoing his reins as well, Peter stood up in the stirrups, looking out ahead. For a moment he saw only hundreds of square miles of sagebrush and sand, and then he saw the line of green about a mile or so up ahead of them. It was the tops of trees.

"So do we stop there for the night?" Brannan said.

"No," Smith replied. "It's barely one o'clock. The Big Sandy is only another twenty miles more I think."

"The horses need some time out of this heat," Peter said. Since becoming an ox-team driver, he had learned that caring for your animals was one of the secrets to success on the trail.

"Of course."

It was as though the horses could smell the water. Without any urging they began walking more briskly. Fifteen minutes later, as they came around a low hill, the valley of the Green River came fully into view below them. It was a welcome sight. Peter stretched, ready to get out of the saddle for a time. Suddenly he stiffened, leaning forward. He blinked twice to clear his vision, then shaded his eyes, even though the sun was at his back. "Sam. Charlie."

But Charlie Smith had already seen it too. "Wagons!" he cried.

They pulled up, coming up alongside one another. "Look at that," Brannan said. "That's got to be the biggest company we've seen so far. There must be seventy or eighty wagons."

"Do you think it could be them?" Peter blurted, not daring to hope.

Smith shook his head slowly. He was trying to stay casual, but Peter heard the touch of excitement in his voice. "No way to know but to go find out."

Nathan and Derek were working in rhythm with the axes, cutting down a cottonwood tree with a trunk about two feet thick. It was long enough and straight enough that they could get the two "canoes" for their division's raft from the same trunk. They worked smoothly and in perfect synchronization. The chips were flying and the bite in the trunk was deepening quickly.

"Riders coming!"

They turned in surprise to see who had shouted it. A few feet away, Willard Richards and Heber Kimball were trimming off the branches of a tree they had already felled. They stopped, squinting as well. Everyone was looking around now to see where the caller was and what he was seeing. And then Heber gave a low cry and pointed to the west across the river. "There," he said.

They turned and saw three dark figures and a small cloud of dust coming toward them.

Brigham, who had been working with a group sawing boards for the ferry's floor, left the two-man saw and trotted to his horse. In a moment he returned with his telescope and brought it up to his eye. It took him a few seconds to find the riders and focus the glass more sharply. "Three riders," he called. "With a couple of packhorses. They've seen us. They're coming at a steady lope."

Suddenly Brigham gasped. "Oh my word!" he exclaimed. He moved a few steps and steadied himself against a tree, then brought up the telescope again. "I declare!"

"What?" Heber called. "What is it?"

"I think that's Sam Brannan."

"Sam Brannan?" Heber blurted. "Are you sure?"

Brigham looked again. "I'm certain it is." Then, after a moment, again there was a quick intake of breath. This time he lowered the glass and turned to stare at Derek and Nathan. Then he held out the instrument toward them. "Derek, you'd better come take a look."

Kathryn was standing at the back of their wagon, putting away the dishes from the noon meal. It had been a cold meal, since Brigham didn't want to make camp on this side of the river if they could get the rafts done in time to start ferrying across. Her crutches were in the wagon, but she used them now only when she had some distance to walk. For getting around camp she almost always used only her cane. Now, with the wagon to steady her, even that was set aside.

She heard a noise and turned around to see Nathan appear from between their wagon and Robert Crow's. At the look on his face, she turned fully to face him. "What is it, Nathan?"

He came forward slowly. "I think you'd better sit down, Kathryn."

There was a sudden clutch of fear. Her first thought was of Nicole, but she was asleep in the wagon. Kathryn had just checked on her a few minutes before. Then she took a quick breath. Rebecca had taken Leah and the two boys down to watch the men work. "Has something happened?" she cried.

He shook his head slowly and now he was smiling. He came over and took her gently by the arm, getting her cane for her. He pointed to the small wooden stool they used when they were camped. "Just come and sit down."

She allowed herself to be led to the stool and sat down

slowly. His smile was reassuring, but her heart was still racing. "What, Nathan? Tell me."

He stepped back. Just then, Derek appeared. Strangely, he was wet to his neck, but he too was smiling broadly. "Good," he said. "You're sitting down."

"*What?*" She nearly shouted it at them.

"This," Nathan said, turning and pointing.

For almost a full two seconds, Kathryn just stared at the figure that stepped out from between the wagons. The first thing that registered in her mind was the fact that this person too was dripping wet. And then her hands flew to her mouth as it dropped open in total astonishment. Beneath the beard . . .

"Hello, Kathryn," Peter said, smiling.

In one instant her eyes filled with joyous tears. "Peter?" she gasped.

He stepped forward, grabbing her hands and lifting her to her feet; then he enveloped her in his arms and with infinite tenderness reached down and kissed her.

Derek and Nathan turned without a word and quietly slipped away to go find Rebecca. Neither Peter nor Kathryn was aware they had left. They clung to each other fiercely for almost a full minute as Kathryn whispered over and over in disbelief, "It's you. It's you. It's you."

Finally, she let him go and stepped back. He kissed her again, shaking his head. "I'm sorry. Look at you. I've gotten you all wet." He laughed. "We were swimming our horses across but Derek couldn't wait; he jumped in the river and swam out to meet me."

"You think I care about that?" she said.

He was staring at her, letting his eyes caress every feature of her face. "I can't believe this. I was planning to go all the way to Pueblo to get you, and here you are."

She just shook her head, unable to speak. Then, after a moment, she took his hand. "Come here. There's someone I want you to see."

He followed her to the wagon. She pulled back the canvas,

letting the light flood in on Nicole, who was sleeping on her back, her head tipped toward them, her arms spread wide above her head. Kathryn had planned for weeks to say something cute and clever at this moment; but then she heard Peter's sharp intake of breath. He leaned forward until his body was half inside the wagon and he was looking down on his daughter. "Oh," he whispered in quiet awe. Kathryn smiled. That was enough. There was nothing more she needed to say.

When Peter awoke the next morning, for a moment he was disoriented. There were no stars above him, and his first thought was that it was overcast and there would be a chance of rain today. Then he realized that the sky above him was really the tent's canvas ceiling with the first light of dawn turning it gray.

He turned his head. Kathryn was up on one elbow watching him, smiling softly. "Good morning."

He felt his whole body relax as he fully realized now where he was. "Good morning."

She reached out and pushed his hair back away from his forehead. "It's gotten so long. Between that and the beard, I hardly recognized you."

He nodded. "We haven't seen many barbershops in the last two months."

She lay down again, snuggling in closer. He lifted an arm and put it around her. She closed her eyes. "Do you know how long I've waited for this?" she murmured. "I still can't believe that you're really here."

He nodded. "Do you realize that today is the first of July? It was one year ago on the fourth that we decided to take you back."

"I remember that very clearly."

"One whole year. I never dreamed it would be that long."

"Is it true what Brother Brannan was telling the Twelve?" she said, her eyes clouding now. "About the Donners?"

He nodded, his face grim. "Yes."

"But the Reeds are all right. You're sure?"

He had assured her of that last night. "Yes. They looked pretty bad, but they came out of it all right. And the Breens. They all made it through as well."

"But the Donners? Uncle George and Father Jacob?"

He looked away. "Gone. And Tamsen too. She refused to leave George, who was pretty far gone by that time. She could have gotten out on two different occasions but she wouldn't leave him."

"I always liked Tamsen," Kathryn said, her voice sorrowful.

"So many are gone. Every time I think that you could have been with them, I—" He stopped and just held her more tightly.

"You were inspired, Peter. I don't have any question about that. It was the Lord who blessed us both. And then to have Rebecca and Derek show up at Pueblo, it was more than we could have hoped for. It made the winter pass so much more quickly for me."

"It's ironic, isn't it? You find Derek and Rebecca in Pueblo, and I find Will and Alice in California."

"I'm so anxious to see them again. Is their baby cute?"

"Yes. He's a little darling. He looks so much like Will, and all you've got to do to make Will bust his buttons is tell him that." He turned and looked toward the small hand-made crib in the corner. "And Nicole. She is so beautiful, Kathryn."

"I know," she said joyfully. "Do you like the name, Peter? We can change it. I wasn't sure what you'd want."

"I love Nicole. It seems to fit her perfectly, with her dark hair and that little button of a nose."

"I think so too."

They fell silent, each comforted deeply by the warmth and closeness of the other. After a long time, Kathryn pulled back. "You don't think Brother Brannan is going to convince Brother Brigham to go to California, do you?"

He shook his head. "Brigham didn't seem too impressed by the proposal, no matter how passionately Brother Brannan made it. I think that's why he went off in a bit of a huff last night."

"I'm glad."

"You are?" he asked in surprise. "You don't want to go to California?"

She shook her head. "I want only three things, and in this order. First, I want to be with you."

"That's first for me too."

"Second, I want to be with the family. It was so good to see Nathan and Matthew again. I've been surprised at how much I've missed them."

"I agree again. I wish Matthew had come on with you. I'd love to see him again."

"And third, I want to be with our people. If Brigham says it's California, then I could be very happy there. If not, then I'll go where he's taking us."

"I feel exactly the same way," he said, laying his hand on her cheek. Then he laughed and reached up to kiss her nose. "Ah, Kathryn," he whispered, "I've missed you so."

The tears came again. "Not any more than I have missed you, my love," she whispered. "I think this is the happiest day of my life."

Chapter Notes

There is no record that Brigham Young ever tried to make Jim Bridger pay up on his wager about the bushel of corn. Eventually the Church purchased Fort Bridger and used it as a way station for their emigration and communication routes. Two days after Bridger's visit, while stopped on the east side of the Green River to build rafts to take their wagons across, the Pioneer Company was astonished when Sam Brannan and two other men rode in from the west.

Chapter Forty-Four

"What is it, Mama?"

Jessica looked at her daughter and shook her head. "I'm not sure, Miriam. We'll know in a moment."

The wagons of the Daniel Spencer company had moved in a circle around Brother Spencer and two other men who were standing beside a tall pole with a board nailed to the top. Jessica was on the wagon seat with Miriam perched beside her. With the heaviest of the five Steed wagons, Solomon and Jessica had been given the oxen, and so Solomon always walked alongside the animals. Miriam was almost four now and liked to pretend that it was she who was driving the wagon and not her father. She had listened to him enough that she knew all of the commands for controlling the oxen and was constantly shouting "Gee" or "Haw" or "Whoa, boys" at them. Fortunately, the animals completely ignored her.

At the pole, one of the men reached up with a hammer and knocked down the board nailed on the top. He held it up. "It's a letter," he said. He really didn't need to explain. Scrawled in red chalk on the pole beneath the board were the words "Platte Post Office," and on the board was written: "Open this and you will find a letter."

The people crowded in closer as Elder Spencer took the board and examined it. It had been hollowed out and turned with the opening to the bottom to protect it from the rain. With his pocketknife Brother Spencer withdrew two folded sheets of paper.

He looked them over, reading quickly, then turned to his people. "It's a letter from the Twelve. There's a report on the trail thus far and some rules that the Twelve have drawn up for the camps."

"Read it to us," someone called.

"We will read it in camp tonight. For now, I think we'd better push on." Spencer glanced at the letter again. "But it was dated May ninth, and today is . . ." He looked surprised. "July Fourth. Independence Day."

There was a ripple of surprise. No one had thought about this being a holiday.

"That means we're only about five weeks behind them. That's good."

On the Fourth of July, the Mormon Ferry at the last crossing of the North Platte River ran from dawn until shortly after dark. Among the emigrant camps there were several small celebrations. Among the nine Latter-day Saints who stayed to run the ferry there was nothing. They were too busy to do any more than remember that this was the birthday of their country.

As it grew full dark, they tied up the raft for the last time on the south bank of the river. Matthew Steed spoke to Thomas Grover, his captain. "I'll be back in a little while. I'm just going to take a look around."

"We would know if they had come in today, Matthew," Grover said kindly.

"I know," he answered cheerfully, "but you know me. I always like to check." He waved and moved away. Almost immediately he was amid the wagons, dozens of them, if not hundreds. The sound of many people filled the air—women talking to each other over cooking fires, children playing games, men shouting at their animals or to each other. Dogs barked, cattle lowed, oxen bellowed, horses whinnied. And all of this while waiting for the Mormons to take them across the river. That was something that Matthew had still not grown accustomed to. The emigrant companies journeying to Oregon and California were coming in so quickly that there was now a four- to five-day wait to be ferried across, even though the ferry ran from dawn to dark.

He turned his head and looked at the glimmer of water off to his left. The water level in the river was dropping noticeably each day. Instead of the hundred yards across it had been when the Pioneer Company had first arrived, it was now about half that width, though the water was still too deep and swift for a safe crossing. But that would change soon enough. Once it was safe to ford the river, the boating team, as instructed by Brigham, would cache the ferry, close up the blacksmith shop with its two forges, and head for home. The only problem being, where was home? Currently three of the men planned to go back to Winter Quarters for their families. Matthew and two others would turn west and follow Brigham Young. Three others would go to Fort Laramie and wait for Brigham when he returned to Winter Quarters.

Having encircled the various encampments, Matthew was satisfied that no new companies large enough to be Mormon had come in. He turned in discouragement and started back for their camp. His daily hope was that the company in which his own family was traveling would show up and then he could go with them to the Salt Lake Valley. But at this rate, the ferry would be shut down in two more weeks, three at the most. Then what would he do?

A little over two hundred miles farther west, the ferrying of the Pioneer Company across the Green River was done. They moved about five miles downriver to a better camping site, then made camp to wait out the Sabbath.

The Sabbath, by chance, was also the Fourth of July, Independence Day. Brief mention was made of it during worship services, but other than that the only celebration came when Elder George A. Smith discovered a long snowbank left by the winter winds on the north side of a hill not far from the river. He and some others took his wagon and fetched a load of snow, then mixed sugar with it and they all had a bowl of "ice cream." It was a refreshing treat.

While camped there, the Twelve determined to send a letter summarizing their experience along the trail back to the following companies. Five men were chosen to take the letter back, then serve as guides to their brother and sister Saints. That afternoon, Brigham and three others of the Twelve rode north with the five men to see them safely across the river. While they were gone the camp wrote letters or in their journals, read, rested, and otherwise waited for the Sabbath to pass. The fact that it was Independence Day was barely noted. Tomorrow they would turn west again, heading for the next important landmark on the trail, Fort Bridger.

All of the Steeds were gathered around their campfire, hoping that the smoke would drive off the mosquitoes. They talked quietly with each other, and Peter told them all that had happened since he and Kathryn had split up. Derek suddenly straightened. "Look," he said, "Brother Brigham and the Twelve are returning."

He was looking upriver. When they turned they saw a large party of men approaching the camp.

"Uh-oh," Nathan said. "They must not have been able to get the men across the river." Brigham had taken only three other members of the Twelve with him to see off the five guides, but many more than just four were coming now.

"Wait a minute," Rebecca cried. "Those aren't the same

men. Look, Derek, they have white belts and bandoliers. They're battalion men."

Derek stood slowly, peering forward, seeing what Rebecca had seen. He could scarcely believe his eyes. Battalion men? Out here?

The oncoming men were just fifty or sixty yards away now. One of the men suddenly started jumping up and down and waving. "Derek! Derek!"

"That's Tom Williams," Rebecca exclaimed with joy.

"It is!" Derek nearly shouted it. "It's part of the detachment from Pueblo."

Now cries were going up and down the rest of the camp as they realized that Brigham Young was returning with about a dozen men. Derek broke into a run. Robert Crow gave a cry and sprinted after him. Kathryn and Rebecca started after Derek, Peter helping Kathryn, who hadn't taken time to get her cane. Nathan fell in with them. "These are our friends," Kathryn explained excitedly. "This is who we spent the winter with."

Soon almost everyone in the camp was moving out to greet the newcomers.

On seeing the camp approaching, Brigham Young formed the men into a line with him and the other Apostles at the head. As he did so, Derek, Bob Crow, and the other runners in front slowed to a stop.

Brigham waited until the others had come up as well, then held up his hand for silence. "Brethren and sisters," he said loudly, "imagine our surprise when we took our five brethren to the ferry this afternoon and found thirteen men on the opposite bank. Much to our joy and surprise, they are members of the Mormon Battalion. They are part of Captain James Brown's detachment that wintered at Pueblo. Elder Amasa Lyman and those we sent from Fort Laramie to lead them back have found them and are bringing them along."

"Where's everybody else?" Derek called.

Sergeant Williams answered. "They're about a week behind us."

Brigham glanced at the men behind him, then explained. "They had some horses stolen, and Captain Brown sent thirteen men ahead to recover them, which they have done. But when they learned that we were a short distance ahead of them on the trail, they decided to ride hard to try to catch us."

Derek counted swiftly. There were only twelve of his former companions.

As though he had asked the question, Brigham answered. "One of their number, Brother William H. Walker, learned that his family is with one of the following companies, so he determined to go back with our five guides."

Derek moved over beside Nathan. "Sergeant Williams is the one who first took Josh under his wing and became his teacher and mentor," he whispered. "You'll like him a lot."

"This is a glorious occasion," Brigham proclaimed. "After sending these brethren off to serve almost one full year ago now, they have returned to our midst. I say that this calls for a cheer to welcome them home."

He raised his hand, fist clenched. "Ready? Hip, hip, hurrah! Hip, hip, hurrah! Hip, hip, hurrah!" It came out as a mighty roar as more than a hundred and fifty voices joined in unison.

"I also propose a 'Glory to God' for their safe return," the President shouted when the sound died away. "Ready?"

Now men straightened and removed their hats. On signal, as one voice, they let their gratitude ring. "Hosannah! Hosannah! Hosannah! Give glory to God and the Lamb. Amen!"

With that, the battalion men and the camp members broke ranks and swarmed around each other in joyous welcome.

At Sutter's Fort in Upper California, the observance of the Fourth of July was brief but intense. There was the raising of the flag, an impromptu march around the compound by the children, a few speeches, and a seven-gun salute to independence. It was interesting to Will and Alice that Captain John Sutter and the other Swiss immigrants who had come with him to America and founded New Helvetia, or New Switzerland, participated in the festivities as fully and as enthusiastically as those who were native-born Americans.

But then he decided that wasn't so surprising after all. Derek and Peter came from England. Jenny and Kathryn came from Ireland. And while they still loved their mother country, they considered themselves as fully American now.

Once the celebration—in duration no more than an hour and a half—was over, people resumed their normal activities. Will was back at Sutter's Fort now permanently. They had finished cutting the lumber for the sawmill upriver and were letting it cure. In the fall Sutter planned to hire a full crew to go back and start construction. In the meantime Will was helping bring in the crops. Sutter and Will had gone in partnership and had purchased a small sailing vessel. They would start shipping wheat and vegetables down the Sacramento River to the San Francisco Bay area in another week or two. Will would captain the boat but for now was helping bring in the goods that would serve as his freight.

Alice had brought Jared out to watch as Will directed a group of about thirty Mexicans and Indians whom Sutter had hired to load the shocks of grain onto waiting wagons. These would be hauled to a threshing floor, and then the wheat would be taken upriver a mile or two to Sutter's new gristmill.

Alice had brought a blanket and found a grassy spot on a nearby creek bank. Jared tried once to venture into the grass, but thereafter seemed content to crawl around his mother or play with some toys she had brought along.

Off to her left a movement caught Alice's eye. Two men on horseback were coming towards them. She turned. Will and his crew were throwing the sheaves of grain onto a wagon and had not seen the approaching men yet. As they drew closer she recognized the gray mare that the lead rider was on. "Will?" she called.

He poked his head around the wagon, now piled almost to its capacity.

She pointed. "I think it's Mr. Sutter."

Will took off his hat, swiping at his forehead with his sleeve as he peered at the two riders. Satisfied that it was John Sutter, he said something to the other workmen, then came over to stand beside Alice. Jared immediately crawled to Will and started pulling himself up on his trousers. Will picked him up, talking softly to him.

The second man with Sutter was a big man with a thick beard but a pleasant-looking demeanor. They swung down and both men came over to where Will and Alice waited. Sutter spoke even as they approached. "Will Steed, I'd like you to meet Thomas Rhoads from up on the Consumnes River."

Will shifted Jared to his left arm and held out his hand. "How do you do, Mr. Rhoads."

Sutter had an amused look on his face. "I thought you called each other 'Brother.' "

That took Will aback for a moment as he looked more closely at the man. "You're a Latter-day Saint?"

"I am. I think you know my two boys—John and Daniel."

"Ah," Will said, understanding now. John and Daniel Rhoads had been two of the heroes in the rescue of the Donner Party, and Peter had told him they were Latter-day Saints. "I do know them," he said. "And two fine sons they are, Brother Rhoads."

"Thank you. They're good boys."

"This is my wife, Alice, and this is our son, Jared."

Rhoads touched the brim of his hat in acknowledgment.

Sutter came in again. "Tom has come down from the Consumnes to do some trading. He was asking about you."

"Oh?" Will said.

"Yes," Rhoads said. "You probably know about the colony of New Hope."

Will nodded. New Hope was the name Sam Brannan had given his attempt to establish a colony near the junction of the San Joaquin and Stanislaus Rivers. He had taken twenty families from the *Brooklyn* there to start farming the rich land.

Unfortunately, like so much, it seemed, of what Sam Brannan put his hand to, the colony had refused to be governed any longer by Brannan's rules, feeling that they were set up primarily to enhance his own position. Brannan had lobbied hard to get Will to join them, but thankfully Will had started in with John Sutter by then.

"Well, Tom Stout—he's the leader at New Hope—and a couple of other men came by my place the other day hoping to trade for some wheat and produce." He reached in his pocket and withdrew an envelope. "They brought this and asked if I would bring it down here the next time I came."

"It's for me?" Will asked in surprise.

"Yes." He handed the letter to Will, who took it eagerly. He looked at the name on the back, then turned to Alice in amazement. "It's from Private Josh B. Steed of the Mormon Battalion."

"It's from your father?" she exclaimed in amazement.

"No, not Joshua, Josh. My cousin." He opened the letter and skimmed the page quickly, then turned it over. "It *is* from Josh. Can you believe it? He's here in California too. Down at a place called Pueblo de Los Angeles."

He turned back to Rhoads. "We just learned the other day about the Mormon Battalion. I was going to write down there and see if by chance any of my family had come. Now I don't have to."

He handed the letter to Alice. "Brother Rhoads, thank you. This is wonderful news." Then he turned to Sutter. "I may have to ask for some time off, Mr. Sutter. If we've got family down there, I'd like to go and find them."

Thomas Rhoads was shaking his head.

Will stopped. "Why not?"

"Because Brother Stout got another letter, this one from one of the officers of the battalion. They're coming this way as soon as they are discharged."

"Really?" Will exclaimed. "And when will that be?"

"Their discharge date is in less than two weeks. Then it just depends on how fast they get themselves up here."

In Pueblo de Los Angeles the celebration of Independence Day started at dawn. The whole command—the Missouri Volunteers, the New York Volunteers, the soldiers of the regular army, General Kearny's Dragoons, and the Los Angeles detachment of the Mormon Battalion—lined up in formation, then paraded inside the fort as the sun came up. The New York Volunteers furnished a regimental band from their ranks. It played "The Star-Spangled Banner" as the flag was raised over the fort. To Josh Steed's surprise, in spite of all that the government of the United States of America had done to—or rather had not done for—his people, he was deeply stirred at the sight of the flag rising slowly to catch the breeze and snap crisply over the stockade. He saluted proudly as it rose to the top of the pole. Then he and all the rest of his Mormon companions in arms joined in lustily when one of the officers led them in a series of nine cheers.

They sang "Hail, Columbia!" and then the First Dragoons gave a thirteen-gun salute to the country. They broke for breakfast in a cheerful and festive mood. At eleven, they assembled again, this time before a large audience of Spaniards and Indians, and marched around the parade ground for a second time. Once again they sang "Hail, Columbia!" A lieutenant from Kearny's Dragoons read the Declaration of Independence—another thing that stirred Josh as it never had before. Colonel Stevenson, the fort commander, gave a short patriotic address. Then the Band of Ciudad de Los Angeles (or City of the Angels) played "Yankee Doodle," much to the Americans' great delight. In a final blast of celebration, the men shot off their guns twenty-eight times, one for each of the states in the Union.

Finally, shortly after noon, the men were dismissed and, except for those on duty, were given the rest of the day off.

The town was still filled with raucous celebration. As Josh

looked in the saloons and cantinas, it was clear that "celebration" in the minds of most of the soldiers meant one thing: spend as much money as you had on rum, ale, or whiskey and drink yourself into a stupor. Josh watched two men stagger by, holding on to each other and laughing so hard that tears streamed down their faces. "And this is their idea of fun?" he said to Tuttle.

"They say it is," the older man said thoughtfully, "but I've always wondered if they really do think so. I guess they do. They certainly come back to it time after time."

"Say," Josh said, "do you think there would be anyone at the post office on a holiday?"

Tuttle laughed shortly. "Well, since the post office is in the general store and cantina, my guess is that it is open. Why?"

"I wrote a letter a couple of months ago. It probably never made it, but I'd like to see if anyone has written back."

"Who in the world were you writing to?"

"Remember how about the first of April we learned that the ship *Brooklyn* had arrived in Yerba Buena? My cousin and his wife came on that voyage."

"Yeah, I do remember now."

"It's a long shot. I didn't even know where to send it for sure. But I'd like to make sure there's nothing."

Tuttle shrugged and changed directions, cutting across the street to where there was a small store and cantina all tucked into one flat-roofed adobe building. "There it is. Let's go find out."

They crossed the road quickly, dodging a passing cart filled with turnips and carrots, then ducked into the store. An older Mexican man with a beautifully long, thick mustache was in the cantina portion of the building. When he saw them come in, he wiped his hands on his apron and came out to greet them. "Sí, señores, may I help you?"

"My name is Joshua Steed," Josh said. "I was wondering if a letter has come for me."

"No, señor Steed. Nothing for you."

Josh's face fell. "Are you sure?" The man hadn't even checked the row of pigeonholes behind him where there were several letters showing.

The Mexican smiled, revealing bright white teeth beneath his mustache. "We receive only one or two letters a month, señor. Believe me, if one had come for you, I would know it."

"Okay." It was hard not to show his disappointment. "Thank you anyway."

"With which group of the *americanos* are you, señor?"

"The Mormon Battalion."

"Ah." He seemed pleased. "And are you *mormones?*"

They both nodded.

"I shall bring a letter out to you if one should come. I know where you are camped." The grin flashed again. "In the meantime, I think it would not do much good to invite you into my cantina to celebrate along with the others."

The two Latter-day Saints laughed easily. "I don't think so," they said, "but thank you anyway."

Chapter Notes

Since Daniel Spencer's company was the first of the Big Company to leave the Elkhorn, it is likely that his company found the "North Platte Post Office" first. If they were making a little better time than the Pioneer Company, which seems to be the case, they would have reached the spot where the letter was deposited sometime around the Fourth of July.

It was while the Pioneer Company was camped at Green River on 4 July that thirteen men from the Mormon Battalion came to the camp. One returned with the five guides sent back by Brigham Young; the rest went on with the Pioneer Company to the Valley.

The description of the Independence Day celebration held by the Mormon Battalion is only for the group that was at Los Angeles, which consisted of Companies A, C, D, and E (see *MB*, pp. 157–58). Company B was still in San Diego on that day but had already received orders to march to Los Angeles, where they would be discharged with the rest of the battalion (see *MB*, p. 140).

It is a little confusing to have two leaders with the same last name associated with the Pueblo group. *John* Brown was the original captain of the Mississippi company who led them to Pueblo. Then he returned to Mississippi. He came to Winter Quarters and traveled west with the Pioneer Company. The second sick detachment of the Mormon Battalion sent back to Pueblo was put under command of Captain *James* Brown. John Brown continued on with Brigham Young. James Brown brought the main Pueblo company to the Valley.

Chapter Forty-Five

It was the twelfth day of July, their fourth day out of Fort Bridger, and they were definitely into mountain country now. The first day out of Bridger they had come to a steep hill that dropped so precipitously that they had to lock the wagon wheels and put several men on ropes tied to the back of each wagon. That had been the steepest slope thus far, but it had been only a harbinger of what was to come. Two days before, as they crossed a ridge beneath the shadow of a peak they named Aspen Mountain, Elder Orson Pratt's barometer registered 7,315 feet above sea level. After passing below the peak's brooding presence, where snow was still visible even though it was mid-July, they discovered that the other side of the mountain was very much steeper than what they had already come up and over. As William Clayton put it, it was like "jumping off the roof of a house." The problem was that wagons were not great jumpers. Here they not only locked the wheels but hooked up block and tackle to each wagon and, for the heavier ones, also harnessed teams to ropes tied on the back. They had made it without incident, but it had been a harrowing experience.

Finally, though there were mountains on every side, they had entered a gently sloping canyon easily manageable by the teams. For the moment, the Steeds were about midway in the column of wagons, which was moving not in a single line but spread out four across to keep the dust down. Nathan and Derek were walking alongside the wagon while Peter drove, with Kathryn and the baby beside him. Christopher and Benji were walking beside their father. Rebecca had taken Leah with her and went back to walk with Elizabeth Crow.

"Well, at least the road is not crowded anymore," Derek said, breaking the silence.

"That's for sure," Peter answered. "By now the word is out on the Donners. Only a fool would take the Hastings Cutoff now."

"Present company excepted," Nathan drawled.

Peter laughed. "I meant all the way across."

Nathan nodded, knowing what he had meant from the beginning. "It is good not to have to compete with a hundred other companies for feed for the teams."

They fell silent again as they trudged along. They were now into their third month on the trail, and the days were too long to try to keep up a conversation at all times. After several minutes Kathryn spoke up. "Peter, do you think President Young sent Sam Brannan back because he was tired of hearing about California?"

Peter chuckled softly at the thought. "To be honest, I wondered that myself."

At Fort Bridger, Brigham Young had learned from Bridger's partner that the rest of the way was pretty mountainous. The five guides he had sent east from the Green River had specific instructions to find the main companies coming from Winter Quarters and to let the Pueblo group come on by themselves. After hearing the report Brigham changed his mind. To be safe, he sent Sergeant Williams back to find the Pueblo company, and then to everyone's surprise—no one more than Brannan himself—he asked Samuel Brannan to accompany him.

"I don't know," Nathan said. "Elder Brannan didn't seem to mind too much."

Before they could respond to that, they heard hoofbeats. Turning, they saw Heber C. Kimball approaching from behind them. "Pull up, folks. I've got an announcement."

All around him wagons pulled to a stop and people moved to where they could see him. When it was quiet the Apostle went on. "Those of us who stayed behind where we nooned haven't left yet. President Young is too ill to travel."

"Mountain fever?" Kathryn asked.

"I'm sure it is. It's what all the others have—a blinding headache, aching joints, fever and chills." He dropped his eyes. "He's even been a little delirious. We're going to stay there at Pudding Rocks and see if more rest will help him."

They nodded. The camp had nooned on a small creek they called Coyote Creek. Just to the north of them on a rocky ridge there had been a curious set of rock formations. They were strange columns made up of layers of rocks which looked as though some giant child had carefully let drops of thick pudding plop one on top of the other until they were thirty and forty feet tall. When someone noted the resemblance to pudding, the pioneers had immediately dubbed the place "Pudding Rocks."

"How many wagons are still back there?" Nathan asked.

"We have eight. It's mostly my company. Go on ahead and find a good camping place. We'll try to catch you by nightfall."

"We've got both Derek and Peter with our wagon now, Brother Heber," Nathan spoke up again. "Would you like me to come back and help with your group?"

Heber started to shake his head, then changed his mind. "Maybe that would be wise. The President is in so much pain, several of us have to lift him each time he needs to move."

"Done," Nathan said. "Let me get my rifle."

Elder Orson Pratt, who was leading the column, had seen Heber come up and now came back to join them. "Do you want the other members of the Twelve to come back with you, Heber?"

"No. The President wants you to push on for now. Let us see how he does. Then we'll get word to you."

They found a good camping site and stopped for the night, but the wagons that stayed behind did not come up. A rider came up to report that their President was still very seriously ill.

During the next day they did not move forward but waited, hoping for an improvement in Brother Brigham's health. To pass the time, some men went exploring on horseback and returned to report that they had found a large cave nearby. That excited a great deal of interest, and others, including Peter and Kathryn on one of their horses, rode out to see the cave that afternoon. When they returned, Derek and Rebecca took the horse and also went. When they got back, the family was just starting to prepare supper.

Derek unsaddled the horse, then came over to stand beside Peter. "Any word on President Young?"

He shook his head. "Just after you left, Elder Pratt and Elder Woodruff decided to send two men back to see how Brother Brigham is doing. They haven't returned yet."

Kathryn turned to Derek and Rebecca. "Supper will be ready in a few minutes," she said. "Why don't you two go down to the creek and wash up?"

Peter looked up at the sky, which was quite gray. The temperature was still almost cool. "We'd better hurry," he said. "I think we're going to have some rain."

Just before they were ready to eat, the two men sent back to Brigham Young's camp returned with Elder Kimball. Everyone quickly gathered around Brother Heber, but all he would say was that while the President was feeling better, he was not yet well enough to travel. Heber, as second in seniority to Brigham Young, called for the other members of the Twelve to meet with him in consultation about what to do.

As they met in Elder Woodruff's wagon, the first drops of rain started to fall. There was a rumble of thunder overhead that seemed to roll up the canyon toward them like a booming cannon. Peter's head came up sharply. "Hey," he said, looking toward the west. The wide canyon they were in gradually began to narrow down below them.

"Hey what?" Kathryn asked, surprised at his sudden reaction.

"That's Echo Canyon down there."

"What?" Derek said.

"You'll see. Down the canyon a ways, you get a really strange echoing sound. Some of our group called it Red Fork Canyon, but the Reed children and I called it Echo Canyon."

The thunder rumbled again, sounding as if it were coming from a barrel. "We'd better get inside the wagon," Rebecca said, "or we'll all be eating in the rain. Derek, go find the boys."

The thunderstorm rolled around them for almost twenty minutes, dumping a pretty heavy rain shower, but it quickly passed. Once it was gone, the Steeds bailed out of the wagon and they continued their preparations for supper. A few minutes later they saw the Apostles climbing down out of Elder Woodruff's wagon. Immediately all talking in the camp stopped and every eye turned to the Apostles.

"Brethren and sisters," Heber began in a loud voice, "as you know, President Young is still too sick to be moved. Albert Rockwood and others are also quite ill. But as you also know, today is July thirteenth. The growing season is already half gone. Every day we delay here is one day less that the seeds will have to mature before first frost. Therefore, President Young has recommended that we split the company."

No one spoke, but several nodded.

"In council we have decided to send Elder Pratt forward with an advance company of twenty-three wagons and forty-two men. We'll meet with the captains shortly and give them the names. We know from the report of Brother Peter Ingalls and

Brother Brannan and from reports in the newspapers that Mr. James F. Reed took another route over the Wasatch Mountains that bypasses the hazards of Weber Canyon. Elder Pratt has been asked to go to the Weber River and try to find Reed's route."

Now many heads were bobbing up and down. This was a wise course of action.

"The rest of the company shall remain here, resting and recruiting their teams until we can bring President Young up to join you. Then we shall proceed together, following the trail that Elder Pratt's company has scouted for us." He stopped. "Any questions?"

"Is the advance company to go all the way to the Valley?" That was John Brown.

"For now we only want them to find Mr. Reed's trail, if that is possible, and then we shall make further decisions at that point."

He looked around. There were no more questions. "All right, you captains of tens, if we can meet with you, we'll give you the names of those who are going. We want to move swiftly. We'd like the advance company to be on the road by three p.m."

As the various captains started moving over toward where the other members of the Twelve were, Heber motioned to Orson Pratt to join him and then came over to the Steed wagon. "Peter?"

"Yes?"

"A matter of some debate in our council was whether to send you on with Brother Orson here. After some discussion we decided against it."

"Oh?" He hadn't expected that.

"We've already taken Nathan back with us. You have two women and four children. That's a lot of responsibility to put on Derek alone. We're going to send Brother Crow and his wife and children ahead so that not all the families are in one company. That means we think you need to stay with Derek."

"All right."

"What we'd like you to do is tell Elder Pratt all that you can about where that trail takes off to the south. Can you remember it that well?"

"I remember it as if it were yesterday," Peter said softly. "Yes, I can tell you exactly where to look."

There was no morning roll call and no guards mounted at Pueblo de Los Angeles on the sixteenth day of July, 1847. That alone said much about the fact that this was going to be a very unusual day. Along with the others, Private Josh Steed spent the day quietly in his tent, cleaning his weapon, polishing his boots (newly issued since they had arrived at Los Angeles), and collecting his gear.

At half past two, word circulated that they were to assemble in half an hour. When the courier had gone, Josh turned to Sergeant Luther T. Tuttle. "Do you think that will be it?"

Tuttle shrugged and got up off his cot. "Could be. This is the day, and the day is rapidly coming to an end."

They lined up by companies. Company A took the front position. Company B, which had arrived from San Diego just the day before, started about three paces behind them. Then came Companies C, D, and E. They lined up in silence, no one speaking, everyone watching carefully. When all were finally in place, Lieutenant Andrew J. Smith stalked out of the nearest barracks. Lieutenant Smith was now an officer with General Kearny's First Dragoons, but this was the same Lieutenant Smith who had taken over command of the battalion back on the Santa Fe Trail after Colonel James Allen had died. This was the same Lieutenant Smith who had worked in harmony with Doctor George Sanderson—"Doctor Death"—and wreaked so much havoc on the men with his martinet ways and his raging tempers. He despised the Mormons and was equally despised by them. The men made no secret of the fact that they considered Smith's replacement by Colonel Cooke a direct answer to prayers.

The lieutenant looked a little ragged. The spit-and-polish West Pointer who had ridden out from Fort Leavenworth to take command was gone. The shoulders of his uniform were dusty, his boots were scuffed, his sword handle tarnished. He stalked out of the officers' barracks and approached the assembled men. Without even a pause to formally acknowledge their presence, he started walking down the first row of them, scanning their faces. All were at attention and no one looked at him. Down the first row, up the second, down the third, up the fourth. He walked slowly, eyes glittering with malice, hands clasped firmly behind his back.

When he finished he walked just as slowly back to the front of Company A. For a moment Josh thought he was going to turn and walk away without uttering a single word, but then his head lifted. In a low voice he said, "You are discharged." Then he spun on his heel and went back to his barracks.

For a moment the men just looked at each other. Finally Captain Hunt, the senior Mormon officer, stepped out of ranks. He looked a little confused.

"Isn't anyone from the regular army going to speak to us, Cap'n?" someone called out.

"Evidently not. I guess we are now officially discharged."

For some it seemed anticlimactic, but Josh didn't care. As the companies began to fall out of line, he reached up and took off his hat. "*Ya-hoo!*" he shouted, and sent his hat sailing through the air. That did it. For the next two or three minutes, the three hundred seventeen remaining men of the Mormon Battalion went wild, cheering, laughing, clapping one another on the shoulders, and tossing their hats in the air. When they finally subsided, they picked up their equipment, went to the armory, and received their mustering out supply of twenty-one rounds of ammunition. Then, carrying the gear that was theirs to keep, they left the fort and marched to a new campsite three and a half miles up the San Pedro River. There they began making plans for heading east to find the rest of the Latter-day Saints.

No one at that moment knew where Brigham Young and the

rest of the Mormons were, but that was all right. The members of the battalion were now free to go and find out for themselves.

As the wagons reached the point where Echo Canyon suddenly opened up on the Weber River, Peter stopped and looked back. The huge massifs of red stone were lined up like gigantic sentinels guarding the way.

Kathryn, riding on the wagon seat beside Derek, saw Peter turn and turned back as well. "It's beautiful, isn't it?"

"Yes," he murmured. "Spectacular." Actually, he wasn't thinking about the canyon very much; rather, he was remembering the day that he had taught Virginia and James Reed, Jr., and some of the Donner children how to hear their own echo. And with that, a sudden sadness had swept over him. Some of those Donner children were now dead.

"I loved it how the thunder boomed in the canyon this morning," Christopher said, beaming happily as he too looked back. "It made me jump, but I liked it."

Peter smiled, pleased that another child was here to remind him of better days. "I thought it was wonderful, too, Christopher," he said. "Though the horses and the oxen don't like it much."

"Nathan! Peter!"

They turned. Elder Kimball was on his horse near the last few wagons where President Young was riding. Once the advance company had gone ahead under the direction of Elder Orson Pratt, the rest of them had waited two more days for Brigham to get well enough to move on. Finally he rejoined the main company, but the sick group traveled at the rear of the train so as to let the others soften the road as much as possible. The Steeds had dropped back so that Nathan could be there to help whenever he was needed.

"Coming," Nathan called. He and Peter both turned and trotted back as Elder Kimball hollered at others as well.

Once they were assembled, he jumped right in. "Brethren, President Young is still not doing well. He had a bad night last night and this road is just pounding him to pieces. I don't think he can endure traveling any farther. We've scouted out a suitable campsite about a mile ahead on the Weber. Instead of nooning here, we'll go on that far, then stop and remain there for the Sabbath tomorrow."

Heber was very sober. "This afternoon the Twelve and a few others are going to hold a special prayer for President Young and the others who are sick. We would appreciate it if all of you would unite your hearts in prayer in their behalf as well."

"Any further word from the advance company?" Peter asked.

Elder Kimball shook his head. "Not since yesterday. We assume they're moving forward with all dispatch."

Peter nodded. At least Elder Pratt's group had found the road the Donner Party had taken the year before. Porter Rockwell had ridden into camp the previous day while they were nooning to report that while the road was faint and mostly overgrown again, they had definitely found it.

"Brethren," Heber concluded, "soon we enter the mountains again. The road will be very rough. The advance company is trying to prepare it as much as possible, but if President Young doesn't get better, there is no way that we can start again. You can imagine how that makes him feel, so brethren, we need your faith and prayers in his behalf."

When Nathan stepped out of his tent the next morning, Sunday, the first thought he had was that it had snowed. Snow on the eighteenth of July? With a closer look, however, he saw that it had just been a heavy frost that left the ground white. But even then it brought Jim Bridger to his mind. Perhaps the mountain man was right. Maybe there was frost every month of the year in these mountain valleys.

He saw movement out of the corner of his eye and turned his head. It was Heber C. Kimball and Willard Richards walking slowly along, deep in conversation. Nathan walked over to join them. "How's President Young this morning?" he asked.

Willard Richards shook his head slowly. "Better, but still very ill."

Heber nodded in confirmation. "We're calling a meeting for ten a.m. this morning. Nathan, I'd like to build a small, temporary bowery in which to meet. Could you and Derek and Peter give me a hand?"

"Of course. I'll get them right now."

It turned out to be surprisingly effective. They picked a place opposite the wagons in a patch of shrubbery, then cut off the tops of the small trees and stuck them into the ground to form an enclosure that was shady and cool. With forty-three of their number ahead with the advance group, the rest of them fit comfortably into the enclosure. Heber opened the meeting with prayer, then immediately got to their purpose for meeting.

"Brethren and sisters, as you well know, sickness has invaded our camp, and several of our numbers are suffering. The Lord has not seen fit to spare our President from this affliction, and he suffers as greatly as any of the rest of us. This is the Sabbath day. I would like to suggest that instead of scattering off as you do on a normal day—some hunting, some fishing, and some climbing the mountains in exploration—we stay in camp in an attitude of fasting and prayer. I should like to propose that we meet together and exhort one another to faithfulness, asking the Lord to turn away the sickness which has come upon us, and especially that he would heal our beloved President Young."

He stopped and looked around. Many were nodding their assent at that recommendation.

"Next," he continued, "in consultation with the President, we would like to propose that tomorrow the whole camp move on. I doubt that President Young will be well enough to travel by then, so we will keep eight or ten wagons back with enough men to help care for our sick. The rest of you are to proceed over the mountains, following the trail of our brethren who have gone ahead. It shouldn't be that far to the Salt Lake Valley. When you find a suitable place there, you will immediately set to work to plant potatoes, turnips, buckwheat, and other crops which will mature quickly. The season is well advanced and there is little time to spare. We cannot delay further or we will have no food to see us through the winter."

Again he stopped and looked around. "All in favor of that proposal?" he asked after a moment. Every hand immediately rose.

"Good. We will meet again at two p.m. and will administer the sacrament to the camp. In the meantime, let us turn our hearts to God and petition him in our behalf."

Chapter Notes

The details of the Mormon Battalion's discharge by their old nemesis, Lieutenant Smith, are found in *MB*, pp. 159–60.

Pudding Rocks—or the Needles, as they are now called—are near the present-day Utah-Wyoming border just a few miles south of I-80. It was near there that President Young contracted mountain fever and became too ill to move on. There is no way to know for sure what disease or illness this was, but many speculate that it was what is now called Colorado Tick Fever, a disease transmitted by ticks, which are common in the sage- and oak-covered mountains of Wyoming and Utah (see Jay A. Aldous and Paul S. Nicholes, "What Is Mountain Fever?" *Overland Journal* 15 [Spring 1997]: 18–23).

When Brigham Young continued to be too sick to travel, the main company stopped a short distance outside the mouth of Echo Canyon, a little bit above, or east, of the present site of Henefer. By then the advance company was deep into the Wasatch Mountains, following the trail cut by the Donners the year before. On Saturday, 17 July, members of the Twelve and a few other leaders went to a site about two miles from camp and climbed a hill where they could find privacy in order to pray. Near that spot were strange formations of rocks rising out of an otherwise smooth hillside. Now called Witches Rocks, these formations are still easily seen as one travels along I-84, just east of the town of Henefer.

It is interesting to note that once the prayer was completed, as the brethren started down again a bit of the boy in each of them took over. William Clayton reports: "On returning they rolled down many large rocks from the top of the mountain to witness the velocity of their descent, etc. Some would roll over half a mile and frequently break to pieces."

Chapter Forty-Six

Though Brigham Young had greatly improved in health when the company awakened on Monday morning, it was decided that fifteen wagons would come along more slowly with the sick and that the rest would forge ahead. From somewhere up front, the bugle sounded the order to move out. The lead teamster shouted to his horses and there was the creak of wood and the rattle of wheels on stone. The main camp was on its way.

Kathryn, Peter, Rebecca, and Derek were standing beside Nathan. His wagon stood back with the others that wouldn't be moving this morning. At the sound of the bugle, Nathan nodded. "You'd better mount up. You're on your way."

Rebecca gave her brother a kiss on the cheek. "You shouldn't be too far behind us."

"A day or two at most," he agreed.

"We'll watch for you," Derek said, sticking out his hand.

Nathan grinned. "Actually, I'm getting the better part of the deal. You and Peter are going to become road-gang workers these next few days."

The main company forded the Weber River on the morning of July nineteenth, then after a mile or so turned south toward the mountains, following the road the Donner-Reed group had made the year before. The Steeds' two wagons were near the rear of the column, and as they approached the turn, they saw that Erastus Snow was there giving directions.

"Did you find the way over Reed's Pass?" Peter asked as they came abreast of him.

"We did," Brother Snow responded, "though we have renamed it Pratt's Pass, in honor of Elder Pratt." He blew out his breath. "I can't believe you made that road with only thirty or so laboring men in your company."

Peter nodded grimly. "Neither can I."

"Well, what you did is a great blessing to us. Even though much of the trail has grown over again, your work is going to save us days of time."

"Good."

"Well," Brother Snow said, reining his horse around, "Elder Richards has given me a letter to carry to Elder Pratt, so I shall leave you now. We'll see you in camp." And with that, he galloped forward to catch up with the lead wagon.

Derek and Peter left Rebecca and Kathryn to drive the team and went ahead to clear the road. They were now climbing what the advance company had named Big Mountain. They were in a heavy forest of fir, aspen, balsam, and cottonwood, but it was not as terrible as what they had come through the last two days since leaving the Weber River. Here at least they were out of the thickets of willows and gooseberry and brambles. And here they didn't have to cross the creek eleven times in one day, as they had done yesterday.

The advance company had improved the road greatly, but it still needed lots of work. With the greater manpower they had, the main company took the work further. They pried big rocks out of the way, pulled up stumps, and leveled out the roughest places. They moved slowly up the long hillside—Big Mountain was an appropriate name—but what they left behind them was a steep but decent road for the wagons to follow.

Shortly after midday, up ahead of them there was a sudden cry. They stopped and looked forward. A man appeared out of the trees waving his arms. "Come and look!" he yelled.

Leaving their picks and shovels, the two dozen men went forward. The steepness of the slope began to level off. Then suddenly they were out of the trees in a large space where there were no trees. They were not on the very top of the mountain—that was another three or four hundred feet above and behind them—but they had come around the shoulder of the hill onto a bald knob. Ahead, the mountain dropped off steeply again. But that was not what caught their eyes. They had ascended hills before, only to see row after row of additional mountains stretching out ahead of them. There were still plenty of mountains to see from this vantage point, but directly ahead of them to the southwest, there was a V-shaped opening in the mountain wall. And there, hazy in the heat of summer, they could see a broad, flat valley and a treeless plain.

"It's the Valley!" Peter cried, gripping Derek's elbow. He remembered with perfect clarity when the Donners had reached this same spot the year before. Joy had infused their company as well, but for different reasons. Peter had been stirred with excitement that day too, but now? To his utter surprise, his throat suddenly tightened and there was a burning in his eyes. The Donner Party had been excited because it meant they were almost through with the endless nightmare of the Wasatch Mountains. But for the Saints it meant far more. There, clearly seen directly ahead of them, was their stopping place. After almost two years and fourteen hundred miles of exile, they were now within sight of their final destination. "It's the Valley, Derek," he said again, his voice strained.

Derek turned and looked into his eyes deeply, and Peter saw that his eyes were glistening too. Derek swallowed hard, then could only nod.

"It's home," Peter whispered. "We're almost home."

"Let's go get Rebecca and Kathryn," Derek finally managed. "I want them to see this."

Derek raced back down the road and found their wagon about two-thirds of the way up Big Mountain. Without giving an explanation, he climbed up and took the reins from Rebecca, then urged the horses forward at a faster pace.

As they approached the end of the trees, Derek turned and parted the wagon flap. "Kathryn? You boys? This is something you'll want to see."

In a moment, the three of them were behind him, looking over his and Rebecca's shoulders. As they came out onto the bald knob where the other wagons were stopped, Derek looked for Peter but couldn't see him in the crowd of people that lined the edge of the drop-off. Seeing that their view was blocked, he swung the wagon around to the left and pulled into a spot where no one else was standing.

"Oh, it's beautiful!" Rebecca blurted when she saw the panorama that lay before them. Then suddenly she stiffened. Her eyes had lifted from the steep canyon below them, lifted higher than the next series of hills, and stopped on the V-shaped cut in the hills where there were no more mountains to be seen. She leaned forward, peering intently, not sure that she was seeing right. Behind him, Derek felt Kathryn clutch at his shoulder.

"Is that . . . ?" Rebecca turned. "Is that what I think it is?" she whispered.

He nodded. "Yes. You are looking at the Valley of the Great Salt Lake."

He turned to see if Kathryn was looking at the right place. She was, and tears were streaming down her cheeks. Suddenly Peter's words seemed like the only appropriate thing to say at this moment. "It's home," he said softly. "We're almost home."

Going down the west side of Big Mountain proved to be far more difficult and dangerous than coming up the east side. The slope was almost at a forty-five degree angle, and they had to lock the wheels and chain up the oxen and horses to the backs of the wagons. Once down, they were back into thick underbrush along the creek beds.

They moved on another four and a half miles from Big Mountain before they came out into a beautiful, gentle valley. Here they found a spring with wonderfully cold water and plenty of grass for their animals. By then their teams had been in the harness for almost ten hours and were clearly tiring. They stopped to rest, but the excitement of knowing their goal was now in reach was too strong to resist. At the spring the road turned sharply to the right, or west, and went almost straight up another ridge. It wasn't even half the challenge of Big Mountain, but with spent teams it would be challenge enough. They dubbed it Little Mountain, probably more out of sheer optimism than good sense, and made their decision. Exhausted, filthy, blistered, and battered, the majority of the camp voted to press on, at least to the top of Little Mountain.

It took them almost an hour and a half to cover half a mile. They rested their animals every seventy-five to a hundred yards and double teamed where they had to. One by one they reached the top and fell out of line in an exhausted stupor.

Then a cry went up. One of the men had walked over to where Little Mountain dropped into another canyon. Suddenly he started shouting. "There they are!"

The men raced over. For a moment they weren't sure they were seeing correctly. But the white tops of wagons in the bottom of the canyon amid the trees were unmistakable. Then

Elder George A. Smith confirmed it. "It's the advance company," he said.

And with that, the decision was made. They would push on one more time.

Actually, the main camp stopped short of where the advance camp was. The two companies were quite large, and with all of their stock, they needed separate grazing room for them. Elder Smith called for the main company to stop about a mile upstream from the advance group, then sent word ahead to let the others know that they were there.

It was just after seven p.m. when they finally called a halt and began to unhitch their teams. They had come fourteen miles, and it had taken them thirteen grueling hours. It was the kind of day that no company could repeat very often without destroying both men and animals, and the weariness lay heavily on the camp. But there was also a euphoric joy that left the camp buzzing with excitement. Tomorrow they would enter the Valley. Of that there was no doubt. They were no more than three or four miles from the canyon's mouth.

Just after getting their fires started, Colonel Stephen Markham, captain of the guards for the Pioneer Company, rode down the canyon and into their camp. He had stayed behind with the wagons bringing along President Young and the rest of the sick, so his appearance brought a quick response from the camp. Everyone moved to the lead wagons, where the members of the Twelve were camped, to hear what he had to say.

Though they had started supper, Rebecca and Kathryn set the kettles off the fire, got Leah and Nicole, and went along with Derek and Peter to hear the report on their President. When they got there, Elder Willard Richards was conversing quietly with Brother Markham. The Apostle kept looking up as the people arrived, but waited until all in the camp had assembled before he spoke. "Brother Markham, can you give us a report on President Young's health?"

"He's doing better but is still having a difficult time," Markham reported. "The roads are so rough that he can't stand a full day's travel. The problem is, we have developed new cases of sickness, and that is slowing us down as well."

"How far behind us are you?" Elder Benson wanted to know.

"We laid over on East Canyon Creek today in consequence of the sick. So we're probably about two days behind you now. Maybe a little more. With a limited number of men, we're making a little slower time than you are."

"But Brother Brigham is better?" Elder George A. Smith spoke up.

"Yes. He is still weak, but the prayers have helped him a great deal. I think—"

Suddenly there was a shout from behind them. They all turned to see two riders coming up the canyon from the advance camp. Elder Richards squinted for a moment, then grunted in satisfaction. "It's Elder Pratt and Brother Snow."

They all turned and watched as the two men rode up and dismounted. Elder Pratt strode forward and warmly embraced his fellow Apostles, then turned to Brother Markham and asked for a report. When it was finished he nodded in satisfaction. Then it was as though his face lit up. He leaned forward, almost breathless now. "We entered the Valley today."

"You did?" several exclaimed.

"Yes." It came out in pure exultation.

"It was glorious," Brother Snow said, clearly as excited as his companion.

"I rode ahead this morning to scout the road," Elder Pratt went on. "I came up and over Little Mountain and down here into Last Creek Canyon."

"*Last* Creek?" Markham cut in. "Oh, I like the sound of that."

"Yes, that's what we call it. Our company was moving very slowly, clearing and fixing the road. Then Erastus arrived with your letter, Elder Richards, telling us to find a place for planting crops. So the two of us decided to ride ahead and do some scouting."

"My horse was exhausted," Brother Snow broke in, "so we rode double on Elder Pratt's."

Elder Pratt, his face flushed from the excitement that was on him, continued. "We rode to the mouth of the canyon and found the way blocked with trees and boulders. We had to go up and over a very steep ridge."

"Yes," Peter cried. "That's the way we went last year and nearly ruined our teams."

"We saw that," Elder Pratt noted, sobered suddenly. "We could scarcely believe that teams could negotiate that hill. We think there is a better way, but I'll come to that in a minute. When we reached the top of the ridge, there, to our amazement, the whole valley lay before us."

Now he looked away and his mouth began to tremble a little. He half closed his eyes, remembering. "Brethren and sisters," he finally went on, his voice ringing like the sound of a clarion, "the sight was overwhelming. Can you imagine what we felt? After our being shut up in these mountains for so many days, there lay the whole Salt Lake Valley before us. It was astonishing." He looked at Erastus Snow, who was nodding. "We could not refrain from giving a shout of joy the moment this grand and lovely scene presented itself to our view."

"Only four and a half miles more?" someone from behind Peter said in awe.

"Yes," Elder Pratt said fiercely. "Tomorrow we shall all be in the Valley."

"Even though we had only one horse between us," Brother Snow said, "we made about a twelve-mile circuit of the Valley before returning to camp a short time ago. We found a place where we think it will be propitious to plow and plant our crops. There is a creek there. The soil is very dry and hard, but with water we think it will be rich and productive."

"Wonderful," Elder Richards said. He looked at Orson. "And what of this other route of which you spoke?"

"Ah, yes," Elder Pratt answered. "Tomorrow we should like to explore a little further, but instead of taking our teams up and over that ridge, we think that with a little work we can cut through along the creek bed."

"Yes," Peter said beneath his breath. "Now, there's someone who's using his head."

Beside him, Rebecca turned to Kathryn. Her eyes were shining with excitement. "Tomorrow, Kathryn," she said softly. "We'll be in the Valley tomorrow."

Peter removed his hat and took out a bandanna from his pocket and wiped his brow. He leaned on his shovel, looking back on their work, shaking his head. A year ago he had argued to have the Donners and Mr. Reed try to build a road down the creek bed to the canyon's mouth, as the Pioneer Company was doing now. He had failed, and they had instead gone up and over the precipitous ridge now behind where he stood. What a difference having a full company of men made! If only— He caught himself. It was easy to wish now, but it made no difference. What was done was done.

He heard the rattle of wheels and the sounds of wagons approaching. Turning, he saw the lead wagon appear around the bend, coming steadily down the new road they had just completed. Cheered at the sight, he looked at Derek. "Looks like we're done here. Let's go find Kathryn and Rebecca."

When they saw the two women bringing along their wagon, Derek and Peter walked to it, put their shovels in the racks on the side of the wagon box, then fell in alongside. Kathryn hardly noticed them. Her eyes were large and luminous with excitement. She watched the road ahead intently. As they started up again, she turned to Peter. "How much farther until we're out of the canyon?"

"Just right around that next bend."

Christopher's head popped out of the opening in the wagon cover. "Are we there, Papa?"

"Not quite, son. But close."

As they rounded the bend and the trees gave way to open

land, Kathryn suddenly grabbed Rebecca's arm. "Rebecca, stop the wagon."

Rebecca reined in. "What?"

"Peter, come help me."

Peter trotted over. "What's the matter?"

"Help me down, please." Then she turned. "Christopher, will you hand me my crutches please?"

He ducked back in the wagon and in a moment returned with her crutches. Kathryn handed them to Peter, then climbed down with his help. He looked puzzled. Derek, who had been walking ahead watching for rough spots, came back as well. "What's wrong?"

Kathryn just shook her head, put the crutches under her arms, then started forward, maneuvering carefully over the rocky road they had just cut. She turned her head, grinning at Peter. "I don't want to ride into the Valley, Peter. We've come a thousand miles and I want to walk this last little way on my own two feet."

At that, Rebecca tossed the reins to Derek. "Children. Come out of the wagon now. Leave the babies. Kathryn's right. We are going to walk into this valley."

Without anyone telling them to do so, the company ground to a halt as they came out of the canyon and up the small rise that took them up about fifty feet or so above the creek bed. One by one they dismounted and walked forward to where the brush gave way to an open view of the valley. Peter twice suggested that Kathryn and Rebecca should get back in the wagon and ride up that hill once they had made their symbolic entry on foot, but neither would hear of it. As they reached the top and stopped the wagons, Peter climbed in the back and got Nicole. She stretched and her eyes fluttered for a moment, but then, as Peter cradled her in his arms, rocking her back and forth, she went back to sleep. Derek and Rebecca moved forward with their children. "I'm so excited," Kathryn said as they approached the others.

Peter nodded, surprised at the emotions he was suddenly feeling. They were once again as intense as what he had felt at the top of Big Mountain.

"It's huge," Howard Egan was saying as they came up with the rest of the group. "It must be twenty-five or thirty miles long."

"And fifteen or so wide," Robert Crow said in awe. "There's no question about whether it's big enough to hold all of us."

Beside him, his wife, Elizabeth, had a look of dismay. "But there are no trees."

Kathryn had to nod at that. After Nauvoo and the vast forests of the East, this looked like desolation itself. There were a few ribbons of green meandering down from the mountains to what looked like a river that ran north and south the length of the valley, but other than that, it was one vast field of sagebrush, dry grass, and the occasional low-growing cactus plant whose needle-like leaves could pierce a person's shoe.

"Maybe we should go on to California."

Kathryn turned, not sure who had said it. One of the women or older girls of the Crow group probably.

"No!" It came out sharply, and Kathryn turned back the other way. William Clayton stepped forward. "Look!" he commanded. "Look along the creeks. See those large green patches? That must be where the water has spread out some. Look at how rich they are. The soil isn't barren. It just needs water."

Howard Egan had a hand up, counting methodically, moving his arm from north to south. "Seven, eight." He turned. "There must be a dozen or more streams coming down from the mountains. We can easily turn them onto the soil. See how gently the land slopes? The water can be sent about anywhere."

"It is so big!" Christopher said to his mother.

She nodded, still a little overwhelmed at the vastness herself—that and the sheer emptiness.

"There's only one objection," William Clayton came back in, "and that is lack of rain. But God can send moisture in season if we are faithful."

Another woman was pointing to the north. "The lake is so beautiful. How can the water be undrinkable?"

Peter could answer that one. "Because there is no outlet. That's what we were told. And I can testify that it is so briny that one swallow can almost cause strangulation." He shook his head. "There won't be any using of that water for our purposes."

Rebecca had been silent through all of this. Now she looked at her brother-in-law. "Peter, what about California? Is it this barren?"

He reached out and put his arm around Kathryn's waist, sensing that she was now experiencing some misgivings too. "No. It is rich and verdant and has a pleasant climate." He took a breath. "And is rapidly filling up with Gentiles."

Kathryn looked at him, not sure that that was what she wanted to hear. They were all reeling a little from the shock of seeing how totally empty and barren the Valley was. As they had crossed the desert country that stretched from the last crossing of the North Platte to Fort Bridger, she had asked herself over and over, *What if this is what it's like where we're going?* But then they had entered the mountains, and things began to look more like home again, and her concerns had subsided. Now this lay before them.

Elders Orson Pratt and George A. Smith had stood back, letting the people react to the sight of their new home. Now Elder Pratt spoke. "I hope you all heard what Brother Ingalls said just now. That is why we are not going on to California. The Lord has led us here because here we shall not be disturbed by our enemies. Here we have a place that is totally unpopulated by others. Here we will at last be safe."

William Clayton spoke one last time. "Brethren and sisters, I must say that I am happily disappointed in the appearance of the Valley of the Salt Lake."

That brought a chuckle from several of the party.

"But I have no fears but that the Saints can live here and do well if we will do what's right."

"We can get timber from the mountains," Howard Egan

added eagerly. "And I'll bet there's coal up there somewhere too."

"There's only one question to ask," Elder Smith said with finality. "Is this the place where God wants us to stop?"

Orson Pratt spoke up, his voice filled with conviction. "President Young thinks it is, so until he says differently, we have work to do. I suggest we get back in our wagons and go find that spot that Brother Snow and I think will be the best place to put in our plows."

As the people turned and started back for their wagons, Kathryn didn't move. She let her eyes roam again across the whole length of the valley before them. Peter watched her closely. "Are you all right, Kathryn?"

She looked at him, and then slowly nodded. "Elder Smith is right. That *is* the only question." She glanced to the west once more, then managed a wan smile. "Will you plant me some trees, Peter?"

He laughed. "I will. Dozens of them."

Now her smile spread and filled her eyes as well. "Then we're home, Peter. And that's all that matters."

It was nearly sundown on the other side of Big Mountain, but Nathan could see none of it. The bulk of the mountain left their campsite in deep shadows. The sun had gone down behind Big Mountain more than half an hour before. Nathan stood beside the creek, absently swatting mosquitoes as he stared up at the massive slope before him. That slope would be their task tomorrow. The reports were encouraging. Though it looked daunting, the riders who had come back from the main party assured them that the soil was soft and would be an easier ride for the sick.

He heard footsteps and turned. Brother Wilford Woodruff was coming from upstream, his fishing rod in his hands. Nathan chuckled. At Fort Bridger, Elder Woodruff, who had brought some so-called "flies" from England and a special lightweight fishing rod, had gone out to try "fly fishing." Some of the men had found this highly amusing. Imagine, thinking you could get a fish to strike a cluster of hair wrapped around a hook floating on *top* of the water. But when he came back with more trout than all the rest of them together, everyone stopped laughing. Now every time they rested alongside a stream of any consequence, the Apostle went out to try his hand again.

"Any luck?" Nathan asked as he came up to join him.

Wilford rattled the creel he had over his shoulders and there was a soft thumping sound. "Of course," he grinned.

Nathan smiled, and then once again, without conscious thought, his eye was drawn to the mountain that towered over them.

Wilford watched him for a moment, then turned to survey the same scene. "So this is the last big one," he said quietly.

Nathan nodded. "From the top they say we can make it into the Valley in one day."

"Hardly seems real, does it?" the Apostle mused.

Again Nathan nodded. "I still find it hard to believe that in a day or two it will all be over."

There was a soft chuckle. "No," Elder Woodruff said, "in a day or two it will all be beginning."

"Private Steed?"

Josh turned around. "Yes, Sergeant?"

Luther Tuttle reached out and boxed his ears playfully. "Hey, boy! What are you doing answering to the title of private? You're not a private anymore and I'm not your sergeant. Do you hear me?"

"Sorry, Mr. Tuttle, sir."

"Don't call me sir," Tuttle started automatically. "I'm not an officer. I work for a living." It was the standard answer noncommissioned officers gave when young privates called them sir. But then he stopped, looking sheepish as he realized that he had just contradicted himself. "I guess you can call me sir if you'd like."

Josh laughed. They were like children. It had been one week since their release, but the euphoric mood was still on them.

"Captain Hunt has already left, you know."

Josh sobered. "Yes. I don't understand it. Why can't we all go together?"

"Because Captain Hunt is convinced that going up the coast by way of Monterey and San Francisco Bay will be faster and safer than going up the central valley."

"Do you think it will?"

"Well, it's longer, but El Camino Real is an established road. It links all of the Catholic missions, so it's well traveled and well maintained."

Josh gave him a severe frown. "That's not what I asked you."

He shrugged. "Hunt is going to Sutter's Fort. We're going to Sutter's Fort. We'll see which is the faster route when we get there."

"Is that what the army did to you?"

"What?"

"Make it so you can't give a man a straight answer?"

Tuttle laughed. "And is that what the army did to you?"

"What?"

"Made you such an insolent pup?"

"See, you did it again," Josh howled in protest. "You don't have a plain yes or no in you."

Just then the flap to their tent opened. It was Levi Hancock. "You two ready?"

"Yep," Tuttle sang out cheerfully. "Soon as I get this young pup housebroke."

Hancock laughed, knowing full well how these two bantered with each other. "Well, we're moving out in half an hour. Better break down your tent."

"Yes, sir," they both said in happy unison.

On the morning of July twenty-fourth, Nathan left his wagon for one of the other men to drive, borrowed a horse from

Brigham Young, then set out with Heber C. Kimball to scout ahead of the lead wagon, carefully scrutinizing the road for particularly rough spots so that they could warn the drivers to watch for them. There was great concern in the camp about the ability of the sick to hold up under another day of travel. After the previous day, those suffering from mountain fever, including President Young, were nearly exhausted. They had started out at six forty-five in the morning. Up and over Big Mountain they went. By the time they made the treacherous descent, they had to stop and rest for a couple of hours. Then they had pushed on. Like the ones who had come this way two days before, they were not content to stop at the logical campsites. When they reached the cold springs at the bottom of Little Mountain, they too made a decision. They hitched up their suspenders, spit on their hands, then went up and over the top of that last ridge. By that time, the sick could stand no more and they had to camp at the head of Last Canyon, six miles short of their destination.

It was a disappointment in a way. Messengers had brought back the word that the main party had entered the Valley two days before. Nathan sighed, and then shrugged. So it would be July twenty-fourth and not July twenty-second for him. What were two days in the grand scheme of things?

"There it is."

Nathan's head came up. He had not been paying attention and suddenly realized that they had come to the canyon's mouth and that the Valley lay before him. He reined in, stunned by the sudden openness.

"Whoa," Heber said softly to his horse, which seemed to have picked up the group's excitement. He looked at Nathan. "I'd say that's big enough."

At the sound of a wagon, they turned. Wilford Woodruff's light wagon was just emerging from the canyon. Nathan was a little surprised that he was that close behind them. Then he smiled. No, not really. In the back of Wilford Woodruff's wagon was a bed. And in that bed was President Brigham Young. It was he who was urging Elder Woodruff ahead with all speed, of that

Nathan was sure. Last night Brigham had wanted to ride his horse into the Valley, but over his protests the brethren had prevailed upon him to stay in his bed for at least one more day.

"It looks like they went that way," Heber said, pointing to a gentle ridge above them. The wagon tracks were clearly evident.

They turned and rode to the top, then stopped to wait for their President. In a moment, Elder Woodruff could be heard urging his team up the hill. Thus far, none of the other wagons had appeared behind him, suggesting again that President Young had urged Elder Woodruff to proceed with full haste.

As Elder Woodruff's wagon came up behind them, Nathan saw that someone had rolled up the canvas partway on both sides of the wagon, then tied it in place, allowing Brigham to see out either side. Now Nathan saw that Brother Brigham was up on one elbow, craning his neck to see better.

"I can't see that much, Brother Wilford," Brigham called out as they reached the spot where Brother Kimball and Nathan were waiting.

"Turn the carriage around, Wilford," Heber suggested.

Wilford nodded and swung the wagon around in a large circle. When he stopped, the side of the wagon faced to the northwest. Wanting to hear Brigham's reaction to what lay before them, Nathan nudged his horse closer. As the wagon stopped, both Elder Kimball and Elder Woodruff got down and moved to their companion. Reaching through the open canvas, they helped Brigham into a half-sitting position.

There was not a sound other than the stamping of horses and the soft jingling of the harnessing. For a long time, Brigham gazed out over the Valley. Nathan could not take his eyes from off the chief Apostle's face. He was wrapped in concentration. His eyes were open and yet they did not sweep back and forth to take in the width of the scene before them. It was as though he were seeing something directly before him, something of such wonder that nothing else could draw his attention.

It seemed to go on for several minutes. No one spoke or moved. Finally, Nathan saw Brigham's body relax somewhat. He sank down a little and turned to Elder Woodruff. There was a soft smile now and his eyes were filled with pleasure. "It is enough, Wilford. This is the right place. Drive on."

Chapter Notes

Orson Pratt and Erastus Snow were the first to enter the Salt Lake Valley on Wednesday, July twenty-first. The main company entered the Valley the next day about four p.m. Brigham Young did not enter until about midday on the twenty-fourth of July. Because it was his vision that had guided the Saints to this place, the twenty-fourth became the official day of entry.

While the conversation of the Saints on seeing the Valley is based on actual comments written later by those who were there, most of what is said here does not come directly from the journals. William Clayton's "happily disappointed" comment does come from his 22 July journal entry.

On the day Brigham Young entered the Salt Lake Valley, Wilford Woodruff wrote in his journal, "President Young expressed his full satisfaction in the Appearance of the valley as A resting place for the Saints & was Amply repayed for his Journey." It was in a conference much later that Elder Woodruff gave more details: "When we came out of the canyon into full view of the valley, I turned the side of my carriage around, open to the west, and President Young arose from his bed and took a survey of the country. While gazing on the scene before us, he was enwrapped in vision for several minutes. He had seen the valley before in vision, and upon this occasion he saw the future glory of Zion and of Israel, as they would be, planted in the valleys of these mountains. When the vision had passed, he said: 'It is enough. This is the right place, drive on.' " (Cited in B. H. Roberts, *A Comprehensive History of The Church of Jesus Christ of Latter-day Saints, Century I*, 6 vols. [Salt Lake City: The Church of Jesus Christ of Latter-day Saints, 1930], 3:224.)

It is an interesting coincidence that though they had no way of knowing it, the main body of the Mormon Battalion left Pueblo de Los Angeles on the twenty-third of July at the very time when the Saints had finally reached the Salt Lake Valley.

Today, Big Mountain and Little Mountain still carry the same names. What the Pioneers called "Last Canyon" is now Emigration Canyon. The famous This Is the Place Monument stands not far from the mouth of that canyon. Those interested in following this portion of the Mormon Trail can find interpretive signs or historical markers at Echo Canyon (beside the westbound rest stop on I-80), Henefer, Hogsback Summit (the current name for Pratt's Pass or Reed's Pass), Mormon Flats (at the eastern base of Big Mountain), on the top of Big Mountain, at the summit of Little Mountain, and at the site of the last camp in Emigration Canyon. There is also a small monument just a short distance up Emigration Canyon noting what has come to be called Donner Hill.

The Donners took approximately sixteen days to cut a road from Henefer into the Salt Lake Valley. The next year the Saints would cover the same distance in four days. Thus, though their journey ended in tragedy, the Donner Party proved to be a great blessing to the Pioneer Company.

Chapter Forty-Seven

As they dismounted at the base of the rounded hill, Nathan watched President Young carefully. He climbed gingerly down from Elder Woodruff's wagon, looking pale and tired. Nathan saw his hands trembling a little as he held on to the tail-gate of the wagon. Nathan and Elder Woodruff exchanged looks, but the Apostle gave a slight shake of his head and Nathan decided it was not his place to say anything. Brigham stood there for a moment, as though collecting his strength, and then he looked up.

Nathan let his eyes follow. They had ridden north about a mile and a half from the encampment on City Creek to where the foothills started rising above the north end of the Valley. This one rounded peak—or better, this knob, for that was what it was—stood apart from the others. It reminded Nathan of the head of a Franciscan monk with his bald pate and a ring of hair around his ears. In this case, the baldness was the rounded top of the peak itself. The hair—really only on one side—was an outcropping of rocks on the west side of the hill.

"I'd like to go to the top."

Several heads jerked around. "President," Heber C. Kimball said, "are you sure you are strong enough to climb?"

"Yes, yes," he said impatiently, waving his hand. "I'm forty-six, brethren, not eighty-six. Don't wait for me. You go on up and I'll get there as soon as these old knees will carry me."

Heber motioned for the others to go. "I'll come up with him. You go on."

From the top the view was spectacular. Directly west, like an azure mirror placed on a brown-gray tabletop, the Great Salt Lake stretched northward as far as the eye could see. Its south end was directly west of them, but in the other direction they could not see where it ended. To the south, the great emptiness of the Valley lay before them. The only thing in the whole expanse that drew the eye was the encampment. There the cluster of wagons was lined up along the first dark squares of the plowed fields. Nathan squinted a little, seeing the tiny figures of horses and men starting on a new plot, and wondered if one of them was Derek or Peter.

The main company had entered the Valley on Thursday. By the time Brigham Young's group came in about midday on Saturday, they had more than five acres plowed and planted in potatoes, and had what they were calling City Creek dammed and turned into furrows to water the fields.

They had rested yesterday and joined in worship services, which primarily were services of thanksgiving. Today, Monday, the plowing was under way again, with sowers bringing in the other crops—oats, buckwheat, beans, anything that would grow rapidly—right behind them.

Nathan turned and walked to the north side of the knob and looked down. Brigham Young was coming slowly, following the trail the others had made, Heber Kimball on one arm, Willard Richards on the other. Brigham was using Elder Richards's walking stick, and he leaned on it heavily as they moved along. Nathan watched until they reached the top; then, along with the other men, he moved over to join those who were waiting.

Brigham took almost five minutes to catch his breath, standing on the edge of the hill on the south side, gazing out across the Valley. The others in the exploration party said nothing but just stood back and waited.

Finally, their President turned and came back to join them. "Brethren, gather in close. There are some things I would like to say before we continue on with our task today."

The men edged in closer, anxious to hear. He motioned to Heber, who, seeming to know what Brigham was after, withdrew a Bible from the bag he had carried up the hill. He handed it to the senior Apostle. Brigham immediately began leafing through the book until he found the place he was looking for. He closed the book with his finger in it and turned back to the men.

"Centuries before the birth of Christ, the prophet Isaiah foretold great things which were to come on the earth in the latter days. Some of those things are now found in the Book of Mormon. Other things Isaiah said were quoted by the angel Moroni when he came that first night to the Prophet Joseph Smith back in September of eighteen twenty-three. Let me read one of the things Moroni quoted from Isaiah. This is in chapter eleven." He opened the book and began to read in a loud voice. " 'And it shall come to pass in that day, that the Lord shall set his hand again the second time to recover the remnant of his people, which shall be left. . . . And he shall set up an ensign for the nations, and shall assemble the outcasts of Israel, and gather together the dispersed of Judah from the four corners of the earth.' "

He closed the book again and looked from face to face. He still looked pale, but his voice was strong and filled with power. "Brethren, we have come to our new gathering place, and in fulfillment of Isaiah's words, uttered so long ago, I would here like to raise an ensign to the nations. Brother Heber."

To Nathan's surprise, Heber already had a large handkerchief out of his pocket. He began to tie it to one end of Willard Richards's walking stick. When he was done, he held it up high and waved it back and forth in the air.

"There is our ensign, brethren," Brigham continued, standing straight, his eyes fired with new energy. "It is the banner which signals to all the nations of the earth to come home to their God. From this place we issue the call for all to gather to the house of Israel."

The only sound now in the afternoon air was the snapping of the cloth as the makeshift banner was caught by the hot wind.

"Brethren," Brigham went on after several moments, "I feel to share with you an experience. After the death of Joseph Smith, when it seemed as if every trouble and calamity had come upon the Saints, we of the Twelve sought the Lord to know what we should do, and where we should lead the people for safety. I knew of Joseph's vision of the Rocky Mountains. As you know, he was preparing an expedition to go to the Rocky Mountains when he was called back to Nauvoo and then went on to Carthage to give his life. But I did not know what we should do once he was killed. Were we to continue to plan to go west?

"While I and others of the Twelve were fasting and praying daily on this subject, one night I had a vision of Joseph Smith. He showed me a mountain, a peak. While I gazed upon it in vision, an ensign fell upon that peak. Even as I watched, Joseph said to me, 'Build under the point where the colors fall and you will prosper and have peace.' "

Nathan felt as if his whole body were tingling. And he had thought they came up here simply to get a grand overview of the Valley.

"We had no professional pilot or guide. Many wanted to show us the way, but we did not engage them, even though none among us had ever been in this country or knew anything about it. However, as I have said on many occasions when you have asked me where we were going, 'I shall know it when I see it.' Well, brethren, two days ago I reached this valley. I had Elder Woodruff turn his carriage so I could see better. And do you know what I was looking for?"

He watched them as he saw comprehension dawn. "Yes, my brethren, I was looking for this very peak. This is what I saw in vision that night, and the moment I saw it day before yesterday I *knew* that this was the right place. That is why I wanted to come here today."

There was a faint smile as he saw the reaction of his brethren. Like Nathan, they had had no idea what his intentions had been.

"This is Ensign Peak, brethren," Brigham said softly. "Now, go where you will. Send out your exploring parties to the east and west, to the north and south. You will always return and say this is the best spot to build our city, just as Brother Joseph showed me before we ever left Winter Quarters."

Matthew was sitting beneath the shade of a huge oak tree that spread its branches wide over the flatlands near the last crossing of the North Platte River. He was watching two wagons from one of the emigrant companies that had arrived the previous night. They were not at the ferry; they were directly in front of him, just approaching the main channel of the river. The North Platte was no longer a fearsome sight. Down to no more than twenty or thirty yards across now, it was no deterrent to these two families.

One man stepped out into the river with a pole about six feet long. He was probing to see how deep the water was. Halfway across he was still only up to his waist. He waved and yelled something to his partner. The second man climbed up into the lead wagon and picked up the reins to his two huge mules. The driver snapped the reins and the wagon started forward slowly.

Mules did not like water and were much more difficult to

control during a fording operation than either horses or oxen. But these were evidently well trained and went into the river with only minimal signs of agitation. Matthew stood, then stepped out from beneath the tree, wanting to see better. The water was deep enough that it reached the bottom of the wagon box, but the driver was experienced and headed the mules at an angle into the current so that the water didn't push directly on the wagon bed. In five minutes it was over. There was a shout of triumph as the second wagon started after the first.

Matthew nodded slowly, then turned and walked swiftly toward their camp. When he arrived, Thomas Grover and Appleton Harmon were standing beside the ferry, looking downriver. Matthew saw that they had watched what he had just watched. He didn't need to say anything.

"Appleton and I were just talking," Grover said. "I think we'll keep the ferry open for a few more days, then close it down."

Matthew nodded. It was time. In the first place, it was the twenty-eighth of July. The number of emigrants moving along the trail this late in the season was minimal. In the second place, it was clear that not many were going to be anxious to pay a dollar fifty cents for a ferry when they could ford the river without much danger.

Appleton Harmon turned to Matthew. "Well, we can decide all that in a day or two. Luke Johnson and I are headed back to Deer Creek to get some more coal for the forges. You interested in coming?"

Matthew nodded without hesitation. Life here was about to get very boring. "Sure. Let me get some things."

For Mary Ann, the camp at Deer Creek was one of the most pleasant places they had stopped along the entire trail. Their campsite was in a grove of tall, stately cottonwoods along the creek, not far from where it emptied into the North Platte. The trees provided deep shade, and there was plenty of grass for the animals in spite of all the other companies that preceded them. Several days before, the five guides sent east by Brigham Young had brought a letter giving details of the trail. One of the things William Clayton had noted about Deer Creek was that there was excellent fishing in the stream. Joshua, Solomon, and Carl had tested that bit of knowledge out and found it to be true. The whole family had feasted on fried trout for supper, a welcome change after hardtack, beans, and occasional antelope stew.

The children were off playing hide-and-seek among the trees. She could hear their calls and an occasional shriek as they tried to beat someone "home." Carl and Melissa had gone over to visit with the Wellesley family. That was good too. David Wellesley had brought his family across from England in time to arrive in Nauvoo after the main body of the Church had left. During the final days of Nauvoo, David and Carl had become acquainted. They had fought together in the Spartan Band and become good friends. It had been good for Carl that the Wellesleys had also ended up in the Daniel Spencer company.

The other thing Clayton had told them about was the coal bank to the south of their campsite a short distance. Always after fuel to fire the bellows, the blacksmith had announced he was going after some coal. Intrigued by the description of an open coal bank, Solomon and Joshua volunteered to help.

Mary Ann found that idea strange too and decided she would walk out there in the morning and see it for herself before they started out again. But for now she was content to just sit and enjoy the pleasant evening. The supper dishes were cleaned up, the tents were pitched, and there was really nothing else that needed doing. Jenny was reading stories to the children in preparation for bedtime. Lydia, Jessica, and Caroline had gone for a walk along the river. They had invited her, of course, but Mary Ann was finding that at nearly sixty-one, she did not have the endurance that she had once enjoyed. There was another half an hour before dark, and she would simply sit and enjoy it.

Jenny came out of the tent, combing out her hair and humming softly to herself.

"Asleep?" Mary Ann asked.

"Finally." Jenny came over and sat down beside her, still humming the song.

"Is that an Irish tune?" Mary Ann asked with a smile.

Jenny ducked her head. She had barely been aware of the fact that she was making any sound. "Yes. My mother used to sing it to us when we were small."

"I love it. Are there words?"

She shrugged. "If there are, I don't remember them."

"It's beautiful."

"It reminds me of Ireland, what little I can remember of it." She smiled with some sadness. "More important, it reminds me of my mother."

"She was a good woman, Jenny."

"I know." She looked away. "It also reminds me of Kathryn." She sighed. "I miss her so, Mother Steed."

"I do too. And Peter. It's funny, but I think of the four of you—Derek and Peter and you and Kathryn—as if you were my own children."

Jenny impulsively reached out and touched Mary Ann's hand. "And you seem as much like my mother as my own mother did." How she loved this good woman! So much of her had been passed on to her youngest son. That was partly why Matthew was so easy to love.

They fell silent, each lost in her own thoughts, neither knowing that the other was thinking of the same person that she was.

There was a noise and then they saw three figures coming toward them through the trees. Mary Ann looked up. "It's Joshua and Solomon." She looked more closely. The light was behind them and she couldn't make out their faces. Who was the third person?

Suddenly Jenny gasped and one hand flew to her mouth. That gait was something she would recognize anywhere.

The figure broke into a run, waving. "Jenny! Mother!"

"Oh!" It came out as though Mary Ann had been struck;

only it was an exclamation of pure joy, not pain. She rose to her feet, staring in total disbelief.

The hairbrush fell from Jenny's fingers as she jumped up and darted forward, running hard, her hair flying out behind her.

Mary Ann's hand shot out to steady herself. "Matthew?" she cried.

Jenny had reached him now and they were holding each other tightly. Joshua walked swiftly over to join his mother. She was on her feet now, but her knees felt weak. She gave Joshua an astonished look, as if to say, "Can this really be?"

"Can you believe it?" he laughed. "When we got to the coal bank, there he and two other brethren were, digging out coal like they'd been there forever." He laughed aloud. "I almost fell off my horse."

Matthew sat on a stool that was placed between his wife and his mother. Betsy Jo, at five, was too big to sit on his lap now, but she did so anyway, her arms around Matthew's neck. Emmeline, now two, sat on one knee. Jenny held his free hand. The rest of the family was gathered around him, beaming as they watched this favorite uncle and brother with his family.

"So Kathryn has a baby now?" Lydia said, shaking her head. She turned to Mary Ann. "Yet another grandchild for you."

Caroline smiled. "Did you ever think that if Will and Alice have a baby too, that will be Mother Steed's first *great*-grandchild?"

"That's right," Matthew said. "I hadn't thought about that."

Lydia's Emily came forward to stand as close to Matthew as she could. It was all she could do not to move in beside Betsy Jo and put her arm around her uncle. There was only twelve years' difference between her and Matthew, and he had been more like a brother to her and Josh when they were growing up than an uncle. She was nearly as happy to see him as Jenny and Grandma Steed were. "I'll bet they do have a baby," she said. "It's been almost two years since they were married."

Caroline looked suddenly sad. "And there's been no word of them?"

"No," Matthew answered. "Hopefully, when Peter got to California, he found them. But there's no word of Peter either yet."

Joshua was as sharply disappointed at the lack of news of their son as Caroline was. "Maybe Peter, Will, and Alice have already started back and will be in the Valley waiting for us."

"Well," Matthew answered, "knowing both Peter and Will, there'll be no stopping them once they learn where we are." Then Matthew noticed Lydia, who sat quietly through all this. "And Josh. The battalion has been discharged by now. They're on the way too, I'll bet."

Lydia smiled her thanks at him.

"Derek and Rebecca couldn't say enough good about your son, Lydia. You would have thought he was their own boy."

Mary Ann leaned forward, breaking in. "Do you know what I've been thinking these last few minutes?"

They all turned to her. "What, Grandma?" Rachel asked.

"Years and years ago—clear back when we were still in Far West—I had a dream. I remember it so vividly because it came at the darkest hour of our troubles in Missouri. I was walking through this great wilderness, a great open plain. It was beautiful but I was all alone. In the far distance there was a beautiful city, and somehow I knew that that was where I was going. Then one by one my family started to join me. It was wonderful. We were so happy. We sang and talked and laughed. We were all going toward the city together."

Jessica was nodding slowly, thoughtfully. "I remember that Father Steed was bothered by the fact that he wasn't with you."

"Yes," she admitted. "But I wasn't worried about it because I knew he was already in the city waiting for us." She straightened. "And then I awoke. I was puzzled by it all, but it left me with a great feeling of peace." She reached out and touched Matthew's arm. "Now the dream is coming true. One by one my family are coming together. When I saw you just now, I felt that same wonderful peace. That's what reminded me of the dream."

"Well," Jenny said, blushing furiously as she took her husband's hand. "Mother Steed has talked about reunions. And this has been glorious, Matthew. But there's one more we haven't told you about yet."

"What?" Matthew asked.

She took his hand and laid it on her stomach. "Matthew, I'd like you to meet the very newest of the Steed clan."

"Why didn't someone tell us that once we were out of the army we still had to keep on marching?"

Sergeant Luther Tuttle laughed. "Why? Would you have been tempted to reenlist?"

Josh removed his hat and wiped the sweat away from his eyes with his bare hand. "If they promised me that I didn't have to march anymore, I may have."

"You just got soft lying around Pueblo de Los Angeles."

Josh grunted something incomprehensible, put his hat back on, and moved ahead again. Maybe he had gotten soft down there, but in the over four weeks since they left Los Angeles, every ounce of softness had been wrung out of him. Four weeks and they were still more than a hundred miles from their destination. In the summer heat, once again as it had happened on so many occasions on their march to the Pacific, men began to fall by the wayside. Once again, the strongest would march on until they found water, then go back with full canteens to help their brethren. Once again they were wearing the boots off their feet. Once again their clothes were falling apart, unable to withstand the combination of pushing through heavy brush, fording rivers, the sun, the dust, pouring sweat, and sleeping fully dressed at night.

As they moved north and finally reached the foothills of the Sierra, water became more plentiful, but they still paid a frightful toll as they inched their way northward. They were now eight days north of the Kings River and moving steadily toward Sutter's Fort and the California Trail.

"Hold it for a minute."

The call from up front brought Josh's head up. Levi Hancock and Sergeant Daniel Tyler had their hands up in the air, motioning for the men to stop. Then, squinting against the brightness of the sun, Josh saw why. Two riders were coming in at a lope.

"Looks like Captain Averett," Tuttle said beside him.

Josh nodded. Captain Jeduthan Averett, like Josh, had been a private in Company D. But on their discharge, Levi Hancock had appointed him as a captain of one of the divisions and given him primary responsibility for scouting the way ahead. To see them coming on the run in the afternoon's heat was unusual, so the men crowded forward to see what was of such urgency.

Averett dismounted even before his horse came to a stop and trotted over to Levi Hancock. "Brother Hancock, you'll never believe what we just found."

"What?"

"A colony of Mormons."

"What?" several men exclaimed.

"Yes. About three miles ahead on the Stanislaus River. There are twenty families from the ship *Brooklyn*. Brother Sam Brannan sent them out here to start a colony called New Hope."

"The *Brooklyn?*" Josh called out, feeling a thrill shoot through him. "I have a cousin who came on the *Brooklyn*. Did you get to meet any of them?"

Averett turned. "We only met their leader, a man by the name of Thomas Stout. But they have invited us to stay with them tonight." He grinned broadly. "In addition to fresh fruit and vegetables, they have five washtubs where we can bathe."

"New Hope?" someone said with a laugh. "Are you sure it's not called New Heaven?"

Josh didn't even wait for the company to be shown where to make their camp. As soon as they reached the village, he sprinted ahead. The sixty or so people at New Hope had come out to meet the Mormon Battalion, lining the road, women and children waving their scarves and handkerchiefs, the men their hats. Racing up to the nearest man, Josh stuck out his hand in eager excitement. "Hello. My name is Josh Steed. I—"

"Brother Quartus Sparks, Brother Steed. We're so delighted to see you. We heard you might be coming this way."

"I have a cousin who came over with you on the ship. Will Steed and his wife, Alice."

"Oh yes, of course."

"Are they here?"

He shook his head. "No. They didn't come upriver with us." He turned to the woman beside him. "This is Sister Sparks, Brother Steed." She did a little curtsy and Josh stuck out his hand. "Do you know if Will and Alice Steed are still in Yerba Buena, then?" he asked.

She shook her head. "I'm not sure."

By now the rest of the men had come up and the villagers were swarming around them. Sparks cupped a hand to his mouth. "Anyone here know where Will Steed is by now?"

A large, burley man swung around. "Will Steed?"

"Yes," Josh said eagerly. "He's my cousin. Do you know where he is?"

"Yes. He and his wife and baby are living up north of here. He's working for Captain John Sutter."

"At Sutter's Fort?"

"Last I heard, and that was just a few days ago."

"And they have a baby?"

"Little boy, from what I hear," the man said, then turned back to the others.

Josh turned to see that Luther Tuttle had heard all of that. "That's wonderful. It looks like you've found them at last."

Chapter Notes

The first encampment of the Saints in the Salt Lake Valley was near the site of the current City and County Building between State Street and First East Street and Fourth and Fifth South Streets in Salt Lake City. The place of plowing for the potato field and other crops was probably about Third South and State Street.

On 26 July, just two days after reaching the Valley, Brigham Young asked to be taken to the top of what would be called Ensign Peak, where a banner was raised in symbolic fulfillment of the words of Isaiah (see B. H. Roberts, *A Comprehensive History of The Church of Jesus Christ of Latter-day Saints, Century I*, 6 vols. [Salt Lake City: The Church of Jesus Christ of Latter-day Saints, 1930], 3:271). It was President George A. Smith who, in a discourse, gave the details of Joseph's vision of Ensign Peak and Brigham's recognition of it when the pioneers came to the Valley (see *Journal of Discourses*, 26 vols. [London: Latter-day Saints' Book Depot, 1854-86], 13:85–86).

Deer Creek is near the site of present-day Glenrock, Wyoming, about twenty miles east of the site of the Mormon Ferry on the North Platte River.

The returning Mormon Battalion members reached the Mormon colony of New Hope on 21 August 1847. New Hope was located near the confluence of the Stanislaus and San Joaquin Rivers a little north of present-day Modesto, California. (See *MB*, p. 172.)

Chapter Forty-Eight

The Pioneer Company had started out with one hundred and forty-eight people—one hundred forty-three men, three women, and two children. With the addition of Robert Crow's party of seventeen at Fort Laramie, that number jumped to one hundred sixty-five, but then Brigham Young sent Amasa Lyman south with three others to get the rest of the Pueblo group, which left one hundred sixty-one. That was not to be a stable number. Sam Brannan showed up at the Green River. Then on July fourth, thirteen members of the Mormon Battalion from the Pueblo group came ahead looking for stolen horses. Twelve of those stayed with the pioneers while one went back with five men Brigham sent east to guide the companies that were following. Then at Fort Bridger, he sent Sam Brannan and Sergeant Tom Williams back to serve as guides to the Pueblo group. As near as Nathan could calculate, they had finally entered the Valley with about one hundred and sixty-five people. When the Pueblo group guided by Brannan and

Williams arrived five days later, that more than doubled the number of the little colony.

Now their numbers were diminishing again.

By the first of August, Brigham was putting plans in place for the winter. A major concern for him was the Mormon Battalion members who were in California. He suspected that by now they had heard that the Saints were in the Salt Lake Valley and were on their way to join them. That was a problem. The first winter was going to be a very difficult one. The crops they planted were doing fine, but with no more than five or six weeks to grow, they would be limited. Most of those who had come to the Valley had all but exhausted their supplies getting there. They didn't need another three hundred men coming in with nothing but what they wore on their backs.

After several meetings on the matter, the members of the Twelve wrote a letter to the battalion members in California asking that only those who had sufficient supplies to see them through the winter should come on to the Valley. The rest should turn back to California—or stay there if they had not yet left—and work until spring to get money and supplies, then come on in the spring of 1848.

Sam Brannan, bitterly disappointed that Brigham could not be persuaded to continue on to California, prepared to leave. The Twelve decided that they should have Captain James Brown and a few other battalion members accompany him and carry the letter to the battalion. To Kathryn's great disappointment, but not to anyone's real surprise, Brigham asked Peter Ingalls to accompany the group. Peter had already turned down an opportunity to live in California, and Brigham felt that he would provide a countering voice to Sam Brannan's passionate conviction that California was the promised land for the Saints. They left on the sixth of August, less than a week after Sam Brannan had returned with the Pueblo contingent.

From the beginning, Brigham had planned that many of those in the Pioneer Company who had families back in Winter Quarters, including himself, would return before winter. Within a few days of their arrival, those who were going back prepared to leave. Elder Ezra T. Benson and Porter Rockwell started back with a small group on August second. Two weeks later, Tunis Rappleye and Shadrack Roundy left with a group of seventy-one men and thirty-three wagons. William Clayton, who had left his family behind at Winter Quarters with only a half hour's notice, left with them.

Then on the twenty-sixth day of August, after only one month in the Valley, Brigham Young and Heber C. Kimball and two others of the Twelve started east as well. With them went one hundred eight men and thirty-six wagons. The Valley population that had swelled to over four hundred when the Pueblo group arrived was cut in half, as those who stayed settled in to wait for the arrival of the Big Company.

When the knock sounded on the door, Alice looked up. Will was at the wash basin, still lathering up before dinner. She laid Jared down in his crib. "I'll get it," she said.

When she opened the door, she had to look up a little. The man standing there was a full head taller than she was. But strangely, he held his hat in front of the lower half of his face so that it covered all but his eyes.

"Mrs. Steed?"

"Yes?"

"Alice Samuelson Steed?"

Her eyes widened a little. Who around here knew her maiden name? "Yes, that's my name."

The hat dropped away to reveal a huge grin. "Well," he said in a slow drawl, "my name is Joshua Benjamin Steed. And I wuz wund'rin if y'all might know of a place I could stay for the night."

Joshua pulled on the reins and turned his horses aside. Caroline, who was walking alongside holding three-year-old Livvy's hand, looked up in surprise. Charles and Savannah were a little behind them, walking with Melissa's Caleb and Sarah. They trotted up to see what was going on. Today the Steeds had the rear guard of the company. Their five wagons were at the back, and they had deliberately fallen behind to let the clouds of dust settle a little.

In a moment the other four wagons pulled up on one side or the other of him. "Trouble?" Carl asked.

"No. I just wanted to point something out to the children."

The other cousins—both those who were riding and those who had been walking—came up to see what was going on.

"What is it, Papa?" Savannah asked, climbing up on the wagon wheel so she could see better.

"See where the road forks there?"

They looked ahead. It wasn't a challenge. In the miles of open nothingness there was only one thing to see, and that was where the wagon track split off to the right and left just ahead of them. "To the right, the road goes over the Greenwood Cutoff to Fort Hall and on to Oregon. To the left is the road to Fort Bridger and the Great Salt Lake Valley."

Caroline was looking at him closely, surprised at his knowledge.

He looked sheepish. "I've been reading that letter President Young sent back for our information. It's been fascinating to me to see how accurately William Clayton has described things for us." He looked around at the young sunburned faces looking up at him. "So how do we know which road we are supposed to take?"

Charles blurted out the obvious answer. "Because that's the way the other wagons are going."

"Well, yes," Joshua said. They could still see the dust and the white tops that indicated that those ahead of them had clearly taken the left fork. "But how did the lead wagon know which way to turn?"

The children were thinking hard, but no one wanted to venture a guess. Finally, Lydia raised her hand. Joshua nodded at her.

"Because our leader, a prophet, told us this is the way."

"Exactly," Joshua said, pleased that she had seen it. "And how did President Young know this was the right way?"

Now his little Livvy was hopping up and down, her hand in the air.

"Livvy?"

"Because Jesus told him."

He felt a sudden lump in his throat at the simple innocence of that answer. "Yes, Livvy. That's exactly right. And when we follow Jesus, and try to do what he says, then we'll know which way to turn."

Suddenly he was embarrassed. He cleared his throat. "Well, sorry for the delay. I just didn't want us to pass by this important point on the trail without the children seeing it."

As they started back to their wagons, Mary Ann leaned forward so she could see him better. "Thank you," she mouthed.

He nodded. Then he turned and looked at Carl, who was on the other side of him, sitting on his wagon seat. "Sorry for the sermon, Carl. I just thought it was worthy of note."

"No apology necessary, Joshua," Carl said slowly. "Any time you want to teach my children about following Jesus, that's all right with me."

As they started the wagons going again, Daniel Spencer, their wagon captain, came riding back toward them. As he reached them, Joshua called out. "We're all right, Brother Spencer. We just stopped for a little lesson of life."

"Oh," said Spencer, "I wasn't worried about you. I just thought you'd want to know."

"Know what?" Caroline asked.

"The lead wagons just reached the Big Sandy, and guess who was there waiting for us. Another one of the companies headed back to Winter Quarters."

"Another one?" Jessica said. They had already met two companies going east. "Who is leading this one?"

This was the surprise that Brother Spencer had been holding back. "President Young and three other members of the Quorum of the Twelve."

Brigham Young stepped out of the darkness and into the firelight. The bugle had already blown for evening prayers, and they were only a few minutes away from lights out. The babies and younger children were already bedded down and asleep, and the adults had gathered around the fire for family prayer, then stayed to talk about the exciting developments of the day.

They all rose to their feet as President Young appeared. A moment later, Elders Heber C. Kimball, Wilford Woodruff, and George A. Smith came out of the darkness as well. There were warm greetings as the four of them went around the fire, shaking hands and hugging their longtime friends. When he reached Mary Ann, Brigham took both of her hands and held them without letting go. "Dear Mary Ann, how good it is to see you here with your family."

"It is so good to see you again, President Young."

He put his arms around her and pulled her to him for a moment. Then he kissed her on the cheek. "That is from Nathan and Derek and Rebecca and the children." He hesitated for a moment, the smile filling his eyes. "And Kathryn. And, of course, Peter."

Matthew jerked up. "Peter? You've found Peter?"

He laughed softly, enjoying his little surprise, knowing that this would come as a shock even to Matthew, since he had been left behind at the ferry at the last crossing of the North Platte. "Yes, even Peter." He told them quickly about the surprise appearance of Peter and Sam Brannan at the Green River and about sending Peter on to California to meet the battalion.

Lydia stepped forward, clenching her hands. "Do you think Josh will come with the battalion to the Valley?" she asked anxiously.

Brigham shrugged, explaining his instructions about who should come on and who should return to California for another season. But then, seeing he hadn't helped her much, he smiled kindly. "Knowing that wonderful son of yours, I would guess they'd have to hog-tie him to a horse and drag him back to California."

There were instant tears in Lydia's eyes. "I can't believe I could actually see him again."

Brigham nodded, then looked around at all of them. "This is our ninth day since leaving the Valley, but with all your cattle, I'd guess it will take you a full two more weeks."

"Tell us about the Valley," Jenny said. "Is it wonderful?"

For a moment Brigham seemed caught off guard by the question. Then a slow smile stole across the face. "It is the right place, dear Jenny. Of that I can testify without reservation."

For the third time in his life, Peter was within sight of Truckee Lake in the Sierra. The first time he and James Reed had passed here going west, on their way to Sutter's Fort and help for Reed's family. The second time he and Sam Brannan and Charlie Smith had ridden past it going east. Later, they had learned that when General Kearny brought a detachment of soldiers through in mid-June on their way to Fort Leavenworth, they had taken time to go to the site of the camp where the tragedy had occurred and given the scattered and grisly remains a decent burial. There was now only the remains of the cabins and the stumps of trees cut off by the emigrants for firewood. The fact that the stumps loomed some twenty feet above the ground attested to the depths of the snow when the Donner group had been there. The snow was gone now. The mountains were bright in their fall colors, and Captain Brown and the others rode over to see the site that was now becoming famous—or infamous—throughout America. Even though the bodies had been buried, Peter once again refused to go. He did not want any visual images, even of their campsites, to go with the stark and terrible memories he already harbored.

Now, the next morning, as they moved slowly on, the deep blue waters of the lake offered a serene contrast to the horrors that had taken place at its eastern end. Even though horrible remains had long since been put away, the men were still deeply sobered by knowing they were this close to real tragedy. They rode in single file, content for the moment to stay within their own thoughts.

Then as they were nearly past the lake, one of the men spoke to Captain Brown. "What do you suppose Sam Brannan will tell them when he reaches them?"

Brown's shoulders lifted and fell, and then he shook his head. "Well, he can say what he wants about me, but he'd better not mislead them about President Young's letter."

Peter nodded. He didn't think Brannan would, but in his current fit of temper, he couldn't be sure. From the time they left Great Salt Lake City, Samuel Brannan nursed a sour temper. The leader of the *Brooklyn* Saints was deeply hurt that Brigham Young had given the letter written by members of the Twelve to the Mormon Battalion to James Brown to carry instead of to Brannan. After all, Brannan was the head of the Church in California, and it was his right to carry the word back to his people. Or so Brannan argued. But Brigham had been adamant that it was a letter to the Mormon Battalion members and Brannan had no standing there. Among other things, the letter contained the power of attorney for Brown to collect the final pay of the soldiers that was due them.

Brannan and the captain had clashed again and again as they moved westward. When Brannan started making comments that perhaps Brother Brigham was no longer under the inspiration of heaven—otherwise, he would have kept coming on to California—Brown, Peter, and the others had reacted sharply. It finally reached the point where two nights before, Brown had sharply suggested that it might be Brannan who was out of touch with the Lord rather than President Young. In one instant Brannan was on his feet flailing at his counterpart. The men had finally pulled them apart, and the leader of the *Brooklyn* Saints had gone off in a huff, sleeping apart from the others. The next morning when they arose, he was gone. They had found his trail and his campfire and knew that he was still only about a day ahead of them, but a day was enough. Wherever the battalion was, he would find them first.

But for all of Brannan's wounded pride and pricked ego, Peter still felt that the man would not deliberately lie. He would put his own twist on things, especially the importance of returning to California, but he wouldn't lie about things. He was—

"Captain Brown!"

Peter came out of his thoughts. The man in the lead had reined in and was pointing. "Campfires ahead of us, sir."

They leaned forward, searching the depths of the forest up ahead. Then Peter saw it—several thin columns of smoke rising almost vertically from the trees.

"Good," Brown exclaimed. "That could be the battalion. Let's go!" He spurred his horse forward and the rest fell in behind him. Peter slapped his reins across the horse's rump, feeling a quick shot of adrenaline surge through his body. If Brown was right, and all was as he hoped, Peter was about to meet Josh Steed for the first time in over a year.

"People comin'," a voice cried out. It was as though someone had made the call to arms. All around the camp, the ex-battalion men leaped to their feet. Some ran toward the lake's edge where the trees thinned and they could see better. Others started tucking shirttails into trousers and pulling on their boots. Levi Hancock started shouting orders as he raced for his rifle.

Josh Steed had Jared on his lap, letting him play with the lid of his canteen. The toddler had not slept well during the night, and Josh was letting Will and Alice sleep a little longer. Or so he thought. As the camp erupted into action, both of them came bursting out of their tent. Will was hopping, pulling on his second boot as he came. Alice was tying on her apron.

"I think it's the men Elder Brannan told us about," Josh explained. "There seems to be several riders." Sam Brannan had ridden in the day before and told them that Captain Brown and others were just a day behind him. Then, refusing their invitation to stay, he rode on.

"Give me Jared," Alice said to Josh. "You and Will go."

They tore off, following the men who were all running forward now. As they approached the lake where the trees thinned, they saw the riders coming on a run toward them. With a whoop of delight, Josh recognized the third man back. He started waving his arms wildly. "Peter! Peter!"

Peter reined in hard, leaped off his horse, and shoved the reins at one of his companions. Then in three great leaps he and Josh met. They grabbed each other and whirled around, pounding each other on the back, laughing and shouting. Finally, Peter stopped and pushed Josh back at arm's length. "Let me look at you," he said. "I can't believe how tall you are. I'll bet you've added two hand spans since I saw you last."

"And about thirty pounds, I think," Josh said, submitting to the scrutiny happily. "But look at you too. You're all tan and lean. Will told me that you had become a bullwhacker."

"Kind of hard to believe, isn't it? From poet to bullwhacker. Who would ever—?" He stopped as another figure stepped out from among the swarm of men. "Is that Will?" he exclaimed.

"It is. He and Alice are with us."

Will came running up, grinning like a boy with a new horse. "Well, well, well," he chortled. "You did come back."

"Told you I would, didn't I?" Peter said, punching his arm lightly. Then he sobered. "I was afraid you'd still be at Sutter's place waiting for me to come back for you."

"What? You think we would stay behind when there's a group of Mormons headed for home?"

"So Alice and Jared are with you?"

"Waiting at the tent. Come on." He took Peter's arm and started moving away. The two groups were in chaos now as former companions in arms celebrated their reunion, and they had to push their way through.

"Is it true, Peter?" Josh asked as they walked swiftly back

toward the camp. "Are you in the Valley now? Do we really have us a home?"

"Yes, Josh. Your father is there waiting for you. Your mother and the rest of the family are coming with the main companies, but will likely be there by the time we get back."

Will's voice had turned wistful. "Can it really be? That sounds so good."

Suddenly reality set in. "Well, yes, but there's one problem."

"What?"

"Captain Brown has a letter from Brigham Young. It asks anyone who doesn't have a good stock of supplies to turn back to California."

"We know. Elder Brannan told us about that last night."

"Oh." Peter had forgotten about Brannan for the moment. He tried to explain. "Things in the Valley are very limited. There's nothing there. Nothing. We had to bring in every button, every seed, every tool. We can't add three hundred men who are destitute and will need to be supported. The President wants only those who won't be a burden. The rest will turn back and come next season."

Will brushed that aside. "That's all decided, Peter. Sutter paid me and Alice in horses and supplies. We're better off than most."

Peter couldn't help but look at Josh, whose clothes were so worn and shabby that he couldn't have much of anything to his name.

Will watched, savoring this next part. "And we also had company about a month ago."

Peter turned. "Who was that?"

"James Reed. He brought you your pay for bullwhacking." Grinning, he took out a leather pouch and jingled it up and down. "It's only five hundred dollars."

Astonished, Peter just stared at him. "Five hundred dollars?"

Will laughed aloud and tossed him the bag. "Yep. Think that's enough to qualify Josh to go with us too?"

On September twentieth, not quite a full two months after the arrival of the pioneers in the Valley of the Great Salt Lake, all work came to a halt. It was not the Sabbath, nor was it a formal holiday of any sort. It was a Monday, and there was still an enormous amount of work to be done as the weather turned colder. The mountains were now turning a brilliant red and orange, and twice already the peaks had been dusted with white. It was not because there was nothing urgent to do, but all work stopped anyway. Foundations for new cabins were left partially undone. The meager crops brought in hastily the previous few days were left in the wagons. The stone walls of the fort to the west of the Grand Encampment were nearly done but still needed a few more feet to be completed. The fort lay deserted, the stone masons' hammers and trowels set aside for the moment.

At ten o'clock the bugle sounded, and men, women, and children ran for their wagons. Dogs barked, oxen bellowed, children screeched, women called excitedly to each other, and men shouted at their teams. Then in one grand movement, the first wagons began to roll. One by one the half dozen wagons that were still in the Valley fell into line and started moving in a southeastward direction, up the gently sloping landscape toward what the new settlers were already calling the "benchland." They followed the track they had made some two months before, but in the opposite direction. They were headed for that opening in the mountain face to the south and east of them. They were headed for the mouth of Last Canyon.

Without anyone specifically directing them, when they reached the canyon's mouth, one by one they pulled off the road, some to the right and some to the left. They lined up facing each other, with the wagon track between them. Suddenly quiet now, the people gathered behind the wagons. The adults stood in small groups, talking quietly. The few children in the company were allowed to play quietly, but were quickly shushed if they got boisterous. There were about two hundred people there, but they made no more noise than a dozen or so.

One of those small groups that stood together consisted of Nathan Steed, Derek and Rebecca Ingalls and their three children, and Kathryn Ingalls and her baby, Nicole. They spoke quietly of other things, but as they talked, their eyes would continually turn toward the canyon. Heads would jerk around at the sound of a horse's whinny or the stamp of an ox's hoof. Then, when there was nothing, they would return to their conversations.

At about ten minutes past noon, one of the men nearest the mouth of the canyon suddenly called out in a loud voice. "Quiet, everyone."

An instant hush swept over the assembly. Ears strained toward the east, listening intently. For a moment, there was nothing except the twitter of birds and the soft rustle of leaves as the breeze stirred them. And then there was something else. It was the jingle of harnessing and the rattle of a steel-rimmed wagon going over rocky ground.

People edged forward, trying to see. For another two or three minutes there was nothing, though the sound of wagons was unmistakable now.

"There they are!" It was a child who shouted it. He was jumping up and down, pointing. A yoke of oxen appeared, followed by another, and then the white top of a wagon. As perfectly unified as if given a signal, a great cheer went up and down the line of waiting pioneers. Now it was not just the children who were dancing up and down and waving their arms.

"Oh, Derek," Rebecca said softly, "what if they're not with this first company?"

"They may not be," he said. "You heard what the rider said. There are nine companies in all. This is only the first."

"How far behind are the others, Papa?" Christopher asked.

"A week," Derek said without enthusiasm. "Maybe as much as ten days."

Kathryn groaned. "I absolutely shall die if they are not here."

The first wagon was fully in view now, and then the second team, this time mules, appeared. A man on a horse rode out from between the two wagons. When he saw what was waiting for them, he took off his hat and began to wave it as he spurred forward.

"Can you tell who it is?" Rebecca asked Nathan.

Nathan was already staring at the approaching rider. "It's Daniel Spencer," he said.

Now the cheering and the shouts and the applause were deafening. Women were weeping and grown men had suddenly lost their ability to speak. Brother Spencer smiled broadly, waving his hat and calling out greetings to those he knew. A third wagon and then a fourth came into sight. There was no longer any question. The first of the following companies had finally arrived.

It was the order of the trail that the companies rotated their position in the train on a regular basis. The company of ten that led out one day would drop to the rear the next, then gradually work their way forward again. That way the terrible dust suffered by those at the rear was shared by all. On the day they had reached the Parting of the Ways, the Steeds' group of ten had been at the rear. In the two weeks since, they had rotated once through completely and were now halfway back.

In the narrow canyon, the rattle of the wagons, the crack of whips, the shouts of teamsters, and the bellowing of the cattle filled the air with noise. In this last stretch of canyon, the road was so rough that they had put everyone in the wagons to ride. Joshua was in the lead, with Caroline at his side. Luke Griffith was driving Lydia's wagon, and Emily and Lydia were seated beside him. Next came Matthew and Jenny and Mary Ann, followed by Solomon, Jessica, and Rachel, then Carl and Melissa and their family.

Beside him, Caroline gripped Joshua's arm. "I can hardly breathe, Joshua."

He laughed. "The dust isn't that bad, dear."

She poked him. "You know what I mean. Do you think they'll be waiting for us?"

He shook his head, poker-faced. "They've got too much to do to come out and wait for a ragtag group like us."

She almost hit him again. Then, seeing his face, she laughed in delight. "You're as excited as I am, you faker!"

"Yes," he admitted. His pulse was racing, and he kept staring forward trying to see past the wagon ahead of them.

And then suddenly the trees opened up, the canyon walls fell away, and a broad expanse of sky assaulted their eyes. At the same instant the wave of sound hit them, drowning out the noise of the wagons and teams and people.

To Joshua's intense surprise, he found himself suddenly unable to see anything except a blur of people waving and dancing around on both sides of the track. Completely caught off guard by his reaction, he quickly wiped at his eyes with the back of his hand. Savannah, standing behind her parents, suddenly started pounding Joshua's shoulder. "There's Kathryn. I see Kathryn."

"There they are!" It was Nathan. He slapped Derek on the back. "Look, there's Joshua and Caroline." He leaped up and down, waving both arms. "Joshua! Joshua!"

Caroline was on her feet, hanging on to Joshua's shoulder, waving wildly and shouting back at them. Suddenly a figure jumped down from the wagon behind Joshua's and darted forward. With the dust, Nathan couldn't see for sure who it was. He saw it was a person in a dress and bonnet, but could see nothing more. Then he heard the shout. "Papa! Papa!"

"Emily?" It came out as a choked cry. Nathan took a step forward, his eyes burning with sudden tears. A great sob constricted his chest, making it in that instant difficult to breathe. "Emily!" He lunged forward, racing around a passing wagon. "Emily! Emily!"

She hurled herself through the air over the last few feet and flew into his arms. "Papa, it's you!"

He buried his face in her hair and stood there, his whole body shaking as he held her tightly. Then, kissing her tear-stained cheeks, he moved her aside, and strode forward. Before the second wagon even stopped, he reached up for Lydia. With a cry of joy, she leaped from the wagon into his arms.

By now any order had completely disappeared. Some groups stood back, disappointed to learn that their families were not in this company. But everywhere else, wagons pulled out of line and people jumped down and into each other's arms.

The Steeds formed one of the largest groups, with over thirty people trying to get to one another. Christopher and Benji and Leah were mobbed by their cousins. The women fell on each other's necks and wept joyously, then cried out at the sight of Kathryn holding Nicole. In an instant she was surrounded. The men somberly shook hands and then embraced, too overcome to say anything of what they were feeling.

Finally, as things began to settle down, Nathan went over to stand beside his mother. She was standing back now. She had been given the first turn with Nicole. Now the others were cuddling her and cooing at her.

"This is the day, Mama! Reunion time."

"Yes," she whispered. There were two wet streaks in the dust on her cheeks.

"If only Papa were here," he said softly. "That would make it complete."

"He's here, Nathan," she said, smiling through the tears. "Do you really think he would miss a day like today?"

Nathan threw back his head and laughed aloud at the joy that that thought brought him. "No," he answered. "Of course not."

Chapter Notes

On July twenty-eighth, just four days after his arrival, Brigham Young selected the spot where the Salt Lake Temple now sits by marking a spot in the dirt with his cane. Before leaving again for the east, he also directed that the city be laid out perfectly square, with broad streets running north and south, east and west. (See Leonard J. Arrington, *Brigham Young: American Moses* [New York: Alfred A. Knopf, 1985], p. 146.) The site for the fort the pioneers built is now Pioneer Park in Salt Lake City and is found between Third and Fourth West Streets and Third and Fourth South Streets.

The Mormon Battalion stayed with the Saints from the *Brooklyn* at the colony of New Hope for a short time. They also met Thomas Rhoads and his family, who lived about twenty miles from New Hope. They then continued north to Sutter's Fort, arriving on 26 August, the same day that Brigham Young left for Winter Quarters.

Once the battalion was discharged and split up into various groups to start back, it is hard to determine exact numbers of who went with each group. There were about two hundred who started over Donner Pass with Levi Hancock and who met Sam Brannan and James Brown near Truckee Lake. In the end, about half of them returned to California while the rest came on. (See Norma B. Ricketts, "The Forgotten Pioneers: Part Two," *Crossroads* 8 [Fall 1997]: 8, for a list of those who came on to the Valley with Hancock's group in 1847.) Captain Brown went back to California with them to collect their back pay from the army and brought back almost five thousand dollars in gold in 1848. About fifty of those who returned to California were hired by John Sutter to build his sawmill on the American River. Thus they were there helping to dig the millrace for that mill when James Marshall, Sutter's foreman, noticed the glint of shiny gold metal in the water. The California gold rush was on. (See *MB*, pp. 169–77.)

For some time the exact date of the discovery was not known, but it was the journal entry of Henry Bigler, a battalion member, that proved it happened on 24 January 1848 (see *MB*, pp. 197–98).

The California gold rush became a major influence in U.S. history, and those from the battalion who were in the area became part of that history. Ironically, John Sutter, who was situated as well as any man to capitalize on the gold rush, ended up being ruined by the discovery. Sutter said that the Mormons were the only ones who didn't desert him. They stayed and finished the work they had contracted to do. Then he added: "Paid off all the Mormons which have been employed by me. . . . All of them made their pile and some of them became very rich and wealthy but all of them are bound to the

Great Salt Lake and [will] spend their fortunes there to the glory and honor of the Lord." (As cited in *MB*, p. 203.)

Sam Brannan went back to San Francisco, where he became prominent in northern California history. When the gold rush broke out, his mercantile business made him wealthy (some say he was California's first millionaire). Some accused him of using tithing money which he had collected from the *Brooklyn* Saints for his own uses. Disillusioned with the Church for not sharing his vision of California, he drifted away from the faith and eventually was disfellowshipped. He became a heavy drinker. His fortunes changed, and he lost huge amounts of money in land development schemes, reaching a point where he even sold pencils on the streets of Nogales, Mexico. Eventually, however, he gave up drinking, repaid some of his debts, and lived out the rest of his life quietly. He died on 6 May 1889, almost forty-three years after the *Brooklyn* sailed through the Golden Gate and anchored near Yerba Buena. (See *CS*, pp. 219–24; Paul Bailey, *Sam Brannan and the California Mormons* [Los Angeles: Westernlore Press, 1943], pp. 129–35.)

Chapter Forty-Nine

The roughly two hundred members of the Mormon Battalion who met Captain James Brown at Truckee Lake the first week of September divided themselves, half continuing eastward, half turning back with Captain Brown to spend another winter in California. For Peter, the return trip passed swiftly. This was the fourth time he had journeyed on the trail across the vast emptiness, but this time would be the last. He knew full well that Kathryn had resigned herself to the fact that he would not return until next summer. As he himself had. Now, not only was he returning, but he was bringing with him Josh, Alice and Will, and the baby no one else in the family had yet seen.

They made steady if not remarkable progress. At Sutter's Fort, Will had purchased a wagon for Alice and Jared, who were the only woman and child in the company. The men also had a couple of wagons to carry their tents and supplies, but all except the wagon drivers walked. They left Truckee Lake on the eighth of September. After coming out of the Sierra, some of the men who felt like they weren't moving fast enough asked their leaders for permission to go on ahead. If their families were not in the Valley, then they would still have time to press on to Winter Quarters to find them. The Indians who had caused so much grief for the Donner Party attempted to harass the group, now split into several smaller companies, but with the travelers' manpower, the Indians posed no real threat other than the loss of animals.

As Peter and Sam Brannan had done earlier that year, they determined that they would not risk taking the Hastings Cutoff and the more direct route to the Salt Lake Valley. They turned north, rejoined the Oregon Trail at the Snake River, and continued east to Fort Hall, reaching there on October sixth, not quite a month after splitting up. They purchased a few supplies at Fort Hall and then, after resting for a short time, turned south, heading for the Valley of the Great Salt Lake.

Peter ran forward to where Josh Steed and William Hendricks were walking together near the front of the line of straggling men. He touched Josh on the shoulder. "Look. See that knobby hill up ahead?"

Josh slowed his step and looked up, staring dully ahead. Then he gave Peter an incredulous look. It was now more than thirty days since their group had split and this half had left Truckee Lake and started down the east slopes of the Sierra. Eleven days ago they had left Fort Hall and turned south toward the Valley of the Great Salt Lake. It was exactly fifteen months after their official mustering in and three months since their discharge. They had marched a total of almost three thousand miles. They were footsore, blistered, sunburned, and windchapped. They were mentally, emotionally, and physically exhausted. And he was supposed to get excited over the sight of some knobby hill?

Peter grabbed his arm and shook it. "Look, Josh. See there, where the mountains come down to meet the plain? Just to the left there's a hill that looks like a monk's bald head."

Finally, Josh straightened and peered ahead more carefully. Others around him lifted their heads as well. Peter's excitement was too much to ignore. Will and Alice were farther back in the company. Will gave Alice the reins, jumped down from the wagon, and hurried forward. A short distance ahead of where they were, Levi Hancock, the spiritual leader of the group, and Captain Jefferson Hunt, the senior officer of the battalion, both turned. "What is that again?" Hunt asked.

"That's Ensign Peak."

They just stared at him, as though he had spoken in a foreign tongue.

Realizing his mistake, Peter rushed on. "Ensign Peak is where Brigham Young raised the ensign to the world two days after we arrived in the Valley." Peter looked around, bursting with energy now. "Don't you understand? We're there. Great Salt Lake City is just about a mile from that peak."

Captain Hunt was nodding, his eyes bright now. He looked around. "Men, we have come a long way. We have endured much." He let his eyes sweep across them with bitter irony. "And we look it."

That brought a weary laugh from several.

"But we are about to march into the Valley of the Great Salt Lake, where our people await us. Are we going to go in like a pack of mangy hounds, or are we going to march in like the soldiers we are?"

To Peter's surprise, men began to straighten. They started to tug at their broad, white belts, about the only thing which remained of their original army "uniforms." Hunt turned to Brother Hancock. "Levi, with your permission, I'd like to find a pole and break out the colors."

Levi Hancock looked at his counterpart for a long moment. There had been many a disagreement between these two men over the months, but all of that was gone now. "I think that would be most appropriate, Captain."

And then the captain had a second thought. He turned to Josh. "Private Steed?"

Josh came to full attention. "Yes, sir?"

"You think you could find us an empty bucket?"

"Yes, sir."

"I think that would make a fine drum with which to mark cadence."

Forgetting that he was no longer a soldier, Josh snapped off a sharp salute. "*Yes, sir!*"

By mid-October, the Valley of the Great Salt Lake could no longer be said to be uninhabited except by the Ute Indians, or what many of the Oregon and California emigrants called the Utah Band. Nine full companies—more than five hundred wagons and almost fifteen hundred men, women, and children—had come in with the Big Company, the last arriving on October sixth. The population of the Salt Lake Valley was now at a whopping eighteen hundred Latter-day Saints.

By that time, the little colony had seen their first birth of a white female, their first birth of a white male, their first death (a boy had drowned in City Creek), a temple site selected, the regions round about explored, and the plan for a city—to be known as Great Salt Lake City—laid out, and surveys begun. Before departing for Winter Quarters, Brigham Young instructed the Saints to build a fort to the west of where they had plowed and planted. It was now completed, and extensions on both the north and south were under way to accommodate the larger numbers. The first settlement outside Great Salt Lake City—known as Sessions Settlement—was established about ten miles north of the city.

With the arrival of the Big Company, cutting and bringing timber from the nearby canyons commenced in earnest. Nearly four hundred cabins were completed or under construction. Sam Brannan had shown the Saints how to make adobe bricks like the ones they used in California, and numerous dwellings had been constructed using hardly any timber at all. But whether it was log cabins, adobe huts, willow lean-tos, tents, or wagons, there was no question but what the Valley of the Great Salt Lake now had permanent inhabitants.

Frost was occurring almost every night now, and a sense of urgency gripped the settlement as they raced to prepare for the first of the lasting snows. In addition to their meager harvest, the pioneers identified local roots and plants which could be eaten—sego lily bulbs and the roots of the thistle being the most popular. An infestation of field mice was dealt with by taking a wooden paddle with rounded handles and laying it across the top of a bucket filled with water. The paddle was smeared with grease. When the mice ventured onto the paddle to get the grease, it would flip and dump them into the water, where they drowned. Literally thousands of mice were killed in this manner. The one cat someone had brought across the plains became the pampered—and fat!—heroine of the settlement.

All of this was on Mary Ann Steed's mind as she walked through the gate of the fort and saw the bustle that filled the large courtyard.

"Mother?"

She turned. Lydia, Emily, Jessica, and Rachel were coming toward her. They had been to the simple store that had been erected inside the fort to provide some means of commerce among the Saints.

"Oh, hello."

"We were just coming over to see you," Lydia said.

"What for?"

"Why don't you come and have supper with us tonight?" Jessica said.

"Nonsense. Don't feel like you have to have me every night for supper. I'm perfectly capable of cooking a meal for myself." When they first arrived, she had moved into the same cabin as Matthew and Jenny. Then, knowing her need for independence and knowing that she would never express it, her sons and sons-in-law built a one-room extension on the back of Matthew's cabin with its own fireplace.

Lydia gave her a look of mock severity. "Now, Grandmother

Steed. You know that the children are all still clamoring to have you spend time with them." She smiled now. "This is part of your duty as a grandmother."

Before Mary Ann could respond, there was a shout from outside the gate. They turned as a rider came racing in and pulled to a halt in a spray of dust. He leaped from his horse. "Elder Taylor! Elder Pratt!"

From the building that was serving as a temporary Council House, the two Apostles who had brought in the Big Company appeared. "Yes?" Parley Pratt said.

"There's a group of men coming in from the north. I think it's the Mormon Battalion."

At that, a great cry went up, racing from mouth to mouth, house to house, and wagon to wagon. Men, women, and children came popping out as everyone started running toward the gate of the fort. Lydia turned to Emily. "Go get Jenny and Kathryn and Melissa."

Jessica nudged her daughter. "Rachel, go tell your father."

As they raced away, Lydia took Mary Ann's arm. "Oh, Mother Steed, it could be Peter and Josh."

Mary Ann gently pried her hand away. "Go, Lydia. Don't wait for me. Go find Josh."

With a cry of excitement, she nodded and started forward, pulling off her bonnet and flinging it aside.

As Mary Ann came out of the gate, all around her people were sprinting past, calling and shouting with excitement. Mary Ann strained to see, and then in a break in the crowd she spied what it was the rider had seen. About half a mile away there was a double column of men approaching. As she looked closer she could see that one of the two at the front of the column carried a long pole from which fluttered the American flag.

Jenny, Kathryn, and Melissa came rushing up, herding the younger children. Jenny was carrying Nicole so that Kathryn could use her crutches and keep up with them. "Where are they?" Kathryn exclaimed.

Mary Ann just pointed.

Then Solomon, Matthew, and Carl came on the run. Just behind them were Nathan and Joshua. The first three went by without seeing her. But Nathan saw her, and he and Joshua changed direction and ran up to her. "Mother," Nathan blurted. "It's the Mormon Battalion coming in."

She smiled and nodded. "I know."

"Come on. Let's go see them. Josh could be there."

"And Will and Alice," Joshua cried. "Come on, Mother. We'll help you."

She shook her head. "You go on. I'll be along."

"Mother!" Nathan exclaimed, surprised at her calmness.

"No. They're your children. Get up there. There will be time enough for Grandma later." When they still hesitated, she gave Nathan a gentle shove. "Go on. Mind me, now."

Sensing that she really meant it, they spurted away, joining the crowds streaming northward.

To her pleased surprised, she had gone only a short distance when she saw that the crowd had stopped. They were divided into two groups now, forming a wide path for the incoming column to pass through. Everything went silent as a great sense of anticipation swept across the waiting Saints. And then Mary Ann heard it. It was the sound of a drum. It sounded tinny and had a high pitch, but it was a drum nevertheless, and it was beating a steady cadence.

In two or three minutes, as the drumbeat grew louder, the column appeared. Now she could see the flag clearly and that one person—perhaps their commander—marched to one side of the first row of men. She also saw that the men in the columns carried muskets on their shoulders and each wore a wide white belt and bandolier. Though they were only thirty or forty yards now from the first of the people, no eyes pulled away from staring straight ahead; no heads turned to the right or to the left. The right hands held their muskets, but their left ones swung back and forth in perfect rhythm. Every foot lifted and fell at precisely the same moment. This wasn't a group of individuals walking in; it was a company of infantry,

Reunion

marching as one man to the beat of their makeshift drum.

In an instant Mary Ann Steed's eyes filled with tears. It was not that she had seen one of her family members coming in. It was not that she was stirred by the sight of them marching in such perfect order, though that was indeed a stirring sight. It was that in one brilliant burst of emotion, the memory of her dream came back to her, and with it came that same sense of incredible peace she had felt that first night that the dream had come to her.

She blinked quickly, trying to clear her vision, but then gave up. It didn't matter if she could see who was there or not. She didn't have to see them to know. She knew with perfect certainty that Peter and Josh were there, and that Will and Alice and the great-grandson she had never seen had come with them.

"Bat-tal-*yun!*" Captain Jefferson Hunt called out, his voice ringing out like a trumpet. "*Halt!*"

As one, the two columns came to a stop in the midst of the waiting onlookers. Still no eye flickered; no head budged as much as a fraction of an inch all up and down the long columns.

Hunt, still facing forward, withdrew his sword from its scabbard and lifted it high in the air. "*Bat-tal-yun!*" This time he let the word hang in the air for what seemed like forever. Then the sword flashed as he dropped it sharply. "*Dis-missed!*"

With a mighty roar the men broke ranks and threw themselves into the waiting crowd. Now Mary Ann could stand it no longer. With a cry of joy she rushed forward, aiming directly at where she saw a tall bearded young man pick Lydia up and begin to swing her around and around.

Joshua leaned forward, putting his arms around Caroline's waist. "It's not quite the same as Steed Row, is it?"

She turned, smiling at him, and shook her head.

The full Steed clan had come together, but there was no cabin big enough to hold them all. Not that such a simple thing would deter them. The Steeds were reunited, and even if they didn't have a large porch on which the adults could sit and a grass-filled yard where the children could play, they were going to have their evening together.

Once supper was done, they brought out every stool, every bench, every box and barrel and bag they could find to provide seats, and then gathered for another "night on Steed Row." First they asked Josh Steed to tell them the story of the Mormon Battalion. He was a natural storyteller, and by the time he had finished with the story of the Battle of the Bulls, the smaller children had moved closer to their parents to be safe. He finished to wild applause and a tearful, joyful kiss from his mother.

Now Will and Alice were telling about their voyage and the year they had spent in California. Grandma Steed held Jared on her lap while his parents spoke. As they talked about storms and miracles and the struggle it had been for the first few months after landing, Joshua was transfixed. His son and his bride had left as young newlyweds—naive, vulnerable children. Now they were mature, confident young parents. Alice was especially enchanting as she teased Will about his love of the sea and the difficulty of learning to walk on land again.

None of the children had been put to bed. This was a night for exceptions, and now Joshua was glad. They sat wide-eyed and totally enthralled, still perfectly content after almost an hour together. He was glad this next generation was hearing what their parents, uncles, aunts, and cousins had done.

When Will and Alice sat down, again to enthusiastic cheers and wild jubilation, the family fell quiet. It was past nine o'clock now and getting cold. They sensed it was time to end the day, but weren't sure just how to do it. After a moment, Joshua looked at Nathan and motioned for him to get up. Nathan looked surprised. "I'm not the eldest here," he said easily. "You get up."

Joshua was nonplussed. "But you're the head of the family," he protested.

"No," Nathan said slowly. "I was for a time, but that was before Joshua Steed became a man of the covenant. You're the eldest."

Looking around, flustered by this unexpected turn of events, Joshua wasn't sure what to do. He had taken the lead on the trail but only because Nathan had gone ahead. Then he looked at his mother. She nodded. "Nathan's right, Joshua. You're the eldest."

Caroline turned, her eyes glowing. "Go on," she murmured. "You know what to do."

He stood slowly, feeling awkward and embarrassed. His eye caught Carl's, and he felt a sudden warmth as he saw Carl nod his encouragement. Then, as he looked from person to person, he saw that same support and encouragement on every face before him. He took a breath and began, speaking slowly, trying to collect his thoughts.

"This morning, as I was walking back from the creek, I was looking around at our little home in the wilderness. Suddenly I was struck by the fact that this was, in many ways, just like it was in Winter Quarters. It was as though we had changed locations but not our situation. We are still living in crudely built cabins or, in some cases, the backs of wagons. We have little money"—he grinned—"except for Peter, who now has more money than all the rest of us put together."

They all laughed at that as Peter blushed. What no one but Kathryn knew as yet was that the five hundred dollars that James Reed had given him had already been turned over to Elders Parley Pratt and John Taylor to use as they saw fit.

"There is no doubt," Joshua went on, quite serious now, "but what this winter will be very much like our last one—inadequate housing, scarcity of food, unsanitary conditions, sacrifice, suffering, and yes, perhaps even death." He took a deep breath. "All of that was on my mind as I looked around today.

"But then suddenly I had a different thought. Yes, there were many things that were the same, but then I realized we have changed much more than our location. For one thing, we won't spend the winter preparing to leave in the spring. This time we won't abandon our homes and our fields and our city. Our homes are meager now, yes. But in time the wagons will become tents, the tents will become cabins, the cabins will become homes.

True, the streets will be filled with traffic, but it won't be headed west. The empty lots that are now no more than stakes in the ground will become neighborhoods. We will build churches, schools, businesses, maybe even a theater again as we had in Nauvoo."

The family listened intently to his every word. Several, including Carl, were nodding thoughtfully.

Joshua felt his face burn a little. "I didn't mean to give a speech, but . . ."

"Give us a speech, Joshua," Nathan said quietly. "This is a great day. It deserves a speech."

"Hear! Hear!" Matthew called out.

"Well, I'll tell you what else I was thinking today." He looked at Savannah, who was watching him with adoring eyes. "I realized suddenly that there was another way in which we had done much more than simply change locations from Winter Quarters to Great Salt Lake City. For almost four months on the trail I kept thinking of the Valley as being the end of the journey. Now I realize it is only the beginning. Think what this valley means for Savannah. For Rachel and Emily. For Mark and Luke and David and Sarah. The nearest mob is now more than a thousand miles away. Our littlest ones—Emmeline, Livvy, Betsy Jo, the two babies—these children will never know a Far West, a Haun's Mill, a Carthage Jail. They may go to bed hungry this winter, but *they will not go to bed afraid.*"

He stopped, very thoughtful now. "The Valley represents much more than that, though. Like Israel of old, we have come through the wilderness and entered a land of promise. Not a promise of milk and honey—though I suspect those shall come too—but a promise of renewal, of growth, of vision—of Zion. Think of this. Our children will raise up children who have never known any life but life in this valley. Think of that"—his voice dropped suddenly—"and rejoice.

"Well," he said, smiling, feeling a little chagrined at the passion he had shown. "We have come many, many miles from those first days in Palmyra. We have come by many paths and at different speeds. Some—like Papa, Olivia, and Mary Melissa—were buried along the way. But the rest of us came on. Think for a moment how remarkable that is. One of those many paths went by way of a ten-thousand-mile sea voyage. Another took a shortcut that proved to be the longest and most tragic possible way. Some went by way of the Santa Fe Trail, some by way of Pueblo and Sutter's Fort and Independence Rock."

He straightened, knowing it was time to finish. "But now those paths have converged again. From here and there, from near and far, they have come together right here, on this very night and at this very campfire."

He looked at his mother and now his eyes were filled with the deepest of joy. "Mama, the dream you had so long ago has at last become a reality. All is well. Our family has come home."

The Story Before the Work and the Glory!

"Without the freedoms guaranteed by the Constitution and the unique climate of religious tolerance found in the United States, the seeds of the restoration of the Church of Jesus Christ would have fallen upon infertile or sterile ground. Truly the episodes that led to the establishment of this nation were a prelude to the Restoration and part of God's work and glory for the good of all mankind."

Gerald N. Lund

Prelude to Glory, Vol. 1: Our Sacred Honor
HARDCOVER $19.95 AUDIO BOOK (16 CASSETTES) $39.95

If you enjoyed *The Work and the Glory* series, you are sure to enjoy the new historical fiction series *Prelude to Glory*. In epic style, this book chronicles the miraculous events that gave birth to a new nation. In *Our Sacred Honor*, the first volume in the series, master storyteller Ron Carter presents the early events of the Revolutionary War through the eyes of common people. Through fictional as well as real-life characters, *Prelude to Glory* powerfully depicts a great story!

The Work and the Glory Collectors Set
$199.95

All nine volumes are bound in beautiful and durable simulated leather. This unique keepsake set is a collection you are sure to cherish.

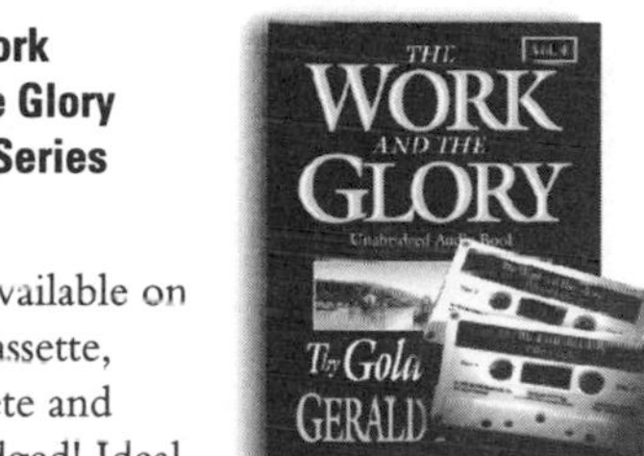

The Work and the Glory Audio Series
$39.95

Now available on audiocassette, complete and unabridged! Ideal for commuters, business travelers, fitness enthusiasts, or those who simply prefer the audio version. Each volume's price has been standardized at only $39.95 suggested retail price, which reflects a discount of over 65% off a comparable national price.

The Music of the Work and the Glory
Volume 1 and Volume 2
EACH CASSETTE $10.95 EACH COMPACT DISC $15.95

These music selections capture the spirit of the Steed family and their experiences with the restoration of the gospel.

BOOKCRAFT

Available wherever LDS products are sold

OREGON
IDAHO
Snake River
Oregon Trail
Greenwood Cutoff
Fort Hall
California Trail
Truckee (Donner) Pass
Great Salt Lake
Humboldt R.
Truckee (Donner) Lake
Johnson's Ranch
Humboldt Sink
Lake Tahoe
Hastings Cutoff
Utah Lake
Sutter's Fort
Truckee River
Wasatch Range
Green River
Yerba Buena (San Francisco)
New Hope
Sierra Nevada
Nevada
Utah
Monterey
Colorado
River
California
Arizona
Pueblo de Los Angeles
Colorado
San Diego
Gila
River
San Pedro River
Tucson
Battle of the Bulls